Lecture Notes of the Institute for Computer Sciences, Social Informatics and Telecommunications Engineering

346

More information about this series at http://www.springer.com/series/8197

Bo Li · Changle Li · Mao Yang ·
Zhongjiang Yan · Jie Zheng (Eds.)

IoT as a Service

6th EAI International Conference, IoTaaS 2020
Xi'an, China, November 19–20, 2020
Proceedings

 Springer

Editors
Bo Li
Northwestern Polytechnical University
Xi'an, China

Mao Yang ⓘ
Northwestern Polytechnical University
Xi'an, China

Jie Zheng
Northwest University
Xi'an, China

Changle Li
State Key Laboratory of ISN
Xidian University
Xi'an, China

Zhongjiang Yan ⓘ
School of Electronics and Information
Northwestern Polytechnical University
Xi'an, China

ISSN 1867-8211   ISSN 1867-822X   (electronic)
Lecture Notes of the Institute for Computer Sciences, Social Informatics
and Telecommunications Engineering
ISBN 978-3-030-67513-4   ISBN 978-3-030-67514-1   (eBook)
https://doi.org/10.1007/978-3-030-67514-1

This Springer imprint is published by the registered company Springer Nature Switzerland AG
The registered company address is: Gewerbestrasse 11, 6330 Cham, Switzerland

Preface

IoTaaS is endorsed by the European Alliance for Innovation, a leading community-based organization devoted to the advancement of innovation in the field of ICT. The 6th International Conference on IoT as a Service (IoTaaS) aims to contribute to the discussion on the challenges posed by the Internet of Things (IoT). The IoTaaS conference aims to bring together researchers and practitioners interested in IoT from academia and industry. IoTaaS attendees present novel ideas, exchange points of view, and foster collaborations. Even, faced with the difficulties of COVID-19, IoTaaS 2020 still received a large number of manuscripts and was successfully held with great help from all authors, reviewers, TPC members, and organization committees.

IoTaaS 2020, consisted of 2 technical tracks and 3 workshops: 2nd Workshop on Edge Intelligence and Computing for IoT Communications and Applications, Workshop on Satellite Communication Networks for Internet of Things, Workshop on Satellite Communications and Spatial Information Network. IoTaaS has become one of the major events in these areas in the Asia-Pacific region. It has been successful in encouraging interactions among participants, exchanging novel ideas and disseminating knowledge.

Following the great success of the past IoTaaS 2014–2019, IoTaaS 2020 received 136 submitted papers, out of which 69 papers were selected for presentation. The Technical Program Committee did an outstanding job in organizing a diverse technical program consisting of 14 symposia that covered a broad range of research areas in IoT technologies. Under the excellent leadership of TPC Co-Chairs Prof. Changle Li, Prof. Zhongjiang Yan, and Prof. Mao Yang, TPC members handled the reviews of papers, with each paper receiving more than 3 reviews on average.

The technical program featured two outstanding keynote speakers, who presented their vision of IoT in theory and practice: Prof. Baoming Bai, Xidian University, China; Prof. Guizhong Liu, Xi'an Jiaotong University, China.

We would like to thank the TPC Co-Chairs, TPC members, all the reviewers, the Workshops Chair, the Web Chair, the Publications Chair, the Local Chair, and all the members of the organizing committee for their assistance and efforts to make the conference succeed. The continuing sponsorship by EAI and Springer is gratefully acknowledged. We also express our appreciation to the conference keynote speakers, paper presenters, and authors.

Bo Li

Conference Organization

Steering Committee

Imrich Chlamtac   Bruno Kessler Professor, University of Trento, Italy
Bo Li   Northwestern Polytechnical University, China

Organizing Committee

General Chair

Bo Li   Northwestern Polytechnical University, China

General Co-chairs

Baowang Lian   Northwestern Polytechnical University, China
Yingzhuang Liu   Huazhong University of Science & Technology, China
Zhenyu Xiao   Beihang University, China

TPC Chair and Co-chairs

Changle Li   Xidian University, China
Zhongjiang Yan   Northwestern Polytechnical University, China
Mao Yang   Northwestern Polytechnical University, China

Sponsorship and Exhibit Chair

Xiaoya Zuo   Northwestern Polytechnical University, China

Local Chair

Zhongjiang Yan   Northwestern Polytechnical University, China

Workshops Chair

Zhong Shen   Xidian University, China

Publicity and Social Media Chair

Zhongjiang Yan   Northwestern Polytechnical University, China

Publications Chair

Jie Zheng   Northwest University, China

Web Chair

Mao Yang   Northwestern Polytechnical University, China

Tutorials Chair

Jie Zheng   Northwest University, China

Technical Program Committee

Zhengwen Cao	Northwest University, China
Zhengchuan Chen	Chongqing University, China
Nan Cheng	Xidian University, China
Hua Cui	Chang'an University, China
Yongqian Du	Northwestern Polytechnical University, China
Rongfei Fan	Beijing Institute of Technology, China
Yongsheng Gao	Northwestern Polytechnical University, China
Chen He	Northwest University, China
Yongqiang Hei	Xidian University, China
Yilong Hui	Xidian University, China
Bin Li	Northwestern Polytechnical University, China
Guifang Li	Northwestern Polytechnical University, China
Zhan Li	Northwest University, China
Ni Liu	Chang'an University, China
Wei Liang	Northwestern Polytechnical University, China
Zhanwen Liu	Chang'an University, China
Zhongjin Liu	Coordination Center of China, China
Hao Luan	Xidian University, China
Xin Ma	Northwestern Polytechnical University, China
Evgeny Neretin	Moscow Aviation Institute, Russia
Laisen Nie	Northwestern Polytechnical University, China
Yong Niu	Beijing Jiaotong University, China
Xiaoyan Pang	Northwestern Polytechnical University, China
Bowei Shan	Chang'an University, China
Jiao Shi	Northwestern Polytechnical University, China
Xiao Tang	Northwestern Polytechnical University, China
Jing Wang	Chang'an University, China
Jun Wang	Northwest University, China
Wei Wang	Chang'an University, China
Jian Xie	Northwestern Polytechnical University, China
Mingwu Yao	Xidian University, China
Daosen Zhai	Northwestern Polytechnical University, China
Yongqin Zhang	Northwest University, China
Xuan Zhu	Northwest University, China
Jiang Zhu	Zhejiang University
Min Zhu	Xidian University, China
Xiaoya Zuo	Northwestern Polytechnical University, China

Contents

**Edge Intelligence and Computing for IoT Communications
and Applications**

Satellite Communication Networks for Internet of Things

Communications

Image and Information

Algorithm and Information for Wireless Network

Approximation of DAC Codeword Distribution for Equiprobable Binary Sources Along Proper Decoding Paths

Nan Yang and Yong Fang[(⊠)] [ID]

School of Information Engineering, Chang'an University, Xi'an, Shaanxi, China
{nyang,fy}@chd.edu.cn

Abstract. Distributed Arithmetic Coding (DAC) is an effective implementation of Slepian-Wolf coding. To research its properties, the concept of DAC codeword distribution along proper decoding paths has been introduced. For DAC codeword distribution of equiprobable binary sources along proper decoding paths, the problem was formatted as solving a system of functional equations. However, in general cases, to find the closed form of DAC codeword distribution still remains a very difficult task. This paper proposes an approximation method for DAC codeword distribution of equiprobable binary sources along proper decoding paths: polynomial approximation. At rates lower than 0.5, DAC codeword distribution can be well approximated by a polynomial. Some simulation results are given to verify theoretical analyses.

Keywords: Slepian-Wolf coding · Distributed arithmetic coding · Codeword distribution · Polynomial approximation

1 Introduction

1.1 Background

Consider the problem of Slepian-Wolf Coding (SWC) with decoder Side Information (SI), i.e. the encoder compresses discrete source X in the absence of Y, discretely-correlated SI. Slepian-Wolf theorem states that lossless compression is achievable at rates $R \geq H(X|Y)$ [1], where $H(X|Y)$ is the conditional entropy of X given Y. Conventionally, channel codes, e.g., turbo codes [2] or Low-Density Parity-Check (LDPC) codes [3], are used to implement the SWC.

Ever since a long time ago, Arithmetic Coding (AC) has been proposed as the successor of Huffman coding to implement source coding and shows near-entropy performance [4–6]. Recently, the AC is applied to implement the SWC. One approach is to allow overlapped intervals, which mirrors the work in [7]. Such examples include Distributed Arithmetic Coding (DAC) [8,9] and Overlapped Quasi-Arithmetic Coding (OQAC) [10]. Another approach is to puncture some bits of AC bitstream, e.g. Punctured Quasi-Arithmetic Coding (PQAC) [11],

B. Li et al. (Eds.): IoTaaS 2020, LNICST 346, pp. 3–13, 2021.
https://doi.org/10.1007/978-3-030-67514-1_1

which mirrors the work in [12]. There are also some variants of the DAC. The symmetric SWC is implemented by the time-shared DAC (TS-DAC) [13]. The rate-compatible DAC is proposed in [14]. Furthermore, decoder-driven adaptive DAC [15] is proposed to estimate source probabilities on-the-fly.

To analyze the properties of the DAC, [16] introduces the concept of codeword distribution. DAC codeword distribution is a function defined over interval $[0, 1)$. For equiprobable binary sources, both codeword distribution along proper decoding paths and codeword distribution along wrong decoding paths are researched. For codeword distribution along proper decoding paths, the problem is formatted as solving a system of functional equations including four constraints [16]. It is affirmed that rate $R = 0.5$ is a watershed: when $R > 0.5$, DAC codeword distribution is an unsmooth function; while when $R \leq 0.5$, DAC codeword distribution is a smooth function. Especially, a closed form is obtained at $R = 0.5$. In spite of these achievements, it remains a very difficult task to find the closed form of codeword distribution along proper decoding paths in general. Though a special closed form of $f(u)$ is found in [16], the procedure is very complex. As a universal approach, a numeric method for finding $f(u)$ was proposed in [17].

1.2   Contribution

This paper makes some advances on the work in [16]. An approximation method is proposed for codeword distribution of equiprobable binary sources along proper decoding paths: polynomial approximation. Then comparisons of polynomial approximation with numeric approximation, among them, numeric approximation is a general approach. Proved that at low rates ($R \leq 0.5$), polynomial approximation works well.

This paper is arranged as follows. In Sect. 2, after a brief introduction to binary DAC codec, DAC decoding process is analyzed in detail to show the significance of DAC codeword distribution. Then the investigated problem is formulated in Sect. 3. Section 4 describes in detail polynomial approximation, where simulation results are also reported. Finally, Sect. 5 concludes this paper.

2   Binary Distributed Arithmetic Coding

2.1   Encoding

Consider a binary source $X = \{x_i\}_{i=1}^{I}$ with bias probability $p = \Pr(x_i = 1)$. In the classic AC, source symbol x_i is iteratively mapped onto sub-intervals of $[0, 1)$, whose lengths are proportional to $(1 - p)$ and p, giving rate $R = H(X)$. Instead, in the DAC [8,9], sub-interval lengths are proportional to enlarged probabilities $(1 - p)^\gamma$ and p^γ, where $H(X|Y)/H(X) \leq \gamma \leq 1$, giving rate $R = \gamma H(X) \geq H(X|Y)$. For conciseness, we refer to γ as overlap coefficient hereinafter. More specifically, symbols $x_i = 0$ and $x_i = 1$ correspond to sub-intervals $[0, (1 - p)^\gamma)$ and $[1 - p^\gamma, 1)$, respectively. It means that to fit the $[0, 1)$ interval, the sub-intervals have to be partially overlapped. This overlapping leads to a larger final interval, and hence a shorter codeword. However, as a cost, the decoder can not decode X unambiguously without Y.

Note that when $\gamma \geq 1/C \geq 1$, where C is channel capacity, it becomes the Error Correcting AC (ECAC).

2.2 Decoding

To describe the decoding process, a ternary symbol set $\{0, \mathcal{A}, 1\}$ is defined, where $\mathcal{A}$ represents the ambiguous symbol. Let C_X be DAC codeword and $\tilde{x}_i$ be the i-th decoded symbol, then

$$
\tilde{x}_i = \begin{cases} 0, & 0 \leq C_X < 1 - p^\gamma \\ \mathcal{A}, & 1 - p^\gamma \leq C_X < (1 - p)^\gamma \\ 1, & (1 - p)^\gamma \leq C_X < 1 \end{cases}. \tag{1}
$$

After $\tilde{x}_i$ is decoded, if $\tilde{x}_i = \mathcal{A}$, the decoder will perform a branching: two candidate branches are generated, corresponding to two alternative symbols $x_i = 0$ and $x_i = 1$. For each new branch, its metric is updated and the corresponding interval is selected for next iteration. To reduce complexity, every time a symbol is decoded, the decoder uses the M-algorithm to keep at most M paths with the best partial metric, and prunes others [8,9]. Finally, after all source symbols are decoded, the path with the best metric is output as the estimate of X.

2.3 Analysis

It deserves to point out that during DAC decoding, the metric of each path is indeed the Hamming distance between this path and SI Y. As we know, each DAC codeword defines a set of possible decoding paths and each possible decoding path corresponds to a sequence of decoded symbols. However, among all possible decoding paths, there is one and only one proper path which corresponds to source X. Let $\tilde{X} = \{\tilde{x}_i\}_{i=1}^I$ be a sequence of decoded symbols. Let $D(Y, \tilde{X})$ be the Hamming distance between Y and $\tilde{X}$. Similarly, $D(X, \tilde{X})$ and $D(X, Y)$ are also defined. Obviously,

$$
D(Y, \tilde{X}) \leq D(X, Y) + D(X, \tilde{X}). \tag{2}
$$

The task of a DAC decoder is in fact to find a path X' that minimizes $D(Y, \tilde{X})$, i.e.

$$
X' = \arg \min_{\tilde{X}} D(Y, \tilde{X}). \tag{3}
$$

However, this is not always followed by $D(X, X') = 0$. If $D(X, X') \neq 0$, then a decoding failure occurs. To find the probability of decoding failure, we need to know the distribution of $D(Y, \tilde{X})$ and $D(X, \tilde{X})$.

Though it is very difficult to find the distribution of $D(Y, \tilde{X})$ and $D(X, \tilde{X})$, this problem can be tackled by means of DAC codeword distribution. As shown in [16], if we know codeword distributions along proper and wrong decoding paths, it seems promising to find the number of possible decoding paths and the distribution of $D(Y, \tilde{X})$ and $D(X, \tilde{X})$.

The rest of this paper makes some advances on DAC codeword distribution along proper decoding paths.

3   Problem Formulation

To simplify the analysis, we consider an infinite-length, stationary, and equiprobable binary source $X = \{x_i\}_{i=1}^{\infty}$. As $p = 0.5$, symbols $x_i = 0$ and $x_i = 1$ correspond to sub-intervals $[0, q)$ and $[1 - q, 1)$ respectively, where $q = 0.5^{\gamma}$. The resulting rate $R = \gamma H(X) = \gamma$.

Let C_X be the DAC codeword of X and $f(u)$ $(0 \le u < 1)$ be the distribution of C_X, then

$$\int_0^1 f(u)du = 1. \tag{4}$$

Due to the symmetry, we have

$$f(u) = f(1 - u), \quad 0 < u < 1. \tag{5}$$

Symbols $x_1 = 0$ and $x_1 = 1$ correspond to intervals $[0, q)$ and $[1 - q, 1)$, respectively. If $x_1 = 0$, the remaining sequence $X_2 = \{x_i\}_{i=2}^{\infty}$ will be iteratively mapped onto the sub-intervals of $[0, q)$; If $x_1 = 1$, X_2 will be iteratively mapped onto the sub-intervals of $[1 - q, 1)$. Let $C_{X_2}^0$ be the DAC codeword of X_2 given $x_1 = 0$ and $f_0(u)$ be the distribution of $C_{X_2}^0$, then

$$\int_0^q f_0(u)du = 1. \tag{6}$$

Since X is infinite-length and stationary, $f_0(u)$ must have the same shape as $f(u)$, i.e.,

$$f_0(u) = f(u/q)/q, \quad 0 \le u < q. \tag{7}$$

Similarly, let $C_{X_2}^1$ be the DAC codeword of X_2 given $x_1 = 1$ and $f_1(u)$ be the distribution of $C_{X_2}^1$, then

$$f_1(u) = f_0(u - (1 - q)) = f(\frac{u - (1 - q)}{q})/q, \quad (1 - q) \le u < 1. \tag{8}$$

Due to the symmetry,

$$f_1(u) = f_0(1 - u). \tag{9}$$

The relations between $f(u)$, $f_0(u)$ and $f_1(u)$ can be illustrated by Fig. 1. Obviously,

$$f(u) = \Pr(x_1 = 0)f_0(u) + \Pr(x_1 = 1)f_1(u) = (f_0(u) + f_1(u))/2. \tag{10}$$

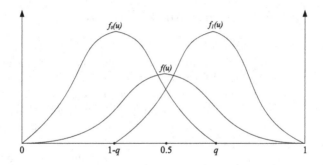

Fig. 1. Illustrations of the relations between $f(u), f_0(u)$ and $f_1(u)$

In [16], we know that $(\sqrt{5}-1)/2$ and $1/\sqrt{2}$ are two watersheds in the interval $(0.5, 1)$ of q. Below the properties of $f(u)$ in different sub-intervals will be analyzed.

A.   When $q = 0.5$, it is the classic AC. Then

$$f(u) = \begin{cases} f(2u), & 0 \le u < 0.5 \\ f(2u - 1), & 0.5 \le u < 1 \end{cases}. \tag{11}$$

This is a uniform distribution, so the classic AC can achieve source entropy theoretically.

B.   When $0.5 < q < 1$, $f(u)$ is a piecewise-defined function, sub-intervals $[0, q)$ and $[1 - q, 1)$ are partially overlapped.

(1) $0 \le u < (1 - q)$: In this interval, $f_1(u) = 0$, so

$$f(u) = f_0(u)/2 = f(u/q)/(2q). \tag{12}$$

(2) $q \le u < 1$: In this interval, $f_0(u) = 0$, so

$$f(u) = f_1(u)/2 = f(\frac{u - (1 - q)}{q})/(2q). \tag{13}$$

(3) $1 - q \le u < q$: In this interval, we have

$$f(u) = \frac{f(\frac{u}{q}) + f(\frac{u-(1-q)}{q})}{2q}. \tag{14}$$

C.   when $q = 1/\sqrt{2}$, it is the closed form of $f(u)$, In [16], only one closed form is obtained at $q = 1/\sqrt{2}$ (i.e. $\gamma = 0.5$)

In addition, it is proved in [16] that when $0.5 < q \le \frac{\sqrt{5}-1}{2}$ (corresponds to $0.6942 \le \gamma < 1$), $f(\frac{q^n}{q+1}) = f(1 - \frac{q^n}{q+1}) = 0, \forall n \in \mathbb{N}$.

4   Polynomial Approximation at Low Rates

Though a special closed form of $f(u)$ is found for $p = \gamma = 0.5$ in [16], the procedure is very complex. As a universal approach for solving this problem, [17] proposes a numeric method for finding $f(u)$.

However, it was affirmed in [16] that $f(u)$ is a smooth function when $q \geq 1/\sqrt{2}$, i.e. $R \leq 0.5$. This property suggests that polynomials may be good approximation to $f(u)$ at low rates ($R \leq 0.5$). Below we propose polynomial approximation to $f(u)$ for $1/\sqrt{2} \leq q < 1$.

To simplify the analysis, we exploit the symmetry and consider only the left half of $f(u)$

$$f(u) = \begin{cases} f(u/q)/(2q), & 0 \leq u \leq (1-q) \\ \frac{f(\frac{u}{q})+f(\frac{u-(1-q)}{q})}{2q}, & (1-q) \leq u \leq 0.5 \end{cases}. \tag{15}$$

We rewrite (15) as

$$f(u) = \begin{cases} 2qf(qu), & 0 \leq u \leq v_1 \\ 2qf(qu) - f(u - v_1), & v_1 \leq u \leq 0.5 \end{cases}. \tag{16}$$

where $v_n = (1-q)/q^n$, $n \in \mathbb{N}$. Note that $v_1 < 0.5$ when $q \geq 1/\sqrt{2}$. Hence, $f(u)$ is a piecewise-defined function over interval $[0, 0.5]$.

At first, in sub-interval $[0, v_1]$, $f(u)$ can be obtained by solving functional equation $f(u) = 2qf(qu)$ [18]

$$f(u) = \phi(u) = \Theta(u)u^\lambda, \quad 0 \leq u \leq v_1, \tag{17}$$

where $\lambda = (1-\gamma)/\gamma$ and $\Theta(u) = \Theta(uq^k)$, $\forall k \in \mathbb{Z}$.

Then, we need to determine $f(u)$ in sub-interval $[v_1, 0.5]$. Because $qu < u$ and $u - v_1 < u$, it is possible to recursively map sub-interval $[v_1, 0.5]$ onto sub-interval $[0, v_1]$ by scaling down or shifting u, over which $f(u)$ has been given by (17), i.e.

$$\begin{cases} f(qu) = \phi(qu), & v_1 \leq u \leq v_2 \\ f(u - v_1) = \phi(u - v_1), & v_1 \leq u \leq 2v_1 \end{cases}. \tag{18}$$

This is the key to solving this problem.

Due to $(u - v_1) - qu = (1 - q)(u - 1/q) < 0$, i.e. $u - v_1 < qu$ for $u \in [v_1, 0.5]$. Hence,

$$f(u) = 2qf(qu) - \phi(u - v_1), \quad v_1 \leq u \leq 2v_1. \tag{19}$$

On solving $2v_1 = 0.5$, we obtain $q = 0.8$. Hereinafter, to facilitate our description, we divide interval $1/\sqrt{2} \leq q < 1$ into two sub-intervals $1/\sqrt{2} \leq q \leq 0.8$ (corresponding to $0.5 \leq 2v_1$) and $0.8 < q < 1$ (corresponding to $2v_1 < 0.5$) (Fig. 2).

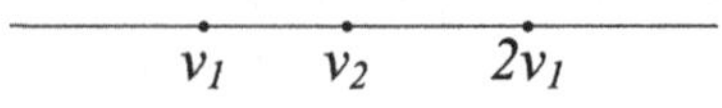

$$v_1 \qquad v_2 \qquad 2v_1$$

Fig. 2. Illustrations of v_1, v_2 and $2v_1$ in the interval $[0, 1]$

4.1 $1/\sqrt{2} \leq q \leq 0.8$

In this sub-interval, since $0.5 \leq 2v_1$, we have

$$f(u) = \begin{cases} \phi(u), & 0 \leq u \leq v_1 \\ 2qf(qu) - \phi(u - v_1), & v_1 \leq u \leq 0.5 \end{cases}. \tag{20}$$

Hence, we need to consider only the term $2qf(qu)$. Depending on the relations between v_n and 0.5, this sub-interval can be further divided into three smaller sub-intervals.

(1) $0.5 \leq v_2$: On solving $v_2 = 0.5$, we obtain $q = \sqrt{3} - 1$, so this sub-interval corresponds to $1/\sqrt{2} \leq q \leq \sqrt{3} - 1$. Since $0.5 \leq v_2$, we have $qu \leq v_1$ for $u \in [v_1, 0.5]$, i.e. $f(qu) = \phi(qu)$. Remember $\phi(u) \equiv 2q\phi(qu)$. Thus

$$f(u) = \begin{cases} \phi(u), & 0 \leq u \leq v_1 \\ \phi(u) - \phi(u - v_1), & v_1 \leq u \leq 0.5 \end{cases}. \tag{21}$$

As affirmed in [16], $f(u)$ is a smooth function for $q \geq 1/\sqrt{2}$. Hence we approximate $\Theta(u)$ by a const c and then obtain

$$f(u) \approx \begin{cases} cu^\lambda, & 0 \leq u \leq v_1 \\ cu^\lambda - c(u - v_1)^\lambda, & v_1 \leq u \leq 0.5 \end{cases}. \tag{22}$$

Now we need to determine c. Let us integrate $f(u)$ over interval $[0, 0.5]$

$$\int_0^{0.5} f(u)du = c\left(\int_0^{0.5} u^\lambda du - \int_{v_1}^{0.5} (u - v_1)^\lambda du\right)$$
$$= \frac{c(u^{\lambda+1}|_0^{0.5} - (u - v_1)^{\lambda+1}|_{v_1}^{0.5})}{\lambda + 1}$$
$$= \frac{c(0.5^{\lambda+1} - (0.5 - v_1)^{\lambda+1})}{\lambda + 1} = 0.5. \tag{23}$$

Thus,

$$c = \frac{0.5(\lambda + 1)}{0.5^{\lambda+1} - (0.5 - v_1)^{\lambda+1}}. \tag{24}$$

Due to $\lambda + 1 = 1/\gamma$,

$$c = \frac{1}{2\gamma(0.5^{(1/\gamma)} - (0.5 - v_1)^{(1/\gamma)})}. \tag{25}$$

(2) $v_2 < 0.5 \leq v_3$: On solving $v_3 = 0.5$, we obtain $q \approx 0.77$, so this sub-interval corresponds to $\sqrt{3} - 1 < q \leq 0.77$. At first, it can be obtained directly

$$f(u) = \begin{cases} \phi(u), & 0 \leq u \leq v_1 \\ \phi(u) - \phi(u - v_1), & v_1 \leq u \leq v_2 \end{cases}. \tag{26}$$

Then, for $u \in [v_2, 0.5]$, we have $qu \in [v_1, v_2]$, i.e. $f(qu) = \phi(qu) - \phi(qu - v_1)$. Thus

$$
\begin{aligned}
f(u) &= 2qf(qu) - \phi(u - v_1) \\
&= 2q(\phi(qu) - \phi(qu - v_1)) - \phi(u - v_1), \quad v_2 \le u \le 0.5.
\end{aligned} \tag{27}
$$

Because $2q\phi(qu - v_1) = 2q\phi(q(u - v_2)) = \phi(u - v_2)$, we obtain

$$
f(u) = \phi(u) - \sum_{i=1}^{2} \phi(u - v_i), \quad v_2 \le u \le 0.5. \tag{28}
$$

Therefore, we can obtain the following approximation

$$
f(u) \approx \begin{cases}
cu^\lambda, & 0 \le u \le v_1 \\
cu^\lambda - c(u - v_1)^\lambda, & v_1 \le u \le v_2 \\
cu^\lambda - c\sum_{i=1}^{2}(u - v_i)^\lambda, & v_2 \le u \le 0.5
\end{cases}, \tag{29}
$$

where

$$
c = \frac{1}{2\gamma(0.5^{(1/\gamma)} - \sum_{i=1}^{2}(0.5 - v_i)^{(1/\gamma)})}. \tag{30}
$$

(3) $v_3 < 0.5 \le v_4$: On solving $v_4 = 0.5$, we obtain $q \approx 0.8$, so this sub-interval corresponds to $0.77 < q \le 0.8$. By iterations, we can obtain

$$
f(u) \approx \begin{cases}
cu^\lambda, & 0 \le u \le v_1 \\
cu^\lambda - c(u - v_1)^\lambda, & v_1 \le u \le v_2 \\
cu^\lambda - c\sum_{i=3}^{2}(u - v_i)^\lambda, & v_2 \le u \le v_3 \\
cu^\lambda - c\sum_{i=1}^{3}(u - v_i)^\lambda, & v_3 \le u \le 0.5
\end{cases}, \tag{31}
$$

where

$$
c = \frac{1}{2\gamma(0.5^{(1/\gamma)} - \sum_{i=1}^{3}(0.5 - v_i)^{(1/\gamma)})}. \tag{32}
$$

4.2 $0.8 < q < 1$

The problem becomes very complex in this sub-interval because $f(u - v_1) = \phi(u - v_1)$ does not hold for $u \in [2v_1, 0.5]$ so that we need to deal with not only $2qf(qu)$ but also $f(u - v_1)$.

Let us consider a simple case first, i.e. $v_1 < 0.5 - v_1 \le v_2$, which corresponds to sub-interval $0.8 < q \le \sqrt{2/3}$. We have $u - v_1 \in [v_1, v_2]$ for $u \in [2v_1, 0.5]$. Hence

$$
f(u - v_1) = \phi(u - v_1) - \phi(u - 2v_1), \quad 2v_1 \le u \le 0.5. \tag{33}
$$

Therefore, the problem becomes

$$
f(u) = \begin{cases}
2qf(qu), & 0 \le u \le v_1 \\
2qf(qu) - \phi(u - v_1), & v_1 \le u \le 2v_1 \\
2qf(qu) - (\phi(u - v_1) - \phi(u - 2v_1)), & 2v_1 \le u \le 0.5
\end{cases}. \tag{34}
$$

Now we need to deal with only $2qf(qu)$, which has been discussed in detail in Sect. 4.1.

For $\sqrt{2/3} < q < 1$, the idea is the same but the procedure becomes more and more complicated as q increases. Therefore, at very low rates, polynomial approximation is not a good choice.

4.3   Simulation Results

Some examples of polynomial approximation have been included in Fig. 3. In the simulation, set numerical approximation parameters $N = 10^5$ and $\delta = 10^{-10}$. Considering the complexity, only the results for $1/\sqrt{2} \leq q \leq 0.8$ are reported. Figure 3 shows that in general, the curves of polynomial approximation fit those of numeric approximation very well. Especially, as q increases, the curves of polynomial approximation almost coincide with those of numeric approximation.

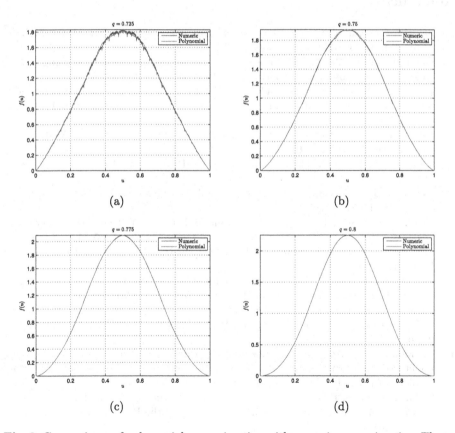

Fig. 3. Comparisons of polynomial approximation with numeric approximation. These results show that polynomial approximation fits numeric approximation very well. Especially, as q increases, polynomial approximation almost coincides with numeric approximation. (a) $q = 0.725$. (b) $q = 0.75$. (c) $q = 0.775$. (d) $q = 0.8$.

In addition, Fig. 3(a) also shows the affirmation in [16] may fail because $q > 1/\sqrt{2}$ does not guarantee smooth $f(u)$. Nevertheless, $f(u)$ does become less irregular as q increases.

5   Conclusion

This paper proposes a polynomial approximation method for DAC codeword distribution of equiprobable binary sources along proper decoding paths. The polynomial approximation fits those of numeric approximation very well.

However, when $0.8 < q < 1$, the polynomial approximation becomes very complicated as q increases. So, the future research direction is to find a simpler approximation method in this interval.

References

1. Slepian, D., Wolf, J.K.: Noiseless coding of correlated information sources. IEEE Trans. Inf. Theory **19**(4), 471–480 (1973)
2. Garcia-Frias, J., Zhao, Y.: Compression of correlated binary sources using turbo codes. IEEE Commun. Lett. **5**(10), 417–419 (2001)
3. Liveris, A., Xiong, Z., Georghiades, C.: Compression of binary sources with side information at the decoder using LDPC codes. IEEE Commun. Lett. **6**(10), 440–442 (2002)
4. Rissanen, J.: Generalized Kraft inequality and arithmetic coding. IBM J. Rese. Dev. **20**(3), 198–203 (1976)
5. Rissanen, J., Langdon, G.: Arithmetic coding. IBM J. Res. Dev. **23**(2), 149–162 (1979)
6. Rissanen, J.J.: Arithmetic codings as number representations. Acta Polytech. Scand. **31**, 44–51 (1979)
7. Boyd, C., Cleary, J.G., Irvine, S.A., Rinsma-Melchert, I., Witten, I.H.: Integrating error detection into arithmetic coding. IEEE Trans. Commun. **45**(1), 1–3 (1997)
8. Grangetto, M., Magli, E., Olmo, G.: Distributed arithmetic coding. IEEE Commun. Lett. **11**(11), 883–885 (2007)
9. Grangetto, M., Magli, E., Olmo, G.: Distributed arithmetic coding for the Slepian-Wolf problem. IEEE Trans. Signal Process. **57**(6), 2245–2257 (2009)
10. Artigas, X., Malinowski, S., Guillemot, C., Torres, L.: Overlapped quasi-arithmetic codes for distributed video coding. In: Proceedings of the IEEE ICIP, vol. 2, no. 2, pp. 9–12 (2007)
11. Malinowski, S., Artigas, X., Guillemot, C., Torres, L.: Distributed coding using punctured quasi-arithmetic codes for memory and memoryless sources. In: Proceedings of the IEEE PCS, Chicago, IL (2009)
12. Sodagar, I., Chai, B.B., Wus, J.: A new error resilience technique for image compression using arithmetic coding. In: Proceedings of the IEEE ICASSP, pp. 2127–2130 (2000)
13. Grangetto, M., Magli, E., Olmo, G.: Symmetric distributed arithmetic coding of correlated sources. In: Proceedings of the IEEE MMSP, pp. 111–114 (2007)
14. Grangetto, M., Magli, E., Tron, R., Olmo, G.: Rate-compatible distributed arithmetic coding. IEEE Commun. Lett. **12**(8), 575–577 (2008)

15. Grangetto, M., Magli, E., Olmo, G.: Decoder-driven adaptive distributed arithmetic coding. In: Proceedings of the IEEE ICIP, pp. 1128–1131 (2008)
16. Fang, Y.: Distribution of distributed arithmetic codewords for equiprobable binary sources. IEEE Signal Process. Lett. **16**(12), 1079–1082 (2009)
17. Fang, Y.: DAC spectrum of binary sources with equally-likely symbols. IEEE Trans. Commun. **61**(4), 1584–1594 (2013)
18. http://eqworld.ipmnet.ru/en/solutions/fe/fe1111.pdf

Research on Multi-UAV Swarm Control Based on Olfati-Saber Algorithm with Variable Speed Virtual Leader

Yanqi Jing[(✉)]

Beihang University, 37 College Road, Beijing, China
jingyq.hi@163.com

Abstract. The high efficiency of control between multiple drones has become a hot topic of research nowadays. Due to the increased demand for combat operations and the increasing number of drones, the efficiency of control between multiple drones has become a hot research topic. Drawing on the principles of some communication in swarm intelligence, it is of great significance for realizing the autonomous cooperative control between UAVs. Learning from the Olfati-Saber algorithm, this paper proposes an optimized algorithm with virtual leaders, in order to make the group speed converge faster and more stable. Then, this paper also shows the impact of variable-speed virtual leaders on complex drone communication systems. Subsequently, two models are simply analyzed and compared with each other in the article. Through the simulation, we prove the effectiveness of certain variable speed virtual leaders for decentralized clusters of complex UAV systems, which improves the application of Olfati-Saber model in practice.

Keywords: Complex UAV network · Variable speed virtual leaders · Swarm intelligence

1 Introduction

Collection Intelligence refers to a group of animals living in groups in nature, which are intelligent behaviors in daily life and actions that are affected by communication between individuals and affect group traits. In nature, bee swarms, ant swarms, wild wolf swarms, bird swarms, geese swarms, fish swarms, etc. are all similar to this rely on the communication between individuals through the layer-by-layer transmission, and thus affect the direction of the entire group, and maintain the formation of the entire group. Once encountering special circumstances, such as obstacles, or natural enemies and other situations that require a change of direction, they can still keep all individuals of the entire group moving forward at a common speed and a common formation.

This work was supported in part by the National Key Research and Development Program (Grant Nos. 2016YFB1200100), and the National Natural Science Foundation of China (NSFC) (Grant Nos. 61827901 and 91738301).

Flocking is used to describe this kind of phenomenon that can quickly affect the group through the exchange of information between a small number of individuals without knowing the status of the group. At the same time, the exchange of information between a few individuals, the strong resistance to environmental noise, and the rapid transformation of group behavior is also an indispensable part of the swarming behavior. Such a magical natural phenomenon has attracted a lot of interest from scholars all over the world. Scholars in biology, computer, physics and other fields have conducted modeling and simulation research in this field, which has further promoted the richness of swarm intelligence algorithms [1, 2].

In 2006, Olfati-Saber innovatively proposed three algorithms. Saber's first algorithm was designed with reference to the three principles in the Boid model, but it does not guarantee that every individual in the group can form a bee colony and move forward together. Saber's second algorithm proposes a swarming algorithm with virtual leaders, which solves the problem of poor clustering effect and the inability to form a stable bee colony in the past. Saber's third algorithm is based on the second algorithm, and more practically considers the situation that contains obstacles, and realizes the intelligent obstacle avoidance of the bee colony in the simulation algorithm [3]. The Saber algorithm provides a profound reference value for many subsequent scholars to study swarm intelligence, and promotes the progress of algorithms in the field of swarm intelligence [4–12].

The structure of this article is summarized as follows: The first chapter introduces the background and source of the subject. Section 2 introduces the system model of swarm intelligence. Section 3 presents the Olfati-Saber second algorithm model. At the same time, the formation of a virtual leader with variable speed was also proposed. By comparing the different results of several simulations, the advantages and disadvantages of the variable speed virtual leader are analyzed in Sect. 4. Finally reached the conclusion of this article.

2 Multi-agent-Aware Network Model

Drawing on the knowledge of graph theory, we define the graph $G(t) = \{v, \varepsilon(t), A(t)\}$ in the algorithm by the vertex set $V = \{v_1, v_2, \ldots, v_n\}$ and the edge set $E(t) = \{\varepsilon_1(t), \varepsilon_2(t), \ldots, \varepsilon_m(t)\}$. The adjacency matrix is $A(t) = [a_{ij}]$. When the value of each element a_{ij} in the adjacency matrix is neither 0 nor 1, the graph $G(t)$ is called a weighted graph.

Assuming that $x_i \in R_m$ ($i \in V$, $m = 2$ or 3) represents the location information of the agent i, it should contain three dimensions in actual situations. According to matrix theory, the position matrix $[x] = col(x_1, x_2, \ldots, x_n)$ is the position matrix of each agent in the figure. Through the position information, the matching of speed information and acceleration information can be completed.

The multi-agent-aware network model is:

$$\begin{cases} \dot{x}_i = v_i \\ \dot{v}_i = a_i \end{cases} \tag{1}$$

Agent perception range: A perceptible range is defined for each agent. This range is a geometric sphere with the agent as the center of the sphere and a radius of r. The geometry of its perception range is expressed as

$$N_i = \{j \in v : \|x_i - x_j\| < r\} \tag{2}$$

3   Optimized Olfati-Saber Algorithm

3.1   Olfati-Saber Second Algorithm

Gradient Expressed with σ Norm. The σ norm is a mapping from R_m to $R \geq 0$, the mathematical definition of the σ norm and its gradient morphology is

$$\|z\|_\sigma = \frac{1}{\varepsilon}\left[\sqrt{1 + \varepsilon\|z\|^2} - 1\right] \tag{3}$$

$$\sigma_\xi = \frac{z}{\sqrt{1 + \varepsilon\|z\|^2}} = \frac{z}{1 + \varepsilon\|z\|_\sigma} \tag{4}$$

where ε is a non-negative parameter that can be set.

Collision Function and Adjacency Matrix. The collision function is a typical scalar function with a domain between [0, 1] and a smooth function. The mathematical expression of the collision function is as follow

$$\rho h(z) = \begin{cases} 1, z \in [0, h) \\ \frac{1}{2}[1 + \cos(\pi\frac{z-h}{1-h})], z \in [h, 1) \\ 0, \text{others} \end{cases} \tag{5}$$

It can be seen from the expression that when $h = 1$, the collision function is a constant function, that is, the value in the interval [0,1] is 1, and the function value in the other intervals is 0.

On this basis, each element in the spatial adjacency matrix $A(x) = [a_{ij}]$ is defined as

$$a_{ij}(x) = \rho h\left(\frac{\|x_j - x_i\|}{r_\alpha}\right) \in [0, 1], j \neq i \tag{6}$$

Potential Energy Function. In order to describe a complete and smooth potential energy function, a force equation $\Phi_\alpha(z)$ is integrated here. According to the definition of the perception range of the agent, the function value of $\Phi_\alpha(z)$ is 0 when the perception range exceeds $z \geq r_\alpha$. In the perception range of the agent, the mathematical expression of the force equation is

$$\varphi_\alpha(z) = \rho h(\frac{z}{r_\alpha})\varphi(z - d_\alpha) \tag{7}$$

$$\varphi(z) = \frac{1}{2}[(a+b)\sigma_1(z+c) + (z-b)] \tag{8}$$

And due to $0 < a < b$, $c = |a-b|/\sqrt{4ab}$, $\Phi(0) = 0$.

It is precisely because of the possible existence of "squadrons" that Saber's second algorithm was born. The algorithm pre-sets a virtual leader with a fixed speed. All other agents in the group need to follow this virtual leader and the team needs to advance together with a geometric structure similar to α lattice. In the mathematical model, the algorithm has been simply improved on the basis of Saber's first algorithm. In addition to the gradient and speed feedback items, the acceleration input also adds navigation feedback items to reflect the role of the fixed speed virtual leader. The new acceleration input is expressed as follows

$$a_i^\alpha = \sum_{j \in N_i} \varphi_\alpha(\|x_j - x_i\|_\sigma)n_{ij} + \sum_{j \in N_i} a_{ij}(x)(v_j - v_i) + f_i^r(x_i, v_i, x_r, v_r) \tag{9}$$

Among them, $f_i^r(x_i, v_i, x_r, v_r)$ is a newly added navigation feedback item, and its mathematical expansion is

$$f_i^r(x_i, v_i, x_r, v_r) = -c_1(x_i - x_r) - c_2(v_i - v_r), c_1 > 0, c_2 > 0 \tag{10}$$

Among them, c_1, c_2 are two non-negative constants. x_r represents the position information of the virtual leader, and v_r represents the speed information of the virtual leader.

3.2   Olfati-Saber Model with Variable Speed Virtual Leader

In order to stabilize and converge the optimized shift leader model, a more complete set of theories must be used to prove and further optimize. In this paper, each agent (including the virtual leader) in the group is subjected to the same form of acceleration input, which can not only ensure the stability of the entire model, but also make the entire movement process convergence speed become faster.

The principle is to input acceleration to the virtual leader in the same form on the basis of the second algorithm of Olfati-Saber. Since the virtual leader itself does not need to be led by itself, the acceleration input of the virtual leader becomes

$$a_i^\alpha = \sum_{j \in N_i} \varphi_\alpha(\|x_j - x_i\|_\sigma)n_{ij} + \sum_{j \in N_i} a_{ij}(x)(x_j - x_i) \tag{11}$$

4 Simulation Results

The number of drones set by simulation is 50, of which the parameter settings are $\varepsilon = 0.1$, $h = 0.9$, $c_1 = 0.1$, $c_2 = 0.2$. The simulation time interval is set to 0.1 s, a total of 1000 cycles. By randomly generating the position and initial speed of the drone, each agent is clustered after each iteration through successive calculations. The blue circle in the figure represents the agent, and the red arrow represents the current direction of the agent. Since the position information and speed information of each simulation are randomly generated, only the results of a certain simulation are shown here.

4.1 Olfati-Saber Second Algorithm

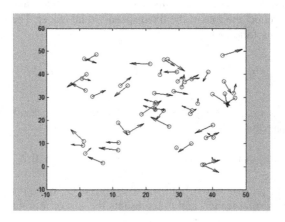

Fig. 1. UAV space arrangement based on Olfati-Saber second algorithm ($t = 0$)

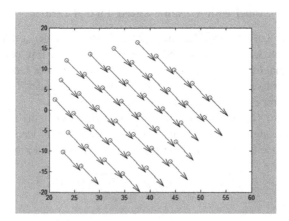

Fig. 2. UAV space arrangement based on Olfati-Saber second algorithm ($t = 1000$)

The speed direction is expressed by the unit vector of speed information, so the range of values in the figure is $[-1, 1]$. Figure 3 shows the x-direction agent's speed following situation, and Fig. 4 shows the y-direction agent's speed following situation. The red horizontal line in the figure represents the speed of the virtual leader at a fixed speed, and the other blue curves represent the speed changes of the remaining 49 agents (Figs. 1 and 2).

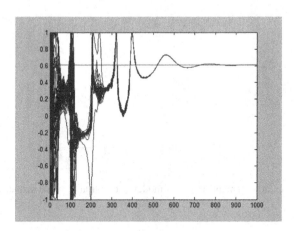

Fig. 3. X-direction agent speed following based on Olfati-Saber second algorithm

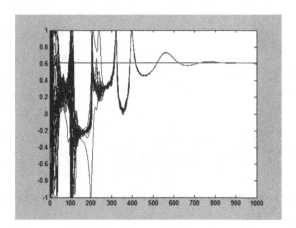

Fig. 4. Y-direction agent speed following based on Olfati-Saber second algorithm

4.2   Olfati-Saber Model Based on Variable Speed Virtual Leader

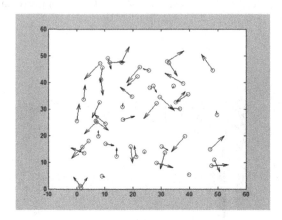

Fig. 5. UAV space arrangement based on model with variable speed virtual leader (t = 0)

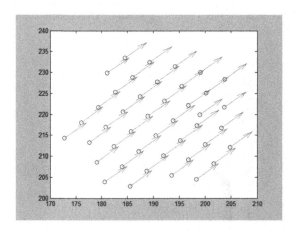

Fig. 6. UAV space arrangement based on model with variable speed virtual leader (t = 1000)

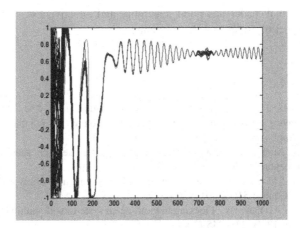

Fig. 7. X-direction agent speed following based on model with variable speed virtual leader

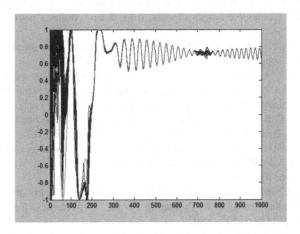

Fig. 8. Y-direction agent speed following based on model with variable speed virtual leader

Through simulation, we can find that the efficiency of the variable speed virtual leader algorithm is much higher than that of the fixed speed virtual leader, and the calculation convergence is fast. It can be seen from the situation that the speed of the agent follows, although the speed of the virtual leader is constantly changing, other agents can still quickly change the direction of the speed (Figs. 5, 6, 7 and 8).

5 Conclusion

In this paper, we proposed an optimized Olfati-Saber algorithm in order to make the group speed converge faster. With the variable speed virtual leader, the new system model is more efficient than before, which proves that the Olfati-Saber algorithm of the variable speed virtual leader has good feasibility and effectiveness, and expands the application prospect of complex UAV systems.

References

1. Chaves-Gonzalez, J.M., Vega-Rodriguez, M.A., Granado-Criado, J.M.: A multiobjective swarm intelligence approach based on artificial bee colony for reliable DNA sequence design. Eng. Appl. Artif. Intell. **26**(9), 2045–2057 (2013)
2. Ok, C., Lee, S., Kumara, S.: Group preference modeling for intelligent shared environments: social welfare beyond the sum. Inf. Sci. **278**, 588–598 (2014)
3. Olfati-Saber, R.: Flocking for multi-agent dynamic systems: algorithms and theory. IEEE Trans. Autom. Control **51**(3), 401–420 (2006)
4. Su, H., Wang, X.F., Yang, W.: Flocking in multi-agent systems with multiple virtual leaders. Asian J. Control **10**(2), 238–245 (2008)
5. Luo, X.Y., Li, S.B., Guan, X.P.: Flocking algorithm with multi-target tracking for multi-agent systems. Pattern Recogn. Lett. **31**(9), 800–805 (2010)
6. Shi, G.D., Hong, Y.G., Johansson, K.H.: Connectivity and set tracking of multi-agent systems guided bu multiple moving leaders. IEEE Trans. Autom. Control **57**(3), 663–676 (2012)
7. Liu, J., Ren, X.M., Ma, H.B.: Adaptive swarm optimization for locating and tracking multiple targets. Appl. Soft Comput. **12**(11), 3656–3670 (2012)
8. Hutchison, M.G.: A method for estimating range requirements of tactical reconnaissance UAVs. In: AIAA's 1st Technical Conference and Workshop on Unmanned Aerospace Vehicles, Portsmouth, Virginia, pp. 120–124 (2002)
9. Szczerba, R.J., Galkowski, P., Glicktein, I.S., et al.: Robust algorithm for real-time route planning. IEEE Trans. Aerosp. Electron. Syst. **36**(3), 869–878 (2000)
10. Jevtić A, Andina D, Jaimes A., et al.: Unmanned aerial vehicle route optimization using ant system algorithm. In: 2010 5th International Conference on System of Systems Engineering (So SE), pp. 1–6. IEEE (2010)
11. Nygard, K.E., Chandler, P.R., Pachter, M.: Dynamic network flow optimization models for air vehicle resource allocation. In: Proceedings of the 2001 American Control Conference, vol. 3, pp. 1853–1858. IEEE (2001)
12. Wei, L., Wei, Z.: Method of tasks allocation of multi-UAVs based on particles swarm optimization. Control Decis. **25**(9), 1359–1363 (2010)

Resource Joint Allocation Scheme Based on Network Slicing Under C-RAN Architecture

Jiajia Chen[1], Jie Gong[2], Xiang Chen[1(✉)], and Terngyin Hsu[3]

[1] School of Electronics and Information Technology, Sun Yat-sen University,
Guangzhou 510006, China
`chenxiang@mail.sysu.edu.cn`
[2] School of Data and Computer Science, Sun Yat-sen University,
Guangzhou 510006, China
[3] Department of Computer Science, National Chiao Tung University,
Hsinchu, Taiwan

Abstract. The upcoming 5G system is considered not only can meet the demand of various services, but also solve the problem that data will grow explosively. Therefore, we need a viable network architecture to support various service demand and realize resources allocation flexibly. C-RAN was considered to be a promising 5G network architecture. And network slicing, which as a promising technology, can provides customized service according to the various business scenarios of 5G. This paper proposed a joint resources allocation scheme of network slicing that based on C-RAN. The scheme not only combine network slicing with C-RAN, but also solve the problem of joint spectrum and computing resource allocation. This paper model the problem into a MINLP problem. Based on the characteristics of the model, the problem will be decomposed into two subproblems respectively to be solved. In order to verify the proposed model, the other two joint resource allocation scheme will be introduced to compare. The simulation results also illustrate the effectiveness of the proposed scheme.

Keywords: Network slicing · Cloud Radio Access Network (C-RAN) · Resource allocation

1 Introduction

In recent years, the exponential growth in mobile data traffic has been triggered by the increasing use of mobile devices [7]. In addition, 5G not only continue to

This work was supported in part by the State's Key Project of Research and Development Plan under Grants 2019YFE0196400, in part by the NSFC under Grant 61771495, in part by the Guangdong R&D Project in Key Areas under Grant 2019B010158001, and in part by the Guangdong Provincial Special Fund For Modern Agriculture Industry Technology Innovation Teams under Grant 2020KJ122.

© ICST Institute for Computer Sciences, Social Informatics and Telecommunications Engineering 2021
Published by Springer Nature Switzerland AG 2021. All Rights Reserved
B. Li et al. (Eds.): IoTaaS 2020, LNICST 346, pp. 23–35, 2021.
https://doi.org/10.1007/978-3-030-67514-1_3

provide stable and high-quality services for traditional mobile communication, but also provide services for other emerging communication types(e.g.., video conferencing, remote monitoring, and smart homing). Besides, different communication typies have different communication requirements. As a promising technology, network slicing is an end-to-end logical network provisioned with a set of isolated virtual resources on the shared physical infrastructure [5]. Through network slicing technology, operators can flexibly and dynamically allocate network resources into logical network slicing according to users' needs, so as to provide services for different types of businesses. However, the deployment of network slicing requires a flexible and programmable physical network architecture, and Cloud Radio Access Network (C-RAN) is a flexible and programmable physical network architecture.

A typical structure of C-RAN includes three main components: Remote Radio Heads (RRHs), fronthaul links, and Baseband Unit (BBU) pool [9]. RRH is responsible for receiving and transmitting wireless signals, and BBU is responsible for baseband processing. Different from the traditional network architecture, in C-RAN, BBU will be decoupled from RRH and concentrated together to form a BBU resource pool. By decoupling RRH and BBU, resource scheduling can be more flexible and network capacity can be improved. By pooling the BBUs together to form a BBU pool, Capital Expenditure (CAPEX) and Operating Expense (OPEX) can be reduced. Moreover, the fronthaul link connecting RRH and BBU pool is usually make up of high-capacity and low-delay optical fiber, which can significantly improve the network efficiency and spectral efficiency. Based on these advantages, C-RAN has become a prospective architecture for 5G. Therefore, this paper combined the network slicing technique with C-RAN.

The most significant advantage of the C-RAN network architecture is the sharing of resources by pooling the BBU together to form a BBU pool. [11] has designed a joint dynamic radio clustering and cooperative beamforming scheme that maximizes the downlink weighted sum-rate system utility. [6] aims at minimizing the system power consumption by jointly allocating the computing and radio resource under the outage Quality of Service (QoS) constraint. Besides, there are many studies on C-RAN and network slicing. [2] has instantiated the network slice under C-RAN by making use of the Open Air Interface (OAI) platform and a specific Software Defined Network (SDN) controller. In addition, in [3,10,14], the resource optimization problem of network slices under the c-ran network architecture is studied. [3] have study the joint optimal deployment of network slicing and the allocation of computational resources in a hybrid C-RAN architecture by taking into account the requirements of the 5G services and the characteristics of the cloud nodes. In [10], it incorporated two typical 5G services, i.e., enhanced Mobile Broadband (eMBB) and ultra-Reliable Low-Latency Communications (uRLLC), in a C-RAN, which is suitable for RAN slicing due to its high flexibility. [14] propose a two-timescale resource management scheme for network slicing in C-RAN, aiming at maximizing the profit of a tenant.

Based on the C-RAN network architecture, this paper proposes a joint allocation scheme of network slicing. The scheme integrates network slicing technology
into the C-RAN network architecture and considers the joint allocation of spectrum resources and computing resources in network slicing. What's more, the
joint allocation of spectrum resources and computing resources will be modeled as a Mixed-Integer Nonlinear Programming (MINLP) problem, which not
only takes into account the different requirements of different types of slices,
but also takes into account the limitation of transmission rate of fronthaul link
in C-RAN. Based on the characteristics of the proposed scheme, the problem
will be decomposed into two subproblems respectively to solved. What's more,
two joint resource scheme will be introduced to varify the effectiveness of the
proposed scheme. The simulation results show that the proposed scheme can
achieve better resource utilization than the other two schemes, thus verifying
the effectiveness of the proposed scheme.

2   System Model and Problem Formulation

As shown in Fig. 1, it is assumed that in C-RAN network, there is a BBU pool
and several RRHs with a set of $\mathcal{K}$. And the RRHs are distributed in an area
with coverage range of R. In the system, the set of total users is $\mathcal{U}$, and the set
of slices is $\mathcal{N}$. What's more, the set of users of slice n ($n \in \mathcal{N}$) is $\mathcal{U}_n$, and we
have $\sum_{n \in \mathcal{N}} \mathcal{U}_n = \mathcal{U}$. In addition, we define the set of users that connect to RRH

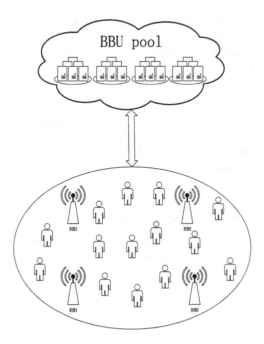

Fig. 1. The system model

k ($k \in \mathcal{K}$) is $\mathcal{U}_k$, and we have $\sum_{k \in \mathcal{K}} \mathcal{U}_k = \mathcal{U}$. Besides, we suppose that the total bandwidth in the network is B, the total computing resources are C, and the limitation of transmission rate of RRH k and the fronthaul link is F_k.

2.1 The Communication Quality Standard of Network Slicing

In this paper, we choose the minimum data transmission rate of users as the communication quality standard of network slicing. We assume that the user u of slice n will connect to the RRH k, then the signal-to-noise ratio (SINR) of the user u is $SINR_{k,u_n}$. According to paper [13], the SINR of user u is

$$SINR_{k,u_n} = \frac{p_k g_{k,u_n}}{\sum_{i \in k, i \neq k} p_i g_{i,u_n} + \sigma^2},$$ (1)

where p_k is transmission power of RRH k, g_{k,u_n} is the channel gain between user k and RRH k, and σ^2 is the white Gaussian noise power. What's more, we assume that b_{k,u_n} is the spectrum resource that allocated to user u. Then according to the Shannon's formula, the spectrum efficiency of the user u is

$$d_{k,u_n} = log_2(1 + SINR_{k,u_n}).$$ (2)

Therefore, the data transmission rate of user u is

$$r_{k,u_n} = a_{k,u_n} b_{k,u_n} d_{k,u_n},$$ (3)

where a_{k,u_n} indicates whether the user u has successfully accessed RRH k. If user u has accessed to the RRH k successfully, then $a_{k,u_n} = 1$, otherwise $a_{k,u_n} = 0$. By defining $r_{n_{min}}$ as the lowest data transmission rate that users of slice n have to satisfy, then we have

$$r_{k,u_n} \geq r_{n_{min}}.$$ (4)

2.2 The Mapping of Computing Resources and Spectrum Resources

The computing resources that consumed in the communication are positively correlated with the spectrum resources that consumed, so the relationship between computing resources and spectrum resources consumed in the system is defined as follow

$$B_{consume} = \omega C_{consume},$$ (5)

where ω is constant. What's more, according to [11] and [8], the computing resources required by users increase with the growth of data transmission rate during the process communication. Therefore, we have

$$c_{k,u_u} = \phi(r_{k,u_n}),$$ (6)

where ϕ is a increasing function.

2.3   The Problem Formulation

In this paper, we aim to maximize the total resource utilization of the network and define the resource utilization as

$$\eta = \frac{r_{sum}}{B_{consume}} = \frac{r_{sum}}{\omega C_{consume}}. \tag{7}$$

Therefore, the resource utilization of this paper is

$$\eta = \frac{\sum_{k \in \mathcal{K}} \sum_{u \in \mathcal{U}_k} r_{k,u_n}}{\beta \sum_{k \in \mathcal{K}} \sum_{u \in \mathcal{U}_k} c_{k,u_n}}. \tag{8}$$

Because the target of this paper is maximizing the total resource utilization, the problem formulation can be expressed as

$$\max_{a_{k,u_n}, b_{k,u_n}, c_{k,u_n}} \eta, \tag{9}$$

s.t.

$$\sum_{k \in \mathcal{K}} \sum_{u \in \mathcal{U}_k} b_{k,u_n} \leq B, \tag{9-1}$$

$$\sum_{k \in \mathcal{K}} \sum_{u \in \mathcal{U}_k} c_{k,u_n} \leq C, \tag{9-2}$$

$$\sum_{u \in \mathcal{U}_k} r_{k,u_n} \leq F_k, \forall k, \tag{9-3}$$

$$r_{k,u_n} \geq r_{n_{min}}, \forall u, \tag{9-4}$$

$$c_{k,u_u} \geq \phi(r_{k,u_n}), \forall u, \tag{9-5}$$

$$\sum_{k \in \mathcal{K}} a_{k,u_n} = 1, a_{k,u_n} \in \{0, 1\}, \forall u. \tag{9-6}$$

Among them, the constraint (9-1) refers that the sum of bandwidth of all the user in the system can not be higher than the total bandwidth of system, constraint (9-2) refers that the sum of computing resource of all the user in the system is not higher than the amount of computing resources in the system, and constraints (9-3) refers that the user's total transmission rate of RRH is not higher than the limitation of the fronthual link. And constraint (9-6) refers that all the users can only connect to one RRH.

3   Joint Resource Allocation Algorithm Based on Network Slice

The problem (9) is a MINLP problem, which can be proved to be a NP-hand problem, so there is no deterministic algorithm to solve it. However, the problem (9) is a multi-variables optimization problem and the variables are correlated. The optimization results of the variables c_{k,u_n} are determined by the optimization results of the variables a_{k,u_n} and b_{k,u_n}. Therefore, this paper will decompose the optimization problem (9) into two sub-problems, including spectrum resource allocation problem and compute resource allocation problem. This two subproblems will be solved by appropriate algorithms respectively.

3.1   The Spectrum Resource Allocation Problem

At first, we assume that variable c_{k,u_n} has been known, then $\beta \sum_{u \in \mathcal{U}} c_{k,u_n}$ can be viewed as a constant. Therefore, the spectrum resource allocation problem can be separated from the problem (9) and expressed as

$$\max_{a_{k,u_n}, b_{k,u_n}} \sum_{k \in \mathcal{K}} \sum_{u \in \mathcal{U}_k} r_{k,u_n}, \tag{10}$$

s.t.

$$\sum_{k \in \mathcal{K}} \sum_{u \in \mathcal{U}_k} b_{k,u_n} \leq B, \tag{10-1}$$

$$\sum_{u \in \mathcal{U}_k} r_{k,u_n} \leq F_k, \forall k, \tag{10-2}$$

$$r_{k,u_n} \geq r_{n,min}, \forall u, \tag{10-3}$$

$$\sum_{k \in \mathcal{K}} a_{k,u_n} = 1, \forall u. \tag{10-4}$$

After decomposition, the subproblem is still a MINLP problem. If the exhaustive search method is used as the solution to this problem, the optimal allocation scheme of spectrum resources needs $|\mathcal{U}|^{|\mathcal{K}|}$ times. [12] has studied the nonconvex optimization of multicarrier system spectrum allocation problem. It has found that when the optimization problem satisfied time sharing conditions, even if the problem is a non-convex optimization problem, the optimum solution of original problem and its dual problem will be the same. Therefore, we apply dual decomposition to solve the spectrum resource allocation problem.

Firstly, the Lagrangian function of (10) is obtained as follows

$$
\begin{aligned}
L(a,&b,\alpha,\beta,\gamma)\\
&= \sum_{k\in\mathcal{K}}\sum_{u\in\mathcal{U}_k} a_{k,u_n}b_{k,u_n}d_{k,u_n} + \alpha(B - \sum_{u\in\mathcal{U}}b_{k,u_n})\\
&+ \sum_{k\in\mathcal{K}}\sum_{u\in\mathcal{U}_k} \gamma_{k,u_n}(a_{k,u_n}b_{k,u_n}c_{k,u_n} - r_{n,min})\\
&+ \sum_{k\in\mathcal{K}}\beta_k(F_k - \sum_{u\in\mathcal{U}_k}a_{k,u_n}b_{k,u_n}d_{k,u_n})\\
&= \sum_{k\in\mathcal{K}}\sum_{u\in\mathcal{U}_k}[a_{k,u_n}(b_{k,u_n}d_{k,u_n} - \beta_k b_{k,u_n}d_{k,u_n}\\
&+ \gamma_{k,u_n}b_{k,u_n}d_{k,u_n}) - \alpha b_{k,u_n}] + \alpha B\\
&- \sum_{k\in\mathcal{K}}\sum_{u\in\mathcal{U}_k}\gamma_{k,u_n}r_{n,min} + \sum_{k\in\mathcal{K}}\beta_k F_k\\
&= \sum_{k\in\mathcal{K}} L_k(a_{k,u_n}, b_{k,u_n}, \alpha, \beta_k, \gamma_{k,u_n}) + \alpha B\\
&+ \sum_{k\in\mathcal{K}}\beta_k F_k - \sum_{k\in\mathcal{K}}\sum_{u\in\mathcal{U}_k}\gamma_{k,u_n}r_{n,min} \qquad (11)
\end{aligned}
$$

where α, β_k and η_{k,u_n} is the dual variables of the constraint in problem (10). What's more, we define

$$
\begin{aligned}
L_k(a,&b,\alpha,\beta,\gamma)\\
&= \sum_{u\in\mathcal{U}_k}[a_{k,u_n}(b_{k,u_n}d_{k,u_n} - \beta_k b_{k,u_n}d_{k,u_n} + \gamma_{k,u_n}b_{k,u_n}d_{k,u_n})] - \alpha b_{k,u_n}.
\end{aligned}
$$

Then, the dual problem of problem(10) is

$$
\begin{aligned}
&\min_{\alpha,\beta,\gamma} g(\alpha,\beta,\gamma)\\
&s.t \quad \alpha \geq 0, \beta \geq 0, \gamma \geq 0
\end{aligned} \qquad (12)
$$

For convenience, the dual problem can be expressed specifically as follow

$$
\begin{aligned}
g(\alpha,&\beta,\gamma)\\
&= \max_{a,b}\sum_{k\in\mathcal{K}} L_k(a,b,\alpha,\beta,\gamma) - \sum_{k\in\mathcal{K}}\sum_{u\in\mathcal{U}_k}\gamma_{k,u_n}r_{n,min} + \alpha B + \sum_{k\in\mathcal{K}}\beta_k F_k \quad (13)
\end{aligned}
$$

When the dual variable are known, $\gamma_{k,u_n}r_{n,min}$, αB and $\beta_k F_k$ can be viewed as constants. Thus, the dual problem can be decomposed into K sub-problems

$$
\begin{aligned}
g_k(\alpha,&\beta,\gamma)\\
&= \max_{a,b} L_k(a,b,\alpha,\beta,\gamma)\\
&= \max_{a,b}\sum_{u\in\mathcal{U}_k}[a_{k,u_n}(b_{k,u_n}d_{k,u_n} - \beta_k b_{k,u_n}d_{k,u_n} + \gamma_{k,u_n}b_{k,u_n}d_{k,u_n}) - \alpha b_{k,u_n}] \quad (14)
\end{aligned}
$$

Assuming that user u will connect with RRH k, which means that $a_{k,u_n} = 1$, we can then obtain the optimal solution to the spectrum resource allocation problem from the following subproblems

$$\max_{b_{k,u_n}} \sum_{u \in \mathcal{U}_k} (b_{k,u_n} d_{k,u_n} - \beta_k b_{k,u_n} d_{k,u_n} + \eta_{k,u_n} b_{k,u_n} d_{k,u_n} - \alpha b_{k,u_n})$$

$$s.t. \quad b_{k,u_n} \geq 0 \tag{15}$$

When the spectrum resources allocated to each user are determined, the user u can obtain the set of transmission rates $\mathbf{R}_{u_n} = \left[r_{1,u_n}, r_{2,u_n}, ..., r_{K,u_n} \right]$ that can be achieved for each RRH connection. According to $\mathbf{R}_{u_n}$, the user can then determine which RRH connection can obtain the maximum data transmission rate and determine a_{k,u_n}

$$a_{k,u_n} = \begin{cases} 1, & \text{if } r_{k,u_n} = arg \max_k \mathbf{R}_{u_n} \\ 0, & \text{else} \end{cases} \tag{16}$$

Finally, we update the dual varialbes by using subgradient method

$$\alpha^{t+1} = [\alpha^t - \rho_1^t(B - \sum_{k \in \mathcal{K}} \sum_{u \in \mathcal{U}_k} b_{k,u_n})]^+ \tag{17}$$

$$\beta_k^{t+1} = [\beta_k^t - \rho_2^t(F_k - \sum_{u \in \mathcal{U}_k} r_{k,u_n})]^+ \tag{18}$$

$$\gamma_{k,u_n}^{t+1} = [\gamma_{k,u_n}^t - \rho_3^t(r_{k,min} - r_{k,u_n})]^+ \tag{19}$$

where ρ_1^t, ρ_2^t and ρ_3^t are appropriate iteration step sizes.

3.2 The Computational Resource Allocation Problem

After the spectrum resource allocation problem is solved, the computational resource allocation problem can be expressed as follows

$$\min_{c_{k,u_n}} \sum_{k \in \mathcal{K}} \sum_{u \in \mathcal{U}_k} c_{k,u_n} \tag{20}$$

$$s.t. \quad \sum_{k \in \mathcal{K}} \sum_{u \in \mathcal{U}_k} c_{k,u_n} \leq C$$

$$c_{k,u_u} \geq \phi(r_{k,u_n})$$

It is clear that the computing resource allocation problem is a convex problem, so there are many ways to solve it. In this paper, we will use the mathematical tools CVX [1] to obtain the optimal solution. Because CVX is a powerful tool to solve the convex optimization problem. It can not only solve the linear programming standards such as quadratic programming problem, also can solve many other complex convex optimization problem.

3.3 The Summary of the Proposed Algorithm

According to the previous content, the algorithm proposed in this paper is shown in Algorithm 1. Firstly, the dual decomposition method is used to solve the spectrum resource allocation algorithm. The system first allocates spectrum resources for the slice users according to the subproblem (15). Based on the result of spectrum resources allocation, the users determine which RRH can get the maximum transmission rate, then update a_{k,u_n}. Next, update the dual variable according to (17) to (19). Then, CVX is used to slove the computing resource allocation problem. Finally, the resource utilization is calculated. This iterates over and over until you find the optimal value for resource utilization.

4 Simulation Results

In this section, the performance of the proposed scheme is evaluated by simulations. In addition to the proposed scheme, we also introduced the other two resource allocation scheme for reference, including the joint resource allocation scheme of network slice under D-RAN and the static resource allocation scheme of network slice under C-RAN. For convenience, scheme 1 refer to the scheme proposed in this paper, scheme 2 refer to the joint resource allocation scheme of network slice under D-RAN, and scheme 3 refer to the static resource allocation

---

Algorithm 1. Joint Resource Allocation Algorithm based on Network Slice

---

Fix step sizes ρ_1, ρ_2 and ρ_3; Initialize dual variables α, β_k and η_{k,u_n}; Set $a_{k,u_n} = 1$ and the number of iterations t=1;

for t **do**

   According to subproblem (15), the spectrum resource allocation b_{k,u_n} is determined;

   According to the spectrum allocation, the user updates a_{k,u_n} according to the formula (16);

   Update the dual variables α, β_k and γ_{k,u_n} according to formulas (17) to (19);

   According to the result of spectrum resource allocation problem, CVX is used to solve c_{k,u_n};

   Calculate resource utilization η according to the formula (8);

   if Resource utilization convergence **then**
     | Break
   else
     | t=t+1
   end

end

---

scheme of network slice under C-RAN. In scheme 2, the spectrum resources and computing resources in the communication system belong to each base station respectively, and the resources between base stations cannot be shared. After the user establishes the connection with the base station, the allocation of computing resources and spectrum resources is determined by the base station. In scheme 3, the allocation of spectrum resources and computing resources is not dynamic, but static segmentation according to the communication requirements of slices.

In the simulation, we consider a C-RAN system, in which the total spectrum resource is 50 Mhz and the computational resource is 50 MIPS. We apply the MATLAB simulation tool for simulation. In this system, there are 4 RRH, the distance between each RRH is 500 m, and the transmission power of RRH is 54 W. In order to calculate the SINR, we need to know the channel condition information and the thermal noise density. Therefore, we set $\sigma^2 = -174$ dBm. What's more, following paper [4], we set the pass loss model to $36.7log(dist) + 22.7 + 26log(f_c)$, where $dist$ refer to the distant between the user and RRH and $f_c = 2.5$ Ghz. In addition, there are three types of slices and several users in the system. The minimum transmission rate of users under each slice is 0.128 Mbit/s, 1 Mbit/s and 10 Mbit/s, and the users are randomly distributed in the system.

When the transmission power of RRH is constantly increasing, the change of resource utilization of the system is shown in Fig. 2, where it is assumed that there are 15 users in the system. It can be seen that with the increase of transmission power RRH, the resource utilization of scheme 1 is the highest. And the resources utilization rate of scheme 2 is the lowest. This is because the computing resources and spectrum resources in scheme 1 and scheme 3 are shared, while the computing resources and spectrum resources in scheme 2 are owned by each base station. And the resources between base stations are not shared, therefore cause the low resource utilization.

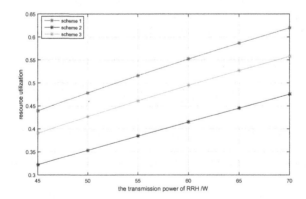

Fig. 2. The change of resource utilization in the system with the increase of RRH transmission power

When the number of users in the simulation increases, the variation of the system's resource utilization is shown in Fig. 3. As can be seen from the Fig. 3, when the number of users in the simulation are increasing, the resource utilization rate of scheme 1 is the highest, and the resource utilization rate of scheme 2 is the lowest. However, in the process of increasing the number of users, the resource utilization of scheme 2 keeps rising and the resource utilization of scheme 3 keeps falling. Moreover, when the number of users in the system reaches 30, the resource utilization of scheme 2 has exceeded scheme 3.

To further explore the performance of the three schemes, we analyzed the number of users that the three schemes could serve when the number of users in the system are increasing, as shown in Fig. 4. As can be seen from Fig. 4, scheme 1 can serve the largest number of users, while scheme 3 can serve the least number of users. According to Fig. 3 and Fig. 4, scheme 1 has the best performance. This is because the resources in scheme 1 are shared together and allocated according to users' requirement, so the resource utilization can be higher and the number of users can be served is larger. However, comparing with scheme 1, scheme 3 is a static resource allocation scheme. The static resource allocation scheme will result in insufficient liquidity of resources, which leads to the resource utilization of scheme 3 is not higher than scheme 1. Comparing with sheme 1, the resources of scheme 2 are owned by each base station, and the resources among base stations cannot be shared, which will definitely lead to the waste of resource. Thus, the resource utilization of scheme 2 is not higher than scheme 1. But, compared with scheme 3, scheme 2 is a dynamic resource allocation scheme. The resource allocation of scheme 2 can be changed according to the number of users so as to increase the number of users it can serve. Moreover, when the number of users in the system is large, the resource utilization of scheme 2 will be higher than scheme 3.

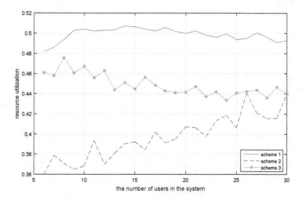

Fig. 3. The change of resource utilization in a system as the number of users increases

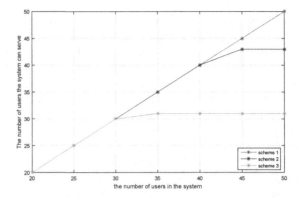

Fig. 4. The number of users that can be served in a system as the number of users increases

5   Conclusion

In this paper, a joint resource allocation scheme based on network slices is proposed under the C-RAN network architecture. This scheme not only solves the problem of joint allocation of spectrum resources and computing resources in the system, but also considers the limitation of transmission rate between RRH and fronthaul link. We models the joint resource allocation problem as a MINLP problem. According to the property of the problem, the joint resource allocation problem of network slicing is decomposed into two sub-problems for solving respectively. In order to verify the effectiveness of the model, we introduced the other two scheme to compare. Numerical simulation shows that the proposed scheme has better resource utilization than the other two schemes and can serves more users.

References

1. Boyd, S., Grant, M.: CVX users' guide (2011). http://cvxr.com/cvx/doc/
2. Costanzo, S., Fajjari, I., Aitsaadi, N., Langar, R.: DEMO: SDN-based network slicing in C-RAN. In: 2018 15th IEEE Annual Consumer Communications Networking Conference (CCNC), pp. 1–2 (2018)
3. De Domenico, A., Liu, Y., Yu, W.: Optimal computational resource allocation and network slicing deployment in 5G hybrid C-RAN. In: 2019 IEEE International Conference on Communications (ICC), ICC 2019, pp. 1–6 (2019)
4. Jian, Z., Muqing, W., Ruiqiang, M., Xiusheng, W.: Dynamic resource sharing scheme across network slicing for multi-tenant C-RANs. In: 2018 IEEE/CIC International Conference on Communications in China (ICCC Workshops), pp. 172–177 (2018)
5. Li, X., et al.: Network slicing for 5G: challenges and opportunities. IEEE Internet Comput. **21**(5), 20–27 (2017)

6. Li, Y., Xia, H., Wu, S., Lu, C.: Joint optimization of computing and radio resource under outage QoS constraint in C-RAN. In: 2017 International Symposium on Wireless Communication Systems (ISWCS), pp. 107–111 (2017)
7. Liu, J., Zhou, S., Gong, J., Niu, Z., Xu, S.: Statistical multiplexing gain analysis of heterogeneous virtual base station pools in cloud radio access networks. IEEE Trans. Wirel. Commun. 15(8), 5681–5694 (2016)
8. Liu, Q., Han, T., Wu, G.: Computing resource aware energy saving scheme for cloud radio access networks. In: 2016 IEEE International Conferences on Big Data and Cloud Computing (BDCloud), Social Computing and Networking (Social-Com), Sustainable Computing and Communications (SustainCom) (BDCloud-SocialCom-SustainCom), pp. 541–547 (2016)
9. Pompili, D., Hajisami, A., Tran, T.X.: Elastic resource utilization framework for high capacity and energy efficiency in cloud ran. IEEE Commun. Mag. 54(1), 26–32 (2016)
10. Tang, J., Shim, B., Quek, T.Q.S.: Service multiplexing and revenue maximization in sliced C-RAN incorporated with URLLC and multicast EMBB. IEEE J. Sel. Areas Commun. 37(4), 881–895 (2019)
11. Tran, T.X., Pompili, D.: Dynamic radio cooperation for user-centric cloud-ran with computing resource sharing. IEEE Trans. Wirel. Commun. 16(4), 2379–2393 (2017)
12. Yu, W., Lui, R.: Dual methods for nonconvex spectrum optimization of multicarrier systems. IEEE Trans. Commun. 54(7), 1310–1322 (2006)
13. Ye, Q., Rong, B., Chen, Y., Al-Shalash, M., Caramanis, C., Andrews, J.G.: User association for load balancing in heterogeneous cellular networks. IEEE Trans. Wirel. Commun. 12(6), 2706–2716 (2013)
14. Zhang, H., Wong, V.W.S.: A two-timescale approach for network slicing in C-RAN. IEEE Trans. Veh. Technol. 69(6), 6656–6669 (2020)

Optimal Thresholds for Differential Energy Detection of Ambient Backscatter Communication

Yuan Liu[1,2(✉)], Pinyi Ren[1,2], and Qinghe Du[1,2]

[1] School of Information and Communications Engineering, Xi'an Jiaotong University, Xi'an 710049, People's Republic of China
yuanaajy@163.com, {pyren, duqinghe}@mail.xjtu.edu.cn
[2] Shaanxi Smart Networks and Ubiquitous Access Research Center, Xi'an 710049, People's Republic of China

Abstract. With wide application of RFID, backscatter communication has become a focus in academy and industry. Specially, ambient backscatter communication has attracted much attention due to its low energy consumption and low cost. In this paper, we study the signal detection of the ambient backscatter communication system and focus on the differential energy detection method. Specifically, we use the off-the-shelf differential encoding model to eliminate the necessity of channel state information (CSI). Differential energy detection method and ML detector are applied as well to make the detecting results more precise and to obtain better performance. Based on them, we improve the approximate threshold and propose optimal thresholds decision algorithm of signal detection, which is proved feasible and efficient. Corresponding BER expressions are derived to estimate the performance of the algorithm. Simulation results are then provided to corroborate the theoretical studies. It can be shown from the results that using two optimal thresholds will improve the performance of the system to some extent, it will also be more tolerant to longer transmitting distance, especially when the channel status are not good.

Keywords: Ambient backscatter communication · Differential energy detection · Maximum likelihood (ML) detection · BER · Two optimal detection thresholds

1 Introduction

Radio frequency identification (RFID), one key technology for Internet of Things (IoT), attracts increasing intention in these years [1]. One typical RFID system consists of a reader and a tag [2]. The reader first generates an electromagnetic wave, the tag receives and backscatters the wave with modulated information bits to the reader [3]. The key communication pattern for RFID system is backscattering.

The research work reported in this paper is supported in part by the National Natural Science Foundation of China under the Grant No. 61941119 and Fundamental Research Funds for the Central Universities, China.

B. Li et al. (Eds.): IoTaaS 2020, LNICST 346, pp. 36–53, 2021.
https://doi.org/10.1007/978-3-030-67514-1_4

Backscatter communication can be divided into three types as in Fig. 1. The monastic backscatter is widely used in RFID and severe round-trip path loss of it will limit the communication distance between the reader and the tag [4–7]. To enlarge the transmitting area, bistatic backscatter technologies were proposed and a carrier emitter is added to the system to reduce the path loss of the signal, which performs better than traditional backscatter [8]. However, it is not always convenient to set an extra facility due to space and cost limit.

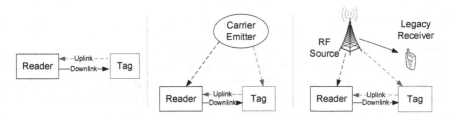

Fig. 1. Three categories in backscatter communication.

Ambient backscatter is a new type of backscatter communication which avoids the above shortcomings. The tags in ambient backscatter communication systems are battery-free devices powered by ambient radio frequency (RF) signals, e.g., wireless fidelity (Wi-Fi) and television (TV) radio. The tags are able to transmit 1 or 0 bit by switching the antenna impedance to reflect the ambient signals or not. After that, some algorithms will be utilized at the reader to detect the transmission status of the tag.

Even though ambient backscatter communication has grasped the intention, the signal processing and performance analysis for it is different from the existing communication and there exist many open problems worth further researching [9]. Several signal detection schemes for ambient backscatter communication systems and their performances are proposed in [10–12]. The ML detector with unknown channel state information (CSI) is presented in [10], it achieves the best performance but the complexity is too high. The joint-energy detector [11] employs the power of received signals in two consecutive intervals, which is simple to operate and requires only channel variances rather than specific CSI. To avoid the estimation of the channel parameters, applying the differentiate energy detector is a good choice. [12] proposes this method and exploits the differences between signal powers in two consecutive intervals, which does not need CSI and training symbols.

In this very work, we focus on the differentiate energy detection and BER performance at the reader. To improve the performance of the detector, we aim to improve the accuracy of the detecting threshold and reanalyze it in mathematical form. We derive that in most cases, there will be two optimal thresholds. As a consequence, new decision standard is developed. BER performance is an essential indicator in evaluating the ambient backscatter communication system, so to validate the efficiency of our standard, the BER expression is derived and analyzed. Finally, numerical simulation results are provided to verify that optimal thresholds will provide better BER performance, be more tolerant to long distances and reduce the complexity, especially when the channel status are not good.

The rest of this paper is organized as follows: Sect. 2 depicts the theoretical model for ambient backscatter communication systems. Section 3 derives the ML detector using the differentiate power and an approximate decision threshold, obtaining corresponding decision region. Section 4 gives optimal thresholds decision algorithm in different scenarios and analyzes the connections between BER performance and parameters. The improvement is also presented. Simulations and results are shown in Sect. 5 and Sect. 6 concludes the paper.

2 System Model

Ambient backscatter communication system is easy to describe since it has a simple structure composed by one reader, one tag and a RF source, this RF source will emit RF signals such as TV signals, Wi-Fi signals and cellular transmissions. The tag in the system modulates this signal and backscatters the processed signal to the reader. Then the detection process begins at the reader.

We assume that RF signal is expressed as $s(n)$, which is the complex baseband equivalent signal and obeys BPSK modulation. Tag receives the RF signal and transmits its own binary signal $B(k)$ to the reader through choosing whether to backscatter $s(n)$ or not. Here we also suppose that the data rate of $B(k)$ is much less than that of $s(n)$. Quantitatively, in one data interval of $B(k)$, the RF source will send out N RF signals.

Tag is a passive device and it will switch its impedance inside its circuit to decide the backscatter state. Specifically, if $B(k) = 0$, little energy of $s(n)$ is reflected. While if $B(k) = 1$, the tag will reflect the whole signal to the reader.

Since we focus most on the backscattered signal from the tag, the final detection is about $B(k)$. However, due to the randomness of the wireless channel, it is hard to get CSI and carry out signal detection with it. At the same time, in order to avoid power-consuming and complexity-increasing training sequences for the battery-free tag operation [13, 14], and also to avoid the high BER at the reader with blind detector [15], we derive an off-the-shelf differential encoding model from [12] at the tag to do some processing in advance. The differential encoding is realized by a differential encoder before the modulator and the model is shown in Fig. 2. Where $A(k)$ is the input and $B(k)$ is the output. They have mathematical connections as

$$B(k) = A(k) \otimes B(k-1), \qquad (1)$$

where $\otimes$ represents addition modulo 2.

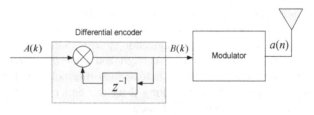

Fig. 2. Differential encoding model.

From the expression, it is easy to get that $A(k)$ stands for the changing-or-not situation of $B(k)$ in two consecutive time intervals: bit "0" for $A(k)$ corresponds to the same states in two intervals before and after, while bit "1" corresponds to the transition from two status. With this model, we will use the detection of $A(k)$ to replace that of $B(k)$ to lower the complexity.

Also, for convenience, we denote the channel between the RF source and the reader as h, the channel between the RF source and the tag as g and the channel between the reader and the tag as ζ. The model is presented in Fig. 3. They are all assumed as slow-fading and will remain unchanged during at least two consecutive intervals of $B(k)$. Furthermore, all these channels are unknown to the reader.

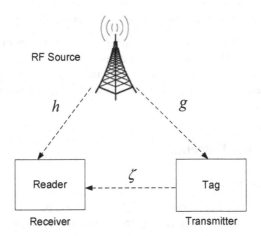

Fig. 3. Channel model of ambient backscatter communication.

With these denotation, we can express the signals sent or received at three devices. Knowing the RF signal is $s(n)$, then the tag receives the transmitted signal

$$x(n) = gs(n). \tag{2}$$

And the signal backscattered by the tag can be expressed as

$$a(n) = \eta B(k)x(n), B(k) \in \{0, 1\} \tag{3}$$

where η is the complex signal attenuation inside the tag. Since the data rate of the RF signal $s(n)$ is N times of that of $B(k)$, $B(k)$ will remain unchanged within N symbols of $x(n)$.

Thus, the passband signal received by the reader is

$$y(n) = hs(n) + \zeta a(n) + w_b(n), \tag{4}$$

where $w_b(n)$ is the zero-mean additive white Gaussian noise (AWGN) with variance N_{wb}.

Though the backscattered signal is superposed on ambient signals at the reader, only the status of reflecting or non-reflecting is aimed to be detected [16], so we have to recover $B(k)$ from the received signal $y(n)$ in case of no CSI knowledge. Note that the ambient backscatter communication system differs from traditional communication systems in that $B(k)$ is hidden in $y(n)$. Consequently, the previous detection methods used in traditional communication systems become invalid and a new detection method must be designed to recover $B(k), k = 1, 2, \cdots K$.

Before the design and implementation of new method, we give some remarks to get a better understanding.

Remark 1: Since the inserted integrated circuit of the tag considered in the ambient backscatter system only consists of passive components and involves at most no signal processing operation, the thermal noise at the tag is normally omitted [17].

Remark 2: Strictly speaking, there exists a time delay τ between the arriving time of $s(n)$ and $a(n)$ at the reader. However, such a delay can be ignored because the communication range among RF-powered devices is limited and the transmission speed of electrical signals inside the on-tag integrated circuit are as fast as light speed [8], the transmitting time is very short.

3 Received Signal Detection

3.1 Format of the Signal

In the former section, we have known that $B(k)$ can be 0 or 1 according to its impedance state. Based on this, we can rewrite the expression of received signal $y(n)$ as

$$y(n) = \begin{cases} hs(n) + \omega_b(n), & B(k) = 0, \\ \mu s(n) + \omega_b(n), & B(k) = 1, \end{cases} \tag{5}$$

where $\mu \triangleq h + \eta \zeta g$ denotes the combined channel information.

In the next step, to detect the signal with differentiate energy, the power of the signals is to be derived. Here we suppose that the tag transmits K symbols in the whole transmitting process so that the reader receives KN signals in total and these signals can be divided into K groups corresponding to K $B(k)$ s. Each group consists of N signals and we compute the average power of them as

$$\Gamma_k = \frac{1}{N} \sum_{n=(k-1)N+1}^{kN} |y(n)|^2, \ 1 \leq k \leq K \tag{6}$$

Based on the expression of $y(n)$, we can easily decompose Γ_k and get the distribution of it in different cases [12]

When N is large,

$$\Gamma_k = \begin{cases} \Gamma_{k,0} \sim \mathcal{N}(|h|^2 P_s + N_{\omega b}, \varsigma_0^2), \\ \Gamma_{k,1} \sim \mathcal{N}(|\mu|^2 P_s + N_{\omega b}, \varsigma_1^2). \end{cases} \tag{7}$$

When N is small,

$$\Gamma_k = \begin{cases} \Gamma_{k,0} \sim \mathcal{N}(|h|^2 P_s + N_{\omega b}, \sigma_0^2), \\ \Gamma_{k,1} \sim \mathcal{N}(|\mu|^2 P_s + N_{\omega b}, \sigma_1^2). \end{cases} \tag{8}$$

where

$$\varsigma_0^2 = \frac{2}{N}|h|^2 P_s N_{wb}, \varsigma_1^2 = \frac{2}{N}|\mu|^2 P_s N_{wb}, \sigma_0^2 = \frac{N_{wb}^2}{N} + \varsigma_0^2, \sigma_1^2 = \frac{N_{wb}^2}{N} + \varsigma_1^2, \tag{9}$$

where P_s is the average power of $s(n)$ and is unknown to the reader.

For the simplicity, we take the first case as an example to analyze the detection process and performance, the corresponding discussions for small N case can be similarly obtained [12].

3.2 ML Detection

We have mentioned the reason for deriving the differentiate encoding in the former section. By using it, the detection of $B(k)$ is transformed into that of $A(k)$, which implies the change of tag signal. This transformation fits the model properly and it can also be reflected in the power change of the received signal at the reader during two transmitting intervals of $B(k)$. So in this paper, we utilize the power difference Φ_k to detect the signal, i.e., to obtain $A(k).\Phi_k$ has the following expression

$$\Phi_k = \Gamma_k - \Gamma_{k-1}. \tag{10}$$

The optimal detector should minimize the error probability, which means that the correct probability should be maximized as much as possible by using this detector, i.e.,

$$\begin{aligned} \hat{A}(k) &= \arg \max_{A(k) \in [0,1]} \Pr(\text{correct decision} | \Phi_k) \\ &= \arg \max_{A(k) \in [0,1]} \Pr(A(k) | \Phi_k). \end{aligned} \tag{11}$$

According to Bayes' rule and the fact that $A(k) = 0$ and $A(k) = 1$ are equal-probable, we will write (11) as

$$\hat{A}(k) = \arg \max_{A(k) \in [0,1]} \Pr(\Phi_k | A(k)). \tag{12}$$

The detectors (12) is well-known as a maximum likelihood (ML) detector.

3.3 Approximate ML Decision Region

Since the tag uses differential encoding, $A(k)$ can be fully determined by $B(k)$ and $B(k-1)$. Based on the distribution of Γ_k, the distribution of Φ_k can be easily checked: $\Phi_{k|0,0} \sim \mathcal{N}(0, 2\varsigma_0^2)$, $\Phi_{k|1,1} \sim \mathcal{N}(0, 2\varsigma_1^2)$, $\Phi_{k|0,1} \sim \mathcal{N}(\delta, \varsigma_0^2 + \varsigma_1^2)$ and $\Phi_{k|1,1} \sim \mathcal{N}(-\delta, \varsigma_0^2 + \varsigma_1^2)$, where the subscript of Φ_k represents different combination of $B(k)$ and $B(k-1)$.

Note that

$$\delta = (|\mu|^2 - |h|^2)P_s. \tag{13}$$

Let $p(\Phi_{k|0,0})$, $p(\Phi_{k|1,1})$, $p(\Phi_{k|0,1})$ and $p(\Phi_{k|1,0})$ denote the probability density functions (PDFs) of the conditional Gaussian distributed random variables above.

We define

$$p_0(x) = \Pr(\Phi_k | A(k) = 0), \tag{14}$$

$$p_1(x) = \Pr(\Phi_k | A(k) = 1), \tag{15}$$

which can be expressed further as

$$p_0(x) = \frac{1}{2}\left((p(\Phi_{k|0,0}) + p(\Phi_{k|1,1}))\right) = \frac{1}{4\sqrt{\pi\varsigma_0^2}}e^{-\frac{x^2}{4\varsigma_0^2}} + \frac{1}{4\sqrt{\pi\varsigma_1^2}}e^{-\frac{x^2}{4\varsigma_1^2}}, \tag{16}$$

$$p_1(x) = \frac{1}{2}\left((p(\Phi_{k|0,1}) + p(\Phi_{k|1,0}))\right) = \frac{1}{\sqrt{8\pi\varsigma_+^2}}e^{-\frac{(x-\delta)^2}{2\varsigma_+^2}} + \frac{1}{\sqrt{8\pi\varsigma_+^2}}e^{-\frac{(x+\delta)^2}{2\varsigma_+^2}}, \tag{17}$$

where

$$\varsigma_+^2 = \varsigma_0^2 + \varsigma_1^2. \tag{18}$$

Subsequently, ML detection rule can be reformulated as

$$\begin{cases} \hat{A}(k) = 0, p_0(x) > p_1(x), \\ \hat{A}(k) = 1, p_0(x) < p_1(x). \end{cases} \tag{19}$$

To clearly distribute the decision region, we have to obtain the decision threshold Th. The detected results in the left and right region of threshold Th are opposite, while the following condition should be satisfied at threshold Th

$$p_0(x) = p_1(x)|_{x=Th}. \tag{20}$$

From the known formulas, this equation has a complex form and does not have a closed-form solution. However, we have two ways to obtain the threshold Th. Firstly, we resort to obtain an approximate solution to replace it; secondly, some approximation methods in certain ranges will be applied to approach the optimal solution. Here we talk about the first method and another one will be discussed in detail in the next section.

We define the approximate threshold as Th^{apx}, which satisfies (30). Assume that δ is very small and $\varsigma_1 = \varsigma_0$, then the following approximation is obtained

$$\tilde{p}_0(x) = \frac{1}{2}((p(\Phi_{k|0,0}) + p(\Phi_{k|1,1})) = \frac{1}{\sqrt{2\pi\varsigma_+^2}} e^{-\frac{x^2}{2\varsigma_+^2}}, \tag{21}$$

$$\tilde{p}_1(x) = \frac{1}{2}((p(\Phi_{k|0,1}) + p(\Phi_{k|1,0})) = \frac{1}{\sqrt{8\pi\varsigma_+^2}} e^{-\frac{(x-\delta)^2}{2\varsigma_+^2}} + \frac{1}{\sqrt{8\pi\varsigma_+^2}} e^{-\frac{(x+\delta)^2}{2\varsigma_+^2}}. \tag{22}$$

Replacing the two terms in (20) with (21) and (22), we obtain

$$T_h^{apx} = \frac{|\delta|}{2} + \frac{\varsigma_+^2}{|\delta|} \ln(1 + \sqrt{1 - e^{-\delta^2/\varsigma_+^2}}). \tag{23}$$

With this approximate threshold, the decision region can be described as

$$\begin{cases} \hat{A}(k) = 0, |\Phi_k| < |Th^{apx}|, \\ \hat{A}(k) = 1, |\Phi_k| > |Th^{apx}|. \end{cases} \tag{24}$$

4 Optimal Thresholds for Detection

4.1 Different Scenarios

In the last section, we have obtained the approximate threshold under the assumption $\varsigma_1 = \varsigma_0$. However, in actual situation, they will not be equal at most of the time, which means there always exist differences between channels. So to make the threshold more robust and be widely applied in all scenarios, we optimize the approximate threshold and obtain an optimal threshold decision algorithm.

To be concrete, when $\delta < \varsigma_+$, we do analysis for $p_0(x)$ and $p_1(x)$: when $x = 0$, $p_0(x) > p_1(x)$ and when $x \to \infty$, $p_0(x) > p_1(x)$, knowing that $p_0(x)$ and $p_1(x)$ are both decreasing in $(0, +\infty)$, we can get the conclusion that they at least have two intersection points, thus two thresholds are obtained in $(0, +\infty)$. According to the relative value of δ and ς_+, three situations are summarized in Fig. 4 and we find their corresponding two optimal thresholds Th^{opt1} and Th^{opt2} respectively.

Case 1: $\delta < \varsigma_+$. In this case, it is clear that both $p_0(x)$ and $p_1(x)$ have only one peak. Thus to get the thresholds, we just have to obtain the intersection points of two PDFs. Since the closed-form solutions are unavailable, we use piecewise dichotomy to approach the solutions. In this method, the determination of demarcation point is very essential and at this point, condition $f(x) = p_0(x) - p_1(x) < 0$ should be satisfied. To get this point, we first consider Th^{apx} and estimate whether it could be the demarcation point. If it satisfies the condition, $(0, +\infty)$ will be divided into two segments: $(0, Th^{apx})$ and $(Th^{apx}, +\infty)$. Then we use dichotomy to get the optimal solutions. If the condition cannot be satisfied at

Th^{apx}, we would rather consider another point Th^{dem} and estimate the feasibility to choose it as the demarcation point in the same way. Th^{dem} is computed as

$$Th^{dem} = \frac{2\varsigma_+^2 \ln 2 + \delta^2}{2\delta}. \tag{25}$$

If condition $f(x) < 0$ is not reached at any point, it will be difficult to get the optimal thresholds and we resort to replace them with $Th^{opt1} = Th^{apx}$ and $Th^{opt2} = +\infty$.

Remark 3: Th^{dem} is obtained from equation $p_0(x) = p(\Phi_{k|0,1})|_{x=Th^{dem}}$ under the condition $\varsigma_1 = \varsigma_0$. Since $p(\Phi_{k|1,0})$ is decreasing in $(0, +\infty)$ and it plays a less important role in determining the value of $p_1(x)$, we omit it and just take $p(\Phi_{k|0,1})$ into consideration to find a threshold.

Case 2: $\delta > \varsigma_+$ and value of δ is moderate. In this case, there are two peaks for $p_1(x)$ in range $(-\delta, \delta)$, the proof is shown in Appendix. As Fig. 4 shows, when the value of δ is modest, the two peaks are at the outside of the peak of $p_0(x)$, $f(x) < 0$ is satisfied at most time when $x = \delta$. At this time, δ can be a demarcation point and then we will obtain two optimal thresholds. However, when it happens that $f(x) > 0$ when $x = \delta$, Th^{apx} and Th^{dem} will be evaluated to be the demarcation point as described in Case 1.

Case 3: $\delta > \varsigma_+$ and the value of δ is very small. Two peaks of $p_1(x)$ are within the peak of $p_0(x)$. The peak of $p_1(x)$ in $(0, +\infty)$ is on the left of $x = \delta$, so we do not know the exact position of δ and whether the demarcation point condition will be satisfied. Thus it is necessary to discuss the positive and negative of $f(x)$ when $x = \delta$. If $x = \delta$ can not be a demarcation point, to get the solution in this case, we make comparison with Case 1 and find that two cases are similar to each other, so the steps in Case 1 are repeated to help us find two optimal thresholds.

Above all, Case 2 and Case 3 both belong to the case $\delta > \varsigma_+$. In this situation, we just have to i) Judge that whether $x = \delta$ will be used to divide the range. ii) If so, use dichotomy to find two optimal thresholds. iii) If not, repeat steps in case 1 to obtain the solutions.

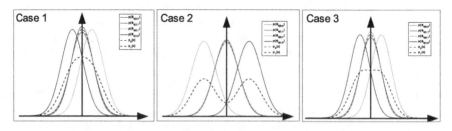

Fig. 4. PDFs of $\Phi_{k|0,0}$, $\Phi_{k|1,1}$, $\Phi_{k|0,1}$, $\Phi_{k|1,0}$ and their combination $p_0(x)$, $p_1(x)$ in three cases.

4.2   Optimal Thresholds Decision Algorithm

To summarize, we discover that δ plays a vital role in distinguishing three cases and determining the segmentation point. When $\delta > \varsigma_+$ and δ is moderate, it is very likely to be chosen as the segmentation point and two thresholds will be in its left and right range. However, when it is too small, it may not be a good choice for dividing two segments. We resort to analyze Th^{apx} and Th^{dem} then obtain the solutions. The algorithm is shown in the following table:

Algorithm 1 Optimal Thresholds Decision

Input: δ、ς_0、ς_1

Output: Optimal thresholds Th^{opt1} and Th^{opt2}

1: **Case 1:** $\delta < \varsigma_+$

2: Compute $f(x)|_{x=Th^{apx}}$.

3: **if** $f(x)|_{x=Th^{apx}} < 0$ **then**

4:　use dichotomy in $(0, Th^{apx})$ and $(Th^{apx}, +\infty)$, obtain Th^{opt1} and Th^{opt2} .

5: **else**

6:　compute $f(x)|_{x=Th^{dem}}$.

7:　**if** $f(x)|_{x=Th^{dem}} < 0$ **then**

8:　　use dichotomy in $(0, Th^{dem})$ and $(Th^{dem}, +\infty)$, obtain Th^{opt1} and Th^{opt2} .

9:　**else**

10:　　$Th^{opt1} = Th^{apx}$，$Th^{opt2} = +\infty$ ·

11:　**end if**

12: **end if**

13: **Case 2:** $\delta < \varsigma_+$

14: Compute $f(x)|_{x=\delta}$ ·

15: **if** $f(x)|_{x=\delta} < 0$ **then**

16:　use dichotomy in $(0, \delta)$ and $(\delta, +\infty)$, obtain Th^{opt1} and Th^{opt2} .

17: **else**

18:　compute $f(x)|_{x=Th^{apx}}$ ·

19:　**if** $f(x)|_{x=Th^{apx}} < 0$ **then**

20:　　use dichotomy in $(0, Th^{apx})$ and $(Th^{apx}, +\infty)$, obtain Th^{opt1} and Th^{opt2} .

21:　**else**

22:　　compute $f(x)|_{x=Th^{dem}}$ ·

23:　　**if** $f(x)|_{x=Th^{dem}} < 0$ **then**

24:　　　use dichotomy in $(0, Th^{dem})$ and $(Th^{dem}, +\infty)$, obtain Th^{opt1} and Th^{opt2} .

25:　　**else**

26:　　　$Th^{opt1} = Th^{apx}$，$Th^{opt2} = +\infty$ ·

27:　　**end if**

28:　**end if**

29: **end if**

Based on the algorithm, the decision regions are shown below

$$\begin{cases} \hat{A}(k) = 0, |\Phi_k| < |Th^{opt1}| \, or |\Phi_k| > |Th^{opt2}|, \\ \hat{A}(k) = 1, |Th^{opt1}| < |\Phi_k| < |Th^{opt2}|. \end{cases} \tag{26}$$

4.3 BER Performance

BER is an important metric to evaluate the performance of system, so here we derive the expression of it to show the connections of BER and parameters clearly.

The BER for the aforementioned ML detector is obtained from

$$P_b = \Pr(A(k) = 1) \Pr(\hat{A}(k) = 0|A(k) = 1) + \Pr(A(k) = 0) \Pr(\hat{A}(k) = 1|A(k) = 0)$$
$$= \frac{1}{2}(\frac{1}{2}P_{b|0,0} + \frac{1}{2}P_{b|1,1}) + \frac{1}{2}(\frac{1}{2}P_{b|0,1} + \frac{1}{2}P_{b|1,0}). \tag{27}$$

where $P_{b|0,0}$ and $P_{b|1,1}$ are obtained by using optimal detecting thresholds and the Gaussian tail probability Q function

$$P_{b|0,0} = \Pr(\hat{A}(k) = 1|B(k-1) = 0, B(k) = 0)$$
$$= 2 \int_{Th^{opt1}}^{Th^{opt2}} p(\Phi_{k|0,0}) d\Phi_{k|0,0} = 2(Q(\frac{Th^{opt1}}{\sqrt{2\varsigma_0^2}}) - Q(\frac{Th^{opt2}}{\sqrt{2\varsigma_0^2}})), \tag{28}$$

$$P_{b|1,1} = \Pr(\hat{A}(k) = 1|B(k-1) = 1, B(k) = 1)$$
$$= 2 \int_{Th^{opt1}}^{Th^{opt2}} p(\Phi_{k|1,1}) d\Phi_{k|1,1} = 2(Q(\frac{Th^{opt1}}{\sqrt{2\varsigma_1^2}}) - Q(\frac{Th^{opt2}}{\sqrt{2\varsigma_1^2}})). \tag{29}$$

Actually, $P_{b|0,1} = P_{b|1,0}$ due to symmetry

$$P_{b|0,1} = P_{b|1,0} = \Pr(\hat{A}(k) = 0|B(k-1) = 1, B(k) = 0)$$
$$= 1 - 2 \int_{Th^{opt1}}^{Th^{opt2}} p(\Phi_{k|1,0}) d\Phi_{k|1,0} = 1 - 2(Q(\frac{Th^{opt1} + \delta}{\sqrt{\varsigma_0^2 + \varsigma_1^2}}) - Q(\frac{Th^{opt2} + \delta}{\sqrt{\varsigma_0^2 + \varsigma_1^2}})), \tag{30}$$

where

$$Q(x) = \frac{1}{\sqrt{2\pi}} \int_x^\infty e^{-\frac{t^2}{2}} dt. \tag{31}$$

Therefore, substituting (28), (29) and (30) into (27), we finally obtain the BER expression as

$$
\begin{aligned}
P_b = & \frac{1}{2}(Q(\frac{Th^{opt1}}{\sqrt{2\varsigma_0^2}}) + Q(\frac{Th^{opt1}}{\sqrt{2\varsigma_1^2}})) - \frac{1}{2}(Q(\frac{Th^{opt2}}{\sqrt{2\varsigma_0^2}}) + Q(\frac{Th^{opt2}}{\sqrt{2\varsigma_1^2}})) \\
& + \frac{1}{2}(1 - 2(Q(\frac{Th^{opt1} + \delta}{\sqrt{\varsigma_0^2 + \varsigma_1^2}}) - Q(\frac{Th^{opt2} + \delta}{\sqrt{\varsigma_0^2 + \varsigma_1^2}}))).
\end{aligned}
\tag{32}
$$

Although BER performance appears different under different thresholds, they have the same trend and connection with parameters, so here we use approximation thresholds under high SNR: $Th^{opt1} = |\delta|/2$ and $Th^{opt2} = +\infty$ to analyze.

Proof: Since

$$
T_h^{apx} = \frac{|\delta|}{2} + \frac{\varsigma_+^2}{|\delta|} \ln(1 + \sqrt{1 - e^{-\delta^2/\varsigma_+^2}}).
\tag{33}
$$

When it is in high SNR, the second term of Th^{apx} is much smaller than the first one, thus can be omitted. So we obtain

$$
Th^{opt1} = \frac{|\delta|}{2}, Th^{opt2} = +\infty.
\tag{34}
$$

Substitute (34) into (32), then we get BER expression as

$$
\begin{aligned}
P_b = & \frac{1}{2}Q(\frac{\Delta_{\mu h}}{4|h|}\sqrt{\gamma N}) + \frac{1}{2}Q(\frac{\Delta_{\mu h}}{4|\mu|}\sqrt{\gamma N}) \\
& + \frac{1}{2}Q(\frac{\Delta_{\mu h}}{2\sqrt{2}\sqrt{\Xi_{\mu h}}}\sqrt{\gamma N}) - \frac{1}{2}Q(\frac{3\Delta_{\mu h}}{2\sqrt{2}\sqrt{\Xi_{\mu h}}}\sqrt{\gamma N}),
\end{aligned}
\tag{35}
$$

where $\gamma = P_s/N_{\omega b}$ and $\Delta_{\mu h} = ||\mu|^2 - |h|^2|$, $\Xi_{\mu h} = |\mu|^2 + |h|^2$.

From this new expression, we can conclude that in ambient backscatter communication system, BER is not only determined by the SNR and channel fading as in traditional communication system, but also by the channel difference $\Delta_{\mu h}$ and the RF signal number N in one group.

4.4   Improvement Analysis

The essence of signal detection is to divide the decision area into different sections. By analysis, we found that the whole decision range is divided into five segments by our two optimal thresholds, in two of them, signals are decided as $A(k) = 1$ while in the other three, signals are detected as $A(k) = 0$. Compared with the previous method which divides three parts, this new algorithm will make detection results more accurate. Especially, when the obtained two thresholds are close to each other, the five segments are more clearly presented and using the earlier detecting threshold will cause mistakes easily if the observed power difference lays in the outside range of Th^{opt2}. So in this case, our optimal two thresholds have a lot to do to decrease BER. In contrast, if two thresholds are very far from each other, it is hard for the power difference to exceed Th^{opt2}, and divided five parts are not so apparent that the significance of our algorithm is just making Th^{opt1} closer to its true value. The improvement exists but is not as great as the former one. The simulation results will testify our analysis in the next section.

5 Simulations and Results

In this section, we resort to numerical examples to evaluate the proposed studies. In our simulations, the noise variance N_{wb} is set as 1 and K is chosen as 100. Since the distance between RF source and tag (or reader) is much larger than that between tag and reader, we generate h and g according to $\mathcal{CN}(0,1)$ and generate ζ according to $\mathcal{CN}(0,10)$ at the beginning. Energies of all channels are assumed to hold unchanged during $K\,B(k)$ s' symbols period. The complex signal attenuation η inside the tag is fixed as 1.1 dB [18]. In order to include as many situations as possible, we do 10^5 Monte Carlo simulations in total.

It need to be mentioned that, to use the received data for detection and avoid training symbols for channel estimation, we can also use $E(|\Phi_k|)$ as an approximation threshold, it also approaches $|\delta|/2$ when K is relatively large. It can be expressed as

$$E(|\Phi_k|) \approx \frac{1}{K}\sum_{k=1}^{K}|\Phi_k|. \tag{36}$$

Figure 5 shows the trend of BER under three different thresholds: $Th^{opt1}\,\&\,Th^{opt2}, Th^{apx}$ and $E(|\Phi_k|)$, with SNR ranging from 5 to 30 dB. Threshold $E(|\Phi_k|)$ is obtained from calculation of power difference and the other two thresholds are the results of algorithm and formula we derived. The number of signals N that RF source sends in one time interval of $B(k)$ is set to be 20 and 50 for comparison. For each SNR, Φ_k is divided into different ranges by thresholds and the signal is detected, then we get corresponding BER. It can be shown that as SNR increases, BER goes down whichever threshold is used. BER performances are similar when using Th^{apx} and $E(|\Phi_k|)$ as the single threshold. However, when two thresholds Th^{opt1} and Th^{opt2} are taken into consideration, there is an apparent decrease in BER due to the accuracy and completeness of the decision threshold. It is also found that larger N will reduce BER to some degree.

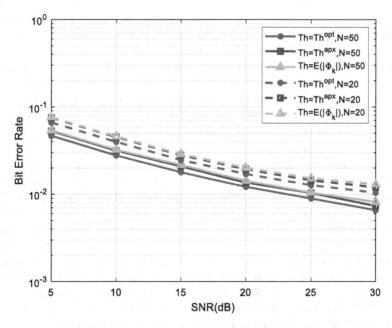

Fig. 5. BER versus transmit SNR under different thresholds and *N*.

In Fig. 6, we change the channel status by changing the variance of *h*, *g* and ζ to 0.1,0.1 and 1, respectively. It means that channel status turn poor. *N* is fixed as 50. What is clearly observed is that BER has an increase due to the poor channel quality.

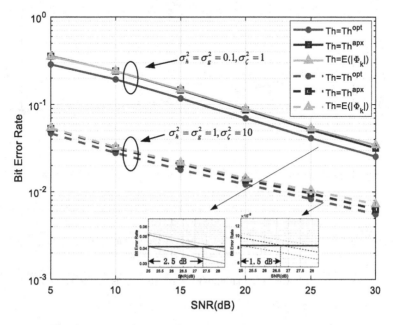

Fig. 6. BER performance improvement in two channel status.

On the other hand, not surprisingly, the result meets our analysis. In this situation, BER performance has a great improvement compared with that in the former case. When the channel status is stable, there is an approximate 1.5 dB improvement, while it has an improvement of about 2.5 dB in average when channel quality is worsened. This is because when the channel status are not good, two optimal thresholds are close to each other, then the detecting results will have great changes, especially when $|\Phi_k| > |Th^{opt2}|$. Results show that our algorithm will provide better performance especially in poor channel status, making the system have strong tolerance to longer distances and obstacles in transmitting path.

Figure 7 shows the curves of BER versus N under three thresholds when SNR = 30 dB. Corresponding BERs are plotted. Clearly, BER decreases as N increases under each threshold. We can also observe from the figure that when N is small, the decreasing trend is very quick, whereas it slows down when N is large and BER curve will tend to be flat when N is larger than 140 or so. This enlightens us to consider the complexity of detection since N is related to the computational complexity. Specifically, it is better to choose a modest N to achieve good BER performance. What is also shown in Fig. 7 is that our two thresholds algorithm greatly improves the performance of the system. When N and SNR are determined, using two optimal thresholds results in lowest BER compared with other thresholds, meanwhile, with the same BER, less RF signals will be sent, thus the computational complexity is reduced.

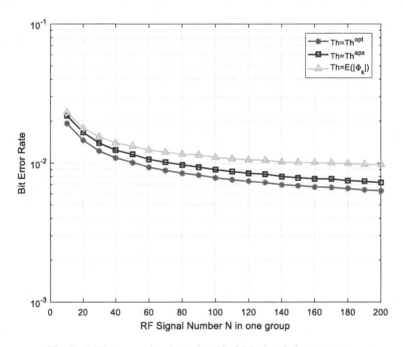

Fig. 7. BER versus signal number N of RF signals in one group.

6 Conclusion

In this paper, we study the signal detection of ambient backscatter communication. Differential encoding model is used at the tag to help the reader implement signal detection. Based on the existing detecting threshold, we do more analysis and propose optimal thresholds decision algorithm. We also find the scenario where this algorithm has the best applicability and improves system performance greatly. Furthermore, we derive BER expressions to connect BER with parameters in the system model. Finally, simulation results are provided to corroborate our theoretical results. The results show that our proposed optimal thresholds decision algorithm will improve system performance to some extent, such as detection accuracy, transmitting distance and complexity, especially when the channel status are poor.

Appendix

The function $p_1(x)$ is expressed as (17) shows. It is the sum of two PDFs of Gaussian random variables whose mean is δ and $-\delta$ respectively and they have the same variance:ς_+^2. Derive function $p_1(x)$ and assume $\frac{dp_1(x)}{dx} = 0$, we will get

$$e^{\frac{2x\delta}{\varsigma_+^2}} = \frac{\delta + x}{\delta - x}. \tag{A.1}$$

Since $p_1(x)$ is symmetry about y axis so we just discuss its properties in $(0, +\infty)$, and whatever δ is positive or negative, the result will be the same, so here we just take $\delta > 0$ into consideration.

The term on the left hand side of the equation is always positive in $(0, +\infty)$, so to make the equation work, there must be $x < \delta$. After deforming the above equation further, we obtain

$$e^{\frac{2x\delta}{\varsigma_+^2}} = \frac{2\delta}{\delta - x} - 1. \tag{A.2}$$

Define

$$a_1(x) = e^{\frac{2x\delta}{\varsigma_+^2}}, a_2(x) = \frac{2\delta}{\delta - x} - 1, \tag{A.3}$$

they are exponential function and negative power function, respectively. Observing (A.2) and we find that $x = 0$ is an absolute solution, which means that there will be a peak at $x = 0$. The appearance of another peak lies in whether another intersection point of two functions exists. When $x \to \delta, a_1(x) \to e^{\frac{2\delta^2}{\varsigma_+^2}}, a_2(x) \to +\infty$, so to find the intersection point, we analyze the trend of them. We obtain the derivation at $x = 0$, when $\frac{da_1(x)}{dx}\big|_{x=0} > \frac{da_2(x)}{dx}\big|_{x=0}$, there must be another intersection point for two functions and its value is smaller than δ. In contrast, when $\frac{da_1(x)}{dx}\big|_{x=0} < \frac{da_2(x)}{dx}\big|_{x=0}, a_1(x)$ will never exceed $a_2(x)$ in $(0, \delta)$ and they will not meet in $(0, +\infty)$.

The derivations are shown as follows

$$\frac{da_1(x)}{dx}\big|_{x=0} = \frac{2\delta}{\varsigma_+^2}, \frac{da_2(x)}{dx}\big|_{x=0} = \frac{2\delta}{\delta^2}. \tag{A.4}$$

Thus we can get the conclusion: when $\delta > \varsigma_+$, function $p_1(x)$ has two peaks and it only has one peak when $\delta < \varsigma_+$.

References

1. Xie, L., Yin, Y., Vasilakos, A.V., Lu, S.: Managing RFID data: challenges, opportunities and solutions. IEEE Commun. Surv. Tutor. **16**(3), 1294–1311 (2014)
2. Dobkin, D.M.: The RF in RFID: Passive UHF RFID in Pratice. Newnes (Elsevier), Oxford (2008)
3. Stockman, H.: Communication by means of reflected power. IRE **36**, 1196–1204 (1948)
4. Griffin, J.D., Durgin, G.D.: Gains for RF tags using multiple antennas. IEEE Trans. Antennas Propag. **56**(2), 563–570 (2008)
5. Boyer, C., Roy, S.: Backscatter communication and RFID: coding, energy and MIMO analysis. IEEE Trans. Commun. **62**(3), 770–785 (2014)
6. Griffin, J.D., Durgin, G.D.: Complete link budgets for backscatter radio and RFID systems. IEEE Antennas Propag. Mag. **51**(2), 11–25 (2009)
7. Griffin, J.D., Durgin, G.D.: Multipath fading measurements at 5.8 GHz for backscatter tags with multiple antennas. IEEE Trans. Antennas Propag. **58**(11), 3694–3700 (2010)
8. Kimionis, J., Bletsas, A., Sahalos, J.N.: Increased range bistatic scatter radio. IEEE Trans. Commun. **62**(3), 1091–1104 (2014)
9. Liu, V., Parks, A., Talla, V., Gollakota, S., Wetherall, D., Smith, J.R.: Ambient backscatter: wireless communication out of thin air. In: Proceedings of the ACM SIGCOMM, Hong Kong, China, pp. 1–13 (2013)
10. Qian, J., Gao, F., Wang, G.: Signal detection of ambient backscatter system with differential modulation. In: 2016 IEEE International Conference on Acoustics, Speech and Signal Processing (ICASSP), Shanghai, pp. 3831–3835 (2016)
11. Qian, J., Gao, F., Wang, G., Jin, S., Zhu, H.: Noncoherent detections for ambient backscatter system. IEEE Trans. Wirel. Commun. **16**(3), 1412–1422 (2017)
12. Wang, G., Gao, F., Fan, R., Tellambura, C.: Ambient backscatter communication systems: detection and performance analysis. IEEE Trans. Commun. **64**(11), 4836–4846 (2016)
13. Dong, M., Tong, L.: Optimal design and placement of pilot symbols for channel estimation. IEEE Trans. Signal Process. **50**(12), 3055–3069 (2002)
14. Xing, C., Ma, S., Zhou, Y.: Matrix-monotonic optimization for MIMO systems. IEEE Trans. Signal Process. **63**(2), 334–348 (2015)
15. Mat, Z., Zeng, T., Wang, G., Gao, F.: Signal detection for ambient backscatter system with multiple receiving antennas. In: Proceedings of the IEEE 14th Canadian Workshop on Information Theory (CWIT), St. John's, NF, Canada, July 2015, pp. 1–4 (2015)

16. Zhang, Y., Qian, J., Gao, F., Wang, G.: Outage probability for ambient backscatter system with real source. In: 2017 IEEE 18th International Workshop on Signal Processing Advances in Wireless Communications (SPAWC), Sapporo, pp. 1–5 (2017). https://doi.org/10.1109/spawc.2017.8227638
17. Wang, G., Gao, F., Dou, Z., Tellambura, C.: Uplink detection and BER analysis for ambient backscatter communication systems. In: Proceedings of the IEEE Global Communications Conference (GLOBECOM), December 2015, pp. 1–6 (2015)
18. Kellogg, B., Talla, V., Gollakota, S., Smith, J.R.: Passive Wi-Fi: bringing low power to Wi-Fi transmissions. In: Proceedings of the 13th USENIX Symposium on Networked Systems Design and Implementation (NSDI), Santa Clara, CA, USA, pp. 1–14 (2016)

Resource Allocation for Multi-UAV Assisted Energy-Efficient IoT Communications with Co-channel Interference

Yanming Liu, Kai Liu, Jinglin Han, Lipeng Zhu, and Zhenyu Xiao[✉]

School of Electronic and Information Engineering, Beihang University,
Beijing 100191, China
{liuyanming,liuk,bxqdl,zhulipeng,xiaozy}@buaa.edu.cn

Abstract. Due to the superiority of high mobility, low labor cost and line of sight (LOS) prominent links of unmanned aerial vehicles (UAVs), UAV-assisted communications are increasingly attractive in emerging Internet of Things (IoT) networks. In this paper, we study the resource (including node association, channel and transmit power) allocation for the multi-UAV assisted IoT network in the uplink, considering the co-channel interference, limited task and channel capacity for the UAV-BSs. To provide long-term services for the IoT nodes, the total transmit power of the IoT nodes is minimized. We decouple the original nonconvex problem into three subproblems, i.e., node clustering, channel assignment, and transmit power control. To find the suboptimal solutions of the first two challenging subproblems, a balanced node clustering algorithm and a *Hungarian-based Channel Assignment* (HCA) algorithm are proposed, respectively. Then, the transmit power control problem turns into a convex problem, which can be calculated within polynomial time. Simulation results are provided to demonstrate the reliability and effectiveness of the overall strategy.

Keywords: Multi-UAV · Energy-efficient Internet of Things · Uplink · Resource allocation · Matching theory

1 Introduction

The Internet of Things (IoT) has been widely applied to many fields, such as military, intelligent transportation, agricultural production and environmental monitoring [1]. Numerous IoT devices which are always small and battery-limited, are usually widely distributed in a big area. Moreover, the transmit power of each device is usually small, such that the devices may not communicate with the

This work was supported in part by the National Key Research and Development Program (Grant Nos. 2016YFB1200100), and the National Natural Science Foundation of China (NSFC) (Grant Nos. 61827901 and 91738301).

common ground base stations (BSs) which are far away. Unmanned aerial vehicles (UAVs) have significant advantages including high mobility, low labor cost and line of sight (LOS) predominant channel [2,3]. Therefore, deploying UAVs as aerial BSs is an efficient and cost-effective approach for providing ubiquitous and long-term services. In the state-of-the-arts, energy-efficient wireless communication has attracted a lot of attention, not only to decrease the operation cost and be greener but also to prolong the battery life of devices [4]. Therefore, it is a crucial challenge to design an effective resource allocation strategy in UAV-assisted IoT networks.

Recently, UAV-assisted IoT communications have been widely investigated [5–8], where UAVs act as a flexible aerial BSs for data collecting or transferring data to the ground sensors. Wu *et al.* [5] aimed at maximizing the throughput of the ground devices with delay and minimal achievable rate consideration, by optimizing the resource allocation and trajectory of a single UAV-BS. Using denoising autoencoder (DAE) neural network strategy, Yu *et al.* [6] studied a spatial data sampling scheme for the UAV-assisted large-scale IoT system for sampling and reconstructing accurate and efficient data. Samir *et al.* [7] investigated the single-UAV routing and the radio resource allocation for collecting data from time-constrained IoT nodes. Considering multi-UAV enabled mobile IoT architecture, Mozaffari *et al.* [8] developed an energy-efficient transmission scheme in order to guarantee the long-term work of the IoT devices, where dynamic clustering and optimal transport theory were exploited.

From the above works, we can see that many works (e.g., [5–7]) only consider a single UAV, which may cannot adapt to latency-sensitive and dense scenarios. Moreover, although some consider multiple UAVs, the abundant spectrum resource is usually assumed and thus there is no inter-cell interference. Besides, load balancing is always neglected.

Therefore, in this paper, we model the uplink transmission problem in a multi-UAV assisted IoT network, considering the balanced task of UAVs, limited channel resource and co-channel interference. To deal with the original nonconvex problem, we design a three-step resource allocation strategy to find a suboptimal solution, including node clustering, channel assignment and transmit power control. Compared with the relevant works, the study in this paper has contributions as follows. First, considering a large-area IoT network with a huge number of nodes, we investigate a multi-user multi-UAV scenario. Second, since massive access to a UAV with the limited capacity will cause network congestion, we consider the task balance of UAVs and proposed a balanced node clustering algorithm leveraging the idea of the K-means method. Besides, since wireless frequency is a scarce resource and the inter-cell interference is serious, we design a heuristic dynamic channel assignment algorithm inspired by matching theory, namely, *Hungarian-based Channel Assignment* (HCA) algorithm, in order to mitigate the inter-cell interference. Furthermore, simulation results display the superiority of the overall solution compared with the random allocation (RA) scheme in terms of convergence, reliability and effectiveness.

The rest of this paper is organized as follows. In Sect. 2 and Sect. 3, we model the system and formulate the problem, respectively. Section 4 propose the solutions to the three subproblems. In Sect. 5, numerical simulation results are presented and discussed. Finally, Sect. 6 concludes the paper.

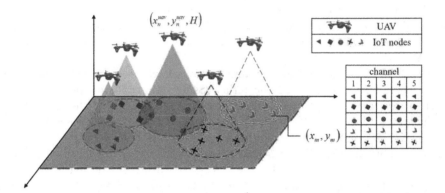

Fig. 1. System model of communications between multi-UAV and IoT nodes in K channels.

2   System Model

The UAV-assisted IoT uplink system is shown in Fig. 1, where M homogeneous and static ground IoT nodes transfer data to N UAVs through. UAVs hover at the same altitude H. The location information of M nodes is already known. Without loss of generality, we allow that several nodes can associate to a same UAV. UAVs utilize the same frequency spectrum to communicate with ground nodes and there are $K \geq \lceil \frac{M}{N} \rceil$ orthogonal channels. The horizontal locations of nodes $m \in \{1, 2, \ldots, M\}$ and UAVs $n \in \{1, 2, \ldots, N\}$ are expressed as $\boldsymbol{x}_m = (x_m, y_m)$ and $\boldsymbol{v}_n = (x_n^{uav}, y_n^{uav})$, respectively. We assume that a UAV is able to communicate with $\lfloor \frac{M}{N} \rfloor$ or $\lceil \frac{M}{N} \rceil$ nodes, and this balanced scheduling can avoid channel waste and network congestion. Thus, the association between UAVs and nodes as well as orthogonal channels should be scheduled. Assume that a channel can be allocated to a node. In the following, we consider the worst condition, i.e., $K = \lceil \frac{M}{N} \rceil$ and the proposed strategy can be applied in the other cases.

2.1   Channel Model

According to [9], we consider a probabilistic LOS channel model, i.e., elevation angle-dependent probabilistic LOS model in an urban environment. The probability of having the LOS link can be modeled as [9]

$$P_{m,n}^{LoS} = \frac{1}{1 + a \exp\left[-b\left(\theta_{m,n} - a\right)\right]} \tag{1}$$

where a and b are modeling parameters. $\theta_{m,n}$ is the elevation angle which is given by $\theta_{m,n} = \frac{180}{\pi} \tan^{-1}\left(\frac{H}{r_{m,n}}\right)$ with the horizontal distance between UAV n and node m expressed as $r_{m,n} = \sqrt{(x_m - x_n^{uav})^2 + (y_m - y_n^{uav})^2}$. Thus, non line of sight (NLOS) probability is $P_{m,n}^{NLoS} = 1 - P_{m,n}^{LoS}$.

The channel power of the LOS and NLOS links are formed as [9]

$$g_{m,n}^{LoS} = \left(\frac{\lambda}{4\pi d_{m,n}}\right)^{\alpha} \eta_{LoS}, \tag{2}$$

$$g_{m,n}^{NLoS} = \left(\frac{\lambda}{4\pi d_{m,n}}\right)^{\alpha} \eta_{NLoS}, \tag{3}$$

where α is path loss exponent, $d_{m,n}$ is the Euclidean distance between IoT node m and UAV n, η_{LoS} and η_{NLoS} are excessive path loss coefficients, λ is carrier wavelength. Thus, the expected channel power from node m to UAV n is expressed as

$$\begin{aligned}
\bar{g}_{m,n} &= P_{m,n}^{LoS} g_{m,n}^{LoS} + P_{m,n}^{NLoS} g_{m,n}^{NLoS} \\
&= \left[P_{m,n}^{LoS} \eta_{LoS} + P_{m,n}^{NLoS} \eta_{NLoS}\right] \left(\frac{\lambda}{4\pi d_{m,n}}\right)^{\alpha}.
\end{aligned} \tag{4}$$

2.2 Interference Model

Then, we model the co-channel interference. Here a set $\{a_{m,n,k}\}$ is defined to indicate the association among node m, UAV n and channel $k \in \{1, 2, \ldots, K\}$. When UAV n associate node m through channel k, $a_{m,n,k} = 1$, otherwise $a_{m,n,k} = 0$. Let $\{p_1, ..., p_M\}$ and σ^2 denote the transmit powers of IoT nodes and the variance of additive white Gaussian noise (AWGN), respectively. Thus, the existing interference for UAV n and node m through channel k can be expressed as

$$I_{m,n,k} = \sum_{\substack{i=1 \\ i \neq m}}^{M} \sum_{j=1}^{N} a_{i,j,k} p_i \bar{g}_{i,n}. \tag{5}$$

Then, the signal-to-interference-and-noise ratio (SINR) of node m is given by

$$\gamma_{m,n,k} = \frac{p_m \bar{g}_{m,n}}{I_{m,n,k} + \sigma^2}. \tag{6}$$

3 Problem Formulation

The total transmit power minimization problem of IoT nodes is formulated as

$$\min_{\substack{\{a_{m,n,k}\}, \\ \{p_m\}, \{v_n\}}} \sum_{m=1}^{M} p_m \tag{7}$$

$$s.t. \quad \sum_{n=1}^{N}\sum_{k=1}^{K} a_{m,n,k}\gamma_{m,n,k} \geq \gamma_0, \forall m \tag{7a}$$

$$\left\lfloor \frac{M}{N} \right\rfloor \leq \sum_{m=1}^{M}\sum_{k=1}^{K} a_{m,n,k} \leq \left\lceil \frac{M}{N} \right\rceil, \forall n \tag{7b}$$

$$\sum_{n=1}^{N}\sum_{k=1}^{K} a_{m,n,k} = 1, \forall m \tag{7c}$$

$$\sum_{m=1}^{M}\sum_{n=1}^{N} a_{m,n,k} \leq N, \forall k \tag{7d}$$

$$a_{m,n,k} \in \{0,1\}, \forall m, n, k \tag{7e}$$

$$0 \leq \sum_{n=1}^{N}\sum_{k=1}^{K} a_{m,n,k}p_m \leq P_{\max}, \forall m \tag{7f}$$

where (7a) demands the minimal limitation of the SINR threshold γ_0 for each node, i.e., the SINR constraint. (7b) is the task capability constraint. (7c) requires that each node communicates with a UAV in a channel, i.e., the association constraint. (7d) indicates that Up to N nodes occupy one channel, i.e., the co-channel node number constraint. Moreover, (7f) constrains the transmit power of each node not exceeding $P_{\max}$.

4   Proposed Solution

In the original problem (7), $\{c_{m,n,k}\}$ is a integer set, and thus all the constraints are integer constraints. In addition, constraint (7a) is nonconvex. Therefore, the problem (7) is a mixed-integer nonconvex problem.

In the following, we decouple problem (7) into three subproblems and find an overall sub-optimal solution. Firstly, a balanced node clustering problem is modeled and an corresponding algorithm is developed inspired by the K-means method. At the same time, the horizontal locations of UAVs are determined. Secondly, based on matching theory, channels are assigned to nodes with the proposed HCA algorithm. Lastly, the transmit power optimization problem transfers into a convex problem and can be solved within polynomial time.

4.1   Node Clustering

Due to homogeneous nodes and distance-based channel power, the K-means method is an efficient strategy in user clustering [8,10]. However, in practical scenario, uneven distribution of nodes with the K-means method may lead to massive access or few access from nodes to a UAV. Correspondingly, there will be the stringent co-channel interference or the idle channel in a cell. Therefore, we propose the balanced clustering algorithm to ensure the full utilization of spectrum resources as well as mitigate the inter-cell interference, and meanwhile, each UAV balances the load.

Without loss of generality, we assume that in the horizontal direction, UAVs are deployed at centers of clusters [10]. Thus, n can denote both "UAV" and "cluster center". Then, we define the association between node m and UAV n as

$$c_{m,n} = \sum_{k=1}^{K} a_{m,n,k}, \tag{8}$$

where we have $c_{m,n} \in \{0,1\}$ according to the model. Thus, the balanced node clustering subproblem can be formulated as

$$\min_{\{c_{m,n}\},\{v_n\}} \sum_{m=1}^{M} \sum_{n=1}^{N} c_{m,n} r_{m,n}^2 \tag{9}$$

$$s.t. \quad \left\lfloor \frac{M}{N} \right\rfloor \le \sum_{m=1}^{M} c_{m,n} \le \left\lceil \frac{M}{N} \right\rceil, \forall n \tag{9a}$$

$$\sum_{n=1}^{N} c_{m,n} = 1, \forall m \tag{9b}$$

$$c_{m,n} \in \{0,1\}, \forall m, n \tag{9c}$$

with $r_{m,n}^2 = \|x_m - v_n\|^2$. In [11], the clustering problem was proven NP-hard. In the following, an three-step algorithm inspired by the K-means method is proposed for the sub-optimal solution of problem (9).

1) **Center Initialization:** First, we initialize centers of clusters by K-means++ to separate centers far from each other.
2) **Association Initialization:** Second, we allocate the M nodes association in sequence to the closest UAV. We define $R = \mod(M, N)$. According to constraint (9a), $\lceil \frac{M}{N} \rceil$ and $\lfloor \frac{M}{N} \rfloor$ nodes are served by R and $(N - R)$ UAVs, respectively. We define the node that is assigned to its closest UAV as *good node*. If a node is going to be assigned to its closest UAV whereas there have been $\lceil \frac{M}{N} \rceil$ nodes served by this UAV, the node will turn to connect the

---

Algorithm 1: Balanced Node Clustering Algorithm

Input: N, M, $\{\boldsymbol{x}_m\}$.

Output: $\{\boldsymbol{v}_n\}$, $\{c_{m,n}\}$.

1 Initialize $R_{clu} = 0$ as the real number of clusters which own $\lceil \frac{M}{N} \rceil$ nodes.
  Initialize $\hat{N}_n = 0$ and $\{c_{m,n}\} = 0$. Initialize $\mathcal{L} = \varnothing$ as the bad node set. Initialize
  R. Compute $\{r_{m,n}\}$;

2 Utilizing K-means++ to initialize cluster center locations $\{\boldsymbol{v}_n\}$;

3 **for** $m = 1$ *to* M **do**

4   **if** $R_{clu} < R$ **then**

5   Get the closest UAV $n^* = \arg\min_{n} \{r_{m,n}\}, n \in \{n \mid \hat{N}_n < \lceil \frac{M}{N} \rceil\}$ and set

         $c_{m,n^*} = 1$. Update R_{clu};

6   **else**

7   Get the closest UAV $n^* = \arg\min_{n} \{r_{m,n}\}, n \in \{n \mid \hat{N}_n < \lfloor \frac{M}{N} \rfloor\}$ and set

         $c_{m,n^*} = 1$. Update R_{clu};

8 **while** *objective function in problem (9) decreases* **do**

9   Update $\{\boldsymbol{v}_n\}$ and $\mathcal{L}$;

10   **for** $i \in \mathcal{L}$ **do**

11   Get UAV $n_1 = \arg_{n} \{c_{i,n} = 1\}$ and UAV $n_2 = \arg\min_{n} \{r_{i,n}\}$. Set

         $\{r_j\} = \varnothing$;

12   **if** $\hat{N}_{n_1} \le \hat{N}_{n_2}$ **then**

13   Compute (11) to get $\{r_j\}$;

14   Compute (12) to get j^*;

15   **if** $r_{j^*} > 0$ **then**

16   Set $c_{i,n_1} = 0$, $c_{i,n_2} = 1$, $c_{j^*,n_1} = 1$ and $c_{j^*,n_2} = 0$;

17   **else**

18   Set $c_{i,n_2} = 1$ and $c_{i,n_1} = 0$;

19 **return** $\{\boldsymbol{v}_n\}$, $\{c_{m,n}\}$.

---

second closest UAV and we call the node *bad node*. In the end, several nodes may be assigned to UAVs which are not the closest UAVs. Furthermore, the execution sequence of nodes affect the association result. Therefore, next we further update clusters to adjust the association from good and bad nodes to UAVs.

3) **Cluster update:** An iterative process is developed to adjust clusters. In each process, we first recalculate each cluster center, which is given by

$$\boldsymbol{v}_n = \frac{\sum_{m=1}^{M} c_{m,n} \boldsymbol{x}_m}{\sum_{m=1}^{M} c_{m,n}}, \tag{10}$$

and the bad nodes is updated. After that, two operations are designed, namely, *exchange operation* and *supply operation* for uncommon nodes in order to improve the clustering performance. Assume that for an bad node i,

n_1 and n_2 denote the associated UAV and closest UAV, respectively. Assume node j associates to UAV n_2 The number of nodes associated to UAV n is denoted as $\hat{N}_n$. In the exchange operation, if $\hat{N}_1 \leq \hat{N}_2$, objective function value in (9) may minish with the exchange for association between UAVs n_1, n_2 and nodes i, j. Furthermore, a fitness set $\{r_j\}$ with $j \in \{m|a_{m,n_2} = 1\}$ is defined as

$$r_j = \left(r^2_{i,n_1} + r^2_{j,n_2}\right) - \left(r^2_{i,n_2} + r^2_{j,n_1}\right), \tag{11}$$

which show the decrease of the objective function. Then, the optimal exchange node j^* with a maximal reduction is got, which is computed as

$$j^* = \arg\max_j \{r_j\}. \tag{12}$$

Note that only when $r_{j^*} > 0$, the association for nodes i and j^* are exchanged. In the supply operation, if $\hat{N}_1 > \hat{N}_2$, node i will be assigned to UAV n_2. The iterative process is stopped when the objective function in (9) does not decrease.

The above process is summarized in Algorithm 1. **Center Initialization** is conducted in Step 2. **Association Initialization** is conducted in Steps 3–7. **Cluster update** is conducted in Steps 8–18. The exchange and supply operations are conducted in Steps 13–16 and Step 18, respectively. In **Cluster update** stage, only if the objective function value decreases, both of the two operations are executed, which guarantee the convergence. The **Cluster update** stage determines the algorithm complexity, which is given by $\mathcal{O}\left(M \lceil \frac{M}{N} \rceil L_1\right)$, where L_1 is the number of iterations.

4.2 Channel Assignment

With the fixed association scheduling $\{c_{m,n}\}$ between UAVs and nodes as well as the horizontal location $\{v_n\}$, the original problem (7) is still nonconvex with uncertain channel scheduling and power control. Thus, in order to minimizing the co-channel interference and get $\{c_{m,n,k}\}$, a channel assignment strategy is designed in the following.

In practical multi-user multi-UAV networks, the co-channel interference is a tricky issue. Specifically, each node can increase the transmit power to improve its SINR, while the SINRs of other co-channel nodes in different cells will decrease. Therefore, a reasonable channel assignment strategy plays a vital part in improving the network performance. Matching theory has been proved to be an effective method for the future wireless communications, especially in channel allocation [12]. Inspired by matching theory, the channel assignment problem in the multi-user multi-UAV network can be modeled as a many-many matching process between channels and nodes. In the following, we design an HCA algorithm to address the channel assignment problem.

Define $\mathcal{P}_k$ as a node set in which the nodes utilize the same channel k and initialize $\mathcal{P}_k = \varnothing$. We assign channels to N clusters (denoted as $\{\pi_n\}$ in which

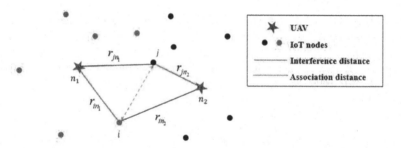

Fig. 2. Interference and association links between two co-channel nodes.

$\pi_n \in \{1, 2, \ldots, N\}$) in sequence. Because of stringent interference between neighbouring clusters, we select the first two clusters as π_1 and π_2, whose centers are closest. According to the nearest distance to the previous clusters, the next cluster π_n, $3 \leq n \leq N$, is selected by

$$\pi_n = \arg\min_{\pi_n} \left\{ \sum_{i=1}^{n-1} \|\boldsymbol{v}_{\pi_n} - \boldsymbol{v}_{\pi_i}\| \right\}. \tag{13}$$

First, we assign nodes in cluster π_1 initially with channels in random, which does not affect the optimality, and $\{\mathcal{P}_k\}$ is updated. Then, we assign channels from cluster π_2 to π_N. The objective cluster is denoted as the cluster where the nodes are required to be allocated channels. Thus, we can model the assignment problem for each objective cluster as a bipartite matching problem, and a heuristic design for the qualification matrix below.

As shown in Fig. 2, assume that the same channel is utilized by nodes i and j which communicates with UAVs n_1 and n_2. r_{i,n_2} and r_{j,n_1} are defined as *interference distance*, as well as r_{i,n_1} and r_{j,n_2} are defined as *association distance*.

Apparently, a higher transmit power of device i is required in case of a larger r_{i,n_1} to make up for a larger channel loss and/or a smaller r_{i,n_1} to counter the more serious interference. Thus, to describe the co-channel interference between any two nodes, we define the fitness set $\{w_{i,j}\}$, in which

$$w_{i,j} = \frac{(r_{i,n_1}^2 + r_{j,n_2}^2)}{(r_{i,n_2}^2 + r_{j,n_1}^2)}. \tag{14}$$

A small value of $w_{i,j}$ can be obtained by both large interference distance and small association distance, indicating small co-channel interference between nodes i and j. Thus, in each objective cluster, we can get the qualification set of channels and nodes, i.e.,

$$\lambda_{i,k} = \sum_{j \in \mathcal{P}_k} w_{i,j}, \tag{15}$$

where $\lambda_{i,k}$ actually indicates the total suffered interference of node i from the other co-channel nodes. We can have $\lambda_{i,k} = 0$ for no co-channel nodes, i.e.,

---

Algorithm 2: HCA Algorithm

Input: $\{x_m\}, \{c_{m,n}\}, \{v_n\}$.
Output: $\{a_{m,n,k}\}, \{\mathcal{P}_k\}$.
1 Initialize $\{a_{m,n,k}\} = 0$, $\{\mathcal{P}_k\} = \varnothing$, the objective clustering list $\{\pi_n\}$ and random channel allocation in objective cluster π_1. Update $\{\mathcal{P}_k\}$;
2 **for** $n = 2$ *to* N **do**
3   Get set $\mathcal{I}_n$ whose element is the node in the objective cluster π_n;
4   Compute $\{\lambda_{i,k}\}$ with (15);
5   Solve matching problem (16) with hungarian method to get $\boldsymbol{S}$;
6   Update $\{\mathcal{P}_k\}$;
7   **for** $i \in \mathcal{I}_n$ **do**
8   Find $k^* \in \{k|s_{i,k} = 1\}$ and set $a_{i,\pi_n,k^*} = 1$;

9 **return** $\{\mathcal{P}_k\}, \{a_{m,n,k}\}$.

$\mathcal{P}_k = \varnothing$. Thus, the matching problem between the nodes of present objective cluster and channels can be given by

$$\min_{\boldsymbol{S}} \sum_{j\in\{m|c_{m,n}=1\}} \sum_{k=1}^{K} s_{j,k}\lambda_{j,k} \tag{16}$$

$$s.t. \quad \sum_{k=1}^{K} s_{j,k} = 1, \forall j \in \{m|c_{m,n} = 1\} \tag{16a}$$

$$\sum_{j\in\{m|c_{m,n}=1\}} s_{j,k} = 1, \forall k \tag{16b}$$

$$s_{j,k} \in \{0,1\}, \forall k, \forall j \in \{m|c_{m,n} = 1\} \tag{16c}$$

Where $\boldsymbol{S}$ is the binary matching matrix and $s_{j,k}$ is the element. The optimal solution can be resolved using hungarian method [13]. $s_{i,k} = 1$ denotes that node i utilizes channel k, and we can have $\mathcal{P}_k = \mathcal{P}_k \cup i$. When the nodes in each objective cluster are allocated channels, the process terminates. Finally, we can get the scheduling among UAVs, nodes and channels, i.e., $a_{m,n,k} = c_{m,n}s_{m,k}$.

In Algorithm 2, we summarize the above process. The hungarian method or fitness set computation in Step 4 determine the algorithm complexity, which is given by $\mathcal{O}\left(\lceil \frac{M}{N}\rceil^2 N\right)$ and $\mathcal{O}\left(\lceil \frac{M}{N}\rceil^3\right)$ [14], respectively. Therefore, the algorithm complexity is $\max\left\{\mathcal{O}\left(\lceil \frac{M}{N}\rceil^3 N\right), \mathcal{O}\left(\lceil \frac{M}{N}\rceil^2 N^2\right)\right\}$.

4.3 Transmit Power Control

After the node clustering and channel assignment with the horizontal locations $\{v_n\}$ of UAVs, relation set $\{a_{m,n,k}\}$ as well as co-channel information set $\{\mathcal{P}_k\}$, original problem (7) can be transferred into a transmit power control problem. The simplified problem is given by

$$\min_{\{p_m\}} \sum_{m=1}^{M} p_m \qquad (17)$$

$$s.t. \quad \frac{p_m \overline{g}_{m,n^{(m)}}}{\displaystyle\sum_{\substack{i \in \mathcal{P}_{k(m)}, \\ i \neq m}} p_i \overline{g}_{i,n^{(m)}} + \sigma^2} \geq \gamma_0, \; \forall m \qquad (17a)$$

$$0 \leq p_m \leq P_{\max}, \forall m \qquad (17b)$$

where $k^{(m)}$ indicates the allocated channel of node m, and $n^{(m)}$ denotes the associated UAV of node m.

Problem (17) is a linear programming (LP) problem. Through interior point method, problem (17) can be addressed within polynomial time [15].

5   Performance Simulations

In this section, the simulation results are provided to verify the performance of the proposed strategy for multi-UAV assisted IoT communications. In the simulations, we consider an urban area of 1km × 1km with 120 randomly distributed IoT nodes and 5 UAVs, and a and b are 11.95 and 0.14 [16], respectively. The carrier frequency is 2 GHz, UAVs hover at 300 m, variance of AWGN is -110 dBm, maximal transmit power of IoT nodes is 300 mW, $\alpha = 2$, $\eta_{LoS} = 3$ dB, $\eta_{NLOS} = 23$ dB, respectively. Our proposed strategy is simulated by MATLAB R2018b.

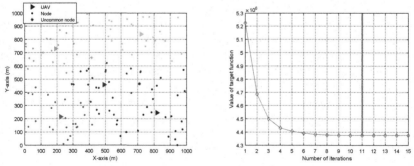

(a) Balanced node clustering using Algorithm 1 with 120 IoT nodes and 5 UAVs. (b) Convergence performance of Algorithm 1.

Fig. 3. Association assignment and convergence in balanced node clustering.

The results in the following Fig. 3(b) and Figs. 4 and 5 are the average results of 2000 independent running. In Figs. 4 and 5, a random assignment (RA) strategy, in which channels are randomly assigned to nodes, acts as a benchmark scheme.

In Fig. 3, with Algorithm 1, we show the balanced node clustering result and convergence of Algorithm 1. Specifically, in Fig. 3(a), 120 IoT nodes are evenly divided into 5 clusters (identified by different colors) and the horizontal locations of the UAVs are fixed at the centers of clusters. What's more, there are 2 bad nodes (indicated by star marks) which are on the boundary of two groups and not communicate with their closest UAVs because of the task and channel constraints. The good nodes are scheduled to their closest UAVs. In Fig. 3(b), the objective function value in subproblem (9) does not decrease after 11 iterations, which show the fast convergence of Algorithm 1.

In Fig. 4, with changing SINR threshold, we show the performance comparison between HCA algorithm and RA strategy, in terms of the system reliability and the transmit power. Reliability denotes the percentage of obtaining feasible solutions. Compared with the RA scheme, we can see that using the HCA algorithm, the reliability is better and the total transmit power is smaller from Fig. 4. As the SINR threshold increases, the reliability becomes worse and more transmit power is needed. With $\gamma_0 = 2\,\mathrm{dB}$, the HCA algorithm has at most 46% improvement of reliability over the RA strategy. In Fig. 4(b), the total transmit power increases by HCA algorithm or RA strategy. In fact, a higher SINR for a node needs more transmit power, but it will produce stronger interference to the co-channel nodes. Therefore, in multi-user multi-cell networks, it is difficult to obtain a very high SINR for nodes with co-channel interference. In Fig. 4(b), there are 23% transmit power reduction at most using HCA algorithm, which verifies the performance.

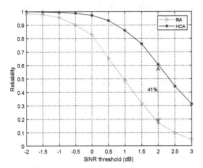 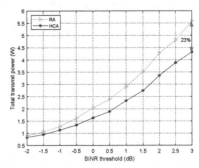

(a) Reliability comparison for different SINR thresholds, where the number of IoT nodes, UAVs and channels is 120, 5 and 24, respectively.

(b) Total transmit power for different SINR thresholds, where the number of IoT nodes, UAVs and channels is 120, 5 and 24, respectively.

Fig. 4. Property with different SINR thresholds.

Figure 5(a) and Fig. 5(b) show the total transmit power of the IoT nodes as the UAV number and the node number change, respectively. From Fig. 5(a), using HCA algorithm, the total transmit power of nodes is reduced by an average of 15% under different number of UAVs and nodes compared with the RA strategy. Furthermore, we can see that the percentage of the performance improvement by using the HCA algorithm will increases with more UAVs, which means that the HCA algorithm will obtain the better performance than the RA strategy with more UAVs. What's more, when the number of UAVs increases, there will be less performance gain using either the RA strategy or HCA algorithm. It reveals that if we take into account the operation and maintenance cost of UAVs, we should not deploy many UAVs to just reduce the total transmit power of nodes but reasonably deploy the proper number of UAVs in practice. From Fig. 5(b), with the increase of nodes, the total transmit power increases linearly. The total transmit power of nodes is reduced by an average of 15% under different number of nodes compared with the RA strategy. We can see that the proposed scheme works well in IoT networks of all sizes.

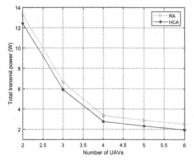
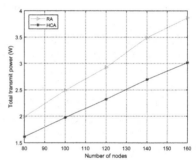

(a) Total transmit power for different numbers of UAVs, where the number of IoT nodes and channels is 120 and 24, respectively, as well as the SINR threshold is 1 dB.

(b) Total transmit power for different numbers of IoT nodes, where the number of UAVs and channels is 5 and 24, respectively, as well as the SINR threshold is 1 dB.

Fig. 5. Total transmit power with different number of UAVs and nodes.

6 Conclusion

In this article, a resource allocation strategy for multi-UAV assisted IoT uplink communication was developed. In particular, we considered the co-channel interference, limited channel resource and balanced task of UAVs. First, the balanced node clustering algorithm was designed. Then, we proposed HCA algorithm to assign channels. Finally, we used CVX to resolve the convex problem of the transmit power control. The proposed solution was verified via the simulations, which showed good convergence and obtained better performance than RA strategy.

References

1. Al-Fuqaha, A., Guizani, M., Mohammadi, M., Aledhari, M., Ayyash, M.: Internet of Things: a survey on enabling technologies, protocols, and applications. IEEE Commun. Surv. Tutor. **17**(4), 2347–2376 (2015)
2. Xiao, Z., Xia, P., Xia, X.G.: Enabling UAV cellular with millimeter-wave communication: potentials and approaches. IEEE Commun. Mag. **54**(5), 66–73 (2016)
3. Zhu, L., Zhang, J., Xiao, Z., Cao, X., Wu, D.O., Xia, X.G.: 3-D beamforming for flexible coverage in millimeter-wave UAV communications. IEEE Wirel. Commun. Lett. **8**(3), 837–840 (2019)
4. Li, B., Fei, Z., Zhang, Y.: UAV communications for 5G and beyond: recent advances and future trends. IEEE Internet Things J. **6**(2), 2241–2263 (2019)
5. Wu, Q., Zhang, R.: Common throughput maximization in UAV-enabled OFDMA systems with delay consideration. IEEE Trans. Commun. **66**(12), 6614–6627 (2018)
6. Yu, T., Wang, X., Shami, A.: UAV-enabled spatial data sampling in large-scale IoT systems using denoising autoencoder neural network. IEEE Internet Things J. **6**(2), 1856–1865 (2019)
7. Samir, M., Sharafeddine, S., Assi, C.M., Nguyen, T.M., Ghrayeb, A.: UAV trajectory planning for data collection from time-constrained IoT devices. IEEE Trans. Wirel. Commun. **19**(1), 34–46 (2020)
8. Mozaffari, M., Saad, W., Bennis, M., Debbah, M.: Mobile Internet of Things: can UAVs provide an energy-efficient mobile architecture? In: 2016 IEEE Global Communications Conference (GLOBECOM), pp. 1–6 (2016). https://doi.org/10.1109/GLOCOM.2016.7841993
9. Zeng, Y., Wu, Q., Zhang, R.: Accessing from the sky: a tutorial on UAV communications for 5G and beyond. Proc. IEEE **107**(12), 2327–2375 (2019)
10. Duan, R., Wang, J., Jiang, C., Yao, H., Ren, Y., Qian, Y.: Resource allocation for multi-UAV aided IoT NOMA uplink transmission systems. IEEE Internet Things J. **6**(4), 7025–7037 (2019)
11. Mahajan, M., Nimbhorkar, P., Varadarajan, K.: The planar k-means problem is NP-hard. In: Das, S., Uehara, R. (eds.) WALCOM 2009. LNCS, vol. 5431, pp. 274–285. Springer, Heidelberg (2009). https://doi.org/10.1007/978-3-642-00202-1_24
12. Gu, Y., Saad, W., Bennis, M., Debbah, M., Han, Z.: Matching theory for future wireless networks: fundamentals and applications. IEEE Commun. Mag. **53**(5), 52–59 (2015)
13. Kuhn, H.W.: The Hungarian method for the assignment problem. Nav. Res. Logist. **52**(1), 7–21 (2010)
14. Kim, T., Dong, M.: An iterative Hungarian method to joint relay selection and resource allocation for D2D communications. IEEE Wirel. Commun. Lett. **3**(6), 625–628 (2014)
15. Boyd, S., Vandenberghe, L.: Convex Optimization. Cambridge University Press, Cambridge (2004)
16. Al-Hourani, A., Kandeepan, S., Lardner, S.: Optimal LAP altitude for maximum coverage. IEEE Wirel. Commun. Lett. **3**(6), 569–572 (2014)

Correlation Based Secondary Users Selection for Cooperative Spectrum Sensing Network

Yifu Zhang[1], Wenxun Zhao[2], Dawei Wang[2,3,4(✉)], Daosen Zhai[2], and Xiao Tang[2]

[1] School of Software, Northwestern Polytechnical University,
Xi'an 710072, Shaanxi, China
`randyzhang@mail.nwpu.edu.cn`
[2] School of Electronics and Information, Northwestern Polytechnical University,
Xi'an 710072, Shaanxi, China
`zhaowenxun@mail.nwpu.edu.cn`, {`wangdw, zhaidaosen, tangxiao`}`@nwpu.edu.cn`
[3] Research and Development Institute of Northwestern Polytechnical University
in Shenzhen, Shenzhen 518057, Guangdong, China
[4] National Mobile Communications Research Laboratory, Southeast University,
Nanjing 210096, China

Abstract. Cognitive radio (CR) can significantly enhance spectrum efficiency by dynamical accessing the licensed spectrum. However, single user spectrum sensing may be inaccurate and the second user (SU) may preempt the channel of the primary users (PUs). The appearance of cooperative spectrum sensing (CSS) can effectively improve the spectrum sensing performance by fusing the results of multiple SUs' decisions to yield reliable decisions. Nevertheless, the communication overhead and the energy consumption of SUs bring a heavy burden for the resource limited secondary network. Therefore, in this paper, we propose a correlation based scheme to select representative SUs based on their correlation by using improved Density-Based Spatial Clustering of Applications algorithm (DSCN). First, we set a threshold to screen out SUs with good channel quality. Then, we propose a improved DSCN algorithm to select SUs that participate in CSS. This algorithm can select representative SUs based on their correlations. Simulation results show that the sensing overhead has been greatly reduced and the probability of detection

This work was supported in part by the National Natural Science Foundation of China under Grant 61941119, Grant 61901379, Grant 61901381, and Grant 61901378, in part by the China Postdoctoral Science Foundation under Grant BX20180262, Grant BX20190287, and Grant 2018M641019, in part by the Natural Science Basic Research Plan in Shaanxi Province under Grant 2019JQ-631, and Grant 2019JQ-253, in part by the National University Student Innovation and Entrepreneurship Training Programs No. 201910699119, in part by Foundation of the Science, Technology, and Innovation Commission of Shenzhen Municipality under Grant JCYJ20190806160218174, in part by the open research fund of National Mobile Communications Research Laboratory, Southeast University under Grant 2020D04.
Y. Zhang and W. Zhao—The first two authors contributed equally to this work.

and the probability of false alarm are better than the traditional spectrum sensing schemes.

Keywords: Correlation · Cooperative spectrum sensing · Improved DSCN · Sensing overhead

1 Introduction

With the rapid development of wireless communication technologies, a large number of equipments require to utilize the spectrum resources. The available wireless spectrum resources is becoming increasingly scarce. However, the researches show that even in hot spots, many of the authorized bands are idle for most of the time in most of the areas [1]. Therefore, due to the lacking flexibility in wireless spectrum resource management, the current spectrum allocation mechanisms can be improved. To enhance spectrum utilization and alleviate the shortage of spectrum resources, cognitive radio (CR) [2] is proposed to sense and utilize the idle licensed spectrum and dynamically access the spectrum.

Spectrum sensing is the main scheme to discover the available spectrum for utilization. Nevertheless, noise uncertainty, shadowing and multi-path fading significantly decrease the spectrum sensing. Noise uncertainty is caused by the time variability and non-uniformity of noise which decreases the accuracy and stability in spectrum sensing. Normally, the antenna beam of the communication ground station is wide, electromagnetic wave is affected by the surface features and landforms. Therefore, the receiver receives the electromagnetic waves produced by refraction, reflection and direct direction, which lead to a serious impact for the spectrum sensing. Large buildings and other objects block the path of the radio waves and inform a semi-blind area in the receiving area of the transmission, which leads to formation of shadowing.

Cooperative Spectrum Sensing (CSS) is proposed to improve the accuracy of spectrum sensing. In general, CSS uses AND and OR fusion schemes. However, during the fusion process, additional sensing overhead will be incurred because of communication and energy consumption. Moreover, extra information will occupy the storage resources of the fusion center. In [3], Meftah et al. proposed wideband CSS schemes based on the multi-bit hard decision, which could help CRN improve the detection of signal in a wide band and save time. In [4], in order to reduce the complexity of processing, Kartlak et al. presented a method based on the cycle-stationarity by selecting optimal relay to communication. [5] considered using double threshold detection method in CSS and determines whether PU is present by comparing double threshold with statistics. In [6], a dynamic spectrum sensing cycle was proposed by using the convex function of the energy detector's threshold to reduce the delay. [7] focused on the optimal number of secondary users in weighted cooperative spectrum sensing to improved the utility of CRN. These methods improve the detection accuracy to some extent, but there are still a great number of SUs which may cause too much sensing overhead.

In this paper, we propose a correlation based SUs selection scheme to select the representative SUs in CSS. In the proposed scheme, the SUs are clustered together in a given area which have the similar geography and communication conditions. Therefore, one secondary user's perceived results can be representative of the others. Density-Based Spatial Clustering of Applications with Noise (DSCN) is a clustering algorithm based on density. However, DSCN is based on the distance and can not completely reflect correlation among SUs. Thus, we proposed an improved the DSCN algorithm in order to select representative SU in a less dense area based on SUs' correlation. Compared with traditional CSS, this method alleviates the spectrum sensing overhead. Moreover, the probability of false alarm (P_f) and the probability of detection (P_d) in the proposed scheme can be improved. The simulation results show that the proposed improved DSCN enhances the detection performances and decreases sensing overhead compared with traditional spectrum sensing schemes.

The rest of this paper is organized as follows. In Sect. 2, we describe the system model. In Sect. 3, we explain CSS scheme for SU selection and propose the improved DSCN. Section 4 provides performance evaluation and simulation results and Sect. 5 concludes this paper.

2   System Model

2.1   Spectrum Sensing Hypothesis

This work considers a centralized CSS system with a primary user (PU), a fusion center (FC) and N SUs. FC is used to collect the perception results of each SU and fuse them. Then FC makes decision and returns the result. SUs detect channel idle condition and look for opportunities to use channel. In the proposed scheme, there is a set $\mathcal{L}\{1, 2, \cdots, L\}$ consisting of L SUs. All SUs are within FC's communication range and FC knows the distances from the SUs to FC. Let distance D from one SU to FC to be $\mathcal{D}\{d_1, d_2, \cdots, d_n\}$.

In CRN, the accuracy of spectrum sensing is to determine whether PU's signals $Si(t)$ appear based on the observed signals $Os(t)$. Therefore, we model it as a binary relationship:

$$Os(t) = \begin{cases} Gsn(t), & H_0 \\ Cg \cdot Si(t) + Gsn(t), & H_1 \end{cases} \tag{1}$$

where $Gsn(t)$ is zero mean additive Gaussian white noise and Cg denotes the channel gain between PU and SU. Hypothesis H_0 represents that PU is idle and hypothesis H_1 indicates that PU is presence. The spectrum sensing algorithm outputs the test statistics Λ from a series of processing of the observed signals in Eq. (1), and determines the availability of the licensed spectrum according to the test statistics Λ and the predetermined decision threshold λ. When $\Lambda > \lambda$, PU is of the presence. Otherwise, the channel is idle.

We use the P_d and P_f to measure performance indicators. They are defined as:

$$P_d = Pr\{E_1|H_1\}, \tag{2}$$
$$P_f = Pr\{E_1|H_0\} \tag{3}$$

where E_1 represents PU is present from the sensing result of the fusion. P_d means when PU signal is present, the probability that SU correctly detects the occurrence of PU signal. Higher P_d means better protection for PU. P_f denotes that PU is absent, the probability that SU incorrectly determines occurrence of PU signal. Higher P_f means lower spectrum efficiency.

2.2 Energy Detector

In this paper, we use energy detector to detect any zero mean and count independent signals. The energy detector determines whether the channel is idle by measuring the strength of the received signal. Equation (4) shows us the received power of user i:

$$P_i = \frac{P_{pu}}{d_i^\alpha}\beta_0 \tag{4}$$

where α is the path loss exponent factor; d_i is the distance between PU and SU_i. β_0 is a scalar and P_{pu} is the PU's signal power. Then the signal-noise ratio (SNR) γ_i of SU_i can be obtained as:

$$\gamma_i = \frac{P_i}{\sigma^2} \tag{5}$$

where σ is noise power. After SU_i obtains the SNR and makes decision whether the channel is idle, they send results to the FC. Section 3 will introduce the proposed scheme about the selecting of the representative SUs.

3 The Proposed Scheme of Improved DSCN

3.1 Fusion Algorithm

In this model, fusion center uses OR rules and AND rules. These two rules will use the same received data to get different results.

OR fusion rule means that the FC will declare that the PU is present as long as at least one SU detects the PU. The equations of P_d and P_f can be derived as [9]:

$$P_d = 1 - \prod_{i=1}^{k}(1 - P_{d,i}) \tag{6}$$

$$P_f = 1 - \prod_{i=1}^{k}(1 - P_{f,i}) \tag{7}$$

where k means total SUs participating in the fusion is k. $P_{d,i}$ is the SUs' detection probability and $P_{f,i}$ is SUs' false alarm probability about the licensed spectrum. AND fusion rule means that the FC will declare the PU is absent unless all of SUs detect the PU. The equations of P_d and P_f can be obtained as:

$$P_d = \prod_{i=1}^{k} P_{d,i} \tag{8}$$

$$P_f = \prod_{i=1}^{k} P_{f,i} \tag{9}$$

3.2 Correction of Shadow Fading

In the transmission receiving area, the large buildings and other objects block the path of the wave and form a semi-blind area, which form the electromagnetic shadow. Due to the shadowing effect, adjacent SUs experience almost the same fading effect, which degrades the performance of collaborative spectrum sensing. To improve spectrum sensing performance, we are required to select a representative SU from SUs with high spatial relevance to participate in the CSS.

First, Eq. (4) shows us that the received power of user i is inversely proportional to the distance d_i. It means that excessive distance causes SNR to be extremely low and significantly decreases SU_i's accuracy of detection. That is to say, the results from FC may be greatly influenced by SUs with low SNR. Therefore, we set a threshold ϵ to remove SUs with a SNR less than ϵ.

Then, according to the Logarithmic Distance Path Loss Model, the average received power decreases logarithmically with distance in both indoor and outdoor. For any send-receive (S-R) distance, the average path loss is expressed as [10]:

$$\overline{PALO}(dB) = \overline{PALO}(d_0) + 10nlog(\frac{d}{d_0}) \tag{10}$$

where d_0 is near ground reference distance determined by the test. n is the path loss index, indicating the growth rate of path loss with distance. d is the distance between receiver and transmitter. Therefore, to model the correlation properties we have used a decreasing correlation function as follows:

$$Crl(d) = e^{-d\theta} \tag{11}$$

where d is distance between two SUs and we define $d_{i,j}$ is the distance between SU_i and SU_j; θ is an environment based parameter and we set $\theta \approx 0.02/m$. When $d_{i,j} = 0$, $Crl(d_{i,j}) = 1$, it means SU_i and SU_j have full correlation. However, SU_i and SU_j have empty correlation if $d_{i,j} \to \infty^+$. Therefore, we set a threshold value δ $(0 < \delta < 1)$ to determine whether there is a good correlation between two SUs. Then we use 0 and 1 to represent the correlation between two SUs and we obtain the equation [11]:

$$Crl'(i,j) = \begin{cases} 1, & Crl(d_{i,j}) \geq \delta \\ 0, & Crl(d_{i,j}) < \delta \end{cases} \tag{12}$$

$Crl(i,j) = 1$ represents that SU_i and SU_j have a good correlation. This method also saves storage space of the FC. Then, we use a $\mathcal{A} \times \mathcal{A}$ matrix ζ to show the relationships among all SUs, it can be obtained as follows:

$$\begin{bmatrix} Crl'(1,1) & Crl'(1,2) & \cdots & Crl'(1,\mathcal{A}) \\ Crl'(2,1) & Crl'(2,2) & \cdots & Crl'(2,\mathcal{A}) \\ \vdots & \vdots & \ddots & \vdots \\ Crl'(\mathcal{A},1) & Crl'(\mathcal{A},2) & \cdots & Crl'(\mathcal{A},\mathcal{A}) \end{bmatrix} \tag{13}$$

3.3 Improved DSCN

DSCN defines the cluster as the largest set of points connected by density and can divide regions with sufficient density into clusters. We improve DSCN so that it can be applied to SUs selection in cooperative sensing mainly reflects in two aspects.

Using Correlation of SUs. Traditional DSCN uses radius of neighborhood to count the number of points that a point contains to determine whether it is a core point or a noise point. However, besides distance, other factors such as shadow fading also affect the detection performance. Therefore, it is better to use correlation to correct shadow fading hereinbefore. Improved DSCN uses correlation of SUs instead of radius of neighborhood. Each radius of neighborhood r corresponds to a unique $Crl(r)$ because Eq. (11) is monotonically decreasing. SU_i and SU_j are considered to be SUs of mutual inclusion if $Crl'(i,j) \neq 0$.

Two-Stage Core Point Judgement Threshold. Traditional DSCN sets a threshold η to determine whether a point is a core point. When considering the actual situation, the SUs who close to PU is denser and SUs who far from PU is looser. Therefore, most of the boundary SUs will be excluded if set a large η. Moreover, there will be very few representative SUs selected internally if set a small η.

Based on the above considerations, we use two-stage core point judgement threshold to solve the problem. When the first judgement is made on a selected point, we set a short η_1 to ensure that most boundary points are also taken into account. Then, we set a large η_1 to avoid too few internal representative points.

Our proposed improved DSCN is summarized in Algorithm 1. This algorithm considers many factors among SUs and selects representative SUs based on the correlation. Moreover, the number of SUs selected can be changed by setting threshold η_1 and η_2, which can significantly improve the accuracy of sensing.

Algorithm 1: Optimal SUs selection

---

1 **begin**
2   **bool** $Visit[m] = false, w[m]$, **int** $Nps[m] = 0, q = 0$
3   **INPUT: Finite set of SUs** $\mathcal{L}$**:** $\{1, \cdots, L\}$ **and** $\mathcal{A}$ **: Set of A SUs' SNR** $> \epsilon$
4   Calculate SNR λ_i of every SU_i using Equation (4)
5   Select SUs based on the SNR and store in $\mathcal{A}$
6   **for** $int\ m = 1\ to\ \mathcal{A}$ **do**
7   **for** $int\ n = 1\ to\ \mathcal{A}$ **do**
8             $Crl(m, n) = e^{-xy}$
9   **if** $Crl'(m, n) < \gamma$ **then**
10                 $Crl'(m, n) = 0$
11   **end**
12   **else**
13                 $Crl'(m, n) = Crl(m, n)$
14   **end**
15   **end**
16   **end**
17   **for** $int\ m = 1\ to\ \mathcal{A}$ **do**
18   **for** $int\ n = 1\ to\ \mathcal{A}$ **do**
19   **if** $Crl'(m, n) \neq 0$ **then**
20                 $Nps[m] + +$
21   **end**
22   **end**
23   **end**
24   **for** $int\ m = 1\ to\ \mathcal{A}$ **do**
25   **if** $Visit[m] = true$ **then**
26   **continue**
27   **end**
28   **else**
29   **if** $Nps[m] < \eta_1$ **then**
30                 $Visit[m] = true$
31                 $w[m] = 0$
32   **end**
33   **else**
34                 $Visit[m] = true$
35                 $w[m] = 1$
36   establish new cluster $C[q + +]$
37   add the neighborhood of the ith point into $C[q]$
38   **for** $int\ n\ in\ C[q]$ **do**
39   **if** $Nps[n] > \eta_2$ **then**
40   add the neighborhood of the nth point into $C[q]$
41   **end**
42   **end**
43   **end**
44   **end**
45   **end**
46   Select SU_T with maximum $Nps[t]$ in $C[t]$
47   add SU_T into $R[t]$
48   **OUTPUT :** T **: Set of selected t SUs**
49 **end**

Selected SUs send decision (H_0 or H_1) to the FC. FC uses OR and AND fusion rules to aggregate the fusion results and make final decision. Then FC sends the decision to SUs that need idle channel and have access to it.

4 Simulation Results

In the simulation, the performance evaluation mainly depends on the sensing overhead (number of participating communication SUs), P_d and P_f in Matlab. Initially, 400 SUs are randomly distributed in a 100 km × 100 km coordinate system. PU is at the center of the coordinate system and can communicate with all SUs. The result is shown in Fig. 1.

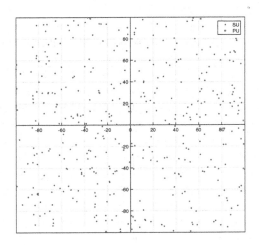

Fig. 1. The distribution of randomly SUs

During the sensing period, the number of received signal samples at each SU is set at 5000 samples. The path loss exponential factor a is set at 3. Set β_0 and P_{pu} to a value so that the SNR of the SUs at 100 km from PU is -16 dB. Then we set threshold ϵ to ensure SUs with good SNR and exclude all SUs with SNR less than threshold. The result is shown in Fig. 2.

In the next phase, we use improved DSCN to select representative SUs. The value of η_1 is set at 5 and η_2 is set at 10. Typically, there are 26 SUs left. The distribute of SUs involved in CSS is shown in Fig. 3.

Next, considering the P_d and P_f, we use AND fusion rule for performance evaluation of P_d because it can reduce the probability of secondary users' interference while primary user is present. OR fusion rule is selected for P_f because when the PU is absent, as long as one SU senses the channel is idle, it can occupy the channel and utilize the spectrum. The simulation considers a total of 100 SUs. Starting from the SU nearest to PU, select SUs by distance from smallest to largest and use improved DSCN and unfiltered SUs for CSS respectively.

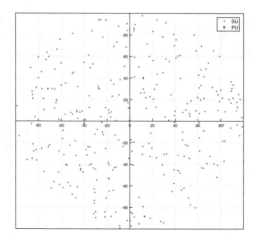

Fig. 2. The distribution after screening SUs with too low SNR

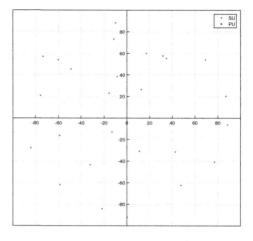

Fig. 3. The distribution of SUs involved in cooperative spectrum sensing

According to the Monte Carlo rule, we run 1000 times simulations and take the mean to evaluate the P_d and P_i of the original CSS method and the CSS method based on improved DSCN. For P_d, target P_i is set at 0.001 and 0.002, the result of simulation is shown in Fig. 4.

The value range of P_d without selection is from 0.1 to 1. Moreover, as the numbers of SUs increases, the value of P_d decreases rapidly. The value range of P_d with selection is from 0.9 to 1, and the downward trend is slow. Furthermore, P_d will increase as the target P_f increases. For P_f, target P_d is set at 0.999 and 0.998, Fig. 5 shows us the simulation result.

The value range of P_f without selection is from 0.08 to 0.1, which increases with the increase of the numbers of SUs. The value range of P_f with selection is

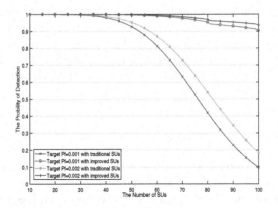

Fig. 4. P_d with Numbers of SUs participating in CSS

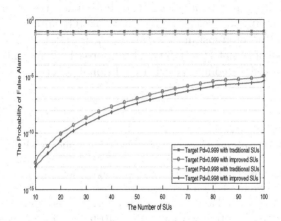

Fig. 5. P_f with Numbers of SUs participating in CSS

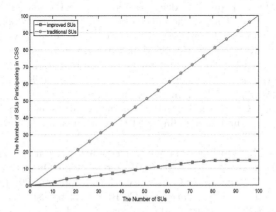

Fig. 6. Numbers of SUs participating in CSS

from 10^{-13} to 10^{-5}, which is much less than the value of P_f without selection. Moreover, P_f will increase as the target P_d grows. In cooperative spectrum sensing, information exchange between SUs and FC result in sensing overhead. Using improved DSCN can greatly reduce the sensing overhead. The simulation result is shown in Fig. 6. For 100 SUs, there are only less than 20 SUs participating in CSS.

5   Conclusion

In this paper, we proposed a correlation based spectrum sensing scheme and designed the improved DSCN to select representative SUs in cooperative spectrum sensing. In the proposed scheme, SUs were selected based on their correlation and the density of distribution. This method could significantly reduce sensing overhead and shadow fading under the premise of ensuring the detection effect. Two-stage core point judgement threshold made the improved SU more representative. Simulation results show that for 100 improved SUs, P_d stays above 0.9 under the circumstance of target $P_f = 0.001$ and P_f is controlled under 0.01 in case of target $P_d = 0.998$. This approach significantly improves the P_d and decreases the P_f compared with traditional spectrum sensing schemes.

References

1. Federal Communications Commission: Spectrum policy task force report, FCC 02-155 (2002)
2. Mitola, J., Maguire, G.Q.: Cognitive radios: making software radios more personal. IEEE Pers. Commun. **6**, 13–18 (1999)
3. Mehdawi, M., Riley, N., Fanan, A., Bentaher, O.: Proposed system model for wideband cooperative spectrum sensing with multi-bit hard decision using two-stage adaptive sensing. In: IEEE 2019 27th Telecommunications Forum (TELFOR), Belgrade, Serbia, pp. 1–4 (2019)
4. Kartlak, H., Odabasioglu, N., Akan, A.: Optimum relay selection for cooperative spectrum sensing and transmission in cognitive networks. In: 22nd European Signal Processing Conference (EUSIPCO), Lisbon, pp. 161–165 (2014)
5. Smriti, Charan, C.: Double threshold based cooperative spectrum sensing with consideration of history of sensing nodes in cognitive radio networks. In: IEEE 2018 2nd International Conference on Power, Energy and Environment: Towards Smart Technology (ICEPE), Shillong, India, pp. 1–9 (2018)
6. Chandrasekaran, G., Kalyani, S.: Performance analysis of cooperative spectrum sensing over $\kappa-\mu$ shadowed fading. IEEE Wirel. Commun. Lett. **4**(5), 553–556 (2015)
7. Yang, J., Shao, X.: Optimal number of secondary users in weighted cooperative spectrum sensing. In: Proceedings of 2011 Cross Strait Quad-Regional Radio Science and Wireless Technology Conference, Harbin, pp. 902–905 (2011)
8. Rifa-Pous, H., Blasco, M.J., Garrigues, C.: Review of robust cooperative spectrum sensing techniques for cognitive radio networks. Wirel. Pers. Commun. **67**(2), 175–198 (2012). https://doi.org/10.1007/s11277-011-0372-x

9. Peh, E., Liang, Y.-C.: Optimization for cooperative sensing in cognitive radio networks. In: Proceedings of the IEEE Wireless Communications and Networking Conference (WCNC), Hong Kong, pp. 27–32 (2007)
10. Gudmundson, M.: A correlation model for shadow fading in mobile radio. Electron. Lett. **27**, 2146–2147 (1991)
11. Dhurandher, S.K., Woungang, I., Gupta, N., Jain, R., Singhal, D., Agarwal, J., et al.: Optimal secondary users selection for cooperative spectrum sensing in cognitive radio networks. In: IEEE Globecom Workshops (GC Wkshps), pp. 1–6 (2018)

The Design Methodology for MAC Strategies and Protocols Supporting Ultra-Low Delay Services in Next Generation IEEE 802.11 WLAN

Bo Li, Ghaleb Abdullah Abdulwahab Mohammed, Mao Yang[(✉)],
and Zhongjiang Yan

School of Electronics and Information, Northwestern Polytechnical University,
Xi'an 710072, China
{libo.npu,yangmao,zhjyan}@nwpu.edu.cn,
abdullahl.ghaleb@gmail.com

Abstract. The next generation WiFi standard needs to consider how to better support ultra-low delay services. There are a lot of works proposed to improve the delay performance of traffic flows in WiFi networks. However, in order to face the high uncertainty of traffic arrival characteristics, it is necessary to explore new methodology to propose feasible Multiple Access Control (MAC) strategies and protocols supporting ultra-low delay services. This paper discusses the design methodology of ultra-low delay MAC strategies and protocols for next generation WiFi. Firstly, a general end-to-end transmission and processing model for an Information Transmission and Processing Network (ITPN) is proposed. The end-to-end delay of an ITPN is analyzed and the expression of the minimum end-to-end delay is obtained. Interestingly, based on the expression of the minimum end-to-end delay, we reveal three key factors that determine the end-to-end delay, namely, the number of processing blocks of the system, the size of information blocks processed and the total processing bandwidth of the system. Furthermore, some key technologies are proposed, which points out the feasible and attractive directions for the follow-up researches. Finally, a general ultra-low delay MAC framework based on the idea of "flexible reservation" is proposed. We believe that apart from IEEE 802.11 WLAN, the MAC framework proposed in this paper can be readily applied to various kinds of wireless networks.

Keywords: Wireless LAN · IEEE 802.11 · Ultra-low delay services · Medium access control · Reservation · Preemption

1 Introduction

WLAN technology regulated by IEEE 802.11 standard is developing continuously. As far as we know, the next generation IEEE 802.11 standard will support higher transmission rate and lower service delay requirements [1].

There are many researches on how to meet the low delay performance requirements for various time delay sensitive traffics in IEEE 802.11 WLAN. In general, the related works can be divided into two categories (see "related work" for details): works to

B. Li et al. (Eds.): IoTaaS 2020, LNICST 346, pp. 80–97, 2021.
https://doi.org/10.1007/978-3-030-67514-1_7

reduce service delay [2–23] and works to eliminate service delay [24–32]. In order to reduce service delay, authors try to improve the performance of service delay by optimizing scheduling strategy [6–13], optimizing queuing strategy [2–5], and distinguishing access priority [14–19]. We believe that these methods are not suitable for supporting the performance requirements of ultra-low delay services. On the other hand, resource reservation and resource preemption are the key methods to eliminate service delay. Because these methods try to eliminate service delay as much as possible, it is believed that they are more suitable for supporting ultra-low delay traffics.

However, considering the uncertainty of traffic arrival characteristics, the medium access strategies based on resource reservation cannot accurately predict the arrival characteristics of a traffic flow, and thus cannot achieve efficient resource reservation. For the medium access strategies based on resource preemption, the preempted traffic flows may be starved by traffic flows with higher priority. Therefore, in view of the uncertainty of traffic arrival characteristics, how to support ultra-low delay service efficiently is one of the key problems to be solved in designing and implementing the next generation WiFi medium access technologies.

This paper discusses the design methodology of ultra-low delay medium access control strategies and protocols for next generation WiFi. The main contributions include:

- A general end-to-end transmission and processing model for an ITPN is proposed. Based on this model, the end-to-end delay of the system is analyzed and the expression of the minimum end-to-end delay is given. Three key factors that determine the end-to-end delay are revealed, that is, the number of processing blocks, the size of information blocks processed and the total processing bandwidth of the system.
- Some key technologies and the core ideas to realize ultra-low delay services are proposed, which points out the feasible directions for the follow-up researches.
- A general ultra-low delay MAC framework based on flexible reservation is outlined. The MAC framework can be applied to various kinds of wireless communication networks including IEEE 802.11 WLAN.

The paper is organized as follows: in Sect. 2, a brief overview of the existing works aimed at improving the service delay performance in IEEE 802.11 networks is given. In Sect. 3, the end-to-end delay in an ITPN system is generalized, modeled and analyzed. In Sect. 4, basic ideas for the key technologies to supporting ultra-low delay are described. In Sect. 5, a MAC framework for supporting ultra-low delay services is proposed. In Sect. 6, some conclusions are given.

2 Related Work

2.1 Latency Reduce Scheme

A. Optimizing Queuing Strategy

Packet queue is an indispensable module in the media access control (MAC) layer of WiFi devices. Packets from the upper layer to the MAC layer often need to be assigned to one data queue. According to Enhanced Distribution Channel Access (EDCA) mechanism specified in IEEE 802.11e, WiFi device always possesses several queues, four or six typically. Each queue corresponds to one access category (AC). It is obvious that packets need to experience queuing delay before being transmitted. Therefore, some studies focus on queuing strategy optimizing for low latency.

Saheb, and et al. [2] propose an enhanced hybrid coordination function (HCF) controlled channel access (EHCCA) scheme. In EHCCA, the packets are queued in MAC based on the traffic deadline. In this case, more urgent packets can be scheduled due to higher priority. Pei, and et al. [3] allows the late arriving packet with low latency requirement to bypass the data queuing. Li, and et al. [4] introduce a new parameter that is related to packet importance index, packet latency, and channel state, where the packet importance index indicated in the IP header can be derived based on gradient of the video QoE function. After that, naturally, the enqueue operation is directly affected by the importance index. Prabhu, and et al. [5] face to the polling based IEEE 802.11 network. The authors analyze that with the increase of STA number, the latency performance is getting worse. Then, two-level priority queues are proposed.

B. Optimizing Scheduling Strategy

Scheduling is quite important for wireless networking and communications. Ahn, and et al. [6] propose a MAC scheme based on Orthogonal Frequency Division Multiple Access (OFDMA) introduced by IEEE 802.11ax. The Access Point (AP) periodically sends trigger frame (TF) to require the associated low latency STAs to send uplink data through OFDMA without access collision. Qian, and et al. [7] introduce an aggregation sliding window for aggregate MAC protocol data unit (A-MPDU) even if some MPDUs aggregated in the A-MPDU exceed the bitmap range. To determine the aggregated MPDU number in the retransmission A-MPDU, the proposed scheme takes the delay requirements into consideration since large A-MPDU duration may lead to large latency. Some other studies also focus on the A-MPDU optimization such as aggregation size, per-MPDU size, and retransmission time [8–11].

Avdotin, and et al. [12, 13] try to enhance the uplink OFDMA random access (UORA) scheme specified in IEEE 802.11ax. The authors propose two schemes. In the first scheme, AP allocates several resource units (RUs) for low latency requirements only. When collision occurs in these RUs, AP polls the low latency STAs one by one in the next several successive TFs. In the second scheme, the low latency STAs are divided into several groups. The STAs in the same group are allocated in one RU. If collision occurs in one RU, AP polls the STAs in the corresponding group in the next few TFs.

C. Distinguishing Access Priority

IEEE 802.11 adopts carrier-sense multiple access with collision avoidance (CSMA/CA). It means contention based channel access is deployed before transmission. Channel access delay cannot be ignored especially when node number is large.

Kim, and et al. [14] modify the channel access rules by introducing "Round". Round is a time duration during which each STA can at most send one frame. They validate that the proposed scheme improves the tail latency for IEEE 802.11 network. Nguyen, and et al. [15] analyze the requirement differences between delay sensitive traffic and throughput sensitive traffic. With the change from delay sensitive to throughput sensitive, both the contention window (CW_{min}) and transmission opportunity (TXOP) limit proportionally increase. Tian, and et al. [16] modify the backoff rule that not only the backoff value is doubled due to transmission failure, but also the backoff value is doubled when the channel is busy. Lin, and et al. [17] model the system performance with all the associated STA's channel access configuration and parameters by using machine learning. Then, based on the trained model, AP optimizes the channel access parameters of each STA and announces these parameters through beacon frame to obtain the delay requirements. Moreover, some studies focus on the contention window size adjusting algorithm [18, 19].

D. Others

Besides the schemes discussed above, some studies try to improve the latency from other perspectives. Some related work introduces redundancy resources to enhance the transmission reliability, thereby improving the latency performance [20, 21]. Moreover, some researchers focus on the static configuration such as operation channel, transmission power, location, and load balance approaches [22, 23].

2.2   Latency Elimination Schemes

A. Channel Reservation

Channel reservation allows the prior transmission piggybacks the transmission time and duration of the subsequent transmissions. Other nodes who successfully receive the reservation information will keep silent during the reserved period. Choi, and et al. [24] propose a reservation scheme named EBA. One node broadcasts the backoff value of the next channel access process. Other nodes obtaining this information avoid selecting the same backoff end time.

Our previous studies extend the channel reservation conception into multi-step channel reservation [25, 26]. We analyze that one-step reservation is not reliable due to channel loss and collisions, resulting in the failed transmission of reservation information. We propose that one packet piggybacks the reservation information of several subsequent packets, named multi-step reservation. This scheme significantly enhances the transmission reliability of reservation information since the reservation information of each packet is transmitted by several times.

Some studies focus on the reservation schemes in the wireless ad hoc network and mesh network. Singh, and et al. [27] pay attention to the periodical traffic. The nodes periodically access the channel, and let other nodes know their periods to avoid the collisions. Sheu and T. Sheu [28, 29] propose two-period reservation MAC protocol.

Nodes in the contention based period transmit data or broadcast the reservation information, while in the contention free period they directly transmit data in the reserved time slot without contention. Moreover, other studies introduce the reservation schemes in synchronized network [30, 31].

B. **Resource Preemption**

Resource preemption allows the intended low latency transmission to pause, stop, or preempt the ongoing transmission. Bankov, and et al. [32] propose an out-of-band announcement based preemption scheme. The STA who has intended low latency transmission firstly sends an announcement frame in a dedicated channel. Then, the sender of the ongoing transmission stops transmission immediately, and meanwhile, other STAs suspend their backoff process. After that, the STA who has intended low latency transmission can send its frame immediately.

3   Modeling and Analysis of End-to-End Delay in Information Transmission and Processing Networks

IEEE 802.11 WLAN is a kind of information transmission and processing network. In order to make the methodology proposed in this paper more general, we summarize a general end-to-end delay model for an ITPN, and analyze the general expression of the end-to-end delay based on it. Then, given the total processing bandwidth of the system, the expression of the minimum end-to-end delay is obtained.

3.1   General System Model of an ITPN

Figure 1 shows a simple ITPN, that is, there are only two nodes (sending node and receiving node) in the system. Furthermore, we can decompose each node into several protocol layers. In other words, information originates from the protocol layer N of the sender and goes through the protocol layers $N, N - 1, \ldots, 1$ of the sender in turn. Then, the information processed by the sender is transmitted into the protocol layer 1 of the receiver, and from the protocol layer 1 of the receiver, it goes through the protocol layers $1, \ldots, N - 1, N$ of the receiver in turn. Suppose that the processing delay of the message to be processed at the protocol layer i of the sender is $T_{ds}(i)$ $(i = 1, 2, \ldots, N)$ and that of the protocol layer j of the receiver is $T_{dr}(j)$ $(j = 1, 2, \ldots, N)$. It can be concluded that the end-to-end delay experienced by the information in this simple ITPN is as follows:

$$T_D = \sum_{i=1}^{N} T_{ds}(i) + \sum_{j=1}^{N} T_{dr}(j) \tag{1}$$

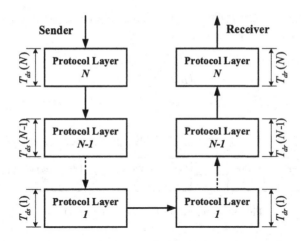

Fig. 1. Two communication terminals with layered protocol stacks

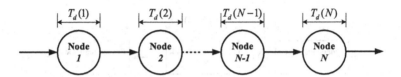

Fig. 2. A multi-hop network composed of several nodes

Figure 2 shows another example of an ITPN, that is, the system contains N adjacent communication nodes, and the information is processed and transmitted hop-by-hop in the way of storage and forwarding. In other words, the information starts from node 1, goes through the processing of the nodes $1, \ldots, N-1, N$ in turn, and finally is output at the node N. If the processing delay of the processed information in the node i is $T_d(i)$ $(i = 1, 2, \ldots, N)$, we can obtain that the end-to-end delay of the information in the system is:

$$T_D = \sum_{i=1}^{N} T_d(i) \tag{2}$$

Above, we only give two examples for ITPN systems (there are still many more). If we generally perceive both "protocol layer" in Fig. 1 and "node" in Fig. 2 as "processing block", we will get a more general end-to-end processing and transmission model for an ITPN as shown in Fig. 3. It can be seen from the model that most of ITPNs can be generally considered as a network system which processes and transmits input information flow from one block to another. Therefore, the delay experienced by the input information in an ITPN can be considered as the superposition of processing delays caused by each processing block

$$T_D = \sum_{i=1}^{N} T_d(i) \tag{3}$$

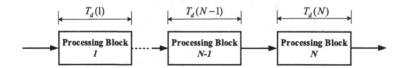

Fig. 3. A general system model for an ITPN

3.2   Modeling of End-to-End Delay

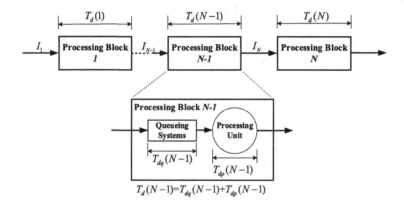

Fig. 4. The decomposition of the end-to-end delay in an ITPN

As shown in Fig. 4, the delay $T_d(i)$ $(i = 1, 2, \ldots, N)$ in each processing block can be further decomposed into queuing delay $T_{dq}(i)$ $(i = 1, 2, \ldots, N)$ and processing delay $T_{dp}(i)$ $(i = 1, 2, \ldots, N)$. Therefore, the end-to-end delay in an ITPN can be expressed as:

$$T_D = \sum_{i=1}^{N} [T_{dq}(i) + T_{dp}(i)] \tag{4}$$

It is worth noting that the queuing delay $T_{dq}(i)$ $(i = 1, 2, \ldots, N)$ is the sum of all the waiting times of the processed information waiting for further processing in the current processing block.

Define the processing bandwidth $b_p(i)$ $(i = 1, 2, \ldots, N)$ of the current processing block as:

$$b_p(i) \triangleq \frac{I_i}{T_{dp}(i)} \tag{5}$$

where, I_i $(i = 1, 2, \ldots, N)$ represents the amount of information to be processed by the current processing block (unit: bits). Combined with (4) and (5), we have

$$T_D = \sum_{i=1}^{N} \left[T_{dq}(i) + \frac{I_i}{b_p(i)} \right] \tag{6}$$

3.3 Minimization of End-to-End Delay

In this paper, we consider how to achieve ultra-low end-to-end delay. If we can take some measures (such as the related technologies described in Sect. 4) to eliminate queuing delays, i.e. let $T_{dq}(i) = 0$ $(i = 1, 2, \ldots, N)$, the end-to-end delay in an ITPN can be simplified as follows:

$$T_D = \sum_{i=1}^{N} \left[\frac{I_i}{b_p(i)} \right] \tag{7}$$

Next, on the basis of Eq. (7), we consider how to minimize the end-to-end delay T_D and what is the value of the minimum end-to-end delay $T_{D,\min}$. It is assumed that the amount of information input into an ITPN remains unchanged after being processed from one processing block to another, i.e. $I = I_i$ $(i = 1, 2, \ldots, N)$. And given the total processing bandwidth of the system to be $B = \sum_{i=1}^{N} b_p(i)$, the optimization analysis of Eq. (7) shows that when the total processing bandwidth of the system is equally allocated to each processing block, the corresponding end-to-end delay reaches the minimum value. That is,

$$T_{D,\min} = \frac{I \cdot N^2}{B} \tag{8}$$

In order to facilitate the readers' understanding, we list some minimum end-to-end delays $T_{D,\min}$ corresponding to different parameters I, N, B in Table 1. Do you think which performance level can be more practically achieved by the current wireless networks?

Table 1. Examples of end-to-end delays achieved

N: Number of processing blocks	I: Size of an information block (bits)	B: Total processing bandwidth (Mbps)	Minimum total end to end delays ($T_{D,\min}$:ms)
100	1,000	10,000	1.0
100	100	1,000	1.0
10	100	10	1.0
10	100	10,000	0.001

4 Basic Ideas of the Key Technologies Supporting Ultra-Low Delay Services

In the previous section, we analyzed and modeled the end-to-end delay in an ITPN, and analyzed the minimum end-to-end delay that can be achieved for an ultra-low delay traffic flows. In the analysis, we assume that the queuing delay of an ultra-low delay traffic flow in each processing block is zero. However, in order to achieve zero queuing delay and minimize processing delay, a variety of key technologies are indispensable. In this section, we will focus on the core objectives of eliminating queuing delay and/or reducing processing delay, and introduce the basic ideas for several key technologies, which is summarized in Table 2.

Table 2. Basic ideas of key technologies

Key technologies	Basic ideas
Traffic identification	When it enters into an ITPN, the corresponding traffic flow will be identified and processed
Simplification of processing tasks	For ultra-low delay traffic flows, fewer processing blocks will be provided as much as possible
Instant processing	The information arriving successively is organized into the information unit with the smallest granularity as possible. The corresponding processing block can start its processing instantly
Resource preemption	When a traffic flow with ultra-low delay requirement arrives at the current processing block, if there is no idle resources for it, it can preempt the processing resources occupied by other delay insensitive traffic flows
Resource reservation	Based on the prediction of the arrival characteristics of an ultra-low delay traffic flow in the future period, corresponding processing resources are reserved for it in advance
Traffic prediction	The possible amount of information to be processed for an arrival traffic flow in a certain future period is estimated in advance

(continued)

Table 2. (*continued*)

Key technologies	Basic ideas
Flexible reservation	Through the efficient combination of resource reservation, resource preemption and resource release, a flexible "exchange" mechanism of occupied resources is introduced (with resource release and resource preemption as the means of exchange) between traffic flows with different performance requirements, and overcomes the intrinsic defects which cannot be easily solved by using only resource reservation or resource preemption
Traffic flexibilization	Reducing the sensitivity of the loss of the utility gain for the recipient of a traffic flow to the loss of partial information in the traffic flow
Grouping based scheduling for traffic flows	The problem to be solved is how to effectively group traffic flows and map specific traffic groups to specific processing bandwidth. The core idea is to organize some class B traffic flows with greater flexibility and some class A traffic flows, which is difficult to accurately predict their arrival characteristics, into some common group to be processed further within a shared processing bandwidth
Collaborative reservation	The basic idea is that when an earlier processing block clearly knows the arrival characteristics of a traffic flow, it informs the subsequent processing blocks to reserve the required amount of processing resources in advance through the signaling system between processing blocks
Adaptive allocation of processing bandwidth	Based on the amount of information to be processed, the corresponding processing bandwidth is allocated adaptively
Optimal configuration of processing bandwidth	Under the given constraints, the end-to-end delay can be minimized by optimizing the allocation of processing resources among all the processing blocks in an ITPN

4.1 Traffic Identification

In an ITPN, it often carries several traffic flows with different performance requirements (i.e. the traffic flows that need to be transmitted and processed by the ITPN). The system needs to take some technical measures for traffic flows with ultra-low delay performance requirements (see the descriptions below). Therefore, it is necessary to identify the traffic flow as soon as it enters the ITPN, so as to configure the processing strategies used by each processing block. In short, the central task of the traffic identification is to identify the traffic flow when it just enters the ITPN, and instruct other processing blocks to properly configure their processing strategies.

4.2 Simplification of Processing Tasks

In an ITPN, a variety of traffic flows need to be processed by several processing blocks, and each processing block brings about a certain delay (including queuing delay and processing delay). It can be seen from Eq. (8) that the minimum end-to-end delay will increase significantly with the number of processing blocks. In order to reduce the delay, an obvious idea is to reduce the number of processing blocks as much as possible for the traffic with ultra-low delay requirements (that is, the fewer processing blocks, the better!). For example, for some ultra-low delay traffic flows, one can consider using a simplified network protocol stack to reduce the number of protocol stacks that must be passed through. As for another example, in a multi-hop ad hoc network, the end-to-end routing with as fewer hops as possible is established for ultra-low delay traffic, so as to reduce the number of "store and forward" links that the traffic must go through in the transmission procedure. In short, the core idea is to provide as fewer processing blocks as possible for ultra-low delay traffic flows, so as to achieve the purpose of reducing end-to-end delay.

4.3   Instant Processing

The information of a traffic flow to be processed in an ITPN is often divided into information units, and then corresponding processing is carried out for each information unit. If the granularity of the information unit is large, it will lead to a large waiting delay before the start of the processing. It can be seen from Eq. (8) that the minimum end-to-end delay will increase linearly with the increase of the size of information units processed by a processing block. In other words, if the size of the information unit can be reduced as much as possible, the end-to-end delay will be reduced accordingly. The basic idea of instant processing is to organize the information flow that reaches the ITPN system successively into information units with the smallest granularity as possible, and start the processing instantly without waiting for a longer period of time. The idea of instant processing can be applied in various scenarios, such as instant framing technology, instant coding technology, and instant medium access control technology and so on.

4.4   Resource Preemption

When an ultra-low delay traffic flow reaches the current processing block, if the processing unit in the processing block has no available processing resources (that is, all its processing bandwidth is occupied by other traffic flows), the ultra-low delay traffic flow can only wait in the queue. The basic idea of resource preemption is that when the ultra-low delay traffic flow arrives, if there is no idle processing resources, it can preempt the processing resources occupied by the other delay insensitive traffic flows. The preempted traffic flows will be temporarily arranged in the queue of processing block, waiting for subsequent resources to be available so as to continue their suspended services. The essence for resource preemption is to reduce the processing delay of ultra-low latency traffic flows at the cost of extending the delay of insensitive traffic flows.

4.5   Resource Reservation

Resource preemption technology has a certain cost, which not only prolongs the delay of the preempted traffic flows, but also causes low priority services to be possibly "starved" by ultra-low delay traffic flows without exerting some proper measures. Moreover, it will cost a certain amount of time to process these interrupts. Resource reservation is a technology that can react faster than resource preemption. Its basic idea is to reserve processing resources in advance according to the prediction of the arrival characteristics of an ultra-low delay traffic flow in the future period (the reserved resources will not be occupied by other traffic flows). In this way, when the ultra-low delay traffic flow arrives, the reserved resources can be used instantly without affecting the processing resources occupied by other services.

4.6   Traffic Prediction

The premise for resource reservation is to accurately predict the ultra-low delay traffic, that is, to estimate the possible amount of traffic arrivals for the corresponding ultra-low delay traffic flow in a certain future period, so as to reserve proper amount of resources accordingly. Generally speaking, the arrival characteristics of most traffic flows are uncertain to some different extent, which makes it an extremely challenging task to achieve accurate traffic prediction. Hence, this implies that it is also very challenging to realize accurate reservation of resources!

4.7   Flexible Reservation

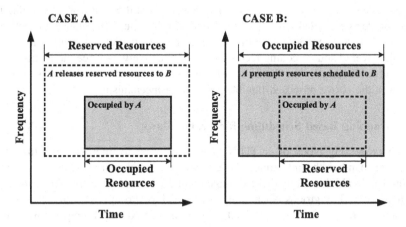

Fig. 5. Flexible reservation mechanism

The basic idea of flexible reservation is to reasonably combine resource reservation, resource preemption and resource release, and introduce an efficient "exchange" mechanism (with resource release and resource preemption as the means for making exchange) for occupied resources between traffic flows with different performance requirements, and then overcome the intrinsic defects that both resource reservation and resource preemption cannot overcome individually. Figure 5 shows the core idea of flexible reservation. For the sake of convenience, we classified traffic in an ITPN into time delay sensitive traffic (class A traffic) and delay insensitive traffic (class B traffic). For a class A traffic flow, it normally relies on resource reservation to enjoy the processing of the system. If the reserved resources are not actually used by it (due to inaccurate traffic prediction), these resources can be released and used by other class B traffic flows (as shown in case A in the figure). On the other hand, for a class A traffic flow, it actually needs to use processing resources that have not been reserved in advance (again due to inaccurate traffic prediction), and in this case it can preempt the resources that are being occupied by some class B traffic flows (as shown in case B in the figure). It can be seen that the flexible reservation mechanism puts much lower requirements on the accuracy for making traffic prediction, which makes it to be more feasible and practical than the above mentioned resource reservation mechanism.

4.8   Traffic Flexibilization

In an ITPN system, the recipient of a traffic flow will get a certain utility gain after receiving a certain amount of information. If not all the information to be received reaches the recipient before the expected time instance (that is, only a part of the information arrives, and the part of information that fails to arrive on time will lose its effectiveness), the utility gain of the recipient will be lost to some extent. The flexibility of a traffic flow means that before the expected time instance, although some information has not reached to the recipient, the loss of the utility gain that the recipient obtained is not large. In other words, the loss of the utility gain at the recipient side is not sensitive to the partial loss of information arriving at the recipient if the traffic flow has some degree of flexibility. The core idea of traffic flexibilization is to reduce the sensitivity of the recipient's loss of the utility gain to partial information losses. For example, layered source coding technology can effectively enhance the flexibility of a traffic flow. The higher the flexibility of a traffic flow is, the more effective it can be applied in the above proposed flexible reservation mechanism.

4.9   Grouping Based Scheduling for Traffic Flows

In each processing block of an ITPN system, in order to improve the utilization of processing bandwidth and reduce the complexity of scheduling resources, the processing bandwidth is usually divided into certain divisions, which are then scheduled to different traffic flow groups (such strategy is called as "grouping based scheduling" in this paper). The problem to be solved in grouping based scheduling is how to effectively group traffic flows and map specific traffic groups to specific processing bandwidth. In order to effectively support the flexible reservation mechanism, the basic idea of grouping traffic flows with various performance requirements is to organize some class B traffic flows with greater flexibility and some class A traffic flows, which are difficult to be accurately predicted (that is, their arrival characteristics have larger uncertainty), into some common groups as far as possible. And, moreover, we can further put some class B traffic flows with less flexibility and some class A traffic flows, which is much more easier to be accurately predicted, into some other common groups. It is believed that grouping based scheduling with such grouping strategy for traffic flows can improve the utilization of the shared processing resources.

4.10   Collaborative Reservation

From the general end-to-end system model of an ITPN, it can be seen that a traffic flow is processed by several cascaded processing blocks. The basic idea of collaborative reservation is that when the earlier processing block clearly knows the arrival characteristics of a specific traffic flow, it will inform the subsequent processing blocks to accurately reserve the required processing resources in advance through the signaling system between processing blocks. It is evident that for the subsequent processing blocks, the uncertainty of the arrival of the traffic flow has been eliminated in advance. Therefore, based on the collaborative reservation mechanism, the resource reservations of the subsequent processing blocks will be more accurate and efficient.

4.11   Adaptive Allocation of Processing Bandwidth

It can be seen from Eq. (7) that in order to reduce the processing delay, the corresponding processing bandwidth should be adaptively allocated according to the amount of information to be processed. That is, the larger the amount of information to be processed, the larger the processing bandwidth should be allocated.

4.12   Optimal Configuration of Processing Bandwidth

Under the given constraints, the end-to-end delay can be minimized by optimizing the allocation of processing resources among all the processing blocks in an ITPN. It is worth noting that in Eq. (8), we obtain the minimum end-to-end delay under the given total processing bandwidth of the system. In fact, considering the various requirements of the actual system, more general and complex conditions can be considered.

5   Design of a MAC Protocol Framework Supporting Ultra-Low Delay Services

In this section, based on the analysis of the end-to-end ultra-low delay of an ITPN system, we propose a general ultra-low delay MAC framework based on the basic idea of the above proposed flexible reservation. Next, we first describe the access strategies for different types of traffic flows in this MAC framework. And then, we describe a general time-frame structure that can effectively support the access strategies. It is worth noting that because of its generality, apart from IEEE 802.11 WLAN, the MAC framework proposed in this paper can be applied to various kinds of wireless communication networks.

94   B. Li et al.

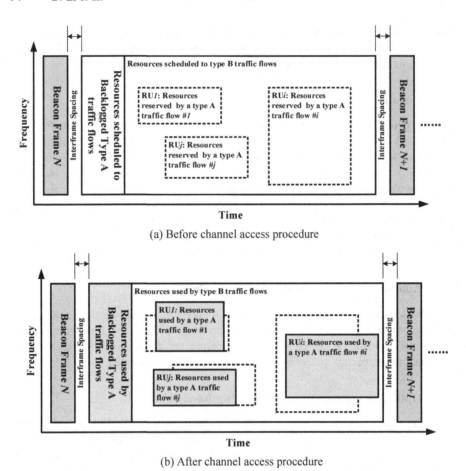

(a) Before channel access procedure

(b) After channel access procedure

Fig. 6. The time-frame structure of the MAC framework

5.1 Basic Access Strategies of the MAC Framework

In the proposed MAC framework, we divide the traffic flows into two categories: delay sensitive traffic (class A) and delay insensitive traffic (class B).

For a class A traffic flow, the system reserves a certain amount of channel resources in an appropriate period of time according to the prediction of its arrival characteristics (i.e. traffic prediction) before its accessing into channel resources. Once the channel resource is reserved, the considered type A traffic flow has the highest access priority for the reserved resources. In other words, if the class A traffic flow needs to access into this part of resources, other traffic flows will not be allowed to use it (unless the considered class A service flow actively releases it). For a class B traffic flow, it can access the channel resources which are not reserved by using either contention-based access or scheduling-based access.

Considering the inaccuracy of traffic prediction, if some reserved resources do not have corresponding class A traffic to carry, it will release this part of reserved resources to other class B traffic flows. On the other hand, if a class A traffic does not have enough access resources reserved for its arrived traffic, it will instantly preempt the channel resources being occupied by other class B traffic flows. The service of the preempted class B traffic flows will be suspended temporarily. In short, the exchange mechanism of channel resources between class A traffic flows and class B traffic flows is introduced in the proposed MAC framework, so as to achieve the win-win performance for both of the two types of traffic flows.

5.2 Basic Time-Frame Structure of the MAC Framework

Figure 6 shows the basic time-frame structure of the proposed MAC framework. In this time-frame structure, the access procedure of the system is divided into one superframe after another. Furthermore, each superframe can be divided into three phases: the transmission phase of beacon frame, the transmission phase of backlogged type A traffic, and the mixed transmission phase of type A and type B traffic. The following is a brief description of the three phases:

A. The transmission phase of beacon frame:
First of all, decisions for the scheduling of backlogged type A traffic, the channel reservations for type A traffic flows and the scheduling for the transmission of type B traffic flows are made. And then, the decisions made are filled into the beacon frame to be transmitted.

B. The transmission phase of backlogged type A traffic:
In this phase, it is necessary to arrange the transmission of backlogged type A traffic which has not yet been transmitted in the previous superframe. The specific actions for channel access and data transmission are executed according to the **scheduling** decision made in the "transmission phase of beacon frame".

C. The mixed transmission phase of type A and type B traffic:
This phase is executed according to the access strategies for the two types of traffic flows described above. Due to the limited space, it will not be repeated here.

6 Conclusions

This paper discusses the design methodology of ultra-low delay MAC strategies and protocols for next generation WiFi. In order to make the proposed design methodology more general, a general end-to-end transmission processing model for an ITPN is proposed. Based on it, the end-to-end delay of the system is analyzed and the expression of the minimum end-to-end delay is obtained. Based on the minimum end-to-end delay expression, we reveal three key factors that determine the end-to-end delay, namely, the number of processing blocks, the size of information blocks processed and the total processing bandwidth of the system. Furthermore, key technologies and their core ideas to realize ultra-low delay services are proposed. Finally, a general ultra-low delay MAC protocol framework based on the idea of flexible reservation is proposed. It is believed that apart from IEEE 802.11 WLAN, the MAC framework proposed can be applied to various kinds of wireless communication networks.

Acknowledgement. This work was supported in part by the National Natural Science Foundations of China (Grant No. 61771390, No. 61871322, No. 61771392, and No. 61501373), and Science and Technology on Avionics Integration Laboratory and the Aeronautical Science Foundation of China (Grant No. 20185553035, and No. 201955053002).

References

1. IEEE 802.11ax Task Group. Project authorization request. Part 11: Wireless LAN Medium Access Control (MAC) and Physical Layer (PHY) Specifications Amendment: Enhancements for Extremely High Throughput (EHT), pp. 1–2 (2019)
2. Saheb, S.M., Bhattacharjee, A.K., Dharmasa, P., et al.: Enhanced hybrid coordination function controlled channel access-based adaptive scheduler for delay sensitive traffic in IEEE 802.11e networks. IET Netw. **1**(4), 281–288 (2012)
3. Pei, C., Zhao, Y., Liu, Y., et al.: Latency-based WiFi congestion control in the air for dense WiFi networks. In: 2017 IEEE/ACM 25th International Symposium on Quality of Service (IWQoS), pp. 1–10. IEEE (2017)
4. Li, M., Tan, P.H., Sun, S., et al.: QoE-aware scheduling for video streaming in 802.11 n/ac-based high user density networks. In: 2016 IEEE 83rd Vehicular Technology Conference (VTC Spring), pp. 1–5. IEEE (2016)
5. Prabhu, H.V., Nagaraja, G.S.: Delay-sensitive smart polling in dense IEEE 802.11n network for quality of service. IUP J. Telecommun. **10**(1), 7–19 (2018)
6. Ahn, J., Kim, Y.Y., Kim, R.Y.: Delay oriented VR mode WLAN for efficient wireless multi-user virtual reality device. In: 2017 IEEE International Conference on Consumer Electronics (ICCE), pp. 122–123. IEEE (2017)
7. Qian, X., Wu, B., Ye, T.C.: QoS-aware A-MPDU retransmission scheme for 802.11 n/ac/ad WLANS. IEEE Commun. Lett. **21**(10), 2290–2293 (2017)
8. Zheng, H., Chen, G., Yu, L.: Video transmission over IEEE 802.11n WLAN with adaptive aggregation scheme. In: 2010 IEEE International Symposium on Broadband Multimedia Systems and Broadcasting (BMSB), pp. 1–5. IEEE (2010)
9. Hajlaoui, N., Jabri, I., Taieb, M., et al.: A frame aggregation scheduler for QoS-sensitive applications in IEEE 802.11n WLANs. In: 2012 International Conference on Communications and Information Technology (ICCIT), pp. 221–226. IEEE (2012)
10. Charfi, E., Gueguen, C., Chaari, L., et al.: Dynamic frame aggregation scheduler for multimedia applications in IEEE 802.11n networks. Trans. Emerg. Telecommun. Technol. **28**(2), e2942 (2017)
11. Azhari, S.V., Gürbüz, Ö., Ercetin, O., et al.: Delay sensitive resource allocation over high speed IEEE802. 11 wireless LANs. Wireless Netw. **26**(3), 1949–1968 (2018)
12. Avdotin, E., Bankov, D., Khorov, E., et al.: Enabling massive real-time applications in IEEE 802.11 be networks. In: 2019 IEEE 30th Annual International Symposium on Personal, Indoor and Mobile Radio Communications (PIMRC), pp. 1–6. IEEE (2019)
13. Avdotin, E., Bankov, D., Khorov, E., et al.: OFDMA resource allocation for real-time applications in IEEE 802.11 ax networks. In: 2019 IEEE International Black Sea Conference on Communications and Networking (BlackSeaCom), pp. 1–3. IEEE (2019)
14. Kim, D., Yeom, I., Lee, T.J.: Mitigating tail latency in IEEE 802.11–based networks. Int. J. Commun. Syst. **31**(1), e3404 (2018)

15. Nguyen, S.H., Vu, H.L., Andrew, L.L.H.: Service differentiation without prioritization in IEEE 802.11 WLANs. IEEE Trans. Mob. Comput. **12**(10), 2076–2090 (2012)
16. Tian, G., Camtepe, S., Tian, Y.C.: A deadline-constrained 802.11 MAC protocol with QoS differentiation for soft real-time control. IEEE Trans. Ind. Inform. **12**(2), 544–554 (2016)
17. Lin, P., Chou, W.I., Lin, T.: Achieving airtime fairness of delay-sensitive applications in multirate IEEE 802.11 wireless LANs. IEEE Commun. Mag. **49**(9), 169–175 (2011)
18. Syed, I., Roh, B.: Delay analysis of IEEE 802.11e EDCA with enhanced QoS for delay sensitive applications. In: 2016 IEEE 35th International Performance Computing and Communications Conference (IPCCC), pp. 1–4. IEEE (2016)
19. Wu, C., Ohzahata, S., Ji, Y., et al.: A MAC protocol for delay-sensitive VANET applications with self-learning contention scheme. In: 2014 IEEE 11th Consumer Communications and Networking Conference (CCNC), pp. 438–443. IEEE (2014)
20. Rentschler, M., Laukemann, P.: Towards a reliable parallel redundant WLAN black channel. In: 2012 9th IEEE International Workshop on Factory Communication Systems, pp. 255–264. IEEE (2012)
21. Halloush, R.D.: Transmission early-stopping scheme for anti-jamming over delay-sensitive IoT applications. IEEE Internet Things J. **6**(5), 7891–7906 (2019)
22. Pei, C., Zhao, Y., Chen, G., et al.: WiFi can be the weakest link of round trip network latency in the wild. In: IEEE INFOCOM 2016-The 35th Annual IEEE International Conference on Computer Communications, pp. 1–9. IEEE (2016)
23. Cheng, Y., Yang, D., Zhou, H.: Det-LB: a load balancing approach in 802.11 wireless networks for industrial soft real-time applications. IEEE Access **6**, 32054–32063 (2018)
24. Choi, J., Yoo, J., Choi, S., Kim, C.: EBA: an enhancement of the IEEE 802.11 DCF via distributed reservation. IEEE Trans. Mob. Comput. **4**(4), 378–390 (2005)
25. Li, B., Tang, W., Zhou, H., et al.: m-DIBCR: MAC protocol with multiple-step distributed in-band channel reservation. IEEE Commun. Lett. **12**(1), 23–25 (2008)
26. Li, B., Li, W., Valois, F., et al.: Performance analysis of an efficient MAC protocol with multiple-step distributed in-band channel reservation. IEEE Trans. Veh. Technol. **59**(1), 368–382 (2009)
27. Singh, S., Acharya, P.A.K., Madhow, U., Belding-Royer, E.M.: Sticky CSMA/CA: implicit synchronization and real-time QoS in mesh networks. Ad Hoc Netw. **5**, 744–768 (2007)
28. Joe, I.: QoS-aware MAC with reservation for mobile ad-hoc networks. In: IEEE 60th Vehicular Technology Conference, VTC 2004-Fall (2004)
29. Sheu, S., Sheu, T.: A bandwidth allocation/sharing/extension protocol for multimedia over IEEE 802.11 ad hoc wireless LANs. IEEE J. Sel. Areas Commun. **19**, 2065–2080 (2001)
30. Ahn, C.W., Kang, C.G., Cho, Y.Z.: Soft reservation multiple access with priority assignment (SRMA/PA): a novel MAC protocol for QoS-guaranteed integrated services in mobile ad-hoc networks. In: Vehicular Technology Conference Fall 2000, IEEE VTS Fall VTC2000, 52nd Vehicular Technology Conference (Cat. No. 00CH37152), vol. 2, pp. 942–947. IEEE (2000)
31. Jiang, S., Rao, J., He, D., et al.: A simple distributed PRMA for MANETs. IEEE Trans. Veh. Technol. **51**(2), 293–305 (2002)
32. Bankov, D., Khorov, E., Lyakhov, A., et al.: Enabling real-time applications in Wi-Fi networks. Int. J. Distrib. Sens. Netw. **15**(5), 1550147719845312 (2019)

Efficient Cluster Head Selection for Multimode Sensors in Wireless Sensor Network

Li Xu[1]([✉]), Xia Luo[1], and Huanzhu Wang[2]

[1] Beijing Research Institute of Telemetry, Beijing 100076, China
xulimouse@163.com, justluoluo219@163.com
[2] School of Electronics and Information, Northwestern Polytechnical University,
Xi'an 710072, China

Abstract. It needs simple and effective network organization to improve the network lifetime in building practical wireless sensor networks (WSNs). As we know, clustering is a classical network model and has been widely used in WSNs, where cluster head (CH) is a manager to control its members and collect sensed data from them. However, in the most of the existing work, the number of cluster heads is stabilized so that the distribution of cluster heads is not reasonable. In addition, they did not consider the dynamic cooperative aware storage and transmission of the sensed data. Therefore, we propose an efficient cluster head selected approach for multimode sensors. First, we select the optimal number of cluster heads based on the approximate distance from the nodes to the sink and the network side length. Second, the nodes that are deployed in the range of cluster head competition radius broadcast their ID, residual energy, location information and distance to the sink node. In the proposed approach, each node competes cluster head according to the number of adjacent nodes and the distance to the sink. Simulation and data analysis show that the proposed approach can efficiently store data and significantly improve the network lifetime.

Keywords: Energy efficiency · Cluster head selection · Target tracking · WSN

1 Introduction

Wireless sensor networks (WSNs) have emerged as an attractive technology that can gather information by the collective effort of numerous sensor nodes [1]. Nowadays this field has attracted the significant attention of many researchers [2–4]. Since sensor nodes always deployed in an unattended environment and it is very difficult to replace their battery after deployed. As a result, energy efficiency is the most critical issues in WSN. It needs simple and effective network organization to improve the network lifetime in building practical wireless sensor networks (WSNs). As we know, clustering is a classical network model and has been widely used in WSNs, where cluster head (CH) is a manager to control its members and collect sensed data from them.

LEACH [5] is one of famous clustering protocols, in which CH is elected randomly and periodically. Cluster can keep only a portion of nodes CHs (cluster heads) active due to high node density in WSN. Except for achieving energy efficiency, clustering is

B. Li et al. (Eds.): IoTaaS 2020, LNICST 346, pp. 98–108, 2021.
https://doi.org/10.1007/978-3-030-67514-1_8

also effective to solve the capacity and scalability problems so as to reduce channel contention and packet collisions, resulting in better network throughput under high load [6, 7]. However, in the most of the existing work, The number of cluster heads is stabilized so that the distribution of cluster heads is not reasonable. And they did not consider the dynamic cooperative aware storage and transmission of the sensed data. In the existing works, although CH is in active state, it can not detect the target on the edge of the cluster since CH always is located at the centre of the cluster. This way causes unnecessary energy consumption and much lower energy efficiency. Thus, it is important to consider the characters of application scenario to optimize the CH selection.

It is assumed that a static WSN and the network has one sink and some randomly distributed sensor nodes $\{Ni\}_{i=1}^{P}$ in an two dimensions field. There is an infinite power supply in the sink, which gathers the sensed data. The nodes are distributed mutually independent random variables and obey a Poisson distribution. The nodes are aware of their locations by GPS and other position algorithm. Let $X_i(x_i, y_i)$, $1 \leq i \leq P$ be the location of node Ni. The network is organized as clusters, as Fig. 1 shows.

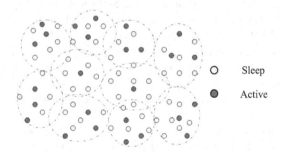

Fig. 1. Illustration of sleep intervals in the different cluster scheme

To solve these problems, we propose an efficient cluster head selected approach for multimode sensors. In the proposed approach, we dynamically choose nodes to play the roles of CHs. First, we select the optimal number of cluster heads based on the approximate distance from the nodes to the sink and the network side length. Second, the nodes that are deployed in the range of cluster head competition radius broadcast their ID, residual energy, location information and distance to the sink node. In the process of cluster head election, a comprehensive evaluation method is used. First, we should determine the weights for each factor. Then, the selected factors of cluster heads are obtained by weighted average with the weight values. In the proposed approach, each node competes cluster head according to the number of adjacent nodes and the distance to the sink. Using the way, the network can keep an optimal number of cluster head and active sensor nodes. Furthermore, in order to balance the energy consumption, an adaptive CH re-selection scheme is proposed to allow each node to take the role of CH different times according to its location and residual energy. As a result, it reduces the energy consumption of data transmitting so as to prolong the network lifetime.

2 Related Works

For cluster-based WSNs, a typical and classical approach is LEACH [5], in which the network is divided into a few clusters and only CHs send the aggregated data to the remote sink directly. The role of the cluster head randomly rotates among the nodes to increase the lifetime of the network. In [8], the authors formulate an optimization problem to maintain an acceptable system blocking probability. For every multicast group to be served, a dynamic cluster of cells is selected based on the minimization of a function that takes into account the traffic in every cell through some weights and the average SINR achieved by the group users. Hybrid Energy Efficient Distributed Clustering (HEED) [9] is a protocol that uses energy and communication cost to elect the cluster head. In [10], the authors proposed a method to decide the final probability of being a cluster head by both the equilibrium probability in a game and a node residual energy-dependent exponential function. In the process of computing the equilibrium probability, new payoff definitions related to energy consumption are adopted.

In [11], the authors propose a novel Raining Energy Cluster Head Selection (RECHS) protocol which is based on a simple Statistical Discrimination (SD) metric which detects collided packets before decoding as well as the Multi-Dimensional Slotted ALOHA (MDSA) MAC protocol which organizes the access to the communication channel. In [12], the tracking strategy is mainly divided into two stages: the cluster head establishes a "neighbor node set" within its communication range, and selects the neighbor node in the "neighbor node set" according to the distance between the node and the target to construct the "intra-cluster member set" to perform the target on the target. Tracking.

Hu et al. [13] focused on the problem of energy saving in moving target tracking scenario in WSN in order to transfer the sleep scheduling of nodes into the selection of the subset. The proposed algorithm uses the energy balance criterion to select a subset of cluster heads and sleep nodes to extend the lifetime of the WSN. However, the strategy only focuses on the "single target tracking" scenario and uses the tracking accuracy as the constraint, which optimization scope is small. At the same time, the limitations of the single life criterion (first node death) [14]. LokMan et al. In this paper, the authors proposed a task aware strategy combined power adaptive and sleep control methods. This strategy enables nodes to work efficiently in different domains and tasks. However, the protocol only verifies the effect in small-scale network, for medium-sized network the effect was not verified.

The above research from the balance of energy consumption, sleep scheduling, topology adjustment and so on. In order to improve the lifetime of WSN, there are still some shortcomings. In some sudden cases, performance and energy saving should be considered and flexible adjustment should be carried out. The above limitations can be summarized as follows: first, the adaptability of life criterion is not enough; second, it has insufficient activity and is not suitable for different application scenarios, such as unable to adjust and control the reliability and life index.

3   Efficient Cluster Head Selection Approach

3.1   Selection of the Optimal Number of Cluster Heads in the Network

In the network deployment phase, sink nodes broadcasts a signal to the monitoring area using a certain power. After the sensor nodes in the network receiving the signal, they calculate the approximate distance d_{sn} (sn is the node identified number) to the sink according to the strength of the received signal. After that, the network area side length l, the number of network nodes Q and the maximum (minimum) distance between the sensor node and sink node are aware. According to the reference [12], the optimal number of the cluster head p of a network is given as follow.

$$p = \sqrt{Q/2\pi} * l/d_{sn} * \sqrt{e/e_a} \tag{1}$$

Where e and e_a are the energy consumption of transmitting 1 bit data per unit distance in the free space mode and multi-channel attenuation mode respectively, the optimal number of cluster heads can be calculated by above formula. Then, the average area of one cluster H_c is approximately the ratio of the total area to the cluster head number.

$$H_c = \pi l/\sqrt{\pi p} = l^2/p \tag{2}$$

As a result, the nodes that are deployed in the area with radius $l/\sqrt{\pi p}$ campaign for cluster head.

After that, the nodes that are deployed in the range of cluster head competition radius broadcast their ID, residual energy, location information and distance to the sink node. All the neighbor nodes within the competition radius will receive this information and establish a neighborhood table. The node calculates the distance to all neighbor nodes and the mean distance.

3.2   Selection of Cluster Heads in the Network

In the process of cluster head election, a comprehensive evaluation method is used. First, we should determine the weights for each factor. Then, the selected factors of cluster heads are obtained by weighted average with the weight values. First, the weights for each factor are calculated as follows.

Through the analysis, we should select the nodes that have more residual energy and shorter distance between them and sink as cluster heads. In this paper, the following method is used to calculate weights for each node. The values of the weights are from 0 to 1. The weight of the residual energy is calculated as follow.

$$E_w(sn) = E_r(sn)/E_i(sn) \tag{3}$$

Where $E_r(sn)$ is the residual energy of the node sn, is the initial energy of the node sn. The weight of the distance is calculated as follow.

$$S_w(sn) = \frac{1/d_{sn} - \min 1/d_{sn}}{\max 1/d_{sn} - \min 1/d_{sn}} \tag{4}$$

Where $\max 1/d_{sn}$ and $\min 1/d_{sn}$ are the maximum and minimum value of the reciprocals of the distance from node sn to the sink. The weight of the average distance to neighbor nodes is calculated as follow.

$$S_w(sn-n) = \frac{1/d_{sn-n} - \min 1/d_{sn-n}}{\max 1/d_{sn-n} - \min 1/d_{sn-n}} \tag{5}$$

Where d_{sn-n} is the average distance between the node sn and its neighbors, $\min 1/d_{sn-n}$ and $\max 1/d_{sn-n}$ are the maximum and minimum value of the reciprocals of the average distance from node sn to its neighbors.

Combining the above factors, the comprehensive weight of node sn is obtained as follow.

$$ES(sn) = \begin{bmatrix} E_w(sn) \\ S_w(sn) \\ S_w(sn-n) \end{bmatrix} \tag{6}$$

3.3   The Comprehensive Evaluation Method

$A = (a_1, \ldots a_n)$ is a comprehensive evaluation standard for cluster head election. $B = (b_1, b_2, b_3)$ is the weight set of three parameters. Using the weighted average model, we can obtain the value of A.

$$A = (a_1, \ldots a_n) = B \cdot ES(sn) = (b_1, b_2, b_3) \cdot \begin{bmatrix} E_w(sn) \ldots E_w(sx) \\ S_w(sn) \ldots S_w(sx) \\ S_w(sn-n) \ldots S_w(sx-n) \end{bmatrix} \tag{7}$$

Then the weighted average method is used to get the value of the comprehensive evaluation for each node $(a'_1, \ldots a'_n)$. If a node within the competing diameter has is highest comprehensive evaluation value, it is selected as a cluster head.

3.4   Dynamic Cooperative Aware Storage Method

The method is mainly divided into two parts, dynamic cooperative sensing data and data backup and storage. In the first part, the cluster partition and cluster head selection are used to divide the whole sensing area. The network is divided into several clusters centered on events (see Fig. 2) in order to ensure that the nodes that in each cluster are closest to the event are used to backup and storage data. Then, the nodes in the same cluster can communicate with each other. The nodes who will be able to sense the event are composed a set Ai1 in which all nodes adopt time division collaboration technology to record event data in turn. Since the dynamic change of network topology, the nodes in each set periodically interact with each other. Thus, the added or dead nodes can be added or deleted. Then, we select a new cluster head node based on the principle of maximum residual energy. Finally, the head node redistributes the monitoring sequence and time slot to its member nodes. Using the proposed method, the scalability of the network is enhanced and the memory space of nodes is saved.

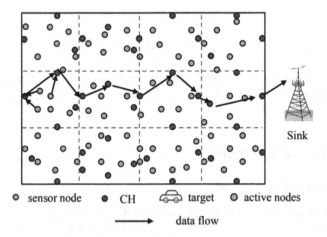

○ sensor node   ● CH   🚗 target   ◎ active nodes

⟶ data flow

Fig. 2. Data transmitting and storage in the proposed approach

In the latter part, the storage data failure caused by node failure is considered. When the monitoring event occurs the source node will first record the event data on the current time slot as independent data blocks. And the event data need to be backup and storage. Then, according to the estimated failure probability of the node, the total number of the data backup is calculated to manage data backup storage.

According to the above discussions, the fault probability of all nodes in the network is assumed as P_n. If the rate P_n is the same for each node, the effective number of backups per data block is b, then the average number of available backups for data blocks is,

$$N_a = \sum_{j=0}^{b} \binom{b}{j} \cdot j \cdot (1 - P_n)^j \cdot P_n^{b-j} = b(1 - P_n) \tag{8}$$

If each piece of data has at least one available data backup, $b(1 - P_n) \geq 1$. Therefore, the optimization model is established to minimize the communication energy consumption of data backup storage. The model can be described as follow,

$$\min Een_r = \sum_{i=1}^{b} H(u, v) \cdot Bp(u, i) \cdot (C_s + C_r) \tag{9}$$

Where $H(u, v)$ is the communication hop from node u to node v, $Bp(u, i)$ is the i-th data copy of node u. Where $b(1 - P_n) \geq 1$ and $bNC_e < nM$, C_e is the total data capacity of each monitoring event. M is the storage space of each node.

Assuming that $H(u, v)$ is a constant, from the above model we can obtain the minimum total energy consumption Een_r of data backup, when the following formula holds,

$$\begin{cases} b = 1/(1 - P_n) \\ P_n < 1 - NC_e/nM \end{cases} \tag{10}$$

In addition, the node is allowed to select the free neighbor in the range of three hops in order to carry the data backup storage. As a result, the delay and energy consumption of data backup are reduced.

4 Performance Evaluation

4.1 Experiment Environment

We assume that there are 200 sensor nodes distributed randomly over an area of 100 m by 100 m. And the sensing range of each sensor node is $r = 12$ m. We also assume each node has an initial energy of 100 J (Joules). Moreover, the position of the sink node is (0, 0) in the network. We also compare our simulation results with LEACH in [5] and RECHS in [11] in terms of total energy consumption, average data collection delay, and network lifetime (Table 1).

Table 1. Parameters

Parameters	Values
Field size	100 m × 100 m
The number of nodes	200
Sensing range	12 m
Data collected frequency	Every 0.6 s
Data packet size	256 bytes
Control message size	8 bytes
Processing data energy	50 nJ/bit/signal
Date storage energy	50 nJ/bit
Amplification coefficients ε_{amp}	100 pJ/(bm^2)
Amplification coefficients ε_{fs}	10 pJ/bit/m^2
The threshold distance d_0	75 m
Initial energy of nodes	10 J
Duty cycle of cluster members	10%
Wireless channel bandwidth	250 kbps
The distance weight	0.3

4.2 Simulation Results

Figure 3 compares the energy consumption of each of the three algorithms in 10 randomly selected rounds through simulation data. LEACH has great randomness in the number and location of cluster heads, and does not consider the residual energy. Therefore, the energy consumption is the largest and the energy consumption of different rounds varies greatly. RECHS gives priority to the nodes with high residual energy as cluster heads, which can achieve the uniform energy consumption among nodes to a certain extent, but this algorithm cannot reduce the energy consumption. The proposed method (TPM) can ensure the appropriate number of cluster heads, thus reducing the energy consumption. According to the residual energy, the number of adjacent nodes, cluster head position and other factors, the proposed algorithm achieves the uniform distribution of cluster heads to a certain extent, so it consumes less energy.

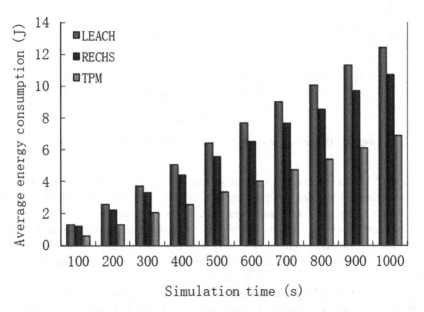

Fig. 3. The average energy comparison

Then, we changed the node number of the network. Figure 4 shows the average residual energy with different node density. From that, we can see the proposed method performs better than the other methods. Clearly, all they tend to decrease, since more nodes can sleep to save energy when the node density is higher. It can be seen that the proposed method can save approximately 25% more energy compared to RECHS because the CH in our algorithm has the most high-energy efficiency. In RECHS, the CH discovery process needs to be executed frequently when the number of nodes increased. Nevertheless, the proposed method transferred the long distance data transmitting into the relative short distance transmitting to save the energy. Unfortunately, in LEACH, the CH has lower energy efficiency. We can see that LEACH approach consumes the most energy since it has a lot of data packets transmitted by long distance.

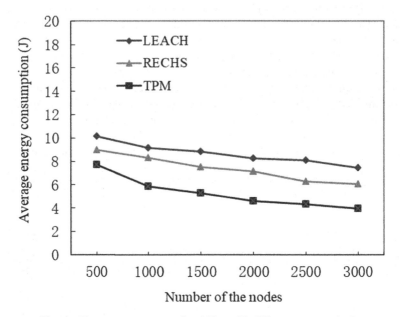

Fig. 4. The average energy after 100 s with different target velocity

Figure 5 shows the average transmission delay comparison of three approaches in our simulation. From that we can see RECHS approach have the longest average transmission delay because it needs to execute the procedure of CH selection and consider many factors inside the network. The proposed method has shorter delay than the other two approaches since it efficiently manages data backup storage and the CHs in the data transmitting chain keep active for the sensed data transmission and the transmitting distance among the CHs is shorter than that in the other approaches. Moreover, the proposed method can reduce the frequency of reconstructing the cluster.

Figure 6 shows the simulation results of the network life cycle of the four algorithms. From the diagram, it is seen that LEACH algorithm has the shortest life cycle. The RECHS algorithm selects CHs from the nodes with more residual energy, and preferentially selects the nodes with more adjacent nodes and the appropriate distance from the selected CH to become the new CHs, which improves the network lifetime. However, because the algorithm cannot reduce energy consumption, due to the uneven distribution of CHs, the improvement of network lifetime is limited. Our proposed method takes into account the uniformity of energy consumption of nodes, which stabilizes the number of CHs and reduces the energy consumption so that it delays the time when nodes begin to die to a certain extent.

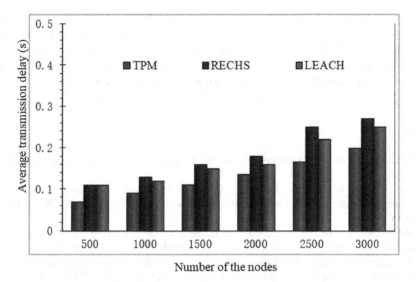

Fig. 5. The data transmitting delay with different number of detecting nodes

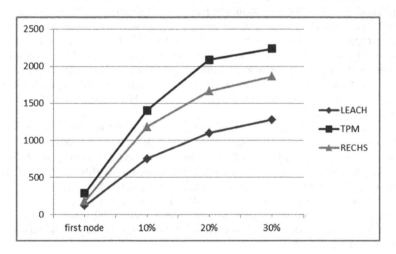

Fig. 6. The lifetime comparison

5 Conclusion

This paper proposed an efficient cluster head selected approach for multimode sensors. We select the optimal number of cluster heads based on the approximate distance from the nodes to the sink and the network side length. Second, the nodes that are deployed in the range of cluster head competition radius broadcast their ID, residual energy, location information and distance to the sink node. In the proposed approach, each node competes cluster head according to the number of adjacent nodes and the distance to the sink. Simulation and data analysis show that the proposed approach can efficiently store data and significantly improve the network lifetime. In addition, each node takes the role of CH different times based on the residual energy of the node. The experiments proved that the proposed approach outperformed the state-of-the-art works by improving the energy cost as well as extending the network lifetime.

References

1. Akyildiz, I.F., Su, W., Sankarasubramaniam, Y., Cayirci, E.: Wireless sensor networks: a survey. Comput. Netw. **38**, 393–422 (2002)
2. Lee, J., Cho, K., Lee, S., Kwon, T., Choi, Y.: Distributed and energy-efficient target localization and tracking in wireless sensor networks. Computer Commun. **29**, 2494–2505 (2006)
3. Shrivastava, N., Mudumbai, R., Madhow, U., Suri, S.: Target tracking with binary proximity sensors: fundamental limits, descriptions, and algorithms. In: SenSys, pp. 251–264 (2006)
4. Vercauteren, T., Wang, X.: Decentralized sigma-point information filters for target tracking in collaborative sensor networks. IEEE Trans. Signal Process. **53**(8), 2997–3009 (2005)
5. Heinzelman, W., Chandrakasan, A., Balakrishnan, H.: Energy-efficient routing protocols for wireless microsensor networks. In: Proceedings of the 33rd Hawaii International Conference on System Sciences (HICSS), Maui, HI, January 2000 (2000)
6. Younis, O., Fahmy, S.: Distributed clustering in ad hoc sensor networks: a hybrid, energy-efficient approach. In: Proceedings of the IEEE INFOCOM, Hong Kong, March 2004 (2004)
7. Younis, O., Krunz, M., Ramasubramanian, S.: Node clustering in wireless sensor networks: recent developments and deployment challenges. IEEE Netw. **20**, 20–25 (2006)
8. Daher, A., Coupechoux, M., Godlewski, P., et al.: A dynamic clustering algorithm for multi-point transmissions in mission-critical communications. IEEE Trans. Wireless Commun. **19** (7), 4934–4946 (2020)
9. Younis, O., Fahmy, S.: HEED: a hybrid, energy-efficient, distributed clustering approach for ad hoc sensor networks. IEEE Trans. Mob. Comput. **3**(4), 366–379 (2004)
10. Wu, X., Zeng, X., Fang, B.: An efficient energy-aware and game-theory-based clustering protocol for wireless sensor networks. ICE Trans. Commun. **E101.B**(3), 709–722 (2018)
11. Alassery, F., Ahmed, W.K.M.: Smart wireless sensor networks powered by remaining energy cluster head selection protocol. In: 2016 IEEE 37th Sarnoff Symposium. IEEE (2016)
12. Shao, Y.: Wireless multimedia sensor network video object detection method using dynamic clustering algorithm. Multimedia Tools Appl. **79**(23), 16927–16940 (2019). https://doi.org/10.1007/s11042-019-7474-y
13. Hu, X., Hu, Y.H., Xu, B.: Energy-balanced scheduling for target tracking in wireless sensor networks. ACM Trans. Sens. Netw. **11**(1), 1–29 (2014)
14. Alhalafi, A., Sboui, L., Naous, R., et al.: gTBS: a green task-based sensing for energy efficient wireless sensor networks. In: Computer Communications Workshops. IEEE (2016)
15. National ICT australia – castalia. http://castalia.npc.nicta.com.au/
16. OMNeT++ Network simulator. http://www.omnetpp.org/
17. Ben-Othman, J., Bessaoud, K., Bui, A., Pilard, L.: Self-stabilizing algorithm for energy saving in wireless sensor networks. In: Proceedings of the IEEE Symposium on Computers and Communications (ISCC 2011), June 2011 (2011)

Pricing Based Resource Allocation Algorithm in Wireless Aeronautics Network Virtualization

Kexiang Wang[1,2], Xueli Zheng[1,2], Mao Yang[3(✉)], Zhongjiang Yan[3], and Bo Li[3]

[1] Science and Technology on Avionics Integration Laboratory,
Shanghai 200241, China
[2] Chinese Aeronautical Radio Electronics Research Institute, Shanghai 200241, China
[3] School of Electronics and Information, Northwestern Polytechnical University,
Xi'an 7100072, China
yangmao@nwpu.edu.cn

Abstract. Wireless aeronautics virtualization enables multiple concurrent wireless aeronautics networks running on the shared wireless network substrate resources. It enhances the resource utilities of spectrum resources, helps for the innovation of physical resources and network services, and improves the QoS guarantee. Resource allocation problem of wireless virtualization, which is how to efficiently assign the physical spectrum resources to several virtual networks, is the primary problem of wireless virtualization. However, the related works generally assume only one physical network, and do not take the economic relationship between infrastructure networks providers (InPs) and service (virtual network) providers (SPs) into consideration. In order to handle this problem, this paper presents a pricing based resource allocation algorithm in wireless aeronautics network virtualization. First, we build up system models under the circumstance of multiple physical networks and multiple virtual networks, and then by using a concave pricing strategy, we present a novel genetic algorithm. Simulation results show our algorithm could provide more revenues for InPs, and show pricing strategy may play an important role on the resource allocation problem in wireless virtualization.

Keywords: Wireless aeronautics network · Wireless virtualization · Resource allocation · Pricing strategy · Genetic algorithm

1 Introduction

With the growing prosperity of intelligent terminals and the increasing demand for communication data, wireless mobile network has become one of the fastest growing technologies that affect people's lives [1]. However, the wireless network is facing its own development dilemma, the first is the 'Spectrum Crisis'. Many operators said that the existing spectrum resources has become increasingly tense

B. Li et al. (Eds.): IoTaaS 2020, LNICST 346, pp. 109–121, 2021.
https://doi.org/10.1007/978-3-030-67514-1_9

is difficult to meet the rapid growth in demand for mobile data including mobile phone [2], however, the father of Martin Cooper (Martin Cooper), many scholars and industry experts said the main reason is the wireless spectrum resource crisis frequency spectrum is not fully utilized [2] resources. A common example, surrounded by people of every kind of wireless network (all operators in GSM, 3G, LTE, WiFi, WiFi and other public enterprise network), but the user can only limited access to a network, even if the poor performance of the access network or other wireless network congestion, or even have a spare the better performance of the resources. Wireless virtualization technology produced in this background, he allowed in one (or more) on the underlying physical wireless network sharing operating multiple parallel virtual wireless network, the wireless network virtual parallel operation, the deployment of different protocols, independent bearer service [1, 3, 4]. Wireless virtualization has been proposed in recent years and has attracted many scholars' attention in a short time. Wireless virtualization can separate operators into physical resource provider (InPs), service (virtual network) provider (SPs), and bring advantages for InPs, SPs and end users (UE). For InPs, wireless virtualization can make use of the physical resources rate more, also can better protect the QoS requirements, so as to improve their income; for SPs, and can provide innovative services focused on, but not restricted to the underlying physical wireless resources, but also conducive to small scale service providers provide specific services, to join the market competition; to the end user (UE), add more service providers to choose more flexibility, can provide the service to choose a more reasonable price, high service quality SPs. Consider the above examples, wireless virtualization, users are no longer limited to the specific physical wireless resources, can choose different virtual network access according to their own needs, so as to improve the quality of service. Therefore, wireless virtualization technology can significantly improve the utilization of radio spectrum resources, and is conducive to the optimization of physical resources and innovation of network services, is conducive to QoS protection and user experience. Aeronautics network is one important type of wireless networks. In this case, wireless virtualization also benefits wireless aeronautics network. Meanwhile, the key problem of wireless aeronautics network is the same as typical wireless networks.

The primary problem of wireless virtualization is the resource allocation problem, that is, how the underlying physical wireless network allocate and schedule its physical resources (spectrum resources) to satisfy the requests of several virtual networks. A number of scholars have carried out research on the allocation of wireless virtualized resources. Document [5] studies the implementation of LTE network virtualization, and simply studies the resource allocation scheme in LTE virtualization. A scheme of Wimax virtualization is proposed in [3], and the way of providing resources is divided into two forms: resource based and bandwidth based, and the corresponding optimal allocation strategy is proposed. Document [6] proposed an overall scheme of resource allocation for wireless network virtualization, but no specific implementation algorithm was proposed. Fu [7] uses game theory to model the supply and demand relationship between InP and SP, and proves that there exists a Nash equilibrium point, and SP needs to truly feedback its own value function. Document [8] addresses the problem of resource allocation in wireless multi hop networks. In this paper, we propose a dynamic allocation algorithm of wireless virtualized resources for [9] Like (Karnaugh-map) in Kano. However, the existing wireless virtualization resource allocation algorithms are relatively simple or straightforward, and assume that the physical resource provider (InP) provides only one physical wireless network. However, the actual situation, there are a number of underlying physical network, and the InP service provider (SP) also affected the pricing strategy, this paper studies the virtual resource allocation strategy based on wireless pricing.

The contribution of this paper is as follows: firstly, this paper puts forward the problem of the use of pricing strategies to study wireless virtual resources allocation, and proposes a new genetic algorithm, the simulation results show that the proposed algorithm outperforms other classical heuristic algorithm, provides a new solution to the problem of virtual wireless resource mapping. Second, for the first time, resource allocation based on virtual network physical wireless aeronautics network under the background of the problem, has more practical significance; third, this paper proposes a virtual network pricing strategy, the simulation results show that the pricing strategy is better than the proportional fair pricing strategy, provides a solution to the problem of resource pricing wireless virtualization.

2 Problem Modeling

2.1 Network Model

Wireless virtualization resource allocation model, such as Fig. 1, is different from previous studies. This paper assumes that there are multiple physical wireless networks, which is closer to the actual situation. This article will alternately use two groups of names: InP and physical network, SP and virtual network.

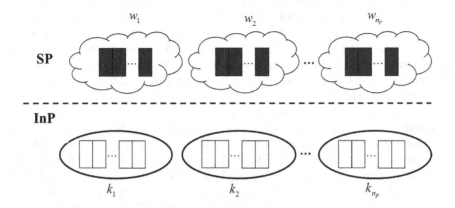

Fig. 1. Resource allocation model map for wireless virtualization

(1) Underlying physical wireless network.

Physical network N^P stands for $N^P = \{N_1^P, N_2^P, \cdots, N_{n_P}^P\}$, where n_p represents the number of physical networks. The number of channels each physical network has is limited, set to $K = \{k_1, k_2, \cdots, k_{n_P}\}$

(2) Virtual network.

The virtual network requests the number of channels to the physical network (InP) according to the service provided by the virtual network. Suppose that the number of virtual networks is n_v, and N^V represents the virtual network, that is, $N^V = \{N_1^V, N_2^V, \cdots, N_{n_V}^V\}$. The requests of each virtual network are independent of each other, so the channel number request of the virtual network can be expressed as $W = \{w_1, w_2, \cdots, w_{n_V}\}$.

(3) Network price.

When the number of virtual networks is large, the requests of some virtual networks will be rejected. Therefore, the introduction of price mechanism can play a role in allocating and stimulating the physical network revenue and the number of virtual network requirements. Setting the price of $P = \{p_1, p_2, \cdots, p_{n_V}\}$., it is clear that the price of each virtual network needs to be related to the number of channels required. Therefore, the pricing of the virtual network by InP can be described as the price of the virtual network

$$p_i = f(w_i) \tag{1}$$

The pricing mechanism will be described in detail in the next section. Previous researches on the allocation of wireless virtualized resources did not take into account the economic relationship between InP and SP, especially when there are multiple physical wireless networks, the relationship can not be ignored.

2.2 Pricing Model

This paper uses pricing strategy to study resource allocation problem. The pricing model of the Internet is divided into static pricing and dynamic pricing in general. The common static pricing includes the monthly payment model (Flat-rate), the Pricing (Usage-based) based on the amount of use (flow), or the combination of the ladder pricing and the pricing based on the use of [10]. Dynamic pricing includes dynamic pricing based on priority, proportional fair pricing, effective bandwidth pricing, etc. According to the quasi real time characteristics of mobile data, Ha proposes a time based pricing strategy in [11]. By setting price discounts, the data at peak time is transferred to the non peak period, so as to reduce the cost of operators. The other pricing models of the Internet are not mentioned in this paper. [12] and other Internet pricing strategies mentioned above are introduced in detail by Ha et al. However, most of these Internet pricing strategies can not be directly applied to the resource allocation problem of wireless virtualization. Unlike the above proportional fair pricing strategy, this paper proposes a concave function pricing strategy. The most typical proportional fair pricing method is linear pricing, that is to say, the bidding of virtual network should be proportional to the number of channel requirements of the virtual network. That is

$$f^{line}(w) = rw \tag{2}$$

Without loss of generality, $r = 1$ can be assumed. The linear pricing strategy does not have a positive stimulating effect on the demand of the virtual network, because the price of the unit channel is certain and has nothing to do with the size of the demand. Concave function has the positive stimulating effect of price, that is, the larger the demand, the lower the unit channel price. Therefore, this paper proposes the use of concave function for pricing, the most common concave function is logarithmic function, so the pricing strategy proposed in this paper is

$$f^{log}(w) = a \log(1 + w) \tag{3}$$

a is the pricing constant. Meet the three basic conditions of the pricing strategy: 1) concave function, said virtual network needs more channel number, channel unit price f^{log}/w lower; 2) $f^{log}(0) = 0$ said that when the virtual network demand is 0, do not need to pay the price; 3) $f^{log}(w)$ for monotone nondecreasing function, this is due to the fact that the source of the physical network is limited, demand for the price increase. In this paper, we will use concave function pricing strategy to represent the pricing strategy proposed in this paper.

In order to compare with the price of linear pricing, this paper assumes that the demand of channel number of each virtual network is independent and identically distributed, and obeys the uniform distribution $[w_{\min}, w_{\max}]$. At the same time, all virtual networks adopt concave function pricing and linear pricing should have the same mean value. Therefore

$$E(\sum_{i=1}^{n_V} f^{line}(w_i)) = E(\sum_{i=1}^{n_V} f^{log}(w_i)) \tag{4}$$

Solution (4) the parameters in the accessible formula (3):

$$a = \frac{r(w_{\min} + w_{\max})(w_{\max} - w_{\min} + 1)}{2 \sum\limits_{w=w_{\min}}^{w_{\max}} \log(1 + w)} \tag{5}$$

2.3 Problem Description

According to the network model and pricing model of the last two sections, we can get the optimal model of the allocation of wireless virtualization resources based on pricing.

$$\max \sum_{i=1}^{n_v} \sum_{j=1}^{n_p} x_{i,j} \bullet a \log(1 + w_i) \tag{6}$$

$$s.t.$$
$$\sum_{j=1}^{n_p} x_{i,j} \leq 1, \quad i = 1, \ldots, n_v \tag{7}$$

$$\sum_{i=1}^{n_v} x_{i,j} \bullet w_i \leq k_j, \quad j = 1, \ldots, n_p \tag{8}$$

$$x_{i,j} = \begin{cases} 1, \text{Physical network j bearers virtual network i} \\ 0 \end{cases} \tag{9}$$

The objective function (6) represents the total revenue of maximizing the physical network. The constraint formula (7) means that each virtual network is carried by a physical network at most. Equation (8) means that the total number of virtual network channels that are loaded in each physical network cannot exceed the total capacity of the physical network. This problem is an integer programming problem with multiple knapsack problem (Multiple Knapsack Problem) is similar, so the problem is NP hard [13–15], there is no optimal solution in polynomial time, and considering the performance of heuristic algorithms, the following section will detail the proposed genetic algorithm.

3   Pricing Based Wireless Virtualization Resource Allocation Genetic Algorithm

In the upper section, the optimization problem has been analyzed as a NP hard problem, so there is no polynomial time optimal solution. Several algorithms for multi knapsack problems can be applied to this problem. The [13] has proposed several heuristic algorithm for knapsack problem, simulation results show that the combination of these heuristic algorithm can achieve better performance, but with some heuristic algorithm will increase the complexity, and it is difficult to guarantee the optimality. Pisinger [14] proposed an iterative and bound method to solve the optimal solution of large scale knapsack problem. However, when the scale of the problem is large, it will take a long time to get the optimal solution completely. Fukunaga [15] proposed a grouping genetic algorithm (Item), items will be placed into the backpack, to perform genetic iteration through the exchange of items in the backpack, but in this process will produce duplicate items appear in more than one backpack, so the performance will be affected. [16] proposes an artificial fish swarm algorithm, which reduces the performance of the algorithm by using random ranking placement rules.

In view of the fact that accurate algorithms require too much time, and the performance of heuristic algorithms is insufficient, this paper proposes a new genetic algorithm to solve the proposed problems. The main idea is that each virtual network assigned to different physical network to go, then through the heuristic algorithm with low complexity of corresponding to each physical network in the virtual network resource allocation (may be part of the virtual network will be rejected), and then through the selection, crossover and mutation to produce new distribution pattern. After several rounds of iteration to obtain an approximate optimal solution. The principle block diagram of the genetic algorithm is shown in Fig. 2, and the process of genetic algorithm is described in detail below.

(1) Coding and initializing populations.

This encoding using integer encoding, each chromosome (code) by n_V genes (integer) composition of $(x_1 x_2 \cdots x_{n_V})$, the value of each gene represents the physical network number, a physical network was randomly selected with probability capacity, i.e.

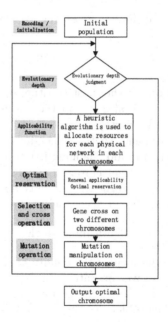

Fig. 2. The principle block diagram of the genetic algorithm is presented in this paper

$$Pro(x_i = n_j) = \frac{k_j}{\sum\limits_{l=1}^{n_P} k_l}, \forall i \in 1, 2, \cdots, n_V, j \in 1, 2, \cdots, n_P \qquad (10)$$

Suppose a chromosome is, then the physical network 1 carries the virtual network 2 and 4, the physical network 2 carries virtual network 1 and 5, and the physical network 3 carries the virtual network 3. In initialization, several sets of initial chromosomes are usually needed, and the number of chromosomes is called the population size. This paper is set up as 20.

(2) Selection and cross operation.

Crossover operation is used to generate the next generation chromosome, and it is the most essential operation in genetic algorithm. Prior to performing cross operation, parent chromosome selection is required. In this paper, the roulette algorithm is used to select the chromosomes, that is, the higher the applicability of chromosomes, the greater probability is selected as mother chromosomes. Because the integer position coding is adopted in this paper, a single point crossover strategy is adopted. The hypothesis is that the chromosome of the stepmother is $X^A = (x_1^A x_2^A \cdots x_{n_V}^A), X^B = (x_1^B x_2^B \cdots x_{n_V}^B)$, and the random crossing position is i, and the new chromosomes are $X^{A'} = (x_1^A x_2^A \cdots x_i^A x_{i+1}^B \cdots x_{n_V}^B)$ and $X^{B'} = (x_1^B x_2^B \cdots x_i^B x_{i+1}^A \cdots x_{n_V}^A)$ respectively. Crossover operation of genetic algorithm is carried out according to crossover probability, and the crossover probability is 0.9.

(3) Mutation operation.

Mutation manipulation is one of the most spiritual operations in genetic algorithms. It is the change of several genes in the chromosome, which produces similar effects in biology. The mutation operation in this paper changes the value of a gene in a chromosome, that is, changing the physical network corresponding to a virtual network and changing it into another physical network to carry it. Suppose that the parent chromosome is $X = (x_1 x_1 \cdots x_{n_V})$, and a random position of i is selected, so the new value is, and the other genes remain unchanged. The mutation rate is 0.1 according to the mutation probability.

(4) Fitness function – heuristic algorithm of single physical network.

Fitness function is used to distinguish the quality of chromosomes, and plays a key role in selection and crossover operation. In this paper, the function of the total income of the physical network in the formula (6) is directly applied to the objective function of the problem, so the fitness function directly reflects the quality of the objective function. However, it is not a simple process to calculate the fitness function in this paper. After considering the above encoding, each physical network will correspond to several virtual network, how these virtual network have a choice (because of the possibility of virtual network demand is greater than the physical network capacity) assigned to the physical network has evolved into an approximate single knapsack problem. The genetic algorithm, the optimal solution has good properties, so the network resource allocation for each physical fitness calculation does not use complex algorithms, but only by the heuristic algorithm with low complexity. The algorithm is divided into two sub algorithms, the initial sub - gamete algorithm and the sub - gamete algorithm, which are described as follows.

In the algorithm of initial gamete, the virtual network will be corresponding to each physical network according to the single channel price (p/w) in descending order, then according to the order of traversing each virtual network, if the network has enough residual physical channel, the virtual network distribution in, or refuse, to analysis the virtual network next. The result of the initial allocation algorithm will get two sets VN_{Succ}, assign a successful virtual network set and assign the failed virtual network set VN_{Rej}.

In the redistribution algorithm, the channel number is assumed at the physical network surplus is R, while VN_{Rej} in each traversal of virtual network for virtual network in VN_{Rej}^i, VN_{Succ} and VN_{Succ}^j makes $R + w_{VN_{Succ}^j} \geq w_{VN_{Rej}^i}$ and $p_{VN_{Succ}^j} < p_{VN_{Rej}^i}$, in line with the conditions of the VN_{Succ} in a minimum of $p_{VN_{Succ}^j}$ from the VN_{Succ} deleted, and the VN_{Rej}^i to VN_{Succ} place, at the same time update the remaining channel number R. That is:

$$VN_{Rej}^i \rightleftarrows \arg\min\{p_{VN_{Succ}^j}|R + w_{VN_{Succ}^j} \geq w_{VN_{Rej}^i}, p_{VN_{Succ}^j} < p_{VN_{Rej}^i}\} \tag{11}$$

$$R' = R + w_{VN_{Succ}^j} - w_{VN_{Rej}^i} \tag{12}$$

Because of the length of the space, the detailed flow of the algorithm is not drawn in this paper. For each physical network, after the resource allocation by the above algorithm, the individual gains of each physical network can be obtained, and then the total revenue of the physical network, namely the fitness function, is obtained.

$$f_{fitness}^X = P^X = \sum_{i=1}^{n_P} p_i^X \tag{13}$$

(5) Optimal reservation strategy.

In order to ensure the convergence speed and the optimal solutions are not missing, this genetic algorithm using optimal preservation strategy, namely, in each iteration, the solution to replace the worst chromosome with the best so far, and in the subsequent selection, crossover and mutation.

4   Simulation and Analysis of Algorithm Performance

In order to verify the performance of the proposed wireless virtualization resource allocation algorithm based on pricing strategy, this section is compared and analyzed by simulation. Firstly, the proposed algorithm is compared with the classical joint heuristic algorithm [13] (MK2+A+I1+I2). In addition, the concave function pricing strategy proposed in this paper is compared with the linear pricing method to further verify the performance of the proposed algorithm.

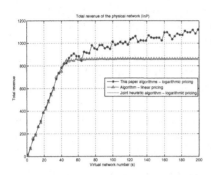

Fig. 3. Total physical network revenue.

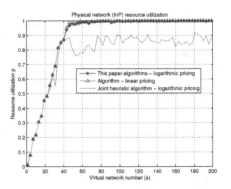

Fig. 4. Resource utilization.

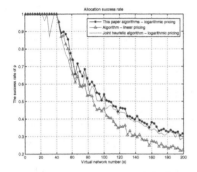

Fig. 5. Virtual network success rate.

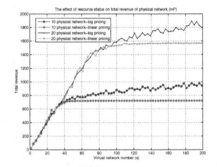

Fig. 6. The influence of resource status on resource allocation.

For InP, this paper assumes that the number of physical nets follows the uniform distribution of [10,15], and that the number of channels in each physical network is independent and identically distributed, and obeys the uniform distribution of [50100]. For SP, this paper studies the performance of the system when the number of virtual networks increases gradually. The number of virtual networks is independent and identically distributed, and obeys the uniform distribution of [10, 30]. For the pricing strategy, without losing generality, the constant factor of linear pricing in the assumed formula (2) can be calculated by formula (5), and the related parameters of concave function pricing are obtained. The genetic algorithm proposed in this paper has a population size of 20, an evolutionary depth of 100, a crossover probability of 0.9, and a variation probability of 0.1.

(1) The genetic algorithm in this paper is better than the joint heuristic algorithm.

As shown in Fig. 3 and 5, in the case of a small number of virtual network, the performance of the algorithm and heuristic algorithm, this is because when the virtual network is small, the two algorithms in the vast majority of virtual network can satisfy the demand. As shown in Fig. 3 and Fig. 4, when the number of virtual networks is small, the total revenue and resource utilization are approximately linearly increased rapidly. However, even at this stage, the proposed algorithm has better performance than the joint heuristic algorithm. In Fig. 5, in the virtual network number in 20 40, a heuristic algorithm of the virtual network obviously declining success rate fluctuations, while this algorithm uses both concave function or linear pricing pricing, are maintained at a success rate of 100%, better than the combined heuristic algorithm.

With the increase of the number of virtual networks, the physical network resources have reached saturation. As shown in Fig. 4, the resource utilization rate of the proposed algorithm is close to 100% regardless of the concave function pricing or linear pricing, while the joint heuristic algorithm is much less efficient than the proposed algorithm. From the perspective of total revenue, as shown in Fig. 3, the total revenue of the proposed algorithm is significantly better than that of the joint heuristic algorithm, and the joint heuristic algorithm has a larger fluctuation than the joint heuristic algorithm. In the virtual network success rate, as shown in Fig. 5, concave function pricing is also used. The success rate of the proposed algorithm is slightly larger than that of the joint heuristic algorithm.

(2) Concave function pricing is better than linear pricing.

As shown in Fig. 3 and 5, concave function pricing is superior to linear pricing in the case of using the proposed algorithm. When the number of virtual network number, the total revenue of linear pricing has been saturated, basically no growth, this is because the linear pricing, total revenue and total channel is proportional to the number of physical network, when resource utilization is saturated (Fig. 4), the total income inevitably tends to be full. For concave function pricing, InP has greater choice, so it can continue to be improved. It can be seen that the total benefit of the joint heuristic algorithm using concave function pricing is also better than the linear pricing algorithm. In the virtual network allocation success rate, as shown in Fig. 5, the success rate of concave function pricing strategy is also significantly greater than linear pricing. Thus, pricing strategy has a great impact on the resource allocation problem of wireless virtualization.

(3) The influence of resource change on performance.

Figure 6 is the impact of physical resource changes on resource allocation results. When physical network number increases, physical wireless resources increase, so the virtual network that can be accommodated will naturally increase, and then the total revenue will increase. In addition, from Fig. 6, it is observed that when the number of physical networks varies from 10 to 20, the saturation point varies from about 40 to about 80, which is very close to the theoretical value of: $10 * (50 + 100)/(10 + 30) = 37.5$ and $20 * (50 + 100)/(10 + 30) = 75$.

Because the genetic algorithm is used in this paper, the computational complexity of each parallel computing module is 1. The complexity of the joint heuristic algorithm is 1. It can be seen that the complexity of each parallel module is lower than that of the joint heuristic algorithm, and the complexity of the algorithm is independent of the number of physical resources.

5   Conclusion

This paper presents a wireless virtual pricing strategy resource allocation algorithm based on InP in multi physical aeronautics wireless network under the background of the concave function pricing strategy, this paper proposes a new genetic algorithm, the performance of the virtual network can effectively meet the demand, at the same time more practical significance. Through the comparison and analysis of simulation algorithm outperforms the classical combined heuristic algorithm is proposed in this paper, also can be seen from the simulation results, the introduction of different pricing strategies, can significantly affect the performance of the total revenue of InP and system. Research on wireless virtualization in recent years has just proposed, and caused widespread concern, the allocation of resources is the primary problem of wireless virtualization, follow-up will further study the wireless virtual resources allocation network under the background of multi physics problems.

Acknowledgement. This work was supported in part by Science and Technology on Avionics Integration Laboratory and the Aeronautical Science Foundation of China (Grant No. 20185553035).

References

1. Yasir, Z., Liang, Z., Carmelita, G., et al.: LTE wireless virtualization and spectrum management. Mob. Netw. Appl. **16**(4), 424–432 (2011)
2. X. C. BRIAN. Carriers Warn of Crisis in Mobile Spectrum[OL]
3. Ravi, K., Rajesh, M., Honghai, Z., et al.: NVS: a virtualization substrate for WiMAX networks. In: Proceedings of the Sixteenth Annual International Conference on Mobile Computing and Networking (ACM Mobicom 2010), Chicago, USA, 20–24 September 2010, pp. 233–244 (2010)
4. Gautam, B., Dipti, V., Ivan, S., et al.: SplitAP: leveraging wireless network virtualization for flexible sharing of WLANs. In: Proceedings of the IEEE Global Telecommunications Conference (GLOBECOM 2010), Miami, USA, 6–10 December 2010, pp. 1–6 (2010)
5. Yasir, Z., Liang, Z., Carmelita, G., et al.: LTE wireless virtualization and spectrum management. In: Proceedings of the Wireless and Mobile Networking Conference (WMNC 2010), Budapest, Hungary, 13–15 October 2010, pp. 1–6 (2010)
6. Keun, M.P., Chong, K.K.: A framework for virtual network embedding in wireless networks. In: Proceedings of the 4th International Conference on Future Internet Technologies (ACM CFI 2009), Seoul, Korea, 17–19 June 2009, pp. 5–7 (2009)
7. Fangwen, F., Ulas, C.-K.: Wireless network virtualization as a sequential auction game. In: Proceedings of the 29th IEEE International Conference on Computer Communications (IEEE INFOCOM 2010), San Diego, USA, 15–19 March 2010, pp. 1–9 (2010)

8. Xin, C., Song, M.: Dynamic spectrum access as a service. In: Proceedings of the 31st IEEE International Conference on Computer Communications (IEEE INFOCOM 2012), Orlando, USA, 25–30 March 2012, pp. 666–674 (2012)

9. Yang, M., Li, Y., Zeng, L., et al.: Karnaugh-map like online embedding algorithm of wireless virtualization. In: Proceedings of the 15th International Symposium on Wireless Personal Multimedia Communications (IEEE WPMC 2012), Taipei, Taiwan, 24–27 September 2012, pp. 594–598 (2012)

10. Prashanth, H., Mung, C., Robert, C., et al.: Pricing under constraints in access networks: revenue maximization and congestion management. In: Proceedings of the 29th IEEE International Conference on Computer Communications (IEEE INFOCOM 2010), San Diego, USA, 15–19 March 2010, pp. 1–9 (2010)

11. Sangtae, H., Soumya, S., Carlee, J.-W., et al.: TUBE: time-dependent pricing for mobile data. In: Proceedings of the ACM SIGCOMM 2012 Conference (ACM SIG-COMM 2012), Helsinki, Finland, 13–17 August 2012, pp. 247–258 (2012)

12. Soumya, S., Carlee, J.-W.S., Sangtae, H., et al.: Pricing data: a look at past proposals, current plans, and future trends. arxiv.org:1201.4197.2012.11.15

13. Silvano, M., Paolo, T.: Knapsack Problems: Algorithms and Computer Implementations, pp. 93–112. Wiley, New York (1990)

14. Pisinger, D.: An exact algorithm for large multiple knapsack problems. Eur. J. Oper. Res. **114**(3), 528–541 (1999)

15. Alex, S.F.: A new grouping genetic algorithm for the multiple knapsack problem. In: Proceedings of the IEEE Congress on Evolutionary Computation (CEC 2008), Hong Kong, China, 1–6 June 2008, pp. 2225–2232 (2008)

Access Algorithm in Software-Defined Satellite Network

Qiheng Gu[1(✉)], Zhen Xu[1], and Xiaoting Wang[2]

[1] School of Electronic and Information Engineering, Beihang University,
Beijing 100191, China
guqiheng@buaa.edu.cn
[2] Beijing Institute of Tracking and Telecommunications Technology,
Beijing 100194, China

Abstract. As the number of satellite constellations increases, a subscriber may be covered by multiple satellite networks simultaneously, and access to different satellite networks can obtain different communication qualities. In this paper, we firstly propose the access network selection algorithm based on analytic hierarchy process (AHP) method in a software-defined satellite network (SDSN) architecture. The weights obtained by AHP method do not consider the real-time changes of the network parameter values, which may result in unbalanced load. In order to solve this problem, two improved algorithms based on AHP-entropy weight method (AHP-EW) and punitive variable weight method (PVW) are proposed, respectively. In the algorithms, the weights can be dynamically modified objectively according to the real-time parameter values of the network index. The simulation results show that the improved algorithms can select the most suitable network and effectively balance the load among the networks on the basis of ensuring the service quality requirements of the subscriber.

Keywords: Software-defined satellite network · Analytic hierarchy process · Entropy weight · Punitive variable weight

1 Introduction

With the rapid development of global information services, subscribers have placed higher demands on the efficiency and diversity of communications. As an important part of the global communication system, a single satellite network cannot meet the development of diversified communication services and quality of service (QoS) requirements. Therefore, multiple satellite networks have become the future development trend. However, as the number of satellite constellations increases, the subscriber may be covered by different satellites networks simultaneously. Due to the relatively high-speed movement between low-orbit satellites and terminals, accessing to different satellite networks will obtain different forwarding path and transmission performance. Besides, the handover will occur immediately which may lead to a longer delay and packet loss when the original access is inappropriate. Under this background, the access algorithm in multiple satellite networks needs to ensure the QoS requirements of subscribers and improve wireless resource utilization rate [1, 2].

B. Li et al. (Eds.): IoTaaS 2020, LNICST 346, pp. 122–134, 2021.
https://doi.org/10.1007/978-3-030-67514-1_10

In order to improve transmission performance and to make better use of satellite channel resources, some existing papers proposed approaches such as longest coverage time, the strongest signal, the number of available channel and the comprehensive weighting algorithm [3, 4, 5]. The single-factor-based access strategy only considers one network performance index and ignores other important network parameters, which is less effective because it cannot take into account both network performance and user service characteristics. The comprehensive weighting algorithm considers multiple performance indicators to make the decision more reasonable. According to the mathematical model adopted by the comprehensive weighting algorithm, it can be divided into access algorithms based on multiple attribute decision making (MADM) [6], utility functions, fuzzy logic [7], game theory [8] and so on.

The algorithm based on fuzzy logic can achieve good performance, but the definition of fuzzy sets and fuzzy criteria is subjective and difficult to construct. Game theory obtains the best access strategy through the bilateral game between networks and users. However, the existence proof of Nash equilibrium point and its solution are complicated. The access algorithm based on MADM can comprehensively consider multiple decision indicators to select the network. The decision result is more convincing and the algorithm complexity is moderate. Therefore, MADM is widely used in network access problems.

The key step of MADM algorithm is to get the right weights. Analytic hierarchy process (AHP) is a commonly used method for getting weights. It sets relative weights on network performance parameters based on user preferences and call quality needs. Since the weights are set by subjective factors and the final weights obtained by the AHP algorithm is a fixed value, it is easy to connect the same type of service request to the same satellite network, resulting in unbalanced load. Therefore, we need to improve the access algorithm.

The aim of our work is to improve the communication quality and balance satellite networks load. Our work is based on SDSN architecture [9]. The main work of this paper is as follows:

In AHP, index weights are only based on the preference of users. Once the weight is determined, it will not change any more. To solve the problem that the weights calculated by AHP are fixed values and does not consider the real-time changes of network parameters, which will lead to an inappropriate result, we use entropy technology to modify network parameter weights. The entropy value is sensitive to the dispersion of the network parameter. Therefore, it makes the judgment result more objective. When the available load of a satellite network is below the threshold, there is a certain possibility that new subscribers still access to this satellite network, which may cause the communication quality deteriorating. On this basis, an optimal comprehensive evaluation model of punitive variable weight is proposed while considering the role and effect of weights and index values. This effect is achieved by making the weights of the indexes change with the index values. Through this model, when the index parameter deteriorates, the impact of this index on the comprehensive evaluation function is increased.

In Sect. 2, we firstly show the SDSN architecture and comprehensive evaluation model. Then the steps to calculate network parameter weights based on AHP are introduced. In Sect. 3, we proposed two improved algorithms based on entropy weight and punitive variable weight. In Sect. 4, We do experiments under the three algorithms and analyze the simulation results. It can be seen that the proposed algorithm can effectively balance the network load while ensuring the QoS requirements of users. And conclusion is given in Sect. 5.

2 Access Selection Algorithm in SDSN

2.1 SDSN Architecture

With the rapid increase in the number of subscriber and the amount of communication data, satellites need more storage space to manage the communication network. However, the storage capacities of satellites cannot meet the requirements of storing. In this paper we use the SDSN architecture proposed in [10] to solve this problem.

The controller plane consists of ground stations and GEO satellites. The ground station is used as the main controller to collect the global status information of satellites and generate access instruction. It analyzes the service characteristics after accepting the access request, executes a corresponding algorithm based on the collected network parameters to select the satellite network, and returns the result to the data plane. GEO satellites serve as local controllers. They monitor the status of LEO satellites, and communicate with the ground master controller in real time. Data plane consists of LEO satellites (Fig. 1).

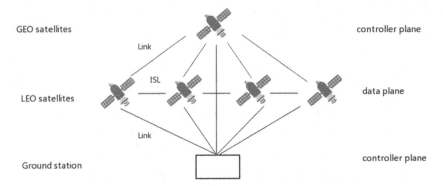

Fig. 1. The SDSN structure

2.2 Access Evaluation Model

The index that affect the selection of satellites are mainly considered from the subscriber preference and network parameters, including transmission reliability, timeliness, throughput, and network load. This paper selects delay, covered time, packet loss rate, transmission rate and load as performance evaluation indexes.

The comprehensive evaluation equation of the access algorithm is as follows:

$$f_i = \sum_{j=1}^{M} w_j * x_{ij} \tag{1}$$

where f_i is the comprehensive evaluation value of the satellite network i, w_j is the weight of the j th index, and x_{ij} is the value of j th index in the satellite network i. If the value of f_i is higher, the possibility of selecting the i th satellite network to access is higher.

In this paper, the standardization process of network parameters is as follows. Assume that there are N satellite networks and M indexes parameters. The evaluation indexes are divided into the cost type and benefit type. If the value of the cost index is smaller, the network is better for users to access. Indexes such as delay, and packet loss rate are cost type. The calculation to standardize the cost index parameter is as follows:

$$y_{ij} = \frac{max_{1 \leq i \leq n}\{x_{ij}\} - x_{ij}}{max_{1 \leq i \leq n}\{x_{ij}\} - min_{1 \leq i \leq n}\{x_{ij}\}} \tag{2}$$

The larger the benefit type index value is, the better networks will be. Indexes such as transmission rate, network available load and covered time are benefit type. The calculation to standardize the benefit index parameter is as follows:

$$y_{ij} = \frac{x_{ij} - min_{1 \leq i \leq n}\{x_{ij}\}}{max_{1 \leq i \leq n}\{x_{ij}\} - min_{1 \leq i \leq n}\{x_{ij}\}} \tag{3}$$

where y_{ij} is the standardized values of x_{ij}.

2.3   AHP Based Access Selection Algorithm

In the mid-1970s, American operations researcher T.L. Saaty formally proposed AHP. AHP is a commonly used decision analysis method, which can solve complex problems with multiple objectives [11]. This method combines quantitative analysis and qualitative analysis, and uses the experience of the decision maker to measure the relative importance between indicators. The index weights of each decision-making scheme are given, and finally the order of each scheme is obtained according to the weights. Because of its practicability and effectiveness in handling complex decision-making problems, it has quickly gained worldwide attention.

It decomposes a complex factor into several different simple factors, and quantitatively considers the dominant relationship between them, and finally forms a multi-level structure.

Establish a Hierarchy Model. According to the relationship, the hierarchy model layers are divided into decision layer, criterion layer and target layer. In this paper, the decision layer is to select the optimal satellite network to access, and the target layer is candidate satellites with different network parameters. The criterion layer is an important indicator that needs to be considered when accessing a satellite network, including network delay, covered time, packet loss rate, optional transmission rate, and network load. The hierarchy model is shown in Fig. 2.

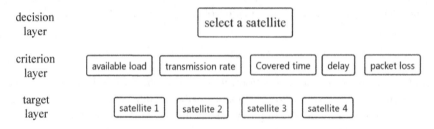

Fig. 2. The hierarchy model.

Constructing the Pairwise Comparison Matrix. Assuming that there are n elements participating in the comparison, a paired comparison matrix $A = (a_{ij})_{n \times n}$ is formed. Each value a_{ij} in the matrix reflects the relative importance between index i and other indexes $j(i, j = 1, 2 \ldots, N; i \neq j)$. The matrix formed by the pairwise comparison results is called the comparison matrix. The comparison matrix has the following properties:

$$a_{ij} = \frac{1}{a_{ji}} \tag{4}$$

Take voice services as example to construct a comparison matrix. Voice services have the highest requirements for real-time transmission. We set the relative importance of the five indicators in Table 1.

Table 1. The comparison matrix $A = (a_{ij})_{5 \times 5}$ of indexes.

Attributes	Delay	Covered time	Loss	Load	Speed
Delay	1	2	4	6	4
Covered time	1/2	1	2	4	2
Loss	1/4	1/2	1	2	2
Load	1/6	1/4	1/2	1	1/2
Speed	1/4	1/2	1/2	2	1

Then we calculate a list of the relative weights of the factors, which is called an eigenvector. We can get the eigenvector ω corresponding with the largest eigenvalue λ_{max} from Table 1:

$$\omega = (0.8309, 0.4384, 0.2575, 0.1165, 0.1938) \tag{5}$$

Consistency Testing. Theoretical analysis shows that if the matrix is a completely consistent pairwise comparison matrix, it should satisfy $a_{ij} * a_{jk} = a_{ik}, 1 \leq i, j, k \leq n$.

In such a case, the w vector satisfies the equation $A\omega = \lambda_{max}\omega$. However, it is impossible to satisfy many of the above equations when constructing a pairwise comparison matrix involving human judgement. Therefore, a certain degree of inconsistency can be allowed for the pairwise comparison matrix.

The difference between λ_{max} and n is an indication of the inconsistency of the judgements. If $\lambda_{max} = n$ then judgements have turned out to be consistent. Therefore, the inconsistency of A can be measured by the value of $\lambda - n$. A consistency index is defined as:

$$CI = \frac{\lambda_{max} - n}{n - 1} \tag{6}$$

λ_{max} is the largest eigenvalue and n is the number of the indexes. We can get $CI = 0.0172$ according to Eq. (6).

RI is called the average random consistency index, and it is only related to the matrix order. RI is the standard for checking the consistency of the pairwise comparison matrix A (Table 2).

Table 2. The standard value of consistency index RI.

n	1	2	3	4	5	6	7	8	9	10
RI	0	0	0.58	0.90	1.12	1.24	1.32	1.41	1.45	1.49

Calculate the random consistency ratio CR of pairwise comparison matrix according to the following equation:

$$CR = \frac{CI}{RI} \tag{7}$$

If $CR < 0.1$, the comparison matrix is considered to have passed the consistency test, otherwise reconstruct the comparison matrix. According to Eq. (7), $CR = 0.0154 < 0.1$. Therefore, the matrix we construct in Table 1 have passed the consistency test. Normalize ω vector and finally get weights:

$$w_{AHP} = (0.4523, 0.2387, 0.1401, 0.0634, 0.1055) \tag{8}$$

According to Eq. (1) and (8), we can select the suitable satellite network with the largest f_i.

3 AHP-EW and PVW Based Improved Algorithm

We can find that index weights are only based on the preference of users in AHP. Once the weight is determined, it will not change any more so that the result can be unreasonable sometimes. Therefore, two improved algorithms are proposed in this section.

3.1 EW Method

According to the explanation of the basic principles of information theory, in the system information is a measure of the degree of order and entropy is a measure of the degree of disorder. According to the definition of information entropy, the entropy value can be used to judge the degree of dispersion. If the information entropy value of the index is smaller, the impact of this index on the comprehensive evaluation is greater. If values of the index parameters are all equal, this index does not play a role in the comprehensive evaluation formula. Therefore, the weight of each index can be calculated according to the actual network parameter value through the concept of information entropy, which provides a basis for comprehensive evaluation of multiple indicators.

Firstly, we calculate the entropy of each index, H_j:

$$H_j = \frac{1}{\ln n} * \sum_{i=1}^{n} y_{ij} * \ln y_{ij} \tag{9}$$

We can get index dispersion degree d_j:

$$d_j = 1 - H_j \tag{10}$$

Finally, we can get the weight w_j:

$$w_j = \frac{d_j}{\sum_{j=1}^{m} d_j} \tag{11}$$

The weights calculated by the EW method are obtained according to the actual network parameter values instead of user preference, which can objectively reflect the influence of network indexes. Combining the entropy weights with the weights obtained by the AHP can improve the problem of excessive subjectivity of AHP.

$$w_{AHP\_EW} = \frac{w_{AHP} + w_{EW}}{2} \tag{12}$$

3.2 PVW Method

According to the previous idea of variable weights, when the value of the index parameter of a network deteriorates, in order to reduce the probability of accessing to this network, the proportion of the index weight in the comprehension evaluation function should be increased. Therefore, this paper adopts punishment variable weight method with hysteresis to modify the weights of the deterioration indexes [12, 13, 14]. When the satellite network normalization parameter y_{ij} is above the threshold y_{th}, priority is given to user preferences to ensure the QoS requirement. When y_{ij} is below to the threshold y_{th}, the index weight will be changed. The flow chart of AHP-EW and PVW based accessing algorithm is as follows (Fig. 3):

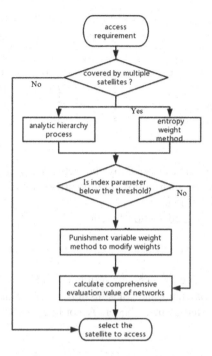

Fig. 3. Flow chart of access algorithm based on PVW method

We first define the weight correction coefficient as

$$k_{ij} = \begin{cases} 1 & y_{ij} > y_{th} \\ e^{-\theta|y_{ij}-y_{th}|} & 0 < y_{ij} \le y_{th} \end{cases} \tag{13}$$

where $k_{ij}(i = 1, 2\ldots, N; \; j = 1, 2\ldots, M)$ is the correction coefficient of the j th index in satellite network i, y_{th} is the threshold and θ is the punishment index. If the value of θ is larger, the punishment will be stronger.

Then, updated weights are as follows:

$$w_{ij} = \frac{w_j * k_{ij}}{\sum_{j=1}^{m} w_j * k_{ij}} \tag{14}$$

$w_{ij}(i = 1, 2\ldots, N; \; j = 1, 2\ldots, M)$ is the weight value of the index j in satellite network i. According to formula (12) and (13), w_{ij} is monotonous declined with y_{ij}, which reflects the punishment for the uneven configuration of indicators.

4 Experimental Simulations

We assume that all the users want maximum speed and covered time, minimum delay and packet loss. The detailed parameters of the satellite networks are shown in Table 3.

Table 3. Simulation parameters of the satellite networks.

	Satellite 1	Satellite 2	Satellite 3	Satellite 4
Delay/ms	40	60	80	60
Loss/ %	0.09	0.08	0.06	0.06
Speed/Mbps	3	2	2.5	1
Covered-time/min	12	10	5	11
Available load/%	30	50	20	80

Assuming that in the area covered by the network overlap, the arrival of new services follows the Poisson distribution and the arrival rate $\lambda \in [0.1, 1]$, the average value of the service time is 60 s.

Here we define the user satisfaction function as

$$u_i = k_1 * y_{delay,i} + k_2 * y_{loss,i} + k_3 * y_{speed,i} \tag{15}$$

u_i is the satisfaction value of accessing to the network. y is the standardized index value of delay, packet loss ratio and transmission speed. If the satisfaction value is higher, it can meet QoS requirement better. According to formula (3) and (14), We have:

$$u_i = \{0.8004, 0.4677, 0.3513, 0.501\} \tag{16}$$

It can be seen that user satisfaction is highest when accessing to network 1, network 4 is the second one and network 3 is the worst. The influence of on variable weight coefficients θ on the comprehensive evaluation value of networks f_i is discussed as follows:

Figure 4 shows the f_i of satellite networks under different θ when the traffic load of network 1 is heavy with 10% available load. Users will choose the network with the maximum f_i to access to.

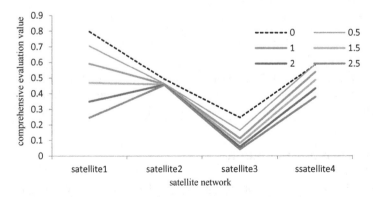

Fig. 4. Comprehensive evaluation values of the satellite networks under different θ.

We can see that when $\theta < 1.5$, network 1 obtains f_1 which is the highest value of f_i even though the user satisfaction value u_i of network 1 is also the highest according to Eq. (15). However, the traffic load of network 1 is heavy and access to network 1 is more likely to cause congestion. The effect of variable weight is not obvious while θ is small.

when $\theta > 2$, the punishment for the load index causes network 1 a low f_i. This will sacrifice QoS to balance the network load. The user will choose network 2 to access, but it is not the optimal option according to Eq. (15) because network 4 has the second highest user satisfaction value u_4. In this paper, we set $\theta = 1.5$, which not only increases the impact of the load index on f_i, but also ensure users' best QoS requirements.

Figure 5, 6 and 7 show the available loads of four satellite networks change with the increase of users under AHP, AHP-EW and PVW algorithm respectively. In Fig. 5, the user first selects the network 1 with the highest comprehensive evaluation value f_1 to access. When the number of users accessing to the network 1 reaches 28, the network 1 has no available load then user begins to select the suboptimal satellite network 4 to access, which may cause network congestion and reduce transmission quality;

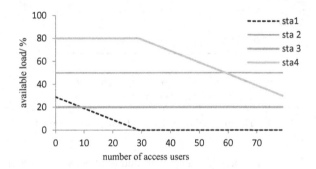

Fig. 5. The trend of available load with the increase of the number of users under AHP.

In Fig. 6, with the AHP-EW algorithm, users select satellite network 1 at first. After 4 users accessing to satellite network 1, the available load of network 1 decreases and the AHP-EW increases the weight of the available load index to increase its influence on f_i. Because the value of f_1 and f_4 are similar, users start to alternately select satellite network 1 and satellite network 4 to access.

In Fig. 7, the comprehensive evaluation value obtained by the PVW is similar as AHP method at first, because the available load of the four satellite networks has not dropped to the threshold and there is no need to modify the network index weight at the beginning. Since the available load of the network 1 drops to the threshold, the network index weights are modified. The additional user subscribers select network 4 to access.

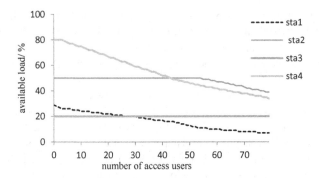

Fig. 6. The trend of available load with the AHP-EW method.

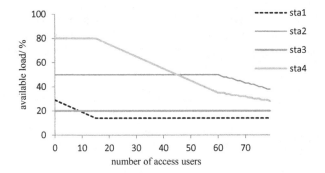

Fig. 7. The trend of available load with PVW method.

From Figs. 5, 6 and 7, since the value of u_3 and f_3 of network 3 are the lowest, that is, the performance indexes of network 3 is not suitable for user to access. Therefore, the available load of network 3 has not changed with the three algorithms.

Figure 8 shows the trend of load variance under three algorithms. We can see that as the number of access users increases, the network load variance of the AHP and PVW algorithms both increase first because the selection result is based on the user's preference. When the number of access users is 18, the load variance value of PVW reaches the maximum value and then decreases. This is because the available load parameters fell to the threshold and the PVW algorithm began to change the weight of the network parameters. When there are few access users, the load variance of AHP-EW algorithm gradually decreases, and the balancing effect is better than AHP and PVW algorithms. When the number of access users exceeds 50, the PVW algorithm has the best balance effect.

Figure 9 shows the relationship between the access blocking rate and the arrival rate of new services under three algorithms. The access algorithm based on AHP_EW and PVW can effectively reduce the blocking rate and ensure the transmission quality while balancing the network.

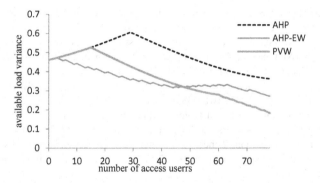

Fig. 8. The trend of load variance with three algorithms

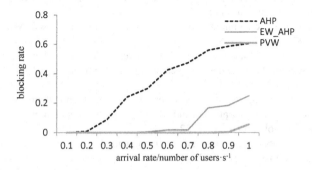

Fig. 9. The trend of the access blocking rate with three algorithms

5   Conclusion

This paper proposed two improved network access selection algorithms based on AHP. The algorithms based on the AHP-EW method calculated the comprehensive weights of the indexes. Then, the PVW method was proposed and the weights of the indexes are dynamically adjusted through the punishment variable weight function to obtain variable weights. The AHP-EW and PVW method not only considered the users' preference, but also considered the actual parameter value of the network to ensure the rationality of the judgment result.

References

1. Wu, J., Li, W., Huang, J., et al.: Key techniques for mobile internet: a survey. Sci. China-Inf. Sci. **45**(1), 45–69 (2015)
2. Wang, L., Kuo, G.: Mathematical modeling for network selection in heterogeneous wireless networks —a tutorial. IEEE Commun. Surv. Tutor. **15**(1), 271–292 (2013)
3. Ma, D., Ma, M.: Proactive load balancing with admission control for heterogeneous overlay networks. Wirel. Commun. Mob. Comput. **13**(18), 1671–1680 (2013)

4. Roy, S., Reddy, S.: Signal strength ratio based vertical hand-off decision algorithms in integrated heterogeneous networks. Wirel. Pers. Commun. **77**(4), 2565–2585 (2014)
5. Qi, Y., Wang, H., Zhang, L., et al.: Optimal access mode selection and resource allocation for cellular-VANET heterogeneous networks. IET Commun. **11**(13), 2012–2019 (2017)
6. Yu, H.-W., Zhang, B.: A hybrid MADM algorithm based on attribute weight and utility value for heterogeneous network selection. J. Netw. Syst. Manage. **27**(3), 756–783 (2018). https://doi.org/10.1007/s10922-018-9483-y
7. Wu, S., Huey, R.: Improved joint radio resource management usage grey fuzzy control in heterogeneous wireless networks. J. Internet Technol. **16**(5), 777–788 (2015)
8. Cai, X., Liu, X., Qu, Z.: Game theory-based device-to-device network access algorithm for heterogeneous networks. J. Supercomput. **75**(5), 2423–2435 (2018). https://doi.org/10.1007/s11227-018-2628-7
9. Xu, S., Wang, X., Huang, M.: Software-defined next-generation satellite networks: architecture, challenges, and solutions. IEEE Access, 1 (2018)
10. Yang, B., Wu, Y., Chu, X., Song, G.: Seamless handover in software-defined satellite networking. IEEE Commun. Lett. 1768–1771 (2016)
11. Saaty, R.: The analytic hierarchy process-what it is and how it is used. Math. Model. **9**(3), 161–176 (1987)
12. Boulahia, L., et al.: Enabling vertical handover decisions in heterogeneous wireless networks: a state-of-the-art and a classification. IEEE Commun. Surv. Tutor. **16**(2), 776–811 (2014)
13. Cai, W., Liu, W., Zhang, N.: Analysis of electromagnetic loop network on loop closing or opening based on model of optimal comprehensive evaluation with punitive variable weight. Power Syst. Technol. **41**(7), 2316–2323 (2017)
14. Li, H.: Factor spaces and mathematical frame knowledge representation (VIII)-variable weights analysis. Fuzzy Syst. Math. (1995)

A Low-Loss Strategy for Network Function Virtualization Multicast Optimization

Muxin Tian[(⊠)]

School of Electronic and Information Engineering, Beihang University,
Beijing, China
tmx5192396@buaa.edu.cn

Abstract. In order to fulfill the multicast task with a service function chain (SFC) requirement and effectively utilize network bandwidth and resources, a low-cost NFV multicast optimization strategy based on Dijkstra's algorithm is proposed for the real-time requirements of wireless network data transmission scenarios. Taking network resource consumption and link bandwidth consumption as evaluation indicators, on the premise of meeting the Service Function Tree (SFT) delay requirements, the Virtual Network Function (VNF) is placed reasonably to realize the embedding of the Service Function Chain (SFC). It creatively proposes the merge rule of VNF in the SFC chain, which reduces the consumption of node resources and link bandwidth while ensuring the connectivity of the network. Experimental results show that the algorithm can effectively reduce the consumption of node resources and link bandwidth under the condition of ensuring low delay, and ensure the real-time and reliability of data transmission.

Keywords: NFV technology · Multicast technology · Network resource consumption · Link bandwidth consumption

1 Introduction

In recent years, the trend of network cloudification has become more and more obvious. Traditional telecommunications services are highly dependent on physical topology and vendor-specific hardware. In order to overcome this problem Software Defined Network (SDN) and Network Function Virtualization (NFV) technologies [1] have been proposed and widely adopted. NFV technology provides an effective solution to the serious hardware and software coupling problem of the 4G core network, which greatly reduces operating time and costs. However, as people's demand for networks further increases, traditional 4G cannot support the surge in mobile data traffic in the future. However, 5G imposes higher requirements on latency and bandwidth [2]. How to improve the network carrying capacity and ensure the real-time performance of data transmission has become an urgent problem to be solved today.

This work was supported in part by the National Key Research and Development Program (Grant Nos. 2016YFB1200100), and the National Natural Science Foundation of China (NSFC) (Grant Nos. 61827901 and 91738301).

B. Li et al. (Eds.): IoTaaS 2020, LNICST 346, pp. 135–142, 2021.
https://doi.org/10.1007/978-3-030-67514-1_11

Under the NFV, multicast is a widely used communication type, which can significantly save bandwidth consumption, and is suitable for real-time data transmission scenarios such as multimedia video sharing and computer cooperative work. Optimizing NFV multicast in SDN can greatly assist 5G research and development. At present, there are studies on this aspect at home and abroad. Literature [3] proposes an approximation algorithm and an online algorithm with guaranteed competition ratio, which realizes the NFV multicast resources supported by SDN under the condition of limited network resource capacity. The rate is the smallest and the network throughput rate is the largest. Reference [4] modeled the deployment and routing of VNF as a linear programming model with the goal of minimizing the number of servers, and proposed a heuristic algorithm based on simulated annealing (SA), which can obtain an approximate optimal solution in a short time. The feasibility is verified by comparing the results of the CPLEX optimizer with the results of the SA algorithm through simulation experiments. The disadvantage of this scheme is that the objective function only considers the computing resources, does not consider the communication resources, and has fewer constraints. Reference [5] studied the optimal SFC embedding problem of NFV multicast. Through the designed two-stage algorithm, the initial feasible solution was generated and the optimized feasible solution was evaluated. The influence of different parameters on the embedded SFT was evaluated. The designed SFT embedding scheme significantly reduces the traffic transmission cost. Most of these studies have focused on optimizing the cost of network resources, and no effective solutions have been proposed for improving bandwidth consumption and latency performance. Therefore, there is an urgent need for a network function virtualization multicast optimization algorithm with low latency, low computing resource consumption, and low bandwidth consumption, which overcomes the deficiencies of the existing technology and adapts to network requirements.

In order to meet the multicast task with service function chain (SFC) requirements, it is necessary to construct a suitable service function tree (SFT) embedded in the shared multicast tree, and use this as a basis for related performance analysis and improvement. The network topology and size of the multicast task are diverse [6], so for a particular NFV multicast task, considering the link bandwidth, VNF setting occupied resources, node resources and algorithm complexity, find the optimal multicast tree in the embedded SFT Is a challenging problem.

This paper presents a network function virtualization multicast optimization algorithm design scheme in the NFV multicast directed network environment supported by SDN. By analyzing the impact of VNF placement on network resource consumption, VNF deployment rules and merge rules are designed to achieve a significant reduction in network computing resources and bandwidth consumption, while ensuring network connectivity. Simulation results show that the NFV multicast optimization scheme proposed in this paper meets the existing network requirements. This is of great significance for improving network performance and ensuring real-time data transmission.

2 Proposed Method

It is known that the NFV multicast resource optimization scheme needs to consider three types of problems in directed network scenarios, namely the placement of VNF, the embedding of SFC, and the determination of VNF merge rules. Through these, optimization of network computing resources and bandwidth consumption is realized. The implementation of the program needs to add NFV elements to the traditional multicast service, set the three types of nodes (source node, intermediate node and target node) of the model reasonably, and perform node calculation resources, link bandwidth (weight) and VNF consumption. The initialization of resources prepares for subsequent algorithm design. Because this paper studies directed networks, the upstream and downstream bandwidths are different, so it is necessary to use the first and the last node serial numbers for effective link naming. Throughout the process, the bandwidth consumed after a certain VNF is not changed by default.

2.1 VNF Layout Rules

The layout problem of VNF is mainly to find the optimal location of VNF without considering the service order constraints. In the process of finding VNF, it is necessary to formulate relevant rules and consider whether node resources and bandwidth can support the placement of VNF. The embedding problem of SFC is more complicated because it requires traffic to traverse a certain number of VNFs in a certain order. Different from the method of placing the VNF first and then finding the appropriate SFC embedding, this paper first finds the shortest path of the source node and the target node through the Dijkstra shortest path algorithm. By judging the node resources and link bandwidth of each node on the shortest path, VNFs are placed in order.Once a certain VNF placed in sequence cannot be placed on the shortest path, it will be stopped, and the capacity is constantly updated during the process. In this step, it is necessary to pay attention to the judgment order of node resources and link bandwidth. According to the actual situation of the data flow, if the bandwidth of the previous link cannot meet the requirements, the shortest path should be disconnected, but if the computing resources of the previous node are not Meet the requirements, you can continue to find the next node that meets the requirements of computing resources.

For unicast tasks with multiple target nodes, the VNF placement results on the shortest path according to the above requirements can be divided into three cases: (1) All VNFs are placed on the shortest path node in sequence. (2) VNF is only partially placed on the node with the shortest path. (3) The first VNF is not placed on the node with the shortest path, that is, no VNF is placed on the shortest path. For case (1), it is only necessary to subtract the initial bandwidth of all links in the shortest path to complete the capacity and bandwidth update. For case (2), the node where the distance between the node where the previous VNF has been placed and the target node is less than two hops. Then select the node with the smallest sum of distances to the two nodes to place the next VNF. If there is a VNF that has not been placed for this SFC, repeat the above operation until it is completely placed. After all VNFs are placed successfully, update the link bandwidth. Once a VNF cannot be placed, the link is broken, and the computing resources previously consumed by placing the VNF are restored. For case (3), first search the network for the point where the distance between the source node and the target node is less than two hops, find the node with the smallest sum of the distance between the two nodes, and place the first VNF. The subsequent process is the same as (2). This completes the VNF placement and SFC embedding process for multi-target unicast. Save the node's consumption of computing resources and link bandwidth at this time, and judge the connection status of SFC and record the number of connections.

2.2   VNF Merge Rule

In existing research, SFC is often embedded in a target network with unicast tasks with multiple targets. For example, maximize the remaining data rate, minimize the number of application nodes, or minimize the traffic delivery delay. The above researches are all SFC embedding problems in unicast tasks, which are both different and related to the research work of this paper. The research in this paper starts with multi-target unicast. After the VNF placement and SFC embedding process is completed, the multi-target unicast scenario will be converted into a multi-cast scenario through VNF merger to achieve VNF and bandwidth sharing, which also greatly reduces the node computing resource consumption.

Before merging, the deployment of each VNF in multi-objective unicast (location and number) is first clarified and calculate the distance between two identical VNF nodes to write into the VNF distance matrix. By calculating the sum of each row of the distance matrix, the distance from the node with the same VNF to all other nodes is obtained. The node represented by the distance and the smallest row is the node to be merged. It is specified that other same VNF nodes with a distance of less than two hops from this node are merged directly, and the rest are not changed. Traverse all VNFs to complete the merge process. At this time, the VNF placement changes. It is necessary to re-judge whether the link bandwidth meets the demand. If not, the link will be disconnected. In the case of leaving only SFCs that satisfy the condition, update the initial values of computing resources and link bandwidth, and save the updated node computing resources and link bandwidth consumption, and determine the number of connected SFC connectivity records.

3   Results and Discussions

The design plan of this paper is to optimize the resource allocation and bandwidth consumption of the multicast service function chain of the entire network. After the VNF placement and SFC embedding are implemented, the data comparison between the multi-target unicast and multicast before and after VNF merge is performed. The network topology (see Fig. 1) has a total of 17 nodes, the initial computing resource cap = [57 58 49 52 55 47 46 42 38 48 50 55 49 48 43 42 51], the initial uplink and downlink bandwidth sum is 5220, and the initial consumption bandwidth $w0 = 20$. Each time, the source node s and the target node di are randomly generated by a random matrix.

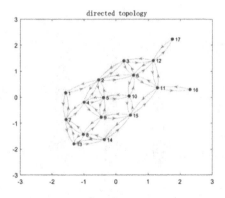

Fig. 1. Directed topology

The results of this paper use computing resource consumption and link bandwidth consumption as indicators to measure its pros and cons. Both show the data capacity and operating speed that the network can carry. Obviously, the smaller the computing resource and bandwidth consumption when a network system implements the same function, the better the network performance.

Each multicast tree is composed of one source node and 6 target nodes, which is equivalent to containing six SFCs. By changing the number of randomly generated SFCs, the running program obtains different results, normalizes the units, and plots the running results in Table 1.

Table 1. Operation result data table.

Number of SFC	Node resource consumption	Link bandwidth consumption	Average bandwidth consumption
24 (before merge)	432	1060	44.1
24 (after merge)	36	900	37.5
48 (before merge)	720	2220	55.5
48 (after merge)	213	1600	48.48
72 (before merge)	792	2700	61.36
72 (after merge)	266	1660	48.82

3.1 Comparison of Computing Resource Consumption

In the process from multi-target unicast to multicast, the VNF merging process is experienced, and the sharing of VNF is realized, which can effectively reduce the consumption of computing resources. Taking 24, 48, and 72 SFCs as examples, a simulation comparison is made. The results are shown in Fig. 2.

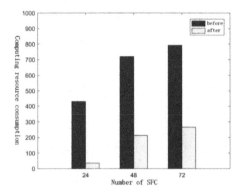

Fig. 2. Compute resource consumption comparison chart

In the figure, the unicast computing resource consumption is 432, 720, 792, and the combined multicast computing resource consumption is 34, 213, and 266 respectively. The gap between the two is obvious. The emergence of multicast significantly saves the node's computing resources Consume.

3.2 Comparison of Bandwidth Consumption

If there are VNFs in the same deployment location and connected in sequence in different SFCs, the repeated paths between these VNFs can be shared and used. Therefore, from multi-target unicast to multicast will definitely reduce the bandwidth consumption, as shown in Fig. 3. Taking 24, 48, and 72 SFCs as examples, the unicast bandwidth consumption is 1060, 2220, and 2700, respectively, and the combined multicast bandwidth consumption is 900, 1600, and 1660, respectively. It is obvious from the figure that at the beginning, the number of SFCs is small, and the link bandwidth and computing resources have little restrictions on the deployment of VNF, and there is not much difference before and after the merger. With the increase in the number of SFCs, within a certain range, the bandwidth savings of multicast is more obvious.

It can be seen from the simulation results that the previous SFC may be broken due to insufficient link bandwidth due to the merge of VNFs, which also partially reduces the bandwidth consumption. Therefore, the total bandwidth consumed by the entire network alone cannot fully explain the problem. By setting the SFC connectivity flag to record the number of SFC connections, and calculate the average bandwidth consumption of each SFC, as shown in Fig. 4. After excluding the impact of the increase or decrease of bandwidth caused by SFC on and off, the difference between the average bandwidth consumption before and after the merger is still increasing. Within a certain range, the more SFCs, the better the optimization effect of average bandwidth consumption.

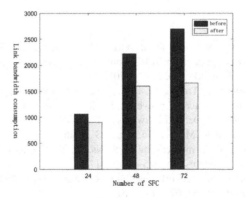

Fig. 3. Link bandwidth consumption comparison chart

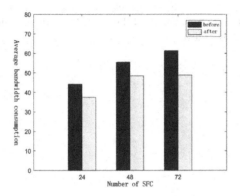

Fig. 4. Average bandwidth consumption comparison chart

4   Conclusions

According to the specific research scenarios, this paper chooses to use the Dijkstra algorithm that can solve the single-source shortest path problem and has a low time complexity to design a network function virtualization multicast resource optimization scheme. VNF deployment, SFC embedding and VNF merge rule design and implementation are completed. Through the analysis of the simulation results, it is known that multicast realizes the sharing of node computing resources and public link bandwidth, which greatly reduces the node computing resources and link bandwidth consumption. It can be predicted from the simulation results that the more complex the network, the more network nodes and links, the more obvious the optimization effect of multicast.

References

1. Rossem, S.V., Tavernier, W., Sonkoly, B., et al.: Deploying elastic routing capability in an SDN/NFV-enabled environment. In: IEEE Conference on Network Function Virtualization and Software-defined Networks, pp. 22–24 (2015)
2. Siddiqui, M.S., Escalona, E, Trouva, E., et al.: Policy based virtualised security architecture for SDN/NFV enabled 5G access networks. In: IEEE Conference on Network Function Virtualization and Software Defined Networks (NFV-SDN), pp. 44–49 (2016)
3. Xu, Z., Liang, W., Huang, M., Jia, M., Guo, S., Galis, A.: Approximation and online algorithms for NFV-enabled multicasting in SDNs. In: IEEE International Conference on Distributed Computing Systems, pp. 625–634 (2017)
4. Li, X., Qian, C.: The virtual network function placement problem. In: IEEE Conference on Computer Communications, pp. 69–70 (2015)
5. Ren, B., Guo, D., Tang, G., Lin, X., Qin, Y.: Optimal service function tree embedding for NFV enabled multicast. In: IEEE International Conference on Distributed Computing Systems, pp. 132–142 (2018)
6. Zhang, S., Tizghadam, A., Park, B., Bannazadeh, H., Leon-Garcia, A.: Joint NFV placement and routing for multicast service on SDN. In: IEEE Network Operations and Management Symposium, pp. 333–341 (2016)

A Deployment Method Based on Artificial Bee Colony Algorithm for UAV-Mounted Base Stations

Chen Zhang, Leyi Zhang, Yanming Liu, Lipeng Zhu, and Zhenyu Xiao[✉]

School of Electronic and Information Engineering, Beihang University,
Beijing 100191, China
{moon_zc,16231001,liuyanming,zhulipeng,xiaozy}@buaa.edu.cn

Abstract. With high mobility and low cost, unmanned aerial vehicles (UAVs) are widely used in wireless communication systems. Especially in emergencies, UAVs can be used as aerial base stations (BSs) to provide wireless communication services for ground users. Aiming to reduce cost, we prefer to minimizing the number of UAVs needed to serve all users. Compared with the existing works, we take the constraints of required quality of service (QoS) and the service ability of each UAV into consideration. To solve the formulated mixed-integer programming problem, we propose a three-step method. First, to ensure each UAV can serve more users, the maximum service radius of UAVs is derived according to users' QoS requirement. Second, we propose an artificial bee colony (ABC) algorithm based clustering method to cluster users into different groups in the horizontal direction. Third, we adjust the positions of UAVs to obtained a better communication performance of the wireless communication system. Finally, the simulation results are presented to demonstrate the superiority of the proposed method.

Keywords: Wireless communication · Unmanned aerial vehicles · Aerial base stations · Three-dimensional deployment

1 Introduction

Because of the high mobility, high agility, and high stability of line-of-sight (LoS) channel [1] of unmanned aerial vehicles (UAVs), wireless communication assisted by UAVs has become more and more popular in recent years [2,3]. Under some circumstances, terrestrial infrastructures are unable to maintain a wireless communication system. For example, earthquakes and floods may destroy those facilities, while concerts and competitions lead to increased traffic exceeding the service ability of the system. It is convenient to apply UAVs to resume wireless

This work was supported in part by the National Key Research and Development Program (Grant Nos. 2016YFB1200100), and the National Natural Science Foundation of China (NSFC) (Grant Nos. 61827901 and 91738301).

B. Li et al. (Eds.): IoTaaS 2020, LNICST 346, pp. 143–155, 2021.
https://doi.org/10.1007/978-3-030-67514-1_12

communication. A solution to use UAVs in emergencies is to apply UAVs as aerial base stations (BSs).

Applying UAVs as aerial-BSs has attracted lots of attention from academia, including several topics. Among all these topics, the deployment of the UAV is a basic one. In [4], the authors maximized the coverage region by optimizing the height of a single UAV. In [5], a three-dimensional (3D) deployment algorithm was proposed, which can maximize the coverage region of each UAV while satisfying the quality of service (QoS) of different users. In [6], a UAV was used as an aerial-BS to serve ground users as many as possible while consuming power as little as possible.

However, as users' number and demands for communication are increasing rapidly, using a single UAV to satisfy all users is becoming more and more difficult. Thus, many studies have discussed the problem of deploying multiple UAVs. In [7], a spiral deployment algorithm was proposed to deploy UAVs in two-dimensional (2D). An algorithm was designed to minimize the number of UAVs needed to serve all the ground users. Similarly, the authors in [8] utilized the elephant herding optimization algorithm [9] to minimize the number of UAVs. In [10], the number of UAVs was minimized in the condition of known and unknown user location. In [11], a low time complexity algorithm was proposed to minimize the number of UAVs and to optimize the 3D positions of UAVs to improve resource utilization.

In this paper, we study a downlink UAV network where multiple UAVs are deployed as BSs to serve the ground users with constraint on service ability. Different from the existing deployment studies, we are committed to using as few as possible UAVs to serve all the ground users and optimize the QoS of users at the same time. As mentioned before, the application of a single UAV is limited because of its finite service region and service ability. Besides, the air to ground (A2G) channel model is decided by the positions of UAVs and users, so the QoS can be improved by adjusting the 3D positions of UAVs.

The rest of this paper is organized as follows. In Sect. 2, the system model is presented and the multiple UAVs deployment problem is formulated. In Sect. 3, the solution to the problem is introduced. In Sect. 4, the simulation performance compared with existing methods is provided to show the superiority of our method. Finally, we conclude this paper in Sect. 5.

2   System Model and Problem Formulation

A downlink wireless communication network assisted by multiple UAVs is shown in Fig. 1, where UAVs are used to transmit data to users randomly distributed in a 2D area $\mathcal{D} = [0, x_{max}] \times [0, y_{max}]$. Users are denoted by $\mathcal{K} = \{1, 2, \cdots, K\}$ and the position of each user is presented by $\boldsymbol{w_k} = [x_k, y_k]^{\mathrm{T}} \in \mathbb{R}^{2 \times 1}$. At the same time, the deployment area of the UAVs is limited to a 3D area $\mathcal{P} = \{[x_m, y_m, h_m] | x_{min} \leq x_m \leq x_{max}, y_{min} \leq y_m \leq y_{max}, h_m > 0\}$. $\mathcal{M} = \{1, 2, \cdots, M\}$ denotes the set of UAVs, and $\boldsymbol{p_m} = [x_m, y_m, h_m]^{\mathrm{T}} \in \mathbb{R}^{3 \times 1}$ represents the position of each UAV $m \in \mathcal{M}$.

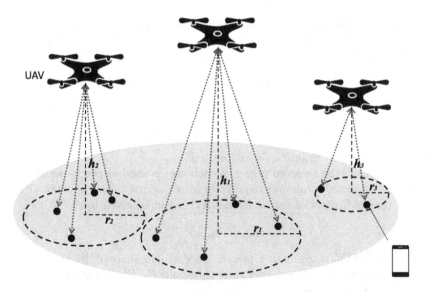

Fig. 1. The considered wireless communication system with UAVs

2.1 System Model

Since some obstacles like trees and buildings may block the link between UAVs and ground users in wireless communication, the channel between UAVs and users is usually a mixture of line-of-sight (LoS) link and none-line-of-sight (NLoS) link. Taking UAV m and user k for example, the large-scale channel gain $\beta_{m,k}$ between them in LoS environments and NLoS environments can be expressed as [12]:

$$\beta_{m,k}(d_{m,k}) = \begin{cases} \beta_0\, d_{m,k}^{-\alpha} & \text{LoS environment,} \\ \kappa\, \beta_0\, d_{m,k}^{-\alpha} & \text{NLoS environment,} \end{cases} \tag{1}$$

In (1), β_0 is the path loss of the reference distance in LoS environments. $\kappa \in (0,1)$ is an attenuation coefficient for NLoS environments. $d_{m,k}$ represents the distance between user k and UAV m, which can be expressed as follow:

$$d_{m,k} = \sqrt{h_m^2 + s_{m,k}^2} = \frac{s_{m,k}}{cos\theta_{m,k}}, \tag{2}$$

where h_m is the height of UAV m, $s_{m,k} = \sqrt{(x_k - x_m)^2 + (y_k - y_m)^2}$ is the 2D distance between user k and UAV m, and $\theta_{m,k}$ is the evaluation angle between user k and UAV m.

Then, the probability of existing an LoS link between user k and UAV m can be given by [12]:

$$P_{LoS}(\theta_{m,k}) = \frac{1}{1 + a\, \exp(-b(\theta_{m,k} - a))}, \tag{3}$$

where a and b are parameters directly related to the environment. Then, the probability of NLoS links can be obtained as $P_{NLoS}(\theta_{m,k}) = 1 - P_{LoS}(\theta_{m,k})$.

Thus, we can obtain the channel gain between user k and UAV m:

$$\bar{g}_{m,k}(d_{m,k}, \theta_{m,k}) \triangleq \mathbb{E}[|g_{m,k}|^2]$$

$$= P_{LoS}(\theta_{m,k})\beta_0 d_{m,k}^{-\alpha} + P_{NLoS}(\theta_{m,k})\kappa\beta_0 d_{m,k}^{-\alpha} \qquad (4)$$

$$= \hat{P}_{LoS}(\theta_{m,k})\beta_0 d_{m,k}^{-\alpha},$$

where $\hat{P}_{LoS}(\theta_{m,k}) = P_{LoS}(\theta_{m,k}) + \kappa P_{NLoS}(\theta_{m,k})$.

In this paper, the received power of each user is used as the measurement of the QoS. The users' minimum required received signal power is denoted by P_0 and the received power of user k from UAV m can be given by:

$$P_{m,k} = \bar{g}_{m,k} \times P_t, \qquad (5)$$

where P_t is UAVs' transmitting power. UAV m can successfully transmit data to user k only when $P_{m,k}$ is larger than threshold P_0. We can get the constraint about $\bar{g}_{m,k}$ according to (5), which can be given by:

$$\bar{g}_{m,k} \geq \bar{g}_0, \qquad (6)$$

where $\bar{g}_0 = \frac{P_0}{P_t}$ represents the minimum channel gain for successful transmission. Only when the channel gain between UAV m and user k satisfies (6), can UAV m possibly serve user k.

2.2   Maximum Service Radius

According to the relationship $\cos\theta_{m,k} = \frac{s_{m,k}}{\sqrt{s_{m,k}^2 + h_m^2}}$, the channel gain $\bar{g}_{m,k}$ can be rewritten as a function of the 2D distance $s_{m,k}$ and UAV's height h_m. The relation is shown in Fig. 2.

Figure 2 shows a typical plot of $\bar{g}_{m,k}$ versus h_m for different $s_{m,k}$ values. It can be seen that when h_m is fixed, $\bar{g}$ decreases with increasing $s_{m,k}$ and finally fails to meet the requirement (6) if $s_{m,k} > r_{max}$, where r_{max} represents the largest service radius of UAV. When $s_{m,k}$ is fixed, $\bar{g}$ increases to the highest point because of the increasing the probability of existing LoS link, and then decreases because of the attenuation of long distance. Therefore, given the minimum channel gain requirement $\bar{g}_0$, the optimal height can be calculated by [4]:

$$\frac{\partial s_{m,k}}{\partial h_m} = 0 \qquad (7)$$

After deriving the optimal height h_m, the largest service radius r_{max} is obtained by solving the following equation [4]:

$$\bar{g}(r_{max}, h_m) = \bar{g}_0 \qquad (8)$$

That is to say, when the 2D distance between UAV m and user k satisfies $s_{m,k} \leq r_{max}$, users k can be served by UAV m. However, if the distance between

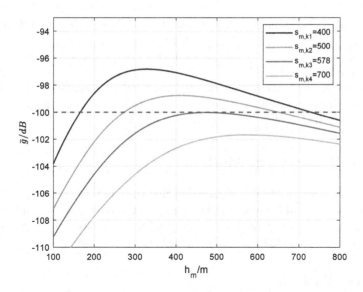

Fig. 2. Curve of channel gain $\bar{g}_0$ as a function of h_m when $s_{m,k}$ is fixed.

UAV m' and user k also satisfies the relation above, whether UAV m should serve user k becomes unclear. In order to solve this problem, we define an indicator function to ensure each user is served by only one UAV:

$$\gamma_{m,k} = \begin{cases} 1, & \text{User } k \text{ is served by UAV } m, \\ 0, & \text{Otherwise,} \end{cases} \qquad (9)$$

where user k is served by UAV m for $\gamma = 1$, and $\gamma_{m,k} = 0$ otherwise.

2.3 Problem Formulation

The number of ground users served by each UAV is limited because of UAVs' limited service ability. N_{max} is used to represent the maximum number of ground users each UAV can serve. By jointly optimizing the connection between UAVs and ground users and the positions of UAVs, the problem for minimization of the number of UAVs is formulated as follows:

$$\min_{\{p_m\}, \{\gamma_k^m\}} \quad |\mathcal{M}| \qquad (10)$$

$$\text{s.t.} \quad \bar{g}_{m,k} \geq \bar{g}_0 \gamma_k^m \quad \forall k \in \mathcal{K}, \forall m \in \mathcal{M}. \qquad (10a)$$

$$p_m \in \mathcal{P} \quad \forall m \in \mathcal{M} \qquad (10b)$$

$$\sum_{k \in \mathcal{K}} \gamma_{m,k} \leq N_{max} \quad \forall m \in \mathcal{M} \qquad (10c)$$

$$\sum_{m \in \mathcal{M}} \gamma_{m,k} = 1 \quad \forall k \in \mathcal{K} \qquad (10d)$$

Constraint (10a) indicates that (6) must be satisfied when user k is served by UAV m. The constraints on the deployment area and service ability of each UAV are shown in (10b) and (10c). Constraint (10d) means that each user can only be served by one UAV.

There are integer and continuous variables in (10), meaning that it is a mixed-integer programming problem, which is difficult to solve [13]. In the next section, a suboptimal solution of (10) will be developed.

3   UAV Deployment Method

In this section, we first design an algorithm that combines the heuristic algorithm in [7] and the artificial bee colony (ABC) algorithm to cluster users into groups. This algorithm can minimize the number of UAVs required to serve all users. Then, we optimize the 3D position of each UAV to improve QoS.

3.1   User Clustering

We reformulate the problem of user clustering as follow:

$$\min_{\{\gamma_{m,k}\}} \quad |\mathcal{M}| \tag{11}$$

$$\text{s.t.} \quad \gamma_{m,k} r_{m,k} \leq r_{max} \quad \forall k \in \mathcal{K}, \forall m \in \mathcal{M} \tag{11a}$$

$$\cdot \sum_{k \in \mathcal{K}} \gamma_{m,k} \leq N_{max} \quad \forall m \in \mathcal{M} \tag{11b}$$

$$\sum_{m \in \mathcal{M}} \gamma_{m,k} = 1 \quad \forall k \in \mathcal{K} \tag{11c}$$

We aim at adjusting the serve indicator variable $\gamma_{m,k}$ to minimize the number of groups, which is also the number of UAVs. To solve (11), an Ordered ABC-based Placement (OAP) algorithm is designed, which combines ABC algorithm and heuristic algorithm. ABC algorithm can effectively find the optimal or suboptimal solution for difficult problem and heuristic algorithm is used to reduce the solution space of ABC algorithm to find the solution more quickly.

The main idea of the iterative algorithm OAP algorithm is to give priority to users located at the outmost periphery of all users. A circle with radius r_{max} is used to cover users, and users covered in each iteration will be clustered into the same group.

In each iteration, we first find users located at the outmost edge of the uncovered users, called boundary users $\mathcal{K}_{U,bo}$, while the other users are called inner users $\mathcal{K}_{U,in}$. In order to ensure that the clustering is performed in an order from outside to inside, a boundary user needs to be selected as the feature user k_0 of each group, so that each clustering work is carried out near the boundary of the uncovered user area. In the first iteration, a boundary user is randomly selected as k_0 from $\mathcal{K}_{U,bo}$, and in each subsequent iteration, the user on the boundary of updated uncovered users that is closest to k_0 in the last iteration will be selected as the new k_0.

After k_0 is selected, calculate the distances between all users and k_0. Boundary users and inner users with a distance of not greater than $2r_{max}$ from k_0 are grouped into the sets $\mathcal{K}_{local,bo}$ and $\mathcal{K}_{local,in}$. Only users in $\mathcal{K}_{local,bo}$ and $\mathcal{K}_{local,in}$ need to be considered when clustering users because users with distances greater than $2r_{max}$ are impossible to be clustered into the same groups. The process above is effective in reducing the solution space of ABC algorithm.

Then, ABC algorithm is applied to determine the cluster's center, trying to cluster as more users as possible into this group. The above iteration continues until all users are grouped. Finally, we derive the center position of each cluster and divide users into different groups. The set of groups is presented as $\mathcal{L} = \{\mathcal{L}^1, \cdots, \mathcal{L}^{|\mathcal{M}|}\}$. Every user k is guaranteed to belong to one subset of $\mathcal{L}$.

Algorithm 1: Ordered ABC-based User Clustering Algorithm

Require:

   User set $\mathcal{K}$, user locations $\{w_k\}$

Ensure:

   The number of groups $|\mathcal{M}|$ and set $\mathcal{L}$

1: Initialize $m = 1$, $\mathcal{L} = \emptyset$, $\mathcal{K}_U = \mathcal{K}$

2: **while** $\mathcal{K}_U \neq \emptyset$ **do**

3:    Find boundary user set $\mathcal{K}_{U,bo} \subseteq \mathcal{K}_U$ and update inner user set
      $\mathcal{K}_{U,in} \leftarrow \mathcal{K}_U \backslash \mathcal{K}_{U,bo}$.

4:    Choose the feature user k_0

5:    For every $k_{U,bo} \in \mathcal{K}_{U,bo}$, calculate the distance between $k_{U,bo}$ and k_0. If the
      distance is not greater than $2r_{max}$, add $k_{U,bo}$ to $\mathcal{K}_{local,bo}$.
      For every $k_{U,in} \in \mathcal{K}_{U,in}$, calculate the distance between $k_{U,in}$ and k_0. If the
      distance is not greater than $2r_{max}$, add $k_{U,in}$ to $\mathcal{K}_{local,in}$.

6:    Use Algorithm 2 to obtain $\mathcal{L}^m$.

7:    Set $\mathcal{K}_U \leftarrow \mathcal{K}_U \backslash \mathcal{L}^m$.

8:    Update $m = m + 1$.

9:    Add $\mathcal{L}^m$ to $\mathcal{L}$.

10: **end while**

11: $|\mathcal{M}| = m$ **return** $\mathcal{L}$.

The process of clustering users into different groups is described in Algorithm 1. Step 6 depicts the process of applying ABC algorithm to decide the center of cluster, which is detailed in Algorithm 2.

ABC algorithm was designed to solve multivariable function optimization problems in 2005 [14]. The algorithm imitates the behavior of employed bees, onlooker bees and scout bees when they are searching for food to find the solution to the problem. The algorithm is presented as follows.

1. *Initialization:* Firstly, the initial solution set is randomly generated as $\mathcal{F}^{(0)} = \{F_1^{(0)}, \cdots, F_{N_p}^{(0)}\}$, where N_p stands for the total amount of solutions. Every

---

Algorithm 2: ABC Procedure

Require: $\{w_k\}_{k \in \mathcal{K}} \in \mathbb{R}^{2 \times 1}$, $\mathcal{K}_{local,bo}$, $\mathcal{K}_{local,in}$, k_0, N_{max}, r_{max}, N_p, T, T_s

Ensure: $\mathcal{L}^m$

1: Randomly initialize the set of possible positions for cluster's center $\mathcal{F}^{(0)}$.
   For $F_{0_i} \in \mathcal{F}^{(0)}$, calculate its distance with feature user k_0. If the distance is
   greater than r_{max} then normalize it.
   Calculate the fitness value of every position, and find the position F_c^m with
   the greatest fitness valuef_c^m
   $t = 0$.

2: **while** $t \neq T$ **do**

3:    Employed bees search for a better solution in the neighbourhood of current
      solution.
      Update the solution set $\mathcal{F}^{(t)}$.

4:    Onlooker bees search for a better solution according to the probability.
      Update the solution set $\mathcal{F}^{(t)}$.

5:    Scout bees generate a new solution if the current remains unmodified
      during T_s iterations.

6:    Calculate fitness value of every solution in $\mathcal{F}^{(t)}$.
      Find the greatest fitness value of solutions in $\mathcal{F}^{(t)}$ and compare it with f_c^m.
      Choose the one with greater fitness value as F_c^m.

7:    Update $t = t + 1$.

8: **end while**

9: Calculate the distance s_{k_i, F_c^m} between F_c^m and every user k_i. If $s_{k_i, F_c^m} < r_{max}$,
   add k_i to $\mathcal{L}^m$.
   return $\mathcal{L}^m$.

---

initial solution $F_i^{(0)} = (x_i^{(0)}, y_i^{(0)}) \in \mathcal{F}^{(0)}$ is a possible location for the center of cluster m.

Then we define a function $s(F_i^{(0)}, k_0) = \sqrt{(x_i^{(0)} - x_{k_0})^2 + (y_i^{(0)} - y_{k_0})^2}$ to represent the 2D distance $s(F_i^{(0)}, k_0)$ between each $F_i^{(0)}$ and k_0. If $s(F_i^{(0)}, k_0) > r_{max}$, which means the cluster cannot cover k_0, the distance $s(F_i^{(0)}, k_0)$ should be normalized to r_{max}. The new position $F_i^{'(0)}$ after normalization is determined as follow:

$$\begin{cases} x_i^{'(0)} = \frac{r_{max}}{s(F_i^{(0)}, k_0)}(x_i^{(0)} - x_{k_0}) + x_{k_0}, \\ y_i^{'(0)} = \frac{r_{max}}{s(F_i^{(0)}, k_0)}(y_i^{(0)} - y_{k_0}) + y_{k_0}. \end{cases} \tag{12}$$

After that, we calculate the fitness value of every solution to find the best position to be the cluster's center. The fitness value is defined as follow:

$$f_{0_i}(x_0, y_0) = \begin{cases} \alpha_1 N_{bo} + \alpha_2 N_{in}, & N_{bo} + N_{in} \leq N_{max}, \\ 0.01, & N_{bo} + N_{in} > N_{max}, \end{cases} \tag{13}$$

where N_{bo} represents the number of boundary users in $\mathcal{K}_{local,bo}$ which are covered by the circle with $F_i^{(0)}$ or $F_i^{'(0)}$ as the center and r_{max} as the radius,

N_{in} represents the number of inner users $\mathcal{K}_{local,in}$ covered by that circle. α_1 and α_2 are weights of N_{bo} and N_{in} respectively and satisfy $\alpha_1 > \alpha_2$. (13) means that if the number of users covered by the circle is no more than N_{max}, the number of covered users increases may lead to the increasing of fitness value and the bigger the fitness value is, the higher probability of $F_i^{(0)}$ to be the optimal solution. However, if the number of users covered by the circle is greater than N_{max}, we have $f_{0_i}(x_0, y_0) = 0.01$, which means that $F_i^{(0)}$'s fitness value is too small to be the optimal solution. By calculating the fitness value of each solution, the initial optimal solution F_c^m with the largest value of fitness function f_m^c can be obtained.

2. *Employed Bees Phase:* The role of Employed bees is to find other possible positions as group centers near the current locations. For every possible position $F_i^{(t-1)}$, an employed bee searches for a new position $F_i^{(t)} = (x_i^{(t)}, y_i^{(t)})$ as follow:

$$F_i^{(t)}(k) = F_i^{(t-1)}(k) + \phi(F_i^{(t-1)}(k) - F_j^{(t-1)}(k)), \qquad (14)$$

where $k = 1, 2$ represents the x or y coordinate of the position, $F_j^{(t-1)}(k)$ represents another position in $\mathcal{F}^{(t-1)}$ differing from $F_i^{(t-1)}(k)$, $\phi \in [-1, 1]$ is a random number. After examining and adjusting the position $F_i^{(t)}$, we can compare its fitness value with $F_i^{(t-1)}$. If $F_i^{(t)}$ has a greater fitness value, $F_i^{(t-1)}(k)$ will be replaced by $F_i^{(t)}(k)$. Finally a new solution set $\mathcal{F}^{(t)}$ will be obtained.

3. *Onlooker Bees Phase:* Every onlooker bee selects a position in $\mathcal{F}^{(t)}$ according to the probability of every solution and starts searching for a better solution in its neighborhood. For every position $F_i^{(t)}$, the probability of being chosen by the onlooker bee is calculated as:

$$P_i = \frac{0.9 * f_i^{(t)}}{max(f_i^{(t)})} + 0.1, \qquad (15)$$

where $max(f_i^{(t)})$ represents the largest fitness value of positions in $\mathcal{F}^{(t)}$. Every onlooker bee generates a random number $rand \in (0, 1)$. If $rand < P_i$, then the onlooker bee chooses $F_i^{(t)}$, and searches for a new position like (14). Then we can adjust its position and calculate its fitness value. If it has a greater fitness value, the current position will be replaced by the new one. Finally, we will get a new set $\mathcal{F}^{(t)}$. The largest fitness value in $\mathcal{F}^{(t)}$ is compared with f_c^m. If it is greater than f_c^m, then f_c^m and F_c^m should be updated.

4. *Scout Bees Phase:* If there is no position better than the current one in its neighborhood after T_s iteration, where T_s represents the largest searching time, the old position will be given up while the scout bee will randomly generate a new position and start its searching. It is an effective process to remove local optimums.

The iteration will be repeated until the iteration time is up to the maximum value T. The position F_c^m with the maximum fitness value is decided as the optimal position for the cluster's center. Users covered by the circle with center F_c^m and radius r_{max} are stored in the set $\mathcal{L}^m$. The algorithm is presented in Algorithm 2.

When operating the proposed user clustering algorithm, Algorithm 2 is called to decide which users should be clustered into a group. In Algorithm 2, the complexity of initialization is $\mathcal{O}(N_p |\mathcal{K}_{local}|)$. The complexity of each iteration is $\mathcal{O}(2N_p |\mathcal{K}_{local}|)$. Thus, the complexity of Algorithm 2 is $\mathcal{O}(TN_p |\mathcal{K}_{local}|)$. In Algorithm 1, the complexity of line 3–5 is $\mathcal{O}(N_0)$ as a whole. Consequently, the total computational complexity of the algorithm is $\mathcal{O}(TN_p |\mathcal{M}| |\mathcal{K}_{local}|+|\mathcal{M}| N_0)$.

3.2   3D Deployment

In the previous subsection, we have divided users into different groups and ensured the number of groups to be as little as possible, which is also the number of UAVs. In this subsection, the 3D position of each UAV will be optimized to improve the QoS of served users and to reduce the total interference of the system. Taking the UAV m and the group $\mathcal{L}_m$ served by UAV m for example, a minimum service region will be derived first to exclude users not belonging to $\mathcal{L}_m$ and normal transmission from UAV m to users belonging to $\mathcal{L}_m$ will be guaranteed at the same time.

To minimize the service region of UAV m, we need a minimum circle to cover all users belonging to $\mathcal{L}_m$. The problem can be formulated as followed:

$$\min_{x_m,y_m} \max_{l\in\mathcal{L}_m} s_{m,l} \tag{16}$$

where $s_{m,l}$ denotes the distance between UAV m and user l in $\mathcal{L}_m$. It has been demonstrated that (16) is a convex optimization problem and can be solved by CVX [5]. The coordinates (x_m,y_m), which are the center of the obtained minimum circle, are also the 2D position of UAV m. The result of (16) r_m is the service radius of UAV m, which is no larger than the maximum service according to the definition, i.e., $r_m < r_{max}$. Thus, we need to adjust the flight height of each UAV next.

According to Fig. 2, when the service radius of UAV m is fixed, there is always an optimal height that can maximize the channel gain of UAV m. That is to say, users belonging to $\mathcal{L}_m$ can get better QoS if UAV is deployed at the optimal height. The optimal height h_m for UAV m to maximize the channel gain can be obtained by solving the following equation:

$$\frac{\partial \bar{g}(r_m, h_m)}{\partial h_m} = 0, \tag{17}$$

where r_m is the real service radius for UAV m.

4   Simulation Results

The simulation results are represented and analyzed in this section. In our simulations, users distribute randomly in a square area and the results in a sophisticated urban environment are considered. The parameters in our simulation are shown in Table 1.

Table 1. Simulation parameters

Parameter	Value
a	11.95
b	0.14
β_0	5×10^{-5}
κ	0.01
T_{pso}, T_{abc}	1000
P_{num}, B_{num}	200
N_{max}	5

According these parameters, we can calculate that $r_{max} = 578\,m$. We choose three other algorithms to compare with the OAP algorithm proposed in this paper, which are Unordered ABC-based placement (UAP) algorithm, Ordered PSO-based Placement (OPP) algorithm and Edge-Prior placement (EPP) algorithm [11]. UAP algorithm picks k_0 randomly from uncovered users, which is different from OAP algorithm. Besides, T_{abc}, T_{pso}, P_{num} and B_{num} denote the maximum iteration times of ABC algorithm and PSO algorithm, the population of ABC algorithm and PSO algorithm, respectively.

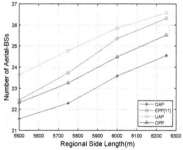
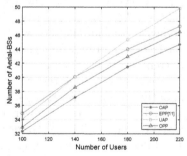

(a) Comparison of required number of UAVs with varying regional area when using different algorithm, where the service ability is 5 and the number of users is 100.

(b) Comparison of required number of UAVs with varying numbers of users when using different algorithm, where the regional side length is 6000m and the service ability is 5.

Fig. 3. Comparison of number of required UAVs when using different algorithm

Figure 3 demonstrates the priority of minimizing the number of UAVs of our algorithm in a general way. Each point is averaged over 100 independent user

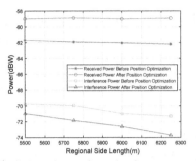
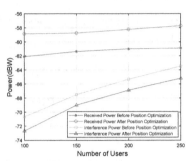

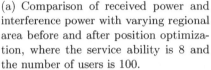

(a) Comparison of received power and interference power with varying regional area before and after position optimization, where the service ability is 8 and the number of users is 100.

(b) Comparison of received power and interference power with varying numbers of users before and after position optimization, where the regional side length is 6000m and the service ability is 5.

Fig. 4. Comparison of received power and interference power before and after position optimization

distributions. In Fig. 3(a), the comparison of the number of UAVs with users distributing in different areas is presented. It can be seen that no matter in which condition, OAP algorithm performs the best. Meanwhile, as the distribution area becomes larger, the density of users becomes smaller, so more UAVs are needed to serve all the ground users. In Fig. 3(b), the comparison of the number of UAVs with different numbers of users is presented. OAP algorithm still performs the best and more UAVs are needed for serving more numbers of users.

Figure 4 shows the effect of our 3D deployment method on improving QoS in a general way. We take the received power and the interference power into consideration with transmitting power $P_t = 30\,dBW$. Figure 4(a) shows the change in received power and interference power before and after position optimization with different users distribution area. It can be seen that the received power always increases and the interference power always decreases obviously after position optimization. With the distribution area enlarging, the received power increases and the interference power decreases. Figure 4(b) shows the change in the received power and the interference power before and after position optimization with different number of users. It is also obvious that the received power increases and the interference decreases after position optimization.

In summary, the simulation results show that compared with other methods, our 3D deployment method performs better on reducing the number of UAVs. After optimizing the 3D position of each UAV, the QoS of wireless communication can be improved obviously.

5   Conclusion

A UAV-mounted wireless communication system was investigated and a 3D deployment method based on ABC algorithm was proposed in this paper. The algorithm could minimize the number of UAVs required to serve all ground users while ensure the QoS requirement of users. We first derived the maximum service radius of UAVs according to the QoS requirement. Then we proposed the OAP algorithm to deploy multiple UAVs, where the number of UAVs was minimized first and then the 3D positions of UAVs were optimized to improve the QoS of the system. Simulation results showed that our method has the superiority of minimizing the number of UAVs and improving the QoS compared with other algorithms.

References

1. Handbook of Unmanned Aerial Vehicles. Springer (2015)
2. Xiao, Z., Xia, P., Xia, X.G.: Enabling UAV cellular with millimeter-wave communication: potentials and approaches. IEEE Commun. Mag. **54**(5), 66–73 (2016)
3. Zeng, Y., Zhang, R., Lim, T.J.: Wireless communications with unmanned aerial vehicles: opportunities and challenges. IEEE Commun. Mag. (2016)
4. Al-Hourani, A., Kandeepan, S., Lardner, S.: Optimal LAP altitude for maximum coverage. IEEE Wireless Commun. Lett. **3**(6), 569–572 (2014)
5. Alzenad, M., El-Keyi, A., Yanikomeroglu, H.: 3-D placement of an unmanned aerial vehicle base station for maximum coverage of users with different QoS Requirements. IEEE Wireless Commun. Lett. **7**(1), 38–41 (2018)
6. Alzenad M., El-Keyi A., Lagum F., et al.: 3D placement of an unmanned aerial vehicle base station (UAV-BS) for energy-efficient maximal coverage. IEEE Wireless Commun. Lett. **PP**(99), 1 (2017)
7. Lyu, J., Zeng, Y., Zhang, R., et al.: Placement optimization of UAV-mounted mobile base stations. IEEE Commun. Lett. **21**(3), 604–607 (2017)
8. Strumberger, N., Bacanin, S., Tomic, M.B., Tuba, M.: Static drone placement by elephant herding optimization algorithm, In: 2017 25th Telecommunication Forum (TELFOR), pp. 1–4. Belgrade (2017). https://doi.org/10.1109/TELFOR.2017.8249469
9. Wang, G.G., Deb, S., Coelho, L.D.S.: Elephant herding optimization. In: 2015 3rd International Symposium on Computational and Business Intelligence. IEEE (2015)
10. Zhao, H., Wang, H., Wu, W., et al.: Deployment algorithms for UAV airborne networks toward on-demand coverage. IEEE J. Select. Areas Commun. **36**(9), 2015–2031 (2018)
11. Qin, J., Wei, Z., Qiu, C., Feng, Z.: Edge-prior placement algorithm for UAV-mounted base stations. In: 2019 IEEE Wireless Communications and Networking Conference (WCNC), pp. 1–6. Marrakesh, Morocco (2019). https://doi.org/10.1109/WCNC.2019.8885992
12. Zeng, Y., Wu, Q., Zhang, R.: Accessing from the sky: a tutorial on UAV communications for 5G and beyond. Proc. IEEE **107**(12), 2327–2375 (2019)
13. Linderoth, J.T., Savelsbergh, M.W.P.: A computational study of search strategies for mixed integer programming. INFORMS J. Comput. **11**(2), 173–187 (1999)
14. Karaboga, D.: An idea based on honey bee swarm for numerical optimization (2005)

Edge Intelligence and Computing for IoT Communications and Applications

Trajectory Optimization for UAV-Aided Data Collections

Hanxin Zhang, Caiyu Zhang, Zixuan Zhang, Changwen Zhou, Yu Zhang, and Congduan Li$^{(\boxtimes)}$ (ID)

Sun Yat-sen University, Shenzhen, Guangdong, China
licongd@mail.sysu.edu.cn

Abstract. The application of the unmanned aerial vehicles (UAV) in future wireless networks is getting more and more popular. This article investigates the flight trajectory optimization problem with minimum energy consumption when the UAVs are communicating with the ground terminals (GT) for data collections. The specific flying speed is determined to minimize the energy consumption of the whole flying process. In addition, the algorithms to find the optimal trajectory are proposed. Experimental results are presented to show the effectiveness of our proposed algorithms.

Keywords: Wireless communication · Energy consumption · Trajectory optimization

1 Introduction

The applications of UAVs have been developed for more than 30 years in the domestic market, gradually expanding from the initial military area to civilian area nowadays [1]. With the wide usage of UAVs, the general public's recognition and demands for UAVs have been significantly increased. It is predicted that the market value of the UAV will reach 70 billion by 2025 [2].

The UAVs began to be used in the military in the 1960s. During the Vietnam War, the United States applied the UAVs to military reconnaissance, air strikes and target destruction. By the end of the 20th century, many countries had developed new UAVs for battlefield [3], intelligence reconnaissance [4], weather forecast, electronic countermeasures and jamming. What's more, in the field of agriculture [5,6], the UAVs technology in Japan has developed more mature after 30 years of improvement. It can be used to supply medicine and add gasoline with high efficiency [7]. Moreover, the UAVs also play an important role in transportation [8].

This work was supported in part by the National Science Foundation of China (NSFC) with grant no. 61901534, in part by the Guangdong Basic and Applied Basic Research Foundation under Key Project 2019B1515120032, in part by the Science, Technology and Innovation Commission of Shenzhen Municipality with grant no. JCYJ20190807155617099. All authors equally contributed to this manuscript.

B. Li et al. (Eds.): IoTaaS 2020, LNICST 346, pp. 159–170, 2021.
https://doi.org/10.1007/978-3-030-67514-1_13

At present, lots of cities in China generally have the road congestion and traffic management problems. With the help of UAVs, the government can conduct area surveillance [9] to ensure the traffic move smoothly. Meanwhile, when emergency happens, it is convenient for relevant departments to carry out urgent rescues [10]. Another common application of UAVs is in data collections, where data from sensors will be collected by a UAV flying by them one by one.

The UAVs have been widely applied in military, agriculture, transportation, photograph, data collections, and so on. However, the energy onboard usually restricts the covering distance and missions of the UAVs. It has been a challenging problem to choose the best trajectory for UAVs to save their energy. Not only the performance of the UAVs should be considered, but also the current surroundings have become a threat to the UAVs. Calculating the optimal trajectory will be beneficial to estimate the prime cost of the flight mission. What's more, it can greatly reduce the flight time, helping the UAVs fulfill those missions more quickly and accurately, and thus speeding up the mission process. At the same time, by designing the most suitable flight speed of the UAVs, the energy consumed by the UAVs can be maximumly saved and the endurance can be greatly improved.

So far, there are not many articles pointing out how to calculate a suitable velocity to get a smaller energy consumption in the flying process. This is one of our research interests. The commonly used model of UAVs' trajectory is that UAVs swerve directly above the GT's center. In this model, the duration of communicating with GT is shortest. In other words, the energy consumption is smaller in communication, but maybe larger in flight, compared to a trajectory that not right above the GT center. In order to reduce energy consumption in flight, one can design that the UAVs change direction while passing through the communication range of GT. This consists of two models: straight or curve trajectory beside GTs. Based on these models, we'd like to go a step further to propose several algorithms to determine the trajectory inside GTs' communication range with different methods to calculate the entry and exit points on the circle of GTs' communication range. By comparing these algorithms, we finally get an optimal algorithm to find the optimal trajectory of UAVs.

This paper mainly addresses the following two issues:

1. The Energy Consumption of the UAVs

It has been a challenge to apply UAVs to communicate with terminals under limited energy has always been a challenge. In order to reduce the consumption of energy for the UAVs, a relatively optimal flight path should be established, and a new energy consumption formula be improved as well. Therefore, in order to minimize energy consumption, variables of easily changeable values should be selected.

2. The Flight Trajectory Optimization Problem

The UAVs usually fly directly above the center of the ground terminals, but they do not need to fly to the exact terminal center to start the communication. They can start communicating once they enter the communication range of a ground terminal. In this way, flight trajectory[11] of the UAVs is optimized to reduce energy consumption.

2   System Model and Energy Minimization

2.1   System Model

It is widely known that the information-interacted distance between GT and UAV is corresponded to the current coordinates of the UAV. For simplicity, we assume that the UAV flies horizontally at a fixed altitude H. On this condition, we can realize a reduction of dimensions in our problem, so that our model is built in a two-dimensional plane rather than a three-dimensional space. In reality, the minimum altitude depends on the environment where the UAV flies in. If altitude H is too low, there may be obstacles such as buildings in the trajectory which will cause collision. In addition, the communication radius of a GT is assumed to be $R = 10$ m. Once the UAV enters the circle with center node and radius R, UAV can communicate with the node without distortion, which strikes a balance between maintaining the superior channel condition and minimizing the propulsion energy consumption. The size of the active range of UAV is set 100 m * 100 m grid. The fixed-wing UAV, as shown in Fig. 1, is considered in this paper. Further, we assume that the UAV's acceleration is taken into account only at the stage where the UAV takes off and lands. The UAV mainly flies with constant velocity for communication between GTs, thus ignoring the acceleration and deceleration stage for ease of analysis and calculation.

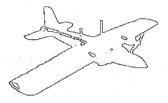

Fig. 1. Structure of a fixed-wing UAV.

The point UAV takes off is marked as point O. For each GT, we choose two points on the circle of radius R centered at GT. Thus, we get two series of points: $A_1, A_2, ..., A_i, ..., A_n$ and $B_1, B_2, ..., B_i, ..., B_n$. A_i is the point that UAV enters the distortion free range of the i'th node, while B_i is the point that UAV move out of the range. Considering the specific characteristics about UAVs while changing flying directions, some more assumptions are made as follows.

– The UAV makes a uniform linear motion when flying out of the communication range, where the flight trajectory of uniform linear motion of the ith GT is the straight line B_iA_{i+1}, as $i = 1, 2, ..., n - 1$. Meanwhile, OA_1 and B_nO are separately the straight line that UAV flies towards the first GT and flies away the nth GT.

- The UAV makes a uniform circular motion when flying within the communication range, where the flight trajectory of uniform circular motion tangent to that of uniform linear motion.
- The UAV makes both two motions with the same speed V.

The demonstration is presented in Fig. 2.

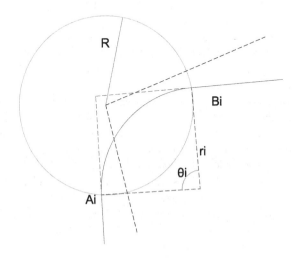

Fig. 2. Demonstration of the flight trajectory at a single GT node.

2.2   UAV Energy Consumption Model and Energy Optimization

In this paper, we choose to ignore the communication energy consumption. Two main reasons are considered. On the one hand, for fixed-wing UAVs, the energy consumption in communication, [12] is quite small compared to the energy expenditure during flight [13], and thus, can be neglected. On the other hand, if we consider the communication energy consumption, then all the algorithms will add a communication energy consumption with the same value. It is equivalent to adding the same value on both sides of the inequality for us to compare which case has the least energy consumption. From these two perspectives, we do not need to consider the communication energy consumption. Furthermore, the total propulsion energy required is a function of the trajectory, which corresponds to the classic aircraft power consumption model known in aerodynamics theory.

The expression [14] is expressed as:

$$E(v(t), a(t)) = \int_0^T [\frac{c_2}{||v(t)||}(1 + \frac{||a(t)||^2 - a^T(t)v(t)^2}{g^2})$$
$$+ c_1||v(t)^3|||dt + \frac{1}{2}m(||v(T)^2|| - ||v(0)^2||), \tag{1}$$

where c_1 and c_2 are two parameters related to the aircrafts weight, wing area, air density, etc. Supposing the UAVs fly at the same speed, the expression(1) can be simplified as:

$$E(V, a(t)) = E_{SLF}(V) + \frac{c_2}{Vg^2}\int_0^T a(t)^2 dt \tag{2}$$

The expression has two components. The first part is the energy consumption of uniform linear motion. In [3], it is expressed as:

$$E_{SLF}(V) = T(c_1 V^3 + \frac{c_2}{V}) \tag{3}$$

The variable T is the time UAV takes to complete uniform linear motion:

$$T = \frac{\Sigma_{i=1}^{n-1}\sqrt{(y_{A_{i+1}} - y_{B_i})^2 + (x_{A_{i+1}} - x_{B_i})^2}}{V} + \frac{\sqrt{(y_{A_1} - y_O)^2 + (x_{A_1} - x_O)^2}}{V}$$
$$+ \frac{\sqrt{(y_{B_n} - y_O)^2 + (x_{B_n} - x_O)^2}}{V} \tag{4}$$

So far, we get:

$$E_{SLF}(V) = (c_1 V^2 + \frac{c_2}{V^2})\left[\Sigma_{i=1}^{n-1}\sqrt{(y_{A_{i+1}} - y_{B_i})^2 + (x_{A_{i+1}} - x_{B_i})^2}\right.$$
$$\left. + \sqrt{(y_{A_1} - y_O)^2 + (x_{A_1} - x_O)^2} + \sqrt{(y_{B_n} - y_O)^2 + (x_{B_n} - x_O)^2}\right] \tag{5}$$

The radius of each communication ranges is:

$$r_i = \frac{VT_0}{\theta_i} \tag{6}$$

With the hypothesis of uniform circular motion, the total function can be expressed as:

$$E(V, a(t)) = E_{SLF}(V) + \frac{c_2 V}{g^2 T_0}\Sigma_{i=1}^n \theta_i^2 \tag{7}$$

As the arc trajectory inside the distortion free range of the i'th GT is tangent to both $B_{i-1}A_i$ and $B_i A_{i+1}$, θ_i is determined by $B_{i-1}A_i$ and $B_i A_{i+1}$:

$$\theta_i = \pi - arccos\frac{(y_{A_i} - y_{B_i-1})(y_{B_i} - y_{A_i+1}) + (x_{A_i} - x_{B_i-1})(x_{B_i} - x_{A_i+1})}{\sqrt{(y_{A_i} - y_{B_i-1})^2 + (x_{A_i} - x_{B_i-1})^2}\sqrt{(y_{B_i} - y_{A_i+1})^2 + (x_{B_i} - x_{A_i+1})^2}} \tag{8}$$

To solve the above equation, we can get some basic formulas:

$$\begin{cases} (x_{A_1} - x_1)^2 + (y_{A_1} - y_1)^2 = 100 \\ (x_{A_2} - x_2)^2 + (y_{A_2} - y_2)^2 = 100 \\ \qquad\qquad\qquad\qquad\vdots \\ (x_{A_n} - x_n)^2 + (y_{A_n} - y_n)^2 = 100 \end{cases} \qquad (9)$$

$$\begin{cases} (x_{B_1} - x_1)^2 + (y_{B_1} - y_1)^2 = 100 \\ (x_{B_2} - x_2)^2 + (y_{B_2} - y_2)^2 = 100 \\ \qquad\qquad\qquad\qquad\vdots \\ (x_{B_n} - x_n)^2 + (y_{B_n} - y_n)^2 = 100 \end{cases} \qquad (10)$$

This problem is difficult to be directly solved. Firstly, it requires to put every pair of points into the formula which is related to the initial settings. What's more, the equation is too complex to find closed-form expressions. As a consequence of the above difficulties, we decide to choose only one point on the communication range to simplify our trajectory.

3   Trajectory Design and Optimization

According to the minimum energy consumption formula above, the energy consumption of UAV is related to the path length. The shorter the path length is, the lower the energy consumption of UAV is. Therefore, in order to get the minimum energy consumption, we need to find the shortest flight path of UAV.

In *Section II*, it is hypothesized that an initial communication radius R is $10m$. The target is to determine where the UAV should change its flying direction towards the next GT after entering the current circle with center node and radius R. There exist infinite combinations of flight paths because there are infinite number of points in each circle, leading to that we cannot find the shortest path by exhausting all the possibilities. In order to figure out the shortest path, we optimize the problem into two steps:

- First of all, take each communication range as a point to find out the sequence of UAV passing through GTs. When each circle is regarded as a point, the *GRASP(Greedy Randomized Adaptive Search Procedures)* [17,18] can be used to determine the flight order. *GRASP* is an iterative process with multiple starting points. Each iteration consists of two stages: one is the construction stage of generating feasible solutions. On the basis of greed, some random factors are added to construct the initial feasible solutions. Secondly, in the local search phase of finding the local optimal solution, neighborhood search is carried out for the initial feasible solution constructed above until a local

optimal solution is found. If the local optimal solution is better than the current optimal solution, the original optimal solution is updated. Before iteration, we construct a solution randomly, and then judge whether it is feasible. If it is not feasible, we will enter the repair function to modify it. The feasible solution is locally searched, and the solution is updated in the local search process. It is worthy of note that the limitation of *GRASP* is that it only applies to precise points.
- Next, based on the sequence, we introduces 5 algorithms whose performances of path length vary from the worst to the best. In Algorithm 5, the arcs and radius corresponding to the shortest flight path on each circle are repeatedly quartered to finally obtain the turning points which determines the shortest flight path within the error range.

The above work realizes the transformation from non-realizable problem to realizable problem in mathematical analysis. We state our algorithms as follows.

Algorithm 1 (Shortest Path Based on Communication Center). The UAV flight trajectory is obtained by visiting the circle centers of the GTs based on *GRASP* [15,16]. Therefore, the shortest flying distance can be calculated by substituting the center of each circle into the formula of the distance between two points.

Algorithm 2 (Shortest Path Based on Minimum Path). It is presumed that the UAV will visit the shortest path points(A pair of shortest path points are the intersection of two arcs and a segment which connects the centers of two circles, abbreviated to SPP) in sequence based on *GRASP* (Algorithm 1) and connect the shortest path points in the same circle with a straight line. As is shown in Fig. 3, where red points are the SPPs and the green lines form the UAV flight trajectory.

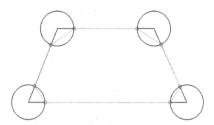

Fig. 3. Rough UAV flight trajectory.

Algorithm 3 (Greedy Algorithm). Regardless of global optimization, we obtain the optimal solution by using greedy algorithm in each step of the solution. For any node except the starting point, the SPP is selected as the hovering point for the UAV. Therefore, the UAV flight trajectory is the current shortest trajectory. Connect the center of the first circle and the second circle, obtain the intersection point of the line and the second circle. Then connect the intersection point and the center of the third circle, obtaining the intersection point of the line and the third circle, and so on. Ultimately, with this method, we go through all hovering points of the UAV. The sum of piecewise paths is the total trajectory length.

Algorithm 4 (Sub-Optimal Algorithm). As is widely known, the limitation of *GRASP* is that there must be exact points. Instead of exact points, a series of circles are identified, so the shortest flying distance calculated by *GRASP* brings some errors. To improve it in Algorithm 4, the circle is divided equally along the arc direction and the radius direction by points (A1, A2, A3, ...) (B1, B2, ...) to find the shortest path (Fig. 4).

Specific steps are as follows:

Step 1: Read in the SPPs according to Algorithm 2 to determine the arcs. Quarter each arc to attain more SPPs.
Step 2: Traverse all possible paths formed by SPPs.
Step 3: Find the shortest 2 paths. SPPs of each circle on these 2 paths determine new arcs.
Step 4: After repeating n times, the simulation points of high precision are regarded as the final SPPs along the arc.
Step 5: Connect each point in step 4 with the center of the corresponding circle. Quarter each segment to attain more SPPs along the radius. Use the same traversing method of the above steps to find the shortest path. Repeat n times.
Step 6: Connect the points in step 5 to attain the final trajectory.

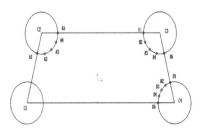

Fig. 4. Segmentation method of Algorithm 4.

Algorithm5 (Newton Iteration). It is out of the question to apply Algorithm 4 to the situations where there are 10 GTs or above. Revisiting the optimization problem, we can first work out the expression of total path length related to the SPP of each circle. Then let the partial derivative of the expression be 0 to figure out the SPPs.

We adopt Newton iteration as a replacement for calculating the analytical solution since the derivative is too sophiscated to compute.

The specific steps are as follow.

Step 1: Express each coordinate with variable θ(relative to the corresponding center). The coordinates of moving points can be determined by θ uniquely since the radius is set.

Step 2: Express the function of the total path length related to coordinates gained in Step 1 with the formula of the distance between two points, say $f(\theta)$.

Step 3: Choose the initial value for each circle. The difference between the initial value and SPP is constrained in $\frac{\pi}{2}$ to ensure that the result of iteration is the shortest path but not the longest.

Step 4: Update θ according to Newton iteration:

$$\theta_{k+1} = \theta_k - \frac{f(\theta_k)}{f'(\theta_k)} \tag{11}$$

Step 5: If the absolute error is within range, break out from the iteration, then gain the shortest path.

Algorithm 5. Newton iteration

Require
a:x-coordinate of center of circles
b:y-coordinate of center of circles
n:number of GTs
r:communication radius of GTs
$theta$:the initial value of the point on the circle

1: $x \leftarrow a + r * cos(theta)$
2: $y \leftarrow b + r * sin(theta)$
3: //the length of the path calculate by x and y
4: $f \leftarrow dis(x, y)$
5: $f_\theta \leftarrow diff(f, 1, theta)$
6: $f_{\theta 2} \leftarrow diff(f, 2, theta)$
7: **for** $i = 1$ to $iteration\_times$ **do**
8:     **if** $max(f_\theta / f_{\theta 2} < 0.01)$ **then break**
9:     **else**
10:         $theta \leftarrow theta - f_\theta / f_{\theta 2}$
11:         Update f_θ and $f_{\theta 2}$ by new $theta$
12:     **end if**
13: **end for**
14: $X \leftarrow a + r * cos(theta)$
15: $Y \leftarrow b + r * sin(theta)$
16: **return** X, Y

---

4 Numerical Results

Simulations of Algorithms 1–3 and Algorithm 5 are performed on 10, 20 and 30 communication nodes.

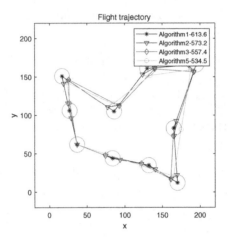

Fig. 5. Flight trajectories of 10 GTs

For 10 GTs (Fig. 5), the path lengths of Algorithm 1–3 and Algorithm 5 are, in order, 613.6, 573.2, 557.4, 534.5. Algorithm 5 can save 12.89%, 6.75%, 4.11% compared with Algorithm 1–3.

For 20 GTs (Fig. 6), the path lengths of Algorithm 1–3 and Algorithm 5 are, in order, 851.3, 769.1, 736.0, 693.9. Algorithm 5 can save 18.49%, 9.78%, 5.72% compared with Algorithm 1–3.

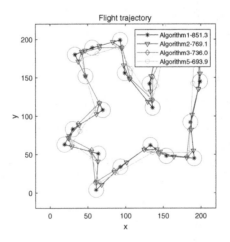

Fig. 6. Flight trajectories of 20 GTs

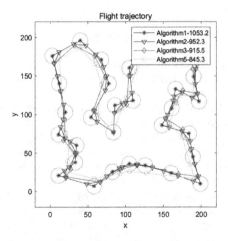

Fig. 7. Flight trajectories of 30 GTs

For 30 GTs (Fig. 7), the path lengths of Algorithm 1–3 and Algorithm 5 are, in order, 1053.2, 952.3, 915.5, 845.3. Algorithm 5 can save 19.74%, 11.24%, 7.67% compared with Algorithm 1–3.

It is convident that the property of Algorithm 5 improves as the number of GTs increases.

As is shown from the figures, Algorithm 5 performs the best, Algorithm 3 is the second, and Algorithm 1 and Algorithm 2 have the worst performance.

5   Conclusion

This paper considers the problem of the UAV energy consumption in data collections. The minimum energy consumption formula is derived with some assumptions. Also, we propose the shortest path algorithm for UAVs trajectory. Effective solutions about reducing the energy consumption of the flight are also proposed. Moreover, compared to the traditional shortest UAV flight path, analogue simulation shows that the solution can reduce about 10% drone flight paths.

References

1. Ping, J.T.K., Ling, A.E., Quan, T.J., Dat, C.Y.: Generic unmanned aerial vehicle (UAV) for civilian application-A feasibility assessment and market survey on civilian application for aerial imaging. In: IEEE Conference (STUDENT), October 2012
2. Canetta, L., Mattei, G., Guanziroli, A.: Exploring commercial UAV market evolution from customer requirements elicitation to collaborative supply network management. In: IEEE International Conference (ICE), June 2017
3. Orfanus, D., de Freitas, E.P., Eliassen F.: Self-organization as a supporting paradigm for military UAV relay networks. IEEE Commun. Lett., 804–807 (April 2016)

4. Jessie, Y.C.: Chen: Effects of operator spatial ability on UAV-guided ground navigation. In: IEEE International Conference Human-Robet Interaction (HRI), March 2010
5. Zhang, Y.: Flight path planning of agriculture UAV based on improved artificial potential field method. In: IEEE 2018 Chinese Control and Decision Conference (CCDC), June 2018
6. Subba Rao, V.P., Srinivasa Rao, G.: Design and modelling of an affordable UAV based pesticide sprayer in agriculture applications. In: IEEE 2019 Fifth International Conference on Electrical Energy Systems (ICEES), February 2019
7. Zhang, Z., Li, C.: Application of unmanned aerial vehicle technology in modern agriculture. Agricultural Engineering, vol. 6 No.4, July 2016
8. Reshma, R., Ramesh, T.K., Sathish Kumar, P.: Security incident management in ground transportation system using UAVs. IEEE (ICCIC), December 2015
9. Reshma, R., Ramesh, T., Sathishkumar, P.: Security situational aware intelligent road traffic monitoring using UAVs. In: IEEE (VLSI-SATA), January 2016
10. Menouar, H., Guvenc, I., Akkaya, K., Selcuk Uluagac, A., Kadri, A., Tuncer, A.: UAV-enabled intelligent transportation systems for the smart city: applications and challenges. IEEE Commun., 22–28, March 2017
11. Wu, Q., Zeng, Y., Zhang, R.: Joint trajectory and communication design for multi-uav enabled wireless networks. IEEE Trans. Wireless Commun. **17**(3), 2109–2121 (2018)
12. Desset, C.: Flexible power modeling of lte base stations[J]. IEEE Wireless Commun. Netw. Conf. (WCNC) pp. 2858–2862 (Apr 2012)
13. Franco, C.D., Buttazzo, G.: Energy-aware coverage path planning of uavs. In: IEEE International on Autonomous Robot Systems and Competitions, pp. 111–117, April 2015
14. Greitzer, E.M., Spakovszky, Z.S., Waitz., I.A.: Thermodynamics and propulsion[OL]. MIT Course Notes, July 2016
15. Raja, M.A.Z.: Technology - Information Technology; Huaibei Normal University Reports Findings in Information Technology (Backtracking Search Optimization Algorithm Based On Knowledge Learning)
16. Sharma, H., Sebastian, T., Balamuralidhar, P.: An efficient backtracking-based approach to turn-constrained path planning for aerial mobile robots. In: 2017 European Conference on Mobile Robots (ECMR), Paris, 2017, pp. 1–8 (2017). https://doi.org/10.1109/ECMR.2017.8098712
17. Chen, E., Sun, Y., Pan, Z., Liu, X.: Discrete particle swarm optimization with greedy randomized adaptive search procedure for linear order problem. In: 2010 Sixth International Conference on Natural Computation (ICNC 2010) (2010)
18. Dharan, S., Nair, A.S.: Biclustering of gene expression data using greedy randomized adaptive search procedure. In: TENCON 2008–2008 IEEE Region 10 Conference

Design and Implementation
of MCU-Based Reconfigurable Protocol Conversion Module for Heterogeneous Sensor Networks

Lei Zhao and Yan Zhang$^{(\boxtimes)}$

Beijing Institute of Technology, Beijing 100081, China
zhangy@bit.edu.cn

Abstract. With the widespread applications of the Internet of Things (IoT), the heterogeneity of communication protocols and data frame formats in the sensor networks has become a significant issue. To address this problem, in this paper we design a reconfigurable protocol conversion module for heterogeneous sensor networks. Based on a microcontroller unit (MCU) hardware platform, the communication protocol conversion among RS232, CAN, and Ethernet is implemented. The upper computer software is developed to receive data from the sensor networks, configure the hardware platform communication parameters, and adjust the monitoring parameters to the normal range. Moreover, aiming to solve the problem of data frame format differences in various IoT applications, we design a reconfigurable scheme to customize data frame formats, enabling the system's support for heterogeneous sensor networks. The experimental results validate the feasibility of the reconfigurable protocol conversion module, and show that the system can transmit, receive, and manage the sensor data effectively.

Keywords: Heterogeneous sensor networks · MCU · Reconfigurable protocol conversion · Upper computer

1 Introduction

In recent years, the unprecedented connectivity in the IoT enables many areas, such as smart factories, smart cities, intelligent homes, and so on [1]. In variable IoT applications, sensor networks play a fundamental role in data acquisition, data transmission, and device monitoring [2,3]. However, as the scale and category of sensors continue to grow, the heterogeneity of sensor networks has become a significant issue to cope with. For sensors with different functions and the same sensors from different manufacturers, different communication protocols and data formats are used to transmit data between sensors and the central controller. As a result, it is difficult for the central controller to acquire data and manage the sensor networks.

© ICST Institute for Computer Sciences, Social Informatics and Telecommunications Engineering 2021
Published by Springer Nature Switzerland AG 2021. All Rights Reserved
B. Li et al. (Eds.): IoTaaS 2020, LNICST 346, pp. 171–181, 2021.
https://doi.org/10.1007/978-3-030-67514-1_14

The problem of heterogeneity in sensor networks exists in many application scenarios. For instance, an intelligent building in [4] needs to monitor the devices under different fieldbuses comprehensively. In the industrial field, gathering data in a heterogeneous sensor network is a challenge for the real-time monitoring center of continuous steel casting [5]. Additionally, for personal healthcare devices [6] or electric power systems [7], communications between different protocols are also a significant issue.

Some studies have been completed to try to tackle this problem. In [8], a heterogeneous network integration module was developed to integrate data transmission in the Zigbee-WiFi hybrid network. Moreover, based on microprocessor control boards, a module was designed in [9] and [10] for communication between the Controller Area Network (CAN) and Ethernet protocols. Additionally, a hardware unit was designed in [11] to take commands and data from transmitter to receiver, working on SPI bus and I2C bus, respectively. Also, conversions between multiple communication protocols are implemented in [12–14], which enables the heterogeneous systems to transfer data freely. Nevertheless, most of the works mainly focused on one-to-one protocol conversion. Even though some studies implemented multi-protocol conversion, these systems only support fixed and limited communication protocols. If an already designed system needs to add some new sensors with new communication protocols, the existing schemes cannot be applied to manage these new sensors directly. Therefore, it is necessary to develop a scalable protocol conversion, which not only supports several fixed communication protocols but also expands to support new protocols when necessary. What is more, different sensors usually use different data frame format to transmit data, which hinders data acquisition, but the differences of transmitted data frame format of different sensors have not been considered in existing studies.

In this paper, taking the smart factories as application scenarios, we design a reconfigurable protocol conversion module (PCM) to deal with data transmission in heterogeneous sensor networks. Both the scalability of communication protocol and the reconfiguration of data frame format are taken into consideration. Specifically, the PCM in this paper consists of MCU hardware platform and upper computer software. The MCU hardware platform is equipped with RS232, CAN bus, and Ethernet protocol interfaces. Meanwhile, the upper computer software is developed to receive data from the sensor networks, configure the hardware platform communication parameters, and adjust the monitoring parameters to the normal range. Besides, the sensors deployed in the factory to obtain variable operating parameters, such as temperature, humidity, etc., can communicate with the hardware platform through RS232, CAN bus interfaces. Then, the upper computer software as a central controller transmits data with the hardware platform using the Ethernet protocol.

The scale of the sensor network and the number of communication protocol types supported by our PCM can be expanded according to needs. In addition, a reconfigurable scheme is designed to customize data frame formats, enabling the system's support for heterogeneous sensor networks. As a result, the PCM can communicate with different sensors in a unified manner, making it easier to manage the whole sensor network.

The remainder of this paper is organized as follows. Section 2 describes the design architecture of the PCM. Section 3 elaborates on the implementation of the system from hardware and software aspects. Experimental results will be illustrated in Sect. 4. Finally, Sect. 5 draws the conclusions.

2   Design of the System Architecture

Given that in a smart factory scenario, many different sensors are deployed in the factory to monitor the environmental parameters, such as temperature, humidity, etc. As the communication protocols and data frame formats that each sensor uses are different, it is necessary to deploy a PCM to acquire data and manage the sensor network as a whole.

The system architecture is shown in Fig. 1, where each sensor in the sensor networks is connected with the PCM through different protocols. The PCM contains an upper computer, a network switch, and many MCU hardware platforms. Moreover, many sensors with different functions and protocols constitute a small heterogeneous network. And the upper computer can communicate with the PCM by Ethernet protocol only, which is widely used in industry and academia.

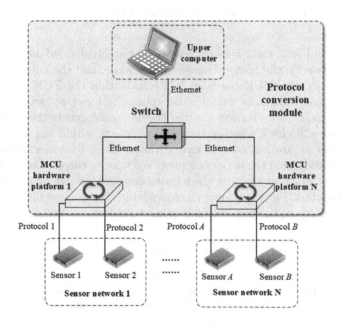

Fig. 1. The system architecture of protocol conversion module, upper computer, and sensor networks.

The details of inside functional blocks of our designed PCM are given in Fig. 2. It is noteworthy that we select the two most commonly used communication protocols in industrial fields as examples for implementation, i.e., RS232 and CAN. RS232 is a standard protocol for serial communications. Besides, CAN bus is a message-based protocol, which supports communications between microcontroller and devices and is widely used in industrial automation and vehicles. However, it should be noted that this architecture can also be used for the conversion between other protocols.

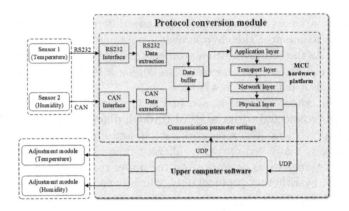

Fig. 2. A functional block diagram of the whole system.

As shown in Fig. 2, the whole system can be roughly divided into three parts: the sensor networks, the protocol conversion module, and the adjustment modules. Specifically, the MCU hardware platform within the PCM receives data from sensors and transmits data to the upper computer software. Then, the upper computer software verifies whether the data conforms to the selected data frame formats and check whether the parameters are within the normal range. If the parameters are out of the normal range, the adjustment modules will receive commands from the upper computer software to correct the environmental parameters. For temperature, the adjustment modules can be a combination of fans and heaters. Likewise, some machines which can change the environmental humidity serve as the humidity adjustment module.

2.1 MCU Hardware Platform Design

To meet the requirements of multi-protocol conversion, the hardware platform is supposed to have multiple communication interfaces, including RS232, CAN, and Ethernet. Thus, a hardware development board in which a microcontroller unit chip and external circuits are embedded is an appropriate option for the implementation of the PCM.

The functional blocks included in the hardware platform and the workflow are presented in Fig. 2. Firstly, RS232 and CAN interfaces embedded in the board receive data from sensor 1 and sensor 2, respectively. The two data flows are transmitted through corresponding communication protocols, i.e., RS232, CAN. Secondly, the data extraction blocks of RS232 and CAN obtain data from RS232 and CAN interfaces and store these data into the data buffer block. Next, a lightweight TCP/IP (lwIP) stack is utilized to transfer the data in the data buffer block to upper computer software through four TCP/IP layers. Additionally, because of its advantages of fast speed and higher security, User Datagram Protocol (UDP) is selected as the transport layer protocol to connect the MCU hardware platform and the upper computer software.

2.2   Upper Computer Software Design

The upper computer software serves as a central controller to receive data from the MCU hardware platform and maintain the environmental parameters within the normal range. Moreover, the upper computer software provides the interfaces by which operators can configure the communication parameters settings.

Typically, different sensors use different data frame formats to transmit data. Only when the data frame formats of sensors are known, the upper computer software can obtain the transmitted data of the sensors. Assuming that the data frame formats of sensors are already known as shown in Fig. 3, four data fields of frame formats are taken into consideration. The details of these data fields are elaborated on as follows.

Fig. 3. The data fields of predefined data frame format.

- *No.* Technically, this is not the data field. Instead, it is the numerical order of the predefined data frame format.
- *Start bit.* The transmitted data will be stored in a buffer data array. And the start bit means where to start inputting data in the buffer data array.
- *Data length.* The length of transmitted data digits.
- *Data type.* Two kinds of data types are considered, i.e., integer and floating-point.
- *Precision.* Precision here means how many digits after the decimal point is retained in the data.

After receiving data through UDP protocol, the upper computer software will verify if the received data meet the requirements of data frame formats of the corresponding sensors. Then, the received data will be displayed on the software graphic user interfaces (GUIs).

As for each environmental parameter in a factory, there must have a normal range. Suppose $T_{\max}, H_{\max}$ are the maximum values of the temperature and humidity, respectively. Similarly, the minimum values of the temperature and humidity are denoted as $T_{\min}$ and $H_{\min}$, respectively. t and h represent the current values of the sensors. If $t - T_{\max} > \Delta T$ or $T_{\min} - t > \Delta T$, the upper computer software sends feedback commands to the adjustment module of temperature to restore the environment temperature to the normal range. Here, ΔT is the maximum offset of temperature. Likewise, the upper computer software is going to do the same thing when the humidity is out of the normal range.

2.3   Reconfigurable and Scalable Design

Considering that in the field of industrial IoT, it is necessary for the network operator and sensors to configure the data format of transmitted data. To establish a reconfigurable protocol conversion system, data frame formats are provided to set. The network operators and sensors are able to configure each data field in the data frame format according to their own needs.

In some scenarios, the monitoring networks need to enlarge the scale due to the addition of new sensors and communication protocols. However, a fixed network hardly supports such a demand. Therefore, it is necessary to develop a scalable protocol conversion system. In our design, the scalability of the network is taken into account from the hardware and software aspects.

As for the hardware, if there is a single sensor network, the upper computer can connect with the MCU hardware platform by the Ethernet protocol directly. Meanwhile, if there are multiple sensor networks, a network switch is needed between the upper computer and the MCU hardware platforms. As long as the new hardware platform has the corresponding protocol interfaces, the network switch can forward the data from different sensor networks to the upper computer without special configurations beyond plugging in cables. As for the upper computer software, it is easy to reserve extended functions for newly added networks.

3   System Implementation

3.1   MCU Hardware Platform Implementation

In order to receive data from different protocol interfaces, an STM32F407 MCU chip embedded development board is used. As Fig. 4 depicted, this board is appropriate for the implementation of multiple protocol conversion since it supports many communication interfaces, such as RS232, RS485, CAN bus, Ethernet, and so on. Thus, commonly used RS232 and CAN are used as physical layer protocols of the sensors in this paper. Besides, with the Ethernet related processor chips and circuits, this board is able to transfer data with the upper computer through TCP/IP protocol.

The hardware mainly consists of four parts. 1. RS232 and CAN interfaces. 2. RS232 and CAN data extraction. 3. Data buffer. 4. Ethernet block. Firstly, initializing the configurations of the RS232, CAN, and Ethernet block. Then,

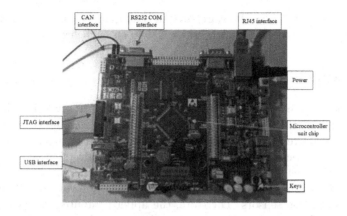

Fig. 4. MCU-based hardware development platform.

with the UART and related chips and circuits, RS232 and CAN nodes receive raw data from corresponding sensors by using interrupt functions. Next, the data extraction block obtains original transmitted data from RS232 and CAN nodes. All data are stored in the data buffer block temporarily, which is made up of arrays. As for the Ethernet block, the physical layer chip LAN8720 should be configured first. After the lwIP kernel is initialized, remote and local static IP addresses and port numbers are ought to be determined because the Dynamic Host Configuration Protocol (DHCP) is turned off here. Finally, data can be transferred from the data buffer block to the upper computer software.

3.2 Upper Computer Software Development

The upper computer software is developed in C# programming language based on Windows Forms, which is a set of libraries designed to develop applications in the .NET framework. The upper computer software will select the same data frame formats as the corresponding sensors from the list of predefined ones, which is given in Table 1.

Table 1. List of predefined data frame formats.

No	Start bit	Data length	Data type	Precision
1	2	3	Integer	0
2	1	6	Floating point	2
3	3	5	Floating point	1
4	4	5	Floating point	2

On the upper computer software side, socket class in C# is selected to implement network communications. After configuring the network parameters, including remote and local IP addresses and port numbers, the upper computer software starts to receive data from the PCM in an asynchronous way.

4   Experimental Results

In this section, some experiments are conducted to validate whether the system realizes the functions of protocol conversion. If the data at the sensors side are accurately transferred to the upper computer software, it means that the system has realized the function of communication protocol conversion successfully.

To customize the data frame formats employed by different sensors, software simulated sensors running on a separate computer are developed to mimic the behaviors of the real sensors. Therefore, the upper computer software can configure the data frame formats according to the known formats on the simulated sensor sides. The simulated sensors transmit data to the MCU hardware platform through the RS232 and CAN interfaces. Moreover, the adjustment modules are integrated into the software simulated sensors to modify the values of parameters when receiving commands from the upper computer.

To start the process of validation, the serial port related parameters should be configured first. As Table 2 presented, the parameter settings of serial ports of the temperature and humidity sensors are given, respectively.

Table 2. Serial port parameter settings of the temperature and humidity sensors.

	Port	Baud rate	Data bit	Stop bit	Check bit
Temperature	COM4	115200	8	2	Even
Humidity	COM1	57600	8	1	None

Table 3. IP addresses and port numbers configurations of the MCU board and upper computer software.

MCU board		Upper computer software	
IP address	Port number	IP address	Port number
192.168.1.30	8089	192.168.1.101	8089

Secondly, as shown in Table 3, the IP addresses and port numbers of the MCU-based hardware development board and the upper computer software need to be determined, respectively.

After selecting a specific data frame format for the two sensors, we can start the process of sending and receiving data. Figure 5 displays the data frame format selections, local area network configurations, and the results of received data. Comparing with the current values of temperature (23.6 °C) and humidity (41%),

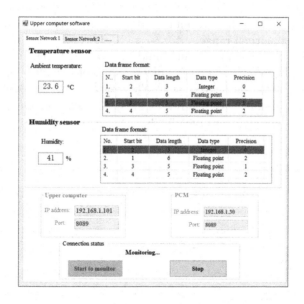

Fig. 5. Screenshot of the upper computer software.

the received data in Fig. 5 are correct. As a consequence, it turns out that the whole system has realized the function of communication protocol conversion well.

Figure 6 presents the changing process of temperature parameter over time. Here, the maximum and minimum values of temperature $T_{\max}, T_{\min}$ are set as 30 °C and 20 °C, respectively. The offset ΔT is 1 °C. As shown in Fig. 6, when

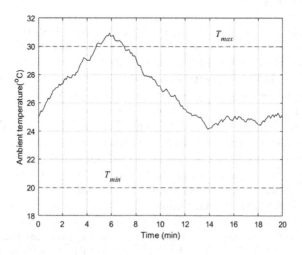

Fig. 6. Temperature parameter changes over time.

the temperature exceeds the maximum and minimum levels, the parameter will be adjusted to the normal range.

Similarly, the changing process of humidity parameter over time is illustrated in Fig. 7. Here, the maximum and minimum values of humidity $H_{\max}, H_{\min}$ are set as 45% and 40%, respectively. The offset ΔH is 2%. As shown in Fig. 7, the humidity parameter will be adjusted to the normal range if the differences between current humidity and maximum or minimum values are greater than ΔH.

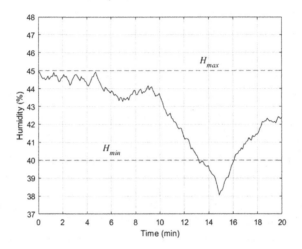

Fig. 7. Humidity parameter changes over time.

5   Conclusions

In this paper, we have designed and implemented a reconfigurable PCM to solve the data acquisition and sensor management problems in the heterogeneous sensor networks. By introducing the predefined data frame formats, a reconfigurable scheme has been designed to customize data frame formats, enabling the system's support for heterogeneous sensor networks. Meanwhile, an MCU-based hardware platform is utilized to implement the multiple communication protocol conversion between RS232, CAN, and Ethernet. Furthermore, the upper computer software has been developed to receive data, configure the communication settings, and adjust the environmental parameters. Finally, validation experiments are conducted to demonstrate that the designed system can realize the function of multiple protocol conversions and ensure that the environmental parameters are within the normal range.

Acknowledgment. This work was supported by the National Key R&D Program of China under Grant 2019YFE010391, the National Natural Science Foundation of China under Grant 61871035, and the National Defense Science and Technology Innovation Zone.

References

1. Paniagua, C., Delsing, J.: Industrial frameworks for internet of things: a survey. IEEE Syst. J. **1–11** (2020). https://doi.org/10.1109/JSYST.2020.2993323
2. Kocakulak, M., Butun, I.: An overview of Wireless Sensor Networks towards internet of things. In: IEEE Annual Computing and Communication Workshop and Conference, pp. 1–6. IEEE, Las Vegas (2017)
3. Kuo, Y., Li, C., Jhang, J., Lin, S.: Design of a Wireless Sensor Network-Based IoT platform for wide area and heterogeneous applications. IEEE Sens. J. **18**(12), 5187–5197 (2018)
4. Xie, J., Gao, Q.: Design and implementation of embedded protocol conversion gateway for intelligent buildings. In: 2019 IEEE 10th International Conference on Software Engineering and Service Science (ICSESS), pp. 1–5. IEEE, Beijing (2019)
5. Zhang, F., Liu, M., Zhou, Z., Shen, W.: An IoT-based online monitoring system for continuous steel casting. IEEE Internet Things J. **3**(6), 1355–1363 (2016)
6. Woo, M.W., Lee, J., Park, K., et al.: A Reliable IoT system for personal healthcare devices. Future Generation Comput. Syst. **78**(2), 626–640 (2018)
7. Zhu, J., Chong, X., Tao, Y.: An electric power system protocol conversion method based on embedded platform. In: 2016 2nd International Conference on Artificial Intelligence and Industrial Engineering (AIIE 2016), pp. 179–182. Atlantis Press (2016)
8. Chen, H.: Heterogeneous network integration based on protocol conversion. In: Proceedings of the 35th Chinese Control Conference, pp. 6888–6893. IEEE, Chengdu (2016)
9. Eum, S.: Implementation of protocol conversion control board for industrial communication. Int. J. Control Automa. **9**(6), 201–208 (2016)
10. Zhang, Y., Feng, X., Guo, Y.: Design of ethernet-CAN protocol conversion module based on STM32. In: International Conference on Future Generation Communication and Networking, vol. 7(1), pp. 89–96 (2014)
11. Trivedi, D., Khade, A., Jain, K.K., Jadhav, R.: SPI to i2c protocol conversion using verilog. In: 2018 Fourth International Conference on Computing Communication Control and Automation (ICCUBEA), pp. 1–4. IEEE, Pune (2018)
12. Ma, S., Liu, F.: Multi-interface gateway protocol conversion method for nearspace-air-vehicle-ground dedicated network. DEStech Trans. Comput. Sci. Eng. CCNT **367–373** (2018)
13. Lou, G., Cai, H.: Research and implementation of ARM-based fieldbus protocol conversion method. In: International Conference on Computer and Communication Technologies in Agriculture Engineering, pp. 260–262. IEEE, Chengdu (2010)
14. Cong, P.-X., et al.: The design of multi-interface protocol adaptive conversion distribution network communication device based on wireless communication technology. In: 2017 IEEE Conference on Energy Internet and Energy System Integration (EI2), pp. 1–4. IEEE, Beijing (2017)

FPGA-Based Neural Network Acceleration for Handwritten Digit Recognition

Guobin Shen[1], Jindong Li[1], Zhi Zhou[2], and Xiang Chen[1(✉)]

[1] School of Electronics and Information Technology, Sun Yat-sen University,
Guangzhou 510006, China
shengb3@mail2.sysu.edu.cn, lijd27@mail2.sysu.edu.cn,
chenxiang@mail.sysu.edu.cn
[2] School of Data and Computer Science, Sun Yat-sen University,
Guangzhou 510006, China
hustzhouzhi@gmail.com

Abstract. Convolutional neural network (CNN) has been widely employed in different engineering fields, as it achieves high performance for enormous applications. However, neural networks are computationally expensive and require extensive memory resource. While still implementing convolutional neural network using relatively few resources but achieving high computation speed has been an active research. In this paper, we propose an FPGA-based handwritten digit recognition acceleration method, applying the Lenet-5 model to the FPGA using Vivado High-Level Synthesis. By using fixed point quantization method, removing data dependencies and applying appropriate pipelining, the accuracy rate reaches 97.6% on MNIST dataset. On Zedboard, we achieve 3.65 times faster than running only on the Processing System (PS) of the same hardware.

Keywords: Convolutional neural network (CNN) · High-Level Synthesis (HLS) · Acceleration · FPGA

1 Introduction

Convolutional Neural Network (CNN) has brought breakthroughs in engineering fields such as signal processing, computer vision and robotics. In recent years, lots of influential Convolutional Neural Network structures have been proposed

This work was supported in part by the State's Key Project of Research and Development Plan under Grants 2019YFE0196400, in part by Industry-University Collaborative Education Program between SYSU and Digilent Technology: Edge AI Oriented Open Source Software and Hardware Makerspace, in part by the Guangdong R&D Project in Key Areas under Grant 2019B010158001, and in part by the Guangdong Provincial Special Fund For Modern Agriculture Industry Technology Innovation Teams under Grant 2020KJ122.

B. Li et al. (Eds.): IoTaaS 2020, LNICST 346, pp. 182–195, 2021.
https://doi.org/10.1007/978-3-030-67514-1_15

[5,6,9,11]. In 1998, Lenet-5 [10] structure proposed by Yann LeCun, achieved an astonishing accuracy of 98% in handwritten digit recognition. In 2012, Alexnet [11], designed by Alex Krizhevsky, significantly improved on the best performance in the image recognition. VGG-16 [9], Google-Net [10] and ResNet [5], also promoted the development of the neural network. However, as the network structure becomes more and more complicated, more computational resources are required. FPGA, a powerful hardware-acceleration architecture, can be used to speed up the computing. Recent study done by Chen et al. [12] presented a CNN accelerator achieving a peak performance of 61.62 GFLOPS under 100MHz working frequency, which greatly improves the traditional GPU accelerator. Lots of research have shown that FPGA has great advantages which still need to be exploited.

When compared with traditional processor architectures, the structures of the FPGA enable a high degree of parallelism. A processor executes a program as a sequence of instructions generated by processor compiler tools, which transforms an algorithm expressed in high level languages into assembly language. While an FPGA converts the program written in Hardware Description Languages (HDL) to a Register-Transfer Level (RTL), it reconfigures the integrated circuits inside the FPGA to best fit the design we need. This architecture can achieve a performance much better than the traditional processor architecture.

However, despite the great advantage of the FPGA architecture, designing a large-scale complex project using low-level hardware description languages is high-cost and inefficient. Figure 1 [2] illustrates the implementation time and achievable performance for different computation platforms. Development time of the FPGA using RTL is quite high, therefore this method has not been widely used.

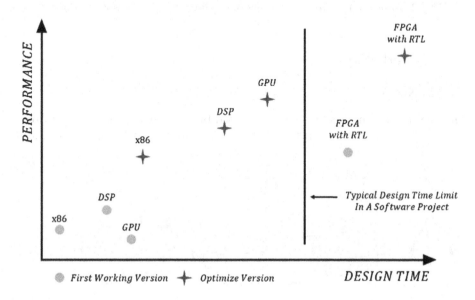

Fig. 1. Implementation time and achievable performance for different computation platforms.

Recently, Xilinx presented the High-Level Synthesis tool, it can automatically convert the high-level language C/C++ to the RTL model and HDL, which remove most of the difference in programing models between a processor and an FPGA. Without degrading the performance achieved by FPGA RTL design flow, FPGA with High-Level Synthesis (HLS) shortens the design time in a software project dramatically. Figure 2 [2] compares the result of the HLS design solution against other processor solutions.

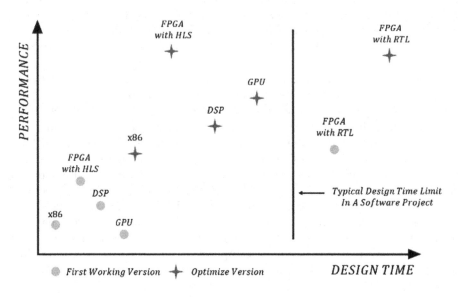

Fig. 2. Result of the HLS design solution against other processor solutions.

2   Related Work

2.1   LeNet-5

The LeNet [10] neural network was proposed by Yan LeCun, the father of Convolutional Neural Networks (CNN). LeNet is mainly used for the recognition

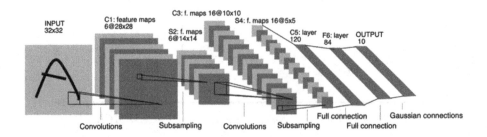

Fig. 3. Network structure of Lenet-5.

and classification of handwritten characters, and has been put into use in American banks. The implementation of LeNet has established the structure of CNN, and now much of the content in the neural network can be seen in the network structure of LeNet. Figure 3 shows the Lenet-5 network structure.

Layer1 is a convolution layer with 6 convolution kernels of 5 × 5, and the size of output feature is 28 × 28; Layer2 is the pooling layer that outputs 6 feature graphs of size 14 × 14. We use average pooling instead of the max pooling. Layer 3 is again a convolution layer with 16 convolution kernels of 5 × 5. Layer4 is similar to layer2, with size of 2 × 2 and output of 16 feature graphs. Layer5 is a convolution layer with 120 convolution kernels of size 5 × 5, and the output size of layer5 is 1 × 1. Then the layer5 is flatten and connects to the fully connected layer6. Using a 120 × 84 weight matrix, an output vector of size 84 is computed, then again using an 84 × 10 weight matrix, we can get the final output feature vector of size 10.

2.2 Design Flow of the High-Level Synthesis

Figure 4 shows the workflow for the FPGA development of Lenet-5 using Vivado HLS.

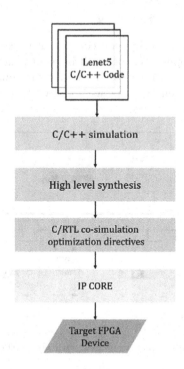

Fig. 4. Workflow for the FPGA development of HLS.

In our work, we used C/C++ as the development language, which is supported by the Vivado HLS. All the kernels and weights parameters are set to use a single fixed-point data type. In the first step, we implemented Lenet-5 using C/C++ and conducted simulation experiments. Once the experimental results met out requirements, the synthesis process converted the C/C++ code to HDL and the RTL model automatically. The synthesis report generated by the HLS gives a detailed information about the utilization of the different resources used in the project, such as Look-up table (LUT), Flip-Flop (FF), DSP Block, and Block Ram (BRAM), and the latency and the number of clock cycle needed. Next, we don't need to write a Verilog testbench code to conduct further verification, as the next C/RTL co-simulation step can do this for us. Furthermore, different FPGA on-chip environments are provided by Vivado HLS to simulate.

3   Optimization Method

HLS does not automatically optimize. In order to increase throughput and reduce the startup interval between operations, we need to choose different optimization strategies according to the characteristics of the task.

3.1   Function and Loop Pipelining

Pipelining allows operations to happen concurrently: each execution step does not have to complete all operations before it begins the next operations. Figure 5 shows the difference between functions with and without pipelining, and Fig. 6 shows the difference between for-loops with and without pipelining.

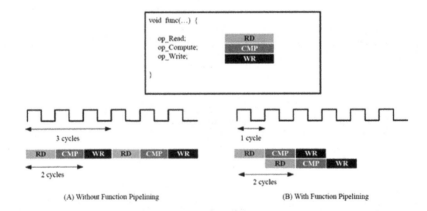

Fig. 5. Difference between functions with and without pipelining

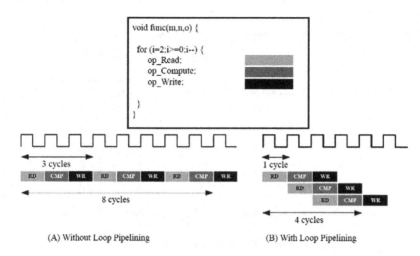

Fig. 6. Difference between for-loops with and without pipelining

3.2   Arrays Partitioning

Arrays are implemented as block RAM which only has a maximum of two data ports. This can limit the throughput of a read/write operations. The bandwidth can be improved by splitting the array into multiple small arrays, effectively increasing the number of ports. Figure 7 shows that array partitioning can be applied in 3 different manners. Figure 8 shows that partitioning dimension can be set when splitting a multi-dimension array.

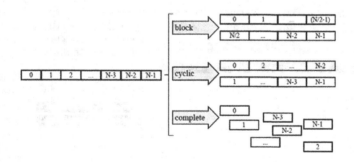

Fig. 7. Method for array partitioning

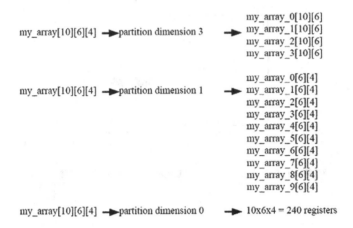

Fig. 8. Multi-dimension arrays partitioning

3.3 Loop Unrolling

In Vivado HLS, loops are kept rolled by default. These rolled loops generate a
hardware resource which is used by each itertion of the loop. This is resource-
efficient, but it can become a performace bottleneck. Using unroll directives,
for-loops can be partially or completely unrolled to improve pipelining. Figure 9
shows how the loop unrolling actually works.

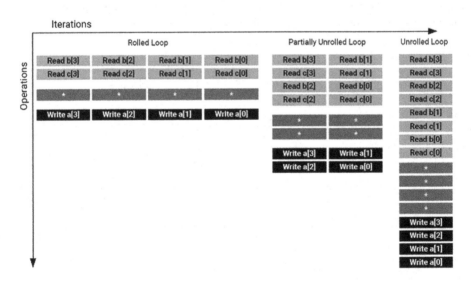

Fig. 9. How the loop unfolds

4   Implementing the Lenet-5 Using HLS

In this section, we discuss the acceleration methods for different modules in the neural network and compare the results.

4.1   Data Quantization

One of the most commonly used method for model compression is the quantification of weights and activations. In common development frameworks, neural network activations and weights are usually represented by floating-point data. Recent work attempts to replace this representation with low-level fixed-point data or even a small portion of training values. On the one hand, using fewer bits for each activation or weight helps reduce the bandwidth and storage requirements of the neural network processing system. On the other hand, using a simplified representation can reduce the hardware cost of each operation. Empirical results [4] also show that when choosing an appropriate method for data quantization, the impact on the accuracy of the model is acceptable. In [8], the optimized solution of a network is chosen layer by layer to avoid an exponential design space exploration. Guo et al. [3] choose to fine-tune the model after the fractional bit-width of all the layers are fixed. In our method, we use linear quantization method to optimize the model.

The selection of data quantization bit width has a great influence on the performance of the model. If the quantization bit width is too short, the weights that cause the model to be close to zero will be determined to be zero, which will cause many effective neurons to "dead", Affecting the performance of the model. If the quantization bit width is large, it will cause the model to consume a lot of resources and have a large latency.

Therefore, we selected the best quantization bit width through experiments. Table 1 shows the accuracy of the model under different quantization bit widths. When the quantization bit width is 9, the model cannot be synthesized due to the limitation of hardware resources. When the number of quantization digits is 7, the accuracy of the model will become very low. So in the end we used 8-bit quantization.

Table 1. Accuracy of the model under different quantization bit widths

Quantization width	7	**8**	9
Accuracy	0.129933	**0.972**	Cannot be synthesized

4.2   Optimization of Convolutional Layer

Figure 10 illustrates how a typical convolutional layer is computed [12].

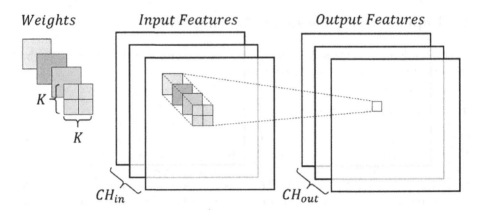

Fig. 10. How a convolutional layer is computed

The convolutional layer receives N input feature maps of size ROW_IN by COL_IN, and gives $N - K + 1$ feature maps of size ROW by COL as output. Each input feature map is convolved by a K by K kernel. The kernel slides through the corresponding input feature map and generates one pixel in the corresponding position in one output feature map. For simplicity, the stride of the kernel window here is set to one. Therefore, the size of each output feature map will be $N - K + 1$. Implementing the computing process of the convolution is basically just nesting 6 for-loops and do the multiplication and accumulation in the innermost loop. The code of a convolutional layer can be written in Algorithm 1.

This algorithm can be synthesized in to RTL model and HDL. Table 2 shows the parameters of this network layer. All the loops are kept rolled and no pipeline directives included. The total latency of this algorithm, latency of each nested loop, and the resources consumed is shown in Fig. 11. This program is resource-efficient, these rolled loops generate a hardware resource which is used by each iteration of the loop. But the total latency of this function is just too high.

Table 2. Parameters of this network layer

IN_CH	OUT_CH	ROW_IN	COL_IN	ROWS	COLS	K
6	16	14	14	10	10	5

Optimization techniques can be applied if we get rid of the data dependencies in this function. In the convolutional layer computing process described above, different input feature maps and output feature maps are independent can be computed in parallel. Pipeline directive can be applied if we just move the output channel loop and the input channel loop into the innermost loop, and partition the array in corresponding dimension. The nested loop inside the

Algorithm 1. Algorithm 1

```
 1: Output_Channel:
 2: for each cho ∈ [0, OUT_CH] do
 3:    Input_Channel:
 4:    for each chi ∈ [0, IN_CH] do
 5:       ROWS:
 6:       for each r ∈ [0, ROW] do
 7:          COLS:
 8:          for each c ∈ [0, COL] do
 9:             Kernel_Row:
10:             for each kr ∈ [0, K] do
11:                Kernel_Col:
12:                for each kc ∈ [0, K] do
13:                   Out[cho][r][c]+ = In[chi][r + kr][c + kc] * W[cho][chi][kr][kc]
14:                end for
15:             end for
16:          end for
17:       end for
18:    end for
19: end for
```

Loop Name	Latency (cycles)		Iteration Latency	Initiation Interval		Trip Count	Pipelined
	min	max		achieved	target		
- Output_Channel	2037344	2037344	127334	-	-	16	no
+ Input_Channel	127332	127332	21222	-	-	6	no
++ Row	21220	21220	2122	-	-	10	no
+++ Col	2120	2120	212	-	-	10	no
++++ Kernel_Row	210	210	42	-	-	5	no
+++++ Kernel_Col	40	40	8	-	-	5	no

Fig. 11. Latency of Algorithm 1

pipeline directive will be automatically unrolled. The revised version of the algorithm is presented in Algorithm 2, and from the synthesis report shown in Fig. 12 we can see that the total latency has been shorten greatly, but it also consumes more resources.

By simply changing the order of the for-loops and applying several directives, the revised version of the algorithm is 102 times faster than the previous one. But still, further optimization method can be used to achieve an initial interval of one. If we notice the warning issued by the HLS complier, some data dependencies stop us from achieving a higher degree of parallelism. Figure 13 shows the RAW dependencies that exists in the nested for-loops. When executing iteration $0(r = c = kr = kc = 0)$, Out[0][0][0] is read and then written into. When executing iteration $1(r = c = kr = 0, kc = 1)$, Out[0][0][0] still needs to be read and written to. The for-loops cannot be fully pipelined if adjacent iteration needs to access the same piece of data.

Algorithm 2. Algorithm 2

1: ROWS:
2: **for** each $r \in [0, ROW]$ **do**
3:    COLS:
4:    **for** each $c \in [0, COL]$ **do**
5:       Kernel_Row:
6:       **for** each $kr \in [0, K]$ **do**
7:          Kernel_Col:
8:          **for** each $kc \in [0, K]$ **do**
9:             Output_Channel:
10:             **for** each $cho \in [0, OUT\_CH]$ **do**
11:                Input_Channel:
12:                **for** each $chi \in [0, IN\_CH]$ **do**
13:                   $Out[cho][r][c] + = In[chi][r + kr][c + kc] * W[cho][chi][kr][kc]$
14:                **end for**
15:             **end for**
16:          **end for**
17:       **end for**
18:    **end for**
19: **end for**

	Latency (cycles)			Initiation Interval			
Loop Name	min	max	Iteration Latency	achieved	target	Trip Count	Pipelined
- Row_Kernel_Row_Kernel_Col	20000	20000	9	8	1	2500	yes

Fig. 12. Latency of Algorithm 2

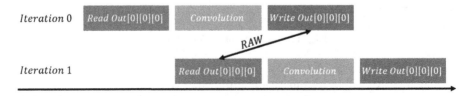

Fig. 13. RAW dependencies that exists in the nested for-loops

Simply changing the order of the for-loops by moving the $Kernel\_Row$ loop and the $Kernel\_Col$ loop to the outermost loop can remove these dependencies, shown in Fig. 14. The final version of the convolution algorithm is shown in Algorithm 3.

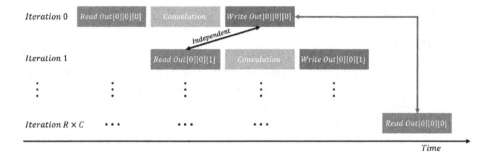

Fig. 14. RAW dependencies disappeared.

From the synthesis report shown in Fig. 15, initial interval of 1 is achieved, and the total latency is shortened to 25us, which is 812 times faster than Algorithm 1.

	Latency (cycles)			Initiation Interval			
Loop Name	min	max	Iteration Latency	achieved	target	Trip Count	Pipelined
- Kernel_Row_Row_Col	2507	2507	9	1	1	2500	yes

Fig. 15. Initial interval of 1 is achieved.

Algorithm 3. Algorithm 3

1: Kernel_Row:
2: **for** each $kr \in [0, K]$ **do**
3:   Kernel_Col:
4:   **for** each $kc \in [0, K]$ **do**
5:     ROWS:
6:     **for** each $r \in [0, ROW]$ **do**
7:       COLS:
8:       **for** each $c \in [0, COL]$ **do**
9:         Output_Channel:
10:        **for** each $cho \in [0, OUT\_CH]$ **do**
11:          Input_Channel:
12:          **for** each $chi \in [0, IN\_CH]$ **do**
13:            $Out[cho][r][c] + = In[chi][r + kr][c + kc] * W[cho][chi][kr][kc]$
14:          **end for**
15:        **end for**
16:      **end for**
17:    **end for**
18: **end for**
19: **end for**

---

5   Experiment

5.1   MNIST

The MNIST dataset [1] (Mixed National Institute of Standards and Technology database) is a large database of handwritten digits collected by the National Institute of Standards and Technology. It contains a training set of 60,000 examples and a test set of 10,000 examples.

5.2   Implementation Details

During training, Our model uses the same structure as [10]. All of the input images are resized to 28×28. Moreover, We use the mini-batch of 8 and stochastic gradient descent (SGD) [7] for network training, the weight decay of 5×10^{-5}, and the momentum of 0.9. The learning rate is set to 0.001 and the iterations are set to 100 epochs.

During evaluation, we use the batch of 1. For each test, we first read the test picture from the disk through the Processing System (PS), and pass the image to the network acceleration module through direct memory access(DMA). In the network acceleration module, the digit in the image will be recognized, and the recognition result will be passed back to the PS through DMA and displayed.

5.3   Result

Table 3 shows the comparison between our FPGA-accelerated neural network and the same model running on PS. In the case of 8-bit quantization, our model loses less than 1% accuracy under the same hardware conditions, but the speed is accelerated by 3.64 times.

Table 3. Model comparison

	Accuracy	FPS
Processing System	0.982	71.43
FPGA-accelerated	0.976	19.62

6   Conclusion

In this paper, we have implemented FPGA-based handwritten digit recognition acceleration. By using data quantization and arrange the loops in an appropriate order, high-speed and low resources consumption are achieved.

References

1. Mnist (1998). http://yann.lecun.com/exdb/mnist/
2. Fpga design with vivado high-level synthesis ug998 (2019)
3. Guo, K., Sui, L., Qiu, J., Yu, J., Wang, J., Yao, S., Han, S., Wang, Y., Yang, H.: Angel-eye: a complete design flow for mapping CNN onto embedded FPGA. IEEE Trans. Comput. Aided Des. Integr. Circuits Syst. **37**(1), 35–47 (2018)
4. Guo, K., Zeng, S., Yu, J., Wang, Y., Yang, H.: A survey of FPGA-based neural network accelerator (2017)
5. He, K., Zhang, X., Ren, S., Sun, J.: Deep residual learning for image recognition (2015)
6. Huang, G., Liu, Z., van der Maaten, L., Weinberger, K.Q.: Densely connected convolutional networks (2016)
7. Lecun, Y., Bottou, L., Bengio, Y., Haffner, P.: Gradient-based learning applied to document recognition. Proc. IEEE **86**(11), 2278–2324 (1998)
8. Qiu, J., et al.: Going deeper with embedded FPGA platform for convolutional neural network. In: Proceedings of the 2016 ACM/SIGDA International Symposium on Field-Programmable Gate Arrays, FPGA 2016, pp. 26–35. Association for Computing Machinery, New York (2016). https://doi.org/10.1145/2847263.2847265
9. Simonyan, K., Zisserman, A.: Very deep convolutional networks for large-scale image recognition (2014)
10. Szegedy, C., et al.: Going deeper with convolutions (2014)
11. Xu, M., et al.: Stylize aesthetic QR code (2018)
12. Zhang, C., Li, P., Sun, G., Guan, Y., Xiao, B., Cong, J.: Optimizing FPGA-based accelerator design for deep convolutional neural networks. In: Proceedings of the 2015 ACM/SIGDA International Symposium on Field-Programmable Gate Arrays, FPGA 2015, pp. 161–170. Association for Computing Machinery, New York (2015). https://doi.org/10.1145/2684746.2689060

Edge Computing Based Two-Stage Emergency Braking in Autonomous Driving

Lian Li[1], Zhan Xu[1,2], Jinhui Chen[1,2]($\boxtimes$), Ruxin Zhi[1,2], and Mingzhe Huang[1]

[1] Beijing Information Science and Technology University, Beijing, China
Jinhui.Chen@bistu.edu.cn
[2] Key Laboratory of Modern Measurement and Control Technology, Beijing, China

Abstract. Emergency braking is a key technology in autonomous driving to prevent collision accidents. In this paper, we propose an edge computing based two-stage emergency braking method (TSEB), which can bring passengers more comfortable experience with emergency braking while avoiding collision. In TSEB, the initial deceleration rate is figured out at the first time point, in terms of motion parameters of the moving vehicle and the moving or static obstacle, and used to set the braking force for the first-stage braking, which can at least avoid serious collision. The second deceleration rate is figured out in terms of the parameters at the second time point and implemented on the vehicle by increasing the braking force in the second-stage braking. With the second-stage braking, the vehicle can stop at a safer distance to the obstacle while the passengers do not feel too much deceleration. The performance of TSEB is evaluated on the simulation platform composed of Prescan, Simulink and Matlab. TIS sensors of long distance and short distance are used to detect the distance between the vehicle and the obstacle.

Keywords: Emergency braking · Autonomous driving · Edge computing

1 Introduction

Emergency braking, as a basic function in autonomous driving, is used to avoid collision accidents, which is critical to vehicle and public safety. V2X in the Internet of Vehicles obtains the information of the stored vehicle through the cloud, and analyzes the data of the vehicle to evaluate the current driving situation, location situation and safety information of the vehicle. When an emergency occurs, relying on the cloud for emergency hedging, the length of the delay is difficult to ensure the success of hedging, and the use of edge computing can achieve extremely low latency and ensure the timely avoidance of the car [1–3].

The development of edge computing is widely used in real-time data processing of public safety, virtual reality, industrial Internet of Things, smart homes,

© ICST Institute for Computer Sciences, Social Informatics and Telecommunications Engineering 2021
Published by Springer Nature Switzerland AG 2021. All Rights Reserved
B. Li et al. (Eds.): IoTaaS 2020, LNICST 346, pp. 196–206, 2021.
https://doi.org/10.1007/978-3-030-67514-1_16

smart cities, and intelligent connected cars and autonomous driving. One of the characteristics of edge computing is the reduction of latency [4]. In edge computing based emergency braking, sensors installed on the vehicles can be used to identify the obstacles in front and to sense the relative distance between the moving vehicle and the obstacles. The obtained parameters are used as input for edge computing to avoid collision [5]. Compared to cloud based decision making, edge computing based emergency baking can perform better in agility and reliability [6].

As a branch of cloud computing, edge computing can marginalize data and make it more efficient and convenient. In this project, edge computing is used. Firstly, information can be put into the cloud as a part of the cloud database to increase the storage data of vehicle networking applications in the later stage. The second point is that when there is a problem with the vehicle identification system, it can be observed and controlled through the cloud as an emergency treatment. The last point is that edge computing has the characteristics of low latency, and can process data quickly, consistent with small devices.

In this paper, we propose an edge computing based two-stage emergency braking method (TSEB), which can bring passengers more comfortable experience with emergency braking while avoiding collision. In TSEB, the initial deceleration rate is figured out at the first time point, in terms of motion parameters of the moving vehicle and the moving or static obstacle, and used to set the braking force for the first-stage braking, which can at least avoid serious collision. The second deceleration rate is figured out in terms of the parameters at the second time point and implemented on the vehicle by increasing the braking force in the second-stage braking. With the second-stage braking, the vehicle can stop at a safer distance to the obstacle while the passengers do not feel too much deceleration. The performance of TSEB is evaluated on the simulation platform composed of Prescan, Simulink and Matlab. TIS sensors of long distance and short distance are used to detect the distance between the vehicle and the obstacle.

2   Two-Stage Emergency Braking

In this section, the processes of collision and emergency braking are formulated and the two-stage emergency braking method (TSEB) is described.

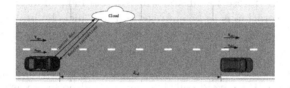

Fig. 1. Top view of parameter identification.

Assume a vehicle moving at velocity v_{ego} and acceleration rate a_{ego} is closing to an obstacle in front moving at v_{obj} and acceleration rate a_{obj}, as Fig. 1 shows. Collision will happen when the following equation holds,

$$v_{ego}t + \frac{1}{2}a_{ego}t^2 = v_{obj}t + \frac{1}{2}a_{obj}t^2 + d_{rel}, \tag{1}$$

where d_{rel} is the distance between the moving vehicle and the obstacle at the time point when v_{ego}, a_{ego}, v_{obj} and a_{obj} are measured. (1) can be written as

$$f(t) = 0 \tag{2}$$

where $f(t)$ is a quadratic function of t

$$f(t) = a_{rel}t^2 + 2v_{rel}t - 2d_{rel}, \tag{3}$$

with

$$a_{rel} = a_{ego} - a_{obj}, \tag{4}$$

$$v_{rel} = v_{ego} - v_{obj}. \tag{5}$$

If the vehicle and the obstacle keep their current speeds and acceleration rates,

1) in the case of $a_{rel} > 0$, i.e., $a_{ego} > a_{obj}$, the vehicle will collide with the obstacle at the time point t_c

$$t_c = \frac{-v_{rel} + \sqrt{v_{rel}^2 + 2a_{rel}d_{rel}}}{a_{rel}}; \tag{6}$$

2) in the case of $a_{rel} = 0$, i.e., $a_{ego} = a_{obj}$, the collision time point is

$$t_c = \frac{d_{rel}}{v_{rel}}; \tag{7}$$

3) in the case of $a_{rel} < 0$, i.e., $a_{ego} < a_{obj}$, $v_{rel} > 0$ and $-v_{rel}^2/a_{rel} \geq 2d_{rel}$, the collision time point is

$$t_c = \frac{-v_{rel} - \sqrt{v_{rel}^2 + 2a_{rel}d_{rel}}}{a_{rel}}; \tag{8}$$

4) in the case of $a_{rel} < 0$, i.e., $a_{ego} < a_{obj}$, and $-v_{rel}^2/a_{rel} < 2d_{rel}$, we have that $f(t) < 0$ for all $t \geq 0$ and thus there is no risk of collision.

For avoiding the foreseen collision which would happen at the time point T_0 in Case 1–3, deceleration is to be enforced to the vehicle by braking. Denote the deceleration rate by b_{ego}. In terms of (3), we have the function

$$g_1(t) = -(b_{ego} + a_{obj})t^2 + 2v_{rel}t - 2d_{rel}. \tag{9}$$

In the light of Case 4, to avoid collision, b_{ego} should be set so as to

$$b_{ego} > \frac{v_{rel}^2}{2d_{rel}} - a_{obj}. \tag{10}$$

In our TSEB method, the sensors on the vehicle measure the speeds and acceleration rates of the vehicle and the obstacle and their distance, denoted by $v_{ego,1}$, $a_{ego,1}$, $v_{obj,1}$, $a_{obj,1}$ and $d_{rel,1}$, when an obstacle in front is sensed. If there is a risk of collision, the first deceleration rate $b_{ego,1}$ is calculated as

$$b_{ego,1} = \frac{v_{rel,1}^2}{2(d_{rel,1} + \Delta d)} - a_{obj,1} \tag{11}$$

where $\Delta d \geq 0$ is a relaxing distance value, and

$$v_{rel,1} = v_{ego,1} - v_{obj,1} \tag{12}$$

At the first stage of emergency braking, the braking force F_1 which can generate the deceleration rate $b_{ego,1}$ is enforced on the vehicle.

After time Δt, the sensors measure the speeds and acceleration rates of the vehicle and the obstacle and their distance again, denoted by $v_{ego,2}$, $a_{ego,2}$, $v_{obj,2}$, $a_{obj,2}$ and $d_{rel,2}$. The vehicle will stop at the time point with the time point when the sensors do the second measurement as the reference time point,

$$t_{ego,2} = \frac{v_{ego,2}}{b_{ego,2}}. \tag{13}$$

Then, if there is risk of collision, the second deceleration $b_{ego,2}$ is calculated as

$$b_{ego,2} = \max \left(\frac{v_{ego,2}^2}{2(d_{rel,2} - \Delta d_s)} - a_{obj,2}, \frac{-v_{ego,2}a_{obj,2}}{v_{obj,2}} \right) \tag{14}$$

where Δd_s is the required minimum distance between the vehicle and the obstacle during the emergency braking process.

The second term in the bracket of (14) comes from the inequality

$$t_{ego,2} \geq \frac{v_{rel,2}}{b_{ego,2} + a_{obj,2}} \tag{15}$$

At the second stage of emergency braking, the braking force F_2 which generate the deceleration rate $b_{ego,2}$ is enforced on the vehicle, which means the incremental braking force $\Delta F = F_2 - F_1$ is implemented.

The TSEB method is used to increase the braking force in two steps, which can improve the passenger's experience on inertia and thus increases the comfort of the ride.

3   Simulation Platform

3.1   Control Principle

The automatic emergency braking system is a cyclic closed-loop system composed of a perception system, an operation control system and an execution system. The system is based on real-time detection data of on-board TIS sensors, and uses target feature extraction algorithms to calculate distance and relative speed to the front target [7,8]. Operation control calculates the data information, performs function judgment, and performs three-level operation of the component to evaluate whether there is a collision. Danger; According to the collision danger level, the actuator prompts an alarm and controls the braking module to make an emergency braking response. The control principle diagram is shown in Fig. 2.

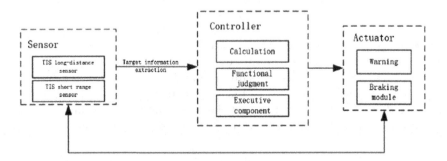

Fig. 2. Control principle diagram.

3.2 Simulation Scheme

The design of the main simulation scene includes the car, obstacles, track design and sensor module, *etc.* The scene information is obtained through the sensor environment perception. The sensed data is transmitted to the module of the control decision algorithm, the control command is given to the actuator by the algorithm and the actuator controls the engine, rotation, steering structure and brake structure module, etc. Finally the state of the vehicle is transmitted to the scene to form a closed loop.

In our simulation, a 5-lane environment is used. A white obstacle vehicle is set in the middle lane. The movement trajectory of the moving car is set and a simulated down-view human eye perspective is set directly above the car for observation.

TIS sensors of long distance and short distance are installed on the car [9]. The long distance sensor is used to detect the distance of the obstacle vehicle in front, and the short distance is used to detect the range of obstacles. As shown in Fig. 3.

In the prescan system, the car dynamics model is set to facilitate the subsequent operation of the brake system of the car dynamics module in MATLAB. The .slx file is compiled and generated based on the characteristics of prescan and designed in MATLAB. The .slx file includes the corresponding car model generation, TIS sensor module, dynamics model module, road control module,

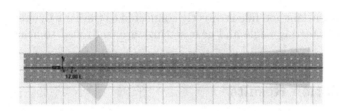

Fig. 3. TIS sensor scene settings.

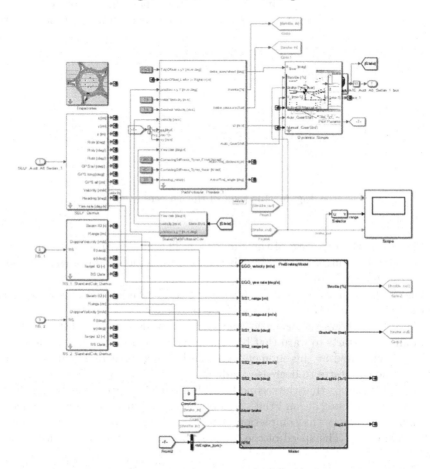

Fig. 4. Configuration interface

and the most important plug-in design parking control module [9]. Figure 4 shows the designed configuration interface.

The corresponding car information is input into the corresponding interface, and the range data recognized by the sensor is connected to the corresponding parking analysis module to analyze when to start the operation of the braking module. The parking module is directly connected to the car's dynamics module. The braking, steering angle and gear settings are controlled to achieve parking of the car.

4   Simulation Results

By running the program, we can observe in 3Dviewer that the car travels smoothly on the road according to the setting. When the sensors detect the obstacle, it prompts warning and starts the emergency braking process with TSEB.

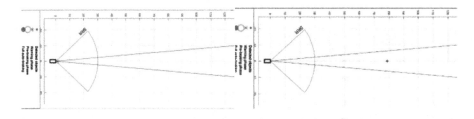

Fig. 5. Top view of the car sensor.

Figure 5 is the top view of the car sensor. The pink area is the short-range sensor detection range, and the blue is the long-range detection range. The blue star is the detected object.

On the GUI, as shown in Fig. 6(a), the speed, braking force, and angle of rotation of the car at a constant speed are presented.

Figure 6(b) shows the scenario that the vehicle detects the obstacle at the beginning, and starts to warn that braking is required. The first stage emergency braking is executed at this moment and the braking force F_1 is enforced. The speed of the car starts to decrease gradually.

Figure 6(c) shows that the second level of braking is started, the braking force reaches hundred percent, and the speed of the car begins to drop more quickly.

Figure 6(d) shows the completion of braking. The braking force is displayed as the maximum. The speed of the car is zero and the angle of rotation is also zero.

Figure 7, Fig. 8, Fig. 9 show the comparison simulation results of TSEB and One-Stage Emergency Braking. In the Fig. 7, it shows the speed curve of the trolley during the whole process. We can see that the speed of the trolley has two different accelerations in TSEB to accelerate the speed of the trolley, while OSEB accelerates to zero with the same acceleration. Figure 8 shows the distance between the car and the obstacle detected by the TIS sensor. We can see that the final distance from the obstacle in OSEB is about 2.9 m, and the final distance from the obstacle in the TSEB is about 2.3 m.Fig. 9 shows the amount of braking force obtained by the car. We can see that there is a stepped increase in braking

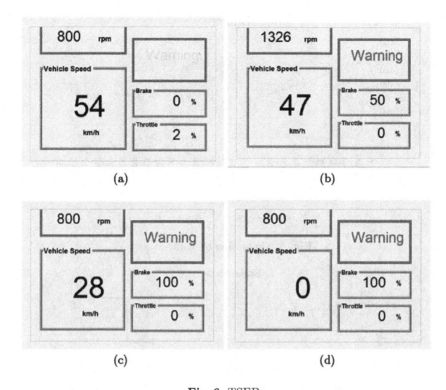

(a)   (b)

(c)   (d)

Fig. 6. TSEB

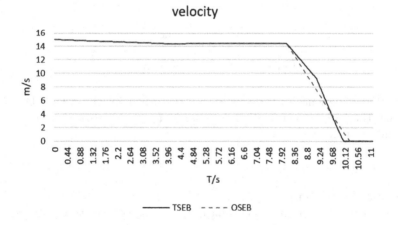

Fig. 7. Simulation of speed.

force in TSEB, so that the car gets two different accelerations to decelerate. The
second braking starts from 9.1 s, and the braking force is 150 N. In OSEB, the
one-time braking maximization is used to achieve the ability to quickly brake
the car. In OSEB, the function is realized only by a single braking, which makes

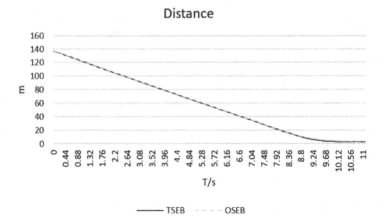

Fig. 8. Simulation of distance.

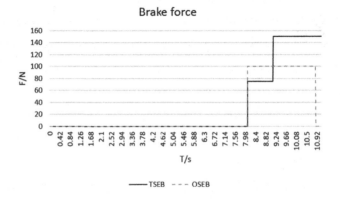

Fig. 9. Simulation of braking force.

the comfort experience of the vehicle and the driver relatively low. The driver feels that the parking inertia will have a larger forward inertia, thereby reducing the comfort of the experience.

For the driver in the process of driving at a constant speed, the body has always maintained the same speed as the vehicle. When the braking starts, the vehicle is given a small braking force, so that the vehicle obtains a small deceleration and begins to decelerate initially. In this process, the driver starts driving at the same speed as the vehicle. When the vehicle starts to decelerate, it has a forward momentum. Since the force is relatively small compared with the force of one braking, the driver will feel less momentum.

In the secondary braking, the braking is performed based on the first braking, so the relative braking force should be the difference between the two braking. After the first braking, the driver should recognize that emergency braking has begun, so he will be more psychologically prepared for the second braking. Compared with a single braking, the driver feels a greater continuous deceleration and is triggered suddenly without preparation. The shock felt will be greater than that of the secondary braking, so the secondary braking will be relatively more comfortable.

5   Conclusion

In this paper, we propose an edge computing based two-stage emergency braking method (TSEB), which can bring passengers more comfortable experience with emergency braking while avoiding collision. In TSEB, the initial deceleration rate is figured out at the first time point, in terms of motion parameters of the moving vehicle and the moving or static obstacle, and used to set the braking force for the first-stage braking, which can at least avoid serious collision. The second deceleration rate is figured out in terms of the parameters at the second time point and implemented on the vehicle by increasing the braking force in the second-stage braking. With the second-stage braking, the vehicle can stop at a safer distance to the obstacle while the passengers do not feel too much deceleration. The performance of TSEB is evaluated on the simulation platform composed of Prescan, Simulink and Matlab. TIS sensors of long distance and short distance are used to detect the distance between the vehicle and the obstacle.

Regarding the choice of braking force, it is temporarily impossible to fully simulate the braking effect of the human body. Only a simple two-stage braking is used as an example to show that multi-stage braking will improve the comfort of emergency braking, which can be further studied in the future. Begin by gradually increasing the braking force, but gradually increasing the braking force will also mean expanding the detection range and further increasing the detection threshold, which will make the distance between the vehicles farther and not suitable for practical applications. This needs to be solved with further research.

Acknowledgement. This work was supported by the Beijing Science and Technology Project (No. Z191100001419001), Key Laboratory of Modern Measurement & Control Technology, Ministry of Education, Beijing Information Science & Technology University (No. KF20201123201), the Shipei Plan of Beijing Information Science & Technology University (2020), the Beijing Excellent Talent Support Program (No. 2016000026833ZK08), and the Support Plan for the Construction of High Level Teachers in Beijing Municipal Universities (No. CIT&TCD201704065).

References

1. Gallego, F.V., et al.: Demo: a mobile edge computing-based collision avoidance system for future vehicular networks. In: IEEE INFOCOM 2019 - IEEE Conference on Computer Communications Workshops, INFOCOM Workshops 2019, Paris, France, 29 April– 2 May 2019, pp. 904–905. IEEE (2019). https://doi.org/10.1109/INFCOMW.2019.8845107
2. Liu, S., Liu, L., Tang, J., Yu, B., Wang, Y., Shi, W.: Edge computing for autonomous driving: Opportunities and challenges. In: Proceedings of the IEEE, vol. 107, no. 8, pp. 1697–1716 (2019). https://doi.org/10.1109/JPROC.2019.2915983

3. ElBamby, M.S., et al.: Wireless edge computing with latency and reliability guarantees. Proc. IEEE **107**(8), 1717–1737 (2019). https://doi.org/10.1109/JPROC.2019.2917084

4. Guleng, S., Wu, C., Liu, Z., Chen, X.: Edge-based V2X communications with big data intelligence. IEEE Access **8**, 8603–8613 (2020). https://doi.org/10.1109/ACCESS.2020.2964707

5. Moubayed, A., Shami, A., Heidari, P., Larabi, A., Brunner, R.: Edge-enabled V2X service placement for intelligent transportation systems, CoRR, vol. abs/2001.06288 (2020). https://arxiv.org/abs/2001.06288

6. Zhou, H., Xu, W., Chen, J., Wang, W.: Evolutionary V2X technologies toward the internet of vehicles: challenges and opportunities. Proc. IEEE **108**(2), 308–323 (2020). https://doi.org/10.1109/JPROC.2019.2961937

7. Zhang, J., Letaief, K.B.: Mobile edge intelligence and computing for the internet of vehicles. Proc. IEEE **108**(2), 246–261 (2020). https://doi.org/10.1109/JPROC.2019.2947490

8. Okuda, R., Kajiwara, Y., Terashima, K.:A survey of technical trend of ADAS and autonomous driving. In: Technical Papers of 2014 International Symposium on VLSI Design, Automation and Test, VLSI-DAT 2014, Hsinchu, Taiwan, April 28–30, 2014, pp. 1–4. IEEE (2014). https://doi.org/10.1109/VLSI-DAT.2014.6834940

9. Cho, M.: A study on the obstacle recognition for autonomous driving RC car using lidar and thermal infrared camera. In: Eleventh International Conference on Ubiquitous and Future Networks, ICUFN 2019, Zagreb, Croatia, July 2–5, 2019. IEEE, 2019, pp. 544–546 (2019). https://doi.org/10.1109/ICUFN.2019.8806152

Cache Resource Allocation in D2D Multi-layer Social Network

Xianglin Kong[1] , Pingping Chen[1], Zhijian Lin[1(✉)], Ying Wang[1],
and Yongcheng Yang[2]

[1] Fuzhou University, Fuzhou 350116, Fujian Province, China
zlin@fzu.edu.cn
[2] Jimei University, Xiamen 361000, Fujian Province, China

Abstract. In cache-enabled device-to-device (D2D) cellular networks, efficient utilization of mobile terminal cache storage reduces peak traffic demands and has a substantial impact on network performance. The combined impact of centrality value and cache memory size of user equipment (UE) are two crucial factors in D2D network, which are ignored in the existing researches. In this paper, an optimization algorithm is proposed to calculate the value of effect centrality (EC) to maximize the cache storage utilization considering various locations and preference of UEs. Firstly, users are clustered according to location, and users in the cluster form a multi-layer social network according to the preference of the requested content. Then based on the user's location, the effect centrality value is calculated, and the general mathematical expressions for the optimization of cache storage utilization with the constraints of effect centrality value and total cache storage is obtained. Subsequently, a Cache Storage Allocation (CSA) algorithm is proposed to obtain the cache storage utilization by taking the value of effect centrality as a variable. Simulation results show that the size of the effect centrality value will affect the utilization of the user's cache storage. Compared with the other two traditional methods, the proposed CSA can achieve the highest cache storage utilization.

Keywords: Cache storage · Centrality value · D2D · Social-aware · Edge caching

1 Introduction

With the widespread popularity of smart devices, a large number of emerging multimedia services are also booming. And services small video, live broadcast and other services meet most of the needs of mobile users for learning and entertainment. It is estimated that by 2020, a person will need more than 5 million years to watch the amount of video flowing through the global IP network every month [1]. Users have higher and higher requirements for video quality. At present, in the personal video on demand traffic, the percentage of ultra high definition (UDP) to IP video on demand (VOD) will rise from 1.6% in 2015 to 20.7%. The traditional wireless network architecture has great limitations, with the development of the times, it has been insufficient to meet the user's requirements for low latency and high reliability. With

© ICST Institute for Computer Sciences, Social Informatics and Telecommunications Engineering 2021
Published by Springer Nature Switzerland AG 2021. All Rights Reserved
B. Li et al. (Eds.): IoTaaS 2020, LNICST 346, pp. 207–221, 2021.
https://doi.org/10.1007/978-3-030-67514-1_17

the maturing 4G standardization, technological research on 5G network is underway in both academia and the industrial community [2].

One method proposed by the researchers is to improve the coding and communication technologies related to the transmission of information [3], in order to save wireless resources in a coding manner for communication. In this way, the utilization of wireless resources has been improved, but it still cannot meet the rapidly increasing demand for wireless traffic in the future. One promising technology adopted by the fifth-generation cellular network is edge caching. Cache files that users may request to the edge of the network, when users request files, they can be obtained directly without going through the server, saving a lot of network resources [4]. Perino D et al. studied the system evaluation of the applicability of existing routers for network-supported caching [5]. Popular content is cached in the router, when the user requests the file, the file can be directly obtained from the router, which can save the backhaul link. In practice, caching content in routers requires a lot of cost. A router with flash memory capacity and a cache space of 10 TB will cost $ 300,000. and the power of the router is also very large. Cooperative caching in D2D networks is an effective solution to the problem of expensive hardware [6]. Cooperative caching network is a promising technology that can meet the rapidly growing demand for mobile data traffic.

D2D communication allows neighboring devices to communicate directly with each other, and smart caching strategies need to be developed in mobile cellular networks[7–9], thereby promoting proximity services with high-speed requirements, so that data can be provided through nearby content Providers visit, which can help improve resource utilization and network capacity, for example, content sharing and distribution. In [10], D2D communication is regarded as a major technology to overcome the upcoming shortage of wireless capacity and achieve novel application services, jointly considering the attributes of the physical layer and the social layer, and constructing the content of the user's online social network according to the Indian Buffet Process. In [11], the author studied the problem of data offload in cache-enabled network, based on the machine learning framework, a novel algorithm for predicting file caching was proposed to solve the problem of active caching in the network. In [12], C. Yen et al. Studied the problem of collaborative caching in ultra-dense cellular networks, where the limited cache space is considered, predicting the popularity of unknown content. In [13], the author proposed a novel method of calculating the centrality value to reflect the importance of the node, and then based on the centrality value, a cache space allocation scheme was proposed, the allocated cache space size was proportional to the centrality value. In a cache-enabled network, how to use the effective cache space of the user terminal more efficiently is called one of the main challenges of whether the caching network is feasible in the future.

In a community, we can use the centrality attribute to select the user node to cache the content. The centrality of a node indicates how close a node is to other nodes in the network, and also indicates the importance of the node in the network. In [14], Z. C. Song et al. proposes a new measure of centrality based on the topology of the path of information transmission between nodes in the network, called "load centrality", because it focuses on the load the nodes bear in the network. The authors briefly reviewed the complex network concept and concentration. Four widely used measures of centrality, the degree centrality, the closeness centrality, the betweenness centrality, and information centrality, are introduced [15], K. Zhang et al. studied the calculation method of closeness centrality in complex networks, which is expressed by the total reciprocal of the sum of the path distances from a certain node to other nodes in the network. In [16], the author proposed the concept of K-hop centrality to represent the importance of nodes in a multi-hop D2D network. It can be calculated locally by adjusting the maximum multi-hop K value in the network, thereby reducing the complexity greatly increases the feasibility. In the pioneer work, many researches are based on the four measures of centrality earlier, David A. Bader [17] proposed a parallel algorithm for network centrality measurement, which is optimized for scale-free sparse graphs.

Recently, the measurement method of centrality of multi-layer social networks means that users form multiple social layer networks according to different request preferences, and the user node preferences in the same social layer are highly the same. In this work, a new metric named EC is defined to reflect the importance of the node. Then the caching performance of multi-layer social network has been carried out with consideration on the size of individual mobile user terminal. Finally, the cache storage quota allocated to user terminal is further optimized based on CSA algorithm, rather than proportional to the centrality value.

Based on the weights between nodes, we proposes an EC for D2D multi-layer social networks. With this EC, the centrality of each node in a multi-layer social network can be measured. Next, we propose a CSA based on the EC value. This is a fundamental outlook of our proposed methodology, which we will further discuss in Sect. 3. In order to verify the proposed method, we simulate it in a multi-layer social network and compared the performance with other two commonly used cache storage allocation methods.

The rest of this paper is organized as follows: Sect. 2 presents the definition of EC. In Sect. 3, we analyses the EC and applied CSA algorithm to allocate cache space. In Sect. 4, the evaluation results are provided. We conclude the paper with future work in Sect. 5.

2   System Model

2.1   Social Layer Model

In recent years, the social attributes of users in the network have attracted extensive attention from researchers in various fields [18, 19]. D2D social network refers to the social network established by users of terminal devices with different social attributes based on supporting D2D communication. In the world, all mobile devices are related to each other in many ways. Users with similar request preferences constitute the same layer of social network, and the attributes of the social network are also constituted by the social attributes of the users. User nodes often have multiple social attributes, and multiple users establish communication at different social layers, called cross-layer social networks or multi-layer social networks. Simple social networks assume that users have only one social attribute, but for the real world, this assumption ignores a lot of valid information. Practically, social network presents different levels due to its sociability, such as layer of interests and hobbies. For instance, in a social network, common node interacts with others through sports program, comedy, technology channel and so on in a social network.

2.2   User Distribution Model

In this section, we first introduce two-tiered caching system illustrated in Fig. 1. As shown in the figure, the physical layer distribution and social network layer distribution of nodes are divided into two layers of social networks according to the social attributes between nodes. Red users belong to social-layer1, blue users belong to social-layer2, black users have two social attributes and belong to a common-layer. Nodes with the same social attributes can communicate with each other, while nodes with different social attributes cannot directly establish D2D links. The nodes that exist in common-layer are the black dots in the figure above, which are also the bridges between the two layers of social networks.

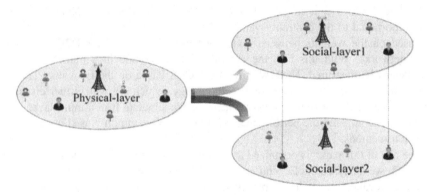

Fig. 1. Example of a multi-layer social network. Red users belong to social-layer1, blue users belong to social-layer2, and black users belong to common-layer at the same time. (Color figure online)

When requesting a file, the user first searches whether other users in the cluster have cached target files. If so, you can directly establish a D2D link between nodes for communication without going through the base station. If not, the user requests the target file from the base station.

2.3   Several Common Calculation Methods of Centrality

This section gives a simple review of the measures of centrality. In [14], four basic centrality calculation methods are introduced. The EC proposed in this paper is mainly combined with the shortest path-based measures of centrality, that is, closeness centrality and betweenness centrality, which will be briefly introduced next.

Closeness Centrality. Closeness centrality was originally proposed by Sabidussi [20] in 1996. The key factor affecting the data transmission volume and speed in the network system is the distance between the data provider and the data requester. Closeness centrality holds that the closer the nodes are, the faster they can reach other nodes.

$$C_i^C = \frac{N-1}{\sum\limits_{j\in N, j\neq i} d_{ij}}. \tag{1}$$

In this expression, $N-1$ represents the number of nodes other than itself in the network, and d represents the distance between two nodes. The closer the distance between the nodes, the greater the calculated centrality value.

Betweenness Centrality. The number of communication paths between any two nodes in the network passes through a certain node, which is expressed as the betweenness centrality value of the node. It emphasizes the importance of nodes when connecting other nodes [21]. The betweenness centrality of a node i can be defined as:

$$C_i^B = \frac{\sum\limits_{\substack{j,k \in N \\ j \neq k; j,k \neq i}} \frac{n_{jk}(i)}{n_{jk}}}{(N-1)(N-2)}. \tag{2}$$

The network assumes that the nodes communicate with each other along the shortest path. The centrality value of the nodes in the network is obtained by accumulating the number of paths through the changed nodes, and the value is divided by $(N-1)(N-2)$ to normalize the process to facilitate comparison of centrality values.

The commonly used measures of centrality in topology diagrams are directed or undirected, weighted or unweighted. However, the social network environment in this paper is D2D communication, which is different from the previous network topology. Under the same layer of network, two nodes are connected to each other, and the nodes of different layers communicate through common nodes. Combined with the characteristics of centrality measure, the EC is proposed in this paper. The EC value of a node is obtained by accumulating the value of closeness centrality between the nodes at the same layer and the betweenness value between nodes across layers. Details of which are shown in 3.1 of Sect. 3.

3 Cache Storage Allocation Based on the Value of Effect Centrality

In this section, we discussed the definition and detailed calculation steps of EC and CSA algorithm in multi-layer social networks.

3.1 Node Importance Metric: Effect Centrality

The EC measure of nodes gives the influential power of the points in a given network. If the centrality of a node is large, it indicates that the node can transmit information to other nodes along a closer path, and can be used more efficiently of the cache space. Social network presents different layers due to its sociability, such as stratification by interest [22]. In D2D communication network, the cache storage of mobile devices is limited. By combining the cache storage size, offline social relations, user interests and hobbies, etc., the size and type of cache contents can be determined by automatically calculating the utility index. In this paper, the social network is divided into different layers according to the types, and an important direction for calculating the nodes with the optimal influence in a given D2D communication network is provided. In this section, we first describe a cache problem in social-aware network. Then a new metric named EC is defined for measuring the value of node importance along the content delivery path by the request.

Now researchers have defined many methods to calculate the central value of a single-layer network based on information such as topology, but the centrality of computing nodes in multi-layer social networks has not been solved yet. In this article, A new centrality measurement method is presented. Compared with other centrality calculation methods, EC is more suitable for computing multi-layer social network scenarios. It is used to measure the importance of nodes in the network and is called "effect centrality", which calculates the node's closeness degree to other nodes in the multi-layer network, because this method takes into account the influence of same-layer nodes and cross-layer nodes.

Weight Value. In [23], when studying channel coding, it is assumed that in a block-fading channel, the fading gain during each symbol block in the codeword remains constant, while it remains a random variable on different blocks. In this paper, inspired by [23], the fading weight value between users is defined as a constant within the same fading gain range, a simulation environment is built under the coverage of a base station (BS), and D2D communication users are distributed under the coverage of a BS according to poisson point process (PPPs). Since D2D is a short-distance communication, the maximum communication distance of D2D users is set to be 30 m, and the adopted D2D path loss model is:

$$PL(dB) = 79 + 40\log(d) + 30\log(f_c). \tag{3}$$

In the above equation, d is the distance between D2D users, f_c is the carrier frequency of the system, which is set as the default value of 3.3GHZ in this paper.

As the distance between nodes increases, the path loss increases, but the weight value between nodes decreases. As shown in Fig. 2, U_1 and U_2 represent users. Calculate the loss value PL_{sum} from U_1 to the communication radius and divide it into 9 equal parts, denoted as PL_{ave}. The distance of each fading PL_{ave}, as shown in $R_1 \sim R_9$, which is correspondingly weighted from near to far 0.9 $\sim$ 0.1. For example, the node whose distance from U_1 is within R_1 has a weight of 0.9, the weight between U_1 and U_2 is 0.6.

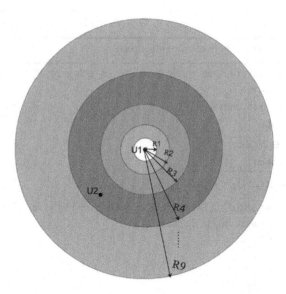

Fig. 2. Schematic diagram of defining weight values according to path loss.

Effect Centrality Algorithm. As far as we know a variety of algorithms have been proposed for finding out the centrality in a single layer social network, our work focused on calculating the centrality value in multi-layer network. The algorithm calculates the centrality level of nodes in D2D social networks. The general formula for closeness centrality is given as follow:

$$C_i^E = \sum_{\substack{j=1 \\ j \neq i}}^{n} W_{ij} \tag{4}$$

Where C_i^E is the EC of node i and $\sum_{\substack{j=1 \\ j \neq i}}^{n} W_{ij}$ is the sum of the weight between nodes.

For a multi-layer social network in this paper, the formula is slightly changed.

In a D2D multi-layer social network, it is assumed that cross-layer nodes cannot communicate with each other directly, they are able to communicate with each other through common nodes. If node j and node i are not in the same layer, an optimal common node k is needed to be a relay between node j and i.

Algorithm 1 Pseudocode of effect centrality algorithm

Input: Coordinate matrix of nodes within the cluster, $N_1 \in layer1, N_2 \in layer2, N_3 \in$
    $common - layer$

Output: Value of effect centrality C_i^E

1: **for** each $i \in N_1$ **do**

2:    **for** each $j \in N_1$ **do**

3:        **if** $j \neq i$ **then**

4:            $d = \sqrt{(i_x - j_y)^2 + (i_y - j_y)^2}$

5:            $w = weight(d)$: (The weight value w is given by the defined weight
            function according to the distance d)

6:            $C_i^1 = C_i^1 + w$

7:        **end if**

8:    **end for**

9:    **for** each $j \in N_3$ **do**

10:        $d = \sqrt{(i_x - j_x)^2 + (i_y - j_y)^2}$

11:        $w = weight(d)$

12:        $C_i^3 = C_i^3 + w$

13:    **end for**

14:    **for** each $j \in N_2$ **do**

15:        **for** each $k \in N_3$ **do**

16:            calculate d_{ik} and d_{jk}, and get w_{ik} and w_{jk}

17:            $w_{ij}(k) = w_{ik} * w_{jk}$

18:        **end for**

19:        $w = \min [w_{ij}]$

20:        $C_i^2 = C_i^2 + w$

21:    **end for**

22:    $C_i^E = \frac{N_1}{N_1+N_2+N_3} * C_i^1 + \frac{N_2}{N_1+N_2+N_3} * C_i^2 + \frac{N_3}{N_1+N_2+N_3} * C_i^3$

23: **end for**

24: **return** C_i^E

25: Similarly, the centrality value of each node in other layers is calculated

---

The formulation for cross layer EC is given as:

$$C_i^E = \gamma \sum_{\substack{j \in N_1 \\ j \neq i}} W_{ij} + \beta \sum_{k \in N_3} W_{ik} + (1 - \gamma - \beta) \sum_{n \in N_2} W_{in}, \tag{5}$$

where C_i^E gives the cross-layer EC value of node i. W_{ij} is the weight of the node i to node j which belongs to social-layer1, W_{ik} is the weight of the node i to node k that belongs to common node, and W_{in} is the weight of the node i to node n that belongs to social-layer2. γ and β is a tuning parameter, which balances the importance of edge within the layer or across the layer. The formulas are as follows:

$$\gamma = \frac{N_1}{N_1 + N_2 + N_3}, \tag{6}$$

$$\beta = \frac{N_3}{N_1 + N_2 + N_3}, \tag{7}$$

$$1 - \gamma - \beta = \frac{N_2}{N_1 + N_2 + N_3}, \tag{8}$$

where N_1 is the number of nodes in the social-layer1, N_2 and N_3 represent the number of nodes in the social-layer2 and the common-layer, respectively.

Algorithm 1 gives the detailed calculation process of EC, which is mainly divided into two steps. First, calculate the weight value between nodes, and then calculate the EC value through the cumulative weight value.

3.2   Cache Storage Allocation Algorithm

In order to allocate users' cache storage more efficiently and reasonably, our goal is to maximize the cache storage utility function. Therefore, we first proposed the CSA algorithm of the basic water-filling algorithm, and then proposed the cache storage utility function of the D2D multi-layer social network, which represents the gain of the cache space used by the node to cache files to the system performance.

Cache Storage Value Function. The cache storage value indicates the system performance that the node can achieve. The optimal CSA that maximizes the cache storage utility function for a multi-layer social networks can be formulated as:

$$\max E_u = \sum_{n=1}^{N} \log(1 + \frac{s_n(c_n)^2}{N_0}), \tag{9}$$

$$s.t. \sum_{n=1}^{N} S_n = S_{sum}, \ n = 1, 2, \ldots, N. \tag{10}$$

Where E_u represents the total cache storage value of the system, N represents the number of nodes that need to be allocated cache storage, S_n represents the cache storage allocated for the n_{th} node, C_n represents the EC value of the n_{th} node, N_0 represents the adjustment parameter, and S_{sum} represents the total cache storage requested by the system.

The optimization problem is a convex optimization problem, and the global optimal solution can be obtained by Lagrange multiplier method.

$$\zeta(\lambda, S_1, S_2, \ldots, S_N) = \sum_{n=1}^{N} \log(1 + \frac{S_n(C_n)^2}{N_0}) + \lambda(\sum_{n=1}^{N} S_n - S_{sum}), \qquad (11)$$

if

$$\frac{\partial \zeta}{\partial S_n} = \frac{\partial \zeta}{\partial \lambda} = 0, \qquad (12)$$

the optimal storage allocation scheme of the solution is:

$$S_n^* = (\frac{1}{\lambda} - \frac{N_0}{|C_n|^2}). \qquad (13)$$

In terms of constraints $\sum_{n=1}^{N} S_n - S_{sum}$, we can get:

$$\lambda = \frac{N}{S_{sum} + \sum_{n=1}^{N} \frac{1}{C_n}}. \qquad (14)$$

Then substitute the calculated value back into Eq. (13), the optimal cache storage allocation is:

$$S_n^* = (\frac{1}{\lambda} - \frac{N_0}{|C_n|^2})^+, \qquad (15)$$

where $(\bullet)^+$ means non-negative.

We observe that the importance of nodes is measured by the EC value in the D2D multi-layer social network. Important nodes are allocated more cache space to achieve higher practical value of cache storage. Less data is sent through the cellular network, thus saving a lot of network communication resources.

4 Simulations

In this section, we provide some numerical results to verify our analysis and compare the performance with other two baselines, which are average allocation and equal proportion allocation. Parameter settings are described in Table 1.

Table 1. Default parameter setting

Parameters	Value
D2D communication range	30(m)
Base station transmission range:	200(m)
The density of node in social-layer1:	0.05
The density of node in social-layer2:	0.01
The density of node in common-layer:	0.005
The total cache storage:	0.1T/0.5T/1T/3T/10T

As shown in the Fig. 3, the social-layer1 nodes, social-layer2 and common-layer nodes, nodes are spatially distributed according to three mutually independent homogeneous PPPs with density λ_1, λ_2 and λ_3, respectively.

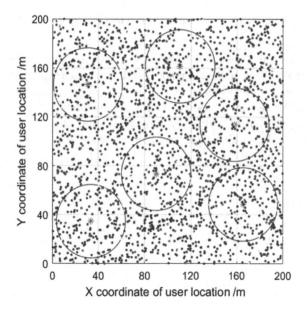

Fig. 3. Node distribution diagram. (Color figure online)

The points in Fig. 3 are the location of user's devices. There are three colored points, namely blue, red and yellow. The blue points represent the nodes in social-layer1, the yellow points represent the nodes in social-layer2, and the red points represent the common nodes in the system.

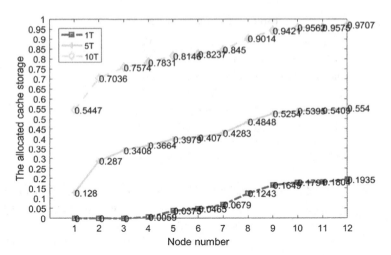

Fig. 4. The cache storage allocation results obtained by CSA algorithm. (Color figure online)

Figure 4 shows the CSA results using the CSA algorithm under different total cache spaces. The blue line at the top represents the total cache space of 10T. the green line represents the total cache storage of 5T, and the red line represents the total cache storage of 1T. Through the proposed allocation algorithm, each node is allocated according to the size of its EC value. The three curves show the same trend. The larger the EC value is, the larger allocated cache storage is, and vice versa.

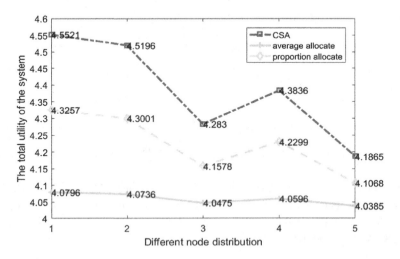

Fig. 5. Cache storage utility values obtained by three allocation algorithms. (Color figure online)

In this section, allocation algorithm numerical results are presented to verify our analysis and performance comparisons among the proposed allocation algorithm with average allocation and proportion allocation. As shown in Fig. 5, three curves represent the cache storage utility value obtained by different algorithms. The blue line represents the value allocated by CSA algorithm, the value on the red line in the middle represents the value allocated by proportion allocation, and the green line below represents the average allocation. The five points on each curve represent five different system node distributions. It can be seen from the figure that CSA algorithm outperforms two other existing methods. The cache storage utility value of CSA algorithm is about 11% higher than that of average allocation and 7% higher than that of proportional allocation.

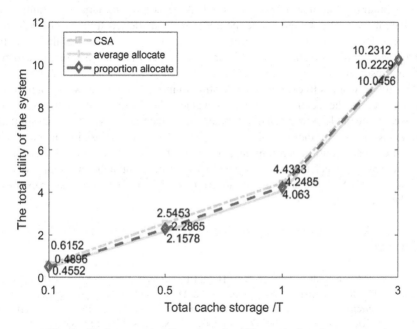

Fig. 6. Cache storage utility values for different total cache storage.

Figure 6 shows the performance implementation and comparisons of the proposed allocation algorithm. The graph shows the cache storage utility value function curves of the three allocation methods under the condition of the same user distribution and different total cache storage, the x-axis indicates that the total cache storage is 0.1T, 0.5T, 1T and 3T from left to right. In addition, we see that when the curve is at the positions of 0.1T and 3T, the cache storage utility value functions achieved by the three distribution methods are relatively close, while the curve is at the position of 0.5T and 1T, the three cache storage utility value are quite different. When the cache storage is moderate, our proposed algorithm achieved improved performance compared with the other two methods; on the contrary, the performance gain is correspondingly small. The CSA proposed in this paper allocates cache storage based on the EC value of the node. The higher the EC value, the more important the node is in the network and the closer it is to other nodes. Compared with the two basic allocation algorithms of average allocation and proportional allocation, CSA can allocate more cache storage to important nodes to achieve higher system performance.

5   Conclusion

In this paper, we first propose a new method to calculate the importance of nodes, named EC. In addition, an optimal CSA approach is proposed to optimize the performance of D2D multi-layer social network. Specifically, the CSA problem for the social network is formulated as a difference of convex (DC) problem and solved by the DC programming. Simulation results show that the nodes with larger centrality value will share more cache storage, while the nodes with smaller centrality value will share less space. By exploiting CSA algorithm for allocation, numerical results show that cache storage utility functions are 11% and 7% higher than that of average and proportional respectively.

Our future work is to extend this algorithm to more complex networks, not only to take into account the location of the node consider other factors in the network, such as the size of the node's own cache storage, the remaining power and the similarity between users, etc. Another line of investigation is the joint optimization of cooperation between clusters, multi-hop communication and scheduling techniques. In the case of mobility, smarter mechanisms are needed to balance computational complexity and content sharing. Also, we are planning to keep our aim to other structural properties of multi-layer networks.

References

1. San Jose: Mobile Video Delivery With Hybrid ICN, Cisco, CA, USA, pp. 1–14 (2017)
2. Lin, Z., Du, X., Chen, H., Ai, B., Chen, Z., Wu, D.: Millimeter-wave propagation modeling and measurements for 5G mobile networks. IEEE Wirel. Commun. **26**(1), 72–77 (2019)
3. Chen, P., Xie, Z., Fang, Y., Chen, Z., Mumtaz, S., Rodrigues, J.P.C.: Physical-layer network coding: an efficient technique for wireless communications. IEEE Netw. **34**(2), 270–276 (2020)
4. Ding, Q., Pang, H., Sun, L.: SAM: cache space allocation in collaborative edge-caching network. In: IEEE International Conference on Communications (ICC), pp. 1–6. IEEE, Paris (2017)
5. Perino, D., Varvello, M.: A reality check for content centric networking. In: ACM SIGCOMM Workshop Information-Centric Networking, pp. 44–49. Association for Computing Machinery, Toronto (2011)
6. Zhang, M., Chen, X., Zhang, J.: Social-aware relay selection for cooperative networking: an optimal stopping approach. In: IEEE International Conference on Communications (ICC), pp. 2257–2262. IEEE, Sydney (2014)
7. Wang, L., Wu, H., Wang, W., Chen, K.: Socially enabled wireless networks: resource allocation via bipartite graph matching. IEEE Commun. Maga. **53**(10), 128–135 (2015)

8. Ma, C., Lin, Z., Marini, L., Li, J., Vucetic, B.: Learning automaton based distributed caching for mobile social networks. In: IEEE Wireless Communications and Networking Conference, pp. 1–6. IEEE, Doha (2016)
9. Zhu, K., Zhi, W., Zhang, L., Chen, X., Fu, X.: Social-aware incentivized caching for D2D communications. IEEE Access **4**, 7585–7593 (2016)
10. Zhang, Y., Song, L., Saad, W., Dawy, Z., Han, Z.: Exploring social ties for enhanced device-to-device communications in wireless networks. In: IEEE Global Communications Conference (GLOBECOM), pp. 4597–4602. IEEE, Atlanta (2013)
11. Baştuğ, E., Bennis, M., Debbah, M.: Social and spatial proactive caching for mobile data offloading. In: IEEE International Conference on Communications Workshops (ICC), pp. 581–586. IEEE, Sydney (2014)
12. Yen, C., Chien, F., Chang, M.: Cooperative online caching in small cell networks with limited cache size and unknown content popularity. In: 3rd International Conference on Computer and Communication Systems (ICCCS), pp. 173–177. IEEE, Nagoya (2018)
13. Cui, X., Liu, J., Huang, T., Chen, J., Liu, Y.: A novel metric for cache size allocation scheme in content centric networking. In: National Doctoral Academic Forum on Information and Communications Technology 2013, pp. 1–6. IEEE, Beijing (2013)
14. Song, Z., Duan, H., Ge, Y., Qiu, X.: A novel measure of centrality based on betweenness. In: Chinese Automation Congress (CAC), pp. 174–178. IEEE, Wuhan (2015)
15. Zhang, K., Li, H., Qin, L., Wu, M.: Closeness centrality on BBS reply network. In: International Conference of Information Technology, Computer Engineering and Management Sciences, pp. 80–82. ITM, Nanjing (2011)
16. Niu, J., Fan, J., Wang, L. Stojinenovic, M.: K-hop centrality metric for identifying influential spreaders in dynamic large-scale social networks. In: IEEE Global Communications Conference, pp. 2954–2959. IEEE, Austin (2014)
17. Bader, D.A., Madduri, K.: Parallel algorithms for evaluating centrality indices in real-world networks. In: International Conference on Parallel Processing (ICPP'06), pp. 539–550. ACM, Columbus (2006)
18. Li, Y., Wu, T., Hui, P., Jin, D., Chen, S.: Social-aware D2D communications: qualitative insights and quantitative analysis. IEEE Commun. Mag. **52**(6), 150–158 (2006)
19. Rao, J., Feng, H., Yang, C., Chen, Z., Xia, B.: Optimal caching placement for D2D assisted wireless caching networks. In: IEEE International Conference on Communications (ICC), pp. 1–6. IEEE, Kuala (2016)
20. Sabidussi, G.: The centrality index of a graph. Psychometrika **31**(4), 581–603 (1966)
21. Freeman, L.C.: A set of measures of centrality based on betweenness. Sociometry **40**(1), 35–41 (1977)
22. Mittal, R., Bhatia, M.P.S.: Analyzing the structures of clusters in multi-layer biological networks. In: First International Conference on Secure Cyber Computing and Communication (ICSCCC), pp. 502–507. IEEE, Jalandhar (2018)
23. Fang, Y., Chen, P., Cai, G., Lau, F.C.M., Liew, S.C., Han, G.: Outage-limit-approaching channel coding for future wireless communications: root-protograph low-density parity-check codes. IEEE Veh. Technol. Mag. **14**(2), 85–93 (2019)

Enhanced Frame Break Mechanism for ALOHA-Based RFID Anti-Collision Algorithm

Xiangjian Zeng, Jiyun Qiu, Xijun Wang, and Xiang Chen[✉]

School of Electronics and Information Technology, Sun Yat-sen University,
Guangzhou 510006, China
153600351@qq.com, 764636216@qq.com, wangxijun@mail.sysu.edu.cn,
chenxiang@mail.sysu.edu.cn

Abstract. Radio frequency identification (RFID) technology is a kind of non-contact identification technology, which has been widely applied in logistics management, access control system and other fields. However, when multiple tags response the RFID reader simultaneously, the superposition of signals will deduce reader's incorrect reception, which is called collision. Dynamic frame slotted ALOHA (DFSA) algorithm is a effective anti-collision algorithm in RFID system, but its' high system efficiency relies on the reliability of the tags' number estimation. Some researches propose a frame break policy for ALOHA-based RFID system, which breaks the frame early when judging that the current frame length is not appropriate through slot-by-slot estimation of number of tags and is called SbS-DFSA. Here, we find some improvement space of SbS-DFSA, and make it more efficient by modifying some details. The simulation shows that our modification is efficient and improves the performance practically.

Keywords: Radio frequency identification technology · Anti-collision algorithm · Dynamic frame slotted ALOHA · Frame break

1 Introduction

Radio frequency identification (RFID) is a technology that uses radio frequency signal to automatically identify target objects and obtain relevant information.

This work was supported in part by the Guangdong Provincial Special Fund For Modern Agriculture Industry Technology Innovation Teams under Grant 2020KJ122, in part by the Collaborative Education Project of Industry University Cooperation (No.201802016050), in part by the State's Key Project of Research and Development Plan under Grants 2019YFE0196400, in part by the NSFC under Grant 61771495, and in part by the Guangdong R&D Project in Key Areas under Grant 2019B010158001.

B. Li et al. (Eds.): IoTaaS 2020, LNICST 346, pp. 222–233, 2021.
https://doi.org/10.1007/978-3-030-67514-1_18

As a key technology to build the Internet of things (IoT), RFID has been widely used in transportation, manufacturing, security and other fields. In recent years, More and more industries have used this technology to improve logistics efficiency and service level.

The implementation of RFID system consists of two hardware entities (reader and tag) and corresponding software. Reader is a active device, responsible for reading and writing the data stored in tag, and powering the passive tag. Passive tag needn't battery and gets energy through the wireless signal transferred by reader. With the advantage of small size and low cost, passive tag is used more widely than active tag, which need independent battery.

In a typical environment with one reader and multiple passive tags, the reader send wireless signal, multiple tags are energized and backscatter their modulation signal to the reader simultaneously, and then collision occurs, as the Fig. 1 shows. This means we have to design specific algorithm and mechanism to identify the each tags respectively.

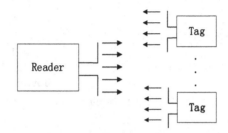

Fig. 1. Typical RFID system with passive tag

An-collision problem is not unique to RFID system and widely exists in the system which need to support access of multi-target through a common channel. In the field of RFID, time division scheme is relatively more appropriate because of its low-complexity in hardware, which is important for tag, especially passive tag.

The anti-collision algorithm in RFID system can be divided into two main branches: tree algorithm and ALOHA-based algorithm.

Tree algorithm essentially create a binary-tree structure to divide tags into different time slots for transmission, related algorithms include Binary Tree Splitting [1], Adaptive Binary Tree Spliting [2,3], Query Tree [4], Binary Search [5] and Bitwise Arbitration [7–9].

ALOHA-based algorithm is based on a scheme that when the collision occurs, tags that participate in the transmission will set a delay time, within which they can't transmission again. Based on this mechanism, Slotted ALOHA [10] and Static Frame Slotted Frame ALOHA [11] are proposed. Slotted ALOHA limits tags' transmission in a time slot with boundary and avoid the partially collision. Frame Slotted ALOHA specifies that a frame consists of multiple time slots and each tag can only transmission once in a frame. It can be proved mathematically that in Frame Slotted ALOHA, the maximum throughput is reached when the number of tag is equal to the frame length (the number of time slots in a frame) [12,13]. Static Frame Slotted ALOHA set a fixed frame length, while Dynamic Slotted ALOHA [5] estimates the number of tags in the end time slots of each frame, and set the next frame length to the estimated number of unidentified tags to achieve better performance.

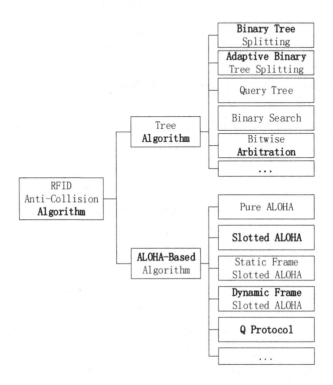

Fig. 2. RFID anti-collision algorithms

Further, some researchers propose slot-by-slot estimations of number of tags, which break the limit that estimation is only made in the end of a frame. This make it possible for reader to break the frame early when the frame length is far from the result of slot-by-slot estimation.

Based on these slot-by-slot estimation methods, a frame break policy for ALOHA-based algorithm [6] was proposed, which is called SbS-DFSA. However, In this paper, we find some irrationalities of SbS-DFSA. To fix the problem, we propose the correction and improvement scheme for SbS-DFSA and call it Enhanced-SbS-DFSA. Simulation results show that Enhanced-SbS-DFSA surpasses the performance of SbS-DFSA shown in [6].

This paper is organized as follows. In section two, we give a brief introduction of DFSA and SbS-DFSA. In section three we point out the defects of SbS-DFSA and propose our Enhanced-SbS-DFSA. In section four we show the simulation results and section five is conclusion part.

2   Related and Basic Work

2.1   DFSA Algorithm

In Frame Slotted ALOHA, the reader can divide the time slots into three types— empty time slot, successful time slot and collision time slot, with none, one and more than one tags response to the reader respectively. Here we use L to stand for the frame length, and use E, S, C to stand for the number of empty time slots, successful time slots and collision time slots in a frame respectively. Universally, the estimation algorithms in DFSA use L, C, S, E to estimate number of tags.

Vogt [12,13] is a high-accuracy estimation method in DFSA, which is based on the minimum mean square error criterion. The formula for Volt estimation is show in (1), where $a_t^{L,k}$ is the expected number of time slots that t tags response to reader when frame length is L and number of tags is k. Note that here we set the search range to 1 to 10L, which avoid the unreasonal estimation result in the case $C = L$ [14]. However, one disadvantage of Volt algorithm is that it needs to use some iterative or traversing method to solve this optimization problem, so that its calculation cost is very high, which induces high requirements to the hardware and software of reader.

$$V olt\_Estimation(L, E, S, C) = \arg \min_{k \in (1, 10L)} \left\| \begin{pmatrix} a_0^{L,k} \\ a_1^{L,k} \\ a_{\geq 2}^{L,k} \end{pmatrix} - \begin{pmatrix} E \\ S \\ C \end{pmatrix} \right\|^2$$

$$a_t^{L,k} = L \binom{k}{t} \left(\frac{1}{L} \right)^t \left(1 - \frac{1}{L} \right)^{k-t}, a_{\geq 2}^{L,k} = L - a_0^{L,k} - a_1^{L,k} \tag{1}$$

Estimation method based on maximum likelihood criterion [15] is shown in (2), where $N(k, S)$ is number of ways to distribute k tags to S slots and $N(k - S, C)$ is number of ways to distribute k-S tags to C slots. Similarly, the calculation cost is very high too. To reduce the calculation cost at the price of decreasing estimation accuracy, it is simplified to formula (3), which is called improved linearized combinatorial model (ILCM) [16].

$$Maximum\_Likelihood\_Estimation(L, E, S, C)$$
$$= \arg \max_k P(E, S, C \mid k, L)$$
$$= \arg \max_k \frac{N(k - S, C)N(k, S)}{L^k} \frac{L!}{E!S!C!} \tag{2}$$

$$k = max\{\frac{C}{\left(\frac{L}{-2.282-0.273L}\right)C + (4.344L - 16.28)} + 0.2407\ln(42.56 + L), 0\}$$

$$l = (1.2592 + 1.513L)\tan(1.234L^{-0.9907}C)$$

$$ILCM\_Estimation(L, E, S, C) = kS + l \text{ when } c \neq 0, \ S \text{ when } c = 0 \quad (3)$$

It should be emphasized that frame length should be limited to integer power of 2. Therefore if the estimation number of identified tags is x, we should set the next frame length to f(x) and function f is defined in (4). Compared to the scheme without limit to frame length, this reduces hardware requirements for tag, which is important for passive tag. This limit has been adopted by EPC RFID G2 UHF protocol [18].

$$f(x) = 2^{round(log_2(max(1,x)))} \quad (4)$$

2.2   SbS-DFSA Algorithm

We define system efficiency as the number of tags divided by the number of time slots costed during the identified process, as showed in (5), which is the main index used to measure the performance of RFID anti-collision algorithm.

$$System \ efficiency = \frac{Number \ of \ tags}{Number \ of \ time \ slots \ costed} \quad (5)$$

The maximum system efficiency of DFSA is almost 0.368 [17], but it is hard to reach because the estimation error of number of tags. Especially, when the estimation result is far from the real value, the large estimation error can't be revised until the end of this frame, which seriously affect the system efficiency. Fortunately, several slot-by-slot estimation methods were proposed, such as SbS-Volt [19] whose formula is shown in (6) and SbS-ILCM [6] whose formula is shown in (7). Here, i is index of time slot, whose range is 1 to L. Definition of e,s,c are similarly to E,S,C, but they are only counted within time slot 1 to time slot i.

$$a_{t,i}^{L,k} = i\binom{k}{t}\left(\frac{1}{L}\right)^t\left(1 - \frac{1}{L}\right)^{k-t}, a_{\geq 2,i}^{L,k} = L - a_{0,i}^{L,k} - a_{1,i}^{L,k}$$

$$SbS\_Volt\_Estimation(L, i, E, S, C) = \arg\min_{k\in(1,10L)}\left\|\begin{pmatrix}a_{0,i}^{L,k}\\a_{1,i}^{L,k}\\a_{\geq 2,i}^{L,k}\end{pmatrix} - \begin{pmatrix}E\\S\\C\end{pmatrix}\right\|^2 \quad (6)$$

$$k'(i) = max\{\frac{c}{\left(\frac{i}{-2.282-0.273i}\right)c + (4.344i - 16.28)} + 0.2407\ln(42.56 + i), 0\}$$

$$l'(i) = (1.2592 + 1.513i)\tan(1.234i^{-0.9907}c)$$

$$SbS\_ILCM\_Estimation(L, i, e, s, c) = k'(i)s + l'(i) \text{ when } c \neq 0, \frac{SL}{i}\text{when } c = 0$$

$$(7)$$

Based on these slot-by-slot estimation methods, a mechanism that the frame is stopped early when slot-by-slot estimation value is far from the frame length is proposed [6], which is called SbS-DFSA. The complete pseudocode of SbS-DFSA using SbS-ILCM estimation is shown in algorithm 1. SbS-DFSA can also be combined with other slot-by-slot estimation methods by modifying row 2 of algorithm 1. For example, if we change algorithm 1 row 2 to '$R(i) = max(1, SbS\_Volt\_Estimation(L, i, e, s, c))$', this algorithm will become SbS-DFSA using SbS-Volt estimation. Note that in SbS-DFSA using SbS-Volt estimation, $SbS\_Volt\_Estimation(L, i, e, s, c) = \frac{2.39cL}{i}$ when $c = i$, which we doesn't adopt in Enhanced-SbS-DFSA using SbS-Volt estimation.

Algorithm 1: SbS-DFSA with SbS-ILCM

1: **while** Reader is working **do**
2:    $R(i) = max(1, SbS\_ILCM\_Estimation(L, i, e, s, c))$
3:    $R_Q(i) = f(R(i))$
4:    **if** $(i > 1)$ *and* $(|R(i) - R(i-1)| \leq 1)$ **then**
5:       $P_1 = \frac{R(i)}{L}(1 - \frac{1}{L})^{R(i)-1}$
6:       $P_2 = \frac{R(i)}{R_Q(i)}(1 - \frac{1}{R_Q(i)})^{R(i)-1}$
7:       **if** $(LP_1 - s) < (R_Q(i)P_2)$ **then**
8:          $R_Q(i) = f(R(i))$
9:          $i = 1$ *and start a new frame with* $L = RQ(i)$
10:       **else**
11:          $i = i + 1$
12:       **end if**
13:    **else**
14:       $i = i + 1$
15:    **end if**
16:    **if** $i == (L + 1)$ **then**
17:       $i = 1$ *and start a new frame with old* L
18:    **end if**
19:    *Send message to tags*
20:    *Update* e, s, c
21: **end while**

---

3   Enhanced-SbS-DFSA Algorithm

3.1   Defects of SbS-DFSA

Although paper [6] claimed that SbS-DFSA shows better performance than traditional DFSA accordingly to simulation results, it is easy for us to find following unreasonable places in SbS-DFSA.

First, the judging rule of convergence is unreasonable, which we can see in algorithm 1 row 12. Specifically, the judging rule of convergence in SbS-DFSA is that the difference between estimation value of this time slot and that of last time slot is less than or equal to one. Typical convergence cases of slot-by-slot estimation are shown in Fig. 3 and obviously the judging rule of convergence in SbS-DFSA can't recognize them easily.

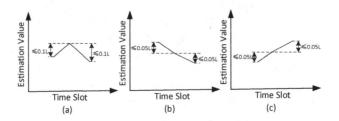

Fig. 3. Typical convergence cases of slot-by-slot estimation

Second, the judging rule of frame break at convergence is unreasonable, which we can see in algorithm 1 row 15, where P_1 is the probability that a time slot is a successful time slot in this frame and P_2 is the probability that a time slot is a successful time slot in next frame whose length is denoted by slot-by-slot estimation, under the assumption that the estimation value is equal to the real value. Therefore, $LP_1 - s$ is the expected number of tags identified successfully in remaining time slots of this frame and $R_Q(i)P_2$ is the expected number of tags identified successfully in next frame. Obviously, the judging rule of frame break that $LP_1 - s$ is lower than $R_Q(i)P_2$ is not intuitively proper.

Third, when number of time slots is small, information reader gets is not enough to give a accurate estimation, which may induce a unreasonal frame break in SbS-DFSA.

Forth, when reader decide to break the frame, if new frame length is equal to the old one, this frame break is meaningless.

Fifth, when the estimation value doesn't converge during the whole frame, SbS-DFSA set next frame length equal to the prior one, which may maintain a improper frame length for many frames.

3.2   Enhanced-SbS DFSA Algorithm

To overcome the deficiencies of SbS-DFSA we mentioned before, we propose several improvements for it and call the new method Enhanced-SbS-DFSA. The complete pseudocode of Enhanced-SbS-DFSA using SbS-ILCM estimation is shown in algorithm 2. Enhanced-SbS-DFSA can also be combined with other slot-by-slot estimation methods by modifying row 3, row 3 and row 28 of algorithm 1. For example, if change row 3, row 7 and row 28 of algorithm 1 to '$R(i) = max(1, SbS\_Volt\_Estimation(L, i, e, s, c) - s)$', this algorithm will become Enhanced-SbS-DFSA using SbS-Volt estimation.

First, change the judging rule of convergence. $R(i-2)$, $R(i-1)$ and $R(i)$ represent the slot-by-slot estimation value of time slot i-2, i-1 and i respectively, while $R_Q(i)$ stands for $f(R(i))$. To deal with the situation like cases shown in Fig. 3, we design a judging rule of convergence shown in algorithm 2 row 9 to row 15. Compared to SbS-DFSA, it uses information of three time slots (SbS-DFSA only uses information of two time slots), sets the convergence threshold dynamically according to the frame length, and propose a scheme to recognize the slight fluctuation of slot-by-slot estimation value shown in (a) of Fig. 3.

Second, change judging rule of frame break at convergence. For Enhanced-SbS-DFSA combined with SbS-ILCM, when estimation value converges, the reader stops the frame early if LP_1 is lower than $R_Q(i)P_2$, which is an empirical conclusion and can be seen in algorithm 2 row 19.

Third, set a start point for slot-by-slot estimation. The start point can be set by setting the value of M in algorithm 2 row 6. For Enhanced-SbS-DFSA using SbS-ILCM estimation M takes 3, while for Enhanced-SbS-DFSA using SbS-Volt estimation M takes 8.

Forth, Enhanced-SbS-DFSA won't break a frame with a new frame length that is equal to the old one, while SbS-DFSA will. This mechanism is integrated into the judging rule of convergence of Enhanced-SbS-DFSA.

Fifth, when the estimation value doesn't converge during the whole frame, Enhanced-SbS-DFSA will set next frame length to the last estimation value. Compared to SbS-DFSA which doesn't change frame length in such a situation, Enhanced-SbS-DFSA ensures that improper frame length won't be maintained for many frames when estimation value doesn't converge. This mechanism can be seen in algorithm 2 row 3 to row 5.

Algorithm 2: Enhanced-SbS-DFSA with SbS-ILCM

1: **while** Reader is working **do**
2:    **if** $i == L$ **then**
3:       $R(i) = max(1, SbS\_ILCM\_Estimation(L, i, e, s, c))$
4:       $R_Q(i) = f(R(i))$
5:       $i = 1$ *and start a new frame* $(L = R_Q(i))$
6:    **else if** $i > M$ **then**
7:       $R(i) = SbS\_ILCM\_Estimation(L, i, e, s, c)$
8:       $R_Q(i) = f(R(i))$
9:       **if** $(R_Q(i) \neq L)$ *and* $(|R(i) - R(i-1)| \leq max(1, 0.1L))$ *and* $(|R(i-1) - R(i-2)| \leq max(1, 0.1L))$ *and* $(((R(i) \geq R(i-1))$ *and* $(R(i-1) \leq R(i-2)))$ *or* $((R(i) \leq R(i-1))$ *and* $(R(i-1) \geq R(i-2))))$ **then**
10:          $FLAG = 1$
11:       **else if** $(R_Q(i) \neq L)$ *and* $(|R(i) - R(i-1)| \leq max(1, 0.05L))$ *and* $(|R(i) - R(i-1)| \leq max(1, 0.05L))$ **then**
12:          $FLAG = 2$
13:       **else**
14:          $FLAG = 0;$
15:       **end if**
16:       **if** $(FLAG == 1)$ *or* $(FLAG == 2)$ **then**
17:          $P_1 = (R(i)/L)(1 - 1/L)^{R(i)-1}$
18:          $P_2 = \frac{R(i)}{R_Q(i)}(1 - \frac{1}{R_Q(i)})^{R(i)-1}$
19:          **if** $LP_1 < RQ(i)P_2$ **then**
20:             $i = 1$ *and start a new frame* $L = R_Q(i-1)$
21:          **else**
22:             $i = i + 1$
23:          **end if**
24:       **else**
25:          $i = i + 1$
26:       **end if**
27:    **else**
28:       $R(i) = SbS\_ILCM\_Estimation(L, i, e, s, c)$
29:       $i = i + 1$
30:    **end if**
31:    *Send message to tags*
32:    *Update* e, s, c
33: **end while**

---

4   Simulation Results

The relationship curve of system efficiency versus number of tags is influenced by initial frame length. Specifically, the peak of system efficiency will appear at the place where the number of tags is equal to the initial frame length. We set initial frame length to 2^4 and get the simulation results of DFSA with ILCM estimation, DFSA with Volt estimation, SbS-DFSA with SbS-ILCM estimation, SbS-DFSA with SbS-Volt estimation, Enhanced-SbS-DFSA with SbS-ILCM estimation, Enhanced-SbS-DFSA with SbS-Volt estimation and DFSA with ideal estimation. Here, we use function 'fminbnd' of MATLAB R2014a to solve the optimization problems in Volt and SbS-Volt estimation. DFSA with ideal estimation assumes that estimation value is equal to real value, which is impossible in realistic. Note that owing to the limit to frame length to integer power of 2, the system efficiency can not reach 0.368 even if we assume the estimation is deal, as Fig. 4 shows.

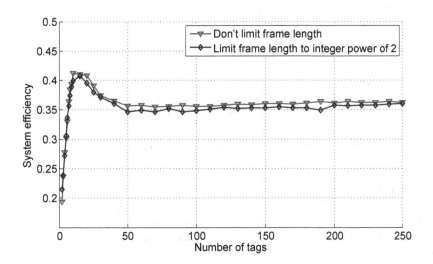

Fig. 4. Performance of DFSA with ideal estimation

The simulation results with the initial frame of 2^4 is shown in Fig. 5. In order to make the performances of different algorithms more differentiated, here we give relationship curve of number of time slots costed versus number of tags, which can be equivalent to relationship curve of system efficiency versus number of tags. From the simulation results we can know Enhanced-SbS-DFSA shows better performance in system efficiency than DFSA, and shows higher system efficiency than SbS-DFSA whether the estimation algorithm used is SbS-Volt or SbS-ILCM. Under the limit that frame length must be integer power of two, Enhanced-SbS-DFSA almost achieves the performance of DFSA with ideal estimation in system efficiency.

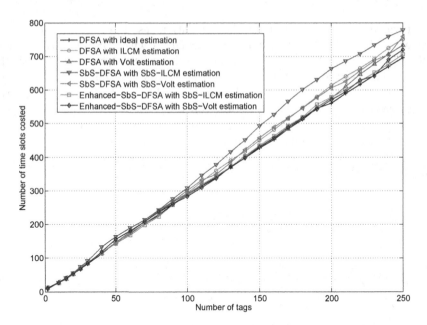

Fig. 5. Simulation results when initial frame length is 16

5   Conclusions

In this paper, focus on the field of RFID anti-collision algorithm, we find several defects of SbS-DFSA and propose some improvements in the aspects of judging rule of convergence, judging rule of frame break at convergence and so on. Simulation results show that our algorithm achieve higher system efficiency than DFSA and SbS-DFSA, no matter we use Volt, SbS-Volt, ILCM, SbS-ILCM as our estimation method. Under the limit to frame length adopted by EPC RFID G2 UHF protocol, in aspect of system efficiency our algorithm almost achieves the performance of DFSA with ideal estimation, which is highly meaningful and proves its application value.

References

1. Hush, D.R., Wood, C.: Analysis of tree algorithms for RFID arbitration. In: The IEEE International Symposium on Information Theory, Mexico City, USA, p. 107 (1998)
2. Myung, J., Lee, W.: Adaptive binary splitting: a RFID tag collision arbitration protocol for tag identification. In: IEEE BROADNETs, Boston, MA, USA, pp. 347–355 (2005)
3. Myung, J., Lee, W., Srivastava, J.: Adaptive binary splitting for efficient RFID tag anti-collision. IEEE Pers. Commun. 10(3), 144–146 (2006)

4. Law, C., Lee, K., Siu, K.-Y.: Efficient memoryless protocol for tag identification (extended abstract). In: Proceedings of the 4th International Workshop on Discrete Algorithms and Methods for Mobile Computing and Communications, Toronto, CA, pp. 75–84 (2000)

5. Finkenzeller, K.: RFID Handbook: Fundamentals and Applications in Contactless Smart Cards and Identification, 2nd edn. John Wiley and Sons Ltd., Hoboken (2003)

6. Solic, P., Radic, J., Rozic, N.: Early frame break policy for ALOHA-based RFID systems. IEEE Trans. Autom. Sci. Eng. **13**(2), 1–6 (2015)

7. Bo, F., Jin-Tao, L., Jun-Bo, G., Zhen-Hua, D.: ID-binary tree stack anticollision algorithm for RFID. In: Proceedings of 11th IEEE Symposium on Computers and Communications, Sardinia, Italy, pp. 207–212 (2006)

8. Jacomet, M., Ehrsam, A., Gehrig, U.: Contact-less identification device with anticollision algorithm. In: Conference on Circuits Systems, Computers and Communications, Athens, Greece (1999)

9. Kim, S.H., Shin, M.K., Park P.: A new tree-based tag anticollision protocol for RFID systems. In: International Conference on Communications in Computing, Nevada, pp. 83–86 (2006)

10. Schwartz, M.: Telecommunication Networks Protocols, Modeling and Analysis. Addison-Wesley, Boston (1988)

11. Zhen, B., Kobayashi, M., Shimizu, M.: Framed ALOHA for multiple RFID objects identification. IEICE-Trans. Commun. **E88–B**, 991–999 (2005)

12. Vogt, H.: Multiple object identification with passive RFID tags. In: The IEEE International Conference on Systems, Man and Cybernetics, Tunisia, pp. 6–13 (2002)

13. Vogt, H.: Efficient object identification with passive RFID tags. In: IEEE PerCom, TX, USA (2002)

14. Knerr, B., Holzer, M., Angerer, C., Rupp, M.: Slot-wise maximum likelihood estimation of the tag population size in FSA protocols. IEEE Trans. Commun. **58**(2), 578–585 (2010)

15. Šolić, P., Radić, J., Rožić, N.: Algorithm for deriving optimal frame size in passive RFID UHF class1-gen2 standard using combinatorial model boundaries. AUTOMATIKA **51**, 255–263 (2010)

16. Solic, P., et al.: Improved linearized combinatorial model (ILCM) for optimal frame size selection in ALOHA-based RFID systems radio. In: Proceedings of the IEEE International Conference on Communications Workshops (ICC), Budapest, Hungary, pp. 1092–1097 (2013)

17. Chen, W.-T.: An accurate tag estimate method for improving the performance of an RFID anticollision algorithm based on dynamic frame length ALOHA. IEEE Trans. Autom. Sci. Eng. **6**(1), 9–15 (2009)

18. EPCglobalInc.: EPC Radio-Frequency Identity Protocols Generation-2 UHF RFID. EPCglobal (2015)

19. Knerr, B., Holzer, M., Angerer, C., Rupp, M.: Slot-wise maximum likelihood estimation of the tag population size in FSA protocols. IEEE Trans. Commun. **58**(2), 578–585 (2010)

Improved Intelligent Semantics Based Chinese Sentence Similarity Computing for Natural Language Processing in IoT

Jiahao Ye[3], Lin Zhang[3], Ping Lan[1], Hua He[2], Dan Yang[2,4], and Zhiqiang Wu[1,2(✉)]

[1] College of Engineering, Tibet University, Lhasa 850000, China
`lightnesstibet@163.com`
[2] Center of Tibetan Studies (Everest Research Institute), Tibet University, Lhasa 850000, China
[3] School of Electronics and Information Technology, Sun Yat-sen University, Guangzhou 510006, China
[4] Beijing Foreign Studies University, Beijing 10089, China

Abstract. It is desired in the Internet of Things (IoT) networks to apply natural language processing (NLP) technology to complete the information exchange tasks such as text summary or text classification between IoT devices. To achieve higher precision for the NLP of Chinese sentences, in this paper, we propose to utilize the deep neural network (DNN) to compute the semantic similarity of Chinese sentences. The proposed DNN consists of the input layer, the semantic generation layer, the concat layer, the dropout layer, the hidden layer, and the output layer. We propose to train the intelligent semantic similarity calculator sequentially to extract the semantic feature and the context information feature. After the offline training, the resultant configured intelligent semantic similarity calculator could evaluate the semantic similarity of Chinese sentences. Furthermore, we provide numerical analysis to demonstrate the improved similarity calculation precision and the consistency of the calculation accuracy in different fields.

Keywords: Similarity computing · Chinese sentences · Deep neural network · Semantics

1 Introduction

Along with the increasing demands of Internet of things (IoT) devices for extracting the feature from the texts, the sentence similarity calculation technology has been widely applied in natural language processing (NLP). With the aid of the sentence similarity evaluation, IoT devices could provide information retrieval in search engines [10], generate the web page text summary [3], and implement the text classification [5], etc.

© ICST Institute for Computer Sciences, Social Informatics and Telecommunications Engineering 2021
Published by Springer Nature Switzerland AG 2021. All Rights Reserved
B. Li et al. (Eds.): IoTaaS 2020, LNICST 346, pp. 234–246, 2021.
https://doi.org/10.1007/978-3-030-67514-1_19

According to the classification strategy of data sources, the scheme of text similarity can be divided into two categories: (1) the calculation scheme based on the knowledge base; and (2) the calculation scheme based on the neural network. On the one hand, the similarity calculation based on the knowledge base, such as the ontology database [12], can quantify the semantic similarity between words by evaluating the shortest phrase semantic distance of words in the tree knowledge base, the shallowest common parent node depth, and the node density. Then the preliminary sentence similarity could be calculated with the weighted sum of word similarity since all sentences are composed of words. Subsequently, the sentence similarity could be evaluated with the consideration of the length, grammar, and location of words to achieve semantic disambiguation [12]. On the other hand, the similarity calculation scheme based on the neural network uses the neural network to learn and extract the context information features of the data set to generate the distribution probability of word semantics. This kind of intelligent similarity calculation method uses the context information in the comparison sentences to judge the specific semantics of words in the sentences and quantify the similarity of words. In [1], the authors propose to calculate the similarity of sentences via a weighted average of the word vectors to obtain the sentences vector, and the singular value decomposition is applied to remove the irrelevant singular value to achieve higher accuracy of similarity calculation.

The first method has the advantage of being capable of providing consistent calculation accuracy in different fields. However, the ontology knowledge base might not be renewed in time, thereby leading to lower similarity calculation accuracy. By contrast, the second method provides higher calculation accuracy, but it has the disadvantage of inconsistent calculation accuracy in different fields.

Against this background, in this paper, we propose to utilize the preliminary semantic similarity calculation results as the data set for further evaluation with the deep neural network which consists of the input layer, the semantic generation layer, the concat layer, the dropout layer, the hidden layer, and the output layer.

In our design, we first apply the encoder to generate the sentence coding results, wherein we quantify the semantic similarity between words by evaluating the shortest phrase semantic distance of words in the tree knowledge base and the shallowest common parent node depth. Then we compose the deep neural network (DNN) based on the long short-term memory (LSTM) [8] to generate a normalized classification probability vector via the multi-layer perception(MLP), the dropout layer, and the softmax function, which determines the sentence similarity. At the offline training stage, the mixed semantics of the text are used to train the neural network to calculate the sentence similarity. The similarity of sentences at the online deployment stage is sequentially calculated by the encoder and the DNN.

Thus with the aid of the sequential processing for Chinese sentences with the serially concatenated siamese neural network encoder and the DNN, the consistency of the similarity calculation can be improved to achieve higher accuracy. Subsequently, we use the large-scale Chinese question matching corpus

(LCQMC) [7] as the dataset. Then we analyze and compare the performances of the proposed design, including the accuracy, precision, F1 score, and recall with counterpart systems.

Briefly, the main contributions of this paper include:

1. The output of bidirectional encoder representation from transformers (BERT) constructed in this paper is the encoding of all tokens of input text, while traditional BERT encoder is the rough semantic representation of the input text under the constraint of the downstream task model. Compared with the traditional output method, our scheme could achieve a better semantic representation.
2. To evaluate the length of the input text, in our design, except for the evaluation of the semantics, the length feature of the input text could also be provided. By contrast, no length feature could be identified in the traditional BER encoder.
3. The output mode constructed in this paper is input to the downstream task model in a sequential manner, which includes the position feature of the text. In the traditional BERT encoder, the length of a token output by the encoder cannot express the position feature of the input text.

The remaining part of the paper is organized as follows. The proposed similarity calculation model is detailed in Sect. 2, followed by results and the associated analysis in Sect. 3. Conclusions are given in Sect. 4.

2   System Model

In this section, we will present the similarity calculation details, including the sentence input vector generation, the training of the encoder, the similarity calculation, and the classification.

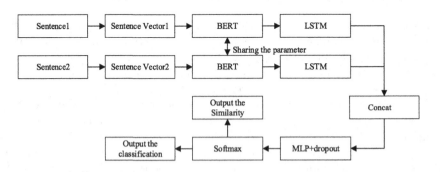

Fig. 1. The framework of the proposed sentences similarity calculation scheme.

As illustrated in Fig. 1, the proposed intelligent sentence similarity calculator is serially concatenated by the BERT [4] and the LSTM based DNN.

In this calculator, the input sentences are firstly represented as 1×512-dimensional sentence input vectors, which act as the input to the siamese neural network encoder. After the sentences encoding vectors pass through the LSTM module, the corresponding sentence overall information vectors are generated. Subsequently, the proposed calculator splice the whole sentence variables into pieces, and the spliced vectors are input into the MLP and dropout layers. The resultant 1×2-dimensional probability vector is then used for the classification by applying the Softmax function. Finally, the classification probability vector is generated.

Notably, the value of the second element of the classification probability vector represents the obtained similarity calculation results, while the category represented by the maximum value of the elements in the vector denotes the sentence classification result. At the offline training stage, the intelligent encoder and the classifier are trained separately. At the online deployment stage, the similarity of sentences could be evaluated and output to the terminals. More details about how to generate the sentence input vector, train the encoder, calculate the similarity and classify the sentences are given as follows.

2.1 Generation of Sentence Input Vectors

As shown in Fig. 1, the sentences are first converted to sentence vectors. In this model, the input sentence vectors are constructed based on 3500 commonly used Chinese characters in the first level character list of the general standard Chinese character list issued by the Chinese language and character working committee in 2013. The construction method is as follows: first, the input sentence is divided by the punctuation as a separator, and the special characters are deleted to reduce the noise in the sentence. Then, 3500 common Chinese characters are sequentially numbered in the first level character table, and the input sentences are represented by $S = (id_1, id_2, ...id_i, ...id_{512})$, where id_i represents the location of the i_{th} word of the input sentences in the first level character table. When the vector length is greater than the length of the input sentence, "0" will be padded to the end of the sequence, i.e., $id = 0$.

2.2 Offline Training

Since the minimum number of layers of the BERT model is 12, the encoder would need a large amount of training data to use the extracted features to represent the text data. To avoid the data overfitting problem of the large-scale neural network, we adopt four ways to prevent overfitting: building precoding model, fine-tuning, data growth, and adding dropout layer.

Specifically, the training set of the encoder could be divided into two parts: Chinese entry interpretation of Wikipedia, and the train set and verification set in LCQMC.

Figure 2 illustrates the training procedure of the encoder. We propose to concatenate the encoder and the DNN serially to extract the semantic features for

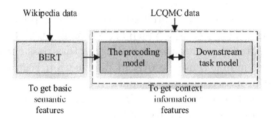

Fig. 2. Offline training of the similarity calculator.

further context information feature extractions. Firstly, we utilize the character interpretation from the Chinese version of Wikipedia to train the encoder to obtain the semantic features. Then we use the precoding model to learn the extracted semantic features. In the downstream model, the data of train set and verification set in LCQMC, as well as the data of train set and the verification set in LCQMC data set, are used to extract the context information features of the text to enable the vectors to extract the specific semantic features.

Unlike the traditional BERT model, whose output is a token length encoding, i.e., the encoding result of the first identifier $[CLS]$ of the sentence, we propose modifying the output of the BERT model to make the encoder output the coding of each token. In our design, the input of the downstream model is transformed into a 512×768 dimensional text semantic vector matrix. Thus the semantic table of the sentences becomes more refined. Then, the encoder outputs the coding results of each token of input sentences 1 and 2 to the LSTM module and performs zero paddings on the coding part that exceeds the input sentence's length.

2.3 Sentences Similarity Calculation and Classification Model

Figure 3 illustrates the intelligent DNN-based downstream model. Considering that the neural network layer number of the BERT encoder is 12, to avoid the overfitting problem of the large-scale model, here, the DNN consists of two LSTM modules, a concat layer, an MLP layer, a dropout layer, and a softmax layer. The details about how to calculate the similarity in each layer are given as follows.

Semantic Generation Layer. In this model, the LSTM module reads the output of the encoder sequentially. It generates the full semantic information on the premise of retaining the input text information by using the memory network characteristics of the LSTM. The parameters of the LSTM module used in the scheme are as follows: $BatchSize$ is 64, $NSteps$ is 512, $Inputdimension$ is 768, $Hiddendimension$ is 768, $Outputdimension$ is 768.

The coding results of the first token into the LSTM are regarded as the initial memory state C_0, and then the LSTM reads the remaining token coding results in turn as the input at a time. Namely, the coding result of the input sentence is expressed as $(C_0, X_1, X_2, ...X_t, ...X_{511})$, where X_t represents the input at time t. X_t would pass through the forget gate in the LSTM module to determine the importance of the last moment's memory state and whether it needs to forget part of the content.

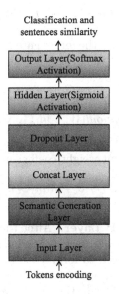

Classification and
sentences similarity

Output Layer(Softmax Activation)

Hidden Layer(Sigmoid Activation)

Dropout Layer

Concat Layer

Semantic Generation Layer

Input Layer

Tokens encoding

Fig. 3. The intelligent DNN-based downstream model.

At time t, the expression in the forget gate is presented as:

$$f_t = sigmoid(W_f * [h_{t-1}, X_t] + b_f) \tag{1}$$

where W_f is the weight matrix of the forget gate, $*$ is the matrix multiplication operation, h_{t-1} is the output state of the previous time slot, b_f is the offset coefficient of the forget gate. In addition, the sigmoid function is given by:

$$sigmoid(x) = \frac{1}{1 - e^{-x}}. \tag{2}$$

Next, X_t passes through the input gate to determine the importance of the X_t in order to determine the extent to which the current input needs to be updated into C_{t-1}, The expression of updating the coefficient i_t is given by:

$$i_t = sigmoid(W_i * [h_{t-1}, X_t] + b_i) \tag{3}$$

where W_i is the weight matrix of the input gate, b_i is the offset coefficient of the input gate. In addition, the memory state C_t^* of the input gate can be expressed as:

$$C_t^* = tanh(W_c * [h_{t-1}, X_t] + b_c) \tag{4}$$

where W_c is the weight matrix to calculate the update memory state, b_c is the offset coefficient to calculate the update memory state, and the function $tanh(\cdot)$ is given by:

$$tanh(x) = \frac{e^x - e^{-x}}{e^x + e^{-x}} \tag{5}$$

It is evident that the greater the value of i_t, the higher the update degree of C_{t-1}.

Finally, with the outputs from the forget gate and the input gate, the memory state C_t and output state h_t at time t can be calculated jointly by:

$$C_t = f_t * C_{t-1} + i_t * C_t^* \tag{6}$$

$$o_t = sigmoid(W_o * [h_{t-1}, X_t] + b_o) \tag{7}$$

where W_o is the weight matrix of the output gate, b_o is the offset coefficient of the output gate, o_t is the output weight coefficient, and h_t is

$$.h_t = o_t * tanh(C_t). \tag{8}$$

Concat, Dropout and MLP Layer. After the encoding results of the two input sentences are generated by the LSTM module, the semantic expressions of the two input texts are spliced to form a 1×1536 dimensional splicing vector as the inputs to the MLP and dropout layers, where the dropout rate is 0.1.

The process of splicing vectors in the MLP layer is carried out as follows:

1. With the aid of the weight matrix in the MLP layer, the dimension degree of splicing vectors is reduced to 1×768 to complete the transfer from the input layer to the hidden layer.
2. After the vector of the hidden layer is processed by the activation function (sigmoid function), the dimension degree drops to 1×2. The transfer from the hidden layer to the output layer is completed, and the classification probability vector between input sentences is obtained.

Output Layer. Last, the output layer will process the resultant data from the MLP and dropout layers by using the Softmax function to obtain the normalized probability vector. In the normalized probability vector, the second element represents the similarity between the input sentences, and the category represented by the maximum value of the elements is the classification result. Additionally, the Softmax function is defined as follows:

$$P(S_i) = e^{g_i} / \sum_{k}^{n} e^{g_k} \tag{9}$$

where i is the category of the text classification, g_i represents 0 or 1.

3   Performance Analysis

In this section, we will evaluate the performance of the proposed scheme with the LCQMC data set and compare the accuracy, recall, precision, F1 score and cross-entropy loss performances of the proposed design with the counterpart systems. In the performance analysis, the learning rate is set as 10^{-5}, the epoch is 2, the batch size is 64, the amount of data in the train set is 238766, the amount of data in the verification set is 8802, and the amount of data in the test set is 12500.

3.1   Definitions

To evaluate the performance of the proposed design, we provide the following definitions.

Table 1. Classification of similarity evaluation precisions

	Predicted label(class 0)	Predicted label(class 1)
Ture label(class 0)	True Positive	False Negative
Ture label(calss 1)	False Positive	True Negative

Accuracy. Accuracy reflects the classification performances, and we define it as the correctness of the classification as below:

$$Accuracy = \frac{TP + TN}{TP + FN + FP + TN} \tag{10}$$

where TP represents the true positive (the predicted label of the sample is class 0, and the true label is class 0), TN represents the true negative, FP represents the false positive, FN represents the false negative.

Recall. Recall reflects the ability of the model to recall target categories in the research field. We define it as:

$$Recall = \frac{TP}{TP + FN}. \tag{11}$$

Precision. Precision reflects the ability of the model to precisely capture the target categories in the research field:

$$Precision = \frac{TP}{TP + FP} \tag{12}$$

F1-Score. F1-score reflects the comprehensive ability of the model:

$$F1 - score = \frac{Recall \times Precision \times 2}{Recall + Precision}. \tag{13}$$

Loss. Loss reflects the deviation degree between the overall predicted value and the overall real value of the model:

$$Loss = \frac{1}{N}(\sum_{0}^{N}(-[y_i \times log(p_i) + (1 - y_i) \times log(1 - p_i)])) \tag{14}$$

where N is the total number of samples, y_i is the label of the samples, p_i is the text-similarity between samples.

Last but not least, to analyze the accuracy, recall, precision, and F1-score, in Table 1, we apply four classification samples for similarity computations based on the real classification results and the prediction classification results of test samples.

3.2   Similarity Evaluation Performance Analysis

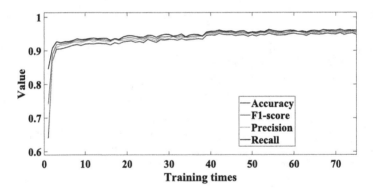

Fig. 4. The similarity evaluation performances versus the training times with the training set.

Similarity Computation Precision. First of all, we investigate the similarity evaluation performances versus the training times when applying the training set at the online deployment stage. As illustrated in Fig. 4, with the increase of training times, the accuracy, F1 score, accuracy, and recall of the scheme are improved. When the training times reach 3, the scheme's four performance indexes are all enhanced to be larger than 0.9. Moreover, it is clear that when the training times are larger than 42, little performance enhancement could be observed, and the similarity evaluation precision approaches 1.

Next, we investigate the loss versus the training times when applying the training set. As illustrated in Fig. 5, with the increase of the training times, the loss decreases rapidly. It is noticeable that when the training times reach 3, the loss drops to 50. Moreover, it is evident that the loss decreases and approaches 0 when the training times are larger than 42.

Robustness Analysis. Subsequently, to evaluate the robustness, we analyze the similarity computation performances when applying the verification set. As illustrated in Fig. 6, with the increase of the training times, the accuracy, F1 score, and precision all increase rapidly. However, the recall fluctuates when the verification set is used at the online deployment stage. When the training times reach 3, the four performances are around 0.84. When the training times are greater than 40, the four performances remain approaching 0.9. The reason is that the LCQMC verification set is aggregated data set, wherein the data with the same label category are not scattered.

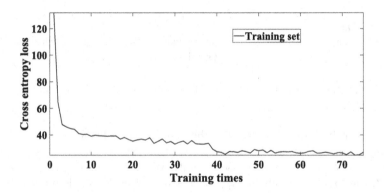

Fig. 5. The loss of the scheme versus the training times with the training set.

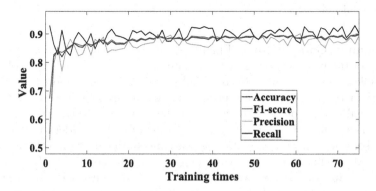

Fig. 6. The similarity evaluation performances versus the training times with the verification set.

We could also notice from the figure that the four performance indicators of the scheme have relatively high values with the verification set, and it converges rapidly. The reason is that the input sentences are processed by the encoder and the LSTM module; hence the obtained sentence semantic expression has higher accuracy than that of the traditional scheme. This also leads to a higher sentence similarity calculation accuracy than that of the traditional scheme. Meanwhile, we could also see that the construction of the siamese neural network architecture accelerates the scheme's convergence speed.

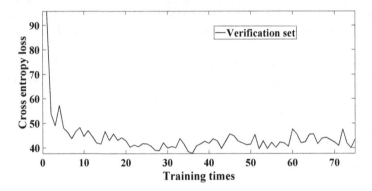

Fig. 7. The loss of the scheme versus the training times with the training set.

Subsequently, Fig. 7 investigates the loss of the scheme with the increase of training times when applying the verification set. It is clear from the figure that the cross-entropy loss decreases rapidly. When the training times are larger than 37, the loss of the scheme approaches 0. Furthermore, thanks to the high similarity evaluation accuracy, the classification precision of the proposed design is also very high, and the classification results of the scheme deviate only slightly from the real one.

Performance Comparisons. Finally, we compare the similarity evaluation accuracy of the proposed design with counterpart schemes. It could be observed from Table 2, the accuracy, F1 score, and precision of the proposed scheme are higher than those of the counterpart schemes. According to the rules of 2018 ant financial's NLP competition, we select the accuracy and the F1 score as the performance indicators for the classification models. It is evident that the proposed scheme's similarity evaluation performances are better than those of other schemes. Meanwhile, the accuracy of the proposed scheme with the LCQMC verification set and the test set are almost identical, demonstrating that our proposed scheme can effectively alleviate the problem of the inconsistent accuracy of the neural network model in different fields.

Table 2. Scheme performance comparisons with LCQMC data set

Scheme	Validation set's accuracy	Test set's accuracy	Test set's F1 csore	Test set's precision	Test set's recall
WMD [7]	*	0.706	0.734	0.67	0.812
C_WO [7]	*	0.707	0.706	0.611	0.887
S_COS [7]	*	0.703	0.716	0.601	0.889
CBOW [7]	*	0.737	0.774	0.679	0.899
CNN [7]	*	0.728	0.757	0.684	0.846
BILSTM [7]	*	0.761	0.789	0.706	0.833
BIMPM [7]	*	0.834	0.85	0.776	0.939
DSSM [2]	*	0.6334	*	*	*
ABCNN [2]	*	0.7992	*	*	*
ESIM [2]	*	0.818	*	*	*
DIIN [2]	*	0.8447	*	*	*
NEZHA [11]	0.8964	0.8710	*	*	*
CHARTEST [6]	0.8443	0.8618	*	*	*
ERNIE [9]	0.897	0.874	*	*	*
Proposed scheme	0.8761	0.8843	0.8890	0.8549	0.9258

4   Conclusions

In this paper, we propose to serially concatenate the encoder and the DNN to compute the similarity of Chinese sentences for enhanced performances jointly. In our proposed scheme, we use the BERT to extract the semantic feature for further context information feature extraction with the DNN. We construct the DNN, which is composed of the input layer, the semantic generation layer, the concat layer, the dropout layer, the hidden layer, and the output layer. At the offline training stage, the Wikipedia data and the LCQMC data are used as the data set to configure the neural networks. Subsequently, we evaluate the similarity of Chinese sentences at the online deployment stage with the obtained parameters and structure. Furthermore, we investigate the accuracy, precision, F1 score, recall, and cross-entropy loss of the proposed design to evaluate its robustness. The results demonstrate that by applying the serially concatenated BERT and LSTM aided DNN design, the similarity computation performances could be improved. Therefore, with higher similarity evaluation accuracy, the proposed scheme could be integrated with IoT devices to provide better NLP services such as searching, data mining, or text classifications.

Acknowledgements. This work was supported in part by the State Key Program of National Social Science of China (No. 18AZD035), the Key Research & Development and Transformation Plan of Science and Technology Program for Tibet Autonomous Region (No. XZ201901-GB-16), the Special Fund from the Central Finance to Support the Development of Local Universities (No. ZFYJY201902001) and the National Natural Science Foundation of China (No. 71964030).

References

1. Arora, S., Liang, Y., Ma, T.: A simple but tough-to-beat baseline for sentence embeddings. In: 5th International Conference on Learning Representations, ICLR 2017 - Conference Track Proceedings, Toulon, France (2019)

2. Bshoter, J.: Text-matching. https://github.com/BshoterJ/Text-Matching
3. Gunes, E., Dragomir, R.: LexRank: graph-based lexical centrality as salience in text summarization. J. Artif. Intell. Res. **22**(1), 457–479 (2011)
4. Devlin, J., Chang, M.-W., Lee, K., Toutanova, K.: BERT: pre-training of deep bidirectional transformers for language understanding. In: Proceedings of the 2019 Conference of the North American Chapter of the Association for Computational Linguistics: Human Language Technologies, vol. 1, Minneapolis, Minnesota. Association for Computational Linguistics, Germany, January 2019
5. Ko, Y., Park, J., Seo, J.: Automatic text categorization using the importance of sentences. In: Proceedings of the 19th International Conference on Computational Linguistics, COLING'02, USA, vol. 1, pp. 1–7. Association for Computational Linguistics (2002)
6. Li, X., Meng, Y., Sun, X., Han, Q., Yuan, A., Li, J.: Is word segmentation necessary for deep learning of Chinese representations? In: Proceedings of the 57th Annual Meeting of the Association for Computational Linguistics, Florence, Italy, pp. 3242–3252. Association for Computational Linguistics, July 2019
7. Liu, X., et al.: LCQMC: a large-scale Chinese question matching corpus. In: Proceedings of the 27th International Conference on Computational Linguistics, Santa Fe, New Mexico, USA. Association for Computational Linguistics, Germany, July 2018
8. Sepp, H., Jürgen, S.: Long short-term memory. Neural Comput. **9**, 1735–1780 (1997)
9. Sun, Y., et al.: Ernie: Enhanced representation through knowledge integration (2019). https://arxiv.org/abs/1904.09223v1
10. Varelas, G., Voutsakis, E., Raftopoulou, P., Petrakis, E.G., Milios, E.E.: Semantic similarity methods in wordnet and their application to information retrieval on the web. In: Proceedings of the 7th Annual ACM International Workshop on Web Information and Data Management, WIDM'05, Bremen, Germany, pp. 10–16. Association for Computing Machinery, New York (2005)
11. Wei, J., et al.: Nezha: Neural contextualized representation for Chinese language understanding (2019). https://arxiv.org/abs/1909.00204
12. Zhao, Q., Qi, J.: A method for calculating the similarity of short texts based on semantic and syntactic structure. Comput. Eng. Sci. **40**(283), 145–152 (2018)

Statistical Feature Aided Intelligent Deep Learning Machine Translation in Internet of Things

Yidian Zhang[3], Lin Zhang[3] (ORCID), Ping Lan[1], Wenyong Li[2,4], Dan Yang[2,5], and Zhiqiang Wu[1,2(✉)]

[1] College of Engineering, Tibet University, Lhasa 850000, China
lightnesstibet@163.com
[2] Center of Tibetan Studies (Everest Research Institute), Tibet University, Lhasa 850000, China
[3] School of Electronics and Information Technology, Sun Yat-sen University, Guangzhou 510006, China
[4] School of Business Administration, Southwestern University of Finance and Economics, Chengdu 611130, China
[5] Beijing Foreign Studies University, Beijing 10089, China

Abstract. Internet of Things (IoT) networks have been widely deployed to achieve communication among machines and humans. Machine translation can enable human-machine interactions for IoT equipment. In this paper, we propose to combine the neural machine translation (NMT) and statistical machine translation (SMT) to improve translation precision. In our design, we propose a hybrid deep learning (DL) network that uses the statistical feature extracted from the words as the data set. Namely, we use the SMT model to score the generated words in each decoding step of the NMT model, instead of directly processing their outputs. These scores will be converted to the generation probability corresponding to words by classifiers and used for generating the output of the hybrid MT system. For the NMT, the DL network consists of the input layer, embedding layer, recurrent layer, hidden layer, and output layer. At the offline training stage, the NMT network is jointly trained with SMT models. Then at the online deployment stage, we load the fine-trained models and parameters to generate the outputs. Experimental results on French-to-English translation tasks show that the proposed scheme can take advantage of both NMT and SMT methods, thus higher translation precision could be achieved.

Keywords: Neural machine translation · Statistical machine translation · Neural network · Statistical feature extraction

1 Introduction

Internet of Things (IoT) networks enable the machines or devices to communicate with each other as well as humans. With IoT, humans could communicate

B. Li et al. (Eds.): IoTaaS 2020, LNICST 346, pp. 247–260, 2021.
https://doi.org/10.1007/978-3-030-67514-1_20

with machines, learn the machine's status, and achieve the intelligent control of IoT devices such as the fridge, the air conditioner, or the microwave ovens. These IoT services provide interactions between IoT devices and humans, while machine translation enables such interactions via providing the human-machine interaction interfaces for users.

Machine translation (MT) involves how to recognize the task of translation between two natural languages through a computer, which has been widely applied to the increasing social demands among people speaking different languages [11].

As a research branch of natural language processing (NLP), the MT systems confront the following difficulties: 1) The variability and the ambiguity of natural language: the same words, phrases, and sentences may represent different meanings in different contexts, while words, phrases or sentences with different or even opposite meanings can sometimes express the same meanings in the same context. Moreover, the mixed-use of new words and typos is also the major obstacle for the computer to understand natural language. 2) The difficulty of modeling: even if a unified linguistic rule can be provided to update and correct new words and typos promptly, it is challenging to build a mathematical model that can fully contain the above rules and meet the computer's affordability. 3) The corpus quality requirements: what kind of corpus can fully reflect the characteristics of language and how to collect such corpus are essential issues to be considered.

The neural machine translation (NMT) and statistical machine translation (SMT) are two main translation methods for achieving high-quality results. On the one hand, the deep learning network has been widely adopted in various research areas, such as the information retrieval [7], image processing [5] and speech recognition [2] etc. Based on the encoder-decoder architecture, the NMT method utilizes the deep learning network and models the translation process as "encoding & decoding".

The deep learning network could effectively adapt to the variability and ambiguity of natural languages and demonstrate outstanding performances to implement MT tasks. However, the NMT has to address the following issues: 1) Translation coverage [8]: a predetermined symbol (such as "EOS") is used as the end marker in the NMT process. The NMT model will finish the decoding process when the decoder generates this symbol, which cannot guarantee that all words in the source sentence can be translated, thereby inducing the problem of the "over-translation" or "under-translation". 2) Translation inaccuracy caused by the decoder [1]: attention mechanism is used in the NMT model, and the result of NMT is usually smoother than that of the SMT model thanks to the smoothing effect of attention weights. However, the smoothing processing may induce the loss of the sentence semantics. 3) Limited vocabulary [4]: the computation cost of the embedding layer in the encoder and the softmax layer in the decoder is directly proportional to the vocabulary. Therefore, the NMT model only uses limited words with higher generation probability and uses a

UNK symbol to represent other words. The occurrences of UNK symbols might result in the semantic truncation of both the input and output sentences.

On the other hand, SMT models the translation relationship between two languages by applying the statistical feature extraction technology, which could address the issues confronted by the NMT models. However, the SMT methods have the following defects: 1) Large model size: the SMT requires a lot of memory to store the statistical features extracted from the corpus, which leads to a larger model size than the NMT aided system. 2) Lack of fluency in results: due to the use of the invariant probability mapping, the SMT often produces accurate but not fluent results.

Against this background, in this paper, we propose to establish and realize a hybrid machine translation system by integrating the SMT model and the NMT model to improve the translation performances.

Different from existing methods, in our design, we propose to use the SMT model to score the generated words in each decoding step of the NMT model, instead of directly processing their outputs. These scores will be first converted into the generation probability corresponding to words by classifiers, and then be utilized to generate the output of the hybrid MT system.

Briefly, the major contributions of this paper include:

1. We propose to establish the unigram based word scoring system and the bigram based word scoring system based on the SMT model to unify the decoding granularity with the NMT model.
2. We propose establishing the communication channels between SMT and NMT models to unify the translation progress and realize the decoding guidance through these two word scoring systems.
3. We propose to construct classifiers and weighting units to integrate the decoding guidance and the generation probability into the NMT model.

The remaining part of this paper is organized as follows. Section 2 presents the details of our proposed system, including the framework of the proposed hybrid MT system model, the DL network structure and the word scoring system, and so on. Then Sect. 3 provides experimental results to validate our design. Finally, we conclude our findings in Sect. 4.

2   The Proposed Hybrid SMT-Aided NMT System

In this section, we will present the hybrid MT system model, and then introduce the word scoring systems and describe the classifier and the weight units.

Figure 1 illustrates the framework of our proposed hybrid MT system. In this system, we use the SMT model to provide the word generation guidance for the NMT model. Then we propose to use the unigram based word scoring system and the bigram based word scoring system to generate the word guidance. In the decoding process, the SMT model combines the attention weights shared by the NMT model to calculate word scores of each step and finally perform the decoding of the hybrid system with classifiers and the weighting unit.

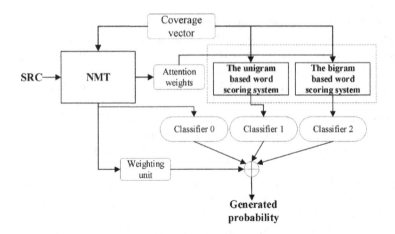

Fig. 1. The framework of the proposed hybrid MT system model.

2.1   Deep Neural Network for Hybrid MT System

In this hybrid SMT-aided NMT system, we proposed to apply the deep neural network (DNN) to achieve the MT. As illustrated in Fig. 2, the source sentence (SRC) is used as the input data set for both SMT and NMT models, while the output of this system is the sequence of word generation probabilities. The deep neural network consists of the input layer, the embedding layer, the recurrent layer, the hidden layer, and the output layer. Then for the DNN-based intelligent MT system, we utilize the word generation guidance of the SMT to combine the attention weights of NMT. Thus the reference output is the target sentence at the offline training stage and is a zero vector when the system is used for MT at the online deployment stage of the translation.

Moreover, to unify the NMT and SMT models' decoding progress, we introduce a coverage vector to mark the translated part of SRC explicitly. The length of the coverage vector is equal to that of the SRC, while elements in the vector are aligned with words in the SRC in order, which indicates that a word is untranslated when its corresponding element is 0 and is translated when the element is 1. To be more explicit, after each decoding step, if the generated word belongs to the word generation guidance, the corresponding element in the coverage vector will be updated to 1 following the setting given in [10].

2.2   The Unigram Based Word Scoring System

Figure 3 shows the unigram-based word scoring system, wherein the SRC is divided into discrete words and sent to the pre-scoring module. This module will calculate the pre-score of generated words according to the following equation:

$$SMT_1(y_t \mid y_{<t}, x) = \sum_{m=1}^{M} \lambda_m H_m(y_t, x_t) \tag{1}$$

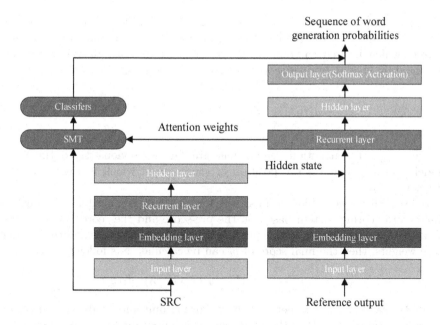

Fig. 2. The deep neural network of the proposed hybrid MT system model.

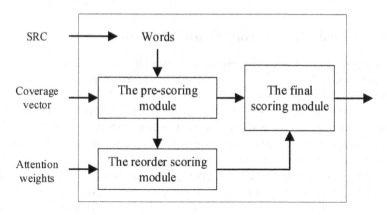

Fig. 3. The diagram of the unigram based word scoring system model

where x_t refers to the untranslated word in the SRC by the coverage vector, and y_t corresponds to the best n_{local} results to reduce the calculation burden of subsequent modules. H_m is a feature function used in the log-linear framework [6], and λ_m is the corresponding weight.

Considering that discrete words might result in the loss of word order, we propose to construct the reorder scoring module in the unigram based scoring system, which is used to compute the reorder score. With the same method presented by [9], the reorder score is calculated as follows:

$$d_1(y_t) = -\sum_{j=1}^{T_x} \alpha_{t-1,j} |sp_{y_t} - j - 1| \tag{2}$$

where $\alpha_{t-1,j}$ is the attention weights generated in the previous step of the NMT model, and sp_{y_t} denotes the position of source word which is aligned to the target word y.

Subsequently, we could establish the final scoring module for the unigram based word scoring system based on the pre-score and the reorder score of y_t. We apply a weighting unit in this module to adjust the pre-score and the reorder score weights, then the final score of y_t can be calculated as follows:

$$score_1(y_t) = \lambda \cdot SMT_1(y_t) + (1 - \lambda) \cdot d_1(y_t) \tag{3}$$

where $\lambda \in [0, 1]$ is the parameter of the weighting unit and needs to be used for the offline training. At last, the final score will be output to the classifier 1 for further processing.

2.3   The Bigram Based Word Scoring System

To retain richer semantics of bigrams in SRC and improve the fluency of the SMT word generation guidance, we propose a bigram based word scoring system.

Unlike the unigram-based word scoring system, the source sentence x of length T_x is first divided into $(T_x - 1)$ bigrams in the bigram based word scoring system. Also, since the SMT model's output length corresponding to input bigram is not necessarily 2, the output will be complemented as a bigram when it is a unigram and keep only the first two words when its length is larger than 2.

To reduce the computational complexity, the output and the input bigram will adopt the alignment assumptions as given in Fig. 4. Namely, the first word in the output is generated at the first step and aligned with the first word of the input. The second word in the output is generated following the first word in the second step and aligned with the second word of the input.

To be more explicit, Fig. 5 presents the details of the alignment between the output sequence and the SRC, wherein y_t in the output sequence may be generated with two input bigrams. Next, we will present how to apply the above two assumptions to the bigram based word scoring system.

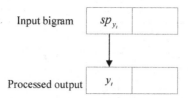

(a) y_t is the first word of the proposed output

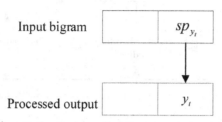

(b) y_t is the first word of the proposed output

Fig. 4. The alignment assumptions for the input bigram and the output.

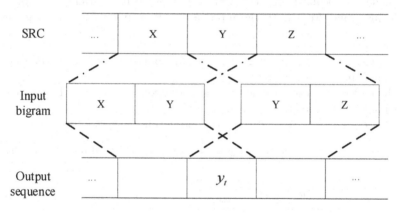

Fig. 5. The alignment between the output sequence and SRC

Figure 6 illustrates the framework of the bigram based word scoring system. Similar to the unigram based word scoring system, this system also consists of the pre-scoring module, the reorder scoring module, and the final scoring module, wherein the final score of the word is calculated based on the two assumptions.

For the first assumption, the pre-score is calculated by a similar method as that in the unigram based word scoring system:

$$SMT_{2-1}(y_t \mid y_{<t}, x) = \sum_{\langle y_t, \_ \rangle \in n-\text{best}} \sum_{m=1}^{M} \lambda_m H_m(\langle y_t, \_ \rangle, \langle x_t, \overrightarrow{x_t} \rangle) \tag{4}$$

where $\langle \cdot \rangle$ means the connections of the words in the brackets as the bigram, $\overrightarrow{x_t}$ is the last word of x_t in the SRC. $\langle y_t, \_ \rangle$ indicates that the first word of the output

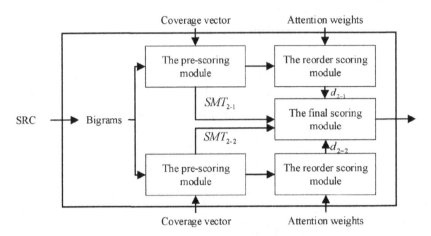

Fig. 6. The diagram of the bigram based word scoring system model

is y_t, while the second is limited by the coverage vector. Coverage vector limits the scoring range from both the input and the output, the limitations are as follows:

1) If the element in the coverage vector corresponding to x_t is 1, then $\langle x_t, \overrightarrow{x_t} \rangle$ does not meet input requirements.
2) If the element in the coverage vector corresponding to $\overrightarrow{x_t}$ is 1, then $\langle x_t, \overrightarrow{x_t} \rangle$ does not meet input requirements.
3) $\langle y_t, \_ \rangle$ only needs to meet the corresponding input $\langle x_t, \overrightarrow{x_t} \rangle$ limitations.

In this case, the reorder scoring is the same as Eq. 2, which is expressed as:

$$d_{2-1}(y_t) = -\sum_{j=1}^{T_x} \alpha_{t-1,j} |sp_{y_t} - j - 1| \tag{5}$$

For the second assumption, i.e., y_t is the second word of the output bigram, we calculate the pre-scoring based on the segment $y_{<t-1} = y_1, y_2, \cdots, y_{t-2}$ that has been generated in the previous step. Moreover, we revise the pre-scoring equation as:

$$SMT_{2-2}(y_t \mid y_{<t-1}, x) = \sum_{\langle \_, y_t \rangle \in \text{n-best}} \sum_{m=1}^{M} \lambda_m H_m(\langle \_, y_t \rangle, \langle \overleftarrow{x_t}, x_t \rangle) \tag{6}$$

where $\overleftarrow{x_t}$ is the previous word of x_t in the SRC, $\langle \_, y_t \rangle$ indicates that the second word of the output is y_t while the first one is limited by the coverage vector. It is worth mentioning that the limitations on scoring range are as follows:

1) If the element in coverage vector corresponding to x_t is 1, then $\langle \overleftarrow{x_t}, x_t \rangle$ does not meet input requirements.

2) If the current state of the element in coverage vector corresponding to $\overleftarrow{x_t}$ is not 1, then $\langle \overleftarrow{x_t}, x_t \rangle$ does not meet input requirements.

3) If the previous state of the element in coverage vector corresponding to $\overleftarrow{x_t}$ is not 0, then $\langle \overleftarrow{x_t}, x_t \rangle$ does not meet input requirements.

4) If the previous output of the hybrid system is $\bar{y}_{t-1}$, then $\langle \text{-}, y_t \rangle$ which first word is not $\bar{y}_{t-1}$ does not meet the output requirements.

In this case, the reorder scoring module uses $\overleftarrow{x_t}$ as the basis for calculating the distance. Moreover, considering that the previous decoding step is occupied by the first word, the reorder score is calculated as follows:

$$d_{2-2}(y_t) = -\sum_{j=1}^{T_x} \alpha_{t-2,j} |sp_{y_t} - j - 2| \tag{7}$$

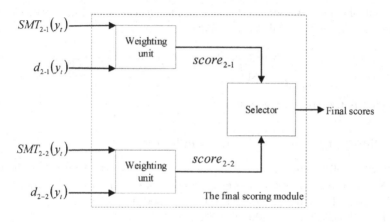

Fig. 7. The final scoring module.

Based on the above two sets of pre-scores and reorder scores, we propose a final scoring module for the bigram based word scoring system. As shown in Fig. 7, in the final scoring module. $score_{2-1}$ and $score_{2-2}$ are respectively calculated by weighting the two sets of scores as follows:

$$score_{2-1}(y_t) = \lambda \cdot SMT_{2-1}(y_t) + (1 - \lambda) \cdot d_{2-1}(y_t) \tag{8}$$

$$score_{2-2}(y_t) = \lambda \cdot SMT_{2-2}(y_t) + (1 - \lambda) \cdot d_{2-2}(y_t) \tag{9}$$

where λ is shared by the final scoring module in the unigram based word scoring system.

Finally, the selector will select the larger one of $score_{2-1}$ and $score_{2-2}$ as the final score of y_t. In particular, when y_t only appears in one assumption, the score under this case will be directly used as the final score of y_t.

2.4   Classifier and Weighting Unit

To unify the output structure of word scoring systems, we separate the Softmax layer from the NMT model and record it as the classifier 0. Moreover, we propose to denote the classifiers corresponding to the unigram based word scoring system and the bigram based word scoring system as classifiers 1 and 2. Furthermore, to match the output form of classifier 0, in both classifiers 1 and 2, we also adopt the Softmax function.

Moreover, to reduce the burden of the Softmax module, thereby decreasing the decoding complexity of the hybrid system, the classifier 1 first sorts all candidate words according to their final scores and only retains the best n_{global_1} results. Afterward, these scores will be mapped by the Softmax function, to achieve the conversion of the generated score to the generated probability. Additionally, the classifier 2 carries out the similar operations, while the only difference is the number of retained results, which is represented by n_{global_2}.

Besides, we propose to construct the weighting unit to control the weight of the output of each classifier, while each weight β_i corresponding to the classifier i is time-varying and calculated as follows:

$$\beta_i = \frac{\exp(g_i(s_t, y_{t-1}, c_t))}{\sum_{j=0}^{2} \exp(g_j(s_t, y_{t-1}, c_t))}, \quad i = \{0, 1, 2\} \tag{10}$$

where $g_i(\cdot)$ is the *sigmoid* function.

2.5   Offline Training and Online Deployment

At last, we briefly introduce the training and the online deployment of the SMT aided NMT system. The parameters shared between the proposed system and the NMT model are initialized by the fine-trained model. The other parameters of the hybrid system are randomly initialized.

After that, all parameters will be trained to minimize the negative log-likelihood of the variables:

$$L(\theta) = -\frac{1}{N_{train}} \sum_{n=1}^{N_{train}} \sum_{t=1}^{T_y} \log(p(y_t{}^n \mid y_{<t}{}^n, x)) \tag{11}$$

where N_{train} is the number of bilingual sentence pairs in the training data and T_y is the length of expected output y.

Then at the online deployment stage, with the trained DNN model, the proposed intelligent MT system could output the translation results in real-time.

3   Numerical Results and Analysis

In this section, we provide numerical results to analyze the performances of the proposed intelligent MT system with the paired French-to-English data sets. In the analysis, the parameter settings are given as follows.

In the numerical analysis, we use WMT2013 as the development set; then, we test the proposed system on newstest2008, newstest2009, newstest2010, newstest2011 in WMT2012. We then use Moses and RNNSearch as the benchmark systems for translation performance comparisons for the proposed intelligent SMT aided NMT system. For Moses, the preprocessing of the bilingual corpus adopts the default method, and use KenLM [3] to train a 4-gram language model by exploiting the target corpus and then realize the grammatical control of the output. Besides, We run Giza++ for word-aligning ours parallel corpus, and carry out the RNNSearch with an open-source NMT system GroundHog, wherein the system setting follows that given in [9].

Additionally, in the unigram based word scoring system, n_{local} is set to 5. That is to say, for each input, the pre-scoring module keeps only the best 5 results. In the bigram based word scoring system, n in $n-best$ is set to 3, while n_{global_1} in classifier 1 is set to 20 and n_{global_2} in classifier 2 is set to 10.

3.1 Translation Performance Analysis

We first analyze the translation performances of the proposed system and compare them with the benchmark RNNSearch system. As shown in Table 1, we compared three examples generated by RNNSearch and the proposed system. In the first example, the fragment "Am érique du nord" at the end of SRC means "North America". From the translation results, it can be seen that RNNSearch

Table 1. Translation examples generated by the RNNSearch and the proposed systems

SRC	Hrafnsson réagissait manifestement aux déclarations faites en Amérique du nord
RNNSearch	Hrafnsson was clearly reacting to statements from North America in the north
The hybrid system	Hrafnsson was clearly reacting to statements from North America
SRC	Les hommes qui ont l'index plus long que l'annulaire sont exposés à un risque moindre d'avoir un cancer de la prostate
RNNSearch	Men who hand around the longer longer than ring finger face may lower off prostate cancer
The hybrid system	Men who have taken a longer index finger than ring finger are at lower risk of prostate cancer
SRC	Un homme et une femme d'une taille de 180 cm ont donc besoin d'un lit de 210/220 cm
RNNSearch	Man and woman with a height of about future gains need a bed of UNK cm
The hybrid system	Man and woman with a height of about 180 cm then need a bed cm

Table 2. Statistics of the percentages of UNK symbols for RNNSearch and the proposed systems

System	newstest2008	newstest2009	newstest2010	newstest2011	Average
RNNSearch	4.93%	5.18%	5.33%	5.38%	5.21%
The proposed system	3.81%	4.24%	4.52%	4.42%	4.25%

has the over-translation problem due to the excessive interpretation of the meaning of "north", while the proposed intelligent MT system demonstrates better control of the translation performances. In the second example, the RNNSearch based MT system still suffers from the over-translation and inaccuracy problems, while the proposed system achieves higher accuracy of translations. For the third example, we could notice that the proposed system is capable of expanding the vocabulary while retaining more SRC semantics. To be more explicit, in this example, "180 cm" is retained in the result of the hybrid system but not appearing in the output of the RNNSearch based system.

Furthermore, Table 2 compares the statistics of the UNK symbols in the proposed systems with that of the benchmark RNNSearch based system by using the test sets. It can be noticed from the table that both RNNSearch and our systems suffer from the limited vocabulary problem. It is worth pointing out that the UNK symbols in the proposed system are significantly fewer than those in RNNSearch system. This fact indicates that the proposed intelligent SMT aided NMT system could effectively mitigate the limited vocabulary effects on the performances of the intelligent DNN aided design.

Table 3. The BLEU results on French-to-English translation task

System	newstest2008	newstest2009	newstest2010	newstest2011	Average
Moses	21.04	23.60	24.88	20.48	22.50
RNNSearch	21.00	23.47	25.14	21.48	22.77
The proposed system	23.41	26.64	28.63	23.83	25.63

Moreover, Table 3 compares the BLEU results for completing the French-to-English translation task. It could be observed that the proposed system outperforms the benchmark RNNSearch system and the benchmark Moses system by 3.13 BLEU points and 2.86 BLEU points.

Table 4. Details of BLEU scores on newstest2011

System	1-gram	2-gram	3-gram	4-gram	BLEU
Moses	57.1	26.5	14.2	8.2	20.48
RNNSearch	50.4	25.0	16.4	12.2	21.48
The proposed system	52.9	28.1	19.7	15.6	23.83

Finally, Table 4 shows details of BLEU scores on newstest2011. It can be seen that both 1-gram and 2-gram scores of Moses are higher than that of RNNSearch, which are 6.7 and 1.5, respectively, reflecting the higher accuracy of Moses in unigrams and bigrams. Meanwhile, RNNSearch's 3-gram and 4-gram are higher, which are 4.2 and 4.0, respectively, reflecting its higher fluency in translation. The proposed system fully combines the advantages of accurate translation of Moses and smoother translation results of RNNSearch, except for 1-gram score is lower than Moses, other scores are higher than those of both Moses and RNNSearch, and the highest BLEU score is obtained finally.

4   Conclusions

In this paper, we propose an intelligent deep learning machine translation mechanism based on the extracted statistical feature to achieve the human-machine interactions for IoT devices. In the proposed MT system, the SMT subsystem combines the current state to calculate the word generation score for each decoding step and guides the translation process. Namely, we employ the SMT to score the generated words and then convert the scores to the generation probability. After the offline training, the resultant well-configured neural networks could output the translation results at the online deployment stage. The experimental results demonstrate that our proposed SMT aided intelligent MT system can effectively improve the translation performances. With the proposed design, IoT devices could achieve more effective interactions with humans, thereby greatly enhancing user-friendliness performances.

Acknowledgements. This work was supported in part by the State Key Program of National Social Science of China (No. 18AZD035), the Key Research & Development and Transformation Plan of Science and Technology Program for Tibet Autonomous Region (No. XZ201901-GB-16), the Special Fund from the Central Finance to Support the Development of Local Universities (No. ZFYJY201902001) and the National Natural Science Foundation of China (No. 71964030).

References

1. Arthur, P., Neubig, G., Nakamura, S.: Incorporating discrete translation lexicons into neural machine translation. In: Proceedings of Conference on Empirical Methods in Natural Language Processing (2016)
2. Dahl, G., Yu, D., Deng, l., Acero, A.: Context-dependent pre-trained deep neural networks for large-vocabulary speech recognition. IEEE Trans. Audio Speech Lang. Process. **20**(1), 30–42 (2012)
3. Heafield, K.: KenLM: faster and smaller language model queries. In: Proceedings of the Sixth Workshop on Statistical Machine Translation, WMT 2011, pp. 187–197. Association for Computational Linguistics, USA (2011)
4. Jean, S., Cho, K., Memisevic, R., Bengio, Y.: On using very large target vocabulary for neural machine translation. In: Proceedings of 53rd Annual Meeting of the Association for Computational Linguistics. 7th International Joint Conference on Natural Language Processing, Beijing, China, vol. 1, pp. 1–10. Association for Computational Linguistics, July 2015

5. Krizhevsky, A., Sutskever, I., Hinton, G.: ImageNet classification with deep convolutional neural networks. In: Proceedings of Advances in Neural Information Processing Systems, pp. 1097–1105 (2012)
6. Och, F., Nev, H.: Discriminative training and maximum entropy models for statistical machine translation, pp. 295–302. Association for Computational Linguistics, Philadelphia (2002)
7. Palangi, H., et al.: Deep sentence embedding using long short-term memory networks: analysis and application to information retrieval. IEEE/ACM Trans. Audio Speech and Lang. Process. 24(4), 694–707 (2016)
8. Tu, Z., Lu, Z., Liu, Y., Liu, X., Li, H.: Modeling coverage for neural machine translation. In: Proceedings of 40th Annual Meeting of the Association for Computational Linguistics, pp. 76–85 (2016)
9. Wang, X., Tu, Z., Zhang, M.: Incorporating statistical machine translation word knowledge into neural machine translation. IEEE/ACM Trans. Audio Speech and Lang. Process. 26(12), 2255–2266 (2018)
10. Wang, X., Lu, Z., Tu, Z., Li, H., Xiong, D., Zhang, M.: Neural machine translation advised by statistical machine translation. In: Proceedings of AAAI Conference on Artificial Intelligence (2016)
11. Zhu, X., Yang, M., Zhao, T., Zhu, C.: Minimum Bayes-risk phrase table pruning for pivot-based machine translation in internet of things. IEEE Access 6, 55754–55764 (2018)

An Automated Method of Identifying Incorrectly Labelled Images Based on the Sequences of Loss Functions of Deep Learning Networks

Zhipeng Zhang[1]([✉]), Wenhui Shou[1], Wengting Ma[1], Dongjia Xing[1], Qingqing Xu[1], Li-Qun Xu[1], Qingxia Fan[2], and Ling Xu[2]

[1] China Mobile Research Institute, Beijing 100032, China
zzp_zzp2002@aliyun.com, shouwenhui@chinamobile.com
[2] Shenyang He Eye Hospital, Shenyang 110034, China

Abstract. Deep learning has been widely applied to medical image analysis tasks. Since the labelled medical images are the foundation of the training, validation, and test of deep learning classification models, the quality of labelling process could directly affect the performance of the models. However, it was estimated that up to ten percent of manually labelled medical images may be incorrectly labelled. In this paper, by utilizing the sequences of loss functions of deep learning classification networks through multiple training epochs, an automated method of identifying incorrectly labelled medical images was proposed. For those identified images, their labels could be further reviewed and updated by senior and experienced physicians, ultimately improving the quality of labelled medical image datasets, as well as the performance of the deep learning models.

Two experiments were carried out to validate the effectiveness of the proposed method, based on a specific fundus image dataset for referable diabetic retinopathy screening. a) In the first experiment, the effectiveness of the method to accurately identify the incorrectly labelled samples from the whole labelled dataset was verified. For a fundus image dataset comprising 10788 samples with gold-standard labels (5394 non-referable diabetic retinopathy samples and 5384 referable diabetic retinopathy samples), the labels of a small part (6%, 648) of the images were intentionally changed to the opposite, in order to simulate the real-world situation. By utilizing the proposed method, 75.31% (488) of the incorrectly labelled samples were successfully identified, and only 4.85% (492) of the correctly labelled samples were wrongly identified as the incorrectly labelled ones. b) In the second experiment, by further reviewing those 980 samples (only 9.1% of the whole dataset) that were identified as incorrectly labelled from the dataset and updating their labels to the correct ones, the deep learning classification model for referable diabetic retinopathy screening was retrained. Tested on an independent test dataset with completely correct labels (700 non-referable diabetic retinopathy samples and 700 referable diabetic retinopathy samples), the best accuracy of the model was increased from 95.93% (trained on the dataset with 6% incorrectly labelled samples) to 96.50% (trained on the revised dataset with 1.5% incorrectly labelled samples), approaching the ideal value 96.57% (trained on the original dataset with 0%

B. Li et al. (Eds.): IoTaaS 2020, LNICST 346, pp. 261–269, 2021.
https://doi.org/10.1007/978-3-030-67514-1_21

incorrectly labelled samples), demonstrating the effectiveness of the proposed method to improve the performance of the deep learning models.

Keywords: Deep learning · Medical image classification · Incorrectly labelled sample identification

1   Introduction

Artificial intelligence (AI) has drawn intense interests around the world. In the healthcare industry, self-diagnostic symptom checkers and clinical decision support systems become a research topic and deep learning techniques-enabled medical image analysis has been applied to almost every medical specialty [1–6]. To realize this vision, it is necessary to obtain a large amount of medical images which were dedicatedly labelled by a group of physicians. These images would be used as either the training samples to construct a deep convolutional neural network (CNN) model, or the validation and test samples to verify the performance of the model.

However, when physicians manually label the medical images, especially a large amount of real-world images with varying levels of image quality, which were taken by different types of medical devices in different clinical and screening settings, it is inevitable that there will be incorrectly labelled samples. The main reasons were as follows:

(1) For the medical image labelling tasks, lesions sometimes occupy a small portion of pixels in the images, such as the microaneurysm (Fig. 1a) and indentation in the arteriovenous crossing (Fig. 1b) in fundus images. The physicians may omit them due to fatigue or limited expertise, making the labels of the images incorrect.

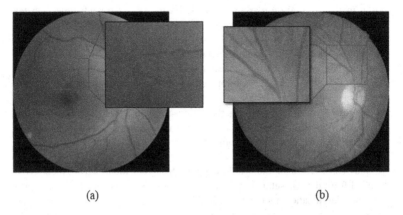

(a)   (b)

Fig. 1. Fundus images with small lesions such as the microaneurysm and indentation in the arteriovenous crossing

(2) The boundaries between the different categories were sometimes illegible in medical images. For example, for the fundus images with high myopia,

peripapillary atrophy appears as a middle stage between normal with leopard pattern and visible sclera, which is the clinical feature of pathologic myopia. It is hard for ophthalmologists to agree on whether an image with the peripapillary atrophy (Fig. 2a) should be labelled as pathologic myopia or non-pathologic myopia. Thus, those challenging samples may be marked with opposite labels, reflecting the inconsistent opinions of different ophthalmologists. Another case is the identification of age-related macular degeneration (AMD) in fundus images, where drusen usually starts to appear at 1 optic-disc-diameter away from the center of macular (Fig. 2b). However, it is hard to accurately quantify the distance and make a correct and consistent labelling decision.

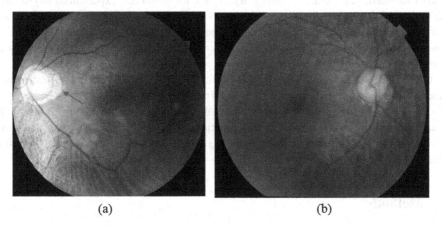

(a)   (b)

Fig. 2. Fundus images in the intermediate state of high myopia and age-related macular degeneration

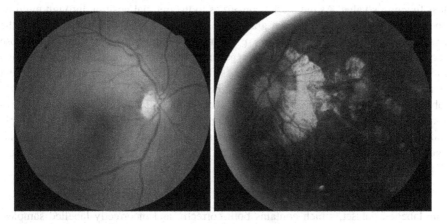

Fig. 3. A fundus image hard to be labelled as gradable or un-gradable

(3) In some situations, labelling standards for medical images are not absolutely objective and measurable [7], resulting in poor consistency on those ambiguous images. For example, the standard of labelling a medical image as gradable (good quality) or un-gradable (poor quality) differs from that of other kinds of images, because it is more focused on whether the target lesion is clear and prominently photographed, as shown in Fig. 3. So the manual labelling process introduces subjective factors unavoidably.

If the incorrectly labelled images were partitioned into the training set, the model would be misled and the performance would be affected. If they were partitioned into the validation set or the test set, the performance of the model could not be authentically evaluated. In general, it is necessary to look for senior and experienced physicians to review all the initial labelling results to ensure the results' reliability, which is time- and energy-consuming. If the incorrectly labelled samples can be automatically identified by an algorithm, the senior and experienced physicians simply need to review a small portion of the images for corrections, which greatly improves the efficiency of data preparation, lays a reliable foundation for the training, validation and test of the deep learning model, and improve the performance of the model.

In this study, a novel automated method of identifying incorrectly labelled medical images based on the sequences of loss functions of deep learning networks was proposed, and its feasibility and effectiveness were evaluated in a fundus image dataset for diabetic retinopathy classification.

2   Methods

In deep learning networks, loss functions measure the discrepancy between the true probabilities and the estimated ones [8]. During the training procedure, optimization algorithms are often used to update the parameters of a model so as to minimize the loss function's value. As the model converges to the optimal position through multiple epochs, the loss value goes down gradually. For those correctly labelled samples, the sequences of loss functions always present a similar decreasing trend. For those incorrectly labelled samples, since their 'ground-truth' were wrong, making the trained model very confused, the sequences of loss functions often show completely different trends from the correctly labelled samples. For example, the loss values of incorrectly labelled samples may maintain at a high level, or present fluctuation changes. Therefore, based on the sequences of loss functions of deep learning networks in multiple training epochs, we can extract the features and cluster all the samples into two categories, one of which represents the correctly labelled samples and the other represents the incorrectly labelled samples.

1) Model training for multiple epochs

The labelled dataset, which contains both correctly and incorrectly labelled samples, was used to train a deep learning network pre-trained on ImageNet dataset [9] through N ($N > 2$) epochs for the target disease classification task. Before the training process, all the images can be resized to a predefined size and data augmentation methods can be used to promote the diversity of the dataset. For each training epoch, we saved each sample's loss value based on the loss function, i.e. cross-entropy loss, and the learning rate was 5e−5. Thus a sequence of loss function with a length of N was obtained for each sample.

2) Feature extraction

As mentioned above, the sequences of correctly labelled samples always present similar decreasing trends, thus six features were extracted to describe the characteristics of the trends.

F1: The mean value of the sequence (with a length of N), representing the global level of the sample's loss;

F2: The mean value of the first P ($1 <= P < N$) terms of the sequence, representing the local level of the sample's loss during the early stage of model training;

F3: The position Q ($1 <= Q < N$) in the sequence, which experiences the biggest decrease level between the Qth term and the (Q + 1)th term;

F4: The mean value of the first Q terms of the sequence, representing the local level of the sample's loss before the significant decrease;

F5: The mean value of the last N-Q terms of the sequence, representing the local level of the sample's loss after the significant decrease;

F6: F4 minus F5, representing the extent of the significant decrease.

3) Clustering

Based on the six features of each sample in the dataset, k-means clustering method [10] was used to cluster the samples into two categories ($k = 2$), one of which represents the correctly labelled samples and the other represents the incorrectly labelled samples. The stopping criteria of the method includes the maximum number of iterations (300), and the relative tolerance with regards to inertia to declare convergence (1e−4). Those incorrectly labelled samples identified by the method could be further reviewed by senior and experienced physicians, in order to improve the quality of the labelled dataset and the performance of the model.

3   Results

The proposed method was validated on a fundus image dataset (denoted as A) for referable diabetic retinopathy (defined as the presence of moderate and worse diabetic retinopathy) screening. Most images of the dataset were obtained using different types of fundus camera during the eye disease screening programs conducted by the He Eye Hospital Group. The rest images were randomly extracted from the training set of Kaggle's Diabetic Retinopathy Detection challenge [11], in order to improve the diversity of the dataset. All the images were labelled and reviewed deliberately by a group of physicians and each image had a ground-truth label, either non-referable diabetic retinopathy (Label = I) or referable diabetic retinopathy (Label = II), as shown in Table 1. The labels were reviewed deliberately by a group of senior and experienced ophthalmologists for more than 3 times, thus each image was considered as a correctly labelled one.

Table 1. The label distribution of the gold-standard dataset (A), the synthetic dataset (A′), and the refined dataset (A″)

Dataset	Label	Number	Correctly labelled	Incorrectly labelled
A	I (non-referable diabetic retinopathy)	5394	5394	0
	II (referable diabetic retinopathy)	5394	5394	0
	Total	10788	10788	0
A′	I (non-referable diabetic retinopathy)	5394	5070	324
	II (referable diabetic retinopathy)	5394	5070	324
	Total	10788	10140	648
A″	I (non-referable diabetic retinopathy)	5394	5284	110
	II (referable diabetic retinopathy)	5394	5344	50
	Total	10788	10628	160

In order to simulate the real-world labelled dataset including incorrectly labelled samples, a synthetic dataset (denoted as A′) was created, through intentionally changing the labels of a small part (6%) of the images, making those correctly labelled samples become incorrectly labelled.

In the first experiment, the effectiveness of the method to accurately identify the incorrectly labelled samples from the whole labelled dataset was examined. The synthetic dataset A′ was used to train the Inception-v3 network [12] pre-trained on ImageNet dataset and the number of epochs was 8 (N = 8). In the pre-processing phase, all images were empirically resized to a predefined 550 × 550 pixels. Figure 4 shows the sequences of loss function of 20 typical correctly labelled samples and 20 typical incorrectly labelled samples respectively. Six features were further extracted based on the sequence of loss function of each sample (P = 4 for F2) and k-means clustering method was used to cluster the samples into two categories. The sensitivity of incorrectly labelled sample identification was 75.31% (=488/648), and the specificity was 95.15% (=9648/10140).

Typical incorrectly labelled samples which were not identified by the method were shown in Fig. 5. Figure 5a shows six images with referable diabetic retinopathy, which were labelled as non-referable diabetic retinopathy in the dataset A′. However, due to either the poor image quality or the limited area of lesions, they looked similar to those images with non-referable diabetic retinopathy, which means it is difficult to identify them successfully among the samples with non-referable diabetic retinopathy. Figure 5b shows six images with non-referable diabetic retinopathy, which were labelled as referable diabetic retinopathy in the dataset A′. Because of the noise such as water spots, reflections and lens stain, they looked similar to those images with referable diabetic retinopathy, which means it is difficult to identify them successfully among the samples with referable diabetic retinopathy.

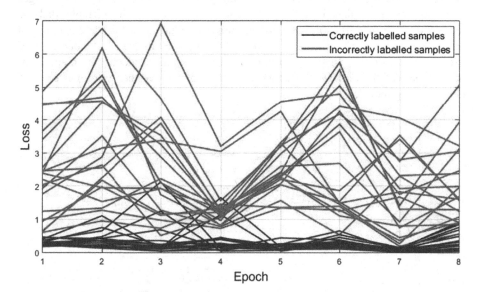

Fig. 4. The loss sequences of 20 typical correctly labelled samples in the synthetic dataset A′

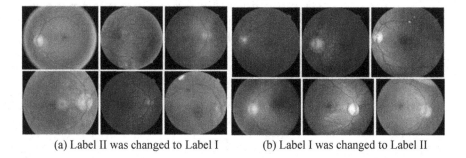

(a) Label II was changed to Label I   (b) Label I was changed to Label II

Fig. 5. Typical incorrectly labelled samples which were not identified by the method

In the second experiment, in order to verify the effectiveness of the proposed method to improve the performance of the deep learning models, the labels of those 980 samples (only 9.1% of the whole dataset) that were identified as incorrectly labelled were reviewed and updated as the correct ones, forming a refined dataset A″ with 1.5% incorrectly labelled samples (as shown in Table 1).

Based on the dataset A″, the deep learning classification model for referable diabetic retinopathy screening was retrained using the same network architecture and the performance of the model was compared to the model trained on the dataset A and the model trained on the dataset A'. As shown in Fig. 6.a and Fig. 6.b, compared to the model trained on A', the accuracy of the model trained on A″ was increased and the average loss was decreased at each training epoch, which was tested on an independent dataset B including 1400 fundus images with completely correct labels (700 images with non-referable diabetic retinopathy and 700 images with referable diabetic retinopathy). During 30 epochs, the best accuracy was increased from 95.93% (model trained on A') to 96.50% (model trained on A″), approaching the ideal value 96.57% (model trained on A), which demonstrates that the automated identification and manually review of the incorrectly labelled samples can improve the performance of the deep learning models.

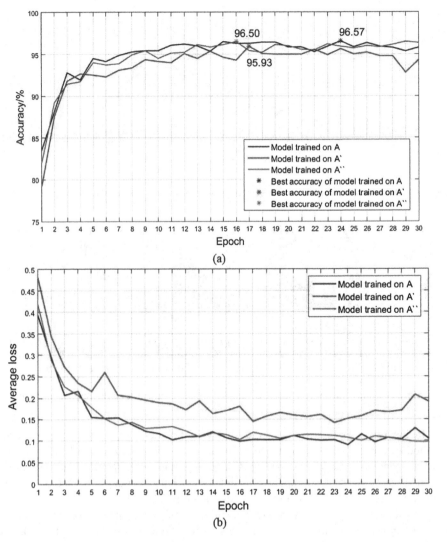

Fig. 6. The accuracy and average loss of the models trained on the dataset A, A' and A″ through 30 epochs, tested on an independent dataset B

4 Conclusions

An automated method of identifying incorrectly labelled medical images based on the sequences of loss functions of deep learning networks was proposed. Through the accurate identification of those incorrectly labelled samples and the further review procedure, the consistency and reliability of dataset labelling can be effectively improved, which lays a better foundation for network training, and ultimately increases the performance of the deep learning models. Further research is necessary to validate the effectiveness of the method for multi-class classification and segmentation tasks.

References

1. Litjens, G., Kooi, T., Bejnordi, B.E., et al.: A survey on deep learning in medical image analysis. Med. Image Anal. **42**, 60–88 (2017)
2. Esteva, A., Kuprel, B., Novoa, R.A., Ko, J., Swetter, S.M., Blau, H.M., et al.: Corrigendum: dermatologist-level classification of skin cancer with deep neural networks. Nature **542**, 115–118 (2017)
3. Hoochang, S., et al.: Deep convolutional neural networks for computer-aided detection: CNN architectures, dataset characteristics and transfer learning. IEEE Trans. Med. Imaging **35**, 1285–1298 (2016)
4. Gulshan, V., et al.: Development and validation of a deep learning algorithm for detection of diabetic retinopathy in retinal fundus photographs. JAMA **316**, 2402 (2016)
5. Yang, W., et al.: Cascade of multi-scale convolutional neural networks for bone suppression of chest radiographs in gradient domain. Med. Image Anal. **35**, 421–433 (2016)
6. Ghafoorian, M., et al.: Non-uniform patch sampling with deep convolutional neural networks for white matter hyperintensity segmentation. In: IEEE International Symposium on Biomedical Imaging, pp. 1414–1417 (2016)
7. Roach, L.: Artificial intelligence: the next step in diagnostics. EyeNet Mag. 77–83 (2017)
8. Shen, Y.: Loss functions for binary classification and class probability estimation. University of Pennsylvania (2005)
9. Deng, J., Dong, W., Socher, R., Li, L., Li, K., Li, F.: ImageNet: a large-scale hierarchical image database. In: IEEE CVPR 2009, pp. 248–255 (2009)
10. Hartigan, J.A., Wong, M.A.: Algorithm AS 136: a k-means clustering algorithm. J. Roy. Stat. Soc. Ser. C (Appl. Stat.), **28**, 100–108 (1979)
11. Kaggle Diabetic Retinopathy Detection competition. https://www.kaggle.com/c/diabetic-retinopathy-detection. Accessed 28 Sept 2018
12. Szegedy, C., Vanhoucke, V., Ioffe, S., Shlens, J., Wojna, Z.: Rethinking the inception architecture for computer vision. In: IEEE CVPR 2016; pp. 2818–2826 (2016)

Low-Latency Method and Architecture for 5G Packet-Based Fronthaul Networks

Yang Liu, Zunwen He, Yan Zhang, and Wancheng Zhang[✉]

Beijing Institute of Technology, Beijing 100081, China
zhangwancheng@bit.edu.cn

Abstract. The design of fronthaul link has become a challenging task in the 5th Generation Mobile Network (5G). In this paper, in order to reduce 5G fronthaul delay and jitter, a multi-thread scheduling receiving method based on interrupt and polling mode is introduced. Considering diverse application scenarios in 5G, we present a new scalable and flexible 5G fronthaul architecture to manage high data traffic flows efficiently. In the end, a hardware system is built to verify the method and fronthaul architecture. Experiments show that delay and reliability can meet the requirements of 5G fronthaul design. Besides, the designed architecture can be used in other distributed high-speed transmission systems to increase their flexibility and efficiency.

Keywords: 5G · Delay requirement · Multi-thread scheduling method · Fronthaul architecture

1 Introduction

Nowadays, with a continuous increase in data traffic and users, 5G has become a hot research topic. Compared with 4G Long-term Evolution (LTE) networks, 5G will provide three main applications: Enhanced Mobile Broadband (eMMB), Ultra-Reliable Low-Latency Communications (uRLLC), and Massive Machine-Type Communication (mMTC), which can support higher data rate, lower latency, and wider access [1]. Therefore, the strict requirements of time delay, reliability, bandwidth, and diversity service are huge challenges to mobile communication technology.

When it comes to solutions, one popular implementation is the Cloud Radio Access Network (C-RAN) architecture [2]. Unlike traditional radio access networks, C-RAN separates remote radio unit (RRU) from base band units (BBUs) to implement flexible and reconfigurable network, and the BBU is divided into a central unit (CU) and many distributed units (DUs) to flexibly adapt to network traffic changes in 5G. The BBU pool can share and dynamically allocate BBUs, offering energy and multiplexing gain.

Although C-RAN architecture can meet various needs of 5G well, some key obstacles still need be taken into consideration for its application. One is the fronthaul link, a low-latency and high-speed communication link between the RRU and BBU pool. Because of the centralization of BBUs, requirements of capacity and delay over the fronthaul link are becoming stricter, which is a key obstacle in the deployment of C-RANs. In 4G LTE, one RRU is connected to one BBU, so the bandwidth and data rate requirements are easy to meet. However, in C-RAN architecture, multiple RRUs

B. Li et al. (Eds.): IoTaaS 2020, LNICST 346, pp. 270–281, 2021.
https://doi.org/10.1007/978-3-030-67514-1_22

connected to one BBU multiple links are combined into one link, raising a huge challenge to 5G fronthaul bandwidth and delay [3]. At the same time, it is also difficult to manage multiple high data traffic flows efficiently. To solve these problems, several works have been carried out on the 5G fronthaul network. In [4], the authors discussed bandwidth usage of the fronthaul link and proposed two methods to reduce the use of bandwidth. The resource scheduling algorithm was studied in [5–8] based on multiple traffic to improve the delay of fronthaul. An erasure coding method was proposed in [9] for MAC frames to reduce delay. Authors in [10] and [11] paid attention to delay and jitter and proposed new fronthaul architecture.

However, most of studies (e.g., [5, 6, 8, 9] and [11]) were based on theoretical simulation and might ignore some influencing factors like clock synchronization and rate matching, which can occur during actual deployment in the 5G fronthaul link. Furthermore, [7–11] concerned delay in the multiple traffic scheduling algorithm and transmission process, but they did not consider delay optimization at the receiving side. In [12], the author proposed a poll-mode method at the receiving side to reduce delay. However, this method in [12] requires the central processing unit (CPU) to always listen, therefore CPU has no time to handle other things. In the 5G mMTC scenarios, this method cannot meet the requirements of intermittent data transmission and low power consumption. Moreover, these studies did not consider the effects of delay and packet loss rate simultaneously. In addition, aforementioned methods focus on a specific scene like optical transport network (OTN) or passive optical network (PON), so they are not able to be generalized to more application scenes. There remains strong demands to design the fronthaul to meet the requirements of delay and loss rate at the receiving side and to adapt to diverse scenes in 5G.

In this paper, a multi-thread scheduling receiving method is proposed, which combines the interrupt and polling methods. This method is suitable for diverse scenes because of generality at the receiving side. Based on this method, a new 5G fronthaul system architecture is designed. Based on the proposed method and architecture, a compact baseband processing unit is implemented, which can support Ethernet-based fronthaul and 10 Gigabit Ethernet interface. With radio frequency (RF) board as well as power and controller board integrated together, the baseband processing unit can support high energy efficiency and lightweight design.

In the remainder of this paper, Section 2 introduces the 5G fronthaul architecture. In Sect. 3, details of the receiving method and new fronthaul architecture are described. Section 4 introduces hardware implementation based on the proposed method and architecture. In Sect. 5 performance of our method is evaluated. Finally, conclusions are drawn in Sect. 6.

2 Fronthaul Architecture

Currently, the fronthaul link is realized through the Common Public Radio Interface (CPRI) by transporting IQ data samples. With the applications of 5G techniques like massive multi input multi output (MIMO), both the bandwidth and the number of antennas become very large. The CPRI interface bandwidth is proportional to numbers of antennas. For example, Table 1 shows the CPRI line rate requirement for

20 MHz/100 MHz bandwidth with different antenna numbers. Using the CPRI interface limits the development of centralized RAN because of the sharply increasing rate.
When a large number of BBUs form a BBU pool, it needs huge fronthaul bandwidth,
so CPRI is no longer applicable because of implementation difficulty. Furthermore, the
transmission efficiency of CPRI is not high. CPRI transport is designed with a constant
transmission rate and has nothing to do with actual network traffic. Even when there is
no traffic on the network, the CPRI link rate is still fixed and not flexible. In order to
promote the evolution of 5G C-RAN, the fronthaul interface needs to be redesigned to
meet more stringent requirements of delay, data rate, and flexibility.

Table 1. CPRI line rate requirement.

Channel BW/MHz	2T2R /Gbps	4T4R /Gbps	8T8R /Gbps	64T64R /Gbps
20	2.4576	4.9152	9.8304	78.6432
100	12.288	24.576	49.152	393.216

As the fronthual link rate requirement continues to increase, the fronthaul architecture is changing. The architectures of traditional RAN, C-RAN, and 5G C-RAN is
shown in Fig. 1. In the 5G C-RAN network, BBUs are divided into a CU and many
DUs which connect RRUs over the fronthaul link to support flexible network architecture. It can be seen from the figure that receiving method is used for DU to reduce
delay and fronthaul architecture design is between DU and RRU in 5G C-RAN to
increase flexibility.

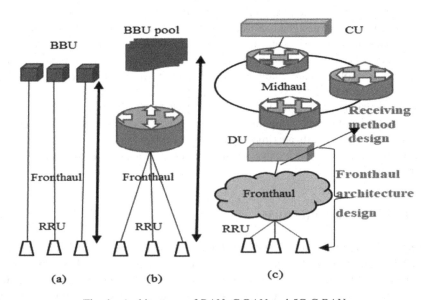

Fig. 1. Architectures of RAN, C-RAN and 5G C-RAN.

3   Fronthaul Design

3.1   Receiving Method Design

Figure 2 shows a general flow of receiving a packet. For high-speed data streams, not only CPU interrupt will be triggered frequently, but CPU usage will be too high. CPU may lose packets with a high error rate due to slow CPU processing. New methods need to be proposed to meet requirements of delay and accuracy [12].

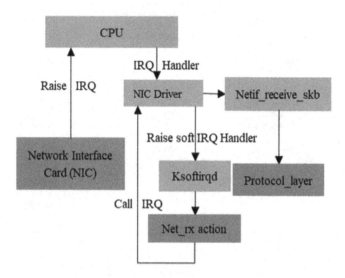

Fig. 2.   General receiving procedure.

In this paper, a new method based on multiple-thread mode is proposed to solve above problems firstly. Delay and accuracy can be effectively improved by using multiple CPUs to simultaneously process data packet. Moreover, multi-queue mode, which receives packet data simultaneously, can be adopted to reduce receiving pressure. However, for resource-constrained BBU pools, an increasing number of threads not only reduces resource utilization but also affects reception performance. Thus, it is important to get appropriate numbers of threads and queues.

The flow diagram depicted in Fig. 3 illustrates the procedure of the receiving method with multi-thread interrupt mode. The details of the parameters are given as follows. T_num: thread numbers used in processing; Q_num: queue numbers used in receiving; T_delay: maximum allowable delay; hashtable: divide traffic to different queues for multi-thread reception according to a hash value. In this method we choose MAC address or IP address according to hashtable value; T_best and Q_best: numbers of threads and queues when delay is minimum; delay: delay measured during the receiving process; Flag: identification for suitable value. Multi-thread receiving method can be summarized in the following steps.

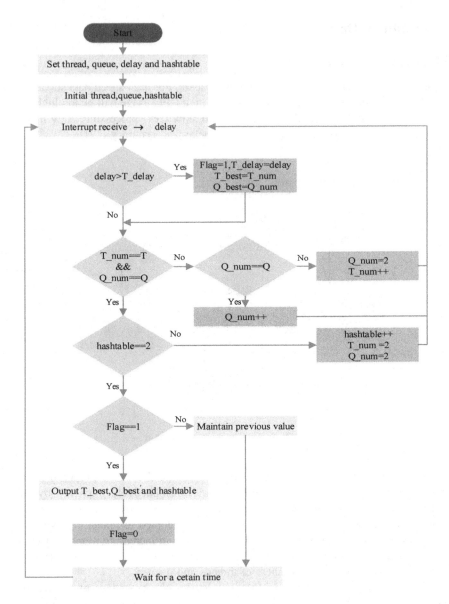

Fig. 3. Flow diagram of multi-thread receiving method.

Step 0: Set T_num, Q_num, T_delay and hashtable to T, Q, 250 microseconds and 2 respectively.

Step 1: Init T_num, Q_num, and hashtable to 2, 2, and 1.

Step 2: Measure delay with multi-thread and multi-queues.

Step 3: Compare measuring delay and setting delay to choose T_best and Q_best. Then, determine the delay for the next comparison. After T_num and Q_num reach T and Q, hashtable value is changed to 2 to divide traffic according to MAC address rather than IP address.

Step 4: When traversal completes, suitable threads and queues can be determined according to T_best, Q_best, and Flag.

Step 5: After DU runs for a certain time with T_best, Q_best, and hashtable, this flow can be run again to obtain new T_best and Q_best.

In order to measure fronthaul delay, a call back mechanism is designed. When DU running on x86 server sends a specific command to RRU, it returns a specific frame data after baseband processing, so delay and loss rate can be measured.

The above method is implemented by using the multi-thread interrupt. Furthermore, a better method of receiving data packet combining interrupt and polling mode is proposed. The method of getting thread and queue numbers is consistent with the method in Fig. 3. When a data packet arrives at DU, the hardware interrupt is triggered. Then the polling mode is used to receive data packet for a setting time. At this time, multiple CPUs always monitor the channel. Packets sent to the NIC will be sent directly to multiple queues and received by multiple CPUs simultaneously rather than sent by a soft interrupt.. The polling time setting is related to different channel environments. For high traffic transmission, polling time can be set longer, whereas, for intermittent low traffic transmission, polling time needs to be reduced to increase resource utilization and reduce energy consumption.

3.2   Fronthaul Architecture Design

Based on proposed method, a new 5G fronthaul architecture is designed as illustrated in Fig. 4. In the new fronthaul design, the goal is that DU sends each data frame with a timestamp to RRU, then the data is written to corresponding random access memory (RAM) address according to DU timestamp. Finally, RRU will send data from the corresponding RAM address according to local RRU time. RRU does not care where data comes from and just sends data from specific address, so it is better for data traffic management through this design. In this way, multiple channels of data from different DUs can be received for transmission to increase flexibility and scalability. To implement the fronthaul design, some aspects should be considered.

A. Clock Synchronization

The strict clock synchronization between DU and RRU is required to meet clock requirements for transmission and reception. Unlike traditional CPRI link, delay can be estimated due to the fixed transmission rate. While the Ethernet-based is used, because of queue delay, frame packing delay and changed link rate, it's difficult to implement clock synchronization scheme between DU and RRU. In this design, in order to get synchronized, timestamps are maintained on both sides of gNodeB and baseband board to mark each local clock, in addition, data is sent according to the timestamp order. For the downlink, when gNodeB sends data frame, FPGA will put data into the specified address of ring RAM according to data frame timestamp. On the other hand, FPGA fetches data from the corresponding address according to local timestamp and sends it. Taking transmission and processing delay into consideration, gNodeB needs to transport data in advance to send correct radio data at the right time on the RF module.

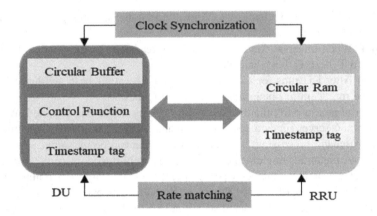

Fig. 4. Fronthaul architecture.

In this way, FPGA doesn't care where data comes from and just sends data according to local clock at FPGA. Therefore, it can provide a better way for scalability and management.

B. Rate Matching

At RRU, the size of circular RAM is limited, and the sending rate at DU and RRU are different. To prevent data at circular RAM from being overwritten, rate control is important for normal data transmission. RRU sends the local timestamp to DU, then DU compares its time with RRU timestamp to get rate relationship between DU and RRU. If time at DU is ahead a lot, which means sending rate at DU is faster and lots of data in circular RAM is waiting to be sent at RRU, DU should pause sending for a while to match rate.

C. Control Function

In addition to the ARM module (PS), gNodeB should also be able to configure the baseband processing unit, so the Ethernet-based network can simultaneously transmit user data as well as control data. The control data is mainly used to configure registers, such as address configuration, control register configuration for receiving and transmitting to achieve uplink and downlink switching. When the link has no network traffic, the corresponding receiving module can be turned off to save energy.

4 Hardware Implementation

In this design, ZYNQ 7000 chip is chosen as System on Chip (SoC) architecture, which includes PS and programmable logic module (PL). The block diagram of the baseband board is shown in Fig. 5, which is connected to Software-Defined Network (SDN) gNodeB running on the x86-64 server over the 10GE fronthaul link. The data transmission control process is realized by PS module, and the design of 10GE interface is completed on the FPGA side with data baseband processing function.

The RF chip AD9371 is configured by PS module. Unlike the traditional Low Voltage Differential Signal (LVDS) interface between FPGA and Analog-to-digital (AD) module, JESD204B high-speed serial interface is used between FPGA and AD module for data transmission because of the high sampling rate of AD module.

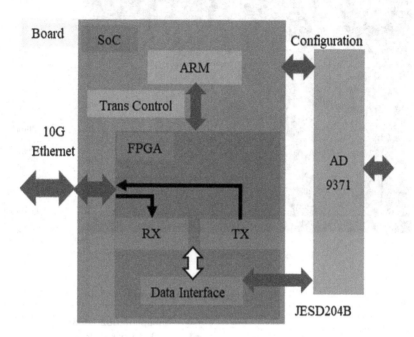

Fig. 5. Block diagram of the baseband board.

A simple sinusoidal signal test is shown in Fig. 6. In this design, the center frequency of AD9371 chip is set to 2.5 GHz and IQ sample data rate is set to 122.88 MHz. It can be seen from the figure that test result is consistent with theoretical result that there is a peak at frequency of 2.5 GHz.

5   Evaluation

Performance of the proposed method and architecture is evaluated in the section. CPRI basic frames are encapsulated in Ethernet payload before transmitted over the fronthaul link, so different Ethernet payload sizes will affect delay and packet loss rate.

Figure 7 shows the result of delay and packet loss rate with different Ethernet payload sizes (64, 256, 512, 1024, and 1480 bytes). As expected, with Ethernet payload sizes increasing, encapsulation delay increases. On the other hand, numbers of interrupts are decreased because of reduced packet numbers under the same traffic, so packet loss rate decreases. Because of increases in processing delay and queuing delay, fronthaul delay increases as the Ethernet payload size increases.

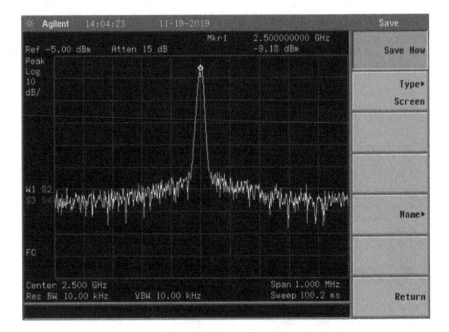

Fig. 6. The test result of spectrum analyzer.

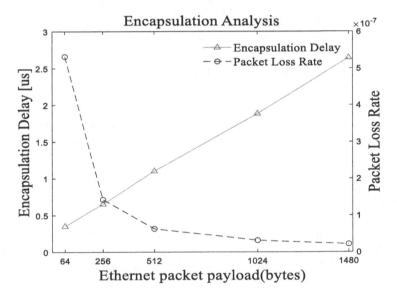

Fig. 7. Analysis of delay and packet loss rate.

Moreover, although encapsulation delay, queuing delay, and processing delay decrease with smaller numbers of payload sizes, a larger packet loss rate results in more retransmissions and has an impact on fronthaul delay. In 5G applications, it is necessary to balance the effects of delay and packet loss rate. Appropriate payload sizes can be selected according to different application scenarios and service requirements to achieve optimal performance.

Delay cumulative distribution function (CDF) diagram is used during the experiment to compare delay performance from DU to RRU. Figure 8 shows the result of delay test using general interrupt, polling method and multi-thread method. The maximum delay of general interrupt is greater than 250 us. Compared with the polling method [12], multi-thread method has shorter delay, which is 160 us and 200 us respectively. Delay requirement of next-generation fronthaul Interface (NGFI) is 250 us when using options 7 and 8 [13], so multi-thread method can meet requirements well. Furthermore, the order of packet loss rate during reception is 10^{-8}, which meets the requirement that NGFI packet loss rate does not exceed 10^{-7} [14].

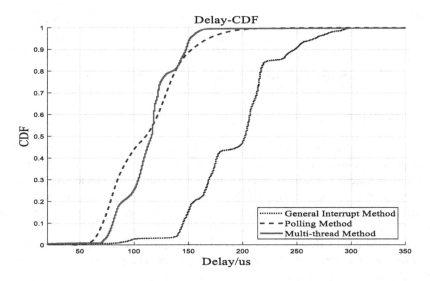

Fig. 8. Delay test result of interrupt, polling and multi-thread methods.

Figure 9 shows delay test result of new method and multi-thread method. By combining interrupt and polling method, lower delay can be achieved with a maximum delay of 110 microseconds, and this method can adapt various application scenarios by adjusting polling time. In addition, flexibility and energy efficiency can be easily achieved by using the method and fronthaul architecture.

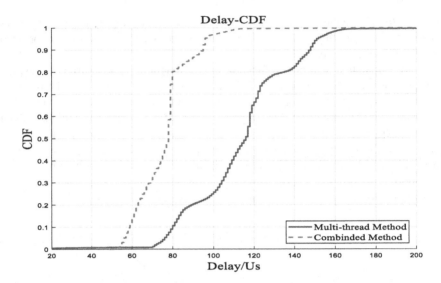

Fig. 9. Delay test result of multi-thread and combined methods.

6 Conclusion

In this study, a multi-thread scheduling receiving method was proposed based on interrupt and polling mode. Based on the method, new scalable and flexible 5G fronthaul architecture was presented to manage data traffic flow efficiently. In the end, an experimental 5G fronthaul platform was built to verify proposed method and architecture based on SDN/NFV technology and 10 Gigabit Ethernet. Delay and reliability can meet requirements of the 5G fronthaul link by using the method and new fronthaul architecture. Besides, the effect of Ethernet payload sizes on delay and packet loss rate was analyzed. With payload sizes increasing, encapsulation delay increased but packet loss rate decreased.

Acknowledgement. This work was supported by the National Key R&D Program of China under Grant 2020YFB1804901 and the National Natural Science Foundation of China under Grant 61871035.

References

1. Chih-Lin, I., et al.: RAN revolution with NGFI (xhaul) for 5G. J. Lightwave Technol. **36**(2), 541–550 (2018)
2. Checko, A., et al.: Cloud RAN for mobile networks - a technology overview. IEEE Commu. Surv. Tutor. **17**(1), 405–426 (2015)
3. Chih-Lin, I., et al.: Toward green and soft: a 5G perspective. IEEE Commun. Mag. **52**(2), 66–73 (2014)
4. Hinrichs, M., et al.: Experimental investigation of new fronthaul concepts for 5G. Kurzfassung, pp. 56–60 (2017)

5. Liu, Y., et al.: Flow Scheduling with low fronthaul delay for NGFI in C-RAN. In: ICC 2019 - 2019 IEEE International Conference on Communications (ICC), pp. 1–6 (2019)
6. Halabian, H., Ashwood-Smith, P.: Capacity planning for 5G packet-based front-haul. In: IEEE Wireless Communications and Networking Conference, WCNC, April 2018, pp. 1–6 (2018)
7. Chitimalla, D., et al.: 5G fronthaul-latency and jitter studies of CPRI over ethernet. J. Opt. Commun. Network. 9(2), 172–182 (2017)
8. Tonini, F., et al.: A traffic pattern adaptive mechanism to bound packet delay and delay variation in 5G fronthaul. In: 2019 European Conference on Networks and Communications (EuCNC), vol. 2, pp. 416–420 (2019)
9. Mountaser, G., et al.: Reliable and low-latency fronthaul for tactile internet applications. IEEE J. Sel. Areas Commun. 36(11), 2455–2463 (2018)
10. Mountaser, G., et al.: Latency bounds of packet-based fronthaul for cloud-RAN with functionality split. In: ICC 2019 - 2019 IEEE International Conference on Communications (ICC), pp. 1–6 (2019)
11. Waqar, M., et al.: A transport scheme for reducing delays and jitter in ethernet-based 5G fronthaul networks. IEEE Access 6(2018), 46110–46121 (2018)
12. Su, S., Wang, W.: 5G fronthaul design based on software-defined and virtualized radio access network. In: 2019 28th Wireless and Optical Communications Conference (WOCC). WOCC 2019, pp. 1–5 (2019)
13. GPP TR38.801: Study on new radio access technology: radio access architecture and interfaces. V1.2.0 (2017-02) (2017)
14. Zhiling, Y., et al.: White paper of next generation fronthaul interface (v1.0). China Mobile Research Institute (2015)

Automated Cataracts Screening from Slit-Lamp Images Employing Deep Learning

Zhipeng Zhang[1]([✉]), Wenhui Shou[1], Dongjia Xing[1], Wenting Ma[1],
Qingqing Xu[1], Wei Wang[1], Li-Qun Xu[1], Ziming Liu[2], and Ling Xu[2]

[1] China Mobile Research Institute, Beijing 100032, China
zzp_zzp2002@aliyun.com, shouwenhui@chinamobile.com
[2] Shenyang He Eye Hospital, Shenyang 110034, China

Abstract. To assess the feasibility and performance using deep learning net-works to automatically detect cataracts from slit-lamp images in large-scale eye diseases screening scenarios. Two datasets were collected using, respectively, the professional Slit-Lamp Microscopes (SLM) and the portable Slit-Lamp Devices (SLD) clipped on a Smartphone, during routine eye disease screening programs in China. The former Dataset-M comprised 4891 images from 1670 subjects and the latter Dataset-D comprised 2516 images from 802 subjects. Each image was then labelled by three ophthalmologists as one of the three classes: 1) un-gradable image, 2) cataract, and 3) normal. For each dataset, two deep learning models were created: one for image quality assessment, and the other for cataracts detection, and the performance of which was assessed by the Area Under a ROC Curve (AUC) and kappa agreement. For the quality assessment models, on Dataset-M (Dataset-D), the corresponding AUC achieved were 0.929 (0.881), with kappa agreements of 0.628 (0.590) and $p < 0.001$, respectively. For the cataract detection models, the corresponding AUC were 0.997 (0.987), with kappa agreements of 0.912 (0.893) and $p < 0.001$, respectively. Furthermore, based on these models we built a practical cloud application that has been trialled in 25 real-world screening settings in China, receiving favourable feedbacks from clinicians, primary care physicians and patients alike.

Keywords: Deep learning · Mobile healthcare application · Automated cataracts screening

1 Introduction

Cataract is the second leading cause of visual impairment and the first leading cause of blindness [1]. According to the Chinese Ophthalmology Society, the prevalence of cataract was 80% among people aged between 60 and 89, and it even reached 90% among people aged over 90. Early screening plays a key role in controlling the disease progression and preventing needless cases of blindness. However, the provision of specialists eye care services are unevenly distributed in China. Primary care physicians at county and lower level hospitals and clinics are generally lack of expensive equipments and necessary expertise in screening and diagnosing common eye diseases,

B. Li et al. (Eds.): IoTaaS 2020, LNICST 346, pp. 282–291, 2021.
https://doi.org/10.1007/978-3-030-67514-1_23

resulting in a large number of patients, especially in resource-limited rural and remote regions, having little or no access to high-quality eye care services.

In recent years, with the cost going down and the use of ophthalmic imaging devices becoming widespread, a large volume of eye images can be available. On the other hand, machine learning technology such as deep learning is advancing very rapidly, which proved to be amenable to various medical image analysis tasks with superior performance [2–5]. Furthermore, the ubiquitous mobile broadband network and cloud computing platform provide unprecedented data acquisition, transmission, storage and processing capabilities. These driving forces make it possible to automatically detect cataracts from slit-lamp images in large-scale eye diseases screening scenarios. Compared to using traditional feature extraction and grading methods to detect cataracts [6], deep learning and convolutional neural network (CNN) methods can be more robust to noises and interferences, and are generally applicable in practical scenarios, which has been shown by Long et al. [7], in the case of diagnosing rare congenital cataracts based on slit-lamp images with diffuse light.

In this paper, an automated system for cataracts screening from slit-lamp images was investigated, which suited for both outpatient and ambulatory scenarios. In outpatient screening scenarios, such as the county and township hospitals, cities' community health service stations and optical vision centres, and even some large rural clinics in China, the professional Slit-Lamp Microscopes (SLM) with single lens reflex (SLR) cameras are available for a technician to take one or more slit-lamp images for each eye of the patient. The images were then uploaded in real-time through 4G-LTE or Wi-Fi hotspots to our cloud platform for detailed analysis using advanced deep learning algorithms in respect of images' quality and cataract presence. On the other hand, in ambulatory screening scenarios such as in remote and rural regions, village doctors, care assistants or trained volunteers were equipped with a cheap option, a portable Slit-Lamp Device (SLD) clipped on a Smartphone, to capture slit-lamp images of the patients anywhere and anytime, and the images were transmitted using the 4G-LTE cellular network to the cloud platform. By taking advantage of this eye diseases screening system, urban and rural communities currently under-served can have equitable access to professional and quality primary eye care services, receiving a fast feedback, diagnosis and/or referral, helping to take a preventive measure or early treatment action as cataracts develop. This would improve quality of life of the patients, save unnecessary medical expenses and get them back to work, thus, relieving illness-related poverty. The feasibility and effective performance of the algorithms and system were investigated and verified.

2 Methods

The slit-lamp images that we used to train, validate and test the methods were acquired during the eye disease screening programs conducted by the He Eye Hospital Group (HEHG) in China between December 2015 and December 2017. Figure 1 shows, respectively, the two typical settings and devices used in the case of outpatients and ambulatory screening scenarios. These were eye hospitals, optical vision centres, community halls and village clinics in Cities of Shenyang, Dalian, Jinzhou, Yingkou, Huludao, and so on across China Northeast Liaoning Province.

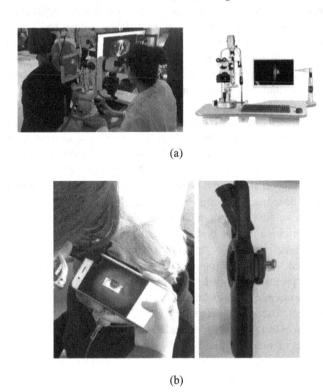

(a)

(b)

Fig. 1. Eye disease screening scenarios and typical slit-lamp devices (a) Outpatient screening scenario and SLM with SLR camera (b) Ambulatory screening scenario and SLD

The images were collected using either professional SLM-KD4, a SLM with SLR camera (Made by Chongqing Ruiyu Instruments and Equipment Co. Ltd, Chongqing, China), or portable SLD prototypes (Built by the HEHG, Shenyang, China) clipped on a Smartphone. Up to six images were captured for each eye by an operator through shifting the focus positions to the front (diffuse light) and side (slit light) of the anterior lens capsule as well as the posterior lens capsule (slit light). Depending on different ophthalmic screening programs, the acquisition of images could have taken place in a darkroom, half-darkroom, or indoor room, all without pupil dilation.

Given that the images taken by the two different types of devices and cameras were largely different in resolution, field of view, brightness, contrast, and other interference factors (Fig. 2), two independent datasets, were created as shown in Table 1. Dataset-M contained 4 891 SLM photographed images and Dataset-D contained 2 516 SLD photographed images.

Each image in the above two datasets was labelled independently, by three ophthalmologists each having at least six years of clinical experience in the HEHG, as one

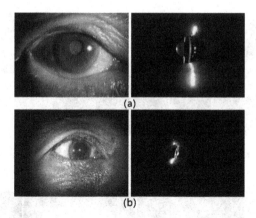

Fig. 2. Examples of slit-lamp images (a) SLM photographed images (b) SLD photographed images

Table 1. Summary of image characteristics and available demographic information in the two datasets

Characteristics	Dataset-M	Dataset-D
No. of images	4 891	2 516
Patient demographics		
No. of individuals	1 670	802
No. of female individuals	1 034	509
Age, mean (SD), y	68.0 (10.7)	62.8 (11.6)
Label distribution		
Label 1	1 216	855
Label 2	1 326	1 246
Label 3	2 349	415

of the three classes: 1) un-gradable image, 2) cataract, and 3) normal. Figure 3 shows a few common examples of un-gradable images, denoted as 'Label 1': no eyeball, no lens, defocused lens, excessive width of slit light, bright ambience, slit light with less than 30-degree angle, and reflective pupil area. Examples of the gradable images, marked as either 'Label 2' (cataracts with lens opacity) or 'Label 3' (normal with clear lens), are shown in Fig. 4. The three ophthalmologists had to discuss to reach a consensus when the labels were in disagreement. After labelling, the distributions of image labels among the two datasets were shown in Table 1.

Deep learning was used to create two models for each dataset, one for image quality assessment, and the other for cataracts detection. In the image quality assessment task, all images were empirically resized to a predefined 650 × 500 pixels, which was based on prior experiments on suitable image sizes; The pixel values were normalized to between 0 and 1. Then, the images with Label 1 were considered as positive samples and images with Label 2 and 3 were negative samples. These images were randomly

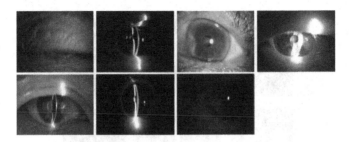

Fig. 3. Examples of un-gradable slit-lamp images

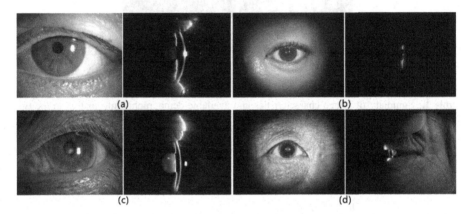

Fig. 4. Examples of normal and cataract (a) Normal – SLM photographed images (b) Normal – SLD photographed images (c) Cataract – SLM photographed images (d) Cataract – SLD photographed images

divided into three parts proportionally according to 8:1:1 as shown in Table 2: a) For training, 80% of the data was used to train the Inception-v3 network [8] (proved to be superior to other popular networks in our experiments) pre-trained on ImageNet dataset [9]; b) For validation, 10% of the data was used to determine the appropriate number of training epochs to avoid the model's over-fitting; and c) For testing, the remaining 10% of the data was used to assess the performance of the final model to unseen data. In the training phase, two separate models for the Dataset-M and Dataset-D were fine-tuned and validated, respectively, incorporating the standard practice of data augmentation. To counter the effect of the data imbalance in positive and negative samples, weighting factors were introduced in the loss function based on binary cross entropy to equally penalize under- or over-represented classes in the training set.

In the cataract detection task, the main processing flow was similar to that of the previous one, including data pre-processing, dataset partition, model training and testing, though the images with Label 2 were considered as positive samples and images with Label 3 negative samples, as shown in Table 3. Considering that the total number of negative samples in Dataset-D was limited (the last row of Table 3), to ensure that the number of images for testing is adequate, we repartitioned the samples to increase the number of testing images.

Table 2. Dataset partition for developing the models for image quality assessment (Positive samples – Label 1; Negative samples – Label 2 & Label 3)

Dataset	Label	Training	Validation	Test	Total
Dataset-M	Positive	974	121	121	1 216
	Negative	2 943	366	366	3 675
Dataset-D	Positive	685	85	85	855
	Negative	1 329	166	166	1 661

Table 3. Dataset partition for developing the models for cataracts detection (Positive samples – Label 2; Negative samples – Label 3)

Dataset	Label	Training	Validation	Test	Total
Dataset-M	Positive	1 881	234	234	2 349
	Negative	1 062	132	132	1 326
Dataset-D	Positive	989	128	129	1 246
	Negative	277	38	100	415

3 Statistical Analysis

The performance of the models on the two test datasets using the consensus of three ophthalmologists as the reference standard was shown in Table 4. For the two image quality assessment models, the AUC were 0.929 (95% CI 0.904–0.951) on Dataset-M and 0.881 (95% CI 0.833–0.925) on Dataset-D, with kappa agreements of 0.628 ($p < 0.001$) and 0.590 ($p < 0.001$), respectively. This shows very strong classification performance of the two image quality models, while the kappa agreements around 0.6 mean a substantial consistency between the test results and the consensus of three ophthalmologists. For the two cataract detection models corresponding to the two datasets, the AUC were 0.997 (95% CI 0.993–0.999) and 0.987 (95% CI 0.975–0.996), with kappa agreements of 0.912 ($p < 0.001$) and 0.893 ($p < 0.001$), respectively. Thus, the classification performance of the two cataract detection models were superb and the consistency proved to be almost perfect.

Table 5 and Fig. 5 compare the performance of the models against that of three individual ophthalmologists, i.e. AJ - junior ophthalmologist, BS - senior ophthalmologist and CS - senior ophthalmologist, for the two datasets, respectively. Except that one of the three ophthalmologists (CS) had a better performance than the model in the image quality assessment task on the Dataset-M, in most cases, the accuracy and kappa agreement of models were superior to ophthalmologists. For quality assessment task, the models can be most valuable to reduce the rate of undetected poor quality

Table 4. The performance indicators (sensitivity, specificity, accuracy, AUC, kappa agreement) of the models for image quality assessment (IQA) and cataracts detection (CPD), using the consensus of three ophthalmologists as the reference standard

Tasks	Sensitivity, % (95% CI)	Specificity, % (95% CI)	Accuracy, % (95% CI)	AUC (95% CI)	Kappa (95% CI)	P-value
IQA on Dataset-M	83.5 (76.5, 89.6)	85.2 (81.5, 89.0)	84.8 (81.5, 88.1)	0.929 (0.904, 0.951)	0.628 (0.548, 0.703)	<0.001
IQA on Dataset-D	80.0 (71.3, 88.2)	81.3 (75.2, 87.2)	80.9 (75.7, 85.7)	0.881 (0.833, 0.925)	0.590 (0.485, 0.689)	<0.001
CPD on Dataset-M	96.2 (93.5, 98.3)	95.5 (91.7, 98.6)	95.9 (93.7, 97.8)	0.997 (0.993, 0.999)	0.912 (0.860, 0.952)	<0.001
CPD on Dataset-D	95.3 (91.3, 98.5)	94.0 (89.0, 98.1)	94.8 (91.7, 97.4)	0.987 (0.975, 0.996)	0.893 (0.832, 0.947)	<0.001

Table 5. The performance of the models vs. that of three individual ophthalmologists for image quality assessment and cataracts detection tasks (AJ – junior Ophthalmologist, BS – senior Ophthalmologist, CS – senior ophthalmologist)

Indicators		Image quality assessment		Cataracts detection	
		Dataset-M	Dataset-D	Dataset-M	Dataset-D
Sensitivity, %	Model	83.5	80.0	96.2	95.3
	AJ	39.7	38.8	40.2	81.4
	BS	43.8	38.8	88.9	83.7
	CS	66.1	41.2	26.1	82.9
Specificity, %	Model	85.2	81.3	95.5	94.0
	AJ	95.1	95.8	98.5	56.0
	BS	92.6	98.2	68.9	63.0
	CS	94.3	98.2	96.2	42.0
Accuracy, %	Model	84.8	80.9	95.9	94.8
	AJ	81.3	76.5	61.2	70.3
	BS	80.5	78.1	81.7	74.7
	CS	87.3	78.9	51.4	65.1
Kappa	Model	0.628	0.590	0.912	0.893
	AJ	0.410	0.397	0.315	0.383
	BS	0.411	0.431	0.593	0.476
	CS	0.639	0.455	0.174	0.260

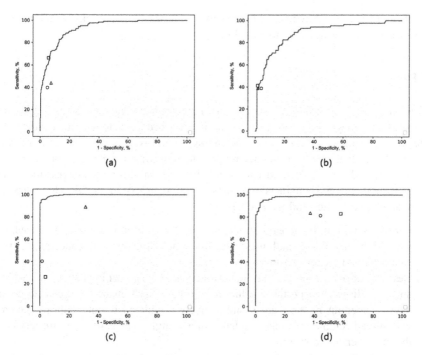

Fig. 5. The performance of the models (ROC curve) and individual ophthalmologists (AJ – circle, BS – triangle, CS – square, as indicated) for image quality assessment and cataracts detection tasks when tested on the two datasets. (a) Image quality assessment on Dataset-M (b) Image quality assessment on Dataset-D (c) Cataracts detection on Dataset-M (d) Cataracts detection on Dataset-D

images in both Dataset-D and Dataset-M. For cataracts detection task, more cataracts cases in both Dataset-D and Dataset-M could be identified accurately by the model than individual ophthalmologists. Overall, the models had achieved high performance in analyzing diverse slit-lamp images obtained in primary care settings, and could be reliably applied to real-world screening.

The deep learning algorithms were integrated with an end-to-end system for large-scale outpatient and ambulatory cataracts screening scenarios. The system consists of a SLM or SLD, a mobile APP running on the android smartphones or tablets, and a cloud-based platform integrating the corresponding models for both Dataset-D and Dataset-M. Slit-lamp images and demographic information such as subjects' gender, age, and personal medical history were acquired and uploaded from the APP to the platform through 4G-LTE or Wi-fi network. By taking advantages of suitable technologies like Graphics Processing Unit (GPU) server cluster and Redis message queue, the system was able to meet the real-world requirements of high concurrency and low latency. Tested on one single GPU server (Alibaba Cloud Computing Co. Ltd., Hangzhou, China), it took 0.3 s to process and analyse a total of six images from one subject. A cluster of 8 GPU servers could support up to 2000 screening settings with a response time of 10 s. The system has been trialled in 25 real-world screening settings in 9 cities of Liaoning Province, China, receiving favourable feedbacks from clinicians, primary care physicians and patients alike.

4 Discussion

To our knowledge, this is the first time that an automated cataracts screening system from slit-lamp images employing deep learning has been developed and validated for large-scale outpatient and ambulatory screening scenarios. Compared to other relevant work applying machine learning techniques to detecting cataracts such as nuclear cataracts [6] and rare congenital cataracts [7] based on slit-lamp images, the image quality assessment and cataracts screening solution proposed in this study has the following characteristics and advantages:

(1) For the benefit of the general public, the target eye disease is age-related cataracts with high prevalence and incidence rate, including nuclear cataracts, cortical cataracts, and posterior subcapsular cataracts.

(2) Besides supporting outpatient ophthalmic screening in settings such as hospitals and eye clinics, the portable solution involving SLD enables large-scale ambulatory screening in rural areas and sparsely populated remote regions, given a widespread cellular coverage available, thus bringing specialist eye care service to the most venerable communities.

(3) Although the images were taken by operators with different knowledge levels using multiple imaging equipment (SLM or SLD) during various acceptable ambient light conditions, the performance of the cataracts detection models tested on gradable images remains unaffected by using sufficient image data to fine-tune deep learning CNNs and data augmentation methods.

(4) Under the close collaboration between scientific researchers and ophthalmologists, the standards of anterior ocular segment image acquisition and quality assessment were innovatively discussed and determined.

(5) The effectiveness of the deep learning algorithms and system has been validated; hence, the system will be ultimately integrated into routine clinical processes and tackle the challenge of real world application scenario.

Further research is necessary to expand the amount and multisource of slit-lamp images to ensure the data heterogeneity, use deep learning algorithms to further grade the severity of lens opacity, and detect other common ocular surface diseases such as corneal disease and pterygium. We have conducted relevant research and the preliminary results are very promising.

Acknowledgements. We acknowledge the help of all the ophthalmologists in HEHG for collecting slit-lamp images during the eye disease screening programs, and Jun Li and Xinghuai Xue in HEHG for image labelling.

References

1. Pascolini, D., Mariotti, S.P.: Global estimates of visual impairment: 2010. Br. J. Ophthalmol. **96**, 614–618 (2012)
2. Esteva, A., et al.: Corrigendum: dermatologist-level classification of skin cancer with deep neural networks. Nature **542**, 115–118 (2017)
3. Hoochang, S., et al.: Deep convolutional neural networks for computer-aided detection: CNN architectures, dataset characteristics and transfer learning. IEEE Trans. Med. Imaging **35**, 1285–1298 (2016)
4. Gulshan, V., et al.: Development and validation of a deep learning algorithm for detection of diabetic retinopathy in retinal fundus photographs. JAMA **316**, 2402 (2016)
5. Zhang, L., et al.: Automatic cataract detection and grading using Deep Convolutional Neural Network. In: IEEE ICNSC 2017, pp. 60–65 (2017)
6. Huang, W., Chan, K.L., Li, H., Lim, J.H., Liu, J., Wong, T.Y.: A computer assisted method for nuclear cataract grading from slit-lamp images using ranking. IEEE Trans. Med. Imaging **30**, 94–107 (2010)
7. Long, E., et al.: An artificial intelligence platform for the multihospital collaborative management of congenital cataracts. Nat. Biomed. Eng. **1**, 0024 (2017)
8. Szegedy, C., Vanhoucke, V., Ioffe, S., Shlens, J., Wojna, Z.: Rethinking the inception architecture for computer vision. In: IEEE CVPR 2016, pp. 2818–2826 (2016)
9. Deng, J., Dong, W., Socher, R., Li, L., Li, K., Li, F.: ImageNet: a large-scale hierarchical image database. In: IEEE CVPR 2009, pp. 248–255 (2009)

System and Hardware

A Flowchart Based Finite State Machine Design and Implementation Method for FPGA

Zhongjiang Yan[(✉)], Hangchao Jiang, Bo Li, and Mao Yang

School of Information and Electronics, Northwestern Polytechnical University,
Xi'an 710072, China
{zhjyan,libo.npu,yangmao}@nwpu.edu.cn

Abstract. The design idea of control and data separation is an effective means to realize the complex communication system, and the control part can usually be designed and realized by means of finite state machine (FSM). However, there is no effective method to realize the complex communication system based on finite state machine in the existing research. Aiming at the problem of the existing FPGA design and implementation methods with complex and non-universal communication protocol and algorithm design, a Flowchart based Finite State Machine (F-FSM) design and implementation method for FPGA is proposed, which significantly improves the FPGA development efficiency. This method takes the flowchart describing the complex communication system as input, divides the communication system into modules, and outputs the finite state machine transition diagram and transition matrix of the control module. This method can effectively shorten the design time of the communication system and its control module. Finally, an IP core encapsulated in FPGA is designed. This method can effectively improve the development efficiency of control module, improve the re-usability of control module and reduce the workload of code development.

Keywords: Flowchart · Finite state machine · FPGA

1 Introduction

Communication systems are important parts of the Internet of Things (IoT). For example, wireless local area network (WLAN) can be used as a low-energy means of IoT communication [1]. With the development of communication technology, the complexity of communication networking protocols in communication systems (such as WLAN, 4G/5G/6G, Bluetooth, ZigBee, etc.) are increasingly high, and how to effectively realize these complex communication systems through Field Programmable Gate Array (FPGA) has become an urgent problem to be solved [2–4]. There are two mainstream FPGA design and implementation methods in existing research, i.e., pipeline design idea [5] and control and data separation idea [6]. The idea of pipeline design is only applicable to communication systems with simple logic and clear functions between modules, while the

© ICST Institute for Computer Sciences, Social Informatics and Telecommunications Engineering 2021
Published by Springer Nature Switzerland AG 2021. All Rights Reserved
B. Li et al. (Eds.): IoTaaS 2020, LNICST 346, pp. 295–310, 2021.
https://doi.org/10.1007/978-3-030-67514-1_24

idea of control and data separation is applicable to complex communication systems, in which the control module can be realized by using finite state machine [7,8], and the finite state machine (FSM) describes the overall working condition of the system.

Combined with the actual system design, the general modular system architecture is shown in Fig. 1. This architecture divides the whole system into several related or independent functional modules, and manages the signal interaction and sequence of each functional module by setting the system main module. In the same way, each function module can be divided into sub-modules, and a functional main module can be used to schedule the functions of the overall function module. This method can also be used if the internal structure of subsequent sub-modules is more complex.

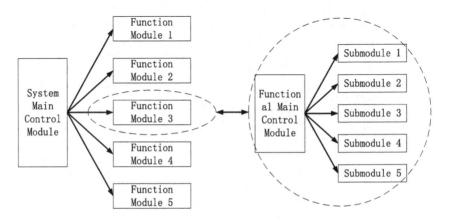

Fig. 1. General modular system architecture

Modular system architecture is very common in practical engineering systems, and its advantages are quite obvious. Ref. [9] applies the modular architecture to design the controller of the machine tool reconstruction. The control module of the top level is responsible for controlling the physical module of the bottom level, and the physical module processes the data. Control is separated from data processing, and this hierarchical control pattern reduces a large amount of overall revalidation. In Ref. [10], IEEE 802.11 multiple access control (MAC) protocol implementation based on FPGA technology divides the entire protocol system into sending and receiving parts, and then realizes the two parts by controlling each function module through main control. Reference [11] applies this architecture to the automatic bag-bagging control strategy based on finite state machine, and verifies the advance of this design method through practical application. In the previously mentioned references on the application of FSM in various fields, the idea of modular system architecture has been used subtly. This paper systematically summarizes this architecture and provides a general design and implementation method for developing a system based on FSM in FPGA.

To reduce the unforeseen problems caused by the redundant circuits, Wen proposed a design method of highly efficient FSM and validated it by the circuit diagrams in Ref. [12]. Chen presented an efficient manner described in Verilog HDL in the design of FSM in Ref. [13], and verifies with a synthesizable example the advantages of the design method of FSM in the area and power consumption. Ref. [14] studied different state encoding styles and Verilog descriptions of FSM. Reference [15,16] found out the advantages and disadvantages on circuit, simulation and stability of different FSMs, which showed that the two-always and three-always method are better than the one-always method. It can be seen that the aforementioned related works study how to optimize and coding the FSM based on Verilog HDL. However, few of existing related works study how to design an efficient FSM for a complex communication system. This motivates us to study this topic.

Although there is no general design method of FSM in the existing research, flowchart is a general method to represent the working mechanism of communication protocol or algorithm. Transforming flowchart into FSM is an idea that has never appeared and is worth studying. Based on this observation, in this paper we propose a flowchart-based FSM (F-FSM) design and implement method for FPGA. The main contributions are listed as follows. The communication system is divided into modules and the state transition graph and matrix of the control module are given. This method can effectively shorten the design time of the communication system and its control module. Finally, an IP core encapsulated in FPGA is designed. This method can effectively improve the development efficiency of control module, improve the re-usability of control module and reduce the workload of code development.

The rest of this paper is organized as follows. Section 2 presents the design principle and modelling methods of FSM, as the theoretical foundations of our proposed method. Section 3 presents the proposed F-FSM method. Section 4 gives the IP core design and implementation of F-FSM method. Section 5 verify the correctness and the efficiency of the proposed F-FSM IP core through functional simulation and mapping. Section 6 concludes this paper.

2 Design Principle and Modelling Methods of FSM

The design principle and modelling methods of FSM are presented in this section, which layout the theoretical foundations of our proposed method. Section 2.1 presents the design principle of FSM and Sect. 2.2 presents three modelling and description methods of FSM, which are state transition diagram, state transition matrix and state transition table.

2.1 Design Principle of FSM

As many theories emerge with the needs of science and engineering, FSM is a theory that provides an approximation for physical and abstract phenomena [7].

By using FSM to describe abstract systems, the internal logic of things can be clearly and completely presented to the analyst or designer. Because FSM is easy to build, it is widely used in life, mathematics, engineering and other fields, for example, early Turing machines, grammatical analysis of English sentences, analysis of three states of water. The system which can be described by the design method of FSM has the following characteristics, which are also possessed by the multi-access protocol in the communication system.

1. The overall logic of the system can be divided into a finite number of states with a definite starting state.
2. At any time instant, the system is only in the unique divided state.
3. The triggering conditions for each state and action are clear.
4. Triggering conditions of the system's actions only depend on the current state and current triggering events.

The mechanism of FSM is that the system is divided into finite states according to certain principles to realize the complete functional actions of the original system. The transition is driven by the occurrence of internal or external events of the system. Extended State Machine (EFSM) is a more perfect and universal form of FSM. Due to its completeness of description, EFSM is often used in the modelling of complex communication systems, such as communication protocols and resource allocation algorithms. Its definition is a six-tuple, as shown in Eq. (1).

$$M = \{S, S_0, I, V, O, T\} \tag{1}$$

S refers to the state set of the state machine, i.e., M, and S_0 is the initial state of the state machine. I is the input set of M, and O is the output set. V is the internal variable set, and T is the state transfer condition set of the state machine. Since the state transition condition contains information such as transition direction and trigger condition, T can be represented in the form of six tuples, as shown in Eq. (2).

$$T = \{S_i, S_j, i, o, P_t, A_t\} \tag{2}$$

S_i is the initial state of M. When the input i and the state transition condition P_t of the current variable value are valid, M is triggered to jump to the end state S_j of the corresponding state transition, followed by a series of operations A_t such as output or assignment, and the output result is o.

2.2   Modelling and Description Methods of FSM

Three modelling methods of FSM are presented in this sub-section, which are state transition diagram, state transition matrix and state transition table.

State Transition Diagram. The state transition diagram of an abstract FSM can be represented by circles representing the finite states and state transition directions (directed arrow) between the states. Figure 2 is a state transition diagram of a three-state FSM with initial state $S1$. This description method is visual and intuitive, which is the most commonly used expression at present. However, with the increase of the number of states and transition conditions, the depicted state transition diagram will be relatively chaotic and no longer applicable.

State Transition Table. In short, a state transition table describes state transitions in a FSM in the form of a table. Table 1 is a state transition table of the FSM state transition diagram shown in Fig. 2. The first row represents all transition conditions between states, and the first column represents all of the finite states of the system. The element at the intersection of a row and a column represents the transition condition from the state indicated by the row to the state indicated by the column. Similar to the disadvantage of the state transition diagram, when the number of states increases, the condition of inter-state transition will increase by a square time, and the number of columns in the state transition table will also increase sharply. Therefore, this description method will no longer be applicable.

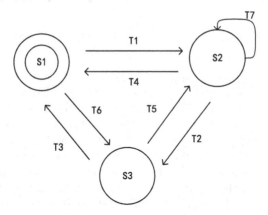

Fig. 2. An example of state transition diagram

Table 1. State transition table

	T_1	T_2	T_3	T_4	T_5	T_6
$S1$	$S2$					$S3$
$S2$		$S3$		$S1$		
$S3$			$S1$		$S2$	

State Transition Matrix. In order to address the shortcomings of the above two methods, the concept of matrix in mathematics is introduced into FSM. Equation (3) shows the state transition matrix of the FSM as shown in Fig. 2. In this matrix, each row and each column represent all states of the system. For each entry of the matrix, the row represents the current working state, and the column represents the state to be transited in the next state transition. The intersection of the row and column represents the trigger condition of the state transition. However, it is not as intuitive as a state transition diagram.

$$
\begin{array}{c}
\begin{array}{ccc} X_1 & X_2 & X_3 \end{array} \\
\begin{array}{c} X_1 \\ X_2 \\ X_3 \end{array}
\begin{bmatrix}
 & T_1 & T_6 \\
T_4 & & T_2 \\
T_3 & T_5 &
\end{bmatrix}
\end{array}
\tag{3}
$$

Above three FSM modelling and description methods are the most commonly used methods in applications, and each has its own advantages and disadvantages. In addition, the combination of the above three methods is also common in FSM modelling and description. In this paper, the FSM is modelled and described mainly by state transition matrix and state transition diagram.

3 Flowchart Based Finite State Machine Designing Method

3.1 Basic Ideas

On the one hand, the modular approach of control and data separation, as shown in Fig. 1, is one that involves the step-by-step splitting of system functions into a number of single functional modules. Among them, the master control module is responsible for implementing the work sequence of these functional modules. On the other hand, flowchart is one of the most common and complete whole project expression method. Therefore, if the flowchart of the judgment conditions can be regarded as state transitions of FSM, and concrete operation can be regarded as the state of FSM, and then connect them with the start and end to form a closed loop, the flowchart can be seen as an FSM state transition diagram. This is the basic idea of the proposed F-FSM. Therefore, the overall engineering design and implementation of FPGA can be carried out based on flowchart.

Figure 3 is the flowchart of the main steps of the proposed F-FSM method. Wherein, the solid frame represents the design step of the method, and the dashed frame represents the finite state machine information obtained by the corresponding step, such as the states and the transition conditions between states. The main steps of the proposed F-FSM is given as follows.

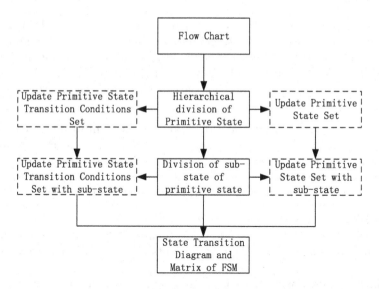

Fig. 3. Main designing flow of F-FSM

1. The flowchart is taken as input.
2. According to the flowchart, the set of primitive state and the set of transfer conditions between the primitive states can be obtained through flowchart division procedures.
3. For each primitive state, the sub-states, each with a single function, can be obtained through flowchart division procedures. And then, the finite state set and the state transition conditions set can be updated by including these sub-states.
4. Run above step 3 iteratively until all of the primitive states are divided into sub-states, which can not be divided any more.
5. Finally, the final state transition diagram of FSM can be drawn, and the state transition matrix can be derived.

The proposed F-FSM provides a modular architecture application method for FPGA system design and implementation, based on the traditional flowchart designing method. Therefore, the proposed F-FSM method is a kind of method for complex logic system based on simple traditional flowchart method. It can greatly reduce the design difficulty, and promote the overall design of the structure of the realizability and maintainability.

3.2 Detailed Description of F-FSM

According to the flowchart of the main steps of the proposed F-FSM method, as shown in Fig. 3, the detailed steps are as follows.

Step 1: According to the top-down principle, partition the complex logic into several functional modules. Networking protocols in communication systems are often a complex set of processes, which can be directly divided into several modules according to their functions. For example, the DTRA protocol can be divided into scanning stage, reservation stage and data sending stage in DTRA. The CSMA/CA protocol can be divided into the sending module and receiving module. The purpose of this step is, not only to reduce the complexity of the single flowchart in Step 2, but also to make the overall structure more intuitive.

Step 2: Comb and draw the flowchart of each module. According to the partitioned functional modules in Step 1, draw the flowchart required by this method after understanding the internal principles of each module. The requirements of the proposed F-FSM method for flowchart are as follows. In the required flowchart, only the following frames or box can be accepted.

– START box and END box.
– A decision box with n, $n \geq 1$, inputs and 2 outputs, known as *decision branch*.
– A multi-process box with m, $m \geq 2$, inputs and 1 output, known as *process branch*.
– A single-process box with one input and one output, known as *single process*.

Up to now, the complex logic system can be modelled and described with the traditional flowchart. The purpose of this step is to normalize the flowchart, with clear transition conditions and complete separation of states and conditions. In addition, this step is also to facilitate the implementation of if-else decision logic based on FPGA hardware language. Figure 4 is an example of a flowchart that conforms to this specification. To facilitate further understanding of this approach, the following steps will be described using this flowchart as an example. This flowchart does not correspond to any actual situation, so there is no specific process operation. However, it will not affect the subsequent operation.

Step 3: According to the obtained flowchart, partition the flowchart into primitive states, and then obtain the set of primitive states and the state transition conditions set. After the primitive states are determined, they are removed from the flowchart so that they do not affect subsequent state partitioning procedures. After the primitive states connected by the decision branch are determined, the transition conditions of these states are also determined. That is, the condition of the establishment of the decision branch is the transition condition of these two states. The detailed flow of this step is as follows.

Step 3.1: Take the boxes of "START" and "END" in the flowchart as the states of $S0$ and $S1$, respectively. If the function of the flowchart is a loop, $S0$ and $S1$ can be merged into state $IDLE$ to form a closed loop. Then go to Step 3.2.

Step 3.2: Find all of the "process branches" in the flowchart, and cut the flowchart with all inputs as cutting points. And then go to Step 3.3.

Step 3.3: After cutting, if the process branch contains "single process", then regard "single process" as a primitive state. It is numbered according to the hierarchy and sequence and counted it into the state set S. If the process branch contains decision branch, then the decision branch can be regarded as the state transition condition. After the states connected to "decision branch" is determined, in terms of the previous states, the post-states and state transition conditions, then the state transition conditions are included in the inter-state transition condition set T. Then go to Step 3.4.

Step 3.4: If there is still a decision branch that is not separated from the flowchart, then look for the first decision branch from "START" following the arrow. And then regard all the inputs and outputs of the decision branch as cutting points. Then go back to Step 3.3. Otherwise, when there are no decision branch, the flowchart partition procedure ends.

The flowchart, as shown in Fig. 4(a), after the primitive states partition is given in Fig. 4(b) according to Steps 3.2 and 3.3. And the flowchart after the partition of primitive state 4 according to Steps 3.3 and 3.4 is shown in Fig. 4(c).

Finally, the state set S and the inter-state transition condition set T are respectively shown in Eq. (4) and (5), where the transition condition is fictitious and is represented by capital letters, i.e., A, B, C and etc.

$$
\begin{aligned}
S &= \{S0, S1, S2, S3, S4\} \\
&= \{S0, S1, S2, S3, \{S4-1, S4-2\}\} \\
&= \left\{ S0, S1, S2, S3, \left\{ \begin{array}{l} \{S4-1-1, S4-1-2, S4-1-3\}, \\ \{S4-2-1, S4-2-2, S4-2-3\} \end{array} \right\} \right\}
\end{aligned}
\tag{4}
$$

$$
\begin{aligned}
T &= \{(S2, S1, A), (S0, S3, B), (S3, S0, C), (S0, S4, \overline{C})\} \\
&= \{(S2, S1, A), (S0, S3, B), (S3, S0, C), (S0, S4-1, \overline{C}+D), (S0, S4-2, \overline{C}+\overline{D})\} \\
&= \{(S2, S1, A), (S0, S3, B), (S3, S0, C), (S0, S4-1-1, \overline{C}+D), \\
&\quad (S4-1-1, S4-1-2, E), (S4-1-1, S4-1-3, \overline{E}), (S4-1-2, S1, F), \\
&\quad (S4-1-3, S2, G), (S0, S4-2-1, \overline{C}+\overline{D}), (S4-2-1, S4-2-2, H), \\
&\quad (S4-2-1, S4-2-3, \overline{H}), (S4-2-2, S2, I), (S4-2-3, S1, J)\}
\end{aligned}
\tag{5}
$$

Step 4: Partition the primitive state into sub-states according to the primitive state functions. There is only a "single process" in the initial state partitioned by Step 3, but it may not achieve the goal of single function requirement of the FPGA module designing and implementation. The primitive state is partitioned into sub-states to achieve the requirement of single function sub-state when the functions of the primitive state are multiple. After that, update the set of the states, i.e., S. In addition, some "single process" can also be combined as one according to the coupling degree of functions. For example, if two single processes with the same functions can be merged as one state. There is no branching condition between the sub-states of an primitive state. That is to say that the internal processes of "single process" are in pipeline form, and the next operation begins immediately after the completion of one operation. Finally, update the set of transition conditions, T.

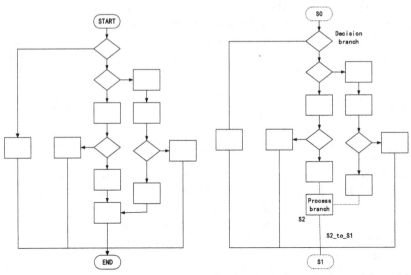

(a) Initial flowchart conforming to the requirements of F-FSM method

(b) Flowchart after procedures of Steps 3.2 and 3.3

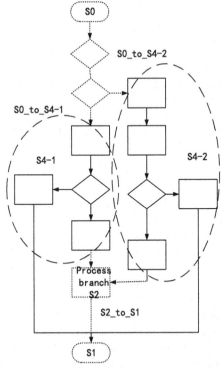

(c) Flowchart after procedures of Steps 3.3 and 3.4

Fig. 4. Example of partition the flowchart into primitive states and sub-states

Step 5: Draw the FSM state transition diagram and derive the FSM state transition matrix. The following steps are helpful to draw and derive the state transition diagram and matrix.

Step 5.1: Draw the tree diagram according to the state set S, as shown in Fig. 5.

Step 5.2: Determine the number of FSM states according to the tree diagram.

In general, it is recommended that a FSM have no more than 9 states since when the number of the states is too large the logic of state transition will be too complex to understand and implement. If there are more than 9 states, the number of states can be reduced based on the hierarchy of the tree diagram.

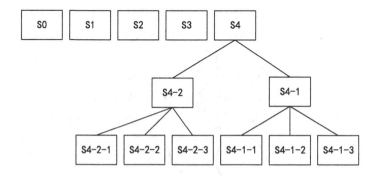

Fig. 5. The tree diagram of the state set S.

As shown in Fig. 5, the first layer has 5 states (namely $S0 - S4$), the second layer has 6 initial states (namely $S0 - S3, S4 - 1$ and $S4 - 2$), and the third layer has 10 initial states (namely $S0 - S3, S4 - 1 - 1/ - 3$ and $S4 - 2 - 1/ - 3$). At this point, $S4 - 1 - 1/ - 3$ can be combined into a state $S4 - 1$ and other states in the third layer can form another FSM, i.e., embedding the new formed FSM into state $S4 - 1$. After that, $S4 - 1 - 1/ - 3$ and the same new state IDLE can be formed into a FSM with four states according to Step 5.2, which can be implemented within $S4 - 1$ in the form of embedding.

Step 5.3: According to the states determined in Step 5.2, the state transition condition set T, draw the FSM state transition diagram according to whether there are transition conditions between states and the direction of state transition. And deduce the transition conditions to output the corresponding position to the state transition matrix.

4   IP Core Design and Implementation of F-FSM Method

The IP core design method of F-FSM is firstly presented in Sect. 4.1 firstly, and then how to use the designed IP core is presented in Sect. 4.2.

4.1   IP Core Design Method of F-FSM

The modular architecture of control and data separation makes the function of the control module become simple, whose function is only to output the enabling signals of other modules according to the changes of input conditions. Therefore, we can design a separate FSM IP core. In the following, we first give the design and implementation principle of the FSM IP core with only 4 states, and then extend it to the design of the finite state IP core with 10 states.

Figure 6 shows an FSM with 4 states and all possible state transitions, where 16 transition conditions can be determined. Table 2 is the parameter definition of the FSM transition condition. In other words, these parameters can be seen as part of the FSM IP core input interfaces.

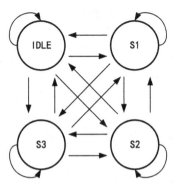

Fig. 6. All possible state transitions in 4-state FSM with $S = \{IDLE, S1, S2, S3\}$, where $S0 = IDLE$.

The inputs of an FSM are directional state transition conditions. That is, a transition from one state to another state. The outputs are enabling signals for corresponding states, indicating that the enabled state module begins to work. Therefore, in the design of the IP core of an FSM with 4 states, the interfaces should include at least the clock and reset signals, 16 transition condition interfaces and 4 state-enabled control signals. Table 2 defines the FSM state transition directions and the state transition parameters. The definition of state transition parameters is named in the direction of the state transition. The state transition condition from $IDLE$ to $S1$ is taken as an example, and its parameter name is *idle-to-s1*.

All of the possible state transition directions and parameters of 4 states can be derived from Eq. (6). Within it, 2 denotes two directional conditions, indicating that any two states among 4 states can jump to each other. 4 means that each state can also transit to itself, so there are altogether 16 transition conditions.

$$2 \times C_4^2 + 4 = 12 + 4 = 16 \tag{6}$$

$$2 \times C_{10}^2 + 10 = 90 + 10 = 100 \tag{7}$$

Table 2. Figure 6's state transition direction and state transition parameter definition

Direction	Parameter	Direction	Parameter
IDLE → S1	idle-to-s1	IDLE → S2	idle-to-s2
IDLE → S3	idle-to-s3	S1 → IDLE	s1-to-idle
S2 → IDLE	s2-to-idle	S3 → IDLE	s3-to-idle
S1 → S2	s1-to-s2	S1 → S3	s1-to-s3
S2 → S1	s2-to-s1	S3 → S1	s3-to-s1
S2 → S3	s2-to-s3	S3 → S2	s3-to-s2
IDLE → IDLE	idle-to-idle	S1 → S1	s1-to-s1
S2 → S2	s2-to-s2	S3 → S3	s3-to-s3

The maximum number of transition conditions that may exist is the number of input ports corresponding to IP core. Therefore, the number of input ports for IP core with 10-states FSM is 100. Due to the excessive number of ports, these ports can be combined and named with certain rules. This is done by merging the 100 ports of the input ports into an input port with a bit width of 100, and similarly merging the output ports into an output interface with a bit width of 10. The corresponding mode of its input and output interfaces is as follows. The transition condition from state i to state j corresponds to the $(10 \times i + j)$th bit of the 100-bit wide input interface, that is, the transition condition from $S2$ to $S3$ is the 23rd bit of the input port. Bit i of the output port with a bit width of 10 is the enabling signal of state i, which controls whether state i is enabled or not.

Figure 7 shows the interface block diagram of 10-state FSM IP core, which encapsulates the traditional three-always style Verilog HDL codes. By combining transition conditions between multiple states as the input interface, the enabling signals of the other functional modules are output. Table 3 is the input/output interface table, where state transition parameters are similar with that defined in Table 2.

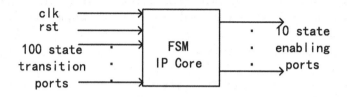

Fig. 7. 10-state FSM IP core interfaces

Table 3. Figure 7's state transition direction and state transition parameter definition

Port name	Width	I/O	Description
clk	1	I	Clock
rst	1	I	Reset
trans-condition	100	I	100 state transitions
state-en	10	O	10 state enabling ports

4.2   System Implementation Method Based on FSM IP Core

According to the modular design architecture of control and data separation idea in Sect. 1, as shown in Fig. 1, the control module and data processing module are effectively separated. The function of the control module is only to control the enabling signals of the other data processing modules and only output the 0/1 control signals of the function modules. Section 4.1 presents the IP core of the designed F-FSM, which can fully meet the single functional requirements of the control module.

In the whole Verilog code implementation process of the system, the design and implementation of the control module can be directly completed by calling the reusable FSM IP core and inputting corresponding state transition conditions, thus reducing a lot of coding time. In addition, the data processing module under the modular architecture is designed as a single functional sub-module. While in different communication systems, some functions are similar or even the same, which makes the functional sub-module under the architecture highly reusable.

5   Performance Evaluation

We implement the proposed F-FSM IP core on FPGA, and verify the correctness and the efficiency of the IP core through functional simulation and mapping.

Figure 8 is the IP core function simulation verification graph of the FSM. In the test case, the state transition conditions between various states were enabled in turn. The functional simulation results show that the implemented F-FSM IP core is correct.

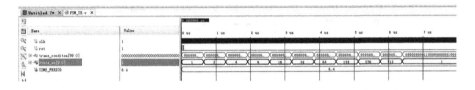

Fig. 8. 10-state FSM IP core functional simulation

Table 4 shows the resource utilization of the implemented F-FSM IP core, among which LUT, register and clock resources account for a relatively low proportion, while input-output interfaces use a large amount of input conditions as the interface in this scheme design.

Table 4. Resource utilization of the implemented F-FSM IP core

Resources	Utilized	Available	Percentage of utilization
Slice LUTs	132	303600	0.04
Slice registers	10	607200	0.00
IO	101	700	14.43
Clocking	1	32	3.12

To sum up, for the implemented F-FSM IP core, the functional simulation result is correct and the resource utilization is low, which meets the design requirements.

6   Conclusion

Finite state machine (FSM) is an important design method of control module in the design of control and data separation modular architecture. However, with the increasing complexity of communication system, how to realize the separation of control and data efficiently and how to design an efficient FSM become a very significant problem. This paper proposes a flowchart-based FSM FPGA design and implementation method for complex communication system, which significantly improves the FPGA development efficiency. This method takes the flowchart describing the complex communication system as input, partition the communication system into modules, and output the FSM transition diagram and transition matrix of the control module. This method can effectively shorten the design time of the communication system and its control module. Finally, an IP core encapsulated in FPGA is designed. This method can effectively improve the development efficiency of control module, and improve the re usability of control module and reduce the workload of code development.

Acknowledgments. This work was supported in part by the National Natural Science Foundations of China (Grant No. 61771392, No. 61771390, No. 61871322 and No. 61501373), and Science and Technology on Avionics Integration Laboratory and the Aeronautical Science Foundation of China (Grant No. 201955053002, No. 20185553035).

References

1. Pirayesh, H., Sangdeh, P.K., Zeng, H.: EE-IoT: an energy-efficient IoT communication scheme for WLANs. In: Proceedings of the IEEE INFOCOM 2019 - IEEE Conference on Computer Communications, Paris, France, 29 April–2 May 2019, pp. 361–369 (2019)
2. Yan, Z., Li, B., Gao, T., et al.: Design and implementation of FPGA-based transmitter memory management system. In: IEEE International Symposium on Consumer Electronics. IEEE (2014)
3. Li, S., Li, B., Yan, Z., et al.: Design and implementation of DSR routing table entries for FPGA. Appl. Electron. Tech. **44**(12), 89–92 (2018)
4. Jiang, H., Li, B., Yan, Z., et al.: Design and implementation of a frequency hopping hybrid multiple access protocol on FPGA. In: 2018 IEEE International Conference on Signal Processing, Communications and Computing (ICSPCC). IEEE (2018)
5. Davis, I.E., Wong, A.: Pipeline method and system for switching packets. United States Patent, 24 March 2015
6. Syed, I., Roh, B.H.: Delay analysis of IEEE 802.11e EDCA with enhanced QoS for delay sensitive applications. In: Performance Computing & Communications Conference (2017)
7. Gill, A.: Introduction to the Theory of Finite-State Machines. McGraw-Hill, New York (1962)
8. Minns, P., Elliott, I.: FSM-based digital design using Verilog HDL (2008). https://doi.org/10.1002/9780470987629:1-22
9. Xu, H., Tang, R., Cheng, Y.: Modular design method for control of reconfigurable machine tools. J. Zhejiang Univ. (Eng. Sci.) **38**(1), 5–10 (2004)
10. Zhang, J.: Design and Implementation of MAC prototype based on FPGA for Wireless Local Area Network. Master Degree Thesis, Northwestern Polytechnical University, Xi'an, China (2015)
11. Ren, P.: Design and implementation of frequency synthesizer based on DDS and PLL. Master Degree Thesis, National University of Defense Technology, Changsha, China (2009)
12. Wen, G.: Design of high efficient state machine based on verilog HDL. Electron. Eng. **32**(6), 4–7 (2006)
13. Chen, Y.: Modelling and optimized design of finite state machine. J. Chongqing Inst. Technol. (Nat. Sci. Ed.) **21**(5), 55–58 (2007)
14. Yu, L., Fu, Y.: Verilog design and research of finite state machine. Microelectron. Comput. **21**(11), 146–148+157 (2004)
15. Luo, X., Li, J., Tian, Z.: Optimization design of FSM based on Verilog HDL. Electron. Qual. **3**(1), 36–38+42 (2012)
16. Feng, K., Li, Y., Zhang, J., Li, J.: Design and implementation of control system based on FSM. Shipboard Electron. Coutermeasure **38**(5), 94–98 (2015)

A Distributed Reservation and Contention Combined TDMA Protocol for Wireless Avionics Intra-communication Networks

Xueli Zheng[1], Zhongwang Zhang[2], Xinyang Yan[1], Zhongjiang Yan[3]($\boxtimes$), Mao Yang[3], and Bo Li[3]

[1] Science and Technology on Avionics Integration Laboratory,
Shanghai 200233, China
1367176109@126.com, yxyhit@126.com

[2] China Aeronautical Radio Electronics Research Institute, Shanghai 200241, China
826371905@qq.com

[3] School of Information and Electronics, Northwestern Polytechnical University,
Xi'an 710072, China
{zhjyan,yangmao,libo.npu}@nwpu.edu.cn

Abstract. To reduce the structural complexity of the cabin avionics communication system and meet the increasing demand for data exchange, Wireless Avionics Intra-Communication (WAIC) networks attract attentions from the academic and industrial researchers. Based on the analysis of the wired cabin avionics bus communication system and the analysis of the short-range wireless communication technologies, this paper firstly shows that Ultra Wideband (UWB) could be taken as the candidate technology of WAIC networks. To guarantee the maximum data transmission delay and improve the channel utilization, this paper proposes a Distributed Reservation and Contention Combined (DRCC) TDMA protocol for WAIC networks. Firstly, AP allocates the time slots to each node to ensure that each node can reserve the channel to transmit data. This can help guarantee the maximum data transmission delay. Secondly, if a node does not have data to transmit in its reserved slot, then the others nodes can contend to access into this time slot with p-probability. Simulation results show that compared to the fixed allocated TDMA and p-CSMA the proposed DRCC protocol can improve the throughput by 5% and 50%, respectively. And the average delay can be reduced by 4% and 10%.

Keywords: Wireless avionics intra-communication · Ultra wideband · Reservation · Contention

1 Introduction

With the increasing interconnection of subsystems in cabin avionics communication system (CACS) and the increasing demand for data exchange, the structural

B. Li et al. (Eds.): IoTaaS 2020, LNICST 346, pp. 311–328, 2021.
https://doi.org/10.1007/978-3-030-67514-1_25

complexity of CACS increases significantly. Avionics full duplex switched ethernet (AFDX) [1] based cabin aviation bus network is used in the new generation of large aircraft. The AFDX aviation bus communication network requires a large number of cables and connectors, which not only increases aircraft weight and integration costs, but also poses structural and fire risks to the wired CACS network, which reduces reliability and increases the difficulty of maintenance in chunks. In recent years, wireless communication technologies such as wireless local area network (WLAN) and Bluetooth have made rapid development, bringing a lot of convenience to people's life and study. However, wireless communication technology has not been widely used in avionics systems.

In 1995, the concept of wireless technology was introduced in specific areas of aerospace and the fly-by-wireless working group was formed in 2007 [2]. This group, which brings together industry leaders from Airbus and the National Aeronautics and Space administration, is discussing the latest applications of wireless communications for aerospace applications. Recently, an avionics communication solution based on wireless technology was proposed to add non-critical onboard functions such as in-flight entertainment network, in-flight communication and aircraft health monitoring. The U.S., France, Germany and other big aircraft manufacturers, as well as the aviation industry and the International Telecommunication Union (ITU), are pushing forward the development of Wireless Avionics Intra-Communication (WAIC) systems. In the early days of the 2015 international radiocommunications conference, the participating countries jointly deliberated and approved a topic to support "spectrum allocation through aviation mobile (airline) services and promote the application and expansion of airborne internal wireless communications in the aviation sector" [3]. ITU-R group and the coherence of the various countries mainly explores the plan to use on WAIC spectrum (4200 MHz to 4400 MHz), to explore with the electromagnetic compatibility problem existing between the airborne radio altimeter. The research results show that after the relevant technical means, WAIC will not produce interference to the existing airborne radio altimeter [3].

Akram et al. devised a CACS network based on WiFi wireless networks [4], which is suitable for ethernet backbone network. Pangun Park and Woohyuk Chang believe that the adaptability of MAC protocol is a key aspect of WAIC network [5]. Literature has proved that the UWB TDMA network with fixed time slot allocation can meet the aviation network communication requirements of a certain scale to determine the maximum delay after reasonable configuration [6].

Although many researchers have been carried out the wireless communication of avionics in airborne cockpit, few valuable research results have been published. At present, it is unknown that there is an onboard cockpit aviation wireless network that has been put into use by the aircraft. Although there are still many difficulties in using wireless in-plane communication in avionics system, with the rapid development of various wireless communication technologies, it has provided possible solutions for in-plane wireless communication.

Aiming at WAIC networks in the demand of low data transmission delay and high network utilization, this paper puts forward a distributed reservation and contention combined (DRCC) TDMA protocol for WAIC networks. The proposed DRCC TDMA multiple access control (MAC) protocol based on ultra-wide band (UWB) is designed. Based on the features of AFDX network, this paper improves the UWB MAC protocol using fixed allocation TDMA, proposes a hybrid TDMA protocol of fixed allocation and competitive allocation, and designs the MAC scheduling process of airborne wireless network based on UWB.

The rest of this paper is organized as follows. Section 2 introduces the advantages and key technologies of the wired airborne networks, e.g., AFDX. And then the airborne wireless networks in cockpit has been carried on the demand analysis, and evaluation of existing short distance wireless communication technology, e.g., UWB. Section 3 presents the system model and motivation. Section 4 introduces the core idea of DRCC-TDMA protocol, then gives the detailed design and protocol flow description, as well as the designed frame structure. Section 5 verifies and analyzes the performance of the proposed protocol through simulation. Section 6 concludes this paper.

2   Related Works

According to the network connection form, the existing airborne in-cabin network can be divided into wired CAC network and wireless CAC (WCAC) network, which will be introduced one by one.

2.1   Wired Cabin Avionics Communication Network

Wired CAC network is also known as airborne in-cabin aviation bus, and the most widely used aviation bus technologies include ARINC429 [7], 1553B [8,9] and AFDX [1].

ARINC429 aviation data bus standard [7] makes clear rules for the format of digital information transmission and requirements between the aircraft airborne avionics and avionics systems. All of the transmitting device and receiving device adopt shielded twisted-pair cable to transmit data between information, transmission mode for one-way broadcasting transmission, modulation method for bipolar three state code modulation. ARINC429 aviation bus structure is relatively simple, and the performance of small network is very stable and has a very strong anti-interference level. Its high reliability in the aviation field has been proved over the past decades. However, the bus bandwidth of ARINC429 is small and the interface does not support the new processor, which leads to the increasing delay. Therefore, with the increasing number of sensors in the new generation of aircraft, the information interaction content is more and more complex. ARINC429 aviation bus has been unable to meet the requirements of the new generation of aviation communication.

1553B aviation data bus [8,9] is a serial, multiplexed based aviation data bus, whose working mode is time-division data/response multiplexing transmission.

The 1553B aviation bus adopts redundant backup bus topology layout, which has the advantages of high timeliness and reliability. Half-duplex is adopted to complete data transmission by Manchester encoding, and its effective data transmission rate is only up to 1 Mbps. The 1553B bus has played an important role in the development of aviation communications over the past decades. Even now, in some indexes, such as real-time, reliability, it still can satisfy the active part of the model. But as the number of a new generation of aircraft sensors increase, the interactive information is exchanged more frequently. Furthermore, because the centralized bus controller for avionics systems may cause the plane's security from a single point of failure, this becomes a serious security threat.

AFDX is an avionic full-duplex switched Ethernet suitable for deterministic network communication in the new generation of avionic systems, which has been officially included in ARINC664 [1]. AFDX can support the transmission rate of physical layer up to 100 Mbps, and the transmission medium can take both optical fiber and coaxial cable. AFDX network is a static network, regardless of the number of nodes in the network or between nodes interconnected, including data transmission path and the flow rate is fixed or is strictly controlled. The AFDX network technology can support a large amount of important data transmission, and the switching is based on its exchange and the concept of Virtual Link (VL), for each of the transmission of data flow to ensure a reservation for the transmission bandwidth.

The realization of VL in AFDX network is based on the transmission mode of Time Division Multiplexing (TDM). In setting up each VL, two important parameters are given as follows: Bandwidth Allocation Gap (BAG) and maximum Frame Size (MFS). Wherein, after the BAG sends out a frame, it needs to wait for at least one BAG to send the next frame, while MFS is the maximum frame length defined in AFDX network that can be transmitted on VL, with the size of 64   1518 Byte. If BAG and MFS are determined, the maximum available bandwidth of VL can also be calculated. Assuming that the maximum bandwidth of link is B_{max}, MFS is denoted by L_{max}, then $B_{max} = L_{max}/BAG$. AFDX network sets BAG and MFS for each VL, which also restricts the maximum bandwidth of VL network. The data that cannot be sent is cached first, and the later data is discarded when the buffer is full.

Even if each end system (ES) sets BAG for all VLs, it may have multiple VLs that need to send data and at the same time have their own sending time. At this time, ES must ask each VL in order according to its scheduling algorithm, and send the data on each VL that meets the sending conditions from the same physical port in turn. This causes a delay in the VL data sent later, known as Jitter. Jitter is unavoidable and is constrained in the AFDX network by setting the maximum permitted Jitter of ES (max jitter, not greater than 500us). If the default max jitter value is exceeded during transmission, the frame is discarded. The avionics system have two sets of each redundancy backup hardware equipment, each of the VL ready to send the data to be copied for exactly two, at the same time sent to the two physical port of backup, and then sent to their respective AFDX network, the destination ES also uses Redundancy Management (Redundancy Management, RM). If it receives two data at the same time, then according to the "first come effective" way of judgment, receives the arrival of the first effective data frames, and then to discard the latter one. This double redundancy network system can guarantee the high reliability of AFDX network data transmission.

2.2   Wireless Cabin Avionics Communication Network

With the development of wireless communication network technology, more and more researchers believe that wireless communication technology in airborne cockpit can meet the communication needs of CAC system. Airborne equipment requiring communication in the cabin is mainly concentrated in the two avionics cabins of the aircraft nose, and the maximum linear distance between any two points in each cabin is less than 6m. Considering the transmission characteristics of airborne equipment and comparing with the existing AFDX airborne network, if wireless communication technology is to be used for communication in the onboard cockpit, the following requirements need to be met in the transmission radius of 6 m.

- Sufficient stable transmission network bandwidth between avionics should be provided
- End-to-end information transmission delay and maximum delay must be guaranteed;
- It cannot tolerate any information errors and must have high reliability.
- It can adapt to electromagnetic compatibility, different temperature and humidity, vibration and other environments in the engine room.

Based on the analysis of application scenarios in airborne cockpit, this paper considers that the wireless network transmission distance in airborne cockpit is relatively short, so we only discuss several possible short-range wireless networks. Through a large amount of research literature [10,11], it can be known that in recent years, short-range wireless networks that have been widely used or studied mainly include Bluetooth, ZigBee, WiFi, UWB and 60 GHz millimeter wave communication technologies.

Bluetooth operates in the 2.4 GHz band and is a time division based full-duplex wireless communication. It has a maximum transfer rate of 1Mbps (higher rate Bluetooth actually uses transport protocols and technologies such as IEEE 802.11). Generally speaking, the effective transmission distance of Bluetooth is within the range of about 10m, but by increasing the transmission power, the maximum transmission distance can reach 100m. In addition to the fact that the working frequency of Bluetooth is in the working frequency band of the avionics wireless equipment, which is easy to interfere with the existing avionics system. Bluetooth is also confronted with such problems as too complex protocol, excessive protocol consumption, low transmission rate and inflexible networking mode, which limit the application of Bluetooth in the cabin wireless communication.

WiFi, like Bluetooth, belongs to a short-range Wireless communication technology used in home or office. IEEE 802.11 protocol group is the protocol standard of Wireless Local Area Network (WLAN). With the development of WiFi nowadays, the transmission speed is fast, but its working frequency is easy to disturb the existing avionics system, which is not suitable for the future development of wireless transmission technology in the cabin.

ZigBee adopts Frequency Hopping Spread Spectrum (FHSS) technology, which works in the 2.4 GHz frequency band and has a transmission rate of only 250 Kbps with a transmission distance of 10 m–100 m. ZigBee's entire network is based on independent nodes, which form a star-shaped, tree-shaped or mesh network through wireless links. Not all nodes have the same function. As a wireless communication technology, ZigBee is characterized by low cost and low power consumption. However, its disadvantages include low bandwidth, large transmission delay, and easy to interfere with the existing avionics system, which is difficult to meet the future needs of wireless transmission technology development in the cabin.

UWB is a new wireless carrier communication technology that uses nanosecond to microsecond non-sinusoidal narrow pulses to transmit data. UWB can support several hundred Megabits per second (Mbps) data transfer speeds in the range of 10m or so, mainly due to its ability to transmit very low power signals over large bandwidth. UWB has strong anti-interference ability, high transmission speed, very large bandwidth, less energy consumption, small transmission power and other advantages, mainly used in indoor communication, high-speed wireless Local Area Network (LAN), security detection, radar and other fields. UWB communication technology has a high transmission rate and good anti-jamming and safety characteristics, which makes it a possibility for future airborne cabin wireless network technology.

As an important short-distance communication technology in the future, 60 GHz millimeter wave communication has the advantages of high transmission rate and wide frequency band occupancy. Many countries have successively opened the spectrum resources of 5–7 GHz near 60 GHz for the research and application of 60 GHz millimeter wave high-speed wireless communication technology. In March 2005, the 802.15.3c working group was established, believing that 60 GHz millimeter wave works in the 57 GHz–64 GHz licensed band, supporting high data transmission applications of at least 2 Gbps. In 2009, the IEEE 802.11ad research working group was established for better research. Benign modifications have been made to IEEE 802.11 (2007) PHY and MAC to enable them to be adapted to transport up to 7 Gbps in the 60 GHz operating band.

Based on Ref. [12,13], the performance and characteristics of several mainstream wireless communication technology are compared, including Bluetooth, ZigBee, WiFi, UWB and 60 GHz millimeter wave (MMW). Comparison results show that UWB and 60 GHz MMW technology and high transmission rate and high security and good anti-interference. These technical indicators can meet the demand of the design of the on-board wireless communication network in cockpit. However, due to the enclosed cabin environment and possible artificial occlusion, airborne cabin wireless communication network needs to be designed with a certain penetration capability in mind. However, 60 GHz MMW has a large attenuation and poor penetration ability during transmission. In addition, the ITU-R group and the relevant national key research plan for airborne in cockpit 4200 MHz to 4400 MHz band and existing problem of electromagnetic compatibility between airborne radio altimeter, the study shows that after a certain technical means, the spectrum airborne equipment communication will not produce interference to the existing airborne radio altimeter [3]. Therefore, it is possible to select UWB as the main technology for onboard cockpit wireless communication network.

3 System Model and Motivation

3.1 System Model

As analyzed in Sect. 2.2, the maximum linear distance between any two points in each airborne cabin is less than 6m, and UWB communication technology can provide a physical layer transmission rate of 200 Mbps over a distance of 6 m. Therefore, the UWB-based wireless network topology in the airborne cockpit can be abstracted as Fig. 1.

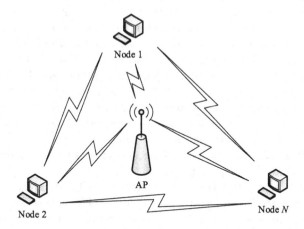

Fig. 1. Wireless network topology based on UWB in airborne cockpit

The entire network is deployed in an airborne cabin confined space within 6m, centered on an access point (AP) responsible for control. There are N terminal systems in the network (referred to as "nodes" in the following description for convenience), and data transmission between terminal systems can be carried out directly at a rate up to 200 Mbps. AP is mainly responsible for time synchronization and slot allocation scheduling, and does not participate in data forwarding between various nodes in the cockpit. The data that needs to be sent from the nodes in the network to the MAC layer does not arrive in cycles, but more in Poisson distribution. At this time, the data that cannot be sent in time will enter the buffer and wait for sending.

In UWB network based on TDMA protocol, time is divided into continuous and periodic frames. In the MAC protocol based on fixed allocation TDMA, since all time slots have been fixed periodically, each node can only send data within the time slots allocated to it. The MAC scheme based on fixed allocation TDMA can guarantee the maximum delay of end-to-end transmission, but the overall network utilization is relatively low.

3.2   Motivation

The traditional UWB network is a competitive wireless network, which can not guarantee the QoS of the wireless network in the cabin. Ref. [14] studies the UWB MAC based on frame, which sets aside 5 MAS and 8 MAS for DRP scheduling in a frame respectively, and obtains the maximum delay of about 300ms and 190ms respectively, indicating that the use of fixed allocation scheduling protocol can effectively reduce the upper bound of delay.

Therefore, Ref. [6] proposed a TDMA MAC protocol based on fixed allocation, the traditional UWB super frame was improved, the entire cycle of super frame TDMA cycle in addition is to be used to synchronize time slot, the rest of the time slots are assigned to all nodes in the network of the fixed, where the network nodes and the time slots are one-to-one correspondence. All of the network node can only transfer data within fixed time slots assigned to it. The whole frame cycle adopts the TDMA scheduling mechanism based on fixed allocation. Therefore, all terminal systems in the cluster are subject to static TDMA scheduling, and fixed time slots have been allocated for each TDMA scheduling cycle of the cycle. In each cycle of TDMA scheduling cycle, each ES can only be assigned to the transfer of information transmission within the TDMA time slot. If there is need to send data, but not assigned to the time slot, or a time slot in the current time remaining is not enough to transfer the information to complete a full, it cannot compete with access networks, and can only wait until assigned to its next time slot transmission.

Therefore, in a network based on fixed allocation TDMA, if the data that the network inner ES needs to be transfer in each TDMA cycle is not uniform, part of the time slot will be wasted and the network utilization will be low. Moreover, with the increase of the network end system and the longer TDMA cycle, the more time slot waste may be caused. This motivates us to design a distributed reservation and contention combined TDMA protocol for airborne cockpit.

4   Proposed Distributed Reservation and Contention Combined TDMA Protocol

4.1   Basic Idea of DRCC-RDMA

The proposed DRCC-TDMA protocol is a combination of traditional fixed allocation TDMA protocol and competitive access protocol. Traditional TDMA protocol for all terminal system based on distribution of fixed distribution based on time of channel resources, can effectively guarantee the maximum time delay, to avoid conflict, but the channel utilization rate is low. The DRCC-TDMA protocol allows other nodes to access the free time slot through p-probability competition, which is beneficial to reduce the waste of idle time slot, in improving the utilization ratio of network at the same time reduce the network system of the whole or part of the node time delay.

In DRCC-TDMA protocol, except AP broadcast time synchronization and slot allocation, the entire frame TDMA cycle is firstly allocated to each node in the network in advance. In the frame TDMA cycle, all nodes in the network are allocated fixed length and time slots, and all nodes are fully synchronized, so that the time of sending data can be determined. All nodes have absolute priority to send data in the time slot assigned to them. However, if a node has no data to send in the time slot fixed to it, other nodes can access the network through p-probability and carry out data transmission in the idle time slot.

4.2   Detailed Description of DRCC-TDMA

Frame Structure. The DRCC-TDMA protocol in this paper is designed based on UWB frame. It should be noted that there are static and dynamic frame structures. Static frame structure refers to the cycle with fixed length allocated by the network system integrator. Dynamic frame structure means that AP dynamically changes the frame length according to the result of slot allocation. Because of the airborne cockpit wireless network studied in this paper, the maximum delay accepted by each node can be determined, and the TDMA scheme based on fixed allocation can ensure the maximum delay. Static frame structure is selected in this paper. As shown in Fig. 2, it is an improved UWB static frame structure based on DRCC-TDMA protocol.

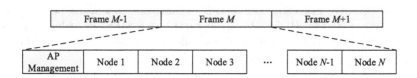

Fig. 2. UWB static frame structure based on DRCC-TDMA protocol

Figure 3 is the schematic diagram of DRCC-TDMA protocol. Since frames are used as the unit of time slot management, this paper defines that each frame consists of N+1 time slot. The first slot 0 of each frame is the management slot issued to AP, and the remaining N slots are used by each node in the network to transmit data business. The number of slots is determined by the total number of nodes in the network. Based on the fixed-allocated TDMA, this protocol allocates one or more fixed-size time slots for each node (in this paper, only one fixed-size time slot is allocated for each node) as the main time slot of this node, which is the Master node of this time slot. Other nodes competing for access to this time slot are called Slave nodes.

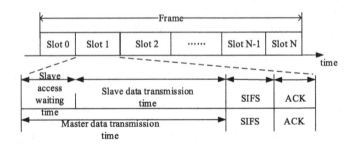

Fig. 3. UWB static frame structure based on DRCC-TDMA protocol

Each TDMA slot is fixed. For the Master, the slot may contain at least one Short Interframe Space (SIFS) and an ACK acknowledgement in addition to the Master data transmission. The maximum value of the data transfer period is the difference between the time slot size and the SIFS and ACK acknowledgement periods. For Slave, the fixed-size time slot can be divided into Waiting time (WT), Slave data transmission time, SIFS and ACK confirmation period, where the maximum value of the time slot is determined as the difference between the time slot and the WT, SIFS and ACK confirmation period. No matter for Master or Slave, the maximum value of the data transmission period is fixed, but the maximum value of the Master data transmission period is greater than the maximum value of the Slave data transmission period.

Slave detection channel busyness is determined according to the channel energy detection. Then only during PLCP preamble when no channel busyness is detected, other nodes can wait for SIFS time to access the network channel with p-probability. Therefore, the setting of Slave access waiting period in this paper is determined by PLCP Preamble cycle and a SIFS. Its value is not less than the sum of the two. Of course, the smaller the value is, the longer the data transmission time of Slave can be.

In order to ensure the reliability of each data in the onboard wireless network, immediately ACK is adopted in this paper. Considering the transceiver conversion and data processing time of the receiving node, a node needs a SIFS waiting time to reply to an immediately ACK frame after receiving the data frame.

DRCC-TDMA Protocol Flow Description. If AP in charge of broadcasting network allocation starts to work, it will occupy the first time slot within the frame cycle, publish the network status and broadcast it to all nodes in the network. Each node gets the current time and slot allocation from the management (MGT) frame released by AP. AP repeatedly publishes MGT frames in each frame cycle.

In each time slot, Master enters its allocated slot, while other Slave nodes enter the waiting period and detect the channel status. Master has absolute priority in this allocated slot. If Master decides to use its allocated slot, the data will be transmitted directly to the destination. The other nodes will not access the network after Master sends out the data. Otherwise if Master does not send data in its allocated slot, other nodes, if there is a need to send, then wait for WT to access into the network with p-probability. In order not to affect the transmission of the next fixed allocation slot, the maximum data that Master or Slave can transmit in this slot cannot exceed the maximum data transmission period that can be allowed.

In the DRCC-TDMA protocol, when a node in the network has a generated information flow that needs to be transmitted, it should first judge whether it is in the main time slot allocated to it. And then determine whether it should send data directly or wait for the end of the access waiting time to access the network. The specific transmission conditions are mainly divided into the following seven categories.

1. Master: A single time slot can complete the data transmission and the transmission is successful.

   Since it is Master, this node can directly monopolize the time slot to send data, and other terminal systems will not access the network after detecting Master sending. This node completes the DATA transmission in this time slot. If the Master receives the ACK frame correctly responded by the destination node after sending the DATA frame, then the DATA transmission is successful and the sending process of this node ends. Figure 4 shows that Master successfully sends the DATA timing diagram. The DATA frame length is variable, and the maximum frame length that can be transferred can be calculated according to the fixed slot size allocated.

2. Master: A single time slot can complete data transmission but the transmission fails.

   When the node does not receive an ACK frame from the destination after sending the DATA frame, it means that the DATA may fail to be sent and the DATA frame needs to be resent. If there is enough time left in the current slot (to complete data sending and receive an ACK frame), the Master can

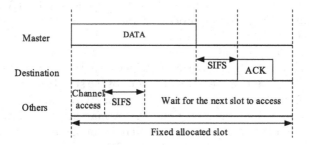

Fig. 4. Timing diagram that Master successfully sends the DATA

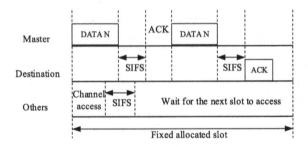

Fig. 5. Timing diagram that Master failed to send but the remaining time of the time slot can complete the retransmission

retransmit in the current slot. Otherwise, Master can attempt to access the idle slot of another node as Slave, or wait for the next allocated slot. Figure 5 is the timing diagram in which Master failed to send but the remaining time of the time slot can complete the retransmission.

3. Master: A single time slot is not sufficient to complete the data transfer.
   This case means that the node still has DATA to send after the exclusive time slot has sent the maximum DATA frame that can be transferred. If the node receives the ACK frame responded by the destination node after sending the DATA frame, it means that the DATA is sent successfully. Otherwise, the DATA frame failed to send and needs to be retransmitted. The remaining DATA to be sent or DATA frame retransmission, the node can use Slave identity to try to access the other node's idle slot or waiting for the next allocated slot.

4. Slave: After successfully accessing into the network, a single time slot can complete the data transmission and the transmission is successful.
   Figure 6 is the timing diagram that Slave successfully sends in a single time slot. As this node is not in its allocated time slot, thus it should detection the channel status. If the channel is not detected to be busy after the WT, the current time slot is judged to be idle, and p-probability is used to randomly access into the network. If the access is successful, i.e. deciding to access, it can use that time slot to transmit data. The node completes DATA transmission in this time slot. If the node receives the ACK frame correctly responded by the destination node after sending the DATA frame, the DATA transmission is successful and the sending process of ends.

5. Slave: After successfully accessing into the network, a single time slot can complete the data transmission but the transmission fails.
   If the Slave successfully accesses into the network, then the node can complete the data transmission in the remaining time of the slot. However, after sending the DATA frame, the node does not receive the ACK frame feedback from the destination node, indicating that the DATA may have failed to be sent and the DATA frame needs to be resent. If there is enough time left in the current slot, then retransmit in the current slot. Otherwise, the node can continue as Slave to try to access the idle slot of another node or wait for the next allocated slot of that node.

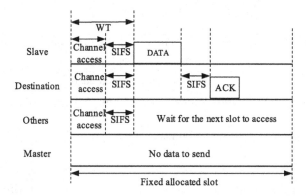

Fig. 6. Timing diagram that Slave successfully sends in a single time slot.

6. Slave: After successfully accessing into the network, a single time slot is not enough to complete the data transmission.
   If the Slave successfully accesses into the network, the node can complete the data transmission in the remaining time of the slot. If the node directly monopolize the time slot to send DATA, after sending the maximum DATA frame that can be allowed to transmit, there are still remaining DATA to send. Then for the remaining DATA to send or DATA frame retransmission, the node can continue to use Slave identity to try to access the idle slot of other end system or wait for the next main slot of the node.
7. Slave: unable to access the network. If it is not in the allocated slot, and the Slave is unable to access the network in an idle slot competition. Then it waits for the subsequent idle slot to try to compete to access, or waits until its own primary slot arrives to send data. If no slot is competed throughout the frame cycle, the worst-case scenario is to wait for the next allocated slot to be sent.

5   Performance Evaluation

In this paper, the performances of the proposed DRCC-TDMA protocol, fixed allocation TDMA (Fixed TDMA) protocol and p-CSMA protocol are evaluated and compared through NS3 simulation software. And the simulation results are presented and analyzed. Simulation parameters are presented in Table 1.

Figure 7 shows the throughput comparison of three MAC protocols under different traffic loads. Simulation results show that when the traffic load is low, the throughput of the three MAC protocols increases as traffic load increase. But the throughputs of Fixed TDMA protocol and DRCC TDMA reach the saturated point when the traffic load is larger than 180 Mbps. However, the throughput of p-CSMA protocol falls down after reaches a maximum peak value at about the traffic load of 140 Mbps, as the increasing of the traffic load. This is because when there are many nodes want to transmit their packets the collision probability

Table 1. Simulation parameters setting

Simulation parameters	Value	Simulation parameters	Value
# of nodes	30	Physical data rate	200 Mbps
Size of data	4096 Byte	Traffic load	170 Mbps
Maximum transmission radius	10 m	Total simulation time	10 s
SIFS	10 us	Waiting time	19.5 us
Lifetime of data	50 ms		

between these packets increase. This can increase the network throughput at a level before the network peak throughput is reached. However, when there are more and more packets are transmitted, the collision probability of the packets continues to increase and thus the network throughput is reduced. Thanks to the carrier sensing capability of p-CSMA, the collision probability will not reach to 1 but to a particular value according to the value of p. And finally, the throughput of p-CSMA become to a constant value when the traffic load is larger than $160Mbps$. In general, the throughput performance of DRCC-TDMA is better than that of Fixed TDMA, and p-CSMA is the worst.

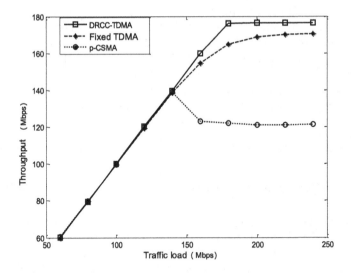

Fig. 7. Throughput comparison under different traffic loads

Figure 8 shows the average delay comparison of three MAC protocols under different traffic loads. The simulation results show that when the network load is small, the competition conflicts between network nodes are small. The delay of p-CSMA is smaller than that of Fixed TDMA. When the traffic load is small, the average delay of p-CSMA and DRCC-TDMA is smaller than that of fixed-allocation TDMA. However, with the increase of the traffic load, the competition among network nodes is gradually intensified. When the maximum throughput of p-CSMA protocol is reached, its delay performance deteriorates sharply, and the average delay is greater than that of DRCC-TDMA and fixed-allocation TDMA. DRCC-TDMA, which combines the advantages of Fixed TDMA and p-CSMA, shows the minimum average delay.

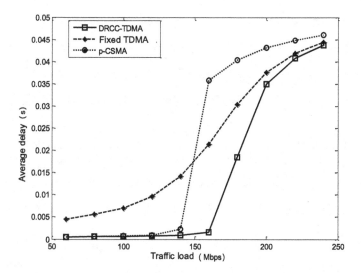

Fig. 8. Average delay comparison under different traffic loads

Figure 9 shows the maximum delay comparison of three MAC protocols under different traffic loads. The simulation results show that the maximum delay of p-CSMA is smaller than that of Fixed TDMA when the service load is small. The maximum delay performance of DRCC-TDMA is smaller than that of p-CSMA when the service load is small. However, with the increase of service load, the competition among network nodes gradually intensified. When the saturation point was reached, the maximum delay of p-CSMA and DRCC-TDMA also increased sharply, and the value of maximum delay was equal to the data life cycle. However, on the whole, the maximum delay of DRCC-TDMA was small.

Figure 10 shows the ratio of packet loss of three MAC protocols under different traffic loads. The simulation results show that when the traffic load is small, the packet loss rate of data transmission under the three protocols is 0, and there is no packet loss. But with the increase of traffic load, the packet loss rate will increase gradually. But DRCC-TDMA has a low packet loss rate among the three protocols. Among them, because the data life cycle is set, when more than 50ms has not been sent, it is destroyed, which also leads to packet loss.

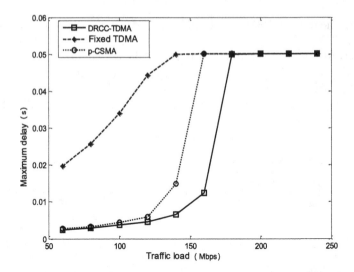

Fig. 9. Maximum delay comparison under different traffic loads

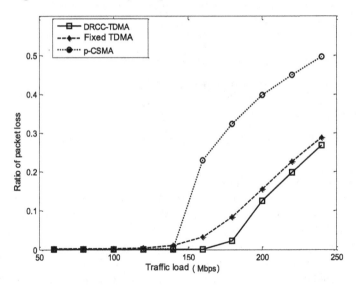

Fig. 10. Ratio of packet loss under different traffic loads

In summary, this paper conducts simulation and analysis on the performance of three protocols under different traffic loads. By comparing the performance of throughput, average delay, maximum delay and packet loss rate, the DRCC-TDMA protocol performs the best on the whole, which also benefits from its combination of advantages of Fixed TDMA and p-CSMA.

6   Conclusion

Wireless Avionics Intra-Communication (WAIC) networks can be used to reduce the structural complexity of the cabin avionics communication system and meet the increasing demand for data exchange. This paper proposes a Distributed Reservation and Contention Combined (DRCC) TDMA protocol to guarantee the maximum data transmission delay and improve the channel utilization. The proposed DRCC-TDMA protocol is a combination of traditional fixed allocation TDMA protocol and competitive access protocol. It allows other nodes to access the free time slot through p-probability competition, which is beneficial to reduce the waste of idle time slot, in improving the utilization ratio of network at the same time reduce the network system of the whole or part of the node time delay.

Acknowledgments. This work was supported in part by Science and Technology on Avionics Integration Laboratory and the Aeronautical Science Foundation of China (Grant No. 201955053002).

References

1. ARINC 664 Part7: Aircraft Data Network Part7 Avionics Full Duplex Switched Ethernet(AFDX)Network [S]. Aeronautical Radio INC. (2005)
2. Elgezabal, G.O.: Fly-by-wireless: Benefits, risks and technical challenges. In: Fly by Wireless Workshop. IEEE (2010). 14-15
3. Raharya, N., Suryanegara, M.: Compatibility analysis of Wireless Avionics Intra Communications (WAIC) to radio altimeter at 4200–4400 MHz. In: 2014 IEEE Asia Pacific Conference on Wireless and Mobile, pp. 17–22. IEEE (2014)
4. Akram, R.N., Markantonakis, K., Mayes, K., et al.: Security and performance comparison of different secure channel protocols for Avionics Wireless Networks. In: Digital Avionics Systems Conference. IEEE (2016)
5. Park, P., Chang, W.: Performance comparison of industrial wireless networks for wireless avionics intra-communications. IEEE Communi. Lett. **PP**(99), 1 (2016)
6. Dang, D.K., Mifdaoui, A., Gayraud, T.: Design and analysis of UWB-based network for reliable and timely communications in safety-critical avionics. Factory Communication Systems, pp. 1-10. IEEE (2014)
7. ARINC 429: ARINC specification 429 [S]. Aeronautical Radio Inc. (2001)
8. Bracknell, D.R.: The MIL-STD-1553B data bus: What does the future hold? Aeronautical J. **111**(1118), 231–246 (2007)
9. Sheffield, G.L., Becnel, R.G.: Wireline communication system and method employing a military standard 1553 bus (2016)
10. Karunakar, P., Anusha, C.: A comparative study of wireless protocols: Bluetooth, UWB, ZigBee and Wi-Fi. Adv. Electron. Electric Eng. **4**(6), 655–662 (2014)
11. Liu, W., Shao, T., Yao, J.: Ultra-wideband and 60-GHz generation and transmission over a wavelength division multiplexing-passive optical network. IEEE/OSA J. Optical Commun. Networking **5**(9), 1076–1082 (2013)
12. Amiribesheli, M., Benmansour, A., Bouchachia, A.: A review of smart homes in healthcare. J. Ambient Intell. Humanized Comput. **6**(4), 495–517 (2015)

13. Park, C., Rappaport, T.S.: Short-range wireless communications for next-generation networks: UWB, 60 GHz Millimeter-Wave WPAN, And ZigBee. Wireless Commun. IEEE **14**(4), 70–78 (2007)
14. Wu, H., Xia, Y., Zhang, Q.: Delay analysis of DRP in MBOA UWB MAC. In: IEEE International Conference on Communications, pp. 229–233. IEEE (2006)

The Automation Tool Development for Aircraft Cockpit Display Systems Verification in Part of Text Data

Sergey Aleksandrovich Dyachenko$^{(\boxtimes)}$ (ID),
Dmitry Mikhailovich Ilyashenko, and Evgeny Sergeevich Neretin (ID)

Moscow Aviation Institute (National Research University), Moscow, 4,
Volokolamskoe Avenue, Moscow 125993, Russian Federation
kaf703@mai.ru

Abstract. Nowadays there are lots of means to automate the aircraft avionics software verification. The model-based software development made a formal verification approach popular (e.g. model checking). Such ways allow to verify the matching of the system model contained the end number of states and requirements expressed in the temporal logic language. However, the software operation in the target platform is out of scope here. Software verification within a hardware-in-the-loop simulation takes into account the target features. In this case, the verification automation tools are capable to simulate the input signals, to check the equipment's feedback by monitoring output signals, to process the captured data, and to generate the verification protocols. At the same time, there are some onboard high-critical systems (e.g. cockpit displays, flight warning) are being required the human-operator during the testing. They generate visual and aural information which has to be perceived by for the crew members. Thus, their verification is complicated to be automated accounting the mentioned aspect that leads to increased time and cost expenses. The paper describes the software tool that has been developed to partially automate the verification of avionics equipment which required human visual checking. The tool performs recognizing of the textual data displayed on the cockpit screens. It allows reducing the time and cost expenses within aircraft testing and recertification.

Keywords: Civil aircraft · Avionics · Software · Verification · Cockpit display · Image recognition · Data processing

1 Introduction

The modern aircraft avionics is a sophisticated intellectual complex. Currently, almost every vehicle system performs its functions using software contained a huge amount of code lines. At the same time, on-board software is one of the most sensitive parts in terms of the errors made during development.

The recent disasters caused by software errors include the crash of Boeing 737 MAX on October 29, 2018 near Jakarta and March 10, 2019 near Addis Ababa. The tragedies were caused by the incorrect operation of the maneuvering characteristics augmentation system. The results of the investigations showed that in both cases, the

B. Li et al. (Eds.): IoTaaS 2020, LNICST 346, pp. 329–335, 2021.
https://doi.org/10.1007/978-3-030-67514-1_26

failure of the angle of attack sensor led to the discordant data issuing which served as the reason for the nosediving (i.e. the described situation was not provided in the software) [1, 2]. Thus, the embedded software development process of aircraft onboard equipment requires the increased responsibility to ensure flight safety. This aspect is especially relevant for high-critical systems which failure can lead to an accident.

The process of onboard systems development is carried out according to V-model regulated by the ARP4754A standard (see Fig. 1) [3] at the current stage of aviation evolution. This approach describes a multi-iterative definition & design and integration & verification cycle with a focus on thorough product testing.

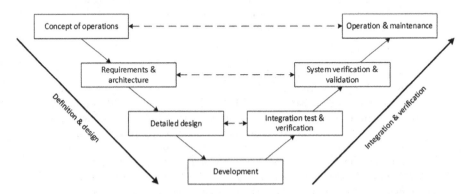

Fig. 1. V-model of aviation onboard systems development.

The listed V-model for the onboard equipment development includes the following nominal levels: aircraft, system, component, hardware, and software. Verification at every level is necessary for the product safe use in subsequent stages since it is aimed to assess the software and established requirements compliance as well as to detect and record errors potentially introduced.

Significant time is being spent on code verification. Taking into account the limited term of modern liner development, it is necessary to reduce the time expenses by using test automation tools for example. Among the such products providers are ScienceSoft (The USA), A1QA (The USA), Kualitatem (The USA), TestingXperts (Great Britain), Oxagile (The USA), AVIAOK (Russia), GosNIIAS (Russia), BugRaptors (India) [4].

There are a sufficient number of ready-made solutions for the software level but there are almost no automation tools for testing at the system level (although the amount of tests at this stage is also significant).

To date, the main necessary information for vehicle handling is displayed by the cockpit display system (CDS) contained the large-format liquid crystal displays placed in the cockpit.

The typical CDS of a modern civil aircraft includes:

- multifunctional displays (MFD);
- control panels;
- head-up display (optional);
- technical vision systems (optional).

The MFD is supposed to display a variety of formats such as:

- primary flight display;
- navigation display;
- engine and warning display (EWD);
- system pages (e.g. fuel, flight control, brake, air, doors), etc.

The EWD is intended to display information about the engines, basic data about onboard systems operation as well as the alerting messages about equipment failures obtained from flight warning system (FWS) (see Boeing 777 EWD example in Fig. 2).

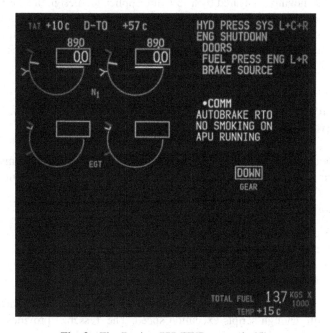

Fig. 2. The Boeing 777 EWD example [5].

One of the most critical EWD zones is the FWS messages zone since it's aimed to warn the crew about the incorrect systems functioning and their failures.

Typically, the following message priority levels are available (from highest to lowest) [6]:

- "WARNING" (highest priority alarms which require the immediate corrective actions of the pilots in a short time);
- "CAUTION" (messages require the immediate crew notification with further corrective actions in a long time);
- "ADVISORY" (notifications that will probably require the pilot's actions without time limitations);
- "MEMO" (lowest priority messages which do not require the pilot's actions and intended to inform the crew about systems operation).

When "WARNING" and "CAUTION" messages appear, crew members have to confirm their reading by pressing the light buttons (master warning & master caution) installed on the dashboard. Unacknowledged messages are indicated on the EWD with a special marker – a symbol (for example, a rectangle) displayed in front of them.

2 Purpose of the Research

The purpose of the research is the tool development to automate the modern and perspective aircraft CDS software verification.

The goal achieving is ensured by a software application design that performing text data recognition (e.g. FWS messages displayed on the EWD). The input data for the tool is photos of CDS screens are being obtained under system verification on the bench. The detailed description of the proposed solution will be given in the next chapters.

3 Software and Algorithms Used for the Task Implementation

Task implementation is carried out through text recognition algorithms. They are applied to images obtained by framing a video stream from a web-camera installed opposite the CDS displays.

The following means were selected for the task implementation:

- Python 3 programming language for software development;
- Tesseract neural network for text recognition in the EWD photos;
- TechSAT ADS2 environment for setting signals values that provide the FWS messages generation.

Python 3 was chosen due to a large number of libraries for optical character recognition with enough scripts execution speed. The Tesseract provides high recognition accuracy by analyzing a lot of image features and hidden relationships between them. The TechSAT ADS2 represents an integrated software environment and hardware platform for prototyping aerospace engineering systems including:

- simulation within systems design;
- high-speed development cycle;
- integration of the leading industry solutions into a common platform;
- support for systems certification according to SAE ARP4754A [3] processes;
- support for interfaces widely used in the aerospace industry (e.g. ARINC 429 [7], ARINC 664 [8], ARINC 825 [9], etc.).

4 Description of Developed Software and Its Use During the Testing

The developed software performing the previously described functionality has a three-component architecture:

- input image processing module;
- logic module;
- output data generating module.

At first, the verifier sets the expected results matrices including the message's color, body, and markers presence. Next, the parameter values are set for generating messages on the EWD. After they are displayed on the CDS screen, the camera catches them in a video stream (see Fig. 3). The received video frames are fed alternately to the developed tool input.

Fig. 3. Avionics integration bench and webcam mounted on it

After, the software provides text recognition of the input image and generates a resulted matrix containing an array of recognized data. After, the comparison of the expected and resulted matrices is performed which allows to conclude the test has been passed or failed.

The webcam should be installed opposite the MFD parallel to the CDS display surface to minimize the optical distortion effects. One of the tasks of the verifier is to configure the camera to ensure minimal distortion in the generated video stream.

The webcam video is converted by the input image processing module to the form necessary for the subsequent recognition. Factually, the following operations are being performed: stream cropping, image rotation (if required), and required area cropping, contrast adjustment.

The processed frame is fed to the logic module which divides the image into text lines sequentially (see Fig. 4) which handled by Tesseract neural network. Markers are recognized by searching for the similar symbols (in particular, rectangles) among the reference images specified a priori. The lines color is determined by matching it to the set color ranges in HSV coordinates.

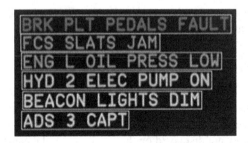

Fig. 4. Example of FWS messages set displayed on EWD

In the output data generating module all recognized messages output to the resulted array line-by-line. Then the expected and resulted matrices comparison is performed and the verification protocol is being generated in HTML or Microsoft Word formats (see Fig. 5).

1. General

Protocol ID: 223-368_20200527-tp
Protocol name: CDS_EWD in part of FWS messages
Date and time of verification performed: 27.05.2020, 09:10
Bench configuration: 96:28:9.2i

2. Tests performed

2.1 Test #1

#	Action	Expectation			Result			Conclusion	Comment
1.	<<RequirementID>>								
1.1	Set parameters	**Marker**	**Body**	**Color**	**Marker**	**Body**	**Color**	PASSED	
	values by uploading	None	FCS SLATS JAM	Amber	None	BRK PLT PEDALS	Red		
	the following files	None	ENG L OIL PRESS LOW	Amber		FAULT			
	placed in the	None	BRK PLT PEDALS	Red	None	FCS SLATS JAM	Amber		
	attachment to		FAULT		None	ENG L OIL PRESS LOW	Amber		
	TechSAT ADS 2:	None	ADS 3 CAPT	White	None	HYD 2 ELEC PUMP ON	Green		
	TEST_1.M.xls	None	HYD 2 ELEC PUMP ON	Green	None	BEACON LIGHT DIM	White		
		None	BEACON LIGHT DIM	White	None	ADS 3 CAPT	White		

Fig. 5. Example of generated verification protocol in Microsoft Word format

5   Testing of the Developed Software

To confirm the developed software operability, a series of about 1120 experiments were carried out. The results have been received show that the text and markers recognition accuracy is 97.19%, the color detection accuracy is 98.26%. Unsuccessful cases were related to the impossibility of detection (wrong recognitions have not been gotten).

Despite obtaining not 100% recognition accuracy, the obtained indicators allow to use the tool during testing. If the test fails, the verificator has to repeat it manually in part of undetected messages.

6 Conclusion

The developed software and the described methodology for its application can significantly reduce the verification time of formats containing text (in particular, EWD) and economic expenses for CDS verification at the system level.

The tool usage within Irkut MC-21 aircraft CDS testing reduced:

- number of manual checks in about 40–45 times respect to fully manual testing;
- verification time in 4 times;
- verification financial expenses in 8 times by reducing the number of verificators.

The mentioned indicators do not take into account neither the time savings are gotten within CDS certification nor an effect from the putting aircraft into exploitation earlier and the cost of errors potentially made by the verifiers during manual testing.

In the future, this project is planned to be finalized to verify not only textual but also graphic (symbolic) information, as well as to automate the FWS verification by recognizing audio signalization.

References

1. KNKT.18.10.35.04 Aircraft Accident Investigation Report. Lion Mentari Airlines. Boeing 737-8 (MAX) PK-LQP. Tanjung Karawang, West Java, Republic of Indonesia. 29 October 2018. Komite Nasional Keselamatan Transportasi Republic of Indonesia, Jakarta, Republic of Indonesia (2019)
2. AI-01/19 Interim Investigation Report on Accident to the B737-8 (MAX) Registered ET-AVJ operated by Ethiopian Airlines on 10 March 2019. Ministry of Transport of The Federal Democratic Republic of Ethiopia, Addis Ababa, Ethiopia (2020)
3. ARP4754A Guidelines for Development of Civil Aircraft and Systems. SAE International, Warrendale, The USA (2010)
4. Top 20 Software Testing Companies in 2019. https://medium.com/@andy_dassan/top-software-testing-companies-in-2019-c418b24f69d0. Accessed 10 June 2020
5. CARE INO III. 3D in 2D Planar Display Project. D4-1: Review of Cockpit Displays Design. EUROCONTROL, Brussels, Belgium (2008)
6. AC 25.1322-1 Flightcrew Alerting. FAA, Washington, The USA (2010)
7. ARINC Specification 429P1-17. MARK 33 Digital Information Transfer System (DITS). Part 1: Functional Description, Electrical Interface, Label Assignments and Word Formats. ARINC, Annapolis, The USA (2004)
8. ARINC Specification 664P1-1. Aircraft Data Network. Part 1: Systems Concepts and Overview. ARINC, Annapolis, The USA (2006)
9. ARINC Specification 825-2. General Standardization of CAN (Controller Area Network) Bus Protocol for Airborne Use. ARINC, Annapolis, The USA (2011)

Design of 'Floating, Medium and Sinking' Pressure Simulation System for Remote Reduction of Pulse Condition in TCM

Wenhui Chen[✉], Xueming Wang, Jiangning Chen, Xiang Yi, Huifang Li, Zhiyong Ding, and Jianying Li

School of Electronic Information, Northwestern Polytechnic University, Xi'an 710072, China
whchen@nwpu.edu.cn

Abstract. In order to solve the problem of simulating 'floating, medium and sinking' in remote diagnosis of TCM (Traditional Chinese Medicine), we designed a set of 'floating, medium and sinking' pressure simulation system which can feedback the remote pulse condition, including automatic pressurization device and pressure detection feedback device. The system uses a piezoresistive sensor to collect the compression force at the bionic prosthetic hand of the pulse recovery terminal and sends it back to the pulse collection terminal. The automatic pressure device at the collection end simulates the TCM doctor to automatically find the appropriate pressure intensity. In this paper, the pulse collection algorithm and pulse reduction algorithm are designed to make the pulse recovery more accurate. Through the collection of a large number of experimental data, and the experience of some professional doctors of TCM, it is believed that the system can well simulate the actual pulse process of 'floating, medium and sinking' pressure.

Keywords: TCM pulse acquisition · Remote reduction of pulse · 'floating, Medium and sinking' pressure feedback

1 Introduction

At present, remote diagnosis of TCM mainly relies on computer and network, sensor and communication to realize the diagnosis of looking, listening and asking, but there are still some difficulties in the study and application of remote pulse diagnosis. Since pulse diagnosis is a contact diagnosis method, the key technology to realize remote pulse diagnosis is to accurately reproduce the pulse signal collected by the pulse reproduction system, to generate the pulse consistent with the human body at the bionic hand of the pulse reproduction system[1,2]. The existing pulse complex system collects the frequency and amplitude of the typical pulse waveform, and then drives the linear motor to move up and down to produce a similar pulse. For example, Zhang Peng's pulse simulator based on voice coil motor designed by Shanghai Jiao Tong University [3]. This complex

© ICST Institute for Computer Sciences, Social Informatics and Telecommunications Engineering 2021
Published by Springer Nature Switzerland AG 2021. All Rights Reserved
B. Li et al. (Eds.): IoTaaS 2020, LNICST 346, pp. 336–346, 2021.
https://doi.org/10.1007/978-3-030-67514-1_27

system can only be used for teaching TCM, but cannot be used for real-time pulse complex. There is another way based on hydraulic and mechanical design by Lv Hao of Tianjin University to use simulated pulsation. This way is to make full use of the advantages of hydraulic and mechanical vibration, to use the hydraulic system to generate blood vessel saturation, and to use the machine to generate simulated pulse pulsation. However, such a system is too limited to transmit pulse signals in real time, and can only extract pulse signals for a period of time for restoration [4].

The innovation of this system design lies in using a hydraulic system and waveform synthesis algorithm to establish pulse information reproduction system [3]. Besides, we designed a set of feedback remote pulse pressure device based on the TCM 'floating, medium and sinking' pressure pulse diagnosis method to make the pulse recovery more accurate. After testing, the system can simulate the radial artery and arterial blood flow of the human body more perfectly, to restore the pulse of the human body more realistically.

2   Pulse Condition Collection

The collection end of the remote pulse system is mainly responsible for collecting pulse information and extracting necessary pulse characteristic values. This system mainly uses the piezoresistive pulse sensor to collect data, displays real-time waveform on the PC display screen at the acquisition end, and then sends pulse characteristic data to the pulse restore terminal through the cloud server. And the pressure data obtained from the restore end is used to drive the automatic pressurization module for real-time automatic pressurization. The overall structure of the acquisition end is shown in Fig. 1.

2.1   Automatic Pressurization Module

The automatic pressure module is the core module to realize the pressure simulation system of 'floating, medium and sinking pressure' [4,5]. It can automatically pressurize to the feedback pressure to realize the simulated pressure of 'floating, medium and sinking pressure'. This module is based on the STM32F103 microcontroller as the core [6], using the drive motor mechanical rotation to control pulse sensor for automatic compression. The process of automatic compression module realization as follow, according to the real-time pulse pressure feedback from the restore end, the automatic compression module drives the motor to drive the pulse sensor to move up and down to realize compression. The piezoresistive pulse sensor can feedback the current static pressure and realize automatic compression through self-pressure correction of the automatic compression module.

Automatic pressure can eliminate many external interference factors, such as human interference factors. For example, in the collection process, the human arm inadvertently shaking. Since there is no professional person at the collection end to locate the pulse collection position, the pulse sensor may be placed in

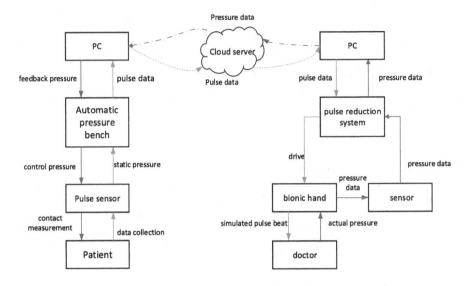

Fig. 1. System structure diagram.

the wrong position, leading to the collection of all wrong pulse signals, which is also a factor of human interference. Automatic compression can make the pulse sensor stable and correct collection. And the pulse sensor can be a stable acquisition. The most important thing is to realize the pulse collection synchronization between the collection end and the reduction end. Since this module is used for measurement in accordance with the pulse reduction module, the pulse pressure collected from the TCM doctor at the pulse reduction end will be feedback to the automatic pressure module through the network, so that the module will apply the same pressure to realize the synchronization of pulse real-time collection. The structure diagram of the automatic pressure module is shown in Fig. 2.

2.2   Pulse Characteristic Value Extraction

Introduction of Pulse. The pulse wave is formed because the vibration of the heart spreads outward along the arteries and blood flow [7]. Previous studies have found that pulse wave is mainly composed of an ascending branch and a descending branch, and the typical waveform is a three-peak wave, including the main-wave B, tidal-wave D and repulse F [8,9]. The ascending ramus and descending ramus constitute the main-wave B, and there is a notch on the descending ramus called isthmus E, which is immediately followed by the recurrent stroke F of isthmus E. Tidal-wave D often occurs between the main-wave B and the descending middle isthmus E, and the fore-wave is also weighed-wave. The schematic diagram is shown in Fig. 3.

Pulse Characteristic Value Extraction Algorithm. The pulse wave shape which has peak and valley is periodic, so we use the eigenvalue extraction method

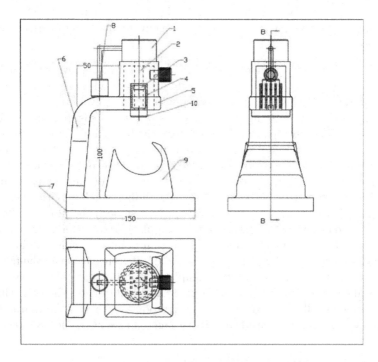

Fig. 2. Structure diagram of the automatic pressure module. (1-stepping motor, 2-motor lead screw, 3-nut, 4-connecting rod, 5-support sleeve, 6-support arm, 7-baseplate, 8-motor drive, 9-hand pillow, 10-pulse sensor)

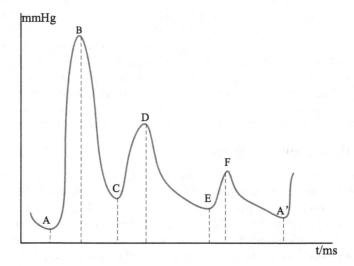

Fig. 3. Pulse waveform.

to process the data. We selects the time point (ms) of point B, C, D, E, F and a pulse period from point A to Point A'as eigenvalue [3]. The algorithm flow of data processing is as follows.

1) Filter the data. The differential method is used to remove some irregular abrupt values in the pulse sensor, which are generated by the data transmission circuit and reflected as the peak points in the waveform.

2) Data smoothing processing. In the process of pulse measurement, noise may be generated due to breathing, arm jitter, which requires data smoothing. In this paper, the method of sliding window filtering is used for data smoothing. Since the data collection frequency 200 Hz, and the pulse frequency of the human body is 1–2 Hz. In order to avoid big error of data, it is verified by experiment that it is better to select the sliding window with width of 5, including 5 data, to calculate the average and smooth the filtering effect.

3) Extract the pulse characteristic value. In a pulse period, after the second part, the curve becomes smooth, and the inflection point (extremum point) of the data can be obtained by using the method of difference between the front and the back of the data so that the complete period of the pulse wave and all the peaks and valleys within the period can be obtained. Then the timer of the main controller is used to get the corresponding time of the characteristic value, and finally, the data frame is packaged and sent to the pulse repeater.

3   Pulse Condition of Reduction

The pulse recovery end includes the simulation feedback module of 'floating, medium and sinking' pressure, which is mainly used to collect real-time pulse pressure data of TCM doctors. The data of 'floating, medium and sinking' pressure can be obtained by stabilizing the pressure data through the simulation algorithm of 'floating, medium and sinking' pressure, and the automatic compression module of cloud server feedback to the collection end can be used to realize remote pulse 'floating, medium and sinking' pressure simulation.

The pulse recovery terminal can receive the pulse data from the transit terminal (cloud server), and the embedded system drives the simulation arm and the hydraulic system uses the pulse recovery algorithm for pulse recovery.

3.1   Hydraulic Bionic System

The hydraulic system [10,11] designed according to the physiological rules of human arteries is mainly composed of motors, hydraulic pumps, solenoid valves, liquid storage tanks, silicone oil, oil pipelines and hoses. The motor and hydraulic pump are combined to drive the silicone oil flow, and there are two sets of motor and hydraulic pump combinations in the reduction equipment for static and dynamic pressure control at the pulsation. The hydraulic pump drives the silicone oil to circulate in the pipeline and hose to simulate the blood flow in the radial artery of the human body.

3.2   Pressure Simulation Feedback Module

The module consists of three piezoresistive sensors, which respectively detect the pressure of TCM doctors on the Cun, Guan, Chi. The module is placed on the position of the reducing end to simulate the Guan, because the Guan has the strongest pulse signal. After the doctor fixed the position, he began to apply pressure. After the pressure was stable, the piezoresistive sensors sent the data, that is, the network feedback was sent to the collection end, and then the automatic compression module was controlled to measure the pulse. The structure diagram of the pressure feedback module is shown in Fig. 4.

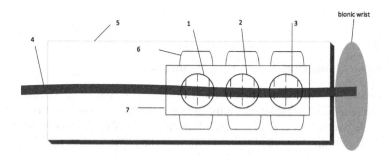

Fig. 4. Structure diagram of pressure feedback module (1,2,3-pulse sensor, 4-simulation of blood vessels, 5-simulation of the arm, 6,7-pulse sensor fixer).

3.3   'Floating, Medium and Sinking' Pressure Simulation Algorithm

In TCM diagnosis, 'floating' pulse lightly on the skin can be felt, the 'medium' is obtained by pressing between the muscles under the skin, the 'sinking' is under the muscles [12]. The above methods are used by TCM for pulse of 'floating, medium and sinking'. However, in the process of remote restoration, machines cannot directly feel pulse like humans, so how to stabilize the pressure and determine the numerical range of pulse of 'floating, medium and sinking' have become a research difficulty.

This paper adopts a pressure simulation algorithm to solve this difficulty. The entry point is to find the best pulse pressure, the best pulse pressure refers to the doctor when the finger feeling is the strongest, the most obvious pulse fluctuations on the pulse channel pressure, it is the doctor to determine the pulse in the main basis [13]. In this paper, the collection end was used to collect pulse data from normal people under nine pressures of 0.25N, 0.5N, 0.75N, 1N, 1.25N, 1.5N, 1.7N, 2.02N and 2.3N. The best pulse pressure (F_g) was the one with the strongest pulse signal.

By analyzing the data of optimal pulse-taking pressure and previous research experience, it can be concluded that the optimal pulse-taking pressure at the is between 0.7N and 1.7N, the floating pulse is less than 0.7N, and the sinking pulse is greater than 1.7N. After the range of 'floating, medium and sinking' pressure is obtained, the system determines that if the error of the collected pressure data does not exceed 0.1N, the data will be stable and sent to the collection end through the network for automatic compression.

The pressure data on the Guan can be obtained as shown in Table 1.

Table 1. Pressure data range.

location	Floating pulse data	Medium pulse data	Sinking pulse data
Guan	<0.7N	0.7N-1.7N	>1.7N

3.4 Pulse Condition Reduction Algorithm

The waveform of the pulse of the human body has a dual wave and three wave. The waveforms are synthesized by using the amplitude of each pulse wave peak and the interval between peaks. According to the data frames received from the acquisition system, the characteristic values of the pulse waveform were obtained by solving the frames. Then, based on the amplitude of the characteristic values, the flow of silicone oil needed to form each wave peak and volley was calculated, denoted as peak flow (V) and volley flow (N), respectively. The total flow in the main wave rising time (T_{AB}) is denoted as the main wave total flow (L_f), and the main wave total flow divided by the main wave peak flow (V_f) can be denoted as the time when the solenoid valve needs to open to form the main wave, denoted as the main wave forming time (T_f). In the above description, the subscript f represents the main wave. The calculation method is as follows.

$$T_f = \frac{L_f}{V_f} = \frac{V_f \times T_{AB}/2}{V_f} = \frac{T_{AB}}{2} \tag{1}$$

Similarly, the waveform synthesis of tide-wave and repulse-wave is consistent with the principle of main-wave synthesis.

4   Experimental Results and Analysis

The pressure simulation system was used to collect the pulse at the 'floating, medium and sinking' pressure at an interval of 5 ms. We collect the actual waveform of the human body and compare it with the pulse reduction waveform under the 'floating, medium and sinking' pressure. Figure 5,6,7 shows the comparison between the actual waveform and the reduction waveform. Among them, the left figure is the actual waveform, and the right figure is the reduction waveform by the reduction system. The horizontal axis represents the data length and the vertical axis represents the pressure in mmHg.

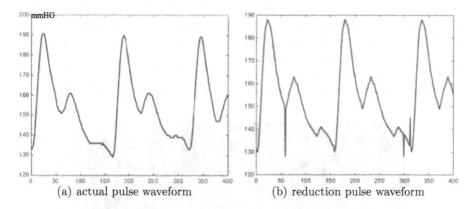

(a) actual pulse waveform   (b) reduction pulse waveform

Fig. 5. Actual pulse wave is compared with the reduction wave under the 'floating'

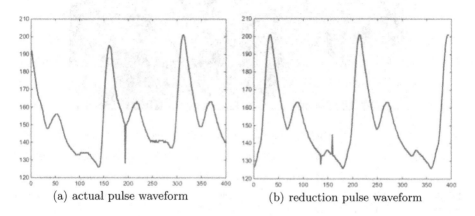

(a) actual pulse waveform   (b) reduction pulse waveform

Fig. 6. Actual pulse wave is compared with the reduction wave under the 'medium'

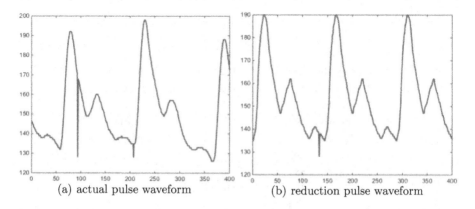

(a) actual pulse waveform   (b) reduction pulse waveform

Fig. 7. Actual pulse wave is compared with the reduction wave under the 'sinking'

By comparing the eigenvalues of the actual waveform and the restored waveform, it is found that the Pearson correlation coefficient of the two groups of data is 0.8678, which proves that this algorithm can restore the pulse with a reduction degree of at least 85%, and it can be seen that the noise of the restored waveform is small and the data is relatively stable.

The pulse measurement photos of the prototype are shown in Fig. 8.

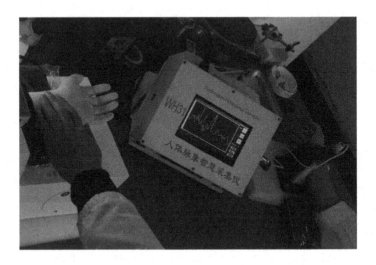

Fig. 8. Pulse collection photograph.

The eigenvalues of the actual waveform and the restored waveform are compared, as shown in Tables 2, 3, 4. It includes three pulse patterns of 'floating, medium and sinking' respectively.

Table 2. 'Floating' comparison of characteristic values of actual pulse and pulse reduction waveform.

Eigenvalue	Actual value	Reduced value	Error value
H_B(mmHg)	195	190	5 mmHg
H_D(mmHg)	140	142	2 mmHg
H_F(mmHg)	111	110	1 mmHg
H_C(mmHg)	128	126	2 mmHg
H_E(mmHg)	109	109	0 mmHg
$T_A B$(ms)	118	113	5 ms
$T_A C$(ms)	295	315	25 ms
$T_A E$(ms)	580	585	5 ms
$T_C D$(ms)	100	110	10 ms
$T_E F$(ms)	50	55	5 ms
T(ms)	750	810	60 ms

Table 3. 'Medium' comparison of characteristic values of actual pulse and pulse reduction waveform.

Eigenvalue	Actual value	Reduced value	Error value
H_B(mmHg)	210	209	1 mmHg
H_D(mmHg)	160	162	2 mmHg
H_F(mmHg)	130	131	1 mmHg
H_C(mmHg)	149	147	2 mmHg
H_E(mmHg)	129	129	0 mmHg
T_AB(ms)	120	115	5 ms
T_AC(ms)	300	315	15 ms
T_AE(ms)	585	580	5 ms
T_CD(ms)	100	110	10 ms
T_EF(ms)	50	55	5 ms
T(ms)	750	800	50ms

Table 4. 'Sinking' comparison of characteristic values of actual pulse and pulse reduction waveform.

Eigenvalue	Actual value	Reduced value	Error value
H_B(mmHg)	230	229	1 mmHg
H_D(mmHg)	169	172	3 mmHg
H_F(mmHg)	142	138	4 mmHg
H_C(mmHg)	150	147	3 mmHg
H_E(mmHg)	129	129	0 mmHg
T_AB(ms)	120	115	5 ms
T_AC(ms)	315	310	5 ms
T_AE(ms)	585	600	15 ms
T_CD(ms)	90	100	10 ms
T_EF(ms)	50	55	5 ms
T(ms)	715	765	50 ms

5   Conclusion

The TCM remote pulse pressure simulation system is designed. The pressure simulation algorithm can accurately feedback on the real-time pulse pressure measurement of TCM doctors at the restoration end of the pulse. The TCM 'floating, medium and sinking' pulse sensing method is combined with modern technology to realize the wisdom of TCM. And the pulse reduction algorithm with the hydraulic system as the core makes the pulse image reduction accuracy further improved. Through the experience of many TCM doctors, the effectiveness of the system's restoring effect is verified, and then the remote wisdom of TCM diagnosis can be realized with the help of the platform.

References

1. He, J., Wang, W., Ding, H.: Development and research of computerized TCM consultation system. Shi Zhen Chin. Med. **21**(9), 2370–2372 (2010)
2. Xuemin, W., Peng, S., Peng, Z., et al.: The pulse complex system of TCM based on multi-sensor technology. J. Sens. Technol. **26**(11), 1604–1609 (2013)
3. Lv, H., Ma, X., et al.: Design of pulse remote recurrence system. China Sci. Technol. Inf. **21**, 70–71 (2019)
4. Zhang, P.: Research and design of pulse wave simulation reproducing system. Shanghai: Shanghai Jiao Tong University (2013)
5. Duan, B., Guo, T., Luo, M., et al.: Mechanical micropump for electronic cooling, pp. 1038–1042 (2014)
6. Wu, L.: Design and Implementation of Portable based on STM32. Hangzhou University of Electronic Science and Technology, Hangzhou (2009)
7. Mingzhen, L.: Discussion and objective study on theory of three portions nine pulse-takings[D]. School of Acumox and Tuina, Guangzhou University of Chinese medicine, Guangzhou (2011). (in Chinese)
8. Yuanlin, H., Xin, L., Wen, W.: Characteristics analysis of flexible diaphragm micropump driven by electrostatic balance metho. J. Sensing Technol. **29**(1), 15–20 (2016)
9. Jiagile, C., Rongjin, Y., Mengfeng, S.: Design of hydraulic virtual experiment system based on Android platform. Exp. Technol. Manage. **36**(11), 153–157 (2019)
10. Liu, X., Li, T., Xie, Y., et al.: Research progress on the position, number, shape and potential of pulse elements. J. Tianjin Univ. Chin. Med. **33**(06), 381–384 (2014)
11. Yuman, Z., Xuemin, W., Peng, S., et al.: Interpretation and verification of optimal pulse taking pressure in TCM based on radial artery blood flow mode. Comput. Appl. Chem. **32**(2), 129–134 (2015)
12. Yan, H., Wang, Y., Li, F., et al.: Discussion on the relationship between the optimal pulse pressure of cunkou pulse inch, Guan pulse and Chi pulse in 264 healthy college students. Chinese J. TCM **25**(09), 1371–1374 (2010)
13. Martin Bland, J., Altman, D.G.: Statistical methods for assessing agreement between two methods of clinical measurement. Int. J. Nurs. Stud. **47**(8), 931–936 (2010)

A Flexible and Scalable Localization System for Off-the-Shelf LoRa Devices

Honggang Zhao, Zuobin Liu, Gui Zhu, Chen Shi$^{(\boxtimes)}$,
and Qingzheng Xu

College of Information and Communication,
National University of Defense Technology, Xi'an, China
hgz_nwpu@163.com, 2551105254@qq.com, zhugui53@163.com,
shishen26@163.com, xuqingzheng@hotmail.com

Abstract. Location Based Service is the key for most of IoT applications, and LoRa-based localization has attracted increasing research interests. The resolution of timestamp provided by LoRa gateway is still the determining factor for LoRa-based localization. Accurate localization is supported well with highly customized LoRa devices, meanwhile the current off-the-shelf LoRa devices have only microsecond accuracy. However, it's impracticable to use many hardware customized LoRa devices in real deployments, in which cost control must be taken into consideration. Therefore a flexible and scalable LoRa-Based localization system has been designed and implemented in this paper. It aims to easily and flexibly build the hardware platform by using off-the-shelf LoRa Devices. Its customized system server consists of LoRa-Network-Server, LoRa-Geo-Server and LoRa-App-Server. All the geolocation computation can be done in LoRa-Geo-Server, and results will be transported to LoRa-Network-Server. This makes the proposed system more scalable to develop specific LoRa-App-Server which will provide more Location Based Services. System test results in different Gateway deployments show that the system localization accuracy is basically within the accuracy range of "LoRaWAN Geolocation Whitepaper" presented by LoRa Alliance. It can provide a good experimental platform support for LoRa Localization technology research.

Keywords: Internet of Things · LoRa · Off-The-Shelf · Localization

1 Introduction

Low–Power Wide-Area Networks (LPWAN) are projected to support a major portion of the billions of devices forecasted for the Internet of Things (IoT) [1], in which Location Based Service is the key for most of applications (e.g., Car Parking [2], Elderly Assisting [3], Endangered Animals Protecting [7], Bus Positioning [14]). LoRaWAN is an open data link layer specification based on LoRa, and is designed from the bottom up to optimize LPWANs for battery lifetime, capacity, range, and cost. Also due to its signal's capability of propagating over long distances and penetrating many infrastructures, LoRa-based localization has attracted increasing research interests. As described in "LoRaWAN Geolocation Whitepaper" presented by LoRa

B. Li et al. (Eds.): IoTaaS 2020, LNICST 346, pp. 347–359, 2021.
https://doi.org/10.1007/978-3-030-67514-1_28

Alliance™ Strategy Committee, LoRa-based localization approaches can be divided into two classes: Received Signal Strength Indication (RSSI) based, for coarse positioning and Time Difference of Arrival (TDOA) based, for finer accuracy [4]. And this paper will study Localization System of TDOA-based approaches.

Fargas et al. [3] designed and implemented a tracking system in order to present accuracy results using LoRa technology. Carvalho et al. [8] designed a LoRa-based test system to study the feasibility of mobile sensing and tracking applications. Podevijn et al. [11] implemented an TDOA-based Localization system to investigate the performance of LoRa geolocation for outdoor tracking. However, because a radio signal translates to around 300 m in 1 μs and the timing resolutions of current off-the-shelf LoRa Gateways have only microsecond accuracy, the above three approaches have poor localization performance when implemented on off-the-shelf LoRa devices. Rajalakshmi et al. [12] designed a multi-band backscatter device which is sub-centimeter sized. Although the study of Rajalakshmi et al. achieves meter-level localization accuracy, the LoRa devices in their study need to be highly customized [13].

Some signal processing approaches have also been studied to improve the localization accuracy. Wolf et al. [6] proposed a multi-channel approach to enable precise ranging for LPWAN radio devices, in which oscillator frequency offsets and multipath influence were also taken into account. Bakkali et al. [5] presented an Extended Kalman Filter based approach to achieve the acceptable level of accuracy, in which particular attention is paid to the processing of outliers. However, it's generally difficult to effectively mitigate the effect of propagation environment and multipath, because it is hard to build an effective path-loss model when the signal propagating across different infrastructures and barriers. Besides, good accuracy results were obtained in literature [9], in which 42 gateways were used in hexagonal layout to improve the results and the signal from the end-node was received by at least 10 gateways. But this will require too much cost of network deployment.

According to the above studies, the resolution of timestamp provided by LoRa gateway determines the accuracy of LoRa-Based localization system. Obviously, the timing resolution of current off-the-shelf LoRa products is not sufficient for implementing accurate localization [10]. It is also impracticable to highly customize hardware of current off-the-shelf LoRa devices, which are originally designed to deployed in low cost scenarios.

So we aim to propose a design of LoRa-based localization system for off-the-shelf devices, with flexible, easy deployment capability and good scalability:

- The system will be designed for off-the-shelf LoRa devices, which means it's easy to build the hardware platform. And system servers will be deployed in Alibaba Cloud [15], which means it's flexible to adjust the servers' configurations.
- A new system server architecture will be proposed based on the ChirpStack [16]. All the geolocation computation can be done in LoRa-Geo-Server component, and results will be transported to LoRa-Network-Server component. This makes the proposed system more scalable to develop specific LoRa-App-Server component which will provide more Location Based Services.

- The TDOA extraction method will be proposed. And the end device's position can be estimated with CHAN algorithm [17]. System test results will be presented to show that it can provide a good experimental platform support for LoRa Localization technology research.

The remainder of this paper is organized as follows. Section 2 presents the proposed system architecture and the detailed design of system server. Section 3 describes how to extract TDOA and to determine End-Device's position in the LoRa-Geo-Server. Section 4 presents the system tests results using off-the-shelf LoRa devices. Section 5 concludes this paper.

2   System Design

The system consists of three parts: LoRa End-Device, LoRa Gateways, and System Server, in which the System Server is comprised mainly of LoRa-Network-Server, LoRa-Geo-Server and LoRa-App-Server. The system infrastructure is illustrated in Fig. 1, wherein the Gateways have only microsecond accuracy. Uplink transmissions from the LoRa End-Device are received and accurately time-stamped by LoRa Gateways, then synchronized LoRa Gateways forward these timestamps to the System Server as part of a frame's metadata, which also includes signal level, signal-to-noise ratio, frequency error, etc. Since a GPS receiver is embedded in the Gateway, the GPS coordinates are transmitted to the System Server by the Gateway periodically.

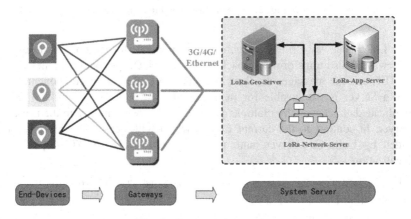

Fig. 1. System infrastructure

The new system server architecture is proposed based on the ChirpStack, and its architecture is illustrated in Fig. 2. The LoRa-Network-Server consists of two components: LoRa Gateway Bridge and LoRa Server, in which the LoRa Server has been highly customized:

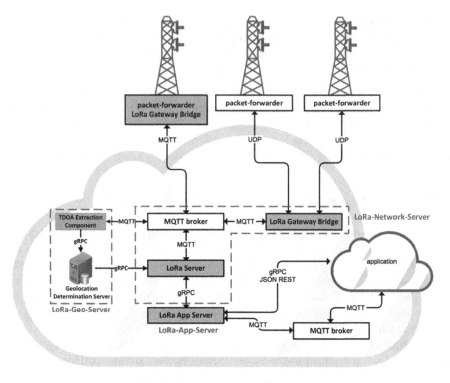

Fig. 2. System server architecture

- The LoRa Gateway Bridge component is responsible for the communication with Gateway. It also transforms the packet-forwarder UDP protocol into message over MQTT, and the messages are then forwarded to LoRa Server component.
- LoRa Server is responsible for managing the state of the network. It also de-duplicate data received by multiple gateways and forward it once to the LoRa-App-Server. In contrast to the current ChirpStack, it will receive the information provided by LoRa-Geo-Server, and no longer subscribe to MQTT topic(s) about localization.

The LoRa-Geo-Server consists of two components: TDOA Extraction Component and Geolocation Determination Server:

- TDOA Extraction Component receives all the events about localization from gateways, by subscribing to corresponding MQTT topic(s). Then TDOAs will be computed and forwarded to Geolocation Determination Server along with Gateways' coordinates, End-Device's short address, etc.
- Geolocation Determination Server will compute the End-Device's position, and transport it to LoRa Server.

The LoRa-App-Server will provide more powerful web-interface and APIs for management of users, organizations, applications, gateways and devices, because End-Device's position can now be provided by LoRa Server. That's to say more Location Based Services can be provided by the LoRa-App-Server.

3 Geolocation Computation in LoRa-Geo-Server

The Geolocation Computation consists of two phases: TDOA Extraction and Geolocation Determination, which are implemented in TDOA Extraction Component and Geolocation Determination Server respectively.

3.1 TDOA Extraction Component

TDOA Extraction Component is implemented in Java, and the detailed TDOA extraction process is illustrated in Fig. 3.

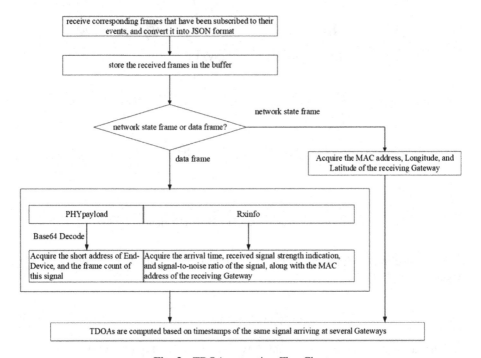

Fig. 3. TDOA extraction FlowChart

Firstly, it will receive all the events about localization by subscribing to its MQTT topic(s). Secondly, necessary information will be acquired, which includes Gateways' MAC addresses, timestamps of one signal arriving at several Gateways, Received Signal Strength Indication, signal-to-noise ratio, Gateways' longitudes, Gateways' latitudes, End-Devices' short addresses, Counts of signals from the End-Devices. Finally, TDOAs are computed based on timestamps of the same signal arriving at several Gateways.

3.2   Geolocation Determination Server

CHAN [17] algorithm will be implemented in Geolocation Determination Server. When TDOAs are acquired, the end-device can be placed on several hyperbolae. Then the end-device can be localized at the intersection of these hyperbolae. This is illustrated in Fig. 4.

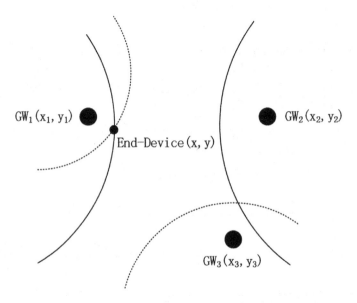

Fig. 4. Localization in CHAN algorithm

As shown in Fig. 4, the distance between End-Device and GW_i is given by Eq. (1), where $i \in \{1, 2, 3\}$.

$$r_i = \sqrt{(x_i - x)^2 + (y_i - y)^2} \tag{1}$$

The distance between GW_i and GW_1 is given by Eq. (2), where $i \in \{2, 3\}$, $C = 3 * 10^8 m/s$, $t_{i,1}$ represents the time difference of the same signal arriving at GW_i and GW_1.

$$r_{i,1} = r_i - r_1 = \sqrt{(x_i - x)^2 + (y_i - y)^2} - \sqrt{(x_1 - x)^2 + (y_1 - y)^2} = t_{i,1} * C \tag{2}$$

Then we can conclude Eq. (3) from Eq. (1) and Eq. (2), where $K_i = x_i^2 + y_i^2$.

$$\begin{cases} r_{2,1}^2 + 2r_{2,1}r_1 = (K_2 - K_1) - 2x_{2,1}x - 2y_{2,1}y \\ r_{3,1}^2 + 2r_{3,1}r_1 = (K_3 - K_1) - 2x_{3,1}x - 2y_{3,1}y \end{cases} \tag{3}$$

Given r_1 is known, the Eq. (3) can be transformed into Eq. (4):

$$\begin{cases} x = p_1 + q_1 r_1 \\ y = p_2 + q_2 r_1 \end{cases} \tag{4}$$

And p_1, q_1, p_2, q_2 in Eq. (4) are represented as follows:

$$p_1 = \frac{y_{2,1}r_{3,1}^2 - y_{3,1}r_{2,1}^2 + y_{3,1}(K_2 - K_1) - y_{2,1}(K_2 - K_1)}{2(x_{2,1}y_{3,1} - x_{3,1}y_{2,1})},$$

$$q_1 = \frac{y_{2,1}r_{3,1} - y_{3,1}r_{2,1}}{x_{2,1}y_{3,1} - x_{3,1}y_{2,1}},$$

$$p_2 = \frac{x_{2,1}r_{3,1}^2 - x_{3,1}r_{2,1}^2 + x_{3,1}(K_2 - K_1) - x_{2,1}(K_2 - K_1)}{2(x_{3,1}y_{2,1} - x_{2,1}y_{3,1})},$$

$$q_2 = \frac{x_{2,1}r_{3,1} - x_{3,1}r_{2,1}}{x_{3,1}y_{2,1} - x_{2,1}y_{3,1}}.$$

Then we can conclude Eq. (5) from Eq. (4) and Eq. (1):

$$ar_1^2 + br_1 + c = 0 \tag{5}$$

And a, b, c in Eq. (5) are represented as follows: $a = q_1^2 + q_2^2 - 1$, $b = -2[q_1(x_1 - p_1) + q_2(y_1 - p_2)]$, $c = (x_1 - p_1)^2 - (y_1 - p_2)^2$.

The r_1 can be obtained by solving Eq. (5). Then by substituting the value of r_1 into Eq. (4), the End-Device's coordinate (x, y) can be obtained.

Through the above steps, the End-Device can be localized when the same signal is received by 3 gateways. And when the End-Device's signal is received by more than 3 gateways, Eq. (6) can be established where $M \geq 4$.

$$\begin{cases} r_{2,1}^2 + 2r_{2,1}r_1 = (K_2 - K_1) - 2x_{2,1}x - 2y_{2,1}y \\ r_{3,1}^2 + 2r_{3,1}r_1 = (K_3 - K_1) - 2x_{3,1}x - 2y_{3,1}y \\ \quad \vdots \\ r_{M,1}^2 + 2r_{M,1}r_1 = (K_M - K_1) - 2x_{M,1}x - 2y_{M,1}y \end{cases} \tag{6}$$

Because the number of equations is greater than the number of unknowns, the least-squares method will be used. Then the End-Device's coordinate (x, y) can be obtained.

4 System Tests in Different Gateway Deployments

This section investigates the performance of the proposed localization system. Several tests have been carried out in different Gateway deployments, to present accuracy results using off-the-shelf LoRa devices.

4.1 Test in Gateway Deployment Case 1

The system is firstly tested in Gateway deployment case 1, which has 3 gateways. Figure 5 illustrates Gateways' and End-Device's geographic positions in the rural area. Figure 6 illustrates the test infrastructure, where the system server has been deployed on Alibaba Cloud [15]. Gateways are connected to the Internet through 4G LTE network. When Gateways receive signals from End-Device, they forward signals to the system server. Each Gateway is placed on a bench, and the antenna of each Gateway is about 1.5 m high.

In Gateway deployment case 1, the tests are carried out 100 times. The detailed localization errors are shown in Fig. 7, the mean localization error is 189.9465 m and the standard deviation is 94.9179 m. Figure 8 shows the estimated positions of End-Device, as well as the real positions of End-Device and Gateways. This verifies that the system localization accuracy is within the accuracy range of "LoRaWAN Geolocation Whitepaper" presented by LoRa Alliance [4].

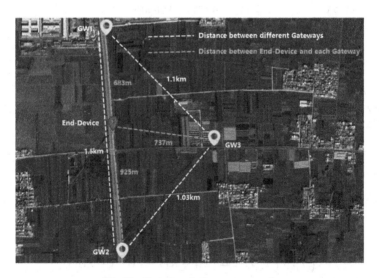

Fig. 5. Gateway deployment case 1

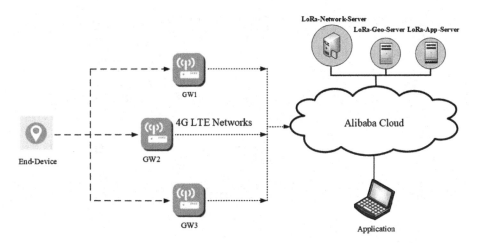

Fig. 6. Test infrastructure

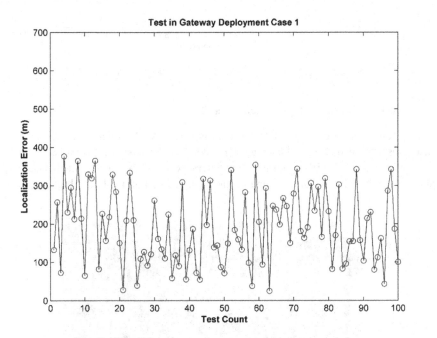

Fig. 7. Localization errors in gateway deployment case 1

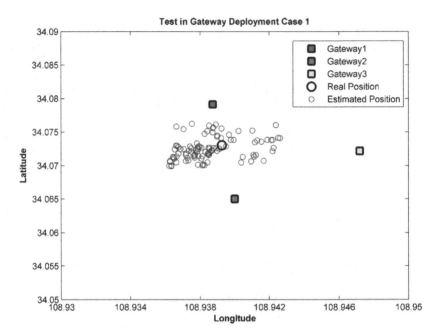

Fig. 8. Estimated positions of End-Device in gateway deployment case 1

4.2 Test in Gateway Deployment Case 2

The system is also tested in Gateway deployment case 2, which has 4 Gateways. In case 2 as shown in Fig. 9, Gateway 4 is added at the basis of case 1, and the End-Device is deployed 150 m north of the intersection of two roads. Each Gateway is placed on a bench, and the antenna of each Gateway is about 1.5 m high.

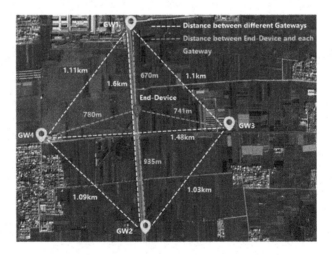

Fig. 9. Gateway deployment case 2

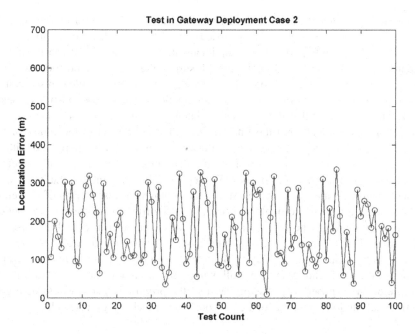

Fig. 10. Localization errors in gateway deployment case 2

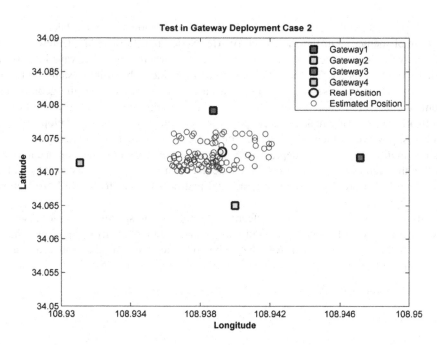

Fig. 11. Estimated positions of End-Device in gateway deployment case 2

In case 2, test infrastructure is similar to case 1 and system server is also deployed on Alibaba Cloud. The tests are also carried out 100 times. The detailed localization errors are shown in Fig. 10, the mean localization error is 176.35785 m and the standard deviation is 88.2780 m. Figure 11 shows the estimated positions of End-Device, as well as the real positions of End-Device and Gateways. We can see that the mean system localization error and standard deviation in case 2 are much less than in case 1. This is because that the number of Gateways is increased, four Gateways are deployed almost squarely and the End-Device is located almost in the center of four Gateways. In other words, the system localization accuracy can be improved with the improved Gateway Deployment. Besides, the deployment case of Port of Barcelona, presented in "LoRaWAN Geolocation Whitepaper" [4], has the similar open environment that case 1 and case 2 have. And in the deployment case of Port of Barcelona, the Gateways' antennas are deployed directly on the rooftops of three-story metallic buildings. By contrast, the height of each Gateway's antenna in case 1and case 2 is much lower. This is the main factor that the system localization accuracy in case 1and case 2 is not good as in case of Port of Barcelona. And because the system localization accuracy in case 1 and case 2 is still within the accuracy range of "LoRaWAN Geolocation Whitepaper" [4], it is proved that the proposed system would be a good experimental platform support for LoRa Localization technology research.

5 Conclusions and Future Work

In this paper, a flexible and scalable LoRa-Based localization system has been designed and implemented. Off-the-shelf LoRaWAN Node and LoRaWAN Gateways are respectively used as the End-Device and Gateways, wherein the Gateways have only microsecond accuracy. This means it's easy and flexible to build the system hardware platform. The system server is customized based on ChirpStack. All the geolocation computation can be done in LoRa-Geo-Server, and results will be transported to LoRa-Network-Server. This makes the proposed system more scalable to develop specific LoRa-App-Server which will provide more Location Based Services. System test results in different Gateway deployments show that the system localization accuracy is within the accuracy range of "LoRaWAN Geolocation Whitepaper" presented by LoRa Alliance. It can provide a good experimental platform support for LoRa Localization technology research.

In the future, we'll propose effective algorithms for specific scenario cases to mitigate the effect of propagation environment and multipath. Customized LoRa-App-Server will be also developed. And they'll be both integrated into the proposed system in this paper.

References

1. Alliance, L.: A technical overview of LoRa and LoRaWAN. White Paper, November 20 (2015)
2. Gotthard, P., Jankech, T.: Low-cost car park localization using rssi in supervised lora mesh networks. In: 15th Workshop on Positioning, Navigation and Communications (WPNC), pp. 1–6. IEEE (2018)
3. Fargas, B.C., Petersen, M.N.: GPS-free geolocation using LoRa in low-power WANs. In: 2017 Global Internet of Things Summit (Giots), pp. 1–6. IEEE, Geneva (2017)
4. Lora Alliance Strategy Committee, et al.: LoRaWAN Geolocation White-paper. LoRa Alliance, January 2018
5. Bakkali, W., Kieffer, M., Lalam, M., et al.: Kalman filter-based localization for Internet of Things LoRaWAN™ end points. In: 2017 IEEE 28th Annual International Symposium on Personal, Indoor, and Mobile Radio Communications (PIMRC), pp. 1–6, IEEE, Montreal (2017)
6. Wolf, F., Villien, C., De Rivaz, S., et al.: Improved multi-channel ranging precision bound for narrowband LPWAN in multipath scenarios. In: 2018 IEEE Wireless Communications and Networking Conference (WCNC), pp. 1–6. IEEE, Barcelona (2018)
7. Martin, B.: Technology to the Rescue. In: Survival or Extinction?, pp. 319–330. Springer, Cham (2019)
8. Carvalho, D.F., Depari, A., Ferrari, P., et al.: On the feasibility of mobile sensing and tracking applications based on LPWAN. In: 2018 IEEE Sensors Applications Symposium (SAS), pp. 1–6, IEEE (2018)
9. Lestable, T., Lalam, M., Grau, M.: Location-Enabled LoRa IoT Network:'Geo-LoRa-ting' your assets. Presentation, September (2015)
10. Dongare, A., Hesling, C., Bhatia, K., et al.: OpenChirp: A low-power wide-area networking architecture. In: IEEE International Conference on Pervasive Computing & Communications Workshops, pp. 569–574. IEEE (2017)
11. Nico, P., David, P., Jens, T., et al.: TDoA-Based Outdoor Positioning with Tracking Algorithm in a Public LoRa Network. Wireless Communications and Mobile Computing **2018**, 1–9 (2018)
12. Nandakumar, R., Iyer, V., Gollakota, S., et al.: 3D localization for sub-centimeter sized devices. In: Proceedings of the 16th ACM Conference on Embedded Networked Sensor Systems (SenSys'18), pp. 108–119. ACM (2018)
13. Gu, C., Jiang, L., Tan, R., et al.: LoRa-Based Localization: Opportunities and Challenges. arXiv: Networking and Internet Architecture (2018)
14. Guan, P., Zhang, Z., Wei, L., et al.: A real-time bus positioning system based on LoRa technology. In: 2018 2nd International Conference on Smart Grid and Smart Cities (ICSGSC), pp. 45–48, IEEE (2018)
15. Alibaba Cloud Homepage. https://www.alibabacloud.com/. Accessed 12 Feb 2020
16. ChirpStack Homepage. https://www.chirpstack.io/. Accessed 12 Feb 2020
17. Ma, L.: Research and application of wireless sensor location algorithm based on TDOA. Shandong University (2012)

Satellite Communications and Spatial Information Network

Research on Optical-Electrical Path Mapping Strategy of Space Hybrid Switches

Wei Liang[✉], Jun Li, Yi Zhang, Jing-ling Li, and Tao Cui

National Key Laboratory of Science and Technology on Space Microwave,
CAST, Xi'an 710100, China
Liangwei86@126.com

Abstract. To solve the problem of heterogeneous path selection, which is caused by the classification, collection, and exchange of multi-layer services in the space information network. An optical-electrical path mapping strategy is proposed. The strategy establishes a normalized identification for the forwarding information and status information, these information are required for each layer switch. The strategy establishes an internal path mapping table. The algorithm enables the services of various granularities in the space to flexibly select internal paths, It can realize the deep integration of multi-layer switching.

Keywords: Hybrid switches · Optical-electrical path · Path mapping table · Space information network

1 Introduce

The structure of the space information network is complex, the information is multi-dimensional, the information representation is diverse, the amount of information is huge, the information relationship is complex, the timeliness, accuracy and reliability of information processing are high. Multi-granularity heterogeneous data exchange at the physical layer (optical layer)/link layer/network layer is required.

In traditional hybrid switching, whether it is in a terrestrial network or in a space network, the optical layer and the electrical layer use different mapping tables to select the internal path [1–3]. The optical switch forwards wavelengths or time slots at the physical layer according to the configuration table. The electrical packet forwards according to the forwarding table and routing table, it adopts two-layer and three-layer switching technology. It is difficult for the tables of different layers to interact, it is not conducive to centralized control of the resources within the switch.

This paper proposes an optical-electrical path mapping strategy in space hybrid switching, this strategy unifies the internal path information and switching matrix state information in the internal path mapping table of the second layer, these information is required by the optical layer and the electrical layer. Various granular switching services can quickly obtains the information of all available paths with this mapping table. The services can flexibly choose different paths, such as optical paths or electrical paths. This strategy not only meets the fast forwarding requirements of each user's data, but also realizes the deep integration of multi-layer switching.

© ICST Institute for Computer Sciences, Social Informatics and Telecommunications Engineering 2021
Published by Springer Nature Switzerland AG 2021. All Rights Reserved
B. Li et al. (Eds.): IoTaaS 2020, LNICST 346, pp. 363–370, 2021.
https://doi.org/10.1007/978-3-030-67514-1_29

2   Space Hybrid Switch Technology

2.1   Space Information Network

There are three main types of links and services that space information network nodes access: one is backbone service links, including GEO-GEO links, GEO-ground gateway station links, etc., these are relatively static links. One is the space nodes and User links, including links between GEO and LEO, aerospace vehicles, nearby space vehicles and other users. The other is the links which is used in some specific situations, such as distributed intra-constellation communications, satellite formation flying, etc. It can be said that space information has the characteristics of diversified services and protocols, and large differences in service quality requirements [4] (Fig. 1).

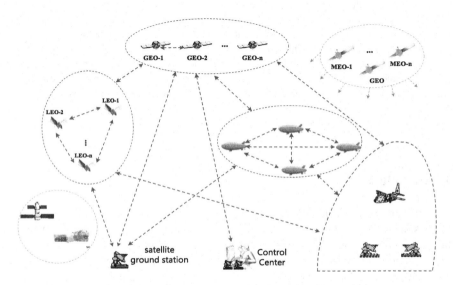

Fig. 1. Conception of the space information network.

The first type of link information only needs to be forwarded transparently in the space node, the second type of link information requires service aggregation and multi-granularity distribution in the space node, and the third type of link information needs to be forwarded quickly, but also needs to be aggregated, distribution. Because of this, there are two forwarding requirements for space information: one is that it only needs to be forwarded transparently, and the other is that it needs to be distributed with multiple granularities. When small-granularity port services are forwarded to large-granularity port services, the unified control is required.

2.2   Optical-Electrical Hybrid Switching

Electrical packet switching technology and optical circuit switching technology are quite different in services granularity, but the integration of optical-electrical switching technology can be achieved in the node, through sophisticated intelligent service management technology (including service aggregation/grooming, optical layer bypass technology, etc.), optical-electrical hybrid switching has multi-granularity switching capabilities, and there are physical layer, two-layer, and three-layer switching at the same time [5, 6]. They implement information forwarding according to physical or logical internal paths (Fig. 2).

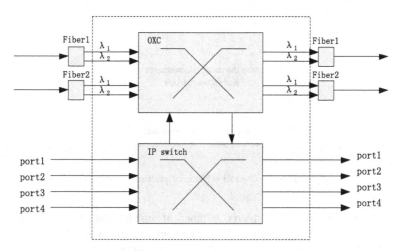

Fig. 2. Optical-electrical hybrid switching unit

Therefore, in order to unify scheduling, aggregation, and distribution of space information, the space hybrid switching needs to establish a unified forwarding basis for all information, thereby shielding the differences between different resources [7, 8].

3   Optical-Electrical Path Mapping Strategy

Whether it is optical or packet switching, this research abstracts the management/ control of data flow through the method of normalizing labels. The normalized label here contains multi-dimensional information of data [9, 10]. For example, optical switching uses available time slots and wavelengths to characterize optical data exchange information, while packet switching uses destination IP addresses to characterize packet data exchange information (Fig. 3).

3.1   Internal Path Mark Mapping

(1) Port mapping

In the optical-electrical hybrid switching node, for the optical switching matrix: if it is wavelength and band switching, assume that n is the number of wavelengths of the optical switching matrix; if it is optical switching matrix switching, assume that n is the

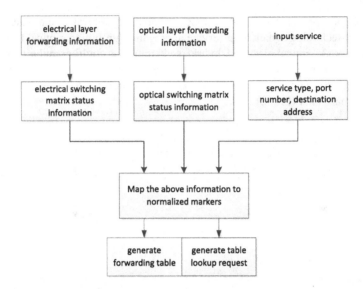

Fig. 3. Overall scheme of path mapping

number of optical switching matrix number of input/output ports. For electrical switching: suppose m is the number of input and output ports of the electrical switching matrix. The following mapping relationships can be established (Fig. 4).

optical switchIng matrix	Value	
	0	
λ_1/ W_1/port1	1	
...	...	n
λ_n/ W_n/port1	...	
electrical switching matrix	n-1	
	n	
Port0	...	
...	...	m
Portm-1	m+n-1	

Fig. 4. Port mapping method

As shown in the figure above, the wavelength/band/port of the optical switching matrix and the port of the electrical switching matrix are mapped to a set of integers, with a value range of $0 \sim m+n-1$, the mapping table is used for fast forwarding, the input and output port number can be mapped to a binary number, and its bit width is m +n, and each wavelength and port are identified by the bit of the binary number.

(2) Switching matrix state mapping

Collect the status information of the optical/electric switching matrix in real time, including the occupancy and congestion of internal paths. If the wavelength/band/port is already occupied, it is marked as "11", and if it is idle, it is represented as "00". If the wavelength/band/port is not occupied, and estimated that it cannot transmit a large number of reports in a short time. It is marked as quasi-idle "01", if the in/out port of this electrical switching matrix is congested, it is marked as "11", otherwise it is marked as "00". The obtained state information is integrated and mapped into two binary numbers with a bit width of 2 (m+n). The above-mentioned identification can be used to generate an internal path mapping table (Fig. 5).

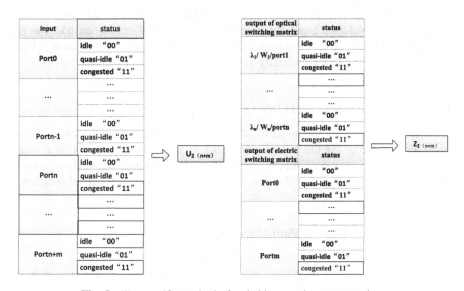

Fig. 5. The specific method of switching matrix state mapping

(3) The internal path mapping of the switch

- Establish the mapping relationship between the destination address and the input/output ports of the switch;
- When a destination address corresponds to a unique output port, set the bit position corresponding to this port to "1", and set the rest to "0". When a destination address corresponds to k output ports, set the bits corresponding to these k ports Position "1", and set the rest to "0";
- Establish a one-to-one correspondence between each input port of the switch and the destination address. If the input port is an optical port, the table entries is generated, and it includes optical input port → optical output port → destination address, optical input port → electrical output port → destination address, optical

input port → electrical input port → electrical output port → All possible paths to the destination address; similarly, if the input port is an electrical port, the table entries is generated, and it includes electrical input port → electrical output port → destination address, electrical input port → optical output port-destination address, electrical input port → optical input port → optical output port → destination address.

- Establish the mapping of multi-dimensional information lookup table request;
- The service type is divided into two parts: multi-dimensional information identification and service type identification. The multi-dimensional information identifier is used to distinguish whether the input data is optical data or packet data, and the service type identifier is used to distinguish the priority of the data packet. Combining the table lookup result of the input data message with the service type, the appropriate forwarding output port and switching granularity can be selected according to different needs;
- Use the input port number and destination address as the read address for quick table lookup. Addra = input port number*the number of destination address. The destination address can be the next hop IP address, MAC address, or a custom label, as long as it can uniquely identify all switches and users in the same network.

(4) Optical\electrical additional information mapping

Establish additional information items of optical/electricity, it is reserved for different needs. For example: for the optical input port, if the switching matrix is a switch matrix, the optical identifier will provide the optical switch path information from the input port to the output port in the switching matrix, it includes all optical switches in use in the occupied path.

3.2   The Table of Internal Path Mapping

Valid bit: Identifies whether the forwarded information is valid;

Optical identification: used to identify the resource occupancy of each port in the optical switching matrix;

Input port number: Input the port number of the optical data packet/input the port number of the packet data packet;

Output port number: the port number of the output port to which the input optical data packet is to be switched, and the port number of the output port to which the input packet data packet is to be switched;

Port status information: used to identify the resource occupation of each port of the switch;

Multicast identifier: indicates the packet data;

Next hop address: Enter the address of the next hop router to be exchanged for data packets (Fig. 6).

Valid bit	Optical identification	Input port number	Output port number	Port status information	Multicast identifier	additional information	Next hop address
...	...	...	...	...	...	...	...
...	...	...	...	...	...	...	...
...	...	...	...	...	...	...	...

Fig. 6. The format of Internal path mapping table

3.3 Create a Table Lookup Request

The services type is divided into two parts: optical/electrical identification and message type identification. Optical/electrical identification is used to distinguish whether the input service is optical data or packet data; the service type identification is used to distinguish the priority of the message, and the result of the table lookup of the input service and the service type can be selected according to different needs. Appropriate forwarding and output ports and switching granularity (Fig. 7).

services type	Input port number	Next hop address

Fig. 7. The format of table lookup request

3.4 Query Steps of the Path Mapping Table

i. When the input message needs search the internal path, firstly, confirm whether the input port is occupied or not, by according to the state information of the switch matrix generated in the previous article. If it is not occupied, perform 2;

ii. According to the destination address in the message of table lookup request, reads the mapping table entry in the memory, and establishes a fast internal switching path according to the output port number and matrix status information of the optical-electrical switch matrix. If the output port queried is Occupied, execute 3

iii. The mapping table are searched in the same clock cycle to find the corresponding entry, for all port numbers except the current message input port number, and then the table entries corresponding to the message destination address are read. According to the information such as the optical-electrical identification and effective bit of the entry, the appropriate entry is selected to establish the optimal internal path.

iv. When the switching matrix performs a message exchange and the status information changes, the internal path mapping table will update in time.

4 Conclusion

Firstly, this paper analyzes the needs of the forwarding and processing for space information network, it gives the principle of space hybrid switching, and it proposes an optical-electrical path mapping strategy for space hybrid switching, This strategy completes some key technical designs, such as port mapping, switching matrix state mapping, and internal path mapping of switches. Optical-electrical hybrid switching is based on this internal path mapping method, it can realize fast forwarding from electricity to light and light to electricity, and can also realize resource integration inside the switch, thus it can concentrates the advantages of the electrical and optical layers, and improves link utilization. This strategy provides technical support for the integration of space optical network and power grid.

References

1. Rui-xin, L., Shang-hong, Z., Zhou-shi, Y.: Research of on-board mixed optical/electric switching of GEO broadband multimedia satellite. Opt. Commun. Technol. **35**(6), 51–53 (2011)
2. Wei, L., Jun, L., Yi, Z.: The study on routing algorithms in hybrid optical/electrical network with the QoS layered-graph model. Opt. Commun. Technol. **43**(3), 54–58 (2019)
3. Hai-yi, Z., Wen-yu, Z., Rui, T.: High-capacity O/E switch. Technology **17**(6), 20–23 (2011)
4. Xifeng, D., Shanghong, Z., Ruixin, L.: Research on laser/RF/packets hybrid switching of space information network. Opt. Commun. Technol. **41**(6), 6–9 (2017)
5. Sato, K., Yamanaka, N., Takigawa, Y., et al.: GMPLS-based photonic multilayer router (hikari router) architecture: an overview of traffic engineering and signaling technology. IEEE Commun. Mag. **40**(3), 96–101 (2002)
6. Zhu, K., Zang, H., Mukherjee, B.: A comprehensive study on next-generation optical grooming switches. IEEE Sel. Areas Commun. **21**(7), 1173–1186 (2003)
7. Bannister, J., Touch, J., Willner, A.: How many wavelengths do we really need? a study of the performance limits of packet over wavelengths. SPIE Opt. Netw. Mag. **1**(2), 1–12 (2000)
8. Shao-bo, Y., Ling-da, W., Xi-tao, Z.: DaaC: an architecture modeling of space information network. J. Commun. **38**(z1), 165–170 (2017)
9. Tao, H., Ying, H., Yiqiang, H.: Wavelength converter information sharing in GMPLS controlled optical networks. Zhongguo Tongxin **07**(5), 77–82 (2010)
10. Jing-ling, L., Jun, L., Wei, L.: Design and processing method of satellite signaling with a mixed optical/electric switching capability. Microelectron. Comput. **35**(06), 112–116 (2018)

Algorithm for Multipath Interference Restraint Based on Blind Source Separation in Passive GNSS-Based Bistatic Radar

Yuanyuan Wen[1(✉)], Lin Bai[2], Xi Zhang[2], She Shang[1], Dawei Song[1], and Shuai Guo[3]

[1] National Key Laboratory of Science and Technology on Space Microwave, Xi'an 710100, China
wyy031980@163.com
[2] Academy of Space Information Systems, Xi'an 710100, China
[3] National Laboratory of Radar Signal Processing, Xidian University, Xi'an 710070, China

Abstract. Passive bistatic radar belongs to passive radar systems and is a variant of bistatic radar that exploit non-cooperative 'illuminators of opportunity' as their sources of radar transmission. Passive bistatic radar has a lot of advantages such as double-base system, silent acceptance, inherently low cost and so on, and hence attractive for a broad range of applications in recent years. The Passive GNSS-Based bistatic Radar system exploits Global Navigation Satellite System as the illuminators of opportunity to detect the potential targets and is inevitable affected by multipath interference due to the reflection effect of mountains and near-earth buildings. If reference signal containing multipath interference is directly used for matching filter processing, the range-Doppler diagram will show the false target formed by matching multipath interference with echo signal. In this paper, a novel blind source separation method is proposed to recovering multipath interference from reference channel data in Passive GNSS-Based bistatic Radar. The elementary reflection matrix is used as a rotation matrix to transform the cumulant matrix to realize the purpose of diagonalization. Finally the direct wave signal and multipath interference signals were separated successfully. Both theoretical analysis and simulation result verify multipath interference can be well suppressed by the proposed method.

Keywords: The Passive GNSS-Based Bistatic Radar · Multipath interference · Direct wave signal · Blind source separation · Elementary reflection matrix

1 Introduction

For nearly twenty years, passive bistatic radar (PBR) has appealed to more and more people to study it at home and abroad because of its unique advantages of double-base system and silent acceptance [1]. The PBR obtains the target information by correlative processing between the target scattering echo signal and the direct wave signal received by non-cooperative transmitters as the illuminators of opportunity, so as to complete the detection, location and tracking of the target. The illuminators of opportunity used

B. Li et al. (Eds.): IoTaaS 2020, LNICST 346, pp. 371–379, 2021.
https://doi.org/10.1007/978-3-030-67514-1_30

include all kinds of wireless signals existing in space (such as FM [2, 3], civil TV [4], mobile communication, Global Navigation Satellite System(GNSS) and other digital video broadcast-terrestrial [5–8]), with good concealment and anti-destruction performance [9]. These systems can realize the features of low-cost network layout [10], wide coverage and flexible layout, and the radar of radiation sources outside the low-frequency segment can also realize anti-stealth, low-altitude detection and anti- "radio silence" [11].

GNSS uses one or more systems in Global Positioning System (GPS) [12], the GLObal Satellite Navigation System (GLONASS) [13], Beidou Satellite Navigation System [14], or Galileo Satellite Navigation System [15] for navigation and positioning. The passive GNSS-based bistatic radar system has many advantages. First, the passive radar is a multi-base radar system, and the stealth equipment cannot absorb microwave signals in the same direction, so passive radar has certain advantages in anti-stealth. Moreover, the passive radar without transmitter has portability and concealment and is difficult to be detected. At present, the worldwide user receives the GNSS by spread spectrum communication signal processing and carrier modulation signal after processing, the launch of the space at the same time, GNSS will remain on the surface of the earth or in the near-earth space of a point to provide 24-hour uninterrupted satellite signal to the world, based on the analysis of these signals using can realize positioning, navigation and timing services [16]. However reference channel of passive GNSS-based bistatic radar system is susceptible to multipath interference. The passive GNSS-based bistatic radar system is inevitable affected by multipath interference due to the reflection effect of mountains and near-earth buildings. When reference channel is affected by multipath interference, reference signals received by reference channel include direct wave signal, multipath interference and channel noise. If reference signal containing multipath interference is directly used for matching filter processing, the range-Doppler diagram will show the false target formed by matching multipath interference with echo signal. How to suppress multipath interference in reference channel of passive GNSS-based bistatic radar has become a difficult problem.

Because the mixed model of multipath interference and direct wave in the channel of the passive GNSS-based bistatic radar system is very similar to the model of blind source separation(BSS), the BSS method can be considered to separate the multipath interference and direct wave [17]. BSS refers to the estimation of each source signal only based on the observed signal received by the receiver when neither the source signal nor the mixed signal can be known [10]. The elementary reflection matrix is used as a rotation matrix to transform the cumulant matrix to realize the purpose of diagonalization and finally the direct wave signal and multipath interference signals were separated successfully.

The rest of the article follows. Section 2 the Passive GNSS-Based Bistatic radar system model is introduced. Section 3 the proposed novel multipath interference restraint algorithm based on BSS in passive GNSS-based bistatic radar is presented in detail. The capability of the proposed algorithm is verified by simulation results in Sect. 4. The conclusions are provided in Sect. 5.

2 Passive GNSS-Based Bistatic Radar System Model

The passive GNSS-based bistatic radar system model is shown in Fig. 1. The GNSS signals are used to detect airborne targets.

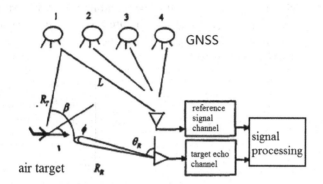

Fig. 1. Passive GNSS-based bistatic radar system model.

Using the traditional GNSS receiver multipath interferences, GNSS direct wave signal and channel noise are received through the reference channel. The signal received by the target channel can be represented as [10, 18, 19]

$$X_{tar}(t) = \underbrace{A_d s(t)}_{\text{directpath}} + \underbrace{\sum_{i=1}^{N} c_i s(t - \tau_{mi})}_{\text{multipathecho}} + \underbrace{a_d s(t - \tau_d) e^{j2\pi f_d t}}_{\text{targetecho}} + \underbrace{n_{tar}(t)}_{\text{noise}} \qquad (1)$$

The signal received by the reference channel can be rewritten as

$$X_{ref}(t) = \underbrace{A_{d1} s(t)}_{\text{directpath}} + \underbrace{\sum_{i=1}^{M} d_i s(t - \tau_{pi})}_{\text{multipath}} + \underbrace{n_{ref}(t)}_{\text{noise}} \qquad (2)$$

where $s(t)$ is the direct wave, A_d and A_{d1} are the coefficient of the direct wave signal; $\sum_{i=1}^{N} c_i s(t - \tau_{mi})$ and $\sum_{i=1}^{M} d_i s(t - \tau_{pi})$ are the multipath signals, N and M are the number of the multipath signals, c_i and d_i are the amplitude of the multipath, τ_{mi} and τ_{pi} are the time delay of the multipath signal; $a_d s(t - \tau_d) e^{j2\pi f_d t}$ is the echo signal, a_d, τ_d and f_d respectively is the amplitude, the time delay and the Doppler frequency of the target echo signal; $n_{tar}(t)$ is the noise at the target echo channel, $n_{ref}(t)$ is the noise at the reference channel receiver antenna, $n_{tar}(t)$ and $n_{ref}(t)$ are independent and uncorrelated of the GNSS signal.

3 Multipath Interference Restraint Algorithm Based on BSS

We consider the multipath interferences suppression in the reference channel. The spectra of the sources are heavily overlapped in the reference channel of the passive GNSS-Based bistatic radar, so array antennas are often used to receive signals. In general, the receiving antenna is assumed to be an arbitrarily shaped array structure. Let's think about the common case that the mixture model of the system is overdetermined, namely, the number of receivers is M, and the number of sources is N (N), the received signals can be rewritten as:

$$
\begin{bmatrix} x_1(t) \\ \vdots \\ x_{M-1}(t) \\ x_M(t) \end{bmatrix} = \begin{bmatrix} \alpha_1(\theta_1), & \alpha_2(\theta_2), & \alpha_3(\theta_3), & \cdots, & \alpha_N(\theta_N) \end{bmatrix} \begin{bmatrix} A_1s(t) \\ d_1s(t-\tau_1) \\ d_2s(t-\tau_2) \\ \vdots \\ d_{N-1}s(t-\tau_{N-1}) \end{bmatrix} + \begin{bmatrix} n_1(t) \\ n_2(t) \\ \vdots \\ n_M(t) \end{bmatrix}
$$

$$(3)$$

we can see that the mixed model of multipath interference and direct wave in the channel of the passive GNSS-based bistatic radar system is very similar to the model of BSS. Therefore, BSS method can be considered to separate the multipath interference and direct wave.

BSS refers to the estimation of N source signal only based on the M observed signal received by the receiver when neither the source signal nor the mixed signal can be known [20, 21].

Suppose an instantaneous linear mixing system in the presence of noise, in which there $M \geq N$. The signal received by the received channel can be expressed as:

$$
x_j(t) = \sum_{i=1}^{N} a_{ij}(k)s_j(t) + n_i(t), \quad j = 1, 2, \ldots, M \tag{4}
$$

where x_j is the j-th observed signal, s_i is the i-th source signal, $a_{ij}(k)$ is the mixed matrix. We assume that the system is a causal finite filter model throughout this article. $n_i(t)$ is the noise. Suppose $S(t) = [s_1(t), \cdots, s_N(t)]^T$ and $X(t) = [x_1(t), \cdots, x_M(t)]^T$ respectively represent the source signals and the observed signals in matrix form. Formula (4) can also be expressed as the matrix form.

Defining $Y(t) = [y_1(t), \cdots, y_N(t)]^T$ represent the estimated signals in matrix form and W is unmixing matrix. By computing the values of the matrix elements of the unmixing matrix W an individual element is mutually independent estimate vector $Y(t)$ of the source signals vector $S(t)$ is computed [22, 23]. The approximate joint diagonalization process of the signals of received channel is the solution process of W.

The elementary reflection matrix is used as a rotation matrix to transform the cumulant matrix to realize the purpose of diagonalization. Finally the direct wave signal and multipath interference signals were separated successfully. Below is the detailed process of diagonalization.

Suppose X be made of matrices $x_1, x_2, \cdots, x_n$ of size $n \times n$. The process of joint diagonalization of X using the elementary reflection matrix can be described to minimize the following equation [24, 25]

$$H'XH = \min \sum \|X - diag(X)\|^2 \tag{5}$$

If $s = 1$, the process of the joint diagonalization is the same as the process of the normal unitary diagonalization. The solution to the matrix H is the process of joint diagonalization of X. And then we make a somewhat rule, through which approximate jointly diagonalizing matrix is realized.

Defining $H = I - 2ww^T$ is the elementary reflection matrix, where $\|w\|_2 = 1$. We can have a 0 in a vector through the elementary reflection matrix. Vector x can be transformed into a new vector that has zero entries except for the first entry.

4 Simulation Results

Let us suppose a simplified model of three inputs and three outputs and three source signals s_1, s_2, s_3 is independent. s_1 is the expected signal, s_2, s_3 is multipath reflection of the expected signal. We artificially mix the three sources via the mixing matrix in the following:

$$H(z) = \begin{bmatrix} 1 + 0.2z^{-1} + 0.1z^{-2} & 0.5 + 0.6z^{-1} + 0.3z^{-2} & 0.3 + 0.6z^{-1} + 0.5z^{-2} \\ 0.5 + 0.6z^{-1} + 0.3z^{-2} & 0.2 + 0.6z^{-1} + 0.2z^{-2} & 0.2 + 0.1z^{-1} + 0.4z^{-2} \\ 0.3 + 0.1z^{-1} + 0.1z^{-2} & 0.5 + 0.2z^{-1} + 0.4z^{-2} & 0.4 + 0.2z^{-1} + 0.3z^{-2} \end{bmatrix} \tag{6}$$

To further measure the separation capability of the proposed method, we evaluate the separation capability of the proposed method using the comparable coefficient. The closer the value of comparable coefficient is to one, the better the capability of the proposed algorithm. The comparable coefficient can be defined as follows:

$$\lambda_{ij} = \lambda(y_i, s_j) = \frac{\left|\sum y_i * s_j\right|}{\sqrt{\sum y_i^2 * \sum s_j^2}} \tag{7}$$

where, s_j and y_i respectively represent two signal vectors; λ_{ij} represents the degree of similarity between two signal vectors.

The original signal and extracted signal are shown in Fig. 2. Figure 2(a) shows the real part comparison of the original signal and extracted signal and Fig. 2(b) shows the imaginary part comparison of the original signal and extracted signal.

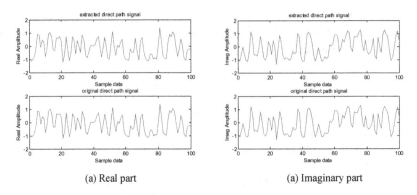

(a) Real part   (a) Imaginary part

Fig. 2. Original signals and extracted direct wave signal.

From the figure above we can see that the waveform of the extracted signal and the original direct wave is very similar. We can further verify the separation capability of the proposed method in this paper by calculating the resemble coefficient under different SNR. The resemble coefficient are shown in Table 1.

Table 1. Comparable coefficient.

SNR/dB	−20	−15	−8	−5	0
Comparable coefficient	0.8543	0.9048	0.9439	0.9789	0.9990

It can be seen from Table 1 that the direct wave signal can be extracted even at a low SNR.

The performance of the algorithm to suppress multipath interference is further verified by comparing the constellations of direct wave signal under different conditions. For the convenience of comparison, this simulation normalizes the direct wave signal under different conditions. When the signal modulus is constant, the signal point trace is distributed as a standard circle with radius 1. When the signal modulus fluctuates with time, the signal point trace distribution is disorganized. By comparing the stray degree of the point trace distribution in the constellation maps, the degree of the signal modulus floating is measured. Therefore, the signal constellation map can directly reflect the distribution of the signal modulus. The comparison results are shown in Fig. 3.

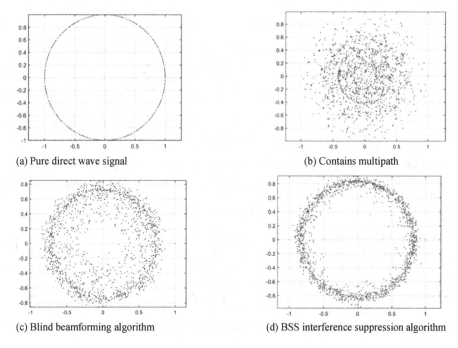

(a) Pure direct wave signal

(b) Contains multipath

(c) Blind beamforming algorithm

(d) BSS interference suppression algorithm

Fig. 3. Comparison of the constellation maps.

As you can see from the Fig. 3 that the stray point trace of the proposed algorithm converges further to the constant modulus circle than the blind beamforming algorithm, which indicating that the proposed method can better suppress multipath interferences.

5   Conclusions

A blind source separation algorithm with the statistical independence of the direct wave signal and multipath interference signals is proposed to suppress multipath signals in the reference channel of the passive GNSS-Based bistatic radar system in this paper. The elementary reflection matrix is used as a rotation matrix to transform the cumulant matrix to realize the purpose of matrix diagonalization and finally the direct wave signal and multipath interference signals were separated successfully. The numerical simulations have demonstrated the validity of the proposed method. Using the proposed method multipath interference signals can also be suppressed at lower SNR and the performance of multipath interference restraint of the proposed method is better than that of the blind beamforming algorithm.

References

1. Guo, S., Wang, J., Chen, G., Wang, J.: Method for multipath interference restraint of the reference channel in passive bistatic radar. J. XIDIAN Uni. **45**(3), 18–23 (2018)
2. Colone, F., Bongioanni, C., Lombardo, P.: Multifrequency integration in FM radio-based passive bistatic radar. Part I: target detection. IEEE Aerosp. Electron. Syst. Mag. **28**(4), 28–39 (2013)
3. Colone, F., Bongioanni, C., Lombardo, P.: Multifrequency integration in FM radio-based passive bistatic radar. Part II: target detection of arrival estimation. IEEE Aerosp. Electron. Syst. Mag. **28**(4), 40–47 (2013)
4. Edrich, M., Schroeder, A., Meyer, F.: Design and performance evaluation of a mature FM/DAB/DVB-T multi-illuminator passive radar system. IET Radar Sonar Navig. **8**(2), 114–122 (2014)
5. Howland, P.E.: Editorial: passive radar systems. IEE Proc. Radar Sonar Navig. **152**(3), 105–106 (2005)
6. Griffiths, H.D., Baker, C.J.: Passive coherent location radar systems. Part 1: Performance predication. IEE Proc. Radar Sonar Navig. **152**(3), 153–159 (2005)
7. Poulin, D.: Passive detection using digital broadcasters (DAB, DVB) with COFDM modulation. IEE Proc. Radar Sonar Navig. **152**(3), 143–152 (2005)
8. Howland, P.E., Maksimiuk, D., Reitsma, G.: FM radio base d bistatic radar. IEE Proc. Radar Sonar Navig. **152**, 107–115 (2005)
9. Nordwall, B.D.: Silent Sentry-A New Type of Radar. Aviation Week & Space Technology (1998)
10. Wen, Y., Sun, W., Shang, S.: Weak signal extraction based on blind source separation in passive radar. In: 2019 International Symposium on Signal Processing, pp. 26–30 (2019)
11. Griffiths, H.D, Long, N.R.W: Television based bistatic radar. Radar Signal Process. **133**(7), 649–657(1986)
12. Navstar IS-GPS-200E, Interface Specification, Science Applications International Corporation, El Segundo, CA, USA. Technical Report IRN-IS-200H-003 (2015)
13. Global Navigation Satellite System GLONASS Interface Control Document (Edition 5 .1), Russian Institute of Space Device Engineering, Nizhnyaya Salda, Russia (2008)
14. BeiDou Navigation Satellite System Signal in Space Interface Control Document, Open Service Signal (Version 2.0). China Satellite Navigation Office, Beijing, China, December 2013
15. Galileo Open Service, Signal in Space Interface Control Document (OS SIS ICD). European Space Agency/European GNSS, Paris, France, November 2015
16. Pastina, D., Santi, F., Pieralice, F.: Maritime moving target long time integration for GNSS-based passive bistatic radar. IEEE Trans. Aerosp. Electron. Syst. **54**(6), 3060–3083 (2018)
17. Colone, F., Cardinali, R., Lombardo, P.: Cancellation of clutter and multipath in passive radar using a sequential approach. In: 2006 IEEE Conference on Radar, Verona (NY), USA, p. 7 (2006)
18. Tsai, P.H.E., Ebrahim, K., Lange, G., Paichard, Y., Inggs, M.: Null placement in a circular antenna array for passive coherent location systems. In: 2010 IEEE International Radar Conference, Washington, DC, USA, pp. 1140–1143 (2010)
19. Feng, B., Wang, T., Liu, C.: An effective CLEAN algorithm for interference cancellation and weak target detection in passive radar. In: 2013 Asia-Pacific Conference on Synthetic Aperture Radar (APSAR), vol. 5, no. 2, pp. 160–163 (2013)

20. Fu, W., Zhou, X., Nong, B., Li, C., Liu, J.: Blind estimation of underdetermined mixing matrix based on density measurement. Wireless Pers. Commun. **104**(4), 1283–1300 (2018). https://doi.org/10.1007/s11277-018-6080-z
21. Li, C., Zhu, L., Xie, A., Luo, Z.: Blind separation of weak object signals against the unknown strong jamming in communication systems. Wireless Pers. Commun. **97**(3), 4265–4283 (2017). https://doi.org/10.1007/s11277-017-4724-z
22. Mohanaprasad, K., Singh, A., Sinha, K.: Noise reduction in speech signals using adaptive independent component analysis (ICA) for hands free communication devices. Int. J. Speech Technol. **3**(22), 169–177 (2019)
23. Liu, S., Gao, X., Qi, W.: Soft sensor modelling of propylene conversion based on a Takagi-Sugeno fuzzy neural network optimized with independent component analysis and mutual information. Trans. Inst. Measur. Control **41**(3), 737–748 (2019)
24. Rader, C., Steinhardt, A.: Hyperbolic householder transformations. IEEE Trans. Acoust. Speech Signal Process. **34**, 1589–1602 (1986). Also in the SIAM Journal on Matrix Analysis and Applications 8(4), 1–5 (1988)
25. Li, Y., Wei, M., Zhang, F., Zhao, J.: Real structure-preserving algorithms of Householder based Transformations for quaternion matrices. J. Comput. Appl. Math. **305**, 82–91 (2016)

Multi-kernel and Multi-task Learning for Radar Target Recognition

Cong Li, Xianyu Wang$^{(\boxtimes)}$, and Xu Yang

Academy of Space Electronic Information Technology, Xi'an 710100, China
lcongxd@126.com

Abstract. In this paper, a multiple kernel and multiple task learning framework (MKMTL) is proposed. To improve the interpretability of input data and adapt to different data sets, a weighted data-dependent kernel function is proposed and extended to multiple kernel functions. To fully reveal and utilize the shared information among different radar targets, multi-task learning framework is proposed. In this paper, a larger class of mixed norm penalty is adopted. It can increase the flexibility of MKMTL model. To verify the performance of the proposed model, measured MSTAR SAR public database is conducted. Experimental results demonstrate that the proposed method can effectively utilize the shared or potential information among different tasks and exhibits a better recognition performance compared with several popular existing recognition methods.

Keywords: Multi-kernel learning (MKL) · Multi-task learning (MTL) · Radar target recognition · Synthetic aperture radar (SAR)

1 Introduction

Based on radar images, automatic target recognition has the ability to produce 24-hour-a-day and robustness towards all-weather condition, which aroused widespread concern among researchers. For the past few years, SAR images have been extensively studied in ATR fields [1–5]. One of the biggest challenges for radar target recognition is that SAR images are highly sensitive to the variation of pose and speckle noise. We still need to study how to recognize the specified radar target. In radar ATR three main stages (detection, discrimination, and classification) are included. Determining the presence and location of the target is completed in the first phase. Then the background clutter is suppressed in the second stage. In the last stage, the category of target is determined by the designed classifier. In this paper, we emphasize features discrimination and classifier design.

Different from the features of optical target, the geometric structure features of radar target hidden in the radar echo are considerably nonlinear and complicated. In order to effectively reveal the nonlinear features of radar targets, the kernel trick is widely utilized [6–10]. By the kernel trick, the input space is mapped into a high-dimensional space, where the linearly indivisible features become separable in the high dimension space. Nevertheless, most of these kernel functions are monotonous and inflexible, which restricts their performances. To adapt to different data sets, a more flexible

B. Li et al. (Eds.): IoTaaS 2020, LNICST 346, pp. 380–391, 2021.
https://doi.org/10.1007/978-3-030-67514-1_31

learning method, called multiple kernel learning (MKL), is proposed [8, 11–13]. Wang et al. propose a discriminative multiple kernel learning (DMKL) method for spectral image classification, where an optimal combined kernel is learned by maximizing separability in reproduction kernel Hilbert space with Fisher criterion (FC) and maximum margin criterion (MMC) [11]. Gu et al. adopt low-rank nonnegative matrix factorization (NMF) and kernel NMF (KNMF) to enhance the ability of unsupervised learning with the predefined base kernels [12]. Besides, Gu et al. propose a multiple kernel sparse representation classification (MKSRC) framework for land cover classification, in which multiple kernel learning (MKL) is embedded into sparse representation classification (SRC) [13]. All the experimental results demonstrate that multiple kernel model is more flexible and can achieve a better recognition performance compared with single kernel. Based on the advantages of multi-kernel learning in ATR field, a weighted data-dependent multiple kernel function is proposed in this paper.

Although multi-kernel learning methods perform well in the field of target recognition, most of these methods are implemented within the framework of single task, which ignores the latent relatedness among multiple tasks. To make full use of the shared information among multi-tasks, a multi-task learning (MTL) framework is proposed [1, 14–19]. Zheng et al. propose a multi-task learning to decrease the within-class distance and increase the between-class scatter for face and expression recognition [18]. Liu et al. propose a method for cells classification by clustered multi-task learning [1]. Dong et al. propose a multi-task learning model for SAR target recognition, where each component of monogenic signal is specified as one single task [19]. These works have provided empirical evidence on the benefit of multi-task framework. Most of the multi-task relationships of these methods are realized by the fixed regularization principle $\ell 1 - \ell 2$. To further increase the flexibility of multi-task model, a larger class of mixed norm penalty $\ell_p - \ell_q$ [20, 21] is applied to this paper.

Inspired by the advantage of multi-kernel and multi-task learning, a multiple kernel and multiple task learning framework (MKMTL) is proposed in this paper and three parts of work have been done. To improve the flexible of kernel function, a data-dependent kernel function [22] is selected as the basic kernel. Based on the basic kernel, the weighted kernel is generated according to Kernel Alignment (KA) measure criterion [23]. Then, the weighed kernel is extended to multikernel by varying the bandwidth parameters. The realization of multi-task learning is the second part of work. In this paper, each of the target recognition or multi-kernel learning is considered as a single task and different tasks to be learned share a common subset of kernel representations. In this paper, a more flexibly mixed norm penalty $\ell_p - \ell_q$ is utilized, where ℓ_p controls the sparsity of the kernel representations across tasks and ℓ_q determines the importance of the task relatedness. To quickly obtain the optimal combinations of model parameters, a genetic algorithm is utilized, which is the last part of work. Lastly, comprehensive experiments on simulated HRRP dataset and measured MSTAR SAR public database are conducted to verify effectiveness of the proposed method.

The rest of the paper is organized as follows. The data-dependent multi-kernel and multi-task learning (MKMTL), and the MKMTL framework for radar target recognition are proposed in Sect. 2. Then the simulation experiments and results analysis based on HRRP and SAR data sets are given in Sect. 3. Finally, conclusions are drawn in Sect. 4.

2 Multi-kernel and Multi-task Learning

2.1 Multiple Kernel Learning (MKL) Based on Data-Dependent Kernel Function

Suppose we are given N samples $\{(x_i, y_i)\}_{i=1}^{N}$, where $x_i \in R^n$ is input vector with the target output $y_i \in \{1, -1\}$. It has been proved that multiple kernels have a better interpretability of the decision function and can improve the performances [8, 11–13]. A convenient and efficient approach is to consider a convex combination of basis kernels

$$K(x_i, x) = \sum_{m=1}^{M} d_m K_m(x_i, x),\tag{1}$$

with $d_m \geq 0$ and $\sum_{m=1}^{M} d_m = 1$. In Eq. (1), $K_m(x_i, x)$ is the basic kernel, d_m is the coefficient of basic kernel function, and M is the total number of kernels. In this paper, a data-dependent kernel is used as the basic kernel K_m and the corresponding weight is defined as the coefficient d_m. To be specific, the data-dependent kernel function [22] can be expressed as

$$K(x_i, x_j) = q(x_i)q(x_j)\tilde{K}(x_i, x_j),\tag{2}$$

where $\tilde{K}(x_i, x_j)$ is defined as the Gaussian kernel. $q(x) = \beta_0 + \sum_{i=1}^{k} \beta_i \hat{K}(x, \widehat{x}_i)$ is the factor function, and $\hat{K}(x, \widehat{x}_i) = \exp\left(-\gamma \left\| x - \widehat{x}_i \right\|^2\right)$, β_i is the combination coefficient, $\{\widehat{x}_i \in R^n, i = 1, \ldots, k\}$ is called the "empirical cores". $q(x)$ is determined by the data itself and can effectively describe the characteristics of different data. Therefore, Eq. (2) is used as the data-dependent kernel. Suppose the kernel matrices corresponding to $\tilde{K}(x_i, x_j)$ and $K(x_i, x_j)$ are denoted by $\tilde{K}$ and K respectively. Then K can be easily expressed as $K = Q\tilde{K}Q$, where Q is a diagonal matrix, whose diagonal elements are $\{q(x_1), q(x_2), \ldots, q(x_N)\}$. Let $q = (q(x_1), q(x_2), \ldots, q(x_N))^T$ and $\beta = (\beta_1, \beta_2, \ldots, \beta_K)^T$, then q can be rewritten as

$$q = \begin{pmatrix} 1 & \hat{K}(x_1, \widehat{x}_1) & \ldots & \hat{K}(x_1, \widehat{x}_K) \\ 1 & \hat{K}(x_2, \widehat{x}_1) & \ldots & \hat{K}(x_2, \widehat{x}_K) \\ \vdots & & & \\ 1 & \hat{K}(x_N, \widehat{x}_1) & \ldots & \hat{K}(x_N, \widehat{x}_K) \end{pmatrix} \begin{pmatrix} \beta_0 \\ \beta_1 \\ \beta_2 \\ \vdots \\ \beta_K \end{pmatrix} = \bar{K}\beta.\tag{3}$$

To evaluate the classification performance of kernel function, the separable measure between two classes is taken as the criterion

$$J = \frac{q^T \tilde{B} q}{q^T \tilde{W} q}, \tag{4}$$

where $\tilde{B}$ and $\tilde{W}$ are the between-class and the within class kernel scatter matrices of basic kernel $\tilde{K}$ respectively. Suppose L tasks are to be learned, then $\tilde{B}$ and $\tilde{W}$ can be denoted respectively as

$$\tilde{B} = \begin{pmatrix} \frac{1}{N_1} K_{11} & 0 & \cdots & 0 \\ 0 & \frac{1}{N_2} K_{22} & \cdots & 0 \\ \vdots & \vdots & \ddots & \vdots \\ 0 & 0 & \cdots & \frac{1}{N_L} K_{LL} \end{pmatrix} - \frac{1}{N} \tilde{K} \tag{5}$$

$$\tilde{W} = \begin{pmatrix} k_{11} & 0 & \cdots & 0 \\ 0 & k_{22} & \cdots & 0 \\ \vdots & \vdots & \ddots & 0 \\ 0 & 0 & \cdots & k_{NN} \end{pmatrix} - \begin{pmatrix} \frac{1}{N_1} K_{11} & 0 & \cdots & 0 \\ 0 & \frac{1}{N_2} K_{22} & \cdots & 0 \\ \vdots & \vdots & \ddots & \vdots \\ 0 & 0 & \cdots & \frac{1}{N_L} K_{LL} \end{pmatrix}, \tag{6}$$

where $K_{ii} \in R^{N_i} \times R^{N_i}$, $(i = 1, 2, \ldots, L)$ is the kernel matrices of $i - th$ class samples. The coefficient β can be obtained by using the standard gradient descent method

$$\beta^{(n+1)} = \beta^{(n)} + \eta \left(\frac{\tilde{K}_1^T \tilde{B} \tilde{K}}{(q^{(n)})^T \tilde{W} q^{(n)}} - J(\beta^{(n)}) \frac{\tilde{K}_1^T \tilde{W} \tilde{K}}{(q^{(n)})^T \tilde{W} q^{(n)}} \right) \beta^{(n)}, \tag{7}$$

where η is a learning rate. Based on the obtained data-dependent kernel $K(x_i, x_j)$, a set of kernels can be easily generated by varying the width parameter of the basic Gaussian kernel function.

To further improve the class separability of multiple kernel functions, the weighted multiple kernels are generated based on the Kernel Alignment (KA) measure [23], where the similarity between the input kernel and ideal kernel are measured. The alignment between the data-dependent kernel K_{data} and the ideal kernel K_{ideal} can be written as

$$KA(K_{data}, K_{ideal}) = \frac{\langle K_{data}, yy^T \rangle_F}{\sqrt{\langle K_{data}, K_{data} \rangle_F \langle yy^T, yy^T \rangle_F}}, \tag{8}$$

where $\langle .,.\rangle_F$ stands for the Frobenius distance $\langle K_x, K_y\rangle_F = \sum_{i,j} K_x(x_i, x_j) K_y(x_i, x_j)$. Then, a proportional weighting is applied as follows

$$\zeta_m = \frac{KA(K_m, K_{ideal})}{\sum_{m=1}^{M} KA(K_m, K_{ideal})} \quad \forall m. \tag{9}$$

The weighted data-dependent kernel function can be written as

$$K_m(x_i, x_j) = \zeta_m k_{data} = \zeta_m q(x_i) q(x_j) \tilde{K}_m(x_i, x_j). \tag{10}$$

where $\zeta_m = d_m$ is the coefficient of basic kernel function. The objective function of MKL based on data-dependent kernel function can be formulated as

$$\begin{cases} \min_d \max_\alpha \sum_{i=1}^{N} \alpha_i - \frac{1}{2} \sum_{i=1}^{N} \sum_{j=1}^{N} \alpha_i \alpha_j y_i y_j \sum_{m=1}^{M} d_m K_m(x_i, x_j) \\ s.t. \quad \sum_{i=1}^{N} \alpha_i y_i = 0, \quad 0 \le \alpha_i \le C, \quad i = 1, 2...N \end{cases}. \tag{11}$$

Equation (11) shows that MKL aims to learn the Lagrange multipliers parameters α and the best weight vector d for the linear combination of base kernels.

2.2 Multiple Task Learning (MTL) Based on Mixed Norm Penalty $\ell_p - \ell_q$

Suppose L classifiers (tasks) are to be trained (learned) from L different datasets $\{(x_{i,1} y_{i,1})_{i=1}^{N_1}, (x_{i,2} y_{i,2})_{i=1}^{N_2}, \dots, (x_{i,L} y_{i,L})_{i=1}^{N_L}\}$ with $\sum_{t=1}^{L} N_t = N$. For the t th task, the decision function is give as

$$f_t(x) = \sum_{i=1}^{N_t} \sum_{m=1}^{M} \alpha_{t,i} d_{t,m} K_m(x_i, x) + b_t. \tag{12}$$

In order to be more data-adaptive, a larger class of mixed norm penalty $\ell_p - \ell_q$ [20, 21] is applied to the regularization term

$$\Omega_{p,q}(f_1, \dots, f_L)^2 = \left(\sum_{m=1}^{M} \left(\sum_{t=1}^{L} \|f_{t,m}\|_{H_m}^q \right)^{\frac{p}{q}} \right)^{\frac{2}{p}}, \tag{13}$$

where ℓ_p controls the sparsity of the kernel representations across tasks and ℓ_q determines the importance of the task relatedness. In the simulation experiments, it was found that $\ell_p (p = 1)$ will produce the desired model sparsity. Thus, $p = 1$ is adopted in the following derivation of MTL model. In Eq. (13), $\ell_p - \ell_q (p = 1, q = 1)$ means that multi-task learning problem boils down to be L independent sub-problems. $\ell_p - \ell_q(p = 1, q > 1)$ denotes that different tasks are jointly learned. In this paper, we focus on the relationships among different tasks and only $\ell_1 - \ell_q(q > 1)$ is studied. The optimization problem of MKL and MTL (MKMTL) can be formulated as follows

$$
\left\{
\begin{array}{l}
\min_{\mathbf{d}} \ J(\mathbf{d}) = \sum_{t=1}^{L} J_t(\mathbf{d}) \\[2ex]
s.t. \ d_{t,m} \geq 0, \ \sum_{m=1}^{M} \left(\sum_{t=1}^{L} d_{t,m}^{q/(2-q)}\right)^{(2-q)/q} \leq 1
\end{array}
\right. ,
\tag{14}
$$

with

$$
\left\{
\begin{array}{l}
J_t(d) = \min_{f_t} C \sum_{m=1}^{M} H(f_{m,t}, y_{m,t}) + \sum_{m=1}^{M} \left(\dfrac{\left\|f_{m,t}\right\|_{H_k}^2}{d_{m,t}}\right) \\[3ex]
= \max_{\alpha_t} \sum_{i=1}^{N_t} \alpha_{t,i} - \dfrac{1}{2} \sum_{i=1}^{N_t} \sum_{j=1}^{N_t} \alpha_{t,i} \alpha_{t,j} y_{t,i} y_{t,j} \sum_{m=1}^{M} d_{t,m} K_{t,m}(x_i, x_j) , \\[3ex]
s.t. \ \sum_{i=1}^{N_t} \alpha_{t,i} y_{t,i} = 0, \ 0 \leq \alpha_{t,i} \leq C, \ i = 1, 2 \ldots N_t
\end{array}
\right.
\tag{15}
$$

where $\{\alpha_t\}$ are the vectors of Lagrangian multipliers.

The problem (15) can be alternatively solved with a block-coordinate descent method [8, 20]. When keeping the matrix d, problem (15) consists of L single-task SVM sub-problems. For the task t, the objective function as following can be easily solved

$$
\left\{
\begin{array}{l}
\max_{\alpha_t} \sum_{i=1}^{N_t} \alpha_{t,i} - \dfrac{1}{2} \sum_{i=1}^{N_t} \sum_{j=1}^{N_t} \alpha_{t,i} \alpha_{t,j} y_{t,i} y_{t,j} \sum_{m=1}^{M} d_{t,m} K_{t,m}(x_i, x_j) \\[3ex]
s.t. \ \sum_{i=1}^{N_t} \alpha_{t,i} y_{t,i} = 0, \ 0 \leq \alpha_{t,i} \leq C, \ i = 1, 2 \ldots N_t
\end{array}
\right.
\tag{16}
$$

When $\{f_{m,t}\}$ being fixed, a closed-form solution $d_{m,t}$ of this problem can be obtained [20]

$$
d_{t,m} = \dfrac{\left\|f_{t,m}\right\|_{H_k}^{2-q} \left(\sum_v \left\|f_{v,m}\right\|_{H_k}^q\right)^{\frac{q-1}{q}}}{\left(\sum_u \left(\sum_v \left\|f_{v,u}\right\|_{H_k}^q\right)^{\frac{1}{q}}\right)} .
\tag{17}
$$

2.3   Radar Target Recognition with Data-Dependent MKMTL Framework

Based on MTL, a MKMTL framework is proposed in this paper. In this framework, multi-kernel learning aims to find an optimal convex combination of different kernel functions and multi-task learning utilize the shared relationships among multiple tasks to improve the classification performance of model. The proposed framework is shown in Fig. 1.

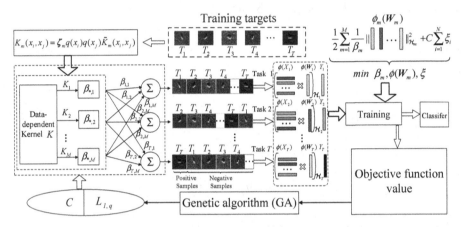

Fig. 1. The framework of proposed MKMTL.

Figure 1 shows the realization process of MKMTL model training. The whole process can be divided into several steps. Firstly, L targets are concatenated as shown in Fig. 1. In this paper, a multiple kernels learning is regarded as an independent task. Based on the concatenated target, the data-dependent kernels are calculated according to Eq. (2), where each kernel has a different bandwidth δ. In other words, the training samples are mapped into different reproducing Kernel Hilbert spaces. After that, the weighted kernel function $K_m(x_i, x_j)$ can be obtained by using Eq. (10). Then, multiple decision functions $f_i(x)$ are jointly learned based on a $\ell1 - \ell q$ mixed norm by Eq. (14). It can be seen that all of these tasks share the same kernels sources, thus the M kernels should be able to interpret the training samples well.

In each task learning, the decision function is obtained by a multi-kernel learning. As shown in Fig. 1, the essence of multi-kernel learning is the choice of different coefficients $d_{*,i}$ according to different kernels. The multi-kernel and multi-task model training will be completed after solving problem (3). Based on the trained mode parameters, the object function value is calculated. A smaller objective function value means a better classification ability of the trained model. In the genetic algorithm, a smaller function value is mapped to a higher fitness. According to the fitness, a combination of C and q in the given range is searched. Then the new combination of C and q are assigned to multi-kernel and multi-task model and a new round of model training is initiated. This is repeated until the maximum genetic iterations is reached. With the nonlinear predictive function Eq. (12), the decision function is reached finally.

3 Experiments and Results Analysis

MSTAR public databases are consisted of SAR images of some targets. Ten targets are to be recognized in the following experiments, and Fig. 2 shows their optical and the corresponding SAR images. The original sizes of SAR images are closed to 128×128 pixels, which are cropped to 64×64 pixels in order to avoid the background clutter. The amplitude of the raw SAR image is used as an input feature. In this paper, the input feature of raw image is reduced to 200 by PCA method. In the following experiments, samples obtained at the operating condition of $17°$ are adopted to train the classifiers and the ones acquired at the operating condition of $15°$ are utilized to test the classifiers. The number of training and testing samples are shown in Table 1.

Fig. 2. The optical and SAR images of ten targets to be recognized.

Table 1. The number of training and testing samples in the ten targets.

Target	2S1	BRDM2	BTR60	D7	T62	ZIL131	ZSU23/4	BRT70	T72	BMP
Training (17°)	299	298	256	299	299	299	299	233	691	698
Testing (15°)	274	274	195	274	273	274	274	196	582	587

In the following simulation experiments, the number of kernel functions is set as 5. In CNN method, the whole net contains 4 trunk layers, including 2 convolutional layers, 1 mean pooling layer and 1 fully-connected layer. The output of the last fully-connected layer is fed to a softmax that plays a classifier role. In two convolution layers, the number of kernels is set as 20 and 120 respectively with size 13 × 13. In the pooling layer, the sampling scale is 4 × 4. In addition, the sample set is augmented by rotating the image clockwise by 60°, 120°, 180° and 240° respectively. The number of iterations of CNN is designed as 100. In this experiment, three targets recognition experiment, the vehicles '2S1', 'BRDM2' and 'ZSU23/4' are selected as the targets and the recognition results are shown in Fig. 3 (Table 2).

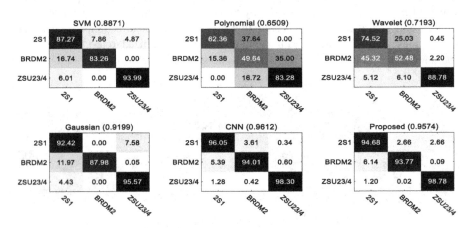

Fig. 3. Confusion matrices of the compared methods.

Table 2. Calculations of different methods.

Methods	Number of multiplications	Number of additions
SVM	$N \cdot n$	$2N \cdot n - 1$
Polynomial	$M \cdot N \cdot (n + l)$	$2M \cdot N \cdot n - 1$
Wavelet	$M \cdot N \cdot [n(n+2) - 1]$	$M \cdot N \cdot [n(3n-1) + 1] - 1$
Gaussian	$M \cdot N \cdot n$	$2M \cdot N \cdot n - 1$
Proposed	$M \cdot N \cdot [n(k+1) + 1]$	$M \cdot N \cdot [2n(k+1) - 1] - 1$
CNN	$C_i^2 \cdot M_{i-1} \cdot M_i \cdot [(I_i^h - C_i + 1)/S_i]$ $\cdot [(I_i^w - C_i + 1)/S_i]$	$(C_i^2 \cdot M_{i-1} - 1) \cdot M_i \cdot [(I_i^h - C_i + 1)/S_i]$ $\cdot [(I_i^w - C_i + 1)/S_i]$

Figure 3 indicates that the average recognition accuracy for the proposed method is 0.9574, compared to 0.8817 for SVM, 0.6509 for Polynomial kernel, 0.7193 for Wavelet kernel, and 0.9199 for Gaussian kernel. It is 7.57%, 30.65%, 23.81%, 23.72% and 3.75% better than the competitors, KNN, SVM, Polynomial kernel, Wavelet kernel, and Gaussian kernel, respectively. These numerical results prove that different kinds of data can be effectively mapped into different RKHSs through the weighted data-dependent kernel, which is generated by the separable measure and Kernel Alignment measure criteria. When compared with CNN deep learning method, the performance of proposed method is slightly worse than CNN. But the complexity of CNN method is much higher than MKMTL method. It can be concluded that the recognition performance of the proposed method is close to deep learning CNN while the calculation amount is lower than the deep learning. To further test the performance of the proposed MKMTL method, the classification experiment of ten targets is implemented and the results are shown in Fig. 4.

Figure 4 shows that CNN and proposed method achieve the ideal recognition rate. The performance of the proposed MKMTL method is 4.69%, 15.42%, 9.71% and

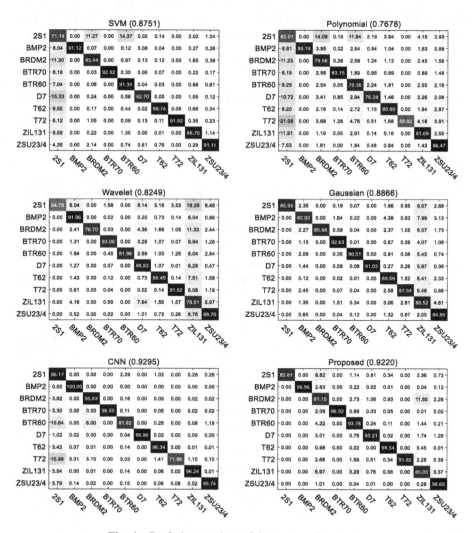

Fig. 4. Confusion matrices of the compared methods.

3.54% better than the competitors, SVM, Polynomial kernel, Wavelet kernel, and Gaussian kernel, respectively. The experimental results show that MKMTL method can interpret the training samples well and fully reveal the relationships among ten tasks. Polynomial kernel and wavelet kernel based methods have a better performance in the case of ten targets recognition. It indicates that more and more information among multiple tasks can be shared with the number of tasks increasing, which improves the performance of model.

4 Conclusion

In this paper, a data-dependent MKMTL framework is proposed to realize the radar target recognition. In order to improve the interpretability of input data, a weighted data-dependent kernel is proposed, which can adapt to different data sets and improve the classification performances. To accurately describe different data sets, the proposed kernel is extended to multiple kernels. Furthermore, multi-task learning framework is proposed to fully reveal and utilize the hidden information among different tasks. To increase the flexibility of multi-task model, a larger class of mixed norm penalty is used. Experiments testify the superiority and practicability of the proposed MKMTL method.

References

1. Liu, A.N., et al.: HEp-2 cells classification via clustered multi-task learning. Neurocomputing **195**(C), 195–201 (2016)
2. Kang, M., et al.: Synthetic aperture radar target recognition with feature fusion based on a stacked autoencoder. Sensors **17**(1), 192 (2017)
3. Wang, S.N., et al.: SAR image target recognition via complementary spatial pyramid coding. Neurocomputing **196**(C), 125–132 (2016)
4. Odysseas, K.S., Nabil, A.: Fusing deep learning and sparse coding for SAR ATR. IEEE Trans. Aerosp. Electron. Syst. **55**(2), 785–797 (2019)
5. Tian, Z., et al.: Classification via weighted kernel CNN: application to SAR target recognition. Int. J. Remote Sens. **39**(3), 1–20 (2018)
6. Su, H.J., et al.: Kernel collaborative representation with local correlation features for hyperspectral image classification. IEEE Trans. Geosci. Remote Sens. **57**(2), 1230–1241 (2019)
7. Wei, C.C.: Wavelet kernel support vector machines forecasting techniques: case study on water-level predictions during typhoons. Expert Syst. Appl. **39**(5), 5189–5199 (2012)
8. Rakotomamonjy, A., et al.: SimpleMKL. J. Mach. Learn. Res. **9**(3), 2491–2521 (2008)
9. Micchelli, C.A., Pontil, M.: Learning the kernel function via regularization. J. Mach. Learn. Res. **6**(6), 1099–1125 (2005)
10. Xu, Y.Y., et al.: An efficient renovation on kernel fisher discriminant analysis and face recognition experiments. Pattern Recogn. **37**(10), 2091–2094 (2004)
11. Wang, Q.W., Gu, Y.F., Tuia, D.: Discriminative multiple kernel learning for hyperspectral image classification. IEEE Trans. Geosci. Remote Sens. **54**(7), 3912–3927 (2016)

12. Gu, Y.F., et al.: Multiple kernel learning via low-rank nonnegative matrix factorization for classification of hyperspectral imagery. IEEE J. Sel. Top. Appl. Earth Obs. Remote Sens. **8** (6), 2739–2751 (2015)

13. Gu, Y.F., Wang, Q.W., Xie, B.Q.: Multiple kernel sparse representation for airborne LiDAR data classification. IEEE Trans. Geosci. Remote Sens. **PP**(99), 1–21 (2016)

14. Karine, A., et al.: Radar target recognition using salient keypoint descriptors and multitask sparse representation. Remote Sens. **10**(6), 843 (2018)

15. Zhang, X.Z., et al.: Two-stage multi-task representation learning for synthetic aperture radar (SAR) target Images classification. Sensors. **17**(11), 2506 (2017)

16. Ozawa, S., Roy, A., Roussinov, D.: A multitask learning model for online pattern recognition. IEEE Trans. Neural Networks **20**(3), 430–445 (2009)

17. Du, L., et al.: Bayesian spatiotemporal multitask learning for radar HRRP target recognition. IEEE Trans. Signal Process. **59**(7), 3182–3196 (2011)

18. Zheng, H., et al.: Multi-task model for simultaneous face identification and facial expression recognition. Neurocomputing. **171**(C), 515–523 (2016)

19. Dong, G.G., et al.: SAR target recognition via joint sparse representation of monogenic signal. IEEE J. Sel. Top. Appl. Earth Obs. Remote Sens. **8**(7), 3316–3328 (2015)

20. Rakotomamonjy, A., et al.: Penalty for sparse linear and sparse multiple kernel multitask learning. IEEE Trans. Neural Networks **22**(8), 1307–1320 (2011)

21. Lounici, K., et al.: Taking advantage of sparsity in multi-task Learning. In: COLT 2009 (2009)

22. Xiong, H., Swamy, M.N., Ahmad, M.O.: Optimizing the kernel in the empirical feature space. IEEE Trans. Neural Networks **16**(2), 460–474 (2005)

23. Cristianini, N., et al.: On kernel-target alignment. Adv. Neural. Inf. Process. Syst. **179**(5), 367–373 (2002)

Information Topology Control Technology of Cluster Satellite Network

Jingling Li[✉], Jun Li, Tao Cui, Wei Liang, and Yi Zhang

National Key Laboratory of Science and Technology on Space Microwave,
CAST, Xi'an 710100, China
ljlspirit@foxmail.com

Abstract. Currently, high dynamic topology and heterogeneous information in cluster satellite network pose new challenges to the topology control at the information level. Because of the topology control of traditional networks can not been directly applied to cluster satellite network, many new topology control technologies used in satellite network have been proposed. Due to the unique flexible networking characteristics of cluster satellite network, further research is needed based on the existing satellite network topology control technology in cluster satellite network. The connotation of information topology control in cluster satellite network is proposed. And based on the in-depth analysis of the characteristics of cluster satellite network, a general information topology model is constructed. Then the existing satellite topology control algorithms are introduced in detail, and its existing problems are analyzed. Finally, according to application requirements, the development trends of cluster satellite network topology control technology are proposed as reference.

Keywords: Cluster satellite network · Information topology control · Heterogeneous information · High dynamic topology

1 Introduction

With the further development of aerospace technology, all kinds of space missions and scientific missions undertaken by satellites are becoming more and more complex. First, from the perspective of solving missions, the traditional space mission solution that relies on a single powerful large satellite is not only expensive, but also inflexible, difficult, and long development time, which cannot fully meet the growing and complex requirements of the new missions; and the currently proposed space networks such as Space-ground integrated network, spatial information network, and so on, have complete functions and large scale, which can deal with space/scientific missions around the world. But these types of network have long deployment period and fixed preset mission requirements. When solving certain needs or responding to certain types of emergencies, the network has limited scalability and flexibility [1, 2]. Secondly, from the perspective of space security, satellite platform or payload damage may cause the satellite to fail to operate normally, and the security and invulnerability of the whole network become weaker.

© ICST Institute for Computer Sciences, Social Informatics and Telecommunications Engineering 2021
Published by Springer Nature Switzerland AG 2021. All Rights Reserved
B. Li et al. (Eds.): IoTaaS 2020, LNICST 346, pp. 392–402, 2021.
https://doi.org/10.1007/978-3-030-67514-1_32

A variety of cluster satellite networks have been proposed for different application scenarios [3–8], among which [3–5] consider the cluster satellite network to be a multi-purpose network composed of heterogeneous satellites, reference [6] considers the cluster satellite network is a system in which multiple small satellites work together. Reference [7] conducts theoretical analysis on small satellite networks with limited resources. Reference [8] believes that cluster satellite networks have loose topological characteristics. And multiple satellite connections with the same or different functions become an organic whole, realizing the dynamic sharing and flexible configuration of information and resources in the cluster.

Due to the advantages of the cluster satellite network in terms of development cost, flexibility and security, it will become an important network system of the space network in the future [8], the schematic diagram of cluster satellite information network is shown in Fig. 1, which includes EOS, DRS and other heterogeneous satellites. For the high dynamic topology and autonomous control characteristics of the cluster network, the topological characteristics of the cluster satellite network are different from other satellite networks and the ground networks. How to optimize the network node status and information connection method is an important basic problem of the cluster satellite network, which is also the main problem solved by topology control technology. The topology control technology of the cluster satellite network includes two levels of connotation: firstly, from the perspective of topology, design and control the spatial layout of network nodes; and secondly, from the perspective of information transmission, for the information topology formed by information transmission perform information logic control. This article mainly discusses the second point of information topology control.

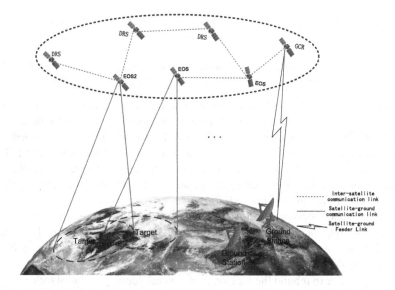

Fig. 1. Schematic diagram of cluster satellite information network

2   Concept and Connotation of Information Topology Control in Cluster Satellite Network

The cluster satellite network mainly includes satellite operating status information (e.g. relative position information, three-dimensional attitude information, relative operating speed, space time/frequency synchronization information, etc.), network control information (e.g. track, track location, etc.) and mission-based data information with large capacity. This article categorizes the satellite control information and status information as basic information, and categorizes mission-related large capacity information as data information. Since basic information and data information have different generation mechanisms, functions, and transmission paths, the two types of information are heterogeneous. As shown in Fig. 2 is a schematic diagram of a satellite heterogeneous information network, in which the satellite basic information is used to ensure the connectivity of the cluster satellite network, and the satellite data information is transmitted according to the mission requirements, which may be the interconnection between some nodes.

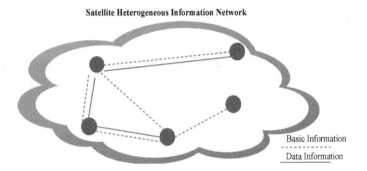

Fig. 2. Schematic diagram of satellite heterogeneous information network

During the process of performing collaborative tasks, the information obtained by each satellite is partial information of their local positions. The information of all satellites in the cluster is merged into global information, which is provided to the decision-making system for task division and Scheduling. When a satellite fails, the cluster satellite system can timely reconstruct the network information topology and dynamically adjust the connection relationship between system members, thereby improving system reliability and fault tolerance.

The information topology control technology in the cluster satellite network is used to connect the relationship between the physical layer and the network layer, which ensures that the network is connected and optimized, as the basis of the upper layer routing protocol. Another important role of topology control is to maintain the generated topology, or to rebuild the topology. In general, topology control technology can optimize the selection method of neighbor nodes according to different application scenarios under the premise of ensuring network connectivity and coverage, and finally form a stable and efficient network structure to complete scheduled tasks.

In order to reflect the "information-oriented" connotation, information topology control can be considered from two aspects. One is to implement topology control based on information of different types of attributes, maintain network connectivity, and optimize network lifetime; the second is to enable the network to better support the transmission of business information and improve network throughput through topology control technology. As shown in the Fig. 3 is a schematic diagram of the complete flow of information topology control technology, where the dotted frame is the content of the topology control technology, and the others are related discovery algorithms and monitoring mechanisms.

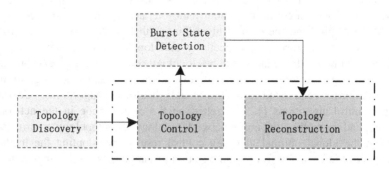

Fig. 3. Schematic diagram of the complete flow of information topology control technology

3   Information Topology Model of Cluster Satellite Network

Since the information topology control technology is strongly related to the information topology of the network, the model of the cluster satellite network needs to be discussed first. In this paper, based on the characteristics of information topology in the cluster satellite network [9, 10], the realization of the comprehensive algorithm, the information topology model of the cluster satellite network is set as follows.

(1) The network contains three types of information: mission information, status information, and control information. Status information and control information are network management and control information that needs to be sensed by the entire network, while task information is only transmitted on specific links.

(2) The network has two types of antennas, omnidirectional antennas are used to transmit status information and control information (low speed); and directional antennas are used to transmit mission information (high speed).

(3) Shared satellite node status information throughout the network: each satellite in the access satellite cluster network regularly shares its status information with other satellite nodes, including the 3-dimensional attitude in the reference system of navigation information, relative position, relative speed and space/time/frequency synchronization information, etc.

(4) The communication protocol on each satellite has an ideal MAC layer, that is, any two satellites can establish a communication link as long as they are within their respective communication ranges.

(5) Each satellite only runs according to its own orbit, which operating status can be predicted.

(6) It does not consider the perturbation effect of celestial bodies other than the earth on the satellite.

4 Analysis of Information Topology Control Technology

There are many different classification methods for network topology control technology. Literature [8] proposed to classify these methods based on algorithm fault tolerance. The control algorithms without fault tolerance are mainly single-connected topology algorithms, and the control algorithms with fault tolerance can be roughly divided into two categories: k-connectivity and topology autonomous restoration. Literature [11] proposed a satellite network topology control strategy based on static or dynamic topology. At present, there are two kinds of mainstream algorithms for topology control: centralized algorithms and distributed algorithms. Centralized topology control algorithms [12–14] relied on the central node in the network for calculating and controlling the entire network topology. This topology control method can obtain the global optimal topology control results, by adopting the method of sending control information from ground station to satellite cluster, it can avoid a large amount of control information overhead and the difficulty of algorithm convergence problems in satellite cluster network. The distributed topology control algorithm [14–16], in which each node can obtain the relevant information of the surrounding nodes, relied on the mutual cooperation between the nodes to complete the topology control, without core node.

The problem faced by this type of algorithm was that the local information obtained by each node cannot optimize the performance of the entire network through topology control, which may lead to deterioration of network connectivity in some cases.

The function and status of each node in the satellite network using centralized topology control technology is different, and the method of hierarchical topology structure can be adopted. And the satellite network using distributed topology control technology can adopt two types of topology control methods: hierarchical and planar (also called non-hierarchical) according to the formed topology, as shown in Fig. 4. Among them, the status of the nodes in the planar topology is the same, while the status of the nodes in the hierarchical topology is different. The hierarchical topology can be further refined into two types: tree topology and cluster topology. Strictly speaking, the cluster topology is also a tree topology, but because of its obvious cluster head nodes, it is classified as a single category.

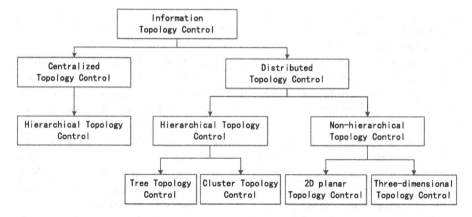

Fig. 4. Satellite network topology control technology classification

4.1 Distributed Satellite Topology Control Technology

The cluster spacecraft network constructed in [17] is similar to the wireless sensor network, and has the characteristics of self-organizing network such as network centerless, multi-hop information transmission, and time-varying topology. Based on the analysis of the advantages and disadvantages of the network hierarchical structure and the plane structure, combined with the characteristics and functional requirements of the cluster spacecraft, the plane structure is used as the basic configuration of the cluster spacecraft research. The paper believes that all modular spacecraft in the network have the same network-wide information routing table. This paper proposes an improved topology control algorithm based on the FLYG algorithm, which combines the expected value of network communication distance with the characteristics of cluster spacecraft. The algorithm optimization goal is to improve the performance of the topology control algorithm, thereby effectively reducing the energy consumption of network data transmission and extend the network life cycle. This paper assumes that the entire cluster spacecraft network is a homogeneous network, and each module spacecraft has the same parameters, including the maximum communication distance, the energy carried, etc., which is not suitable for heterogeneous cluster satellite networks.

Literature [18] describes a distributed cluster satellite network, which can provide flexible space scenarios that guarantee service quality. In such a multi-satellite heterogeneous system, a reasonable power control scheme can improve system performance. This paper establishes a network power control model by analyzing the characteristics of the distributed cluster satellite network and the difficulties of power control, and proposes a power control method based on prediction. The method mainly adjusts the network neighbor nodes by controlling the power of the satellite nodes, and requires the small satellites of the cluster satellite network to have the power adjustable ability, which is difficult to implement.

The cluster spacecraft studied in the literature [19] is a new type of space distributed system, in which the satellites move at high speed in orbit and the inter-satellite links frequently switch, which fully reflects the high dynamics and periodicity of the cluster spacecraft network topology. This paper sets in the network model that each satellite can perceive the dynamic topology of the entire cluster network and the orbit data of other satellites, and can calculate the distance between each other at any time, so each satellite participates in the information topology in real time calculation and maintenance. And from the perspective of network energy consumption balance, the idea of star cluster network management is proposed, the main satellite node selection mechanism is set according to the energy consumption of nodes, and the network topology update strategy of dynamically changing the main satellite is adopted to avoid excessive energy consumption of the main satellite node. However, the network model constructed by this method is too ideal. In the actual network environment, it is difficult to establish wireless links between satellite nodes, and it is not always possible for each satellite to perceive the status changes of the entire network in real time.

In view of the characteristics of laser inter-satellite links, literature [20] takes into account the high-speed communication and high-precision measurement requirements of the navigation satellite inter-satellite links, and makes the link utilization rate, end-to-end transmission delay, link space geometric configuration and other parameters to be the optimization goal of the topology control algorithm. This paper converts the topology planning problem of laser inter-satellite link as a multi-objective function optimization problem under multiple constraints.

The article assumes that if two satellites meet the condition of continuous visibility in a certain FSA state in the network, the two satellites are considered to be visible in this state. By improving the multi-target simulated annealing algorithm (MOSA), a method is designed to avoid the conflicting link cross update algorithm, through the cross conversion of the link building matrix and the visible matrix, prevents the link switching from conflicting with the constraint conditions, and optimizes the multi-source minimum delay routing algorithm to improve the efficiency of the algorithm. When a certain satellite or a certain laser link is unavailable, the topology can still be dynamically optimized, and then the global optimal topology can be solved. However, this algorithm only discusses the solution method of the established function, and there is no specific analysis of the satellite network scenario and specific description of the topology control update mechanism.

4.2   Centralized Satellite Topology Control Technology

Literature [21] elaborated on the topology control scheme of dynamic link establishment of two types of heterogeneous satellites in Walker constellation. Since the movement trajectory and information link of the satellite in the satellite constellation network change periodically, the topology table can be generated on the ground to plan the network topology in advance. Therefore, the ground is used as the topology control center of the network.

Literature [22] is oriented to a heterogeneous satellite network composed of Earth Observation Satellite (EOS), Ground Station Communication Satellite (GSC) and Data Routing Satellite (DRS), and expands the functions of the entire network through the collaborative work between heterogeneous satellites. This paper constructs a three-dimensional satellite information topology model according to the set network scenario, and proposes a centralized topology control strategy. The cluster regularly calculates all possible network links through a satellite, and then distributes the results to other satellites. The process of topology control strategy mainly includes two parts:

(1) Topological matrix calculation and its distribution. The calculation of the topology matrix means that one of the data routing satellites is responsible for analyzing the network link connection and obtaining the topology optimized for reliability;
(2) Information distribution. That is, the satellites with the link relationship distribute the information, and then in a topology update cycle, the network changes the link connection according to the topology matrix.

The disadvantage of this algorithm is that it does not analyze the complexity of the algorithm and the algorithm convergence time, and the centralized algorithm also lacks network robustness analysis. If the central computing node fails, how should the network recover and recalculate the network information topology.

4.3 Hybrid Algorithm Topology Control Technology

Literature [23] is different from the traditional centralized control algorithm and distributed control algorithm. It uses a hybrid method to divide the spatial information network into a series of autonomous domains according to the node attributes. Each autonomous domain adopts an independent control strategy. Different autonomous domains realize the exchange of control information through boundary nodes. Each autonomous domain can be divided into the next level of sub-autonomous domains as needed to build a hierarchical autonomous domain network structure. Through this division, the spatial information network, which is highly dynamic as a whole, is decoupled into a quasi-static sub-network composed of similar types of nodes with weak dynamic changes in its parts, thereby simplifying the complex problems of network topology control.

The spatial information network targeted by this paper has the characteristics of many types of nodes, three-dimensional multi-layer distribution, heterogeneous nodes, and large dynamic differences. Although the cluster satellite network also has high dynamics and heterogeneous characteristics, its network level is not complicated, and its satellites are mostly small satellites, with limited computing power, and are not suitable for overly complex topology control algorithms.

5 Research Direction of Information Topology Control Technology

At present, researches on topology control algorithms in satellite networks such as spatial information networks, navigation satellite networks, constellation networks, and cluster satellite networks have gradually increased, focusing on the characteristics of high dynamics of satellite networks, heterogeneous networking, and limited network energy. The network topology update strategy of dynamically changing the main satellite, the link cross update algorithm to avoid conflicts, the algorithm based on centralized and distributed hybrid control, and many other topology control algorithms with multiple optimization objectives are proposed. Because cluster satellite networks have stronger flexibility and self-organizing characteristics, they face more problems compared with other types of satellite networks and require further research.

(1) First, facing the demand for high-speed transmission, it is necessary to further study the cluster satellite network directional sensing technology to obtain the set of reachable neighbor nodes. Due to the complexity of the satellite link building process, the inter-satellite link resources are very limited. In this case, it is difficult to assume that each satellite can perceive the state of all neighboring nodes and obtain neighbor node information. The literature [24] proposes A neighbor discovery method based on directional antennas, through the Q-Learning mechanism to determine the receiving/transmitting mode of each neighbor scan, and determine the return value according to the current scan result, learn the experience in the scan, and achieve the goal of improving the efficiency of neighbor discovery. However, this method takes a long time to search for neighbor nodes, and further research is needed for the high dynamic characteristics of cluster networks.

(2) Secondly, it is necessary to further study the influence of heterogeneous information on key nodes and topology strategies of the cluster satellite network. Literature [6] proposed to design the distributed satellite system communication network architecture into two logically independent sub-networks, namely the on-orbit operation control data control sub-network (operation control sub-network) and the high-speed load data transmission sub-network (data transmission sub-net). Among them, the operation control sub-net is mainly responsible for the transmission of control data required for network operation, using omnidirectional transmission; the data transmission sub-net is mainly responsible for the transmission of load data, using directional high-speed transmission.

(3) Finally, it is necessary to further solve the problems of self-organized storage, update and calculation of information in the cluster satellite network. The networking trend of cluster satellite network is the form of self-organizing network [8]. It can connect multiple spacecraft with the same or different functions into an organic whole, and can flexibly realize variable tasks by sharing information and resources in the cluster. In the future, topology control technology can be used to spontaneously respond to emergencies, adjust the network task structure or spatial topology structure, and independently maintain network security and dynamic stability. In this case, it is necessary to comprehensively consider the fault tolerance, convergence time and computational complexity of the satellite topology control algorithm. At present, there are few literatures for comprehensive analysis and research on this problem.

6 Conclusions

At present, cluster satellite networks have played an important role in the fields of earth observation, communication, scientific exploration, space surveillance, and space attack and defense. Since the strict distributed configuration of cluster satellite network is very difficult to realize, the future cluster satellite network is more inclined to the network topology form of loosely coupled configuration, which requires higher flexibility and dynamics of information topology. Research on information topology control technology can help accelerate the realization of a new generation of cluster satellite distributed networking, further improve the flexibility, scalability and effective life cycle of the network. In the future, the cluster satellite network will bring greater advantages to specific space applications such as rapid observation and deployment in local areas, rapid assessment of natural disasters, etc.

References

1. Kandhalu, A., Rajkumar, R.(Raj): QoS-based resource allocation for next-generation spacecraft networks. In: 2012 IEEE 33rd Real-Time Systems Symposium, pp. 163–172 (2012)
2. Alvarez, J., Walls, B.: Constellations, clusters, and communication technology: expanding small satellite access to space. In: 2016 IEEE Aerospace Conference. AERO 2016, June 2016
3. Faber, N., et al.: Heterogeneous spacecraft networks: concept for a law-cost, multi-institutional earth observation platform. Submitted to IEEE Aerospace Conferences, Big Sky, MT (2014)
4. Nakamura, Y., et al.: Heterogeneous spacecraft networks: performance analysis for low-cost earth observation missions. Submitted to IEEE Aerospace Conference, Big Sky, MT (2014)
5. Richard, A., et al.: Heterogeneous spacecraft networks: wireless network technology assessment. Submitted to IEEE Aerospace Conference, Big Sky, MT (2014)
6. Shi, F.: The research of networking mechanisms for micro-satellites formation, pp. 27–28. Xidian University, November 2014
7. Liu, R., et al.: An analytical framework for resource-limited small satellite networks. In: ICLEF6 2016, pp. 388–391 (2016)
8. Chen, Q., et al.: Development status and key technology of spacecraft cluster network. J. Harbin Inst. Technol. **49**(4), 1–7 (2017)
9. Dong, F., Wang, J., Yang, J., Cai, C.: Distributed satellite cluster network: a survey. J. Donghua Univ. **32**, 100–104 (2015)
10. Dong, F., Li, X., Yao, Q., He, Y., Wang, J.: Topology structure design and performance analysis on distributed satellite cluster networks. In: Proceedings of the 4th International Conference on Computer Science and Network Technology (ICCSNT), Harbin, China, December 2015, pp 881–884 (2015)
11. Lu, Y., et al.: Routing techniques on satellite networks. J. Softw. **25**(5), 1085–1100 (2014)
12. Ramanathan, R., Rosales-Hain, R.: Topology control of multihop wireless networks using transmit power adjustment. In: IEEE INFOCOM, pp. 404–413 (2000)
13. Yu, J., Roh, H., Lee, W., et al.: Topology control in cooperative wireless Ad-hoc networks. IEEE J. Sel. Areas Commun. **30**(9), 1771–1779 (2012)
14. Li, N., Hou, J.: Localized fault-tolerant topology control in wireless ad hoc networks. IEEE Trans. Parallel Distrib. Syst. **17**(4), 307–320 (2006)
15. Wattenhofer, R., Li, L., Bahl, P., et al.: Distributed topology control for power efficient operation in multihop wireless ad hoc networks. In: IEEE INFOCOM, pp. 1388–1397 (2001)

16. Chiwewe, T.M., Hancke, G.P.: A distributed topology control technique for low interference and energy efficiency in wireless sensor networks. IEEE Trans. Ind. Inform. **8**(1), 11–19 (2012)
17. Chen, Q.: Research on fractionated spacecraft ad-hoc network properties and topology control algorithm, Harbin, June 2014
18. Zhong, X.D., et al.: Power control approach in distributed satellite cluster network based on presetting and prediction. In: 2016 IEEE Information Technology, Networking, Electronic and Automation Control Conference. ITNEC 2016, Chongqing, China, May 2016, pp. 265–269 (2016)
19. Lv, Z.C.: Research On optimal energy management for fractionated spacecraft network topology, Harbin, pp. 12–45, June 2015
20. Dong, M., Lin, B.: Topology dynamic optimization for inter-satellite laser links of navigation satellite based on multi-objective simulated annealing method. Chin. J. Lasers **45**(7), 1–12 (2018)
21. He, J., et al.: Study and simulation of topology control technology based on dynamical inter-ISL linkage in LEO constellation system. J. Syst. Simul. **21**(23), 7540–7548 (2009)
22. Chen, Q., et al.: A topology control strategy with reliability assurance for satellite cluster networks in earth observation. Sensors **17**, 445:1–18 (2017)
23. Zhang, W., et al.: Network model and topology control algorithm based on hierarchical autonomous system in space information network. J. Commun. **37**(6) (2016)
24. Mo, L., Liang, Z.: Simulation of neighbor discovery algorithm in directional antenna ad hoc networks based on OPNET. J. Syst. Simul. **30**(5) (2018)

Application

Smart Home Security System Using Biometric Recognition

Phan Van Vinh[1(✉)], Phan Xuan Dung[2], Pham Thuy Tien[1],
Tran Thi Thuy Hang[1], Truong Hong Duc[1], and Tran Duy Nhat[2]

[1] School of Computing and Information Technology, Eastern International
University, Binh Duong City, Vietnam
{vinh.phan, tien.pham.set15, hang.tran.set15,
duc.truong.set15}@eiu.edu.vn
[2] School of Engineering, Eastern International University, Binh Duong City,
Vietnam
{dung.phan, nhat.tran}@eiu.edu.vn

Abstract. A security system is one of the most important applications of a smart home that protects our home from thieves or potential risks. However, a traditional home security system usually suffers from high costs or does not satisfy the user's needs. Therefore, in this research, we design and implement an IoT-based smart home security system, which not only protects our home from unauthorized access but also saves our life from dangerous situations. In our proposed system, biometric recognition based on the combination of fingerprint and face image is used to identify the homeowners who have permission to access the home. The main door will be opened if the input biometric image matches the one stored in the database. Otherwise, the system will raise an alarm with a doorbell and/or send a notification message to the homeowner. Besides, the system also collects environmental data in the home and notifies the homeowner in case of a dangerous situation, e.g. there was a fire or gas leak. The homeowner can monitor and control their home remotely via a friendly Web-based user interface. All activities happening in the home are recorded in a logging system for further analysis.

Keywords: Smart home · Security system · Fingerprint recognition · Face recognition

1 Introduction

Nowadays, a smart home and its applications becomes more realistic with many advantages for a more convenient and better life [1]. A security system is one of the most essential applications that need to be considered when building a smart home. People usually install a security system in their home to keep safe valuables from burglars and thieves and to protect their family safe from potential risks by fires or leakage of poisonous gas. In a traditional home security system, people usually use a key, password or security cards to unlock the door for entering their home. However, these security methods are easy to break by a thief and do not keep track of the user's information of whom got accessed into the home. To tackle these problems, one

B. Li et al. (Eds.): IoTaaS 2020, LNICST 346, pp. 405–420, 2021.
https://doi.org/10.1007/978-3-030-67514-1_33

approach for the security system is to use human biometrics to identify a person, in which a fingerprint is widely used since the human fingerprint is unique and never changes [2]. However, it takes time to identify multiple people at the same time within closed distance. Moreover, it is not easy for human to recognize a person based on his fingerprint data. Recently, another approach in the security system is face recognition [3]. This technique usually applies computer vision and machine learning to recognize a person based on training data. At this time, the face recognition has significant improvement in accuracy and processing time with the support of IoT edge devices and deep learning technology. Recently, many deep learning algorithms with high performance of accuracy and speed have been proposed, such as Region Convolutional Neural Network (RCNN) [4], Fast RCNN [5], Multi-scale Deep Convolutional Neural Network (MS CNN) [6], Faster RCNN [7], and YOLO [8]. MobileNet-V2 [9] is the state-of-the-art object detection algorithm with the best performance in accuracy. The disadvantage of these algorithms is the hardware cost, requires more processing units than the others. However, face recognition should not be implemented alone in the security system due to the unreliability of the system. User photos or videos can be used to spoof facial recognition system. The face anti-spoofing is an open research and therefore still needs more contributions to provide a concrete solution with better performance. Some approaches take the advantages of both fingerprint and face recognition by using a combinational system [10, 11] to improve the accuracy and reliability of a security system. However, they did not provide a complete system with a friendly user interface that can be applied in practical scenarios.

In this paper, we aim at design and implement a smart home security system with a two-stage verification process of two biometric recognitions to provide higher security level. Face recognition is used in the first phase for fast and fairly reliable verification and then fingerprint recognition can be used to improve the accuracy of the system. Besides, the proposed system can be able to provide a live video stream of the monitoring area, detect human presence and other environmental related information such as humidity, temperature, carbon monoxide (CO), poisonous gas, etc. All activities happening in the home will be kept in a logging system for further analysis. The proposed system can be controlled and managed remotely via a friendly Web-based user interface. In summary, the contribution of this paper is as follows: (1) Design and implement a smart home security system prototype and test it in practical scenarios. (2) Implement a friendly Web-based user interface to control and manage the proposed smart home security system.

In what follows, we present the principle design of the proposed approach in Sect. 2. Section 3 covers the implementation results. Finally, we make concluding remarks in Sect. 4.

2 Smart Home Security System Design

In this section, we present the main design of the proposed smart home security system, including the system architecture, the hardware and software design, and the multi-mode verification process.

2.1 System Architecture

The proposed security system architecture consists of four layers: Sensors/Actuators layer, Controller/Gateway layer, Analytic/Processing layer and User/Application layer, as shown in Fig. 1:

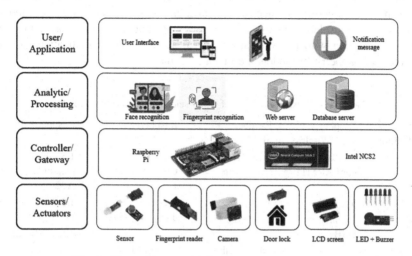

Fig. 1. The architecture of the proposed security system

- *Sensors/Actuators layer*: This layer consists of many types of input devices such as sensors, fingerprint reader, camera, and output devices such as door lock, LCD screen, LED and doorbell (buzzer). Sensors, including temperature and humidity sensor (DHT11), gas sensor (MQ2), motion detection sensor (PIR), are used to get the ambient data in the home and then send these data to the center server for further processing.
- *Controller/Gateway layer*: This is the main layer of the proposed system in which IoT edge devices are used for system control. At this time, there are several kinds of IoT edge devices with different capabilities and performance, such as Raspberry Pi family, Nvidia Jetson family, Google Edge TPU Dev Board. Moreover, Intel Neural Compute Stick 2 (NCS2), a deep learning processor on a USB stick, can be used to accelerate the performance of IoT edge device in image processing.
- *Analytic/Processing layer*: At this layer, biometric images captured from a camera and fingerprint scanner are used to detect the registered user by using face recognition and fingerprint recognition algorithms. The door will be opened or an alarm will be raised, depending on whether the detected person has the right to access or not. While the ambient data from sensors are analyzed by using a fuzzy logic control algorithm to judge whether the target environment is safe or not. All activities happening in the home will be kept in a logging system for further processing.

- *User/Application layer*: The homeowner or admin user can monitor and control all activities in the home via a web-based interface. An alert message will be displayed on the screen monitor or a notification message will be sent to mobile phone to notify the homeowner about an abnormal or dangerous situation.

Currently, there are many types of IoT-enabled devices available in the market. They can have differences in size, performance and cost. Because of project requirements, we are considering to use the Raspberry Pi model, a Linux-based high performance computer with low cost and powerful features. The specifications of some well-known Raspberry Pi models are given in Table 1.

Table 1. The specifications of some selected Raspberry Pi models

Raspberry Pi Platform	Raspberry Pi Zero Wireless	Raspberry Pi 3B	Raspberry Pi 3B+	Raspberry Pi 4B
Processor	1 GHz single-core ARM11	1.2 GHz, Quad-Core Cortex A53	1.4 GHz, Quad-Core Cortex A53	1.5 GHz, Quad-Core Cortex A72
RAM	512 MB	1 GB	1 GB	1/2/4 GB
USB	1x micro USB	4x USB 2.0	4x USB 2.0	2x USB 3.0 +2x USB 2.0
Ethernet	–	10/100 Mbps	10/100 Mbps	1 Gbps
Wi-Fi	802.11n	802.11n	2.4 GHz and 5 GHz 802.11 b/g/n/ac	2.4 GHz and 5 GHz 802.11 b/g/n/ac
Bluetooth	4.1	4.1	4.2	5.0
HDMI	Mini-HDMI	Yes	Yes	2x micro HDMI
GPIO	40 pins	40 pins	40 pins	40 pins

As we can see from Table 1, the Raspberry Pi models with small-sized, Wifi & Bluetooth enabled, and GPIO support can be one of the best options for IoT applications. However, due to the hardware limitation, the Raspberry does not perform well in some real-time image processing applications which require high speed and accuracy. To overcome this problem, one solution is to combine the Raspberry with Intel Neural Compute Stick 2 (NCS2), a deep learning processor on a USB stick (as shown in Fig. 2). With the hardware-optimized performance of the newest Intel Movidius Myriad X Vision Processing Unit (VPU), NCS2 is one of the best combinations with Raspberry Pi in image processing tasks, especially in deep learning applications.

Fig. 2. Raspberry Pi 4 with Intel Neural Compute Stick 2

2.2 Hardware Design

In this section, we describe the hardware design of the proposed security system. The Raspberry Pi model is used as a main controller to connect to all other hardware components, including sensors, LED, buzzer, DC motor, fingerprint module and Pi camera module. The following Table 2 presents all required hardware components of our proposed system.

Table 2. The hardware components of the designed system

Hardware components	Description
Raspberry Pi (3B+, 4B)	Main controller of the system
Intel neural compute stick 2	Deep learning USB device to accelerate edge devices
MQ2 Gas/Smoke sensors	Detecting LPG, Smoke, Alcohol, CH_4
DHT11 sensor	Measuring temperature and humidity
PIR sensor	Detecting a person moving in a given area
Buzzer module	Playing an alarm as doorbell
Pi camera module	Taking video or photo
DC motor	To open/close the main door
L298N motor controller	Driving DC motors to open/close a door
R305 fingerprint module	Sensor for fingerprint recognition
LED	Lights in the house
ADS1115	Analog to digital converter module
CP2102 UART	Connect Fingerprint module to Raspberry
LCD (16 x 4) with I2C module	Display information on the screen

Before going to make the printed circuit board (PCB), hardware and functionality testing need to be performed to make sure that all required components can work well in a concrete model. Figure 3 shows the connection diagram of the required components connected via a breadboard for testing purpose.

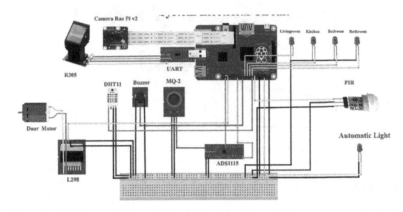

Fig. 3. The connection diagram of required parts of the proposed system

After finishing the hardware testing, we go to the hardware circuit design phase to make the printed circuit board (PCB) of the proposed system. Figure 4 illustrates the schematic diagram of all required component as follows:

- **Power block**: include the voltage reducer circuit with pulse power supply which can have maximum output of 5 V–3A from the input voltage of 5–24 V DC to supply power for other components (e.g. Raspberry Pi, sensors and actuator)
- **Motor driver block**: include Dual H-bridge driver chip L298N which can drive DC motors, control the speed and direction of each DC motor independently through PWM (Pulse Width Modulation). Input voltage is 5–30 V DC and maximum output is 2A for each bridge.
- **Controller block**: Raspberry Pi 3B+/4 is used for control system operations
- **Actuator block**: include DC motor, LCD module, buzzer and LED. The camera module attaches to the CSI interface and the R305 fingerprint module is connected to USB interface of the Raspberry

- **Sensor block**: include DHT11, PIR and MQ2 sensor for environmental data collection

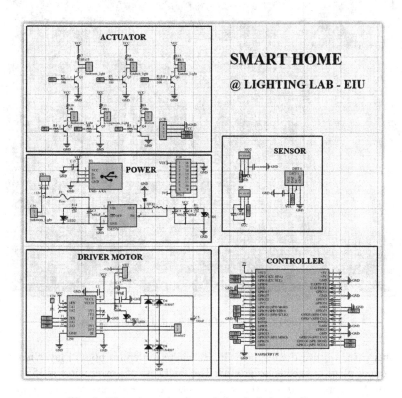

Fig. 4. The schematic view of electrical circuit diagram

The next step is to transfer the schematic diagram into a drawing of PCB (Fig. 5). The schematic will serve as a blueprint for laying out the traces and placing the components on the PCB. In addition, the PCB editing software can import all of the components, footprints, and wires into the PCB file, which will make the design process easier.

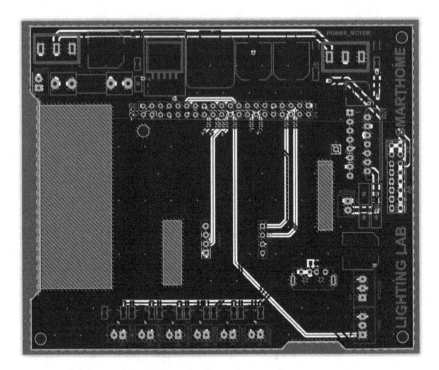

Fig. 5. The PCB layout of the designed system (2D view)

In this case, we use double layer PCB, where the entire bottom layer is covered with a copper plane connected to ground. The thickness of power wires is 35 mil while the one of data wires is 10 mil (0.254 mm). The positive traces are routed on top and connections to ground are made through holes or vias. Ground layers are good for circuits that are prone to interference, because the large area of copper acts as a shield against electromagnetic fields. They also help dissipate the heat generated by the components (Fig. 6).

(a) Front-view   (b) Bottom-view

Fig. 6. The PCB layout of the designed system (3D view)

2.3   User Interface Design

In this project, we design a friendly web-based user interface for monitoring and control all operations of the proposed system efficiently. The web-based user interface is mainly developed by the PHP language and MySQL database. Figure 7 shows the structure of the designed web interface. Users must have an account to access to the system. User's registration can be done via REGISTER page. There are two types of users: *Normal users* who can only see the monitoring data and live-stream image while *Admin users* who have full privileges to manage the whole system. The functionalities of some main pages in the web application are as follows:

– CONTROL page: Users can control all activities in the home at this page, such as: switch the lights ON/OFF, enable/disable camera, video live-streaming, biometric recognition and object detection features; take photo or record video;
– DATA page: Including three subpages, display the recorded videos and photos captured from camera; visualize real-time environmental data acquisition in graph view and tabular view.

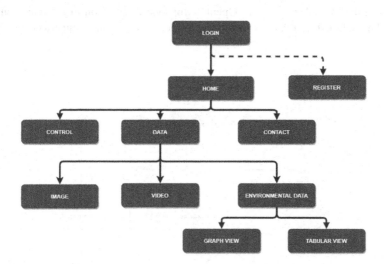

Fig. 7. The structure of the Web-based user interface of the proposed system

2.4   Multimode Verification Process

Only face recognition or fingerprint recognition may not satisfy the needs of security system in term of accuracy and processing time. Therefore, in this project, we take the advantage of using the combination of both biometric recognitions to provide a more accurate and reliable security system. There are two modes of security level for flexible usage as follows:

- *Basic security mode*: This mode provides a fast verification process with an acceptable level of security; therefore either a face recognition method or fingerprint recognition method can be used in this mode.
- *Enhanced security mode*: This mode provides high precision of security by using both biometric recognitions. In the first phase, the face recognition method is used to verify whether a person is authorized or not. This verification is not completely perfect but the achieved results are fairly good with low processing time. If the first phase is passed, the next phase of verification with fingerprint recognition is used to provide more accuracy level of the security system.

a) **The verification process with face recognition**

In this process, we apply a face recognition algorithm with a deep learning technique. Firstly, we need to build a dataset of users who are permitted to access the home. The pre-trained Caffe face detection model is used for face detector. After building the dataset, face embeddings are extracted with a pre-trained OpenFace PyTorch model. The face embeddings consist of a 128-d vector for each face in the dataset. We train a machine learning model on the set of embedding with the support of Support Vector Machines (SVM). Finally, we use the trained model with OpenCV for face recognition in the real scenarios. The detailed verification process with face recognition is illustrated in Fig. 8.

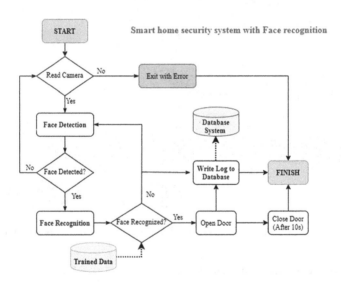

Fig. 8. The verification process with face recognition

b) **The verification process with fingerprint recognition**

The verification with fingerprint recognition in a security system is one of the most reliable and accurate methods. Firstly, fingerprint enrollment is performed to collect a dataset of user's fingerprint. The main step of this process is minutiae extraction in which the image of user's fingerprint is utilized for extracting minutiae points and stored to create a user's fingerprint dataset. In the fingerprint recognition process, the minutiae matching technique is used to compare the input minutiae set with the one in feature set. If a fingerprint match found, the door will be opened. Otherwise, a notification message will be sent to the homeowner to notify the unauthorized access. The detailed verification process with fingerprint recognition is illustrated in Fig. 9.

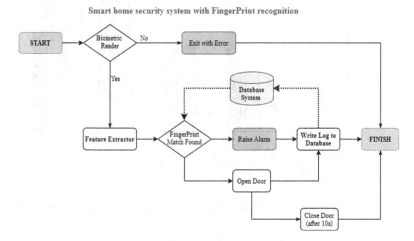

Fig. 9. The verification process with fingerprint recognition

For the notification system, we used the pushbullet application [12], a useful application to send or receive SMS and multimedia message from a computer, mobile phone or embedded device. The homeowner can receive notification messages with images captured by the attached camera. By this way, they can know what happening in their home immediately and then take the right action.

3 Implementation Results

3.1 Inference Benchmarks

In this part, to verify how the Intel NCS2 module can improve the performance of the edge devices in image processing tasks, we conduct some experiments with the inference benchmark testing. The experiments use the SSD Mobilenet-V2 network model and TensorFlow framework, frame size of 400 x 400 with object detection application.

Figure 10 shows the results from deep learning inference benchmarks of some selected Raspberry models, and laptop or desktop computers with or without the Intel NCS2 module attached. As we can see that with the Intel NCS2, the performance of all Raspberry Pi models increase rapidly, especially for the Raspberry Pi 4 with high speed of CPU and USB3.0 port supported. The Intel NCS2 also improves the performance of other hardware platforms, such as laptop or desktop computers which do not have a graphic card inside. However, the upper bound benchmark of the Intel NCS2 is about 20 FPS according to this experiment.

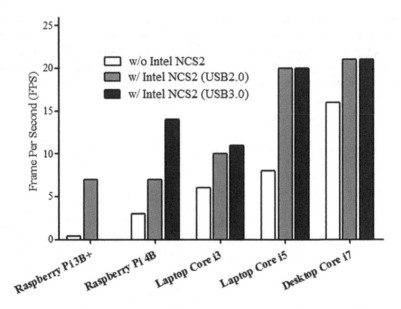

Fig. 10. The comparison of inference benchmarks of some experimental platforms

The Table 3 shows the detailed inference benchmarks and hardware utilization of some selected platforms when running the object detection algorithm. From these results, we can see that the Intel NCS2 not only improves the inference benchmark but also reduce the CPU usage when running deep neural network applications. This allows IoT-enable devices can adapt well to a variety of wide range of IoT applications.

Table 3. Inference benchmarks of some experimental platforms

Platform	FPS	Memory usage	CPU usage
Raspberry Pi Zero	0.03	N/A	N/A
Raspberry Pi 3B+	0.3–0.5	83 MB	342% (*)
Raspberry Pi 4B	3.1–3.3	78 MB	343% (*)
Laptop Core i3	5.6–6.3	103 MB	68%
Laptop Core i5	7.3–8.1	100 MB	77%
Desktop Core i7	14.1–16.3	170 MB	60%
Raspberry Pi Zero with Intel NCS2	DNR	DNR	DNR
Raspberry Pi 3B+with Intel NCS2	6.5–7.5	80 MB	106% (*)
Raspberry Pi 4B with Intel NCS2 (USB 2.0)	8.8–9.7	103 MB	148% (*)
Raspberry Pi 4B with Intel NCS2 (USB 3.0)	13.1–14.3	104 MB	167% (*)
Laptop Core i3 with Intel NCS2 (USB 2.0)	9.4–10.6	107 MB	7%
Laptop Core i3 with Intel NCS2 (USB 3.0)	9.8–10.9	106 MB	6%
Laptop Core i5 with Intel NCS2 (USB 2.0)	18.2–20.1	143 MB	7%

(continued)

Table 3. (*continued*)

Platform	FPS	Memory usage	CPU usage
Laptop Core i5 with Intel NCS2 (USB 3.0)	18.9–20.2	140 MB	7%
Desktop Core i7 with Intel NCS2 (USB 2.0)	19.8–21.3	196 MB	3%
Desktop Core i7 with Intel NCS2(USB 3.0)	19.5–21.2	193 MB	3%

(*): The total CPU usage of multi-core platform in a Linux-based system
DNR (did not run) or N/A: The results occurred due to limited memory capacity or hardware/software limitations.

3.2 Implementation Results

1) Smart Home Security System Prototype

First of all, we build a smart home model for testing purpose. As we can see in Fig. 11, the camera, fingerprint module, LCD module are installed in front of the home, to display user information and open/close the main door with biometric recognitions. People must do security verification before getting into the home. MQ2 – Gas/Smoke sensor is installed in a kitchen room to detect gas/smoke leakage.

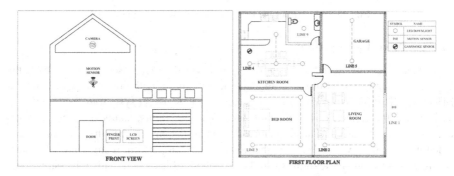

Fig. 11. The layout design of smart home prototype

Figure 12 presents the prototype of our proposed smart home model which is made of 5 mm high quality acrylic sheet with the support of a laser machine in our lab. The home model looks very nice and firmly.

Fig. 12. The prototype of our designed smart home model

2) Web-based User Interface

When accessing to the smart home system via the web-based user interface, the homeowner can take control of the system operation with the full rights. At the MAIN CONTROL page (Fig. 13), users can see much useful system information, such as live streaming data, environmental data, status of lights, status of door, who got accessed to the home, etc. The alarm message can be displayed when the monitoring data reach the threshold value. Besides, the homeowner can perform many kinds of system control, such as switch the lights ON/OFF, enable/disable camera, video live-streaming, enable biometric recognition and object detection features, take photos or record videos.

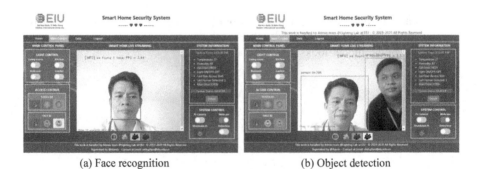

(a) Face recognition   (b) Object detection

Fig. 13. A screenshot of security check with (a) Face recognition and (b) Object detection

At the DATA page, all collected information from the environment can be observed in real-time. Figure 14 shows the screenshot of the DATA page with the real-time monitoring data in a graph view and tabular view.

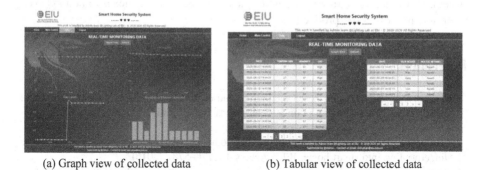

(a) Graph view of collected data   (b) Tabular view of collected data

Fig. 14. A screenshot of the DATA page: monitoring data in graphs

Moreover, at the DATA page, the users can review all photos or record videos as shown in Fig. 15. In some special cases, this information is very helpful to identify what happened in the home or who got accessed to the home without permission.

Fig. 15. A screenshot of the DATA page: the recorded videos or photographs

4 Concluding Remarks

In this paper, we have proposed and implemented a smart home security system with high level of security by using the combination of both biometric recognitions. The real-time face recognition and fingerprint recognition are used to grant access for authorized people while object detection is used to detect intruders who intend to get into the home without permission. Notification messages are sent to the homeowner via

SMS or multimedia application when an intruder tries to access the home or critical situation happens in the home. The smart home control and management activities can be remotely performed via the web-based user interface. Experimental results have shown that the proposed system satisfies requirements of the smart home security system. However, the hardware design of the smart home model needs to be improved when making a realistic product.

References

1. Kumar, P., Pati, U.C.: IoT based monitoring and control of appliances for smart home. In: IEEE International Conference on Recent Trends in Electronics, Information and Communication Technology (RTEICT), pp. 1145–1150 (2016)
2. Jose, A.C., Malekian, R., Ye, N.: Improving home automation security; integrating device fingerprinting into smart home. IEEE Access **4**, 5776–5787 (2016)
3. Pawar, S., Kithani, V., Ahuja, S., Sahu, S.: Smart home security using IoT and face recognition. In: Fourth International Conference on Computing Communication Control and Automation (ICCUBEA), pp. 1–6 (2018)
4. Girshick, R., Donahue, J., Darrell, T., Malik, J.: Rich feature hierarchies for accurate object detection and semantic segmentation. In: IEEE Conference on Computer Vision and Pattern Recognition, pp. 580–587 (2014)
5. Girshick, R.: Fast R-CNN. In: IEEE International Conference on Computer Vision (ICCV), pp. 1440–1448 (2015)
6. Cai, Z., Fan, Q., Feris, R., Vasconcelos, N.: A Unified Multi-scale Deep Convolutional Neural Network for Fast Object Detection (2016)
7. Ren, S., He, K., Girshick, R., Sun, J.: Faster R-CNN: towards real-time object detection with region proposal networks. IEEE Trans. Pattern Anal. Mach. Intell. **39**, 1137–1149 (2017)
8. Redmon, J., Divvala, S., Girshick, R., Farhadi, A.: You only look once: unified, real-time object detection. In: IEEE Conference on Computer Vision and Pattern Recognition (CVPR), pp. 779–788 (2016)
9. Sandler, M., Howard, A., Zhu, M., Zhmoginov, A., Chen, L.: MobileNetV2: inverted residuals and linear bottlenecks. In: IEEE/CVF Conference on Computer Vision and Pattern Recognition, pp. 4510–4520 (2018)
10. Priyadarsini, M.J.P., et al.: Human identification using face and fingerprint. In: International Conference on Intelligent Sustainable Systems (ICISS), pp. 325–329 (2017)
11. Thakre, S., Gupta, A.K., Sharma, S.: Secure reliable multimodel biometric fingerprint and face recognition. In: International Conference on Computer Communication and Informatics (ICCCI), pp. 1–4 (2017)
12. https://www.pushbullet.com/

Internet of Things in the Game of Basketball

Kornel Tokolyi$^{(\boxtimes)}$ and Maher Elshakankiri

University of Regina, Regina, SK S4S 3T1, Canada
{ktw284,maher.elshakankiri}@uregina.ca

Abstract. In this paper, a list of IoT technologies are introduced that are used to help basketball players, coaches and fans get to know more about the game of basketball. Several IoT tools exist to improve player and team development as well as fan experience. IoT goes hand-in-hand with basketball analytics, which has become a central part of basketball philosophy. Three technologies are explained in detail in this paper, each focusing on different areas of the game. Wilson X is strictly a shooting trainer tool, HomeCourt offers shooting, dribbling and agility drills, while the VR system is focusing on basketball tactics. These three technologies are compared in detail on eight different criteria including accuracy, comfort, user-friendliness, cross platform, price, lifetime, memory, and room to improve. By examining these tools and their features, we gain a better understanding about the power and limits of IoT within the field of sports.

Keywords: Internet of things · Basketball · Sensors · Player development · Team development · Analytics · Camera · Virtual reality

1 Introduction

Technology has come a long way since the Turing-machine. The Internet of Things (IoT) is all around us, it surrounds our existence. From smart fridges to smart cars and smart watches, the list of smart devices is endless. These devices make life easier and more efficient for people. This system of devices also connects people all around the globe and it has become one of the most important – if not the most important – network in our world. There are innovations made every day that help the Internet of Things to expand its scope. The world of sports is just one branch on the tree of IoT.

Since the ancient Olympic Games, generations have witnessed the evolution of different sports, old ones were altered, and new ones were created. In the last few years, IoT has been integrated into sports (see Fig. 1). Although, there are plenty of challenges associated with IoT in sports, such as generalized approach, energy consumption, fan interaction, privacy, security and the large amount of data produced [11], many types of sports have benefitted from using devices for player and team development. One of these sports is basketball, which has grown into a global entertainment industry.

B. Li et al. (Eds.): IoTaaS 2020, LNICST 346, pp. 421–435, 2021.
https://doi.org/10.1007/978-3-030-67514-1_34

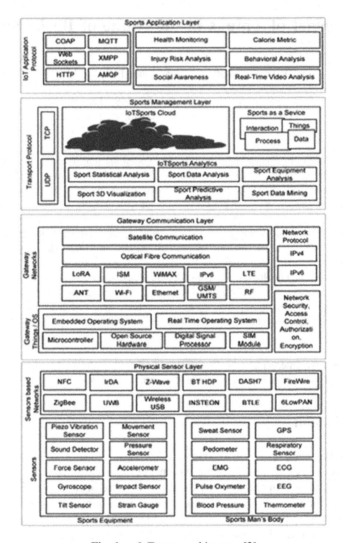

Fig. 1. - IoT sport architecture [2]

When basketball first became a game, there was no three-point line. Every field goal counted as two points. The game did not adapt the three-pointer until 1979 [1]. In recent years, the three-pointer king Stephen Curry has revolutionized the game by pulling up from 30+ feet away from the basket and taking more 3-point shots than anyone ever before. With this game changing new style, basketball analytics and technology have become a focal point of the game. Coaches have changed their game plans and now encourage their players to take more threes than ever before because advanced analytics show that 3-point shots are one of the best ones to take. The growth of IoT and the development of technology have changed the philosophy of the game. The Internet of Things serves as a bridge between basketball and basketball analytics.

Starting from youth basketball, all the way to the professionals in the National Basketball Association (NBA) and in Europe, IoT presents a great set of tools to develop players and analyze teams. Coaches know how to reach the full potential of their teams and fans can experience the game in ways that were not possible before. The game of basketball has grown into a meticulous science and a great entertainment industry. As technology develops, so does the science behind the game. People often forget or just simply not aware of the fact that the mental part of the game is a significant component to success. In basketball, you need to have awareness to see what is going on around you on the court. It is crucial that players are mentally prepared in order to outsmart the competition. Today, load-management is playing an increasing role in NBA circles, which means that players take games off to save their bodies. What if they could play a game on a mental level while resting their bodies?

The purpose of this paper is to investigate several IoT technologies present in the world of basketball including sensor-based, camera-based and Virtual Reality-based systems. In this paper, we take a look at several technologies that are closely related to what the Internet of Things represent – global connections and precise measurements. Furthermore, I have tested one video-based system called HomeCourt and reflected on my experience with the application. Players need to gain confidence from the things they do well on the court, and they need to be aware of their weaknesses in order to become better in those areas. IoT in the sport world helps players to do just that by analyzing motion and creating data, therefore, it helps sports become more sophisticated and competitive.

The rest of this paper is divided into six units. Section 2 introduces two related works. In Sect. 3, a sensor-based tracking system is examined, while Sect. 4 focuses on a camera based system and Sect. 5 talks about virtual reality approaches. Section 6 compares these three areas and Sect. 7 contains the conclusion as well as future work.

2 Related Work

2.1 IoT as a Shooting Aid

Antunes' design science research [3] focuses on the use of IoT to improve the shooting motion. This research introduces IoT Sport and breaks down the motion of a perfect shot. It is crucial to understand the proper motion in order to build a device that recognizes it. A list of existing basketball related IoT technologies are introduced as well as new artifacts are proposed. These artifacts are results of a series of interviews with players and coaches. This collaboration gives inside information for people who understand technology but does not know the game of basketball and vice versa. As a result, innovative ideas were formed for future work, such as an audio instruction system that would help the shooter correct the motion during practice. This dissertation is a great example of how the world of basketball and technology needs to work side-by-side in order to help players work on their game and therefore enrich the game with even more skilled players.

2.2   Three Men Tracker

At a European university, a prototype has been created that can identify basketball plays using sensors [4]. The system is constructed of sensors on players, three receptors placed around the court and optionally one more sensor in the ball. However, the study argues that it is possible to locate the basketball if we know which player has the ball, so the sensor in the ball is negligible. The system uses a three-player attention approach, meaning that even though there are five players on the court, only three of them are heavily involved in the given basketball play. This system is able to recognize basketball plays, such as pick-and-roll, and able to return valuable data to the coaching staff to understand the strengths and weaknesses of their team. On the first test, the proposed system achieved nearly 98% accuracy. I picked this work to survey because the system is not only smart and accurate; it also considers the fact that technology is expensive and offers a more affordable solution than the leading companies do (see Fig. 2).

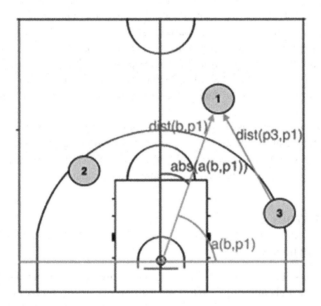

Fig. 2. 4 features from sensor system [4] player 1 distance from basket, distance between player 1 and 3; angle and absolute angle between player 1 and basket

3   Sensor Based Shot Tracker

3.1   Wilson X

Wilson X is a system that involves a basketball with built-in sensor in it and an application. The sensor connects to the smartphone and the data is displayed through the application. This technology was developed to help players improve their shots by measuring made and missed attempts along with the speed and arch of the shot.

The great thing about Wilson X is that the ball feels like a normal basketball. The sensor does not add extra weight to the product and the material of the ball has a great grip, it is not slippery (see Fig. 3).

Fig. 3. - Wilson X basketball and its application [6]

This leads to the next big advantage of Wilson X, which is instant feedback. For example, a player may be shooting, and the coach sees what areas to focus on. This feature allows a player to correct their mistakes as they are shooting, instead of going home and having to watch the recorded video all over again to analyze.

The sensor lasts for a long time - 100,000 shots, which gives more than 300 shots per day for an entire year [6] - but the battery of the sensor cannot be recharged. This means that after the battery dies, it becomes a regular basketball. Longevity is the main area in which Wilson X must improve. Perhaps magnetic charging could be an option. If the ball could be placed on a charging plate – just like newer smartphones – battery life would no longer be a problem.

The other area that needs improvement is the memory inside the ball. As opposed to a smart watch that can record the data from a workout and later synchronize it with the smartphone, the Wilson X basketball cannot store data. The ball needs to be able to connect to the phone throughout the shooting practice in order to record data. This somewhat limits the conditions in which the player can train. It would be beneficial to add a minimal memory to the sensor just as a backup. For example, if the smartphone dies, the new training data gets lost.

The third area of limitation is range. This technology is limited to only measure shots taken 7 feet or further from a regular 10 feet tall rim [6]. To make it realistic and game-like, Wilson X should be usable from any distance and perhaps should recognize dunk attempts - zero range.

4   Camera Driven Application

4.1   HomeCourt

HomeCourt, an iOS application has quickly gained popularity in the past few years in the sports world. This application helps to improve players' jump shots and recommend workout trainings to them based on their needs. As opposed to Wilson X that has a built-in sensor, this application does not require sensors in the basketball or on the player. The only device needed is a iOS product- an iPhone or iPad - which records the workout. Among many other features, the app can count the streak of made shots (see Fig. 4), and calculates the shooting percentage of each sector on the court.

Fig. 4. - Outdoors testing

In order to make the app authentic, Apple worked alongside Steve Nash, probably the most famous and accomplished Canadian basketball player, during the development and promotion process of the application. Furthermore, the NBA and its players have collaborated with, and invested in HomeCourt [8]. The users of the app can do shooting workouts named after and presented by NBA-sharp-shooter Joe Harris and other NBA stars. The app also offers dribbling and agility workouts. The free version allows the player to take one thousand shots a month - enough for people who just shoot the ball as a hobby - and some basic drills are included.

The main reason why this app is so successful is the lack of a big, uncomfortable sensor. With no sensor, players are able to keep their natural shooting motion and stay in normal circumstances throughout the workout. This is an essential part of integrating IoT into sports: the technology cannot affect the athlete's performance. HomeCourt achieves this goal.

Another advantage of this system is its simplicity. In today's world, most people have their phones on them at all times, which come in handy for HomeCourt. Because the player does not need anything else besides an Apple device, the use of this app becomes highly convenient. For a shooting exercise, the device automatically recognizes the basketball hoop, and prompts an error if it was not found - similar to face recognition in smartphones. The app also shows virtual basketball lines. If the app does not find automatically the actual basketball lines on the court, then it is the player's task to align the virtual lines with the actual lines of the court.

This leads us to the first problem with the app. Because at times the user has to align the virtual lines with the actual lines of the court, there is some room for error with accuracy. Because the app defines the different sectors based on the basketball lines, a precise alignment is crucial. If the alignment is faulty, it may result faulty representation of data - incorrect shooting percentage and accuracy, for example.

Another problem is the size of the screen. For dribbling workouts (see Fig. 5), the routine changes from the shooting drills. Instead of the phone cameras facing the player, now the screen is placed to see the player, who is looking at the screen. The app then recognizes the player and creates target points on the screen for the player to touch. The small screen can make it hard for the player to see the target. For this drill, it is better to use an iPad instead of an iPhone, however not all iPhone owners can also afford an iPad. Perhaps it would be a good idea to offer a cheap monitor that somehow connects to the iPhone, although it makes it more complicated to use the software.

Fig. 5. - Dribbling challenge

After testing this app both indoors and outdoors (see Fig. 4, 5 & 7), it became obvious that the lighting can cause trouble at times. In some cases, the camera recognized the attempt but did not count the shots there were made. As the first screenshot (see Fig. 6) shows, HomeCourt gives the location of every shot taken and missed during the workout. Designated symbols mark makes and misses. On the second screenshot (see Fig. 8), HomeCourt summarizes the total shooting percentages of the day per sectors.

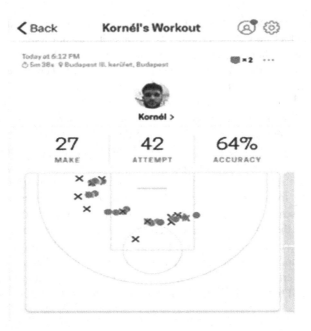

Fig. 6. - HomeCourt shot chart

After the workout, the player can play back his/her workout in the app. This is an important tool for a player who can see the movement as a whole instead of just plain evaluation of the workout in numbers. There are specific highlight types that the app offers, such as how many shots were made in a row or makes/attempt (see Figs. 4 & 7). The video also gives the option to display an orange tracking line feature in the video that shows the path of the ball (see Fig. 4), making it easy to analyze the arch and angle of the shot.

Fig. 7. - Indoors testing

The app also allows users to watch other players around the globe doing their own workouts. This feature represents perfectly the idea of the Internet of Things because it enables people to be connected through their devices regardless of the distance between them and share data with each other. Players can share workout summaries and track each other's progress, much like on a social media site. HomeCourt brings the basketball community closer all over the globe.

Fig. 8. - Shooting zones display

5 Virtual Reality

Virtual reality (VR) is a great aid for the game of basketball. Players, coaches and even fans benefit from the technology of VR. In the NBA, virtual reality enhances fan experience and optimizes the players' performance. Fans that are not able to afford courtside seats are now able to get the experience from their own couch, thanks to virtual reality, and players are now able to rest their bodies by doing mental training with VR. From the fans' perspective, the experience of a basketball game is much more hands-on. Fans can feel more connected to players by buying special jerseys with sensor tags to unlock exclusive highlight videos of their favorite players [10]. VR also enables kids to learn how to play basketball in schools where there is no option to play outside because of the weather or there is not enough space for a basketball court [12].

5.1 Magic Leap

Magic Leap created the Magic Leap One VR system that is composed of a headset, called Lightwear, a controller and a minicomputer called Lightpack. Furthermore, Magic Leap has begun a partnership with the NBA that enables the user of the system to watch live games from home. This device uses spatial computing and augmented reality, which enables the user to watch multiple games or highlights simultaneously [9]. This technology helps the game to become global. There are only twenty-nine active NBA arenas in the world (Clippers and Lakers share an arena in Los Angeles), yet people all over the globe use virtual reality to feel like they are at the game (see Fig. 9).

Fig. 9. - Magic Leap headset [9]

5.2   Tactic Training

Four scholars from National Cheng Kung University, Taiwan have created a prototype of a trainer system to help players learn basketball tactics. The system involves two devices: "a tablet-based digital tactic board (2D BTB)" [5] and a VR system that allows a 3D experience. The idea behind this technology is that the coach – or someone else – draws up a basketball play in 2D on a tablet, this play is converted into a 3D content, and the player can watch the action in 3D with a VR device. In other words, the coach and players do not need to be together to practice the tactics. The unique part of this technology is that the system interprets simple drawings and creates an animated environment for the player. It is a great idea because coaches and players need to be on the same page in order to be successful.

The system offers two perspectives of viewing the play: first-person perspective (1PP) and third-person perspective (3PP). In 1PP, the player sees what he would see if he was running the play. The player is surrounded with four other players. This perspective allows seeing the play from one position. In the 3PP version, the user is viewing the events of the play from the outside. This perspective allows for an overall view, which gives a better picture of the overall flow and rhythm of the plays (see Fig. 10).

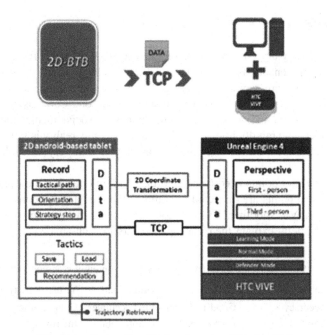

Fig. 10. - Converting 2D drawings into 3D plays [5]

The three kinds of training modes include normal mode, learning mode and defender mode. In normal mode, the play runs regardless which direction the player looks. In learning mode, the player must look at the right direction (which is the direction of the next step in the play from his perspective) in order to the animation to continue. Thirdly, in defender mode, the system adds defenders to the animation, giving the player a real in-game environment to practice the tactics.

The scholars asked 60 subjects to test the system, creating two groups of 30 people. At the end of the test, each player had to fill out a questionnaire to give feedback. The conclusion was that the 3D version makes it easier and more realistic to prepare for the game than looking at a 2D drawing because the player can be "in the game" virtually. However, there are areas such as user-interface that needs to develop before this technology becomes a big hit.

5.3   Virtual Shooting

New technologies are being developed to help players shoot using VR sets. In Covaci's work, the VR system creates a virtual environment to teach the user how to shoot a free throw [7]. This is a perfect prototype for a player who needs to rest, but wants to get in a shooting workout. Players can do that without ever leaving their homes. Just like the first related work above, this technology could use audio feedback to correct the motion of the shooter. With time, the graphics, the accuracy and the overall experience of VR systems will improve.

6 Comparison

In this paper, we analyzed three technological areas within the framework of the Internet of Things: sensor based tracking; camera based tracking and virtual reality. All three of these areas are rapidly improving. Sensors are key components of the IoT world; data is collected by measurement made with sensors. Cameras are the driving force of improvement in mobile computing thanks to social media; the quality of photos and videos are rapidly improving. Moreover, the new reality is virtual reality. In other words, all three of these technologies are unique and very valuable in today's world.

In sports, several points need to be considered when choosing the right device. In this section, these points are dissected to compare the pros and the cons of Wilson X, HomeCourt and VR shooting. Table 1 compares these three technologies in eight categories and briefly explain their main parameters in each area.

Table 1. Comparing the three technologies based on eight common parameters

Categories	Wilson X	HomeCourt	Virtual Reality
Accuracy	Good if 7+feet	Less accurate	Own accuracy
Comfort	Uneven ball	Comfortable	Improving
User friendliness	Easy to use	Good interface	Most potential
Cross platform	iOS & Android	Apple only	N/A
Price	Hardware cost	Free or paid	Expensive
Lifetime	100k shots	Smartphone	Improving
Memory	None in ball	Cloud	Live broadcast
Room to improve	Sensor size	Better cameras	Most potential

6.1 Accuracy

Accuracy is a major aspect of sport data to consider. A sensor-based tracker discussed in this paper, Wilson X, is highly accurate. Although, it has range limitations (7+ feet), the measurements are properly converted into data. The same is not true for camera-based technology. With camera, it is hard to analyze the input as accurately as a sensor can. External factors, such as wind, and foreign objects can cause interruptions in the recording. Virtual reality creates its own world, which prevents real measure of accuracy. The user "lives" in a virtual reality that has its own measuring scale.

6.2 Comfort

The next area that must be considered is the comfort factor. Because athletic movement cannot be limited while measuring, the goal is to get accurate data without affecting the movement of the player. Sensors will give data that are more accurate but will also affect the player to some degree, depending on the size and placement of the sensor. On the other hand, a camera will not be as accurate as a sensor because of reasons mentioned in Sect. 6.1 above, but the player will not be bothered during the workout.

Therefore, accuracy and comfort are contradictory. As opposed to accuracy, where Wilson X performed much better than HomeCourt, the later one is more comfortable because the player is free of restricting devices. Wilson X loses the feel of a true basketball, even though the sensor is very small. Virtual reality has its limits of comfort. Perhaps one day it will be available in the form of contact lens, but until then, we must accept the funky-looking goggles.

6.3   User Friendliness

Wilson X, HomeCourt and Covaci's work [7] all use applications. User friendliness may be the single most important feature to influence and win over customers. VR has the most potential in this area for obvious reasons. Literally, anything can be created in virtual reality so the sky is the limit. HomeCourt is designed for Apple's iOS, which is knows for great user experience. Wilson X has a good interface as well; it is just simply a hard task to compete with Apple in this area.

6.4   Cross Platform

In mobile computing, HomeCourt is the obvious loser of the cross platform aspect as it only runs to Apple devices. Wilson X can be used on both Android and iOS systems. Once again, VR stands alone as it has its own environment.

6.5   Price

At this point, VR is the most expensive technology out of the three. You can use HomeCourt for free – limited number of shots and access of content – or you can pay for unlimited use and access. Purchasing Wilson X cost money – here you pay mainly for a hardware (basketball) and get the software with it to use, as opposed to Home-Court, where you pay specifically for the software.

6.6   Lifetime

Only Wilson X has a limited lifetime because of the hardware component – battery in the basketball. Wilson is currently working on the second version of their ball, which supposedly will have longer lifetime or an option to charge. HomeCourt gets better as cameras improve and the software improvements and maintenance helps the application to stay relevant. Virtual reality is only in the beginning phase of what's speculated as the future of computing.

6.7   Memory

Memory-wise, Wilson X does not have internal memory built into the ball, which can lead to loss of data. Cloud computing is becoming the new standard of storage; HomeCourt takes full advantage of this by storing data on the cloud. This consumes lots of memory space because of the video content. Wilson X does not contain video, whereas Magic Leap and other virtual reality devices can transmit live broadcast.

6.8   Room to Improve

All three technologies compared above and all athletes have room to improve. In this sense, sports and IoT are similar: neither is ever perfected. It is perfection why people in both areas strive daily to make improvements. These two fields not only can work together to strive for perfection but can also help each other along the way.

7   Conclusion and Future Work

Basketball is a complex game and has evolved tremendously throughout the years. Just like the three-point shot changed how basketball has been played throughout the last few years, IoT is changing in the game today. New plays, tactics, systems are being invented and applied constantly based on new data. IoT connects basketball personnel with scientists, allowing them to understand each other and work together to improve the game.

In this paper, we have introduced and compared three technologies: sensor- and camera-based IoT systems as well as virtual reality. Sensor-based technologies, such as Wilson X delivers accurate information, however the sensor can have negative impact on the performance due to its size. HomeCourt was the main camera-based app that we focused on. Due to the lack of sensors, it allows athletes to keep their natural range of movement, however external factors, such as wind, may affect the accuracy of the data collected. Virtual reality has the most potential out of the three technologies. It may become the most user-friendly interface out of the three one day and there is no limit on what can be accomplished with VR.

Perhaps the perfect solution to track basketball movement lies in combining these technologies in some sort of fashion. By pairing two of these three technologies, we can avoid some of the detriment that one of them has and emphasize only the good parameters of each technology.

My future work lies in the field of basketball analytics. It is fascinating to analyze each segment of the game of basketball. By collecting data via IoT, priceless information can be extracted which can point to the future direction of the game.

IoT has already had a tremendous impact on the game of basketball and basketball analytics. Thanks to IoT, advanced stats can be extracted from games that point out the areas to improve from an individual standpoint to a team perspective. Basketball analytics has developed into a game-changer tool; whoever has better analytics most likely has the better chance to win games. IoT represents the bridge between the game of basketball and science, or, in other words, it is the channel of communication between players and scientists.

References

1. The History of the 3-Pointer. (n.d.). https://www.usab.com/youth/news/2011/06/the-history-of-the-3-pointer.aspx. Accessed 22 May 2019
2. Ray, P.P.: Generic Internet of Things architecture for smart sports. In: 2015 International Conference on Control, Instrumentation, Communication and Computational Technologies (ICCICCT), Kumaracoil, pp. 405–410 (2015)

3. Antunes: Use of IoT technologies to improve shooting performance in basketball (Unpublished doctoral dissertation). NOVA Information Management School (2018)
4. Sangüesa, A.A., Moeslund, T.B., Bahnsen, C.H., Iglesias, R.B.: Identifying basketball plays from sensor data; towards a low-cost automatic extraction of advanced statistics. In: 2017 IEEE International Conference on Data Mining Workshops (ICDMW), New Orleans, LA, pp. 894–901 (2017)
5. Tsai, W.-L., et al.: Train in virtual court: basketball tactic training via virtual reality. In: Proceedings of the 2017 ACM Workshop on Multimedia-Based Educational and Knowledge Technologies for Personalized and Social Online Training, pp. 3–10 (2017)
6. Quin, C.: Hands-on Test: Wilson X Connected Basketball. RSS, 17 May 2017. eandt.theiet. org/content/articles/2017/05/hands-on-test-wilson-x-connected-basketball/
7. Covaci, A., Postelnicu, C.-C., Panfir, A.N., Talaba, D.: A virtual reality simulator for basketball free-throw skills development. In: Camarinha-Matos, Luis M., Shahamatnia, E., Nunes, G. (eds.) DoCEIS 2012. IAICT, vol. 372, pp. 105–112. Springer, Heidelberg (2012). https://doi.org/10.1007/978-3-642-28255-3_12
8. NEX Team Inc.: https://www.homecourt.ai/about. Accessed 6 June 2020
9. The new NBA App on Magic Leap is a game changer (2019). www.magicleap.com/en-us/ news/product-updates/nba-app-launch. Accessed 19 June 2019
10. Behr, O.: Fashion 4.0 – digital innovation in the fashion industry. J. Technol. Innov. Manage. 2(1), 1–9 (2018)
11. Ray, P.P.: Internet of Things for sports (IoTSport): an architectural framework for sports and recreational activity[Scholarly project]. In: Academia.edu (2015)
12. Yao, H.-P., Liu, Y.-Z., Han, C.-S.: Application expectation of virtual reality in basketball teaching. Procedia Eng. 29(C), 4287–4291 (2012)

Next Generation Network

Object Recognition Through UAV Observations Based on Yolo and Generative Adversarial Network

Bo Li[1,2(✉)], Zhigang Gan[1,3], Evgeny Sergeevich Neretin[3],
and Zhipeng Yang[1]

[1] School of Electronics and Information, Northwestern Polytechnical University,
Xi'an, China
libo803@nwpu.edu.cn
[2] CETC Key Laboratory of Data Link Technology, Xi'an, China
[3] Moscow Aviation Institute, Moscow, Russian Federation

Abstract. Aiming at the object recognition through UAV, an intelligent object recognition model based on YOLO and Generative adversarial network is proposed in this paper. Firstly, the solution is given, and an object recognition model that can realize intelligent recognition is established. Then, in order to improve the resolution of the identified images, an image resolution enhancement model based on generative adversarial networks is built. After that, the structure and parameters of the recognition model and image resolution enhancement model are adjusted through the simulation experiments to improve the accuracy and robustness of the object recognition. Finally, the object recognition model based on YOLO and generative adversarial network in this paper is verified through UAV.

Keywords: UAV · Machine learning · Object recognition

1 Introduction

In recent years, UAVs have widely used in different types of civilian missions, such as target tracking, wildlife protection, disaster rescue and 3D reconstruction. In view of the rapid development of advanced UAV technology, target tracking is an important research and application direction of UAV. Object recognition technology has huge requirements in areas such as autonomous UAV-guided landing, criminal vehicle or personnel hunting, military target reconnaissance and strike. However, the above tasks have high requirements on the accuracy, stability, and robustness of object recognition. Traditional object recognition can no longer meet the current task requirements. In order to complete the precise recognition tasks, today's more advanced technology must be used. At the same time, there are many difficulties in applying object recognition. For example, complex lighting changes, occlusion between targets and scenes, similar interference in the background, and camera perturbations all make target tracking tasks more difficult.

B. Li et al. (Eds.): IoTaaS 2020, LNICST 346, pp. 439–449, 2021.
https://doi.org/10.1007/978-3-030-67514-1_35

The advantage of the traditional object recognition algorithm is that it can clearly display the recognition features, and if the object is simple, the outline is clear, or the color contrast is sharp, then the traditional object recognition algorithm can be used to identify the target well. However, deep learning methods work well for high-dimensional data. Without manual selection of features, classification results with good effect can be obtained by deep learning methods. Among the object recognition algorithms based on deep learning, models such as the YOLO(You only look once) [1, 4] model and R-CNN have achieved good recognition results. YOLO can detect video very fast basic YOLO model processes images in real-time at 45 frames per second.

Considering the YOLO model's efficient and accurate recognition ability for video images, this article decided to use YOLO to complete object recognition missions. Considering the limited sharpness of object images, this paper uses image enhancement technology based on GAN (Generative adversarial network) [2] to assist object recognition. In terms of image resolution enhancement technology, the traditional problem is that when the magnification of the image resolution is more than 4 times, high-frequency information is missing, and the realism in details is missing. However, SRGAN (Super-resolution generative adversarial network) [3] model, an image resolution enhancement method based on generation adversarial network, can better generate image details when dealing with the enhancement problem with larger resolution magnification.

In this paper, we have combined YOLO and GAN in object recognition to ensure the stability and efficiency of video images recognition and the clarity of UAV recognition images.

The contributions of this paper are summarized as follows:

1. We combined YOLO and SRGAN to propose a new method for object recognition through UAV observations. UAV realizes object recognition through YOLO and enhances the resolution of the recognition images through SRGAN, which can realize the high-quality and fast object recognition.
2. We use YOLO algorithm to achieve object recognition and SRGAN algorithm to enhance the resolution of the recognition image, which can achieve high-quality rapid detection of the target by the UAV.
3. We constructed a UAV platform and verified the effectiveness of our proposed methods on the UAV platform. Through a series of experiments, we show that the UAV can quickly and efficiently complete object recognition and realize the resolution enhancement of the recognized images.

The reminder of this paper is organized as follows. In Sect. 2, this article defines a solution for completing object recognition on UAV, and details the implementation of object recognition and image resolution enhancement. In Sect. 3, this paper trains the recognition model and completes the test on the UAV. Finally, conclusions are presented in Sect. 4.

2 Problem Formulation and Learning Algorithm

2.1 Problem Description

The research body is divided into two parts: UAV and ground laptop. The height advantage and mobile advantage of UAV are utilized to complete the acquisition of ground images, and the acquired images are transmitted to the ground laptop in real time through the image transmission system of UAV [6–9]. The ground laptop completes the object recognition of interest and performs resolution enhancement operations on part of the bounding box of image [10–12]. The process of UAV object recognition is shown in Fig. 1.

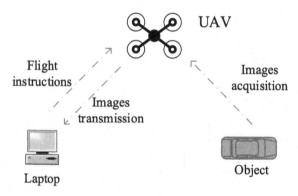

Fig. 1. The process of UAV object recognition

The object recognition process of this paper is as follows. UAV collects images from the ground through the camera and transmits the images to the ground laptop in a real time. The real-time images are input into the YOLO network to complete the object recognition [13–15]. The recognition images are enhanced by generative adversarial network to improve the recognition of object by human eyes. The implementation process is shown in Fig. 2.

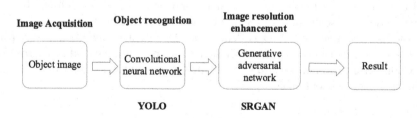

Fig. 2. The implementation process of recognition

2.2   Object Recognition Based on YOLO

Most of the current object recognition algorithms treat the object recognition problems as classification problems. However, the YOLO model abstracts object recognition as regression problems, directly from image pixel input to output boundary box and category probabilities. YOLO is an object recognition system based on a single neural network proposed by Joseph Redmon and Ali Farhadi et al. in the paper You Only Look Once: Unified, real-time Object Detection in 2015 [1].

YOLO is based on the convolutional neural networks to achieve the recognition. YOLO consists of 24 convolutional layers [5] and 2 fully connected layers. The neural networks extract features from the images through the convolution layers, and uses fully connection layers to predict the output probability and the position information of the bounding box.

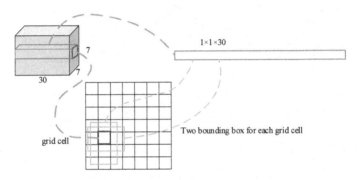

Fig. 3. The process of object recognition by YOLO (Color figure online)

In the YOLO network, the neural network predicts the location and confidence of each bounding box. Confidences includes the confidence of the object in the bounding box and the accuracy of the position prediction of the bounding box. When an image is input into the YOLO, the output is a $7 \times 7 \times 30$ three-dimensional tensor. Figure 2 shows the process of object recognition by YOLO.

As shown in Fig. 3, the red box represents the grid cell, and the yellow boxes represent the bounding boxes. The input image is divided into 7×7 grid cells, each grid cell corresponds to two output bounding boxes predicted by YOLO. 30 in the output tensor represents the position and category of each bounding box.

The loss function of YOLO is defined as (1), which is divided into two parts: position error and classification error. Classification errors include confidence error and probability error. Confidence errors are divided into confidence error with object and confidence error without object.

$$loss = \lambda_{coord} \sum_{i=0}^{S^2} \sum_{j=0}^{B} 1_{ij}^{obj} [(x_i - \hat{x}_i)^2 + (y_i - \hat{y}_i)^2] +$$

$$\lambda_{coord} \sum_{i=0}^{S^2} \sum_{j=0}^{B} 1_{ij}^{obj} [(\sqrt{w_i} - \sqrt{\hat{w}_i})^2 + (\sqrt{h_i} - \sqrt{\hat{h}_i})^2]$$

$$+ \sum_{i=0}^{S^2} \sum_{j=0}^{B} 1_{ij}^{obj} (C_i - \hat{C}_i)^2 + \lambda_{noobj} \sum_{i=0}^{S^2} \sum_{j=0}^{B} 1_{ij}^{obj} (C_i - \hat{C}_i)^2$$

$$+ \sum_{i=0}^{S^2} 1_i^{obj} \sum_{c \in classes} (p_i(c) - \hat{p}_i(c))^2$$

(1)

where, λ_{coord}, λ_{noobj} respectively represent the weights of position information and category information defined in the loss function, i represents the i-th $(i = 0, \ldots, S^2)$ grid cell, j represents the j-th $(j = 0, \ldots, B)$ bounding box, 1_{ij}^{obj} represents j-th bounding box in grid cell i to be predict the object, 1_i^{obj} indicates that the object appears in grid cell i, $(\hat{x}_i, \hat{y}_i)$ represents the center position information of the prediction object position, $(\hat{w}_i, \hat{h}_i)$ represent the width and height of the prediction recognition box, $\hat{C}_i$ represents the classification category for object i, $\hat{p}_i(c)$ represents the confidence for category.

2.3 Image Resolution Enhancement Based on SRGAN

Since the implementation and test platform of this paper is the UAV, the images collected by the UAV are input into the YOLO model to complete the object recognition mission. Considering that the UAV is at high altitude, the clarity of the image information collected from object is limited. Therefore, after the object recognition is completed, the resolution enhancement of recognition image is carried out to improve the recognition effect. This paper uses Generative Adversarial Network (GAN) [2] which has excellent performance in generating images and enhancing image resolution.

In order to enhance the image sharpness of images, this paper decided to use SRGAN (Super-Resolution Using a Generative Adversarial Network), a branch model of generation antagonism network, to achieve image resolution enhancement. SRGAN recovers high-frequency information of images by Perceptual loss and Adversarial loss. SRGAN makes the generated image and target image more similar in style by comparing the features extracted from the convolutional neural network and the features extracted from the target image through the neural network. SRGAN consists of a generation network and a discrimination network. The generation network consists of 5 convolutional layers and 5 layers of residual networks. Convolutional layers are used to extract image features. The residual network can promote the training effect and solve the problems of gradient disappearance and gradient explosion. The discrimination network consists of 4 convolutional layers for extracting input image features. The generation work takes low-resolution images as input and tries to generate high-resolution image data. The discrimination network takes the real high-resolution image and the image generated by the generation network as input, and predicts whether the current input comes from real data or generated image.

The loss function of generation network is defined as, which consists of (3), (4), (5). $g_{contentloss}$ represents the content loss of the generated image, $g_{VGGloss}$ represents the loss after feature extraction, $g_{adversarial}$ represents the training loss of the generation network. (x, y) represents the image pixel coordinates, and r_w, r_H represent the width and height of the image. $\phi_{i,j}(I^{HR})_{x,y}$ is the output of the high-resolution image after the feature extraction, $\phi_{i,j}(G_{\theta_G}(I^{LR}))_{x,y}$ is the output of the generated image after the feature extraction.

$$g_{loss} = g_{contentloss} + g_{VGGloss} + g_{adversarial} \tag{2}$$

$$g_{contentloss} = \frac{1}{rWrH} \sum_{x=1}^{rW} \sum_{y=1}^{rH} (I^{HR} - G_{\theta_G}(I^{LR})_{x,y})^2 \tag{3}$$

$$g_{VGGloss} = \frac{1}{W_{i,j}H_{i,j}} \sum_{x=1}^{W_{i,j}} \sum_{y=1}^{H_{i,j}} (\phi_{i,j}(I^{HR})_{x,y} - \phi_{i,j}(G_{\theta_G}(I^{LR}))_{x,y})^2 \tag{4}$$

$$g_{adversarial} = \sum_{n=1}^{N} -\log D_{\theta_D}(G_{\theta_G}(I^{LR})_{x,y}) \tag{5}$$

The loss function of discrimination network is defined as

$$E_{I^{HR} \sim p_{train}}(I^{HR})[\log D_{\theta_D}(I^{HR})] + E_{I^{LR} \sim p_G}(I^{LR})[\log(1 - D_{\theta_D}(G_{\theta_G}(I^{LR})_{x,y}))] \tag{6}$$

where I_{xy}^{HR}, I^{HR} represent high-resolution images, I^{LR} represent low-resolution images, and $G_{\theta_G}(I^{LR})_{x,y}$ represents the generation results of the generation network. $D_{\theta_D}(I^{HR})$ represents the discriminant result of the discrimination network with high-resolution images as input, $D_{\theta_D}(G_{\theta_G}(I^{LR})_{x,y}$ is the result of the discrimination network with generated images as input, $I^{HR} \sim p_{train}$ is the high-resolution images from the training data set, and $I^{LR} \sim p_G$ represents the generated images from generation network.

When training the generation adversarial network, alternately train the generation network and the discrimination network. Within a period of time, the parameters of the generation network are fixed and the discrimination network is optimized. In the next period of time, the parameters in the discrimination network are fixed and the generation network is optimized. The training process of SRGAN is shown in Fig. 4.

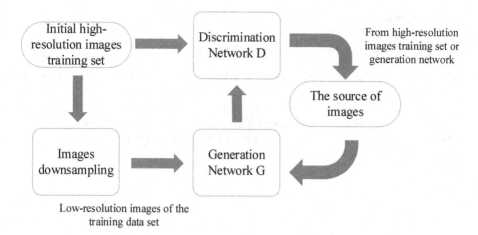

Fig. 4. The training process of SRGAN

The image resolution enhancement algorithm is summarized in Table 1.

Table 1. SRGAN algorithm

Algorithm SRGAN

In generation network G and discrimination network D

for number of training iterations **do**

    for k steps **do**

        Sample minibatch images from high-resolution images $\{x^{(1)}, x^{(2)}, x^{(3)}, ..., x^{(m)}\}$

        Sample minibatch images from low-resolution images $\{z^{(1)}, z^{(2)}, z^{(3)}, ..., z^{(m)}\}$

        Update the discrimination network by ascending its stochastic gradient:

$$V = \frac{1}{m}\sum_{i=1}^{m} \log D(x^i) + \frac{1}{m}\sum_{i=1}^{m} \log(1 - D(G(z^i)))$$

    end for

    Sample minibatch images from low-resolution images $\{z^{(1)}, z^{(2)}, z^{(3)}, ..., z^{(m)}\}$

    Update the generation network by ascending its stochastic gradient.

end for

---

3 Experiment and Analysis

3.1 The Object Recognition Experiment by YOLO

This paper completes the construction and trains the recognition model based on TensorFlow module.

The changes in the loss of the recognition model training process are shown in Fig. 5. It can be seen that the recognition result reaches the expected value after 1,000,000 training steps. The recognition rate of the final recognition model on the test set reached about 86%.

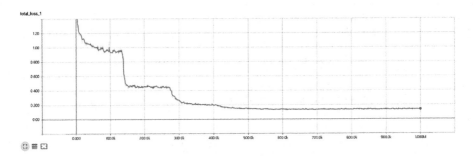

Fig. 5. The loss function during training

When testing on UAV: The experimental procedure is that in the case of low-speed movement of the unmanned vehicle, the UAV is manually operated to take off and fly in the direction of the object. During this period, the camera on the UAV has been collecting the ground images and transmitting them to the ground laptop in real time. While receiving the images, the trained YOLO model has been running. When the unmanned vehicle appears on the screen of the laptop, the bounding box is superimposed on the real-time video, which means the object is found. In order to detect the robustness of the recognition algorithms, pedestrians are introduced as interference during the test.

According to the Fig. 6, it can be seen that the YOLO model can accurately complete the recognition task of the unmanned vehicle moving at low speed at various heights, positions and angles.

3.2 The Resolution Enhancement Experiment by SRGAN

In this paper, the high-resolution image data sets are composed of images similar to the target texture features, while the low-resolution image data sets are obtained from the down-sampling of the high-resolution image data sets.

The loss of generation networks and discrimination networks are shown as Fig. 7. The left graph is the loss of generation network, and the right graph is the loss of discrimination network.

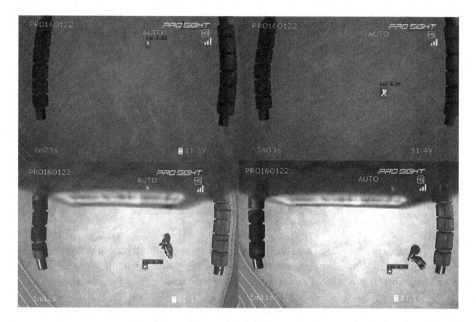

Fig. 6. The recognition results on UAV

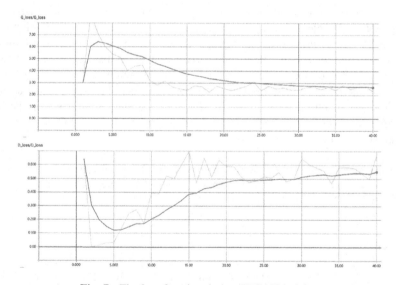

Fig. 7. The loss function during SRGAN training

Due to the poor definition of the image information collected by UAV, SRGAN was used to enhance the resolution after completing the recognition tasks. The results are shown in Fig. 8.

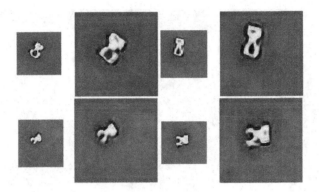

Fig. 8. The results of image resolution enhancement

From the experimental results in Fig. 8, it can be seen intuitively that the sharpness of the unmanned vehicle has been enhanced, which shows that the use of SRGAN technology in UAV platform target detection is beneficial to human observation.

4   Conclusion

This paper proposes a recognition model based on YOLO and generative adversarial network for UAV object recognition. First, we construct a real-time recognition model based on YOLO. Then, in order to improve the resolution of the images, we construct an image resolution enhancement model based on generative adversarial network. Through a series of experiments, we adjust the structure and parameters of the recognition model and image resolution enhancement model to improve the accuracy and robustness of object recognition. Finally, we carry out experiments on the UAV platform, which verify the effectiveness of this paper based on YOLO and generative adversarial network.

Acknowledgments. This research was supported by The Aeronautical Science Foundation of China (No. 2017ZC53021) and The Open Project Fund of CETC Key Laboratory of Data Link Technology No. CLDL-20182101).

References

1. Redmon, J., Divvala, S., Girshick, R., Farhadi, A.: You only look once: unified, real-time object detection. In: The IEEE Conference on Computer Vision and Pattern Recognition (CVPR), pp. 779–788 (2016)
2. Goodfellow, I.J., et al.: Generative Adversarial Networks, June 2014
3. Ledig, C., et al.: Photo-realistic single image super-resolution using a generative adversarial network. In: The IEEE Conference on Computer Vision and Pattern Recognition (CVPR), pp. 4681–4690 (2017)

4. Simon, M., Milz, S., Amende, K., Gross, H.-M.: Complex-YOLO: real-time 3D Object detection on point clouds, September 2018
5. Radford, A., Metz, L., Chintala, S.: Unsupervised representation learning with deep convolutional generative adversarial networks. In: International Conference of Learning Representation (ICLR), January 2016
6. Zeng, F., Shi, H., Wang, H.: The object recognition and adaptive threshold selection in the vision system for landing an Unmanned Aerial Vehicle. In: 2009 International Conference on Information and Automation, pp. 117–122 (2009)
7. Kechagias-Stamatis, O., Aouf, N., Nam, D.: 3D automatic target recognition for UAV platforms. In: 2017 Sensor Signal Processing for Defence Conference (SSPD), London, pp. 1–5 (2017)
8. Ibrahim, A.W.N., Ching, P.W., Seet, G.L.G., Lau, W.S.M., Czajewski, W.: Moving objects detection and tracking framework for UAV-based surveillance. In: 2010 Fourth Pacific-Rim Symposium on Image and Video Technology, Singapore, Singapore, pp. 456–461 (2010)
9. Wang, C., Zhao, R., Yang, X., Wu, Q.: Research of UAV target detection and flight control based on deep learning. In: 2018 International Conference on Artificial Intelligence and Big Data (ICAIBD), Chengdu, pp. 170–174 (2018)
10. Li, X., Yan, B., Wang, H., Luo, X., Yang, Q., Yan, W.: Corner detection based target tracking and recognition for UAV-based patrolling system. In: 2016 IEEE International Conference on Information and Automation (ICIA), Ningbo, China, pp. 282–286 (2016)
11. Sommer, L., Schumann, A., Muller, T., Schuchert, T., Beyerer, J.: Flying object detection for automatic UAV recognition. In: 2017 14th IEEE International Conference on Advanced Video and Signal Based Surveillance (AVSS), Lecce, Italy, pp. 1–6 (2017)
12. Wang, J., Pundit, S.P., Abdelzaher, A.F., Watts, M.: Asynchronous localization of ground objects using a 2-UAV system. In: 2019 IEEE Conference on Multimedia Information Processing and Retrieval (MIPR), San Jose, CA, USA, pp. 316–321 (2019)
13. Zientara, P.A., Choi, J., Sampson, J., Narayanan, V.: Drones as collaborative sensors for image recognition. In: 2018 IEEE International Conference on Consumer Electronics (ICCE), Las Vegas, NV, pp. 1–4 (2018)
14. Zhe, L.I., Jianzeng, L.I.: Analysis of blurred image restoration for small UAV. J. Ordnance Equipment Eng. 40(3), 165–168 (2019)
15. Yang, C., Chen, D., Liu, Z., et al.: Image dehazing method based on deep learning. J. Ordnance Equipment Eng. 40(10), 131–135 (2019)

Soft Channel Reservation Towards Latency Guarantee for the Next Generation WLAN: IEEE 802.11be

Jianfei Cheng, Bo Li, Mao Yang$^{(\boxtimes)}$, and Zhongjiang Yan

School of Electronics and Information, Northwestern Polytechnical University,
Xi'an, China
434321310@mail.nwpu.edu.cn,
{libo,yangmao,zhjyan.npu}@nwpu.edu.cn

Abstract. Real-time applications (RTAs) are a major challenge for wireless networks. The traditional wireless local area network (WLAN) adopts Enhanced Distributed Channel Access (EDCA) in order to differentiate the quality of services (QoS) based on traffic priorities. However, for the high-dense scenario, the collisions frequently occur, thereby deteriorating both throughput and latency. The next generation WLAN standard: IEEE 802.11be aims to efficiently decrease the latency. Therefore, in this paper, we propose a soft channel in-band reservation protocol (SCRP). SCRP introduces channel reservation to alleviate channel collisions since the ongoing transmission piggybacking the predicted next transmission time. Moreover, a soft reservation canceling scheme is introduced to fully reuse the wireless resources. It means if the nodes who reserve the channel does not has packet to send at the reservation time, a low-overhead frame exchange may flexibly cancel the reservation and, in this case, other nodes can contend the channel resources. Simulation results show that SCRP significantly decreases the latency and improves the throughput of the entire network.

Keywords: Low latency · Real-time application · Medium access control · QoS · IEEE 802.11be · Channel reservation

1 Introduction

In recent years, wireless local area network (WLAN) has developed very rapidly [1], and a series of products designed based on the IEEE 802.11 protocol have already penetrated into human lives. WiFi makes up for the shortcomings of the complicated network wiring of cellular networks [2]. In the wireless Internet market, the proportion of WiFi has increased year by year [3]. In 2019, Cisco released the WiFi6 router, marking that the new generation standard IEEE 802.11ax has been officially commercialized. Immediately, in March 2019, the IEEE 802.11 standard working group confirmed the official establishment of the next generation of WiFi, i.e. IEEE 802.11be.

B. Li et al. (Eds.): IoTaaS 2020, LNICST 346, pp. 450–461, 2021.
https://doi.org/10.1007/978-3-030-67514-1_36

IEEE 802.11ax aims at significantly improve the average throughput and efficiency in high-dense scenario. Thus, a series of scenario and technologies are studied such as dense AP scenarios [4], network performance and optimization [5], Orthogonal Frequency Division Multiple Access (OFDMA) [6], and Multi-user Multiple-Input Multiple-Output (MU-MIMO) [7]. In order to achieve the objective of extremely high throughput (EHT), IEEE 802.11be introduces lots of new technical features including multi-AP cooperation [8], multi-band operation [9], spatial multiplexing optimization [9], hybrid automatic repeat quest (HARQ) [10], low-latency solution, and etc. According to the current development of network services, the proportion of multimedia services is getting higher and higher, and the demand for video, games and other services is rapidly increasing. WIFI needs to face a difficult challenge: to ensure the user experience with low latency. Thus, low-latency access has become one of the most important and challenging goals of IEEE 802.11be.

In the current protocol standard, enhanced distributed channel access mechanism (EDCA) can provide priority-based channel access transmission services for different types of services, so that high-priority real-time services in the network can be lower Priority MAC layer transmission with priority for ordinary services. EDCA supports priority QoS and parameterized QoS. However, due to the complexity of network conditions and changes in network scenarios, the static parameter settings in EDCA cannot optimize system performance. Many studies have shown that under high load conditions, due to the network With a high collision rate, the performance of EDCA is not satisfactory. Moreover, many studies focus on dynamically adjusting EDCA parameters to reduce the transmission delay of high-priority services to adapt to complex network environments. Abu-Khadrah et al. [11] proposed a dynamic window adjustment algorithm based on the Markov chain model, which effectively improved the performance of the network. Akinyemi et al. [12] proposed a feedback-based control algorithm that dynamically outputs the EDCA competition window based on the number of active nodes in the network. Rathnakar et al. [13] proposed an algorithm that uses conflict avoidance and adaptively adjusts the competition window. Ahmed Abu-Khadrah et al. [14] proposed an enhanced EDCA protocol that adjusts the contention window based on workload, thereby increasing network throughput while ensuring QoS. Zhong et al. [15] proposed to dynamically adjust the size of the competition window according to the throughput ratio of each business category and the number of active nodes to achieve throughput optimization. Alam et al. [16] proposed a dynamic TXOP transmission parameter protocol for the specific scenario of campus network, which improves QoS performance by reducing end-to-end delay. However, the existing studies are either too inefficient or have high complexity without considering power consumption.

Face to the RTAs problem, in order to improve the latency performance, this paper proposes an enhanced MAC protocol based on flexible channel reservation; called SCRP. In the design of this protocol, a node dynamically reserves channel resources through a channel reservation frame (SRT). In a high-load network scenario, it effectively reduces the network conflict rate and ensures the

QoS of high-priority services. In addition, due to the high Priority services have more transmission opportunities, so the transmission delay will also be greatly reduced. When the high-priority service in the network is not saturated, the node can also cancel the reserved time slot through the SRT frame, so that other services can be transmitted normally, ensuring the fairness of the transmission of other services in the network. In addition, the SCRP protocol does not use complex algorithms, only some simple frame interaction in the network, which means that the SCRP protocol has a low complexity.

The contributions of this article are summarized as follows:

1) A soft channel in-band reservation protocol, named SCRP, is proposed in this paper. SCRP can significantly reduce the transmission delay of high priority services and improve network performance.
2) The complexity of the protocol is low, and the compatibility with the IEEE 802.11 standard is good, which is convenient for engineering implementation.

The rest of this article is organized as follows. In the second section, the deficiencies of the EDCA mechanism are briefly introduced. The third section introduces the SCRP protocol; the fourth section introduces the simulation results and analysis; and the fifth section summarizes this paper and the prospect of future research directions.

2   Motivation

2.1   Related Work Brief Introduction to EDCA

In the IEEE 802.11ac standard, the EDCA mechanism in IEEE 802.11e is adopted to solve the QoS guarantee. As shown in Fig. 1, the EDCA algorithm defines the upper 8 types of service categories and the MAC layer 4 types of access categories AC, 8 types of TC Mapped to 4 types of AC queues, that is, each channel defines 4 access categories, access categories can be expressed as BK, BE, VI, VO, priority from low to high, each access category has an independent send The queue achieves the purpose of distinguishing priorities by assigning different contention parameters for each access category. The meaning of each AC is shown in Table 1.

Table 1. AC vs TC vs traffic type.

Access category	Traffic type	Traffic category
AC_BK	Background traffic	0 and 3
AC_BE	Best effort traffic	1 and 2
AC_VI	Video traffic	4 and 5
AC_VO	Voice traffic	6 and 7

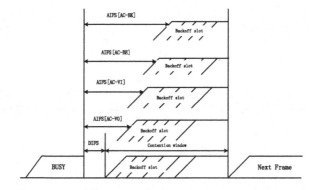

Fig. 1. Enhanced distributed channel access.

Each node has four back-off state machines. The pair of sending queue and the corresponding random back-off state machine is called a virtual internal site QSTA. The node changes the network's completely fair competition by setting different EDCA parameters for QSTA. EDCA parameters include CWmin, CWmax, TXOP, and AIFS. A high-priority QSTA has a smaller contention window (CW), longer TXOP, and shorter AIFS. Therefore, high-priority services have more transmission opportunities than low-priority services.

2.2 Motivation

Under the traditional IEEE 802.11 standard, the EDCA mechanism can well meet the QoS and low-latency access of high-priority services. However, with the popularity of smart phones and the dramatic increase in network load, EDCA has been unable to meet existing network scenarios As shown in Fig. 2, the nodes in the cell are very densely distributed. Although high-priority service nodes 1 and 2 have a smaller competition window, the competition between nodes is very serious. These services still cannot guarantee QoS and Lower access delay. Therefore, we need an enhanced MAC protocol to ensure low-latency access and QoS for high-priority services in a high-density environment.

3   Proposed Flexible Channel Reservation Protocol

3.1   Protocol Design

In order to cope with high load and complex network environment, improve the QoS of high-priority services and reduce access delay, an enhanced MAC protocol SCRP is proposed. As shown in Fig. 3, the main idea of SCRP is to use channel reservation on the entire channel to ensure all nodes'Synchronization, separate transmission of time slots reserved for high-priority services; SCRP protocol defines two transmission modes: implicit reservation mode using DATA-ACK and explicit reservation mode SRT-SRT_RES.

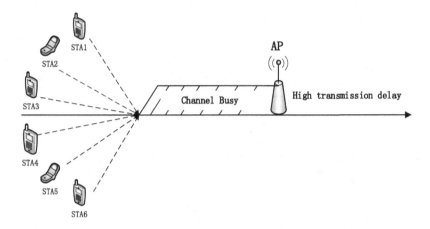

Fig. 2. Densely distributed nodes.

(1) If the current channel is within the time period $\tau_1(t_1, t_2)$, $\tau_1(t_1, t_2)$ has been reserved by the last reservation node; the reservation node monitors the entire channel through carrier sensing until the channel is idle and the back-off is completed.

(2) After the backoff is completed, DATA is sent over the entire channel, and DATA implicitly includes the next reserved time slot $\tau_2(t_1, t_2)$ as a time period for its independent transmission.

(3) The node receiving the DATA obtains the future time slot $\tau_2(t_1, t_2)$, suspends its own back-off state machine within $\tau_2(t_1, t_2)$, and avoids competing with the reserved node for the channel.

(4) The node receiving DATA replies with ACK, and the entire transmission process is internal $\tau_1(t_1, t_2)$.

(5) When the time slot arrives $\tau_2(t_1, t_2)$, the reservation node transmits independently in the current time slot without interference from other nodes, and the process repeats steps 1–4.

Consider a situation where, when the reserved time slot $\tau_2(t_1, t_2)$ arrives in the future, if the reserved node has packet to send, the node can make full use of $\tau_2(t_1, t_2)$ for transmission. But, if the node currently has no packet to transmit, other nodes cannot transmit within $\tau_2(t_1, t_2)$, so the wireless resources are greatly wasted.

In order to overcome this shortcoming, as shown in Fig. 4, the SCRP protocol proposes an soft reservation canceling scheme, the process is as follows:

1) If the current channel is within the time period $\tau_1(t_1, t_2)$, $\tau_1(t_1, t_2)$ has been reserved by the last reservation node; the reservation node monitors the entire channel through carrier sensing until the channel is idle and the back-off is completed.

2) After the backoff is completed, send SRT frames on the entire channel to reserve a future time slot $\tau_2(t_1, t_2)$ as a time period for independent transmission. At the same time, determine whether there is a business in the

current time slot $\tau_2(t_1, t_2)$ that the node needs to send; if there is a business that needs to be transmitted, pass SRT frame clear time slot $\tau_1(t_1, t_2)$ will be used for independent data transmission of this node, otherwise, the reserved time slot will be released explicitly through SRT, and this time slot will be occupied by other services through random competition.

3) The node receiving the SRT frame acquires the future time slot $\tau_2(t_1, t_2)$, sets its own back-off state machine to be suspended in $\tau_2(t_1, t_2)$, and avoids competing with the reserved node for the channel.

4) After the SRT frame is sent, the reservation node sends DATA to the destination node at intervals.

5) The receiving node replies with ACK, and the entire transmission process is inside $\tau_1(t_1, t_2)$.

6) When the time slot $\tau_2(t_1, t_2)$ comes, the process repeats steps 1–5.

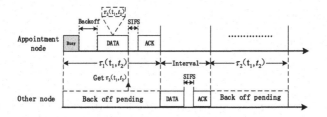

Fig. 3. The procedure of the implicit order.

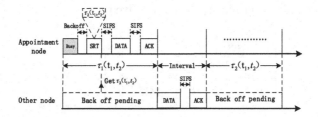

Fig. 4. The procedure of the explicit order.

3.2 Resolved Hidden Nodes

Due to the limitations of wireless transmission, the transmitted signal will rapidly decay in a certain range, and when it exceeds a certain distance, the data will not be successfully received. This range is called the effective transmission range. Similar to the RCS/CTS solution to the problem of hidden terminals, the interaction of SRT frames in the SCRP protocol will also have hidden terminals. As shown in Fig. 5, when the reserved time slot comes, STA1 sends an SRT frame, and all nodes in the range It can correctly receive SRT, including the destination node AP of STA1. However, due to the limitation of the transmission distance, STA2 cannot receive the SRT frame, so STA2 does not know that it has been reserved by STA1; STA2 competes for the channel randomly, and then also sends the AP to the AP Send DATA, which caused a serious conflict of STA1'DATA.

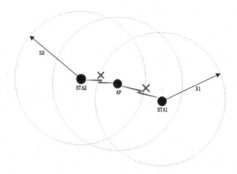

Fig. 5. Hidden nodes problem.

In order to overcome the problem of hidden terminals. As shown in Fig. 6: The SRT frame needs to interact between the AP and the STA; the process is as shown. First, STA1 sends an SRT frame to the AP. After receiving the SRT, the AP replies to SRT_RES. The reserved time slot carried in the SRT_RES frame is the same as the SRT; SRT_RES will inform the AP The time slot of the node within the range has been occupied; through the two-step handshake of SRT and SRT_RES, the hidden terminal problem is solved.

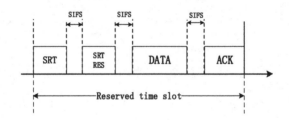

Fig. 6. SRT/SRT_RES Interaction process.

3.3   Frame Design

In SCRP, the frame structure of SRT and SRT_RES needs to be designed. SRT and SRT_RES are similar in function to RTS/CTS, but in SCRP, they also have the function of clearing the current time slot and reserving the next time slot.

In the SCRP protocol, the frame structures of SRT and SRT_RES are as shown in Fig. 7. Both SRT and SRT_RES have 6-byte ST and SE fields, which are used to indicate reserved time slots. The Duration field is used to indicate the occupied length of the current time slot. All nodes need to process SRT1 and SRT_RES frames, so the DA field is the broadcast address. The difference between SRT and SRT_RES is that SRT has a Flag field, which occupies one byte. When Flag is 1, it is clear that the time slot is occupied, otherwise the time slot will be occupied by other services through random competition.

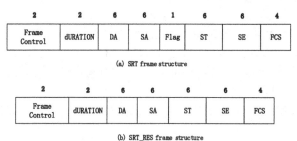

(a) SRT frame structure

(b) SRT_RES frame structure

Fig. 7. Frame structure.

4 Simulation and Analysis

In order to evaluate the performance of our proposed SCRP, we build a simulation platform based on NS3. In order to make SCRP performance easier to evaluate, we assume that the channel is ideal. Nodes are divided into high-priority service nodes and low-priority service nodes, and all services can be considered saturated. High-priority service nodes use the SCRP protocol, and the remaining nodes use EDCA to access. We assume that during the simulation, the appointment period and duration will not be adjusted dynamically. We will evaluate SCRP performance from three aspects: access delay, service packet loss rate and service throughput.

The simulation parameters are as Table 2 shown, we choose the appointment period to be 10 ms and the appointment duration to be 4 ms. As the network load continues to increase, observe the performance comparison of SCRP and EDCA.

Figure 8 shows the change in throughput of high-priority service nodes as the cell load increases. As the network load increases, the throughput of both EDCA and SCRP has decreased. This is because the high collision rate caused by the increased load is inevitable. However, it can be clearly seen that Performance of SCRP protocol is 125% higher than that of EDCA.

The change in the access delay of high-priority service nodes as the cell load increases is shown in Fig. 9. As the network load increases, the access delay of

Table 2. Simulation parameter.

Parameter	Value in simulation
Bandwidth	20 MHz
Package length	1500 Bytes
MCS	9
NSS	1
CWmin of high priority traffic	7
CWmax of high priority traffic	15
AIFS of high priority traffic	34 μs
CWmin of low priority traffic	15
CWmax of low priority traffic	63
AIFS of high low traffic	43 μs
SIFS	16 μs
Slot time	9 μs

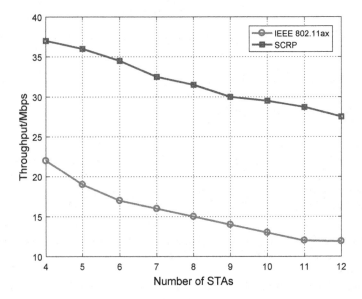

Fig. 8. Throughput varies with the number of STAs.

both EDCA and SCRP has increased. However, it can be clearly seen that SCRP has lower access latency and is more suitable for low-latency access for high-priority services, Compared with EDCA, SCRP protocol reduces transmission delay by 20%.

The change in the packet loss rate of high-priority service nodes as the cell load increases is shown in Fig. 10. As the network load increases, the packet

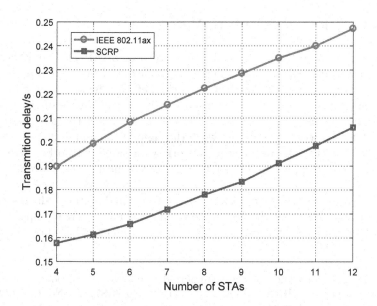

Fig. 9. Number of STAs vs transmission delay.

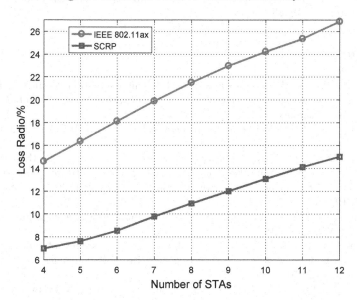

Fig. 10. Number of STAs vs loss radio.

loss rates of EDCA and SCRP both increase. But compared with EDCA, SCRP has a lower packet loss rate, which guarantees QoS well, Compared with EDCA, SCRP protocol reduces packet loss rate by 40%.

5   Conclusions and Future Work

This article proposes the enhanced MAC protocol SCRP based on the IEEE 802.11be standard. Its purpose is to reduce the access delay of high-priority services and improve the throughput of the entire network. Readers can improve the user experience in engineering practice according to the design of the protocol. Simulation research shows that SCRP significantly reduces the access latency of high-priority services, improves network throughput, and guarantees QoS while reducing the packet loss rate of the network. Compared with other algorithms, SCRP has lower complexity. Therefore, this agreement has better overall performance.

In the future, we still have work to do. For the SCRP protocol, the reservation period and the length of the reservation time slot have a great impact on the network performance. We need to optimize the parameters based on the arrival rate of the service.

Acknowledgement. This work was supported in part by the National Natural Science Foundations of CHINA (Grant No. 61771390, No. 61871322, No. 61771392, No. 61271279, and No. 61501373), the National Science and Technology Major Project (Grant No. 2016ZX03001018-004), and Science and Technology on Avionics Integration Laboratory (20185553035).

References

1. Laya, A., Alonso, L., Alonsozarate, J.: Efficient contention resolution in highly dense LTE networks for machine type communications. In: IEEE Global Communications Conference (2016)
2. Bellalta, B.: IEEE 802.11ax: high-efficiency WLANs. IEEE Wirel. Commun. **23**(1), 38–46 (2016)
3. Bankov, D., Didenko, A., Khorov, E., Loginov, V., Lyakhov, A.: IEEE 802.11ax uplink scheduler to minimize delay: a classic problem with new constraints. In: International Symposium on Personal, Indoor and Mobile Radio Communications (IEEE PIMRC 2017) (2017)
4. Bellalta, B., Kosek-Szott, K.: AP-initiated multi-user transmissions in IEEE 802.11ax WLANs (2017)
5. Niu, Y., Li, Y., Jin, D., Su, L., Vasilakos, A.V.: A survey of millimeter wave (mmWave) communications for 5G: opportunities and challenges. Wireless Netw. **21**(8), 1–20 (2015)
6. Bo, L., Qiao, Q., Yan, Z., Mao, Y.: Survey on OFDMA based MAC protocols for the next generation WLAN. In: Wireless Communications & Networking Conference Workshops (2015)
7. Studer, C., Durisi, G.: Quantized massive MU-MIMO-OFDM uplink. IEEE Trans. Commun. **64**(6), 2387–2399 (2016)
8. Yang, M., Li, B., Yan, Z., Yan, Y.: AP coordination and full-duplex enabled multi-band operation for the next generation WLAN: IEEE 802.11be (EHT). In: 2019 11th International Conference on Wireless Communications and Signal Processing (WCSP) (2019)

9. Gao, S., Cheng, X., Yang, L.: Spatial multiplexing with limited RF chains: generalized beamspace modulation (GBM) for mmWave massive MIMO. IEEE J. Sel. Areas Commun. **PP**(99), 1 (2019)
10. Shi, Z., Zhang, C., Fu, Y., Wang, H., Yang, G., Ma, S.: Achievable diversity order of HARQ-aided downlink NOMA systems. IEEE Trans. Veh. Technol. **69**(1), 471–487 (2020)
11. Abu-Khadrah, A.I., Zakaria, Z., Othman, M., Zin, M.S.I.M.: Enhance the performance of EDCA protocol by adapting contention window. Wireless Pers. Commun. **96**(2), 1945–1971 (2017). https://doi.org/10.1007/s11277-017-4277-1
12. Akinyemi, I., Yang, S.H.: Feedback control algorithm for optimal throughput in IEEE 802.11e EDCA networks. Syst. Sci. Control Eng. Open Access J. **5**(1), 321–330 (2017)
13. Lan, Y.W., Yeh, J.H., Chen, J.C., Chou, Z.T.: Performance enhancement of IEEE 802.11e EDCA by contention adaption. In: IEEE Vehicular Technology Conference (2005)
14. Abu-Khadrah, A., Zakaria, Z., Othman, M.A.: New technique to enhance quality of service support for real time applications in EDCA protocol. Int. Rev. Comput. Softw. **9**(3), 541 (2014)
15. Fan, Z.: Throughput and QoS optimization for EDCA-based IEEE 802.11 WLANs. Wireless Pers. Commun. **43**(4), 1279–1290 (2007). https://doi.org/10.1007/s11277-007-9301-4
16. Alam, M.K., Latif, S.A., Akter, M., Anwar, F., Hasan, M.K.: Enhancements of the dynamic TXOP limit in EDCA through a high-speed wireless campus network. Wireless Pers. Commun. **90**(4), 1647–1672 (2016). https://doi.org/10.1007/s11277-016-3416-4

Optimal Four-Dimensional Route Searching Methodology for Civil Aircrafts

Evgeny S. Neretin, Alexander S. Budkov$^{(\boxtimes)}$,
and Andrey S. Ivanov

Moscow Aviation Institute,
4, Volokolamskoe Highway, Moscow 125993, Russian Federation
kaf703@mai.ru, asbudkov@gmail.com

Abstract. The work is devoted to the analysis of problems in the implementation of four-dimensional navigation routes in civil aviation, the determination of the minimum necessary requirements for a decision support system that would provide a solution to these problems, as well as the development of a methodology for optimal four-dimensional route searching to provide the crew with a set of necessary information on possible flight strategies in case of difficult weather conditions. In the course of the work, the analysis of discrete and continuous optimization methods, as well as methods of operational trajectory planning has analyzed. The developed methodology for the optimal four-dimensional route searching is based on the A-star method of graph theory using the cellular decomposition of three-dimensional airspace. The methodology provides solutions for 4 optimization criteria's, takes into account the influence of wind conditions and no fly zones, as well as the aircraft performances. In the conclusion of the work, experimental results are presented that confirm the effectiveness of the proposed method.

Keywords: Decision support system · Flight management system · 4-D navigation

1 Introduction

A key function of four-dimensional navigation is the aircraft's ability to arrive at a required point in space at a required time of arrival (RTA). Existing modern flight management systems already perform such a function. This function is called RTA.

First of all, in order to perform the function, the crew at the stage of pre-flight preparation must enter the following minimum necessary information by the interaction with the human-machine interface:

– waypoint – determine the waypoint in the flight plan with the time restriction;
– RTA – determine the desired arrival time at a given waypoint of the route;
– type of RTA – determine the time limits that must be carried out by the aircraft. Three types of restrictions that are currently supported: AT - at a strictly specified time; AT or Before (AB) - at a specified time of arrival or earlier; AT or After (AA) - at a specified time of arrival or later.

© ICST Institute for Computer Sciences, Social Informatics and Telecommunications Engineering 2021
Published by Springer Nature Switzerland AG 2021. All Rights Reserved
B. Li et al. (Eds.): IoTaaS 2020, LNICST 346, pp. 462–473, 2021.
https://doi.org/10.1007/978-3-030-67514-1_37

Further, after calculating the time profile of the flight during its execution, the function provides continuous time of arrival errors monitoring. Acceptable error is limited by regulatory documentation [1, 2].

During the flight along the route, a situation may occur when the error exceeds the acceptable values. In these cases the system will respond with an information message about the inability to arrive in time. Also, if complex weather conditions or conflict situations arise with the other air traffic participants along the formed route, the reaction of the system will also be just a notification.

Thus, as a result of the analysis of the RTA function principle of operation, we can conclude that in the event of an emergency, the system will respond only a notification that it is impossible to provide the current time limit.

But such functionality may not be enough in the context of global management of four-dimensional trajectories where the world civil aviation community is currently moving.

A system providing four-dimensional trajectories support must be resistant to external disturbances leading to route changes, such as: difficult weather conditions along route sections, conflict situations with other aircraft, restricted areas. The system should simplify the decision-making process as much as possible and provide the crew with the most complete necessary information.

In such situations, today the air traffic controller is responsible for making decisions, as well as maintaining and controlling each aircraft. In conditions of high airspace congestion, such situations will at best lead to a violation of the integrity of the control of the four-dimensional trajectories of each air traffic participant, and in the worst case, catastrophic situations are possible.

2 Decision Support System Functions

To solve the problems identified as a result of the analysis that arise when flying along four-dimensional navigation routes, the proposed decision support system should provide:

- solving the problem of the optimal four-dimensional route searching;
- issuing the necessary information to the information-control field of the cockpit about available flight strategies in a specific typical situation.

Let us consider in more detail the task of finding the optimal four-dimensional route, since it is this function of the system that must solve the navigation problem.

First of all, during the optimal route searching, it is necessary to determine optimization criteria. For the problem under consideration, it is necessary to find four optimal routes according to the following criteria:

- minimization the difference between the RTA at the point and the estimated time of arrival (ETA). This criterion has the highest priority, as it determines the availability of a solution that meets the requirements of four-dimensional navigation [2]. A solution to this criterion does not always exist, therefore, in its absence, a solution is not provided;

- fuel consumption minimization;
- flight time minimization;
- Multi-criteria task: fuel consumption and flight time minimization.

In order to find a solution by the last criterion, the value of cost index (CI) parameter is used. It characterizes the weight of two criteria in relation to each other. The parameter is entered manually by the crew or determined by the airline's strategy. The parameter, as a rule, is determined by a value from 0 to 99. The extreme values of the parameter characterize the criteria of fuel consumption and flight time minimization.

When forming each of the described criteria, the following factors must be considered:

- wind value and direction along the calculated flight path;
- zones of difficult weather conditions or areas of space prohibited for flight;
- aircraft flight performances, especially for the vertical flight profile calculating.

Each of these factors significantly affects the final result, namely, the calculated parameters of the optimal route. Ignoring these factors in the calculations will lead to an erroneous final result, which with a high degree of probability will not be optimal by the desired criterion.

If with forbidden zones everything is quite simple - it is forbidden to cross certain zones of space when constructing a route, with the aircraft flight characteristics - one cannot ignore the capabilities of the aircraft in terms of speed limits, altitudes, masses, set gradients, etc., then in order to show the importance of accounting wind conditions when searching for the optimal route for each of the described criteria, we consider global wind maps at altitudes of approximately 20,000 feet and 35,000 feet, shown in Figs. 1, 2, respectively.

Wind speed scale

0 km/h   80 km/h   160 km/h   360 km/h

Fig. 1. 20,000 feet global wind map

Wind speed scale

      0 km/h   80 km/h   160 km/h   360 km/h

Fig. 2. 35,000 feet global wind map

The following conclusions can be drawn from these figures:

- wind direction is constant only in certain areas;
- with an increase in flight altitude, the wind strength changes significantly (usually increases), and the direction changes only partially.

At the next step of solving the problem of the optimal route searching, it is necessary to calculate the parameters of each of the sections of the route trajectory, such as: fuel consumption, flight time, climb gradient, required climb distance, etc. The calculation of these parameters is performed in the performance database (PDB) [3]. In the PDB for a specific aircraft for all phases of flight, calculation tables of parameters are given depending on the given mode and flight conditions.

Also, during the process of solving the air navigation problem, it is necessary to choose a coordinate system suitable for it, since the accuracy of the calculation of the navigation parameters of the aircraft location, as well as the parameters of the calculated trajectory, depends on its choice. Since when solving the problem, it is necessary to consider ranges of more than 500 km, it must be taken into account that the meridians converge at the poles of the Earth, and, therefore, depending on latitude, the price of dividing the degree of longitude will change in linear terms. To account for these distortions, a transformation in the Gauss-Kruger projection is used. The map sweep in the Gauss-Krueger projection is shown in Fig. 3.

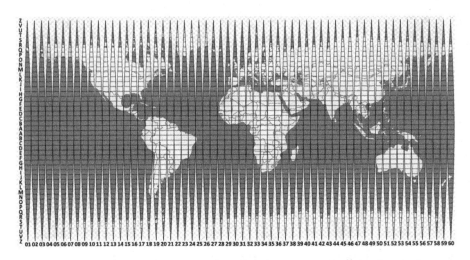

Fig. 3. Map sweep in the Gauss-Kruger projection

The use of the Gauss-Krueger projection provides the possibility of constructing a system of plane rectangular coordinates on the territory of the entire Earth and makes it possible to obtain rather large sections of the earth's surface with almost no distortion. Due to this, graph theory methods become applicable when searching for the optimal route. Also, when forming the vertices of the graph, it becomes possible to calculate the values of the information necessary at the vertices of the graph, for example:

- accessibility of a cell for flight (projection of forbidden zones);
- the value and direction of the wind at each ceil of airspace.

The ability to calculate for each vertex of the graph of meteorological and navigation information makes it possible to solve with high accuracy the task of finding the optimal route according to the given criteria.

3   Methodology of Optimal Four-Dimensional Route Searching

As a result of the analysis of scientific papers [4–7] on the subject of the problem in which various approaches to solving the problem of the optimal route searching are given, the following conclusions are drawn:

- for the task of the optimal four-dimensional route searching, the procedure for planning a three-dimensional trajectory and determining the speed profile is divided into two stages. The first step is to search for the trajectory in the horizontal plane, and then on its basis the optimization of the vertical profile is performed. But even taking into account the influence of all the described factors, such division into two stages will lead to an erroneous result as a result of the search for the optimal trajectory according to the required criteria for four-dimensional navigation.

- for the task of the optimal four-dimensional route searching, only criteria for fuel consumption and flight time minimization are used. This does not take into account the most important optimization criterion for the four-dimensional navigation problem – time delay minimization.

Therefore, it is imperative to have a procedure that would optimize the three-dimensional trajectory in one step, taking into account the factors influencing it.

The methodology that provides the search for solutions to the problem of planning the optimal four-dimensional route must meet the following requirements:

- search for solutions according to four optimality criteria:
  • time delay minimization;
  • flight time minimization;
  • fuel consumption minimization;
  • fuel consumption and flight time minimization.
- consider airspace parameters (wind, restricted zones, zones of difficult weather conditions) and aircraft flight performances;
- ensure the calculation of many existing four-dimensional trajectories in one step without dividing the vertical profile from the horizontal one.

This technique can be represented in the form of an algorithm consisting of 8 consecutive steps.

The block diagram of the developed algorithm for the optimal four-dimensional route searching that satisfies the above requirements is presented in Fig. 4.

At step 1, the input data necessary for the operation of the optimal route search algorithms is entered.

At step 2, the airspace parameters are loaded. By airspace parameters we mean information about the wind in each cell of the space and the presence of restricted zones for flight or zones of difficult weather conditions.

At step 3, the function calculates the parameters of the set of existing four-dimensional trajectories. The function provides a search for a set of trajectories for all acceptable flight speeds, as well as for all acceptable flight levels. This function is based on the algorithm of A-star graph theory methods and is used to solve the problem in the two-dimensional space. In order to take into account the flight capabilities at a different altitude from the initial altitude, the function provides an additional calculation for the climb and descent profiles for the corresponding trajectories. The result of the A-star algorithm for each flight speed and altitude is the calculation of the flight cost function. To calculate the cost of the flight, the CI value is taken equal to 0, which generally corresponds to the criterion of minimum fuel consumption. Thus, the result for each search cycle with a fixed altitude and speed of flight is one of the most fuel-efficient trajectory. And the result of the whole function is a lot of fuel-efficient trajectories for all permissible altitudes and speeds.

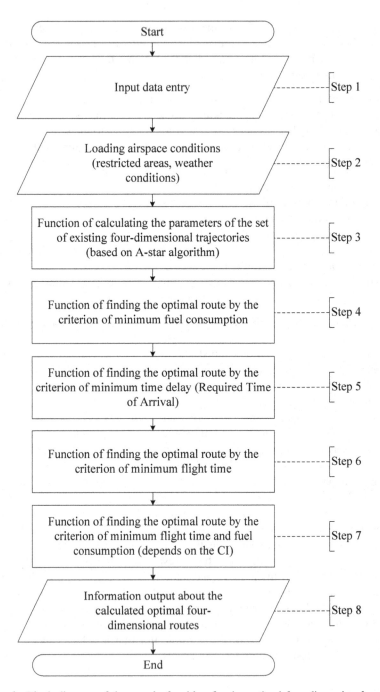

Fig. 4. Block diagram of the search algorithm for the optimal four-dimensional route

For each flight path according to the results of step 3, the following are calculated:

- amount of fuel consumed;
- flight time;
- flight distance;
- the coordinates of each cell in the airspace through which the calculated trajectory passes in the local topocentric and geodetic coordinate systems.

At steps 4–7, the search for the optimal route is performed according to the optimization criteria.

As a result, we get solutions based on four optimization criteria. These results can be provided for decision making to the crew.

4   Experimental Results

In order to confirm the correctness of the algorithm's operation, comprehensive testing was carried out for many different conditions. The main results are given by an example. Let us consider the situation when a zone of difficult weather conditions arises on the cruise phase of flight, which does not allow to fly the predefined route anymore. It is necessary to find 4 optimal routes from the start point with the coordinates of the aircraft position to the final point of the cruise phase (top of descent point). The initial flight parameters are shown in the following Table 1.

Table 1. Initial flight parameters.

Start altitude, ft	Aircraft weight, kg	Start point coordinates	End point coordinates	UTC	RTA
30000	40000	N55° E037°	N55° E044°	21:00:00	21:43:00

In order300 to demonstrate the necessity to take into account each of the requirements for the methodology for finding the optimal four-dimensional route, first of all, we will perform the algorithm without the influence of the wind with the loaded data of the zones of difficult weather conditions.

Information about optimal routes without wind influence is presented in Table 2.

Table 2. Information about optimal routes without wind influence.

Criteria\Info	Altitude, ft	Speed, mach	Distance, NM	Fuel consumption, kg	Enroute time
Minimum fuel	40000	0.74	275	1084	00:38:58
Minimum time	40000	0.78	285	1112	00:38:01
Minimum fuel/time	40000	0.76	282	1096	00:38:29
Minimum delay	40000	0.72	275	1120	00:43:00

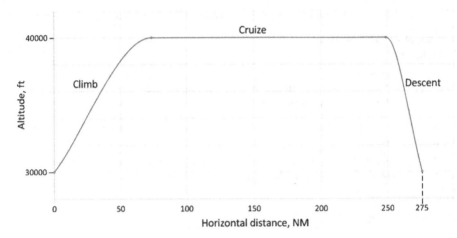

Fig. 5. Vertical profile of the minimum fuel optimal route without wind influence

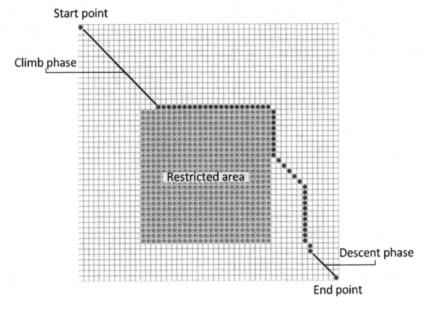

Fig. 6. Horizontal profile of the minimum fuel optimal route without wind influence

As an example, Figs. 5, 6 show the trajectories of the vertical and horizontal profiles of the route, which is optimal according to the criterion of minimum fuel consumption without taking into account the wind influence.

The next step is to perform the algorithm with similar initial data and zones of difficult weather conditions, but with the influence of wind. The direction of the wind is divided into tailwind and headwind zones. Graphical interpretation of the wind for the test is shown in Fig. 7.

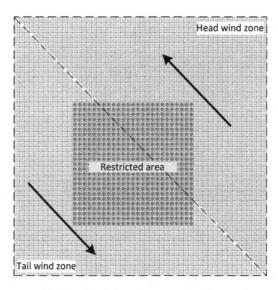

Fig. 7. Wind direction zones for the test

Information about optimal routes with wind influence is presented in Table 3.

Table 3. Information about optimal routes with wind influence.

Criteria\Info	Altitude, ft	Speed, mach	Distance, NM	Fuel consumption, kg	Enroute time
Minimum fuel	36000	0.8	302	1024	00:36:17
Minimum time	36000	0.81	301	1038	00:35:40
Minimum fuel/time	36000	0.8	302	1024	00:36:17
Minimum delay	36000	0.72	302	1065	00:43:00

Figures 8, 9 show the trajectories of the vertical and horizontal profiles of the route, which is optimal according to the criterion of minimum fuel consumption with taking into account the wind influence.

Results of the analysis of two examples show that, despite the distance increasing of the route as a result of the route searching with the wind influence, the fuel consumption has decreased. It can also be seen from the results that in order to obtain a more favorable result, it is necessary to analyze the three-dimensional space, because in the result another flight level has selected as an optimal level.

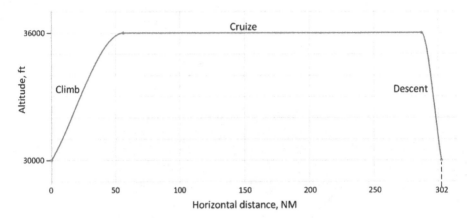

Fig. 8. Vertical profile of the minimum fuel optimal route with wind influence

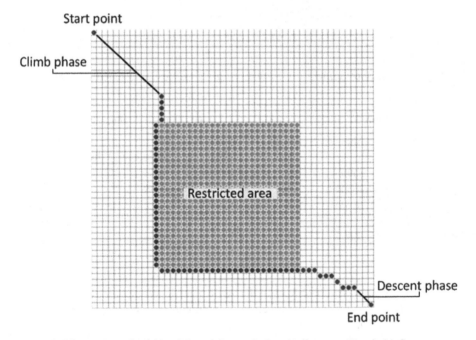

Fig. 9. Horizontal profile of the minimum fuel optimal route with wind influence

5   Conclusion

As a result of the work, the analysis of the problems that arise when performing four-dimensional navigation routes in civil aviation is performed, the requirements for a decision support system that will provide a solution to these problems are identified, and the methodology for the optimal four-dimensional route searching is developed.

The results of the conducted testing confirmed the adequacy of the results of the algorithm, and also confirmed the need to take into account each factor that effects on the searching results for the optimal four-dimensional route.

References

1. RTCA/DO-283 2015 Minimum Operational Performance Standards for Required Navigation Performance for Area Navigation
2. RTCA/DO-236C 2013 Minimum Aviation System Performance Standards: Required Navigation Performance for Area Navigation
3. Eurocontrol: User manual for the Base of aircraft Data (BADA) Revision 3.14, EEC Technical/Scientific Report №17/05/29-143, June 2017
4. Degtyarev, O.V.: Methodical and algorithmic issues of constructing four-dimensional flight routes for long-range aircrafts. J. Comput. Syst. Sci. Int. **45**, 110–124 (2006)
5. Patrón, R.S.F.: Flight trajectories optimization under the influence of winds using genetic algorithms. ETS, Laboratory of Research in Active Controls, Avionics and AeroServoElasticity (www.larcase.etsmtl.ca), Montreal, Quebec, H3C-1K3, Canada
6. Fett, G.D.: Aircraft route optimization using the A-star algorithm, USA, pp. 1–68, March 2014
7. Ramasamy, S., Sabatini, R., Gardi, A., Kistan, T.: Next generation flight management system for real-time trajectory based operations. Appl. Mech. Mater. **629**, 344–349 (2014)

Multi-list Design and FPGA Implementation Method of OLSR protocol

Hongyu Zhang, Bo Li, Zhongjiang Yan[(✉)], and Mao Yang

School of Electronics and Information, Northwestern Polytechnical University,
Xi'an, China
chong@mail.nwpu.edu.cn,
{libo.npu,zhjyan,yangmao}@nwpu.edu.cn

Abstract. Ad Hoc network is a new networking technology that does not rely on preset communication facilities, and is one of the important components of the next generation wireless communication network system. The OLSR (Optimized Link State Routing) protocol is a classic proactive routing protocol in Ad Hoc networks. Most of the existing research is based on software, there has not been a case of using hardware to implement the OLSR protocol. The core of implementing OLSR protocol based on FPGA (Field Programmable Gate Array) is the design of memory management table. This paper proposes a multi-link list design and FPGA implementation method, which effectively avoids the conflicts that will arise when using memory management tables.

Keywords: Ad Hoc · OLSR · FPGA · Memory management

1 Introduction

Ad Hoc network is a new and developing network technology in the current wireless communication field [1], which has the characteristics of no central control node, multi-hop routing, and dynamic topology [2]. It can provide flexible and convenient communication without fixed infrastructure support, which has a very wide range of application scenarios in today's society. A good routing protocol design can improve the overall performance of Ad Hoc networks [3], which is one of the hot spots and difficulties in the research of Ad hoc networks.

The Optimized Link State Routing protocol for mobile Ad Hoc networks is an optimization of the classical link state algorithm tailored to the requirements of a mobile wireless LAN [4], which is a table-driven active protocol. In the protocol, adjacent nodes periodically exchange HELLO packets [5] to realize neighbor discovery and link detection. Then MPR (Multipoint reply) nodes periodically forward TC packets to spread topology information to the entire network. Finally, the route calculation is realized by dynamically establishing and updating network topology. Among them, the addition of MPR mechanism reduces the occupation of bandwidth resources due to the transmission of control packet information [6], which greatly reduces the overhead of network transmission.

Most of the research on Ad Hoc network at home and abroad is based on software. Existing network simulation tools mainly include: OPNET, NS-2, GloMoSim, OMNET++, NS-3, etc. [7], there has not been a case of implementing OLSR protocol based on FPGA.

In the Ad Hoc network, by connecting the hardware and the embedded chip, the power consumption can be reduced while the operation speed is increased, and other operations can be performed at the same time [8]. In addition, using hardware to implement the OLSR protocol can establish calls and change the dynamic topology faster [9]. Therefore, the implementation of OLSR protocol based on FPGA can effectively improve the speed and reduce the power consumption, which will have a great practical use.

The core of implementing the OLSR protocol based on FPGA is the design of the memory management table. The main difficulty is to solve the conflicts caused by "multiple modules simultaneously read or write to the same port of the same memory management table", which are generated during the work of the memory management table based on the "RAM + FIFO" design concept.

2 Implementation Model of Multi-link List Based on FPGA in OLSR protocol

With reference to the introduction of the OLSR protocol in the rfc3626 standard document, this article designs and implements an FPGA-based OLSR protocol. During its implementation, the FPGA-based OLSR project is divided into five parts: packet sending module, packet receiving module, memory management module, expired entry deletion module, and time counter module. Each part can be further divided into several sub-modules, the relationship of them is shown in Fig. 1.

During the work of the OLSR protocol, nodes send and process HELLO or TC packets by the packet sending module and the packet receiving module, which can continuously update the local memory management tables to calculate the shortest path from this node to other nodes, and store them in the local routing table. In order to maintain the local routing table, the expired entry deletion module combines the time counter module to periodically read and delete expired entries in each memory management table. It is not difficult to find that as the core of the OLSR protocol design, the memory management table has close information interaction with every module. The working relationship between each memory management table and other function modules is shown in Fig. 2.

For the memory management table, this article adopts the idea of one-way linked list, and uses two storage structures of true dual-port RAM and FIFO to

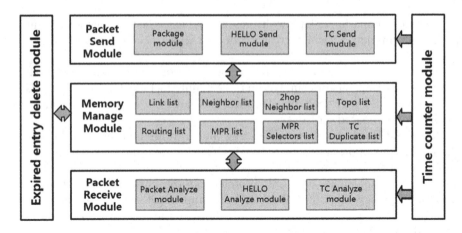

Fig. 1. OLSR routing algorithm module division.

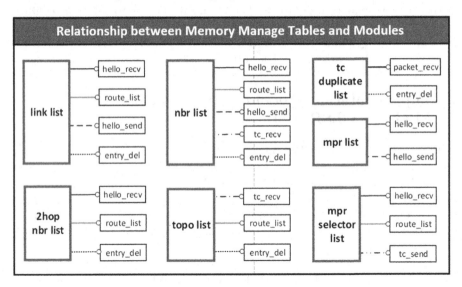

Fig. 2. Relationship between tables and modules.

complete the design. Each storage unit in RAM contains three parts of information: header, key data of this storage table, and address of the previous entry. FIFO is used to store the valid RAM entry addresses. Based on such table structure, referring to the processing idea of the one-way linked list, the modules can add, query, delete, traverse and update the memory management table entries through the read and write operations on the RAM A or B ports.

With reference to Fig. 2 and 3, it can be seen that the memory management table whose main body is true dual-port RAM needs to meet the read and write requirements of multiple modules at the same time. Then, when the read or write demand exceeds the available number of 2, there will be conflicts that have a significant impact on the result. Therefore, in the implementation of the FPGA-based OLSR protocol, the biggest difficulty is how to solve the conflict problem that occurs when "multiple modules in the OLSR project simultaneously read or write to the same port of the same table" in the case of "less RAM ports with more demand".

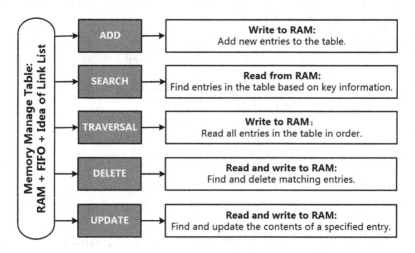

Fig. 3. List function and meaning.

Taking the neighbor table with the most associated modules as an example, the relationship among RAM port, function and module is shown below. As Fig. 4 shows, the arrow on the left indicates whether the A/B port of RAM is read or written when using a function of the table, and the right line connects the function and the module using this function.

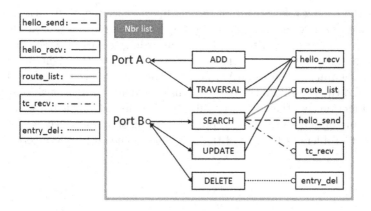

Fig. 4. Port-function-module relationship diagram of the neighbor table.

The port read and write status of the neighbor table RAM is shown in Table 1. It can be seen that the number of read and write requirements of each module in the olsr project for this table greatly exceeds the number of read ports that a true dual-port RAM can provide. In this way, when the situation of "HELLO receive module and route list module use the traversal function of A port at the same time" or "route list, HELLO send, TC receive module use the search function of B port at the same time" occurs, there will be conflicts which can affect the working process of the OLSR protocol.

Table 1. Neighbor table port supply and demand.

Port	Supply	Demand
Port A: read	1	2
Port A: write	1	1
Port B: read	1	6
Port B: write	1	2

3   Solution for Conflicts in the Use of Memory Management

In order to solve the conflict problem that occurs when "multiple modules in the OLSR project simultaneously read or write to the same port of the same table", the following two aspects are considered to improve the memory management module of the original OLSR project.

3.1   Sort Out Timing Relationship

Sort out the timing relationship of the modules associated with each table, and put modules with "clear timing relationship" on the same port. Take the neighbor table as an example. After modifying according to this idea, the "ram port-function-module" relationship changed from the left to the right in Fig. 5. At this time, the function on the RAM port A is only related to the HELLO receive module, and the HELLO receive module has a sequential relationship in the use of these functions, so there is no possibility of conflict. On this basis, if the possibility of modules associated with port B working simultaneously is eliminated, the conflict problem of the use of the neighbor table can be effectively solved.

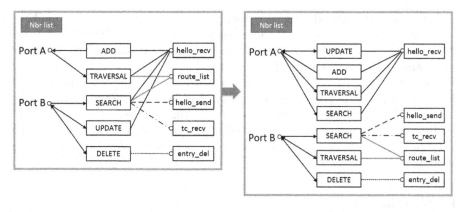

Fig. 5. Port-function-module relationship conversion after time's sorting.

3.2   Add Timing Relationship

If the timing relationship between modules is not clear, add a timing relationship as appropriate. Consequence: bring some performance loss. Considering that it is necessary to ensure that the expired entries can be promptly deleted and the routing table can be accurately updated after the node is moved, the working order of each module is adjusted to:

(1) Periodically start the expired entry deletion module according to HELLO cycle.
(2) After deleting the expired entries, send the HELLO packet and the TC packet successively.
(3) Start the calculation of the routing table.

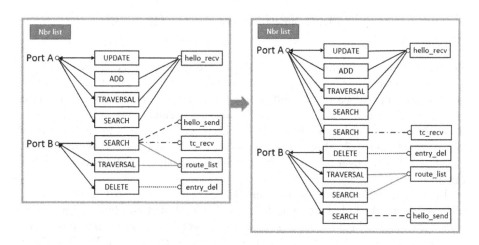

Fig. 6. Port-function-module relationship conversion after adding time relationship.

In this way, the entry delete, route list, HELLO send, and TC receive modules have a sequential relationship, which can basically solve the conflict of port usage of each table. At this time, the port-function-module relationship of the neighbor table can be further transformed as shown in Fig. 6.

For the neighbor table at this time, the three modules associated with port B no longer have the possibility of conflict. Just add the waiting sequence for the HELLO receive and TC receive modules to the read function of port A, all conflicts that may occur in the use of the neighbor table will be resolved. The situation of other tables is simpler than that of neighbor tables. Conflicts can be resolved under the above ideas.

4   Simulation

In this paper, Verilog language is used to design the OLSR project, and the simulation of OLSR project is completed based on virtex-7 device and xc7vx485tfg1157-1 device.

4.1   Functional Simulation and Analysis

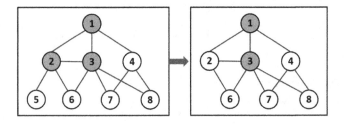

Fig. 7. Simulation scenario of OLSR.

The functional verification scenario of the OLSR project is shown in Fig. 7. According to the protocol content, when nodes 1 to 8 communicate as the neighbor relationship shown on the left, nodes 1, 2, and 3 can be selected as MPR nodes, and their respective routing tables are established. After a period of time (as shown on the right), node 5 leaves and other nodes update their memory management tables. At this time, only nodes 1 and 3 are selected as mpr nodes. This scenario can cover all workflow branches under the OLSR protocolso it has generality.

In the simulation results shown in Fig. 8, there are 7 entries in the routing table of node 1, including one-hop routes to nodes 2, 3, 4 and two-hop routes to nodes 5, 6, 7, 8, which is same as expected. According to the provisions of the agreement on the content of the routing table entry, the symbol ① in the Fig. 8 refers to the address of the local node as 1111aaaa, ② refers to the routing table

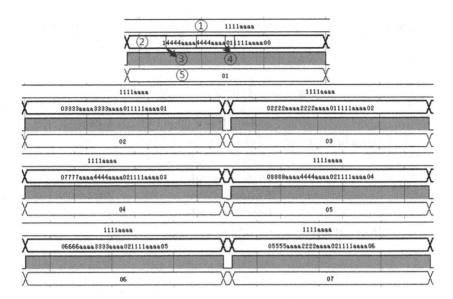

Fig. 8. Routing table of node 1.

entry records the ④ hop route from this node to the node with the address ③, ⑤ refers to the sequence number of the entry in the routing table.

In the scenario on the left side of Fig. 7, the contents of the routing table and mpr table of the 8 nodes are shown in Table 2, and all match the results estimated according to the OLSR protocol.

Table 2. Routing table of 8 nodes.

Node	1hop-route	2hop-route	3hop-route	mpr list
1	2/3/4	5/6/7/8	None	2/3
2	1/3/5/6	4/7/8	None	1/3
3	1/2/6/7/8	4/5	None	1/2
4	1/7/8	2/3	5/6	1
5	2	1/3/6	4/7/8	2
6	2/3	1/5/7/8	4	2/3
7	3/4	1/2/6/8	5	3
8	3/4	1/2/6/7	5	3

Waiting for a period of time, stop the communication between node 5 and other nodes, the scene changes to the right side of Fig. 7. After 2 HELLO sending cycles, the routing tables of 8 nodes are updated correctly. At this time, the storage tables of node 5 are empty, that of the other 7 nodes no longer contain node 5, and the mpr table no longer contains node 2, which are all in line with expectations. So far, the function verification of FPGA-based OLSR project is successful.

Table 3. Utilization results.

	Name	Power (W)	Utilization (%)
Dynamic (0.299 W)	Clocks	0.088	29
	Signals	<0.001	<1
	Logic	<0.001	<1
	BRAM	0.211	70
	I/O	<0.001	0
Device static	0.250 W		

4.2 Performance Simulation and Analysis

There are two power consumption estimation modes. One is the vector mode, which needs to provide SAIF or VCD files; the other is the non-vector mode, which only needs to provide simple parameters. Considering the estimated speed, Xilinx recommends selecting SAIF files in vector mode. At the same time, in order to obtain more accurate power consumption estimates, the performance analysis below is based on functional simulation after implementation.

The total on-chip power consumption is 0.549 W and the module power consumption is 0.299 W, which is shown in Table 3.

The resource usage of each part on the chip is shown in Table 4. Add clock constraint file for the OLSR project, and the highest clock frequency can be estimated to be 96.395 MHz.

Table 4. Utilization results.

Resource	Utilization/Available	Utilization (%)
LUT	17887/303600	5.89
LUTRAM	118/130800	0.09
FF	21854/607200	3.60
BRAM	73/1030	7.09
IO	229/600	38.17

In summary, using hardware to implement the OLSR protocol takes up very few hardware resources and consumes very low power. The integrated circuit can reach a higher clock frequency and a faster calculation speed.

5   Summary

This article proposes a multi-link list design and FPGA implementation method in OLSR protocol, which can solve the conflict problem that occurs when "multiple modules simultaneously read or write to the same port of the same table" in the case of "less RAM ports with more demand". Through platform simulation, the correctness of the method was verified, and the performance of resource utilization and power consumption of the project was analyzed. Since this method sacrifices the accuracy of the route calculation in a short time, the update of the correct route in the mobile scenario will be delayed by 2 HELLO cycles, the maximum clock frequency also needs to be increased. This research will continue to improve in the future, try to test the OLSR project in the multi-node scenario, and strive for lower power consumption.

Acknowledgement. This work was supported in part by Science and Technology on Avionics Integration Laboratory and the Aeronautical Science Foundation of China (Grant No. 201955053002), the National Natural Science Foundations of CHINA (Grant No. 61871322, No. 61771392, No. 61771390, and No. 61501373), and Science and Technology on Avionics Integration Laboratory and the Aeronautical Science Foundation of China (Grant No. 20185553035).

References

1. Xie, W.: Improvement and implementation of OLSR protocol in ad hoc network. Ph.D. dissertation, South China University of Technology (2010)
2. Zarakovitis, C.C., Ni, Q., Spiliotis, J.: Energy-efficient green wireless communication systems with imperfect CSI and data outage. IEEE J. Sel. Areas Commun. **34**(12), 3108–3126 (2016)
3. Xu, Y.: Ad hoc network performance analysis and routing technology research. Ph.D. dissertation, Xidian University (2014)
4. Clausen, T.: Optimized link state routing protocol, Rfc (2003)
5. Li Chen, R.Y., Pingjun Pan, M.H.: Ad hoc high dynamic routing protocol simulation and research. Mod. Defense Technol. **43**(249)(5), 121–125+174 (2015)
6. Chen, Y.: Comparative study and simulation analysis of wireless ad hoc network routing protocols OLSR and AODV. Comput. Knowl. Technol. **014**(8), 22–24 (2018)
7. Shu, W.: Performance simulation of OLSR protocol based on NS-3. Shandong Ind. Technol. **000**(005), 229–229 (2016)
8. Rathinam, A., Natarajan, V., Vanila, S., Viswanath, A., Guhan, M.S.: An FPGA implementation of improved AODV routing protocol for route repair scheme. IEEE Computer Society (2008)
9. Ramakrishnan, M., Shanmugavel, S.: FPGA implementation of DSDV based router in mobile adhoc network. In: India Conference (2006)

Improvement of Contact Graph Routing Algorithm in LEO Satellite DTN Network

Huijuan Zhu[1(✉)], Tao Zhang[1], Qi Wang[2], and Yanan Gu[3]

[1] School of Electronic and Information Engineering, Beihang University,
Beijing, People's Republic of China
616652671@qq.com
[2] Beijing Institute of Tracking and Telecommunications Technology,
Beijing, China
[3] Beijing Institute of Spacecraft System Engineering, Beijing, China

Abstract. As a space network technology, DTN (Delay/Disruption Tolerant Networks) has a wide range of applications in space system networking, and the application of DTN in LEO (Low Earth Orbit) satellite network is also a hot topic. Aiming at the problem of DTN routing technology in LEO satellite network, this paper proposes a routing algorithm for LEO satellite DTN network, which is based on throughput constrained minimum delay backup path of CGR (Contact Graph Routing) algorithm. By comparing the existing routing algorithms, this paper summarizes the problems existing in the application of existing routing algorithms in LEO satellite DTN network, proposes to calculate the shortest delay path of the whole network under the condition of throughput constraints, and select the best transmission path and backup path for data transmission. It solves the problems that the increase of queuing delay caused by the rapid change of network topology, the limited transmission capacity caused by single path transmission, and the active avoidance of node congestion. The simulation results show that compared with the traditional CGR algorithm and ECGR algorithm, the algorithm proposed in this paper is better in average delay and loss packet rate, and more suitable for LEO satellite DTN network.

Keywords: LEO satellite network · DTN · Contact Graph Routing

1 Introduction

In recent years, as the construction of LEO Mobile Communication satellite system in China is developing rapidly, some LEO satellite communication systems have been proposed successively, such as Hongyun and Hongyan [1]. However, the current networking technology of these satellite systems is still based on the ground IP networking technology.

Delay/Disruption Tolerant Networks [2] have the characteristics of intermittent connectivity, large delay and weak processing capacity of nodes, which makes DTN widely used in spatial information networks, such as [3, 4].

The successful application of DTN in space information network proves that DTN can also be used in LEO satellite network.

© ICST Institute for Computer Sciences, Social Informatics and Telecommunications Engineering 2021
Published by Springer Nature Switzerland AG 2021. All Rights Reserved
B. Li et al. (Eds.): IoTaaS 2020, LNICST 346, pp. 484–492, 2021.
https://doi.org/10.1007/978-3-030-67514-1_39

In recent years, the application of DTN in LEO satellite network has attracted more and more attention. However, due to the direct application of DTN, there are a series of problems, especially in the aspect of routing. The existing DTN routing algorithms are designed according to special scenarios. Critical factors in the network (links or nodes) and network traffic are not considered; the drastic change of network topology leads to frequent interrupt of links; the storage capacity and computing capacity of nodes are limited; most of the existing DTN routes are single-path transmissions and so on.

In 2008, NASA(National Aeronautics and Space Administration) proposed CGR algorithm based on DTN Network [5]. CGR algorithm uses the periodicity of spatial network nodes. It generates contact graph through the known contact plan of each transmission node, and then determinies the transmission path of data according to the generated contact graph. Duing to its advantages of occupying less storage and computing resources, CGR algorithm has been widely used in spatial DTN network since it was proposed. [6, 7] have respectively verified the feasibility of applying CGR algorithm to LEO network. However, there are still a series of problems in applying the exsting CGR directly to LEO satellite network.

This paper will focus on the existing CGR routing algorithm and the problems of its application to LEO satellite network, and proposes a CGR algorithm suitable for LEO satellite DTN network, as well as carrys out simulation test on it.

2   CGR Algorithm

CGR is a routing based on prior knowledge. Becaues of the pre-planning and periodicity of the link between communication nodes, and according to the contact plan (connect information and distance information) of each node in the network, the contact diagram is generated. Contact plans include two types: connection messages and distance messages. Each connection message includes the start time, end time of the connection, the node number of the sender, the node number of the receiver, and the planned transmission rate; Each distance message includes the start time of the connection, the end time, the node number of the sender, the node number of the receiver, and the planned transmission distance. Once a connection plan information is obtained, the CGR routing algorithm can be applied.

When a message is sent from a communication node, the CGR algorithm will analyse the contact graph and calculate as well as generate a collection of next-hop nodes. And then it will select the transmission path in the collection. When the data reaches the next-hop node, the CGR algorithm will continue to run the process on the next- hop node [8–10]. CGR is a completely connection plan-dependent routing algorithm that uses less storage and computing resources than other routing algorithms in periodic application scenarios.

In order to avoid the loop and route oscillation caused by CGR algorithm in routing calculation, [11] proposes an improved algorithm–ECGR(Enhanced Contact Graph Routing), which uses Dijkstra algorithm to calculate the shortest path. And it reduces the cost of routing algorithm. It has become the core of CGR algorithm at present. In [12], based on the consideration of reducing the amount of nodes computation, CGR-EB algorithm is proposed and added extension block choreography into packets. In

[13], CGR-ETO(Contact Graph Routing Earliest Transmission Opportunity), the earliest transmission opportunity algorithm, is proposed. Considering the queuing delay of three different priority data, CGR-ETO improve the accuracy of arrival time of each priority bundle, and proposes the Overbooking Management mechanism to deal with the case of over-contact. This algorithm is the most recognized CGR algorithm at present. In [14], MD-CGR(Multi-Destination Contact Graph Routing). It analyse the path coding method and orchestrates the path information into the data. The intermediate node only recalculates the path when the contact changes. Thus, it reduce the calculation amount of the intermediate node in the resource-constrained environment.

These improved CGR algorithm all have their advantages, but the application of CGR algorithm to LEO satellite networks needs to be further improved.

[1]. Due to the high dynamic nature of LEO satellite nodes and the poor connection stability between nodes, it eventually lead to the inconsistency between the connection plan and the actual networking topology. The reliability of the transmission is poor, resulting in unreliable connection plans, and the final computed path may be invalid. At this time, the packet is temporarily stored in the satellite node, which greatly increases the queuing delay of the packet and the possibility of satellite node congestion.

[2]. CGR does not fully consider the state of link and queuing delay in calculation, which may cause packet loss due to excessively large transmission delay or even cache overflow in some special cases.

[3]. In LEO satellite DTN network, there will be some relatively "important" nodes, which exist on many paths and receive many packets at the same time. Under limited processing conditions, many packets will be cached in the nodes, which not only increases the packet queuing delay, but also causes node congestion very easily.

[4]. CGR algorithm is based on a single copy of the satellite, which is the data transmission between the source and destination only exist a transmission path. In this mode of transmission, transmission ability of CGR algorithm is limited. And CGR algorithm can not make full use of network resources, especially in LEO satellite network, which is the node with limited resources. Once the business conflict, the network is likely to cause the network congestion, and even partial paralysis.

Aiming at the above four problems, this paper improves the CGR algorithm, and proposes the Based on Throughput Constrained Minimum Delay Backup Path of CGR Algorithm.

3   Based on Throughput Constrained Minimum Delay Backup Path of CGR Algorithm

Based on throughput constrained minimum delay backup path of CGR algorithm (TCMDB_CGR) is divided into link checking and message forwarding. The link checking process adopts the link checking process of CGR algorithm.

3.1   The Connection Check Process

The connection check process computes the path recursively until a complete path without loops is found. The connection checking process traverses all the connection plan. If the receiving node of the connection plan information is not the destination node, then the node is skipped. For the receiving node of the connection plan information, it is the destination node:

If the sending node is a local node, it is directly added to the alternative node set;

If the sending node is a node in the alternative node set, it is skipped;

If the sending node is neither a local node nor a node in the alternative set of nodes, it is used as the destination node and the connection check process and is performed again;

Until all connection plans are traversed, an alternate set of nodes is obtained.

3.2   The Message Forwarding Process

After obtaining alternative nodes set through link checking process, TCMDB_CGR algorithm consider the link cache and throughput. It will set a threshold τ for the residual capacity of the link. If the residual capacity of the link is less than this threshold, the path will be deleted. In this way, it can reduce queuing delay caused by the heavy load of data packet forwarding to the link, and even avoid the packet loss caused by link overflow.

When there is no overflow in the link, we calculate the throughput according to the link connection time, and compare it with the expected volume of business. If the throughput is less than the expected traffic volume, the path will be deleted. If the throughput can meet the expected requirements, the transmission delay of the packet is considered.

Then, after two "filtering" of alternative nodes set, the total delay of packet transmission is calculated. The total delay sums transmission delay, propagation delay, queuing delay and waiting delay. The specific calculation process is as follows:

[1]. Link throughput:

$$W = \int_{t_{m,n-start}}^{t_{m,n-end}} c_{m,n}(t)dt \qquad (1)$$

t_{m,n_start}: The node of "m" and "n" start contract time; t_{m,n_end}: The node of "m" and "n" end contract time; $C_{m,n}(t)$: The node of "m" and "n" information transmission rate.

[2]. Propagation delay: The propagation delay can be obtained by dividing the physical distance $D_{m,n}$ between the source node and the destination node by the speed of light.

$$t_{m,n} = \frac{D_{m,n}}{c} \qquad (2)$$

$D_{m,n}$: The physical distance between the nodes of "m" and "n"; c: The speed of light
(3*10^8 m/s).

[3]. Transmission delay: the processing time of the link layer.

$$t_{send} = \frac{L_{data}}{BW} \qquad (3)$$

L_{data}: The frame length of the transmitted data packet, Unit: bit; BW: The channel
bandwidth, Unit: bit/s.

[4]. Queuing delay: the sum of all data transmission delays waiting to be forwarded
before forwarding the data.

$$t_q = \sum_{i=0}^{n} \frac{L_{data}}{BW} \qquad (4)$$

L_{data}: The frame length of the transmitted data packet, Unit: bit; BW: The channel
bandwidth, Unit: bit/s.

[5]. Waiting delay: Not all data will be forwarded to the destination node immediately. There is a connection time between the source node and the destination
node. If the current time is not within the connection time range, you need to
wait for the link to connect before forwarding.

$$t_{wait} = \begin{cases} 0 & (t_{contract} \le t_{now}) \\ t_{contract} - t_{now} & (t_{contract} \ge t_{now}) \end{cases} \qquad (5)$$

$t_{contract}$: Two nodes start contact time; t_{now}: The current time.

[6]. Dpath: Total delay time.

$$D_{path} = t_{m,n} + t_{send} + t_q + t_{wait} \qquad (6)$$

According to the above method, the total delay time is arranged the delay in ascending
order. And TCMDB_CGR algorithm will select the two paths with the minimum total
delay. The path with the least total delay is selected as the best transmission path, and
the path with the less total delay is selected as the backup path.

In order to avoid node congestion, TCMDB_CGR algorithm set a threshold set for
each node to receive packets. Judge whether the capacity of the destination node of the
optimal path reaches the threshold or not, and adopt the optimal path to transmit if the
threshold is not reached; Otherwise, judge whether the threshold value of the destination node of the backup path reaches the threshold value. If the threshold value is not
reached, the backup path is adopted for transmission; Otherwise, the two paths are
removed and the new best path and backup path are re-selected from the alternative
nodes set.

This scheme can effectively avoid some nodes with heavy link burden on the basis of guaranteed traffic and select other paths with smaller delay, so as to effectively reduce the impact of queued delay on the whole network performance. And the backup path scheme can reduce the computation of nodes to a certain extent, and it is more suitable for the network with limited resources of LEO satellite nodes.

The flow chart of forwarding decision is as follows (Fig. 1):

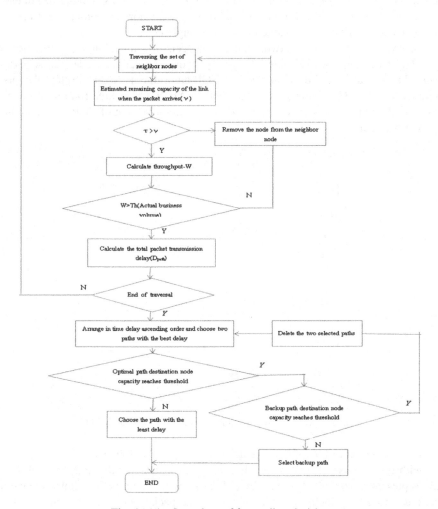

Fig. 1. The flow chart of forwarding decision

4 Simulation Test

The simulation in this paper is based on the SNSim simulation platform independently developed by the laboratory. The DTN nodes model is developed to build the LEO satellite network scenario. And the protocol is added to the node to set the motion trajectory and carry out simulation processing. In this scenario, 48 LEO satellite nodes, one space station node, one cargo spacecraft node, and one ground center node were designed and added. The ground center node transmits the data to the space station node or the cargo spacecraft through the LEO satellite network, and can realize the communication between the ground center node and the space station or the cargo spacecraft. The simulation scenario is initiated by the space station, the cargo spacecraft and the ground center. The transmission rate was 1 Mbps–2 Mbps, and the size of each packet was 1000Byte. In this simulation, all messages are normal (non-critical Bundle), that is, CGR algorithm is forwarded only as a single copy.

Carried out in the above network simulation scenario simulation, this paper realize the CGR based on the LEO satellite DTN network simulation. Under the scenario, packet loss rate and the end-to-end delay of CGR algorithm, ECGR algorithm (the most commonly used CGR routing algorithm) and TCMDB_CGR three routing algorithm has carried on the contrast, and confirmed that the improvement of CGR algorithm has optimal performance (Fig. 2).

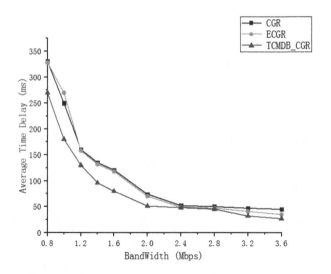

Fig. 2. Relationship between average time and bandwidth

The simulation results of average delay can be seen as follows:

With the increase of link bandwidth, the average delay of the three routing algorithms presents a downward trend. This is because with the increase of link bandwidth, the node processing cache speed is faster, and the packet sending delay and queuing delay are greatly reduced. However, on the whole, the delay curves of CGR algorithm and ECGR algorithm are not significantly different, while the average delay of TCMDB_CGR algorithm is significantly smaller than the above two algorithms. Especially in the case of poor link performance, TCMDB_CGR algorithm can significantly improve the average delay of the whole network. This shows that TCMDB_CGR algorithm has more advantages in network performance under the condition of limited link resources.

This is because the TCMDB_CGR algorithm fully considers the link state and queueing delay. In the case of a link queue with too high occupancy rate or a node with too high cache, it can choose a more "idle" path to avoid a long queued waiting transmission (Fig. 3).

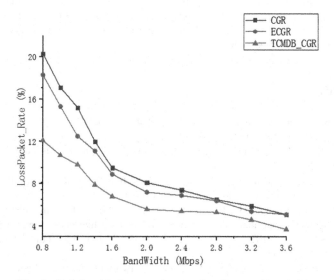

Fig. 3. Relationship between loss_packet_Rate and bandwidth

The simulation results of packet loss rate can be seen as follows:

With the increase of link bandwidth, the packet loss rate of the three routing algorithms decreases. This is because the link bandwidth increases, queue processing speeds up, and the packet loss caused by queue overflow is reduced under the premise of constant node caching capacity. But on the whole, ECGR algorithm and CGR algorithm, the packet loss rate is slightly smaller, but the difference is not big. The packet loss rate of TCMDB_CGR algorithm is much lower than that of the other two algorithms, especially in the case of poor link performance. With the increase of link bandwidth, the packet loss rate of TCMDB_CGR algorithm drops faster.

This is because the TCMDB_CGR algorithm fully considers the link state and the reliability of the connection plan, bypasses the path that may cause congestion and nodes near congestion, makes full use of the entire network resources, and reduces the packet loss caused by cache overflow. At the same time, it avoids the unstable link, ensures the traffic volume of network transmission, increases the reliability of network, and reduces the packet loss caused by packet failure due to queuing delay.

5 Conclusion

In this paper, CGR algorithm based on throughput constraint minimum delay backup path is proposed for LEO satellite DTN network. It is introduced and compared with simulation. Simulation results show that compared with CGR algorithms and ECGR algorithms, TCMDB_CGR has better end-to-end delay and packet arrival rate, which proves that the routing algorithm proposed in this paper is more suitable for LEO satellite DTN network.

Acknowledgment. This work was supported by the National Key R&D Program of China (No. 2016YFB1200100). The National Nature Science Foundation of China (No. 91638301). Science and Technology on Complex Electronic System Simulation Laboratory, Research on Test Technology (No. 1700050369).

References

1. China's two global satellite networks will launch 456 first satellites in the year. https://www.sohu.com/a/224754950_115479, Accessed 08 Sept 2019
2. Burleigh, S., et al.: Delay-tolerant networking: an approach to interplanetary internet. IEEE Commun. Mag. **41**(6), 128–136 (2003)
3. Lin, C., Dong, Y., Dan, Z.: Overview of DTN based spatial network interconnection services. Comput. Res. Dev. **51**(5), 931–943 (2014)
4. Caini, C., Cruickshank, H., Farrell, S., Marchese, M.: Delay- and disruption-tolerant networking (DTN): an alternative solution for future satellite networking applications. In: Proceedings of the IEEE, vol. 99, no. 11, pp. 1980–1997 (2011). https://doi.org/10.1109/JPROC.2011.2158378
5. Scott, B.: Dynamic routing for delay-tolerant networking in space flight operations. In: Spaceops Conference (2008)
6. Caini, C., Firrincieli, R.: Application of contact graph routing to leo satellite DTN communications. In: IEEE ICC Communications Symposium (2012)
7. Apollonio, P., Caini, C., Lülf, M.: DTN LEO satellite communications through ground stations and GEO relays. In: Dhaou, R., Beylot, A.-L., Montpetit, M.-J., Lucani, D., Mucchi, L. (eds.) PSATS 2013. LNICSSITE, vol. 123, pp. 1–12. Springer, Cham (2013). https://doi.org/10.1007/978-3-319-02762-3_1
8. Burleigh, S.: Contact graph routing.https://tools.ietf.org/id/draft-burleigh-dtnrg-cgr-01.txt, Accessed 08 Sept 2020
9. Giuseppe, A., et al.: Contact graph routing in DTN space networks: overview, enhancements and performance. IEEE Commun. Mag. **53**(3), 38–46 (2015)
10. Alaoui, S.E.: Routing Optimization in Interplanetary Networks. University of Nebraska-Lincoln, Nebraska (2015)
11. Segui, J, Jennings, E., Burleigh, S.: Enhancing contact graph routing for delay tolerant space networking. In: Global Telecommunications Conference, pp. 1–6 (2011)
12. Edward, J.B.: Improving graph-based overlay routing in delay tolerant networks. In: IEEE Wireless Days (2011)
13. Bezirgiannidis, N., Caini, C., Montenero, D.D.P., Ruggieri, M., Tsaoussidis, V.: Contact graph routing enhancements for delay tolerant space communications. In: Advanced Satellite Multimedia Systems Conference and the Signal Processing for Space Communications Workshop((ASMS/SPSC)), Livorno, Italy, pp. 17–23 (2014)
14. Birrane, E., Burleigh, S., Kasch, N.: Analysis of the contact graph routing algorithm: bounding interplanetary paths. Acta Astronautica **75**, 108–119 (2012)

Double-Threshold-Based Massive Random Access Protocol for Heterogeneous MTC Networks

Yuncong Xie[1,2], Pinyi Ren[1,2(✉)], and Dongyang Xu[1,2]

[1] School of Information and Communications Engineering, Xi'an Jiaotong University,
Xi'an 710049, People's Republic of China
`qy1z29@stu.xjtu.edu.cn` , `pyren@mail.xjtu.edu.cn` , `xudongyang@xjtu.edu.cn`
[2] Shaanxi Smart Networks and Ubiquitous Access Research Center,
Xi'an 710049, People's Republic of China

Abstract. In this paper, we consider the uplink transmission of a heterogeneous MTC network with massive number of delay-insensitive terminals and URLLC terminals coexistence, and propose a novel double-threshold-based massive random access (DT-MRA) protocol. On the one hand, the proposed DT-MRA protocol allows partial delay-insensitive terminals temporarily preempting URLLC spectrum channels to alleviate the traffic overload, via adaptively tuning access control parameters including ACB factor and traffic offloading factor. On the other hand, a grant-free access mechanism with packet repetition is applied to support the stringent QoS requirements of URLLC. Then, we formulate an optimization problem to maximize the access throughput of delay-insensitive terminals, while satisfying the QoS requirements of each URLLC terminal. Based on the statistical traffic load information, an optimal access control strategy is also developed to solve this optimization problem. Simulation results validate the theoretical analyses and demonstrate the effectiveness of our proposed DT-MRA protocol, in terms of improving access throughput.

Keywords: Random access protocol · Massive machine-type communications (mMTC) · Ultra-reliable and low-latency communications (URLLC)

1 Introduction

The fifth generation (5G) cellular networks is envisioned to support seamless data exchanges among machine-type devices (MTDs), with minimum or no human intervention. Based on the application scenario and design requirement,

This research work is supported in part by the National Science and Technology Major Project under Grant No. 2018ZX03001003-004, and in part by the Fundamental Research Funds for the Central Universities.

B. Li et al. (Eds.): IoTaaS 2020, LNICST 346, pp. 493–509, 2021.
https://doi.org/10.1007/978-3-030-67514-1_40

5G machine-type communication services fall into two main categories [1]. One is the massive machine-type communications (mMTC) with massive connectivity and delay-insensitive traffic. The other is the ultra-reliable and low-latency communications (URLLC), which has a stringent Quality-of-Service (QoS) requirement in end-to-end (E2E) latency bound (e.g., 1 ms) and packet loss probability (e.g., no more than 10^{-5}). With the development of wireless technologies, there appears some emerging use cases with mMTC and URLLC services coexistence. Take the industrial internet-of-things (IoT) as an example, there exists a massive number of delay-insensitive sensors to monitor the factory environment, such as temperature and humidity. Apart from this, there also exists a relatively small number of URLLC sensors to perform mission-critical tasks, such as remote control and alarming [2]. Obviously, how to design the radio access protocol of heterogeneous MTC networks with diverse services is a challenging issue.

In this paper, we focus on the uplink transmission of heterogeneous MTC networks with massive delay-insensitive and URLLC terminals coexistence. Traditionally, LTE cellular networks use the grant-based uplink transmission protocol. Under this protocol, each terminal needs to carry out multiple control signaling exchanges before the uplink data transmission, such as four-step handshaking, scheduling request and scheduling grant [3]. Obviously, the grant-based transmission protocol is not suitable to MTC terminals with sporadic and small packet arrivals, which can be explained in the following two aspects: On the one hand, the massive access of delay-insensitive MTC terminals at the same time will lead to a serious radio access network (RAN) congestion and low access efficiency. In view of this, some congestion mitigating mechanisms, such as access class barring (ACB) [4], group paging [5], and traffic offloading [6], are developed to sustain the successful operation of massive access. On the other hand, the connection-oriented RA procedure induces excessive control signaling overhead and causes a large access delay, which is conflicting with the ultra-low E2E latency requirement of URLLC terminals. To overcome this bottleneck, the authors in [6] proposed a grant-free uplink access scheme with repetition coding, where each URLLC terminal can directly transmits its packets to the BS in a contention-based manner without connection-establishment, and transmits multiple copies of the same packet to achieve target reliability within the given E2E latency bound.

The major contributions of this paper are summarized as follows: Firstly, we propose a novel double-threshold-based massive random access (DT-MRA) protocol, which allows partial delay-insensitive terminals temporarily preempting URLLC spectrum channels to alleviate the traffic overload caused by massive access. Then, an optimization problem is formulated to maximize the access throughput of delay-insensitive terminals, while satisfying the QoS requirements of each URLLC terminal. Based on the statistical traffic load information, an optimal access control strategy is also developed to solve this optimization problem. Simulation results validate the theoretical analyses and demonstrate the effectiveness of our proposed DT-MRA protocol, in terms of improving access throughput.

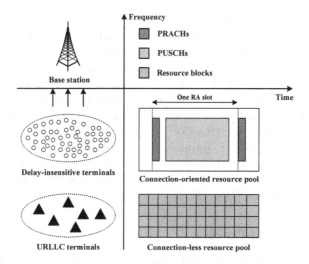

Fig. 1. Graphical representation of the heterogeneous MTC netwotk with delay-insensitive and URLLC terminals coexistence.

2 System Model

As depicted in Fig. 1, we consider a heavy-loaded MTC network consisting of one BS, K delay-insensitive terminals and L URLLC terminals. Time is discretized into slots with a duration of τ, which is the basic time unit of the system. In particular, the QoS requirement of each URLLC terminal is characterized by an E2E latency bound T_{th} and the corresponding maximal allowable packet loss probability ϕ_{th}.

2.1 Time-Frequency Resource Configuration

With the consideration of differentiated characteristics between delay-insensitive and URLLC terminals, the BS prepares two independent spectrum resource pools that equipped with different RA procedures and time-frequency resource configurations. One is called as connection-oriented resource pool, which utilizes the traditional LTE-based RA procedure to support the massive access of delay-insensitive terminals, i.e., each terminal randomly selects one of M available preambles and transmits to the BS over the physical random access channel (PRACH). Note that the PRACH is a certain time-frequency resource blocks (RBs) that appear periodically [7]. Denote the interval between two consecutive PRACHs as one RA slot, whose duration is T_{RA} and contains I_{RA} consecutive slots. The RA procedure is successful when a preamble is only selected by one terminal, and then BS will assigns dedicated physical uplink shared channel (PUSCH) for this terminal to complete the uplink data transmission.[1]

The other is called as connection-less resource pool, which utilizes a grant-free RA procedure to reduce the control signaling overhead and satisfy the ultra-low E2E requirement of URLLC, i.e., each terminal can directly transmits its packets to BS in a contention-based manner. In the connection-less resource pool, the total bandwidth is equally divided into N orthogonal channels, such that there exists NI_{RA} RBs within each RA slot[2]. Due to the small payload characteristic of delay-insensitive and URLLC terminals, we assume that only one RB is required to complete the uplink data transmission. For simplicity, we further assume that transmission errors can only occur in the channel collision, i.e., the impact of noise and other channel imperfections are negligible.

2.2 Packet Arrival Process

To simplify the packet arrival process of delay-insensitive terminal, we assume that newly packet arrivals will only take place at the beginning of each RA slot. Moreover, each delay-insensitive terminal has an infinite-size queue buffer to store newly arrival packets and the number of newly arrival packets per RA slot follows the Poisson distribution with a parameter of $\lambda \in (0, 1)$. One access request will be generated when a new packet is arrived, and each delay-insensitive terminal can sustain at most one ongoing access request, regardless of the number of packets in the queue buffer. Therefore, the data transmission of each delay-insensitive terminal can be modeled as a $Geo/G/1/1$ queue [8].

Due to the sporadic packet arrival characteristic, the newly packet arrival of each URLLC terminal can be modeled as a poisson process with exponentially distributed inter-arrival time, and denote the average number of new arrival packets per slot as $\mu \in (0, 1)$. Since the packet inter-arrival interval in typical URLLC applications is much longer than the E2E delay bound T_{th} (e.g., 1 ms) [9], it is reasonable to assume that the queueing delay is zero because the packets will be immediately dropped once the E2E delay bound expires.

3 Protocol Description and Performance Analysis

3.1 DT-MRA Protocol Description

To effectively support the massive access characteristic of delay-insensitive terminals and the stringent QoS requirement of URLLC terminals, we propose a novel double-threshold-based massive random access (DT-MRA) protocol and the detail is described as follows: On the one hand, the URLLC terminals can

---

[1] This conference paper only focus on the first step of connection-oriented RA procedure, i.e, preamble transmission in the PRACH, and assume that the number of PUSCHs is sufficiently large to complete the data transmission.

[2] Note that one RB in the connection-less resource pool is defined as a time-frequency block with one channel bandwidth and one slot duration.

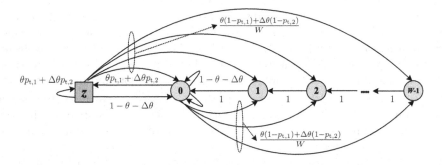

Fig. 2. State transition diagram of each delay-insensitive terminal.

only utilize the connection-less resource pool for the grant-free data transmission to achieve an ultra-low E2E latency. Meanwhile, a packet repetition mechanism is also applied to guarantee the ultra-high transmission reliability, which allows each URLLC terminal transmits the same packet Q_{th} times in consecutive slots, via randomly selects one out of N orthogonal channels at each slot. Based on the time-frequency configuration of connection-less resource pool, we have $Q_{\text{th}} = \lfloor T_{\text{th}}/\tau \rfloor$ to satisfy the E2E latency bound of URLLC.

On the other hand, each delay-insensitive terminal can either perform LTE-based RA procedure in the connection-oriented resource pool, or temporarily utilizes one RB in the connection-oriented resource pool to perform grant-free RA procedure. To realize the function mentioned above, a double-threshold ACB scheme is developed for massive access of delay-insensitive terminals. At the beginning of each RA slot, the BS will broadcast two access control thresholds, including the ACB factor $\theta \in (0,1]$ and the traffic offloading factor $\Delta\theta \in [0,1)$. Then, each delay-insensitive terminal generates a random number $\delta \in [0,1]$ in a non-cooperative manner, and performs the ACB check via comparing it with the given two access control thresholds:

1. If $\delta \leq \theta$, the terminal will attempts to perform the LTE-based RA produce in connection-oriented resource pool, via randomly selects one out of M preambles.
2. If $\theta < \delta \leq \theta + \Delta\theta$, the terminal will performs the grant-free RA produce in connection-less resource pool, via randomly selects one out of NI_{RA} RBs.
3. Otherwise, the terminal is rejected by the ACB check mechanism temporarily and reattempt to initiate access at the beginning of next RA slot.

3.2 Transmission Performance Analysis

In this subsection, we will analyze the transmission performance of each delay-insensitive and URLLC terminal. As depicted in Fig. 2, the transmission behaviour of each delay-insensitive terminal can be modeled as a discrete-time Markov process. At each RA slot t, denote $p_{t,1}$ and $p_{t,2}$ as the successful transmission probability in connection-oriented resource pool and connection-less resource pool, respectively. The data transmission phase is initially in state z, and remain in state z when it passes the ACB check and successfully transmitted with a probability of $\theta p_{t,1} + \Delta\theta p_{t,2}$. When the transmission collision occurs, it randomly selects a integer value between 0 and $W - 1$, where W is the Uniform Backoff (UB) window size in unit of RA slot, and moving to state $s \in \{0, 1, ..., W-1\}$ with equal probability $\frac{\theta(1-p_{t,1})+\Delta\theta(1-p_{t,2})}{W}$, and counts down at each RA slot until it reaches state 0. Otherwise, it shifts to state 0 that implies the terminal is rejected by the ACB check temporarily and reattempt to initiate access at the beginning of next RA slot.

Based on the discussion above, the steady-state probability distribution in Fig. 2 can be obtained as

$$
\begin{cases}
\pi_z = \left(\dfrac{(W-1)(\theta(1-p_1)+\Delta\theta(1-p_2))}{2(\theta p_1 + \Delta\theta p_2)} + \dfrac{1}{\theta p_1 + \Delta\theta p_2} \right)^{-1}, \\
\pi_0 = \dfrac{1-(\theta p_1 + \Delta\theta p_2)}{\theta p_1 + \Delta\theta p_2}\pi_z, \\
\pi_s = \dfrac{(W-s)(\theta(1-p_1)+\Delta\theta(1-p_2))}{W(\theta p_1 + \Delta\theta p_2)}\pi_z, \quad s = 1, 2, ..., W-1,
\end{cases}
\tag{1}
$$

where $p_1 = \lim_{t\to\infty} p_{t,1}$ and $p_2 = \lim_{t\to\infty} p_{t,2}$ is the steady-state success transmission probability in connection-oriented and connection-less resource pools, respectively.

For each delay-insensitive terminal, denote the nonempty probability of data queue as ρ. If one particular terminal performs RA procedure in the connection-oriented resource pool, via randomly selects one of M available preambles. The data transmission is successful only when the behavior of other $K-1$ delay-insensitive terminals satisfies the following conditionals: 1) the data queue is empty, and the corresponding probability is $1-\rho$, 2) the data queue is nonempty, but not transmitting in the connection-oriented resource pool, the corresponding probability is $\rho\big((1-\theta)(\pi_0+\pi_z)+\sum_{j=1}^{W-1}\pi_j\big)$, and 3) the data transmission occurs in the connection-oriented resource pool, but not select the same preamble as the terminal of interest, the corresponding probability is $\rho\theta(1-\frac{1}{M})(\pi_0+\pi_z)$. Based on the analysis above, the mathematical expression of p_1 can be obtained as

$$
p_1 \triangleq \binom{M}{1}\frac{1}{M}\left((1-\rho) + \rho\Big((1-\theta)(\pi_0+\pi_z) + \sum_{j=1}^{W-1}\pi_j + \theta(1-\frac{1}{M})(\pi_0+\pi_z)\Big) \right)^{K-1}
$$

$$
= \left(1-\rho\frac{\theta}{M}(\pi_0+\pi_z)\right)^{K-1} = \left(1-\frac{\rho\theta\pi_z}{M(\theta p_1 + \Delta\theta p_2)}\right)^{K-1},
\tag{2}
$$

where the closed-form expression of ρ is given by [8]

$$
\rho = \frac{\lambda}{\lambda + \pi_z},
\tag{3}
$$

since the value K is large, we have $K - 1 \approx K$ and $(1-x)^K \approx e^{-Kx}$ for $0 < x < 1$. By combining (1) and (3), the mathematical expression of (2) can be approximated as

$$p_1 \overset{\text{when } K \text{ is large}}{\approx} \exp\left(-K\frac{\rho\theta\pi_z}{M(\theta p_1 + \Delta\theta p_2)}\right)$$

$$= \exp\left(-\frac{K}{M}\frac{1}{\theta p_1 + \Delta\theta p_2}\frac{\lambda\theta}{1 + \lambda\left(\frac{1}{\theta p_1 + \Delta\theta p_2}\left(1 + \frac{W-1}{2}(\theta + \Delta\theta)\right) - \frac{W-1}{2}\right)}\right). \tag{4}$$

To evaluate the access performance of all delay-insensitive terminals, we are interested in the average access throughput $\bar{\lambda}_{\text{out}}$ of delay-insensitive traffic, which is defined as the average number of delay-insensitive terminals that successful access to the BS per RA slot. Based on the characteristic of $Geo/G/1/1$ queue model, the mathematical expression of $\bar{\lambda}_{\text{out}}$ can be written as

$$\bar{\lambda}_{\text{out}} = \tilde{\lambda}(1 - \rho), \tag{5}$$

where $\tilde{\lambda} = K\lambda$ is the aggregate data arrival rate of delay-insensitive terminals, the mathematical expression of π_z and ρ are given by (1) and (3), respectively. By substituting (1) and (3) into (5), the average access throughput of delay-insensitive traffic is obtained as

$$\bar{\lambda}_{\text{out}} = \frac{K\lambda}{1 + \lambda\left(\frac{(W-1)(\theta(1-p_1)+\Delta\theta(1-p_2))}{2(\theta p_1 + \Delta\theta p_2)} + \frac{1}{\theta p_1 + \Delta\theta p_2}\right)}. \tag{6}$$

In the following, we analyzes the transmission performance of URLLC: As an analytical tool that indicates the degree of reliability loss, the packet loss probability of each URLLC terminal is defined as the probability that all Q_{th} packets are not successfully transmitted within the E2E latency bound T_{th}. Therefore, the packet loss probability of each URLLC terminal is given by $\phi = p_c^{Q_{\text{th}}}$, where p_c is the collision probability of each individual packet. Since the other $L - 1$ URLLC terminals and K delay-insensitive terminals might collided with the packet of interest, denote the corresponding probability as p_{c1} and p_{c2}, respectively. Therefore, the mathematical expression of packet loss probability can be rewritten as

$$\phi = \left(1 - (1 - p_{c1})(1 - p_{c2})\right)^{Q_{\text{th}}}. \tag{7}$$

In general, the probability that one URLLC terminal has packets to transmit is $p_{\text{ra}} \triangleq 1 - e^{-\mu}$. For each of other $L - 1$ URLLC terminals, the probability that its generated packets not collided with the packet of interest, i.e., randomly selects one out of other $N - 1$ orthogonal channels, is obtained as $p_{\text{access}} \triangleq \binom{N-1}{1}/\binom{N}{1} = \frac{N-1}{N}$. Therefore, the mathematical expression of p_{c1} is given by

$$p_{c1} = 1 - \left((1 - p_{\text{ra}}) + p_{\text{ra}}p_{\text{access}}\right)^{L-1}$$

$$= 1 - \left(\frac{e^{-\mu} + N - 1}{N}\right)^{L-1}. \tag{8}$$

Apart from this, to avoid the collision with the packet of interest, the behavior of K delay-insensitive terminals should also satisfies one of the following conditions:

1) the data queue of delay-insensitive terminal is empty with probability $1-\rho$, 2) the data queue of delay-insensitive terminal is nonempty, but not transmitting in the connection-less resource pool, the corresponding probability is $\rho((1-\Delta\theta)(\pi_0+\pi_z)+\sum_{s=1}^{W-1}\pi_s)$, and 3) the data transmission of delay-insensitive terminal occurs in the connection-less resource pool, but not select the same RB as the packet of interest, the corresponding probability is $\rho\Delta\theta(1-\frac{1}{NI_{RA}})(\pi_0+\pi_z)$. Therefore, the mathematical expression of p_{c2} is given by

$$
\begin{aligned}
p_{c2} &= 1 - \left[(1-\rho)+\rho\left((1-\Delta\theta)(\pi_0+\pi_z)+\sum_{s=1}^{W-1}\pi_s+\Delta\theta\left(1-\frac{1}{NI_{RA}}\right)(\pi_0+\pi_z)\right)\right]^K \\
&= 1 - \left[(1-\rho)+\rho\left(\left(1-\frac{\Delta\theta}{NI_{RA}}\right)(\pi_0+\pi_z)+\sum_{s=1}^{W-1}\pi_s\right)\right]^K,
\end{aligned}
\tag{9}
$$

substituting (8) and (9) into (7), the packet loss probability of each URLLC terminal can be rewritten as

$$
\begin{aligned}
\phi &= \left[1-\left((1-\rho)+\rho\left((1-\frac{\Delta\theta}{NI_{RA}})(\pi_0+\pi_z)+\sum_{s=1}^{W-1}\pi_s\right)\right)^K\left(\frac{e^{-\mu}+N-1}{N}\right)^{L-1}\right]^{Q_{th}} \\
&\triangleq \left[\omega\left(1-\frac{\rho\Delta\theta\pi_z}{NI_{RA}(\theta p_1+\Delta\theta p_2)}\right)^K\right]^{Q_{th}},
\end{aligned}
\tag{10}
$$

where $\omega=\left(\frac{e^{-\mu}+N-1}{N}\right)^{L-1}$, and since the value K is large, we have the approximation $(1-x)^K\approx e^{-Kx}$ for $0<x<1$. By combining (1) and (3), the mathematical expression of (10) can be approximated as

$$
\begin{aligned}
\phi &\overset{\text{when } K \text{ is large}}{\approx} \left[\omega\exp\left(-K\frac{\rho\Delta\theta\pi_z}{NI_{RA}(\theta p_1+\Delta\theta p_2)}\right)\right]^{Q_{th}} \\
&= \left[\omega\exp\left(-\frac{K}{NI_{RA}}\frac{1}{\theta p_1+\Delta\theta p_2}\frac{\lambda\Delta\theta}{1+\lambda(\frac{1}{\theta p_1+\Delta\theta p_2}(1+\frac{W-1}{2}(\theta+\Delta\theta))-\frac{W-1}{2})}\right)\right]^{Q_{th}},
\end{aligned}
\tag{11}
$$

Similar to the theoretical derivations above, the mathematical expression of p_2 is also obtained as

$$
\begin{aligned}
p_2 &= \left[(1-\rho)+\rho\left(\left(1-\frac{\Delta\theta}{NI_{RA}}\right)(\pi_0+\pi_z)+\sum_{s=1}^{W-1}\pi_s\right)\right]^{K-1}\left(\frac{e^{-\mu}+N-1}{N}\right)^L \\
&= \left[1-\frac{\rho\Delta\theta\pi_z}{NI_{RA}(\theta p_1+\Delta\theta p_2)}\right]^{K-1}\left(\frac{e^{-\mu}+N-1}{N}\right)^L.
\end{aligned}
\tag{12}
$$

4   Optimal Access Control Strategy Design

4.1   Problem Formulation

In this subsection, we formulate an optimization problem to maximize the average access throughput of delay-insensitive terminals, while meeting the QoS requirement of each URLLC terminal. Therefore, the optimization problem can be mathematically written as

$$(\textbf{P1}) \max_{\theta,\Delta\theta,W} \bar{\lambda}_{\text{out}} \tag{13}$$

$$\text{s.t.} \quad \phi \leq \phi_{\text{th}}, \tag{14}$$

$$\theta \in (0,1], \ \Delta\theta \in [0,1), \tag{15}$$

$$\theta + \Delta\theta \leq 1, \tag{16}$$

$$W \in \{1, 2, ..., W_{\max}\}, \tag{17}$$

where (14) implies the constraint in packet loss probability of each URLLC terminal, and (15) (16) (17) denote constraints in the values of ACB factor θ, traffic offloading factor $\Delta\theta$ and UB window size W, respectively.

Based on the observation in (6), we can draw the conclusion that $\bar{\lambda}_{\text{out}}$ is crucially determined by the value of p_1 and p_2, which is a function of θ, $\Delta\theta$ and W. By applying $K - 1 \approx K$ and $L \approx L - 1$ to (12), the expression of p_2 can be approximated as

$$p_2 \approx \left[1 - \frac{\rho\Delta\theta\pi_z}{NI_{RA}(\theta p_1 + \Delta\theta p_2)}\right]^K \left(\frac{e^{-\mu} + N - 1}{N}\right)^{L-1}, \tag{18}$$

and then we have $p_2 \approx 1 - \phi^{1/Q_{\text{th}}} \geq 1 - \phi_{\text{th}}^{1/Q_{\text{th}}}$. Plugging (4) and (12) into (13), and performing some manipulations, the problem (P1) can be converted to the following equivalent optimization problem:

$$(\textbf{P2}) \max_{p_1,p_2} \bar{\lambda}_{\text{out}} = -Mp_1 \ln p_1 - NI_{RA}p_2 \ln \frac{p_2}{\omega} \tag{19}$$

$$\text{s.t.} \quad 0 < p_1 \leq 1, \tag{20}$$

$$1 - \phi_{\text{th}}^{1/Q_{\text{th}}} \leq p_2 \leq 1, \tag{21}$$

4.2   Optimal Access Control Strategy

In this subsection, the optimal access control strategy is developed to obtain the maximal average access throughput $\bar{\lambda}_{\max} = \max_{\theta,\Delta\theta,W} \bar{\lambda}_{\text{out}}$ and the corresponding optimal setting of $\theta^*, \Delta\theta^*$ and W^*. Since $\bar{\lambda}_{\text{out}}$ is determined by the value of p_1 and p_2, which is a function of the ACB factor θ, the traffic offloading factor $\Delta\theta$ and the UB window size W, as shown in (4) and (12), respectively. Therefore, the general idea of solving optimization problem is given as follows: In the first step, we aim to solve the optimization problem (P2), and find the optimal setting of p_1 and p_2 that maximizing the access throughput $\bar{\lambda}_{\text{out}}$, which is denoted as p_1^* and p_2^*. In the second step, we aim to find the corresponding optimal solution $(\theta^*, \Delta\theta^*, W^*)$ under given values of p_1^* and p_2^*. Based on the discussion above, we have the following theorem that characterizes the optimal solution:

Theorem 1. In the optimization problem (P2), the global optimal solution is $(p_1^*, p_2^*) = (e^{-1}, 1 - \phi_{\text{th}}^{1/Q_{\text{th}}})$, and the corresponding maximum access throughput is $\bar{\lambda}_{\max} = Me^{-1} + NI_{RA}(1 - \phi_{\text{th}}^{1/Q_{\text{th}}}) \ln \frac{\omega}{1-\phi_{\text{th}}^{1/Q_{\text{th}}}}$, where $\omega = \left(\frac{e^{-\mu}+N-1}{N}\right)^{L-1}$. Furthermore, the corresponding optimal setting of $(\theta^*, \Delta\theta^*, W^*)$ in the optimization problem (P1) should together satisfy

$$\frac{\Delta\theta^*}{\theta^*} = -\frac{NI_{RA}}{M} \ln \frac{1 - \phi_{\text{th}}^{1/Q_{\text{th}}}}{\omega} \triangleq \alpha, \tag{22}$$

$$W^* = 2 \frac{\frac{K\theta^*}{M} - \frac{1}{\lambda}\left(\theta^* e^{-1} + \Delta\theta^*(1 - \phi_{\text{th}}^{1/Q_{\text{th}}})\right) - 1}{\theta^*(1 - e^{-1}) + \Delta\theta^*\phi_{\text{th}}^{1/Q_{\text{th}}}} + 1, \tag{23}$$

$$\theta^* \in (0, 1], \quad \Delta\theta^* \in [0, 1), \quad \theta^* + \Delta\theta^* \leq 1. \tag{24}$$

Proof. In the optimization problem (P2), $\bar{\lambda}_{\text{out}}$ is a convex function of (p_1, p_2). For $0 < p_1 \leq 1$, we have $\frac{\partial}{\partial p_1}\bar{\lambda}_{\text{out}} \geq 0$ when $p_1 \in (0, e^{-1}]$ and $\frac{\partial}{\partial p_1}\bar{\lambda}_{\text{out}} < 0$ when $p_1 \in (e^{-1}, 1]$. For $1 - \phi_{\text{th}}^{1/Q_{\text{th}}} \leq p_2 \leq 1$, we have $\frac{\partial}{\partial p_2}\bar{\lambda}_{\text{out}} < 0$ since $\omega e^{-1} < e^{-1} < 1 - \phi_{\text{th}}^{1/Q_{\text{th}}}$. Therefore, the combination of $(p_1^*, p_2^*) = (e^{-1}, 1 - \phi_{\text{th}}^{1/Q_{\text{th}}})$ is the global optimal solution of (P2), and the corresponding maximum access throughput is $\bar{\lambda}_{\max} = -Mp_1^* \ln p_1^* - NI_{RA}p_2^* \ln \frac{p_2^*}{\omega} = Me^{-1} + NI_{RA}(1 - \phi_{\text{th}}^{1/Q_{\text{th}}}) \ln \frac{\omega}{1-\phi_{\text{th}}^{1/Q_{\text{th}}}}$. Furthermore, the mathematical expressions in (22) (23) and (24) can be obtained via substituting $(p_1^*, p_2^*) = (e^{-1}, 1 - \phi_{\text{th}}^{1/Q_{\text{th}}})$ into (4) and (12), respectively. This completes the proof.

Remark 1. According to the constraint shown in (17), the value of UB window size W should not be less than 1, i.e., $W \geq 1$. Therefore, when $\frac{K\theta^*}{M} - \frac{1}{\lambda}(\theta^* e^{-1} + \Delta\theta^*(1 - \phi_{\text{th}}^{1/Q_{\text{th}}})) < 1$, i.e., $\lambda < \frac{\theta^* e^{-1} + \Delta\theta^*(1-\phi_{\text{th}}^{1/Q_{\text{th}}})}{\frac{K\theta^*}{M}-1} = \frac{e^{-1}+\alpha(1-\phi_{\text{th}}^{1/Q_{\text{th}}})}{\frac{K}{M}-\frac{1}{\theta^*}} < \frac{e^{-1}+\alpha(1-\phi_{\text{th}}^{1/Q_{\text{th}}})}{\frac{K}{M}-1-\alpha} \triangleq \lambda_H$, the maximal access throughput $\bar{\lambda}_{\max}$ cannot be achieved since (23) does not hold for any combination of θ^*, $\Delta\theta^*$ and W^*. That is to say, the maximal access throughput $\bar{\lambda}_{\max}$ can be achieved when $\lambda \geq \lambda_H$, and the corresponding optimal setting of $(\theta^*, \Delta\theta^*)$ and W^* can be adaptively tuning based on (22) (23) and (24).

Since the maximal access throughput $\bar{\lambda}_{\max}$ cannot be achieved when $\lambda < \lambda_H$, the following theorem characterizes the optimal setting of $(\theta^*, \Delta\theta^*, W^*)$ that maximizes the access throughput $\bar{\lambda}_{\text{out}}$ when $\lambda < \lambda_H$:

Theorem 2. On the one hand, the optimal setting of $(\theta^*, \Delta\theta^*, W^*)$ when $\frac{e^{-1}}{\frac{K}{M}-1} \triangleq \lambda_L \leq \lambda < \lambda_H$ should together satisfy the constraint that $\theta^* + \Delta\theta^* = 1$

and $W^* = 1$. On the other hand, the optimal setting of $(\theta^*, \Delta\theta^*, W^*)$ when $\lambda < \lambda_L$ has the unique solution of $\theta^* = 1$, $\Delta\theta^* = 0$ and $W^* = 1$. Denote the maximal access throughput when $\lambda_L \leq \lambda < \lambda_H$ and $\lambda < \lambda_L$ as $\bar{\lambda}'_{\max}$ and $\bar{\lambda}''_{\max}$, respectively. It is proved that $\bar{\lambda}'_{\max}$ and $\bar{\lambda}''_{\max}$ are monotonic increasing functions of λ, and $\bar{\lambda}''_{\max} < Me^{-1} \leq \bar{\lambda}'_{\max} < \bar{\lambda}_{\max}$.

Proof. Based on the idea of reduction to absurdity, assuming that $p_1^* = e^{-1}$ can be obtained when $\lambda < \lambda_L$, then substituting $p_1^* = e^{-1}$ and $\Delta\theta = 0$ into (4), we can get the following mathematical expression that

$$\frac{1}{\theta} + \frac{W-1}{2}(1 - e^{-1}) = \frac{K}{M} - \frac{e^{-1}}{\lambda}, \tag{25}$$

it can be observed that the (25) does not hold when $\frac{K}{M} - \frac{e^{-1}}{\lambda} < 1$, i.e., $\lambda < \frac{e^{-1}}{\frac{K}{M}-1} \triangleq \lambda_L$, which is conflict with previous assumptions. By performing some manipulations that $\frac{\partial}{\partial\lambda}\bar{\lambda}_{\text{out}} > 0$ and $\frac{\partial}{\partial p_1}\bar{\lambda}_{\text{out}} < 0$ for $p_1 \in (e^{-1}, 1)$, we can draw the conclusion that $p_1 > e^{-1}$ is founded when $\lambda < \lambda_L$, and the optimal value of p_1 is $p_1^* = e^{-1}$ when $\lambda \geq \lambda_L$. Similarly, we can also prove that the optimal value of p_2 is $p_2^* = 1 - \phi_{\text{th}}^{1/Q_{\text{th}}}$ if and only if $\lambda \geq \lambda_H$.

Based on the discussion above, we can draw the conclusion that $p_1^* = e^{-1}$ and $p_2^* > 1 - \phi_{\text{th}}^{1/Q_{\text{th}}}$, substituting it into (4) and (12), we can get the following expression that

$$\frac{\Delta\theta^*}{\theta^*} = -\frac{NI_{RA}}{M}\ln\frac{p_2^*}{\omega} \triangleq u(p_2^*), \tag{26}$$

$$\frac{W^* - 1}{2} = \frac{\frac{K\theta^*}{M} - \frac{1}{\lambda}(\theta^* e^{-1} + \Delta\theta^* p_2^*) - 1}{\theta^*(1 - e^{-1}) + \Delta\theta^*(1 - p_2^*)}, \tag{27}$$

it can be observed that the (27) is hold if and only if $W = 1$, since $\lambda < \lambda_H$. Thus, the optimal setting of $(\theta^*, \Delta\theta^*)$ can be mathematically written as

$$\theta^* = \frac{1}{\frac{K}{M} - \frac{e^{-1} + p_2^* u(p_2^*)}{\lambda}}, \quad \Delta\theta^* = \frac{u(p_2^*)}{\frac{K}{M} - \frac{e^{-1} + p_2^* u(p_2^*)}{\lambda}}, \tag{28}$$

and the corresponding maximal network throughput can be obtained as

$$\bar{\lambda}'_{\max} = Me^{-1} + NI_{RA}p_2^*\ln\frac{\omega}{p_2^*}, \tag{29}$$

since $\bar{\lambda}'_{\max}$ and $\theta^* + \Delta\theta^*$ is monotonically decreasing with p_2^*, with the constraint that $\theta^* + \Delta\theta^* \leq 1$, we can draw the conclusion that the value of $\bar{\lambda}'_{\max}$ can be maximized when $\theta^* + \Delta\theta^* = 1$. Substituting $\theta^* + \Delta\theta^* = 1$ into (28) and performing some manipulations, we can get the following expression that

$$\frac{K}{M} - \frac{e^{-1} + p_2^* u(p_2^*)}{\lambda} = 1 + u(p_2^*), \tag{30}$$

which has an unique root of p_2^* that maximizes the value of $\bar{\lambda}'_{\max}$.

Similar to the theoretical analysis above, we have $\theta^* = 1$, $\Delta\theta^* = 0$ and $W^* = 1$ when $\lambda < \lambda_L$, and the corresponding maximal network throughput is $\bar{\lambda}''_{\max} = -Mp_1^* \ln p_1^*$. Substituting $\theta^* = 1$, $\Delta\theta^* = 0$ and $W^* = 1$ into (4) and performing some manipulations, we can get the following mathematical expression that

$$\frac{K}{M} + (1 + \frac{1}{\lambda}p_1^*)\ln p_1^* = 0, \tag{31}$$

which has an unique root of p_1^* that maximizes the value of $\bar{\lambda}''_{\max}$. This completes the proof.

Remark 2. According to Theorem 1 and Theorem 2, we can define the following traffic load regions based on the value of λ_H and λ_L. Then, we can obtain the corresponding optimal access control strategy via comparing the values of λ, λ_H and λ_L.

1. **High Traffic Load Region** (when $\lambda \geq \lambda_H$), in which the maximal access throughput is $\bar{\lambda}_{\max} = Me^{-1} + NI_{RA}(1 - \phi_{\text{th}}^{1/Q_{\text{th}}})\ln \frac{\omega}{1-\phi_{\text{th}}^{1/Q_{\text{th}}}}$, and the corresponding optimal setting of $(\theta^*, \Delta\theta^*)$ and W^* can be adaptively tuning based on (22) (23) and (24). For example, the optimal setting of $(\theta^*, \Delta\theta^*)$ when $W = 1$, which is denote as $\theta^*|_{W=1}$ and $\Delta\theta^*|_{W=1}$, can be written as

$$\theta^*|_{W=1} = \frac{1}{\frac{K}{M} - \frac{e^{-1}+\alpha(1-\phi_{\text{th}}^{1/Q_{\text{th}}})}{\lambda}}, \tag{32}$$

$$\Delta\theta^*|_{W=1} = \frac{\alpha}{\frac{K}{M} - \frac{e^{-1}+\alpha(1-\phi_{\text{th}}^{1/Q_{\text{th}}})}{\lambda}}, \tag{33}$$

Similarly, the optimal UB window size when $\theta + \Delta\theta = 1$, which is denote as $W^*|_{\theta+\Delta\theta=1}$, can be written as

$$W^*|_{\theta+\Delta\theta=1} = 2\frac{\frac{K}{M} - \frac{e^{-1}+\alpha(1-\phi_{\text{th}}^{1/Q_{\text{th}}})}{\lambda} - 1 - \alpha}{1 - e^{-1} + \alpha\phi_{\text{th}}^{1/Q_{\text{th}}}} + 1. \tag{34}$$

2. **Medium Traffic Load Region** (when $\lambda_L \leq \lambda < \lambda_H$), in which the maximal access throughput is $\bar{\lambda}'_{\max} = Me^{-1} + NI_{RA}p_2^* \ln \frac{\omega}{p_2^*} < \bar{\lambda}_{\max}$, where p_2^* is the unique solution of the following mathematical equation

$$\frac{K}{M} - \frac{e^{-1} + p_2^* u(p_2^*)}{\lambda} = 1 + u(p_2^*), \tag{35}$$

where $u(p_2^*) = -\frac{NI_{RA}}{M}\ln\frac{p_2^*}{\omega}$, the optimal setting of $(\theta^*, \Delta\theta^*, W^*)$ cannot be adaptively tuned, and has an unique solution of $\theta^* = \frac{1}{\frac{K}{M} - \frac{e^{-1}+p_2^* u(p_2^*)}{\lambda}}$, $\Delta\theta^* = \frac{u(p_2^*)}{\frac{K}{M} - \frac{e^{-1}+p_2^* u(p_2^*)}{\lambda}}$ and $W^* = 1$, respectively.

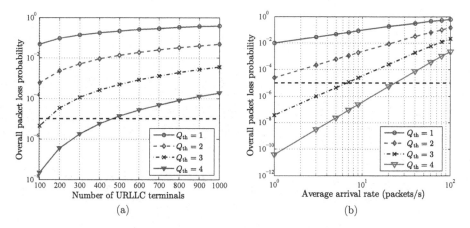

Fig. 3. Transmission performance of URLLC without traffic offloading mechanism (i.e., when $\Delta\theta = 0$): (a) Overall packet loss probability ϕ vs. Number of URLLC terminals L, where the number of channels in the connection-less resource pool $N = 10$ and the average arrival rate of each URLLC terminal is $\tilde{\mu} = 5\,(\text{packets/s})$. (b) Overall packet loss probability ϕ vs. Average arrival rate $\tilde{\mu}$, where $L = 100$ and $N = 10$.

3. **Low Traffic Load Region** (when $\lambda < \lambda_L$), in which the maximal access throughput is $\bar{\lambda}''_{\max} = -Mp_1^* \ln p_1^* < Me^{-1}$, where p_1^* is the unique solution of the following mathematical equation

$$\frac{K}{M} + \left(1 + \frac{1}{\lambda}p_1^*\right) \ln p_1^* = 0, \tag{36}$$

the corresponding optimal setting of $(\theta^*, \Delta\theta^*, W^*)$ cannot be adaptively tuned, and has an unique solution of $\theta^* = 1$, $\Delta\theta^* = 0$ and $W^* = 1$, respectively.

5 Simulation Results

In this section, numerical and simulation results are provided to validate the theoretical analyses and demonstrate the performance gain of our proposed DT-MRA protocol. Consider the uplink transmission of a heterogeneous MTC network with $K = 10000$ delay-insensitive terminals and $L = 100$ URLLC terminals coexistence. The QoS requirement of each URLLC terminal is characterized by an E2E latency bound $T_{\text{th}} = 1\,\text{ms}$ and the corresponding maximal allowable packet loss probability $\phi_{\text{th}} = 10^{-5}$. To support multiple transmission attempts of URLLC, we consider a 5G NR mini-slot structure with unit slot length of $\tau = 0.25\,\text{ms}$ (e.g., each mini-slot contains 7 OFDM symbols, and the subcarrier spacing is $W_0 = 30\,\text{kHz}$ [10]), and thus each URLLC terminal can transmit same packet $Q_{\text{th}} = 4$ times within the E2E latency bound. In the connection-oriented resource pool, there are $M = 54$ available preambles and the duration of each RA

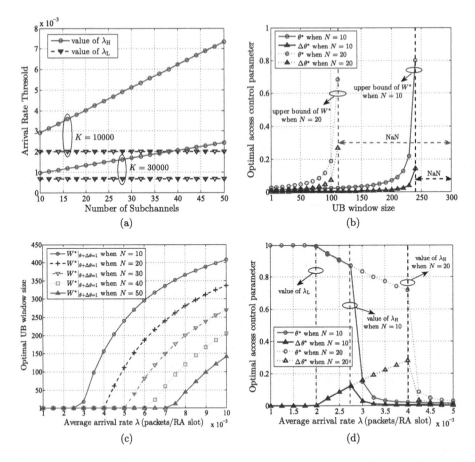

Fig. 4. Illustration of the optimal access control strategy, where the arrival rate of URLLC is $\mu = 10^{-3}$ (packets/slot) and $Q_{\text{th}} = 4$: (a) the value of arrival rate thresholds (λ_H, λ_L) vs. the number of channels in the connection-less resource pool N. (b) the optimal access control parameters $(\theta^*, \Delta\theta^*)$ vs. the UB window size W. (c) the optimal UB window size W^* when $\theta + \Delta\theta = 1$ vs. the average arrival rate of each delay-insensitive terminal λ (packets/RA slot). (d) the optimal access control parameters $(\theta^*, \Delta\theta^*)$ when $W = 1$ vs. the value of λ (packets/RA slot).

slot is $T_{RA} = 5$ ms, which contains $I_{RA} = T_{RA}/\tau = 20$ consecutive slots. Moreover, the maximum allowable UB window size is $W_{\max} = 401$. To achieve reliable numerical results, Monte-Carlo simulations are implemented that all statistical results are averaged over 10^7 RA slots.

As depicted in Fig. 3, numerical results are provided to illustrate the overall packet loss probability ϕ of URLLC when $\Delta\theta = 0$, i.e., the connection-less resource pool is only utilized by URLLC terminals for the grant-free data transmission. In this scenario, the value of ϕ is obtained via substituting $\Delta\theta = 0$ into (11). On the one hand, Fig. 3(a) shows how the overall packet loss probability varies with the total number of URLLC terminals L and the degree of packet repetition Q_{th}. Since the E2E latency bound $T_{th} = 1\,\text{ms}$ is given, the value of $Q_{th} = \lfloor T_{th}/\tau \rfloor$ is determined by the frame structure. For example, $Q_{th} = 2$ implies that the slot length is set to $\tau = 0.5\,\text{ms}$, and then we can further obtain that the average number of new arrival packets per slot is $\mu = \tau\tilde{\mu} = 2.5 \times 10^{-3}$. From the curves in Fig. 3, we can observe that the overall packet loss probability decreases substantially with the degree of packet repetition increases, which validates the viewpoint that the packet repetition mechanism in our proposed DT-MRA protocol is helpful to guarantee the ultra-high transmission reliability of each URLLC terminal.

Figure 4 illustrates how to design the optimal access control strategy, i.e., find the optimal setting of access control parameters $(\theta^*, \Delta\theta^*, W^*)$, based on the statistical traffic load information (λ, μ). In practical networks, the statistical traffic load information can be obtained via designing traffic prediction algorithms, such as the work in [11]. In this conference paper, we assume that the statistical traffic load information can be perfectly estimated without error. Figure 4(a) shows how the value of arrival rate thresholds (λ_H, λ_L) changes as the number of channels in the connection-less resource pool varies. It is not hard to observe that the value of λ_L keeps constant when the value of N changes, and the value of λ_H increases when the value of N increases, which comply well with the theoretical derivations in Theorem 2. Figure 4(b) illustrates how the optimal setting of access control parameters $(\theta^*, \Delta\theta^*)$ and UB window size W^* in high traffic load region adaptively tuning based on (22) (23) and (24), where $\lambda = 5 \times 10^{-3} > \lambda_H$ and the upper bound of W^* can be obtained via substituting $\theta^* + \Delta\theta^* = 1$ into (22) and (23). As a supplementary to Fig. 4(b), Fig. 4(c) shows how the upper bound of W^* changes with the value of λ varies. By comparing with Fig. 4(a), we can observe that the upper bound of W^* can be larger than 1 only when $\lambda > \lambda_H$, and can only be equal to 1 when $\lambda \leq \lambda_H$, which comply well with the conclusions in Remark 2. Moreover, Fig. 4(d) shows how the optimal access control parameters $(\theta^*, \Delta\theta^*)$ when $W^* = 1$ changes with the value of λ varies, we can clearly observe that $(\theta^*, \Delta\theta^*) = (1, 0)$ when $\lambda \leq \lambda_L$ (i.e., low traffic load region), $\theta^* + \Delta\theta^* = 1$ and $\Delta\theta^* > 0$ when $\lambda_L < \lambda < \lambda_H$ (i.e., medium traffic load region), and $\theta^* + \Delta\theta^* \leq 1$ when $\lambda \geq \lambda_H$ (i.e., high traffic load region). Note that the values of θ^* and $\Delta\theta^*$ when $W^* = 1$ are given by (32) and (33), respectively.

Figure 5(a) illustrates how the average access throughput of delay-insensitive terminals $\bar{\lambda}_{out}$ varies with number of channels N in the connection-less resource pool, under different value of data arrival rate λ. Specifically, the relationship between $\bar{\lambda}_{out}$ and N has been discussed in the Theorem 1 and Theorem 2. Based on the observation in the Fig. 5(a), there exists a prefect match between the simulation results and theoretical analysis. Moreover, we can see that the value of $\bar{\lambda}_{out}$ is not vary with N when $\lambda < \lambda_H$, and linearly increases with N thanks to the impact of traffic offloading. Note that the value of λ_H is also linearly increases with N. As depicted in Fig. 5(b), we demonstrate the effectiveness of our proposed DT-MRA protocol, in terms of improving the access throughput.

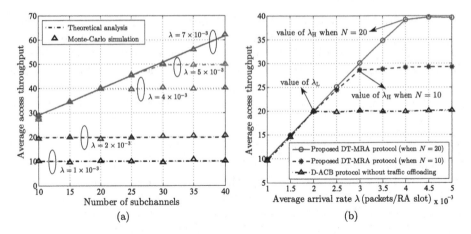

Fig. 5. Monte-Carlo simulation results to validate the theoretical analysis, where the arrival rate of URLLC is $\mu = 10^{-3}$ (packets/slot) and $Q_{\text{th}} = 4$: (a) Average access throughput of delay-insensitive terminals $\bar{\lambda}_{\text{out}}$ vs. the number of channels N. (b) Performance comparison between our proposed DT-MRA protocol and benchmark protocol, in terms of average access throughput $\bar{\lambda}_{\text{out}}$.

To provide comparable numerical results, the D-ACB protocol proposed in [12] without traffic offloading mechanism is specified as a benchmark scheme. On the one hand, we can see that the maximum value of $\bar{\lambda}_{\text{out}}$ is linearly increases with λ when $\lambda < \lambda_H$, and stay constant when $\lambda \geq \lambda_H$. This is due to the value of $\bar{\lambda}_{\text{max}}$ is a constant with λ varies, and the value of $\bar{\lambda}'_{\text{max}}$ and $\bar{\lambda}''_{\text{max}}$ is linearly increases with λ, which has been proved in the Theorem 1 and Theorem 2. On the other hand, when $\lambda > \lambda_L$, our proposed DT-MRA protocol can provide a remarkable performance gain with compare to the benchmark scheme, thanks to the traffic offloading mechanism. Seen from a different perspective, our proposed DT-MRA protocol also has the advantage of low complexity, due to the optimal access control parameters $(\theta^*, \Delta\theta^*, W^*)$ can be determined without the need of real-time load estimation per RA slot.

6   Conclusions

In this paper, we considered a heterogeneous MTC network with massive number of delay-insensitive and URLLC terminals coexistence, and proposed a novel double-threshold-based massive random access (DT-MRA) protocol. On the one hand, the proposed DT-MRA protocol allows partial delay-insensitive terminals temporarily preempting URLLC spectrum channels to alleviate the traffic overload, via adaptively tuning access control parameters including ACB factor and traffic offloading factor. On the other hand, a grant-free access mechanism with packet repetition was applied to support the stringent QoS requirements of URLLC. Then, an optimization problem was formulated to maximize the access throughput of delay-insensitive terminals, while satisfying the QoS requirements of each URLLC terminal. Based on the statistical traffic load information of each terminal, an optimal access control strategy was also developed to solve this optimization problem. Simulation results validated the theoretical analyses and demonstrated the effectiveness of our proposed DT-MRA protocol, in terms of improving access throughput. In future works, we will further investigate the issue of joint random access and resource allocation strategy design under a practical case that the number of PUSCHs is limited, which is still a open issue in the MTC networks with delay-insensitive and URLLC terminals coexistence.

References

1. Jayawickrama, B.A., He, Y., Dutkiewicz, E., Mueck, M.D.: Scalable spectrum access system for massive machine type communication. IEEE Netw. **32**(3), 154–160 (2018)
2. Li, X., Li, D., Wan, J., Liu, C., Imran, M.: Adaptive transmission optimization in SDN-based industrial internet of things with edge computing. IEEE Internet Things J. **5**(3), 1351–1360 (2018)
3. 3GPP TR 36.881 v1.1.0, Study on latency reduction techniques for LTE, June 2016
4. Zhan, W., Sun, X., Li, Y., Tian, F., Wang, H.: Optimal group paging frequency for machine-to-machine communications in LTE networks with contention resolution. IEEE Internet Things J. **6**(6), 10534–10545 (2019)
5. Lin, Y., Huang, J., Fan, C., Chen, W.: Local authentication and access control scheme in M2M communications with computation offloading. IEEE Internet Things J. **5**(4), 3209–3219 (2018)
6. Singh, B., Tirkkonen, O., Li, Z., Uusitalo, M.A.: Contention-based access for ultra-reliable low latency uplink transmissions. IEEE Wireless Commun. Lett. **7**(2), 182–185 (2018)
7. 3GPP TS 36.321 V12.5.0, Evolved universal terrestrial radio access (E-UTRA); Medium access control (MAC) protocol specification, April 2015
8. Gross, D., Harris, C.M.: Fundamentals of Queueing Theory. Wiley, Hoboken (1998)
9. Sun, C., She, C., Yang, C., Quek, T.Q.S., Li, Y., Vucetic, B.: Optimizing resource Allocation in the short blocklength regime for ultra-reliable and low-latency communications. IEEE Trans. Wireless Commun. **18**(1), 402–415 (2019)
10. Sachs, J., Wikstrom, G., Dudda, T., Baldemair, R., Kittichokechai, K.: 5G radio network design for ultra-reliable low-latency communication. IEEE Netw. **32**(2), 24–31 (2018)
11. Xu, Y., Yin, F., Xu, W., Lin, J., Cui, S.: Wireless traffic prediction with scalable gaussian process: framework, algorithms, and verification. IEEE J. Sel. Areas Commun. **37**(6), 1291–1306 (2019)
12. Duan, S., Shah-Mansouri, V., Wang, Z., Wong, V.W.S.: D-ACB: adaptive congestion control algorithm for bursty M2M traffic in LTE networks. IEEE Trans. Veh. Technol. **65**(12), 9847–9861 (2016)

IP Addressing and Address Management of Space-Based Network Based on Geographical Division

Fu Wei[1(⊠)], Xu Zhen[1], and Gao Zihe[2]

[1] School of Electronic and Information Engineering, Beihang University,
Beijing 100191, China
fuwei@buaa.edu.cn
[2] China Academy of Space Technology, Beijing 100094, China

Abstract. In this article, a detailed geographically-based address allocation method in space-based network is designed, which saves address resources, reduces the size of routing tables, and improves data forwarding efficiency. On this basis, an address management method is proposed to reduce the impact of satellite handover on data transmission. The simulation results of the model on the simulation platform show that our address management method can automatically assign addresses and achieve efficient routing addressing. The handover between a satellite and location areas does not affect the terminal node.

Keywords: Space-based network · Addressing · Satellite handover

1 Introduction

The space-based network mainly refers to a network that uses satellites as an access point to provide communication for the ground. It is the main way and method for collecting, processing, and forwarding information or resources obtained in space. It is regarded as an important part of the next generation Internet by many domestic and foreign enterprises and units. Due to the convergence trend of space-based networks and terrestrial Internet, it is necessary to directly use IP protocol in space-based networks to enhance compatibility. In addition, as the cost of terrestrial access terminals decreases, the number of access terminals will continue to increase. Therefore, it is necessary to consider how to better allocate and manage the IP addresses of access users.

Specifically, address allocation management in the network mainly includes two addressing ideas: host-based and link-based. The former is to directly assign an address to a host in the network. The advantage is to save address resources, but it will make the routing table size of the nodes in the network increase linearly with the number of nodes, which in turn leads to an increase in calculation and search. [1] The latter is to configure the address for the host's interface. The advantage is that for the router, only the subnet information aggregated by the gateway node needs to be stored, which greatly improves the routing lookup efficiency. However, the mobility of satellite nodes will cause link periodic disconnection, making this method couldn't be directly applied

B. Li et al. (Eds.): IoTaaS 2020, LNICST 346, pp. 510–525, 2021.
https://doi.org/10.1007/978-3-030-67514-1_41

to the space-based network. [2] According to the existing routing table entry measurement research [3], the main reason for the continuous growth of the routing table is that the aggregation relationship cannot be maintained and the network address fragmentation is excessive. Therefore, the key to addressing space-based networks is how to maintain the hierarchical relationship in the network and realize the aggregation of subnets. A method for segmenting the network based on the ground coverage area of the low-orbit satellite provides idea for how to maintain the hierarchy of nodes in the network during addressing. Although this addressing method has been preliminarily studied, there are still many details that are not perfect for address management and specific implementation [4]. No consideration has been given to the address allocation of the space-based network during deployment, nor the address and link changes caused by the movement of satellite nodes and ground user nodes in the space-based network. Therefore, this article will carry out further research on the IP address management method of space-based network based on geographical division.

The main work of this paper is as follows: in section two, we designed the IP address allocation method of space-based network based on geographic partitioning. This method divides the earth's surface into multiple regions and location areas based on network structure and geographic information. According to the mapping relationship between the partition and the satellite node, we improve routing addressing method, reducing the number of routing table entries. In section three, we propose link and IP address handover management method in space-based networks. By preprocessing before the satellite's corresponding location area changes, the terminal information remains unchanged, thereby ensuring that the terminal address within the area remain unchanged. The timing of switching is determined by the terminal, which reduces the impact of link switching on data transmission. Finally, the space-based network architecture is modeled on the simulation development platform, and joined the ground access terminal to test whether the handover management is realized. We also make the simulation output visualized. Simulation results show that for space-based networks, this address management method can automatically assign addresses, achieve routing addressing, avoid the occurrence of abnormal access terminals, and the handover between satellite and location area will not affect terminal nodes.

2   IP Addressing and Allocation

To achieve better ground coverage, higher communication rates, and lower access delays, the development of a global mobile satellite network based on a low-orbit satellite network has become an international military and civilian satellite system development trend. For a single country, due to geopolitical factors and defense security considerations, satellite ground stations cannot be evenly deployed globally. Therefore, by increasing the number and performance of geostationary satellites, a more space-based network can be created.

2.1   Network Architecture and Addressing Concept

For the purpose of better explaining our addressing concepts and methods, a space-based network model with a three-layer network structure is proposed. The convergence layer node is composed of dozens of satellites running in geostationary orbit, and serves as the main bridge between the space-based network and the ground network. The access layer node is composed of hundreds of low-orbit satellites to provide data transmission capabilities for ground access terminals. The ground network layer is composed of interconnected ground stations and data centers to achieve the connection to the Internet, and is connected to the satellite nodes of the convergence layer by satellite-ground links. Through the interconnection of the ground core network with the Internet and cellular communication networks, the integration of the satellite-ground network can be achieved to meet the needs of commercial and military data access (Fig. 1).

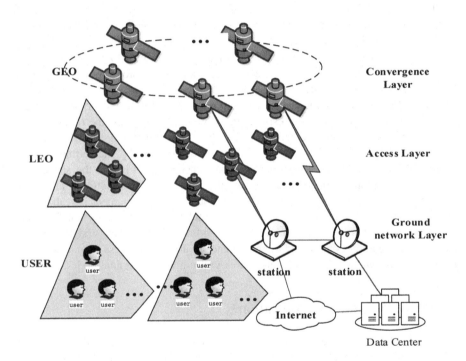

Fig. 1. Space-based network architecture

The network layer is the key to realize the integration between heterogeneous networks. Using IP addressing format is the mainstream method to avoid increasing the redundant traffic due to conversion of address formats. Besides, a unified address allocation method can also improve the throughput and efficiency of data exchange between the stars and the ground. In the network layer, since the existing Internet still widely uses the IPv4 protocol. IPv4-in-IPv6 [5] related tunneling technology has also been studied, which means IPv4 format addresses will easily evolve into IPv6. In the IPv4 protocol, the identifier set for each user consists of 32 binary digits, which can distinguish up to more than 4 billion user terminals.

In order to achieve the aggregation of subnet addresses, for a given IP address segment, we divide it into many subnets that can be aggregated, and then assign the subnet to each ground area [6]. For a low-orbit satellite constellation with P low-orbit satellites orbiting planes and S nodes in each plane, the earth surface coverage area can be divided into M = P × S ground location areas. Each location area corresponds to a satellite at the same time. In addition, the location areas of the same longitude are aggregated into a region, which means that there will be P regions. The geostationary satellite selects its own service area according to its longitude and traffic of the region, and establishes an inter-satellite link with the low earth orbit (LEO) satellite node corresponding to the location area in the region. This method combines link-based and host-based addressing features, which improves routing addressing efficiency through address aggregation and reduces the required address space.

2.2 Address Allocation

The links in the space-based network can be divided into inter-satellite links and satellite-ground links according to different types of nodes, and also can be divided into point-to-point links and spot beam links according to the number of nodes. Our address allocation method will allocate addresses in the order of allocating the satellite-ground link subnet first and then the inter-satellite link subnet (Fig. 2).

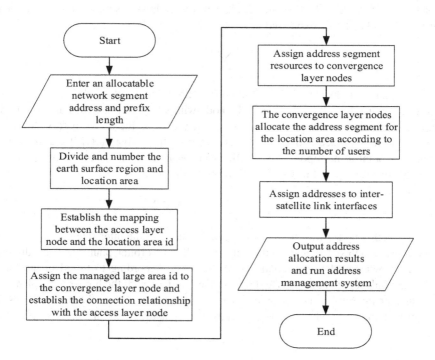

Fig. 2. Main process of IP address allocation

The first step is to divide the given network segment into aggregated subnets. Our project adopts classless addressing scheme which uses variable-length subnet mask (VLSM), and implements address aggregation through classless inter-domain routing (CIDR) [7]. In this method, the network type and network number no longer restrict the address format, and the subnet size can be changed to any size [8]. According to the hierarchical relationship in the space-based network, the address segment is firstly divided into different subnet segments according to the number of regions. Then the subnet segment is subdivided again according to the number of ground location areas.

After completing the division of the subnet, we begin to assign addresses to the satellite-ground links. The interface communicating to ground of the access layer node will be assigned the first IP address of the corresponding subnet segment. The ground access host finds its ground location area, registers in the location area and obtains a host address. The address of the access host when it first accesses the service location area is assigned by the satellite node. According to RFC 3927, the host can choose an address from the 169.254.0.0/16 address segment as a temporary IP address for the initial address application and terminal registration [9].

Then, the address allocation of the inter-satellite link is performed. The subnet mask of a point-to-point inter-satellite link in space can be expressed as 255.255.255.252, indicating that the link can accommodate two interface addresses in addition to the network address and broadcast address, corresponding to the two ends of the link. Therefore, a single point-to-point inter-satellite link needs at least 4 addresses. We divide the links into permanent links and dynamic links according to whether they will change. Since the permanent links are all point-to-point links in the space-based network, the interface addresses of both ends can be directly configured as a subnet, such as 172.22.1.5 and 172.22.1.6, the addresses should be applied for F permanent links can be expressed as:

$$N_{perm} = \sum_{i=0}^{F} f_i = 4F \tag{1}$$

For dynamic links between satellite nodes with different orbit radii, the link subnet address is assigned to the interface of the node with a larger orbit radius, making it the party which actively allocates the address (referred to as the active party), the other address of the interface is dynamically allocated by the active party. If the high-orbit node is a point-to-multipoint link of the spot beam type, the number of addresses required for a group of links with a maximum of d nodes is:

$$n_{dyna} = 2^K \geq d + 2, K \in N \tag{2}$$

For satellite nodes with the same orbit radii, although the inter-satellite links are all point-to-point links, the node links between different orbital planes will be disconnected or switched due to the latitude of the node. According to the id of the track plane, the link subnet address is assigned to the interface with the higher track plane id, and another interface is not assigned an initial IP address. When the dynamic link is established, the party with the address sends its own address, and the party without the initial address first selects a temporary address from the 169.254.0.0/16 address segment as the communication address.

Therefore, the number of addresses required by D dynamic links and the total number of addresses of inter-satellite links are:

$$N_{dyna} = \sum_{i=1}^{D} n_{i-dyna} \tag{3}$$

$$N_{ISL} = N_{perm} + N_{dyna} \tag{4}$$

2.3 Routing Strategy

After accessing the ground location area and applying for an IP address, the ground node can communicate with other nodes in the space-based network or the server in the Internet through the ground network nodes, so the data packets transmitted in the network need to be routed, addressed, and determined the egress interface corresponding to the next hop according to the destination address of the packet. Since only the ground network nodes and the access terminal nodes can send and receive data in the network, other satellite nodes will only forward data packets, and will not generate a lot of application layer information. Therefore, the routing addressing method should target the data packets sent by ground users. In space-based networks, terrestrial user terminals must have a home location area. Through the mapping of the location area and satellite nodes, the data packets will eventually be routed based on the satellite nodes. This method has less cost and higher routing performance, and is more suitable for space-based networks with multiple nodes [10].

Each satellite node has three processing steps for the received data packets:

1. Find the number information of the region and ground location area to which it belongs according to the destination address of the received data packet;
2. Search for the corresponding satellite node in the mapping table between the satellite node and the service location area, according to the number of the ground location area;
3. If the corresponding node is the current satellite node, the ground terminal information is queried and sent to the corresponding terminal; otherwise, the corresponding next hop exit is searched in the node routing table according to the satellite node information, and the data packet is forwarded.

The routing information between the satellite nodes can be calculated and converged by itself at the initial stage of the establishment of space-based network. By mapping the destination address to a specific satellite node, our routing method shields the addressing difficulties caused by link switching, reduces the cost of routing maintenance, and is more suitable for the long-term operation of space-based networks.

3 IP Address Management and Handover

3.1 Address Management of Inter-Satellite Link

Due to the different orbit radii, inclination and phase of the satellite, the inter-satellite link will dynamically switch. Inter-satellite links are mainly composed of links in the same orbital plane, links in adjacent orbital planes and links in different orbital radii, where dynamic links mainly exist between nodes in different orbital planes or orbital heights. If the nodes on the link have the same orbit radii but different orbit planes, address management is performed according to the orbit id, as shown in the following figure. The node with the higher orbital plane number where the node is located manages the address, and the interface of the other party obtains the communication address through the handshake information when the link is established, and resets its interface address after the link is disconnected (Fig. 3).

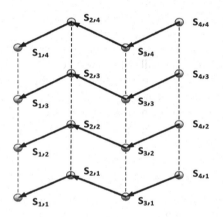

Fig. 3. Address management of links between adjacent orbit planes

For link handover between satellite nodes with different orbit radii, address management is performed according to the operating altitude and the level in the space-based network. For the node interface that may establish a connection, the node closer to the ground network manages the address. For example, when establishing a link with an aggregation layer node, the access layer node selects the aggregation layer node bound to the region for handshake according to the correspondence between the ground location area and the region, and the aggregation layer node allocates the address to ensure its own interface The interfaces corresponding to the aggregation layer nodes are in the same subnet. When the access layer node leaves the area, the link is disconnected, the convergence layer node reclaims the assigned address, and the access layer node interface resets the address to zero.

3.2   Address Handover of the Satellite-Ground Link

The satellite-ground link is mainly composed of the connection between the satellite node and the ground station or the ground access terminal. Since the geostationary satellite is stationary relative to the ground, the satellite-ground link of the ground station will generally not switch. During the operation of the space-based network, as shown in the following figure, the LEO node moves relatively faster than the ground, so the coverage area is also constantly changing. Therefore, we need perform address maintenance for the interface of LEO node connected to the ground access terminal. In order to better distinguish different satellites and their orbits planes, so as to more concisely represent the mapping relationship between satellites and location areas, the LEO nodes are numbered uniformly. Eventually, routing and address management are performed through the correspondence between satellite id and location areas (Fig. 4).

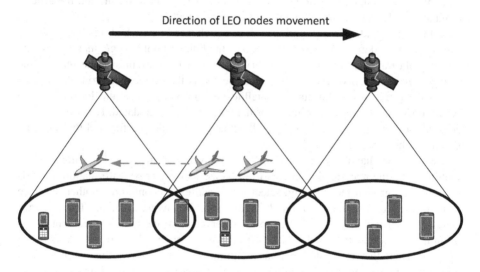

Fig. 4. Movement of LEO nodes

If the LEO's interface initiates link handover and updates the interface address, it will result in a large number of simultaneous interruption of the user terminal's link, affecting data transmission and upper-layer application sessions. Therefore, in order to better ensure that the LEO node smoothly switches the ground-based location area, we consider adding an interface of LEO to ground. One of the interfaces serves the current location area, and another interface forwards the data packets of the adjacent location area. The location area served by the satellite node is simply referred to as the service location area, the forwarded adjacent location area is called the proxy location area, the satellite bound to the ground location area is called the service satellite, and the satellite that forwards the specific location area grouping is called the proxy satellite.

For a location area A, the binding and handover process of its serving satellite is shown in the flowchart. Initially, the relationship between the serving satellite and the location area is determined according to the location information of the satellite node, and then it is periodically checked whether the handover process starts. The average coverage period of the satellite to the location area is obtained through dividing the time of satellite circling the earth by the number of location areas under the orbital plane. The average coverage period of the low-orbit satellites in the same orbital plane is equal. When the location area is served for more than a certain time, the satellite nodes in the same orbital plane start the switching process at the same time, making the rear satellite as the proxy satellite node, which will serve as the new service satellite in the future. Then the current service satellite sends main information of the location area, including geographic location, network resources, and information of connected users to the proxy satellite. At the same time, the current satellite will also broadcast to the connected terminal, indicating that the handover is about to occur, and the ground terminal will decide whether to switch to the new satellite.

On the one hand, if the ground user does not choose to switch at this time, then its address and the address of the opposite end of the link will not change, maintaining the original data transmission. When the service time of the current satellite reaches the average coverage period, the satellite node performs the conversion from the service role to the proxy role. The current satellite no longer serves as the location area's service node, and the user terminal information is no longer updated. However, for the terminals still connected, the satellite will act as proxy node and forward the sent data packets to the new service node.

On the other hand, after receiving the handover start message from the original satellite node, the rear satellite begins to initialize its own proxy information, records the registered ground terminal and select a free address to configure another interface from the network segment of the location area. To avoid conflicts, the interface addresses of proxy and service satellite are reserved from the network segment of the location area, which means the first two addresses can be allocated in the network segment. Then the new satellite node configures its own forwarding strategy and officially becomes the proxy satellite in location area A. After receiving the formal handover message, the new satellite changes the forwarding strategy again and becomes the serving satellite in location area A. The processed data packets are searched in the access terminal information table in location area A according to the routing strategy in Sect. 3 (Fig. 5).

In order to keep the satellite nodes in each orbital plane switching synchronously, the nodes need to broadcast their status of service or proxy to neighboring nodes in the same orbit every short period of time. Through this "heartbeat" mechanism, satellite nodes and service location areas can maintain their correspondence relationship, try to reduce the delay caused by handover, and keep it consistent in all low-orbit satellite nodes, so as to ensure normal routing addressing.

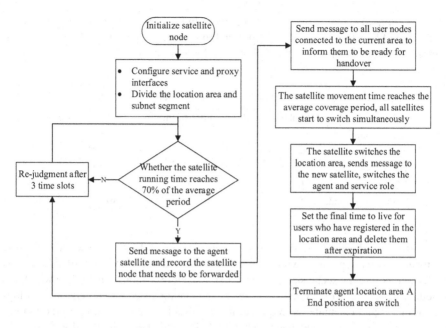

Fig. 5. Process of satellite handover

4 Network Simulation and Visualization

4.1 IP Addressing and Address Allocation Simulation

To simulate our space-based network model, we built a space-based network simulation platform, the overall architecture is shown in the following figure. The simulation platform is mainly composed of four parts: scene maintenance, address management, data transmission and 3D demonstration platform (Fig. 6).

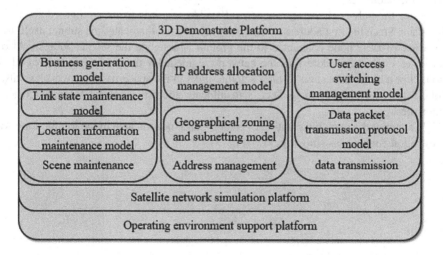

Fig. 6. The overall architecture of space-based network address management simulation

According to actual requirements, the nodes in the space-based network are mainly composed of four types of satellite nodes and three types of ground nodes. The specific number of nodes is shown in the following table (Table 1).

Table 1. Configuration of node in simulation scenario

Node type	Number of node	Number of interface	Node id in scene
IGSO node	3	3	6–8
GEO node	14	6	9–22
HEO node	3	3	23–25
LEO node	110	6	26–135
Ground gate node	5	6	136–140

With the address 172.22.0.0 and the prefix length of 13 as the specified network segment information, the division of the region and the allocation of address are performed before the scene starts to run. First, the address allocation module will check whether the giving network segment meets the existing space-based network topology requirements and calculate the required number of addresses according to the number of node interface types and the number of links, and then start the division of the location area. According to the number of LEO satellite nodes, the surface of earth is evenly divided by latitude and longitude. According to the number of GEO satellite nodes and Eq. (1), the allocable address segment is divided into $2^4 = 16$ subnets of the same size, and the prefix length of each network segment is $13 + 4 = 17$. Each aggregation layer node selects the nearest one or two regions as its own service area according to its longitude information, and assigns a subnet address segment to each location area according to the location area information in the area. Each region requires $2^3 = 8$ subnets, so the network prefix length of the location area is $17 + 3 = 20$, and finally ensure that each location area can support at least 2046 allocable addresses.

After the subnet division, a specific IP address needs to be configured for each interface. Since the first address of each network segment indicates the subnet itself, the interface of LEO node connected to the ground is assigned the second address. Also, we reserve the third address of the network segment for the proxy interface of LEO node. For address allocation of inter-satellite links in the space-based network, we also follow the relevant design in Sect. 3 to allocate address segments for management interfaces.

We output the main information of each ground location area in the log file for easy viewing at runtime, as shown below (Fig. 7).

```
[INFO][0][Print_Grcells_Basicinfo] leo id, startposi, addrinfo:|
[INFO][0][]cell id 0, geo id 11, leo id 134, startposi   -180,    -90, addrinfo 172.23.136.0
[INFO][0][]cell id 1, geo id 11, leo id 135, startposi   -180,-57.2727, addrinfo 172.23.144.0
[INFO][0][]cell id 2, geo id 11, leo id 125, startposi   -180,-24.5455, addrinfo 172.23.152.0
[INFO][0][]cell id 3, geo id 11, leo id 126, startposi   -180, 8.18182, addrinfo 172.23.160.0
[INFO][0][]cell id 4, geo id 11, leo id 127, startposi   -180, 40.9091, addrinfo 172.23.168.0
[INFO][0][]cell id 5, geo id 11, leo id 128, startposi   -180, 73.6364, addrinfo 172.23.176.0
[INFO][0][]cell id 6, geo id 18, leo id 129, startposi      0, 40.9091, addrinfo 172.27.8.0
[INFO][0][]cell id 7, geo id 18, leo id 130, startposi      0, 8.18182, addrinfo 172.27.16.0
[INFO][0][]cell id 8, geo id 18, leo id 131, startposi      0,-24.5455, addrinfo 172.27.24.0
[INFO][0][]cell id 9, geo id 18, leo id 132, startposi      0,-57.2727, addrinfo 172.27.32.0
[INFO][0][]cell id 10, geo id 18, leo id 133, startposi     0,    -90, addrinfo 172.27.40.0
[INFO][0][]cell id 11, geo id 12, leo id 29, startposi   -162,    -90, addrinfo 172.24.8.0
[INFO][0][]cell id 12, geo id 12, leo id 30, startposi   -162,-57.2727, addrinfo 172.24.16.0
[INFO][0][]cell id 13, geo id 12, leo id 31, startposi   -162,-24.5455, addrinfo 172.24.24.0
[INFO][0][]cell id 14, geo id 12, leo id 32, startposi   -162, 8.18182, addrinfo 172.24.32.0
[INFO][0][]cell id 15, geo id 12, leo id 33, startposi   -162, 40.9091, addrinfo 172.24.40.0
[INFO][0][]cell id 16, geo id 12, leo id 34, startposi   -162, 73.6364, addrinfo 172.24.48.0
[INFO][0][]cell id 17, geo id 12, leo id 35, startposi     18, 40.9091, addrinfo 172.27.136.0
[INFO][0][]cell id 18, geo id 19, leo id 36, startposi     18, 8.18182, addrinfo 172.27.144.0
```

Fig. 7. Output record of location area

Due to the need of avoiding address ambiguity, the link-based centralized address allocation method must ensure that the address is in a different subnet segment when the link of interfaces is different. Therefore, it is impossible to aggregate addresses based on the hierarchical relationship of the network. When the satellite nodes in the network are kept unchanged as shown in Table 1 and the number of access terminals is increased, the required IP address resources are shown as the figure below compared with the method based on geographic division. Since the address allocation method based on geographic partition can effectively use the location area for addressing without address ambiguity, the occupied address space can be smaller. The difference is more obvious when there are more terminals (Fig. 8).

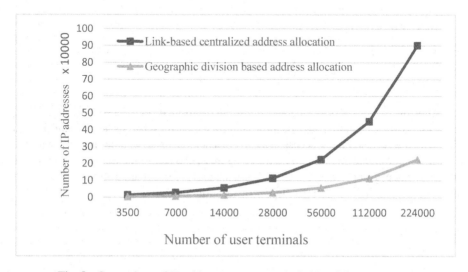

Fig. 8. Comparison of IP address resources occupied by different methods

The overall result of address allocation shows that the designed address allocation method can meet the needs of the space-based network operation, and can ensure that the address resources are saved under the premise of no conflicts, which provides an effective reference for the development of the space-based network.

4.2   Data Transmission and Address Management Simulation

When the address allocation in the network is completed, the nodes in the simulation scenario start to run. LEO nodes broadcast to neighboring satellites according to their own routing tables, and update their own routing tables according to the received information of other nodes. In the case of one broadcast interval, the routing tables of all LEO nodes reach convergence after five broadcast cycles. All interfaces are recorded in the routing table, and the data is shown in the following Fig. 9:

#LEO id: 1				
DstAddr	SubnetMask	NextHop	OutputIntrf	Distance
0.0.0.0	0.0.0.0	172.26.128.1	172.26.128.3	32
172.22.0.141	255.255.255.252	172.22.0.141	172.22.0.142	1
172.22.0.145	255.255.255.252	172.22.0.141	172.22.0.142	1
172.22.0.146	255.255.255.252	172.22.0.154	172.22.0.153	2
172.22.0.150	255.255.255.252	172.22.0.150	172.22.0.149	1
172.22.0.154	255.255.255.252	172.22.0.154	172.22.0.153	1
172.22.0.157	255.255.255.252	172.22.0.150	172.22.0.149	1
172.22.0.158	255.255.255.252	172.22.0.150	172.22.0.149	2
172.22.0.161	255.255.255.252	172.22.0.150	172.22.0.149	1
172.22.0.162	255.255.255.252	172.22.0.154	172.22.0.153	2
172.22.0.165	255.255.255.252	172.22.0.150	172.22.0.149	2
172.22.0.166	255.255.255.252	172.22.0.150	172.22.0.149	3

Fig. 9. Partial routing table of LEO node

After the scene starts to operate, the ground terminal nodes also start to join the network. After calculating the location area to which they belong and establishing a link with the corresponding access layer node. Then they start to communicate with the peer at a random rate after obtaining the IP address, and record the transmission process of some node groups in the log. The log also records a handover of the terminal between the service and proxy satellite of location area.

As shown in the figure below, in the operation of the space-based network, with the assistance of the proxy and the service role, the handover of the satellite to the ground area no longer means that the connection with the terminal in the area will be immediately interrupted, and the terminal can choose proper time to switch according to its own data transmission situation. The application layer session of the ground terminal shields the satellite service and proxy partition changes, so that routing and addressing can still be normally achieved (Fig. 10).

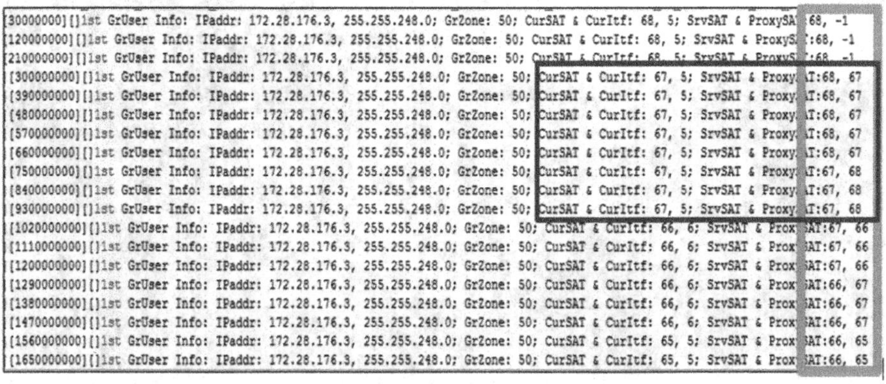

```
[30000000][]1st GrUser Info: IPaddr: 172.28.176.3, 255.255.248.0; GrZone: 50; CurSAT & CurItf: 68, 5; SrvSAT & ProxySA :68, -1
[120000000][]1st GrUser Info: IPaddr: 172.28.176.3, 255.255.248.0; GrZone: 50; CurSAT & CurItf: 68, 5; SrvSAT & ProxyS :68, -1
[210000000][]1st GrUser Info: IPaddr: 172.28.176.3, 255.255.248.0; GrZone: 50; CurSAT & CurItf: 68, 5; SrvSAT & ProxyS :68, -1
[300000000][]1st GrUser Info: IPaddr: 172.28.176.3, 255.255.248.0; GrZone: 50; CurSAT & CurItf: 67, 5; SrvSAT & Proxy T:68, 67
[390000000][]1st GrUser Info: IPaddr: 172.28.176.3, 255.255.248.0; GrZone: 50; CurSAT & CurItf: 67, 5; SrvSAT & Proxy T:68, 67
[480000000][]1st GrUser Info: IPaddr: 172.28.176.3, 255.255.248.0; GrZone: 50; CurSAT & CurItf: 67, 5; SrvSAT & Proxy T:68, 67
[570000000][]1st GrUser Info: IPaddr: 172.28.176.3, 255.255.248.0; GrZone: 50; CurSAT & CurItf: 67, 5; SrvSAT & Proxy T:68, 67
[660000000][]1st GrUser Info: IPaddr: 172.28.176.3, 255.255.248.0; GrZone: 50; CurSAT & CurItf: 67, 5; SrvSAT & Proxy T:68, 67
[750000000][]1st GrUser Info: IPaddr: 172.28.176.3, 255.255.248.0; GrZone: 50; CurSAT & CurItf: 67, 5; SrvSAT & Proxy T:67, 68
[840000000][]1st GrUser Info: IPaddr: 172.28.176.3, 255.255.248.0; GrZone: 50; CurSAT & CurItf: 67, 5; SrvSAT & Proxy T:67, 68
[930000000][]1st GrUser Info: IPaddr: 172.28.176.3, 255.255.248.0; GrZone: 50; CurSAT & CurItf: 67, 5; SrvSAT & Proxy T:67, 68
[1020000000][]1st GrUser Info: IPaddr: 172.28.176.3, 255.255.248.0; GrZone: 50; CurSAT & CurItf: 66, 6; SrvSAT & Prox AT:67, 66
[1110000000][]1st GrUser Info: IPaddr: 172.28.176.3, 255.255.248.0; GrZone: 50; CurSAT & CurItf: 66, 6; SrvSAT & Prox AT:67, 66
[1200000000][]1st GrUser Info: IPaddr: 172.28.176.3, 255.255.248.0; GrZone: 50; CurSAT & CurItf: 66, 6; SrvSAT & Prox AT:67, 66
[1290000000][]1st GrUser Info: IPaddr: 172.28.176.3, 255.255.248.0; GrZone: 50; CurSAT & CurItf: 66, 6; SrvSAT & Prox AT:66, 67
[1380000000][]1st GrUser Info: IPaddr: 172.28.176.3, 255.255.248.0; GrZone: 50; CurSAT & CurItf: 66, 6; SrvSAT & Prox AT:66, 67
[1470000000][]1st GrUser Info: IPaddr: 172.28.176.3, 255.255.248.0; GrZone: 50; CurSAT & CurItf: 66, 6; SrvSAT & Prox AT:66, 67
[1560000000][]1st GrUser Info: IPaddr: 172.28.176.3, 255.255.248.0; GrZone: 50; CurSAT & CurItf: 65, 5; SrvSAT & Prox AT:66, 65
[1650000000][]1st GrUser Info: IPaddr: 172.28.176.3, 255.255.248.0; GrZone: 50; CurSAT & CurItf: 65, 5; SrvSAT & Prox AT:66, 65
```

Fig. 10. Handover between ground terminal and satellite

4.3   Visual Demonstrate

In order to better demonstrate and analyze the operation of the space-based network and the address allocation management method, a three-dimensional demonstration of the scene operation process was developed. During initialization, the visualization platform receives node type and quantity information. When the simulation scene time is greater than 0, the scene platform updates the topology of the space-based network in real time and sends it to the visualization platform. It also updates the location area information and the address information of each node interface.

As shown in the figure below, according to the different orbit radii, the positions of GEO nodes and LEO nodes can be seen, and the links between satellites with different orbit altitudes are hidden to better reflect the operating status of the access layer nodes. When the simulation scenario is running, you can click on the node to view the IP address and routing table information of each interface to observe the address allocation and network operation (Fig. 11).

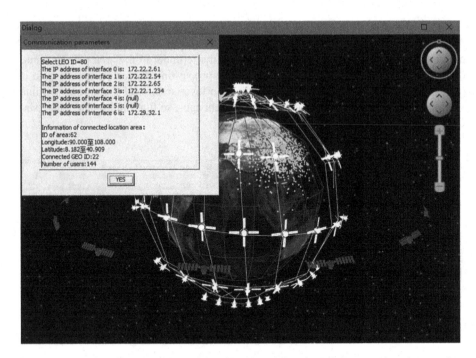

Fig. 11. Visualization of the operation and address allocation of the space-based network

5 Conclusion

In this paper, under the background of continuous development of space-based network technology research, the main methods of address allocation management in the network are studied. We first examined the problems of interface address allocation and access terminal management faced by space-based networks in actual operation. Then, according to the characteristics of the space-based network, a method for address allocation to each node interface in the space-based network is proposed. This method greatly reduces the number of addresses required in the network. Then we propose an address management scheme when the network is running, so that users can maintain a smooth transition at the network layer during satellite switching. Finally, the address allocation and management scheme was developed and verified in the simulation scenario, and the feasibility of network operation was demonstrated through visualization.

References

1. Erunika, O., Kaneko, K., Teraoka, F.: Performance evaluation of host-based mobility management schemes in the internet. In: 2015 Eighth International Conference on Mobile Computing and Ubiquitous Networking (ICMU), Hakodate, pp. 173–178 (2015). https://doi.org/10.1109/icmu.7061062
2. Faraz, S.: Troubleshooting IP Routing Protocols. Cisco Press, Hoboken (2002)

3. Tian, B., Gao, L., Towsley, D.: On characterizing BGP routing table growth. Comput. Netw. **45**(1), 45–54 (2004)
4. Liu, F, Huang, Z.: Design of IP addressing scheme based on satellite network. In: DMCIT, Shanghai (2018)
5. Colitti, L., Battista, G., Patrignani, M.: IPv6-in-IPv4 tunnel discovery: methods and experimental results. IEEE Trans. Netw. Serv. Manage. **1**(1), 30–38 (2004). https://doi.org/10.1109/tnsm.2004.4623692
6. Zhang, T., Liu, L.: Polar low-orbit satellite network IP addressing method and device. China National Intellectual Property Administration. CN201610979071.X (2016). (in Chinese)
7. Mark, S.: IP Routing Fundamentals. Cisco Press Networking Technology, Hoboken (1999)
8. Fuller, et al.: Classless inter-domain routing (CIDR): an address assignment and aggregation strategy. Plant Nutrition. Springer Netherlands (1993)
9. Cheshire, S., Aboba, B., Guttman, E.: Dynamic Configuration of IPv4 Link-Local Addresses. RFC 3927, May 2005
10. Henderson, R., Katz, H.: On distributed, geographic-based packet routing for LEO satellite networks. In: Global Telecommunications Conference, 27 November–December 1,2000, San Francisco, CA, USA, vol. 2, pp. 1119–1123. IEEE, Piscataway, New York (2002)

Artificial Intelligence

A Convolutional Neural Network Approach for Stratigraphic Interface Detection

Jingya Zhang[1], Guojun Li[2], Juan Zhang[2], Guanwen Zhang[1(✉)],
and Wei Zhou[1]

[1] Northwestern Polytechnical University, Xi'an 710072, China
guanwen.zh@nwpu.edu.cn
[2] China Petroleum Logging Co., Ltd., Xi'an 710077, China

Abstract. Making full use of the remaining oil-gas resources is a practical and feasible way to solve the problem of oil shortage. And the most important step of this method is the accurate detection of stratigraphic interface. In this paper, we propose a Convolutional Neural Network (CNN) approach for stratigraphic interface detection from the geophysical well logging data. Our proposed approach can automatically extract representative features from well logs data. It can reduce errors caused by human factors such as manual randomness and lack of experience. First of all, we normalize the data in the form of a single point of the well logging data and convert data points to 2D segment. We then feed segments into the CNN model for training. Secondly, we predict the formation of the well logging data using the trained model. Finally, we introduce a post-processing method to perform the stratigraphic interface detection. The experimental results demonstrate the proposed approach is able to achieve 89.69% of the average accuracy of stratigraphic interface detection. Moreover, the relative error between the predicted boundary points with the ground-truth is only 1%, which indicates the proposed approach satisfy the real-world application requirements.

Keywords: Stratigraphic interface detetion · Geophysical well logging · Convolutional Neural Network

1 Introduction

Nowadays, various high-tech technologies emerge sequentially with the rapid development of the world economy. This is the reason why the consumption of oil in various countries is increasing. To meet the needs of developing of society,

This work was supported in part by the National Key R&D Program of China (No. 2018AAA0102801 and No. 2018AAA0102803), in part of the National Natural Science Foundation of China (No. 61772424, No. 61702418, and No. 61602383), and in part by 13th Five-Year Plan of China National Petroleum Corporation Limited (2019A-3610).

B. Li et al. (Eds.): IoTaaS 2020, LNICST 346, pp. 529–542, 2021.
https://doi.org/10.1007/978-3-030-67514-1_42

further exploration and exploitation of the oil and gas resources is a practical and promising solution. Stratigraphic interface detection is one of the most important tasks for petroleum logging. An automatic stratigraphic interface detection can save human and material resources for the successive development of oil and gas resources.

The well logging data obtained using logging technology contain the formation properties varying with the depth of well. They directly reflect of underground geological features. Therefore, the interface detection of well logs is of great significance for accurately determining the location of the stratigraphy. For a long time, the manual interpretation methods of stratigraphic interface detection is mainly subjective judgments. These methods are mainly based on the morphological transformation characteristics of well logging data, the differences between strata, and the past experience of geologists. These conventional methods not only need huge human and material resources, but also has a relative high detection error. However, the machine learning methods provide an promising solution for automatic detection to solve these problems.

In this paper, we propose a convolutional neural network approach for stratigraphic interface detection. First of all, we normalize the data in the form of a single point of the well logging data, and convert the data points to 2D segment. We then feed segments into the CNN model for training process. Secondly, we use the trained model to predict the formation of the well logging data. Finally, we introduce a post-processing method for the stratigraphic interface detection to fine-gain the detection results. The proposed approach can automatically extract representative features from well logging data. It can reduce errors caused by human factors such as manual randomness, lack of experience, and relatively low proficiency. It can also improve the work efficiency and provide a theoretical basis and foundation for the further development of remaining oil-gas resources.

The contributions of the proposed approach can be summarized as follows. Firstly, we convert single-point well logging data point into segment. Using single points of the well logging data directly will separate the well logging and ignore the relationship between points. So in our manner, the short term temporal information can be fully combined to facilitate subsequent training operations. Secondly, we define stratigraphic interface detection as a classification problem and utilize the formulated segments as input for training CNN model. It is able to extract the effective features of all well logging data. Finally post-processing the prediction results can effectively avoid prediction errors in the prediction process. We evaluate the proposed approach on a real-world oilfield application. The experimental results show that the relative error between our predicted detection result with the ground-truth only 1%, which proves that the proposed approach satisfy the real-world application requirements.

2   Related Work

There are manual interpretation methods and machine learning based methods of stratigraphic interface detection division for well logging. The manual interpretation methods need observing the changes in the shape of the logging data to find out the position of the half point of each section. These methods require export knowledge and experience [20]. These methods also will cause great differences in the stratigraphy results due to differences in personnel experience and proficiency. It will bring a lot of work to the staffs and cause a lot of waste of human and material resources. As the spread of machine learning methods in well logging application, the automatic stratigraphic interface detection methods developed fairly quickly. These methods it can be mainly divided into mathematical statistics methods, non-mathematical statistics methods, and artificial intelligence methods.

Mathematical statistics consists of intra-layer difference methods, ordered cluster analysis and extreme variance clustering methods. Merriam and Hawkins used ordered cluster analysis to stratify a well log firstly [6]. The essence of this method is to seek the optimal cut point to estimate the mutation point. By using the concept of variance in mathematical statistics, the data with close regularity of variance and dispersion is regarded as one category. The data in the two adjacent classes should be obviously different. It is used as the basis for well logging segmentation. Later, they applied the algorithm to multiple well logging application [7]. It can be seen from the methodological perspective that the ordered cluster analysis is very sensitive to the error parameters, and it is easy to lead to overfitting problem. Moreover, the boundary points required by this method only satisfy the minimum intra-layer variance and the maximum inter-layer variance, without considering the geological significance of the interface, i.e., the appearance of false layers. Robert et al. proposed a method based on extreme variance clustering to divide the stratigraphic interface [8,21]. Firstly, they separate the well log roughly, and then they found the segmented point of the precise interface. The cluster analysis method is used to subdivide the layer to realize the merging of the layer interface. This method can maintain the uniformity of the formation and the difference between the layers, but the calculation is very large. It needs to calculate the stratigraphy index for all possible stratigraphy points, and then locates the best stratigraphy interface from these points. If this method is used in the detailed layering step, the amount of calculation will be very huge.

Non-mathematical statistics methods consists of Walsh transform, activity function method, wavelet transform method, Fourier transform and so on. The activity function method was firstly used to calculate the dip angle of microelectrode logging to determine the formation interface [22]. In the process of finding the inflection points of the well log as the stratigraphy point, it can be known that the second derivative at these points is zero. In this manner, the second derivative can be obtained from the well log and the zero point can be found. However, this method is very sensitive to the selection of the window length. The activity curve with a small window length has a poor suppression of interference noise, while the activity curve with a large window length reflects the poor change in the slope of the well logs. Lanning et al. first applied the Walsh transformation to logging data to discover lithological boundaries [24]. Maiti et al. used Walsh transform to perform logging automatic stratigraphy [25].

Pan et al. combined wavelet transform and Fourier transform to achieve logging stratigraphy [26]. Qiao et al. used 3D technology to establish a stratigraphic model [4,5]. They tried to find a consistent method for describing heterogeneity by defining a curved coordinate system that conforms to the sedimentary layer. Non-mathematical statistics methods are simple in principle, with small calculation and fast speed. However, these methods are not easy to integrate multiple well logs information.

Artificial intelligence methods include fuzzy recognition and neural network methods. Hathaway et al. identified the formation interfaces based on fuzzy clustering [9]. Based on the feature vector of each sampling point, they determined the affinity relationship of each sampling point and clustered the sampling points according to this relationship. There is no doubt that this method also has an obvious problem of large amount of calculation. Wu et al. used a simple iterative linear regression model to identify the interface, and used heuristic algorithm to filter to get the stratigraphy [27]. Zhou et al. proposed a machine learning method for stratum series simulation respectively [2,3]. On the basis of the recurrent neural network, a sequence model of stratum types and a sequence model of stratum thickness are established. Shahab et al. [10] applied BP neural network [11,12] to the identification of reservoir lithology. The integrated electrical measurement data is used as input of convolutional neural network to construct the within-group and between-group errors of known classified samples. Then the ratio of the within-group error to the between-group error is used as the objective optimization function to obtain the discriminant function and discriminant criterion. The classification of the flow units of the key wells to be classified is carried out at last. However, although the application of neural network to the lithology identification of reservoirs can greatly increase the calculation speed, this application method is also not suitable for all well logs. Only the well logs with better lithology recognition effect can be used to participate in the training process.

Our proposed approach belongs to artificial intelligence method. Different from the methods mentioned above, we directly process the single-point well logging data. We convert one dimensional data into two dimensions, so that combining the short term temporal information to facilitate subsequent training operations. And we define stratigraphic interface detection as a classification problem. The proposed method can not only solve the problem of large amount of calculation, but also make full use of the information in multiple well logs. The human participation factor in our proposed method is relatively small.

3   Proposed Method

The overview of our proposed approach is shown in Fig. 1. First of all, we converted the data in the form of a single point of the well logging data into 2D segments after standardizing according to the well logging. And these segments are fed into the CNN network as a single-channel picture for training. Secondly, we use the trained model to predict the formation of the well logging data.

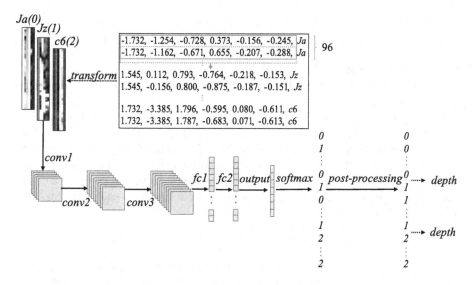

Fig. 1. The overview of our proposed approach

Finally, we detect the stratigraphic interface according to the label changes by post-processing the prediction results. In the following sections, we will present the discussion respectively.

3.1   Data Formulation

There are six features corresponding to each well are given in the form of single point data. These features contains the depth of survey point (Depth), gamma ray (GR), spontaneous potential (SP), acoustic (AC), array induction resistivity (AT90), and array induction resistivity (AT20) that are obtained by different sensors. Each well log data is presented in the form of a single point. The data format of a single well is shown in Table 1.

Table 1. Data format of a single well in dataset.

Wellname	Depth	GR	SP	AC	AT90	AT20	Label
W100	648.000	50.83	40.87	263.05	14.93	15.40	Ja
W100	648.125	53.03	41.73	269.79	13.44	14.54	Ja
⋮	⋮	⋮	⋮	⋮	⋮	⋮	⋮
W100	751.875	84.68	53.91	265.08	17.20	18.04	Jz
⋮	⋮	⋮	⋮	⋮	⋮	⋮	⋮
W100	1807.750	0.00	78.70	237.83	21.47	8.08	c6

Generally, convolutional neural network requires a 2D data as input. At the same time, considering the need to extract all the information of the logging data, we need to convert well logging data points into segment. The continuous data point of the six features within a certain threshold is combined into a two-dimensional segment. And the segment is used as input of CNN model for training process.

We first normalize all data according to the well logging data for the data of a single well with 1 lines of text information. And then we use a window threshold t to slide the window down along the well logging data at intervals of i. Finally, the data of each well in text form is converted into the form of a single-channel segment with a size of $t * 6$. The label corresponding to the segment is the label that appears mostly in the t single-point data selected in each window. The selected label is defined as:

$$label_{pic} = \arg\max(bincount(label[j : j + t])), \qquad (1)$$

where $label_{pic}$ is the label corresponding to the segment, and $\arg\max$ is the label index with the largest number. In Eq. 1, the $bincount$ indicates the number of times each label appears, $label$ is the label corresponding to the single point, j is the line j of the text, and j belongs to $0 < j < l - t$. The final number num of segment converted for each well is defined as:

$$num = (l - t + i)/i. \qquad (2)$$

In Eq. 2, l is the number of lines in for each well logging data, t is the sliding window size, and i is the sliding interval of the sliding window. The whole process of data formulation is shown in the Fig. 2.

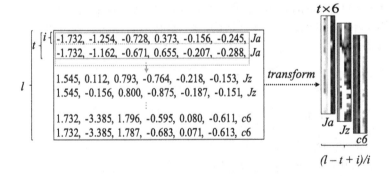

Fig. 2. The process of data formulation.

3.2   Stratigraphy Classification

We formulate the stratigraphic interface detection as a classification problem based on the CNN classification model. The segment obtained as in Sect 3.1

can be used as the input of CNN, and the corresponding label can be used as a specific category of the stratigraphy.

The CNN extracts features from the input segment, and it can obtain a deep feature map through multiple convolution layers. The last fully-connected (FC) layers connect all neurons in the feature maps to perform feature fusion. The output features are used as the input of the multi-class classifier. The proposed CNN model consists of three convolutional layers and two FC layers. The output of the CNN model is a softmax classifier. The details of CNN model structure is summarized in Table 2. During the testing process, the CNN model predict on the basis of segments of the testing well logging data, and output the label corresponding to a single point for each well. The final predicted number of tags for each well num_label is defined as:

$$label_{num} = l - (t - 1), \tag{3}$$

where $label_{num}$ is the number of tags for each well, and t is the sliding window size.

Table 2. The structure of CNN model

Layer	Structure
Input	Size:96 $*$ 6 $*$ 1
Conv1	Kernel size:3 $*$ 3, Filter:64, stride:1, pad:1
Conv2	Kernel size:3 $*$ 3, Filter:128, stride:1, pad:1
Conv3	Kernel size:3 $*$ 3, Filter:256, stride:1, pad:1
FC1	Output number:512
FC2	Output number:512
Output	Softmax,output number:10

3.3   Stratigraphic Interface Detection

We ultimately need to perform stratigraphic interface detection for each well. Therefore, it is necessary to perform a post-processing on basis of the classification results of all the well logging data points.

During the post-processing, we traverse the predicted label $label\_predict$. If a label change is detected, we determine whether the label has appeared. On the one hand, if the label has appeared, the label is defined as incorrect and we correct it to the previous label. On the other hand, if the label does not have appeared, we use a threshold $label\_step$ at this point and select the label $predict\_num$ that appears the most within the threshold. If the two labels are same, the prediction is defined as correct. If they are not same, the label is mispredicted, and the label value is converted to $predict\_num$. The algorithm process is shown in Algorithm 1.

After traversing the processed predicted label, if a label change is detected, the depth corresponding to the label is the stratigraphic interface between two adjacent geological layers. The stratigraphic interface detection error can be obtained by comparing the predicted interface with ground-truth.

Algorithm 1. Results post-processing algorithm

$label\_step = 20$
$label\_predict = result[:, -1]$
$save = [\ ]$
for $label$ **in** $range(len(set(label\_predict)) - 1)$ **do**
  $predict = [\ ]$
  save.append(label)
  for i **in** $range(len(label\_predict))$ **do**
    if $label\_predict[i]! = label$ **then**
      if $label\_predict[i]$ **in** $save$ **then**
        $predict.append(label)$
      else
        $predict\_label\_step = np.array(label\_predict[i : i + label\_step])$
        $predict\_label\_step = predict\_label\_step.astype(np.int)$
        $predict\_num = np.argmax(np.bincount(predict\_label\_step))$
        if $label\_predict[i]! = predict\_num$ **then**
          $predict.append(label)$
        else
          $predict.append(label + 1)$
        end if
      end if
    else
      $predict.append(label)$
    end if
  end for
end for

---

4 Experiment

4.1 Dataset

We choose a well logging dataset from a real-world oilfield application for stratigraphic interface detection. The dataset contains 3000 wells. The logging data information mainly contains the name of the wells, the geographic location of the wells. Each data point has 6 features, and is associated to a specific stratigraphy label. The dataset contains 10 types of stratigraphy, i.e., 'K1z', 'Jz', 'Jy', 'Jf', 'c1', 'c2', 'c3', 'c4+5', 'c6', and 'Ja'.

Since the characteristics of wells with similar geographic locations are similar, we selected 228 wells with similar geographic locations according to the coordinate positions as the dataset. The visualization of geographic locations of the whole 3000 well is shown in left part of Fig. 3, and the visualization of

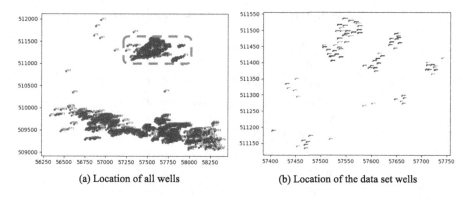

(a) Location of all wells   (b) Location of the data set wells

Fig. 3. Select dataset based on coordinates

geographic locations of the selected the 228 wells is shown in the right of Fig. 3. We randomly select 200 wells as the training set from the selected 228 wells, and use left 28 well as the testing set.

In the data formulation process, we set the window threshold as 96 and set the interval as 1. The resulted segments are used as input for the CNN network. During the training phase, we use 'ReLU' as the activation functions in the network structure, which can increase the nonlinearity of the network [14,15]. We use dropout layer [16] with a parameter of 0.5 after each the FC layers. The dropout layer makes each neuron in the CNN activate with a probability of 0.5 to prevent overfitting during the training process.

We employ the strategy of 'gradual' learning rate, i.e., the initial learning rate is set as 0.01, and is reduce 9*(1e-6) after each epoch. The Adam algorithm [17,18] is employed to optimize the network during training, and the maximum number of iterations is set to 100. We use the earlystop [19] with a parameter of 6 against overfitting. If the loss rate of the verification set does not decrease for 6 consecutive times as the number of training increases, the training willstop.

4.2   Classification Accuracy

After training, we used the trained CNN model to predict 28 test wells. The final average prediction accuracy is able to achieve 89.69%. The statistical information of the classification of 10 wells is summarized in Table 3. As shown in Table 3, the accuracy and recall rate of the stratigraphy classification are all above 85%, which indicates that the proposed CNN model can show a good effect on the classification for stratigraphic interface detection.

Table 3. The stratigraphy classification accuracy

Wellname	Number	Accuracy	Recall
W1615	12484	0.9350	0.90
W1628	12151	0.9486	0.94
W1669	12490	0.9082	0.89
W1675	12597	0.9472	0.93
W1686	12441	0.8898	0.86
W855	12736	0.9112	0.88
W830	12630	0.9425	0.91
W707	12146	0.8636	0.85
W615	13145	0.9253	0.89
W425	13866	0.9152	0.86

4.3   Stratigraphic Interface Detection

In order to evaluate the stratigraphic interface detection accuracy of 28 testing wells, we adopted the method of calculating the relative error between the predicted detection with ground-truth. The average relative error of the 28 testing is 1%. We summary the maximum, minimum, and average relative error results of the corresponding wells in Table 4. As shown in Table 4, the predicted interface is very close to the ground-truth.

Table 4. The stratigraphic interface detection error

Name	Maximum	Minimum	Average
W1615	0.0446	0.0001	0.0072
W1628	0.0095	0.0003	0.0066
W1669	0.0277	0.0002	0.0089
W1675	0.0333	0.0002	0.0081
W1686	0.0246	0.0008	0.0063
W855	0.0281	0.0004	0.0086
W830	0.0291	0.0002	0.0084
W707	0.0213	0.0001	0.0164
W615	0.0326	0.0002	0.0097
W425	0.0547	0.0003	0.0092

4.4   Time Consumption

We evaluate the time consumption of the CNN model using NVIDIA GeForce RTX 2080 Ti. The training and testing time for the well logging data per well is shown in the Table 5. From the perspective of the overall training time and the prediction time of a single well, our classification speed is very fast. With the consideration of the classification accuracy and detection error, the time consumption of our proposed approach is able to satisfy real-world application requirements.

Table 5. The time consumption of training and testing phase.

Phase	Criterion	Consumption
Training	Epoch	211 s
	Total	1.6 h
Testing	Well	3.06 s
	Total	85.83 s

4.5   Ablation Study

In order to evaluate the performance of the proposed CNN model, we built MLP network consisting of two FC layers with 512 nodes and a softmax classifier. For MLP training on single-point datas of well logs, the network parameters during the training process are exactly the same as the CNN training process. The each data point with six features is used as input, and the classification result is output through the 'softmax' classifier. The details of the MLP model structure is shown in the Table 6.

Table 6. The structure of MLP model

Layer (type)	Structure
Inputlayer	Size:6
FC1	Output number:512
FC2	Output number:512
Output	Softmax, Output number:10

We used the MLP trained model to predict 28 test wells, and the final average prediction accuracy rate was 80%. We summary the prediction accuracy and recall rate of corresponding 10 wells in Table 7. As shown in Table 7 and Table 3, the proposed CNN model greatly improve the stratigraphy classification accuracy and average recall rate. This experiment proved that the construction of the convolutional layer in CNN can extract useful features from the well logging data, and eventually improve the results of stratigraphic interface detection.

Table 7. The classification result of MLP method

Wellname	Number	Accuracy	Recall
W1615	12579	0.8599	0.86
W1628	12246	0.8206	0.82
W1669	12585	0.8525	0.86
W1675	12692	0.8875	0.87
W1686	12536	0.9004	0.88
W855	12831	0.6660	0.64
W830	12725	0.8312	0.82
W707	12241	0.6918	0.72
W615	13240	0.7696	0.75
W425	13961	0.7204	0.66

5   Conclusion

In this paper, we propose a CNN approach for stratigraphic interface detection from the geophysical well logging data. First, the data in the form of a single point of the well logging data is normalized according to the well logging. We then select the sliding window threshold to be 96. We Use the size of 1 as the line interval (0.125 depth interval) along the loggings data sliding window. And we convert data points to 2D segment. The segments are fed into the CNN network as a single-channel picture for training. Secondly, we call the trained model to predict the formation of the test wells. Finally, we introduce a post-processing method to perform the stratigraphic interface detection. The experimental results demonstrate the proposed approach is able to achieve 89.69% of the average accuracy of stratigraphic interface detection. Moreover, the classification accuracy and recall rate of most wells are much higher than the MLP single-point training method. For 200 wells and each well with data of more than 1,500 m, the training phase takes no more than two hours. The forecast duration of a single well is only 3.06 s. In addition, the relative error between the predicted boundary points with the ground-truth is only 1%, which indicates the proposed approach satisfy the real-world application requirements.

The method of interface detection based on CNN proposed in this paper only conducted experiments on division of stratigraphic interface. In the future, this method can be applied to the identification of reservoirs, oil, gas, water and lithology. The biggest advantage of CNN is that through a large amount of data analysis, it can autonomously dig out its inherent characteristics. In addition, we convert single-point well logging data point into segment. Our manner can fully combine the short term temporal information to facilitate subsequent training operations. This provides a brand new method for solving the problems of stratigraphic interface detection, reservoir division and oil, gas and water identification.

References

1. Lecun, Y., Bengio, Y., Hinton, G.: Deep learning. Nature **521**(7553), 436 (2015)
2. Zhou, C., Ouyang, J., Ming, W., et al.: A stratigraphic prediction method based on machine learning. Appl. Sci. **9**(17), 3553 (2019)
3. He, M., Gu, H., Wan, H.: Log interpretation for lithology and fluid identification using deep neural network combined with MAHAKIL in a tight sandstone reservoir. J. Pet. Sci. Eng. **194**, 107498 (2020)
4. Qiao, J., Pan, M., Li, Z., et al.: 3D Geological modeling from DEM, boreholes, cross-sections and geological maps (2011)
5. Caumon, G., Mallet, J.: 3D Stratigraphic models: representation and stochastic modelling (2018)
6. Hawkins, D.M., Merriam, D.F.: Optimal zonation of digitized sequential data. Math. Geol. **5**, 389–395 (1973)
7. Hawkins, D.M., Merriam, D.F.: Zonation of multivariate sequences of digitized geologic data. Math. Geol. **6**, 263–269 (1974)
8. McIntyre, R.M., Blashfield, R.K.: A nearest-centroid technique for evaluating the minimum-variance clustering procedure. Multivar. Behav. Res. **15**(2), 225–238 (1980)
9. Hathaway, R.J., Bezdek, J.C.: Local convergence of the fuzzy c-Means algorithms. Pattern Recogn. **19**(6), 477–480 (1986)
10. Shahab, M.: Virtual-intelligence applications in petroleum engineering: part 1-artificial neural networks. J. Petrol. Technol. **52**(9), 64–73 (2000)
11. Hecht-Nielsen, R.: Theory of the backpropagation neural network. Neural Netw. (1988)
12. Rumelhart, D.E., Hinton, G.E., Williams, R.J.: Learning representations by back propagating errors. Nature **323**(6088), 533–536 (1986)
13. Hubek, D., Wiesel, T.: Receptive fields, binocular interaction and functional architecture in the cat's visual cortex. J. Physiol. **160**, 106–154 (1962)
14. Le, Q.V., Jaitly, N., Hinton, G.E.: A simple way to initialize recurrent networks of rectified linear units. Comput. Sci. (2015)
15. Glorot, X., Bordes, A., Bengio, Y.: Deep sparse rectifier neural networks. J. Mach. Learn. Res. **15**, 315–323 (2011)
16. Srivastava, N., Hinton, G., Krizhevsky, A., et al.: Dropout: a simple way to prevent neural networks from overfitting. J. Mach. Learn. Res. **15**(1), 1929–1958 (2014)
17. Kingma, D.P., Ba, J.: Adam: a method for stochastic optimization. Comput. Sci. (2014)
18. Duchi, J., Hazan, E., Singer, Y.: Adaptive subgradient methods for online learning and stochastic optimization. J. Mach. Learn. Res. **12**(7), 257–269 (2011)
19. Chiou-Jye, H., Ping-Huan, K.: A deep CNN-LSTM model for particulate matter (PM2.5) forecasting in smart cities. Sensors **18**(7), 2220 (2018)
20. Xin-Hu, L.I.: Study on well logging curve shape automatic identification method. Pet. Geol. Oilfield Dev. Daqing (2006)
21. Dharmawardhana, H.P.K., Keller, G.V.: Statistical method for the determination of zone boundaries using well log data. In: SPE Annual Technical Conference and Exhibition. Society of Petroleum Engineers (1985)
22. Kerzner, M.G.: An analytical approach to detailed dip determination using frequency analysis. In: SPWLA 23rd Annual Logging Symposium. Society of Petrophysicists and Well-Log Analysts (1982)

23. Kerzner, M.G., Frost Jr., E.: Blocking-a new technique for well log interpretation. J. Petrol. Technol. **36**(02), 267–275 (1984)
24. Lanning, E.N., Johnson, D.M.: Automated identification of rock boundaries: an application of the Walsh transform to geophysical well-log analysis. Geophysics **48**(2), 197–205 (1983)
25. Maiti, S., Tiwari, R.K.: Automatic detection of lithologic boundaries using the Walsh transform: a case study from the KTB borehole. Comput. Geosci. **31**(8), 949–955 (2005)
26. Pan, S.Y., Hsieh, B.Z., Lu, M.T., et al.: Identification of stratigraphic formation interfaces using wavelet and Fourier transforms. Comput. Geosci. **34**(1), 77–92 (2008)
27. Wu, X., Nyland, E.: Automated stratigraphic interpretation of well-log data. Geophysics **52**(12), 1665–1676 (1987)

A Deep Neural Network Based Feature Learning Method for Well Log Interpretation

Liyuan Bao[1], Xianjun Cao[2], Changjiang Yu[2], Guanwen Zhang[1(✉)], and Wei Zhou[1]

[1] Northwestern Polytechnical University, Xi'an 710072, China
guanwen.zh@nwpu.edu.cn
[2] China Petroleum Logging Co., Ltd., Xi'an 710077, China

Abstract. Well log interpretation is an important task in the process of petroleum logging. It is able to help the researchers to determine the residual oil volume and to improve the petroleum productivity efficiency. Well log interpretation requires the synthesis of a large amount of data, and it is difficult to manually browse the data from a global perspective. It is urgent to introduce big data analysis methods to deal with the complex oil well logs data. The accuracy of logging interpretation greatly depends on the logging features selection and representation. However, the conventional methods using expert experiences easily lead to feature incomplete problem and affects the interpretation results. In this paper, we propose a deep neural network based feature learning method for well log interpretation. Firstly, we select original features of the well log data according to the physical characteristics of well logging sensors. And then, we formulate a deep neural network based autoencoder model to explore the intrinsic representation of original features. At last, we utilize linear SVM classifier on well log interpretation problem to evaluate the proposed feature learning method. The experimental results demonstrate that the classification accuracy by using learned feature representation increase to 99.8% compared with that of 74.6% by using original feature representation.

Keywords: Well logging interpretation · Deep neural network · Feature learning · Autoencoder

---

This work was supported in part by the National Key R&D Program of China (No. 2018AAA0102801 and No. 2018AAA0102803), in part of the National Natural Science Foundation of China (No. 61772424, No. 61702418, and No. 61602383), and in part by 13th Five-Year Plan of China National Petroleum Corporation Limited (2019A-3610).

B. Li et al. (Eds.): IoTaaS 2020, LNICST 346, pp. 543–556, 2021.
https://doi.org/10.1007/978-3-030-67514-1_43

1   Introduction

Nowadays, oil has become a strategic material that all countries attach great importance to. However, petroleum energy is facing some problems such as uneven distribution and difficult mining technology. Logging technology is an indispensable method for accurately discovering oil and gas layers and finely describing oil and gas reservoirs, and it is able to help to achieve more efficient production. Logging interpretation requires the synthesis of a large amount of data, and it is difficult to manually browse the data from a global perspective. It is urgent to introduce big data analysis technology to deal with complex oil well logs data. By introducing the artificial intelligence methods into the logging interpretation, the establishment of intelligent logging interpretation will improve the automation and accuracy of logging interpretation. The classification effect of deep learning and machine learning depends on the expressive ability and separability of logging features. Therefore, learning feature representation of logging interpretation is very an important research field.

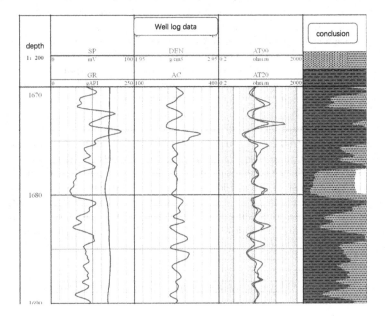

Fig. 1. An example for well logging interpretation application by using manual designed feature representation.

The logging feature representation consists of manual designed feature method and learning feature method. Experts get logging interpretation by drawing intersection diagrams of well logs data, as the example shown in Fig. 1. The well logs data is generally used to determine the main features in the logging. However it greatly requires the expert knowledge and experience, and it easily leads to insufficient use of logging features and inaccurate logging interpretation results. In [22], Liu et al. tested 127 mudstone samples in Shanxi Formation by X-ray diffraction (XRD), scanning electron microscope (SEM), and gas content. They used the logging curve superposition method and reservoir parameter calculation equations to qualitatively identify and quantitatively evaluate gas-bearing mudstone reservoirs in 4 gas wells, and achieved good results. However, this method has the problem of time-consuming data collection and analysis, and the analysis results have large human errors.

In this paper we proposed a deep neural network based feature learning method for well log interpretation. On the basis of deep neural network, we formulate a autoencoder model to explore the intrinsic features of well log data. The encoded feature representation is learned by minimizing the reconstruction error between the original log data and predicted data. The proposed method provides a high-dimensional representation method for well logs data features. The learned feature representation is expected to contribute the linear separability for classification problem in well log interpretation problem. The method proposed consists of three parts. Firstly, we select the original features of the well logs data according to physical characteristics of the logging sensors. And then we construct the encoder network to perform feature learning on the basis of original features. Finally, we utilize linear SVM as a classifier to evaluate the proposed feature learning method. The experimental results demonstrate that the classification accuracy by using learned feature representation has been greatly improved from 74.6% to 99.8% compared with that by using the original well data.

2   Related Work

Logging interpretation produces huge production benefits in the field of oil and gas reservoir exploration. It has become an indispensable part of modern oil and gas exploration [2,7]. The widely used methods in well logging interpretation consists of artificial neural network methods, machine learning methods, statistical analysis methods, etc. [10,13,14]. The latest mathematical analysis knowledge has also been applied to well logging interpretation. These emerging information processing technologies have greatly promoted the vigorous development of the logging interpretation industry [11]. At present, there are two main group methods for presenting features of well logs data, i.e., the manual designed feature method and feature learning methods.

In the group of feature evaluation and selection in well logging interpretation, researchers proposed various method to analyze sensitive factors and to deal with the complex features in well logs data [5,12]. Li et al. used a Relief-F feature selection for processing a large number of high-dimensional data sets [6]. They tried to select sensitive attributes for multiple attributes extracted from logging and seismic data. By comparing the prediction results, they showed the reliability and accuracy of the sensitive factors for the Relief-F feature selection. Principal component analysis (PCA) [21] is very widely used in well logs data for dimensionality reduction and sensitive attribute selection. By mapping highly redundant information to low-dimensional principal component space, PCA simplifies the data model while retaining effective information as well as reducing staff judgment difficulty. Linear discriminant analysis [4] is a supervised learning method. It pays more attention to the distance between different classes, so it is more common to be applied in the dimensionality reduction scenario of the gap between the classifications.

In the group of feature learning method, the autoencoder is also a common method for data feature extraction. Seeun Jo [3] and others used the autoencoder to extract the features of the sample in the spectrum to improve the recognition accuracy. In [1], a new stacked local preserving autoencoder is proposed, which can better preserve the local data structure. The conventional machine learning methods show excellent classification performance on many classification problems [15]. In [16], Wang et al. proposed the application of stacked sparse autoencoders based on PCA and SVM for power system line trip fault diagnosis. A sentiment analysis method based on kmeans and online migration learning was proposed in [8], which achieved good results in error rate and classification accuracy. As an emerging information processing technology, deep neural network has been widely used in many engineering fields. The application of deep neural network in the field of logging interpretation has also achieved convincing performance. It introduce the contribution to the solution of many difficult problems in the field of logging interpretation [9]. Zhang et al. used artificial neural network (ANN) to establish the non-linear correspondence between reservoir lithology, physical properties, and oil-bearing parameters [17]. Their method is able to predict the lithology, physical properties, and oil-bearing parameters of the reservoir. The comparison between the network prediction results and other oil testing and analytical laboratory results shows that the ANN method is feasible and effective. It makes a great reference value for oilfield exploration and development.

Manual designed features have problems that are not conducive to promotion and generalization. The learning feature has the problem of low logging interpretation accuracy. In response to the above problems, this article proposes a method of learning features based on autoencoder. This method can learn the characteristics of the data from the logging data and solve the problem of generalization and promotion of the characteristics. We selected data from a well in Changqing Oilfield to verify the effectiveness of our proposed method. The classification accuracy and clustering effect of this method are greatly improved.

3   The Proposed Method

In the following sections, we first introduce the original features of the well log data with respective to physical characteristics of the logging sensors. And then we formulate a deep neural network based autoencoder model to learn the feature representation for the original features. At last, we demonstrate the application by using the learned features for logging interpretation. The illustration of our proposed method is shown in Fig. 2.

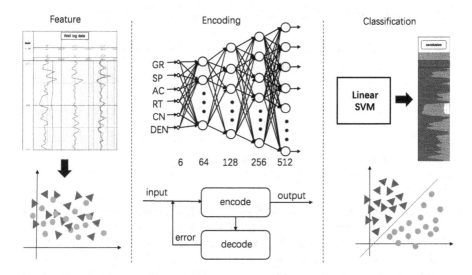

Fig. 2. The illustration of our proposed method. We first select original features for logging data according to the physical characteristics of the sensors. These features are generally linear non-separable. The original features are then used for further feature learning with autoencoder model on the basis of deep neural network. By the minimizing the reconstruction error between original features and predicted features, the learned feature representation is expected to persevere intrinsic distinctiveness of the well log data. The resulting feature representation can therefore contribute the classification for the well log interpretation application.

3.1   Original Feature Selection

There are many original features can be used for well log data representation according to different sensors used in real-world well log application. These various features have different physical characteristics and can be used for different application purposes. With the consideration of generalization and scalability, we choose gamma ray (GR), density (DEN), acoustic (AC), spontaneous potential (SP), compensated neutron (CN), and resistivity (RT) as the original features for well log data representation. These features are summarized in Table 1.

The GR feature is obtained by measuring the intensity of gamma rays emitted during the decay process of naturally occurring radionuclides in the rock formation in the well. The GR feature can be used to judge lithology, stratigraphic comparison, and estimate shale content. The DEN feature is obtained by using an isotope gamma-ray source to radiate gamma rays to the formation, and then using a detector at a certain distance from the gamma source to measure the intensity of the gamma rays that reach the detector after being scattered and absorbed by the formation. The intensity of the scattered gamma rays received by the detector is related to the rock volume density of the formation. The SP feature is a measurement of the potential generated under the electrochemical action of the formation. The "positive", "negative" and amplitude of the

Table 1. The original features for well log data representation.

Original features	Physical characteristics and utilization
GR	Stratigraphic comparison
DEN	Identify lithology
AC	Calculate mineral content
SP	Determine the flooded layer
CN	Determine the gas layer
PT	Depth correction

spontaneous potential polarity are consistent with the relationship between the mud filtrate resistivity Rmf and the formation water resistivity Rw. When Rmf $\cong$ Rw, SP is almost flat; when Rmf > Rw, SP is negative anomaly; when Rmf < Rw, SP is positive anomaly in the permeable layer. The SP feature can be used to divide permeability stratum, determine the resistivity of formation water, determine the water-flooded layer, and study the sedimentary facies. The AC feature is based on the acoustic physical characteristics of the rock to measure the sound velocity of the formation. When the gas-bearing layer appears, the sound wave time difference appears to have cycle jumping phenomenon, or the logging value becomes larger. At large boreholes, the sonic jet difference will increase or jump. The CN feature is a thermal neutron logging using the dual source distance ratio method, which measures the thermal neutron flux caused by the neutron source along the well section. The CN feature can be used to determine the porosity of the formation, calculate the mineral content, and judge the gas layer by overlapping the compensation density curve. The RT feature is a logging curve that studies the electric field distribution in various media. In the measurement, an artificial electric field is first introduced into the medium. The distribution characteristics of this field are determined by the resistivity of the surrounding medium. Therefore, as long as the electric field distribution characteristics in various media are measured, the resistivity of the medium can be determined. The RT feature can be used to divide lithology profile, find the true resistivity of the rock formation, find the porosity of the formation, depth correction, and formation comparison.

3.2   Feature Representation Learning

The proposed autoencoder model is on the basis of deep neural network. It consists of multiple fully-connected (FC) layers. It is proposed to explore the intrinsic representation of well log data. The autoencoder model is trained by minimizing the reconstruction error between the original features and predicted features.

The number of encoder layers needs to be associated with the characteristics of deep neural networks. Increasing the number of FC layers can reduce network errors and improve accuracy. However, more FC layers will make the network much more complex and lead to the overfitting problem. It will also increase the training time of the deep neural network. Generally, increasing the number of neuron in FC layers can achieve a lower reconstruction error, while the training effect is easier to be achieved than that by increasing the number of hidden layers. For a neural network model without hidden layers, it is a linear or nonlinear regression model. According to the cross verification for setting the number of layers of the autoencoder, it can be obtained by comparing with multiple experiments based on well logs data.

The number of nodes in each hidden layer of the encoder needs to be combined with the characteristics of the neural network and the distribution of potential characteristics of the data. In autoencoder model, the choice of the number of neurons in FC is very important. It not only has a great impact on the performance of the established neural network model, but also is the potential cause of the overfitting during training process. However, there is no scientific and universal method of determination in theory. The calculation formulas for determining the number of neurons in FC layer in the literature are proposed for the case of any number of training samples. And most of these methods are used for the most unfavorable situation, which is difficult to be satisfied in general engineering practice and should not be adopted. In fact, the number of neurons in FC layer obtained by various calculation formulas sometimes differs several times or even hundreds of times. In order to ensure sufficiently high network performance and generalization ability, it is crucial to deal with the overfitting problem during training as much as possible. Therefore, the basic principle for determining the number of neurons in FC layers is to use as compact a structure as possible with the consideration for satisfying the accuracy requirements, i.e., using as less neurons as possible. Research shows that the number of neurons in FC layer is related to the size of the input and output in the specific layer. And it is also related to factors such as the complexity of the problem, the type of the transfer function, and the characteristics of the sample data. The number of training samples must be more than the connections of the neural network model. If the number of neurons is too large, the learning ability of the encoder will be improved. But if the number of neurons is too small, the encoder may not be able to learn any information. It is necessary to set a proper number of neurons for the encoder to ensure that the encoder learns effective information. According to experimental verification on well logs data, the number of neurons in each layer is chosen carefully and wisely.

Taking the above factors into consideration, the encoder network structure is set as four layers. The decoder structure is a symmetrical mirror of the encoder. The decoder and encoder structure are only the reverse relationship correspondingly. The network parameters are the settings of the corresponding layers of the encoder are the same. The structure of the autoencoder model is summarized in Table 2.

Due to complex environment of the well logging in real world application, signal noise and machine disturbing are inevitable during data collecting process. There are great amount of random noise, which will affect impact feature

Table 2. The structure of autoencoder model

Layer (type)	Structure
Input	Size: 6
FC Layer 1	Output number: 64, dropout: 0.5, activate: elu
FC Layer 2	Neuron number: 128, dropout: 0.5, activate: elu
FC Layer 3	Neuron number: 256, dropout: 0.5, activate: elu
FC Layer 4	Neuron number: 512, dropout: 0.5, activate: elu
FC Layer 5	Neuron number: 256, dropout: 0.5, activate: elu
FC Layer 6	Neuron number: 128, dropout: 0.5, activate: elu
FC Layer 7	Neuron number: 64, dropout: 0.5, activate: elu
Output	Size: 6

representation learning. Therefore, we use a more robust elu activation function for each neurons. In the different perspective view, the elu activation function can still propagate the gradient under any condition. The elu activation function can prevent the death of neurons and update connection weights, and speed up the convergence of the network.

The reconstruction error is measured between original features and predicted features. In our proposed method, we use the mean square error (MSE) as the loss function. The MSE loss function is defined as:

$$MSE = \frac{1}{m} \sum (y - y')^2, \tag{1}$$

where y is the input original features and y' is predicted features of the decoder, and m is the number of output. We use the Adam optimizer for gradient descent training, due to its stable performance and suitable for large-scale data scenarios.

3.3 Stratigraphic Interface Detection

In this section, we utilize the learned feature representation for well log interpretation application. Log interpretation is to analyze the classification information of each depth point according to the characteristics of the well logs data. Stratigraphic interface detection is the first and important application for in well log interpretation. Experts divide geology into more than 20 types of geological layers. Stratigraphic interface detection purpose is to associate the each well log data with specific geological type. It can then be formulated to use classifier to classify the well log data with different class label. Since linear SVM has the characteristics of fast classification speed and high classification accuracy, we choose linear SVM as the classifier.

Classification is a very important task in the field of data mining. The SVM classifier is a classification algorithm in machine learning. The purpose of SVM is to learn a classification function, such that the classifier can be used to predict unseen sample. The linear SVM classifies data by calculating a hyperplane, which minimizes the classification error and maximizes the classification interval. The classification interval is defined as:

$$L = max\frac{1}{2}||w||^2 - C\sum(y(w \cdot x + b) - 1), \tag{2}$$

where $w * x + b$ is the classification plane, and w is the normal vector of the classification plane. In Eq. 2, C is the penalty coefficient, C represents the degree of attention to the total error during the entire optimization process. A larger value of C leads to a higher the requirement for reducing the error.

4 Experiments

In order to evaluate the performance of proposed feature representation learning method, we choose a well logging data collected in real-world oilfield application. There are total 37761 samples with 8 geological type, containing 'J2z', 'J1y', 'J1f', 'chang1', 'chang2', 'chang3', 'chang4+5', and chang6'. We randomly select 70% of the data for the training and use the remaining data for the testing. We choose the principal component analysis (PCA) and locally linear embedding (LLE) as the baseline. We use PCA to preserve 3 dimension with 95% information on the basis of original features. We use kmeans method for clustering to evaluate the linear separability of feature representation.

4.1 Autoencoder Performance

We divide the input data into a testing set and a training set. We use the training set to train the autoencoder model, and then use the testing set to verify the performance of the network model. After 100 epochs of the training, the accuracy curve and loss curve are shown in Fig. 3.

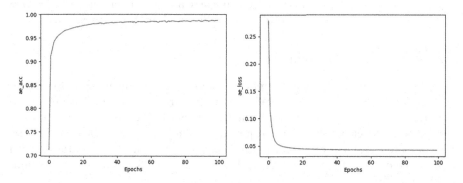

Fig. 3. The accuracy and loss of our proposed autoencoder model during the training process.

As shown in Fig. 3, the reconstruction error reduce rapidly and the training accuracy increases rapidly. After 20 epochs, the loss and accuracy rate remain stable. The accuracy rate achieve 99%, while the reconstruction error between the predicted features and the original features was smaller than 0.04. The learned 512-dimensional feature representation is supposed to contain all the information as that of the original features.

We selected 10000 samples and used the t-SNE [20] method to project the original features and our learned features to 2 dimensions plane for visualization. The result shown in Fig. 4.

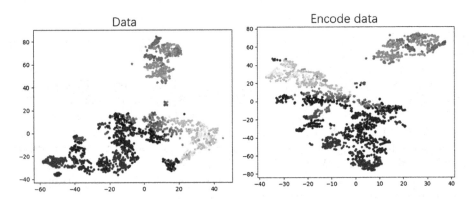

Fig. 4. Visualization of original features and our learned features. Different color indicate different class of geological type.

As the left part shown in Fig. 4, we can see that the samples formulated by original features from different classes are coupled together. It is not easy for a classifier to make classification. As the right part shown in Fig. 4, the learned features reduce the coupling and increases the intra-class variance. It will be easy to achieve better classification using a linear classifier. Therefore, the learned feature representation shows better separability and feature expression.

4.2   Classification Evaluation

In order to evaluate the feature representation, we use linear SVM for stratigraphic interface detection to evaluate the performance of the feature representation. Since the penalty coefficient C of linear SVM has an impact on the classification effect, we use different penalty coefficients during the experiments. We compare classification performance between our feature representation with that of the original features, PCA, and LLE. The classification results are summarized in Table 3.

As shown in Table 3, when the penalty coefficient increases, the classification accuracy of SVM also increases. When the penalty coefficient is set as 100, the classification accuracy of the original features achieves 74.7%, and our proposed

Table 3. The classification results using different C

C	Original	PCA	LLE	Ours
0.0001	0.530	0.485	0.243	0.675
0.001	0.608	0.521	0.243	0.768
0.01	0.686	0.557	0.243	0.865
1	0.739	0.558	0.475	0.979
10	0.744	0.558	0.459	0.994
100	0.747	0.558	0.457	0.998

feature representation is able to achieve 99.8%. Compared with the original features, the classification accuracy has been greatly improved. The experiments indicate that our proposed feature representation has better separability.

When the penalty coefficient increases to 1, the improvement of SVM classification accuracy has stabilized. We summary the statistics of the classification using our proposed feature representation in Table 4:

Table 4. The statistics of classification using our proposed feature representation with different C.

Label	Number	C = 0.0001	C = 1	C = 100
0	1012	0.544	0.934	0.996
1	2755	0.788	0.997	0.998
2	1682	0.758	0.998	1
3	815	0.744	0.963	0.996
4	1372	0.506	0.964	1
5	1700	0.635	0.986	0.996
6	1422	0.559	0.969	0.997
7	560	0.425	0.962	0.997
Total	11318	0.675	0.979	0.998

4.3 Clustering Evaluation

Clustering is one of the commonly used algorithms in machine learning, and the clustering evaluation index can intuitively reflect the feature representation ability. We use the Kmeans algorithm for clustering the data processed by PCA, LLE, and our proposed method. We use adjusting rand index (ARI), adjusting mutual information (AMI), V-measure, homogeneity, completeness, silhouette, and davies bouldin index for comparison [18,19]. The results are summarized in Table 5.

Table 5. Clustering evaluation index comparison

Evaluation indexl	Data	PCA	LLE	Ours
ARI	0.292	0.282	0.239	0.306
AMI	0.395	0.399	0.327	0.430
V-measure	0.396	0.400	0.328	0.430
Homogeneity	0.387	0.396	0.298	0.431
Completeness	0.405	0.404	0.366	0.429
Davies bouldin index	1.081	0.968	0.822	1.144
Silhouette	0.297	0.316	0.305	0.320

As shown in Table 5, we can see that the our proposed feature representation is better than that of the original features, PCA, and LLE through all clustering evaluation. Compared with traditional dimensionality reduction methods, our proposed method has better feature expression capabilities.

5   Conclusion

This paper proposed a data processing method based on autoencoder. According to the characteristics of the well logs data and the problems in the logging process, a feature coding network is set up to upgrade well logs data. We selected a well containing 37761 data, and used linear SVM classification and clustering algorithm to verify the effect of the proposed method. And compared with the commonly used feature extraction methods PCA and LLE to verify the effectiveness of the encoding. The experimental results demonstrate that the classification accuracy by using learned feature representation increase to 99.8% compared with that of 74.6% by using original feature representation,so the encoded well logs data has better separability. From the evaluation index of KMeans algorithm, the encoded data has better feature expression ability than the original data.

Stratigraphic division is only the first step in logging interpretation. Logging interpretation includes tasks such as lithology identification, reservoir division. In the future, we will continue to explore the application of this feature representation method we proposed in these tasks. Provide more methods to improve the efficiency and accuracy of logging interpretation.

References

1. Wang, Y., Liu, C., Yuan, X.: Stacked locality preserving autoencoder for feature extraction and its application for industrial process data modeling. Chemometr. Intell. Lab. Syst. **203**, 104086 (2020)
2. Mathematics - Geometry; Reports from China University of Petroleum (East China) Advance Knowledge in Geometry (Numerical Study of Pore Structure Effects On Acoustic Logging data In the Borehole Environment). J. Math. (2020)

3. Jo, S., Sohng, W., Lee, H., Chung, H.: Evaluation of an autoencoder as a feature extraction tool for near-infrared spectroscopic discriminant analysis. Food Chemistry **331**, (2020)
4. Zhang, L., et al.: Research on image transmission mechanism through a multimode fiber based on principal component analysis. Opt. Lasers Eng. **134**, (2020)
5. Nagarajan, S., Nettimi, S.S.S., Kumar, L.S.. Nath, M.K., Kanhe, A.: Speech emotion recognition using cepstral features extracted with novel triangular filter banks based on bark and ERB frequency scales. Digit. Signal Process. **104** (2020)
6. Li Kai, H., Shaohua, Z.F., et al.: Application of relief F algorithm in attribute optimization. Petrol. Geophys. Explor. **53**(S2), 230–234 (2018)
7. Applied radiation research; new findings in applied radiation research described from China University of petroleum (neutron transport correction and density calculation in the neutron-gamma density logging). Sci. Lett. (2019)
8. Wu, S., Liu, Y., Wang, J., Li, Q.: Sentiment analysis method based on Kmeans and online transfer learning. Comput. Mater. Continua **60**(3), 1207–1222 (2019)
9. Mei, H., Hanming, G., Huan, W.: Log interpretation for lithology and fluid identification using deep neural network combined with MAHAKIL in a tight sandstone reservoir. J. Pet. Sci. Eng. (2020, prepublish)
10. Szabó, N.P., Dobróka, M.: Interval inversion as innovative well log interpretation tool for evaluating organic-rich shale formations. J. Petrol. Sci. Eng. **186**(C) (2020)
11. Geophysics; Research Conducted at National Research Institute Has Provided New Information about Geophysics (Well logging interpretation methodology for carbonate formation fracture system properties determination). Sci. Lett. (2020)
12. Davydycheva, S., Kaminsky, A.: Triaxial induction logging: new interpretation method for biaxial anisotropic formations–Part 1. Soc. Explor. Geophys. Am. Assoc. Petrol. Geol. **4**(2), 151–164 (2016)
13. Viggen, E.M., Merciu, I.A., Løvstakken, L., Måsøy, S.-E.: Automatic interpretation of cement evaluation logs from cased boreholes using supervised deep neural networks. J. Petrol. Sci. Eng. (2020)
14. Tan, M., Bai, Y., Zhang, H., Li, G., Wei, X., Wang, A.: Fluid typing in tight sandstone from wireline logs using classification committee machine. Fuel **271** (2020)
15. Rodríguez-Hoyos, A., Rebollo-Monedero, D., Estrada-Jiménez, J., Forné, J., Urquiza-Aguiar, L.: Preserving empirical data utility in k -anonymous microaggregation via linear discriminant analysis. Eng. Appl. Artif. Intell. **94** (2020)
16. Wang, Y., Liu, M., Bao, Z., Zhang, S.: Stacked sparse autoencoder with PCA and SVM for data-based line trip fault diagnosis in power systems. Neural Comput. Appl. **31**(10), 6719–6731 (2018). https://doi.org/10.1007/s00521-018-3490-5
17. Tao, Z.: Application of BP Neural Network in Logging Interpretation. Northwest University (2010)
18. Osamor, I.P., Osamor, V.C.: OsamorSoft: clustering index for comparison and quality validation in high throughput dataset. J. Big Data **7**(1), 1–13 (2020). https://doi.org/10.1186/s40537-020-00325-6
19. Bhatia, N., Sojan, J.M., Simonovic, S., Srivastav, R.: Role of cluster validity indices in delineation of precipitation regions. Water **12**(5) (2020)
20. Nicola, P., Lelieveldt Boudewijn, P.F., Van Der Maaten, L., Thomas, H., Elmar, E., Anna, V.: Approximated and user steerable tSNE for progressive visual analytics. IEEE Trans. Vis. Comput. Graph. **23**(7) (2017)

21. Xu, S.: The fuzzy comprehensive evaluation (FCE) and the principal component analysis (PCA) model simulation and its applications in water quality assessment of Nansi Lake Basin, China. Environ. Eng. Res. 26(2) (2021)
22. Liang, L., et al.: Reservoir characteristics and logging evaluation of gas-bearing mudstone in the south of North China plain. Sci. Rep. **10**(1) (2020)

Trust Prediction Model Based on Deep Learning in Social Internet of Things

Yuyao Wen⑩, Zhan Xu, Ruxin Zhi$^{(\boxtimes)}$, and Jinhui Chen

Beijing Information Science and Technology University, Beijing 100192, China
wenyuyao163@163.com, zhiruxin@bistu.edu.cn

Abstract. The Social Internet of Things (SIoT) is the result of the development of Internet of Things from intelligence to socialization. In the social internet of things, different nodes can automatically establish social relationships through social networks to obtain the services they need. Trust management is very important to such an open environment. This paper proposes an improved trust management model for social internet of things, which is divided into two parts: the improved node-level trust model and server-level trust model. In this paper, we propose an innovative trust model at the SIoT server-level, by introducing the deep learning model to predict the trust value of the new nodes in the social internet of things, to solve the problem that the network delay may affect the trust value evaluation in the actual social internet of things network. The simulation results show that the model based on deep learning prediction can get more successful transaction experience, and it is still effective against the high proportion of malicious nodes. The system performance is significantly better than the model without deep learning.

Keywords: Social internet of things · Trustworthiness management · Deep learning

1 Introduction

With the rapid development of 5G in recent years, the internet of things is facing greater opportunities and challenges, and has attracted more and more attention [1, 2]. The internet of things makes the social form of human society not only occur to people, but also expand on a wider range of people to things, things to things. Because of this, the internet of things is also known as the future of the Internet. With the connection between a large number of objects and the intelligence of things, it is an inevitable trend to study the interaction method of social form among devices in the internet of things [3–5]. SIoT came into being. It is the combination of traditional internet of things and existing social networks [6].

In recent years, more and more attention has been paid to deep learning and learning model based on neural network. They are widely used in e-commerce, medical and other fields, and have brought great changes in various fields [7]. So is deep learning in 5G communication field. In the application scenario of the internet of things, the communication may not go well because the nodes are too sparse or too dense, which affects task delivery and trust to value evaluation. At this time, some new

B. Li et al. (Eds.): IoTaaS 2020, LNICST 346, pp. 557–570, 2021.
https://doi.org/10.1007/978-3-030-67514-1_44

nodes have little historical information about transaction with other nodes, which makes it difficult for other nodes to get effective trust evaluation. This problem is also known as the "cold start".

The overall structure of this paper is as follows: The second part introduces the related work of this paper; The third part introduces the improved node-level trust model and the SIoT server-level trust model; The fourth part proves the superiority of this model by simulation. The last part summarizes this paper.

2 Related Work

The original internet of things only considers the connection between things, while the concept of owner of each node is added to the social Internet of things. Each node establishes its own social relationship according to its owner's social network, and spontaneously finds other reliable nodes to deliver tasks. Each node can play the role of service provider or service requester. In such a social Internet of things network of frequent social behaviors, some nodes will face the risk of malicious attacks from the bad nodes because of their own interests, so it is important to evaluate the credibility of service providers in the social Internet of things.

There have been some trust models in the social internet of things before [8–11]. In [8], the author puts forward two parts of the trust model: subjective model from social network, each node calculates the credibility of its owner's friends according to its own experience and the opinions of friendly recommenders, and objective model from P2P (peer-to-peer computer network) communication network, in which each node stores the trust value to other nodes. Information is sent to its peers in a distributed hash table structure, so any node can use the same information. On the basis of [8, 12] proposed a new social internet of things model based on [13]. According to this model, a group of objects can be given social forms. For example, equipment in the same area can be defined as friendship, which is like living together or working together. Another type of relationship is defined as the object owned by the same user, which is called ownership object relationship, just like different intelligent devices in the same family owned by the same person, establishing friendship relationship is more convenient for their transaction.

A trust model named TMCOI-SIoT is proposed in [14]. In this model network, there is a SIoT server and several communities. Each community chooses the node with the highest reputation as its administrator according to the actual situation. Different task requester nodes can select the nodes in the corresponding community according to their own interests or task types of task transaction. In this model, all nodes that want to join or leave the community need the consent of the community administrator (that is, nodes with a trust value higher than the threshold value will be allowed to join the community by the administrator, and nodes with insufficient trust value will be kicked out of the community by the administrator, and all nodes must not leave the community without permission). Otherwise, the community administrator will add their information to the "blacklist" and inform the SIoT Servers and other community administrators. In [14], trust models are proposed at node-level and administrator-level. In the node-level trust model, two interactive nodes obtain the trust value evaluation through the previous transaction experience; in the administrator-level, use Kalman filter model to predict and evaluate the trust value of unfamiliar nodes (nodes with insufficient transaction experience).

Based on [14] and deep learning model, this paper proposes an improved trust model for social internet of things, which is divided into improved node-level trust model and SIoT server-level trust model. The main innovations of this paper are as follows:

1) In the node-level trust model, we calculate the trust weight of the friendship nodes that provide indirect trust, that is, the higher the trust degree, the more valuable the advice provided by the nodes. This is more similar to the general situation of network trust calculation.

2) In the trust model of the SIoT server-level, aiming at the "cold start" problem mentioned above, this paper introduces the deep learning model to predict the trust value of the newly added nodes in the community in advance. Simulation results show that under the guidance of this prediction, the trust value convergence of the target node is faster than that without deep learning model, and the transaction success rate is higher in the total transaction process.

3   Trust Model

3.1   The Improved Trust Model of Node-Level

The purpose of trust management is to evaluate the credibility of nodes effectively, so as to find the malicious nodes that may provide malicious attacks in the network. Because different malicious nodes may launch a variety of malicious attacks in different situations, this paper divides the malicious node attacks into three types:

1) Malicious nodes destroy the reputation of a well-behaved node by providing wrong suggestions. And this will reduce the possibility of choosing this good node as a service provider. In this trust model, when a malicious node requests services from a good node, whether the service provided by the good node is good or bad, the malicious node gives it a lower trust value.

2) The malicious node can improve the reputation of another bad node by providing good suggestions, thus increasing the possibility of the bad node being selected as a service provider. This is also a collusive attack, that is, it can work with other bad nodes to improve each other's reputation. In this trust model, when a malicious node requests services from another malicious node, it will give a higher trust value, so as to carry out the collusion attack.

3) A malicious node can enhance its importance by providing a good service so that it can be selected as a service provider, but then it will provide a malicious service in an important transaction. In this model, when a good node requests services from a malicious node, the malicious node will provide good services to increase its trust in transactions of low importance, and provide poor services in important transactions.

In this paper, the trust value of a node is evaluated by the evaluation of node trust obtained by direct transaction between nodes (direct trust) and the reputation obtained by requesting service providers from friends (indirect trust). In this trust model, each node maintains its own set of trust evaluation for other nodes. In the experiment, each node dynamically updates its direct trust value and indirect trust value when interacting with other nodes (Table 1).

Table 1. List of parameters

Symbol	Meaning
i	Service requesting node
j	Service providing node
T_D	Direct trust value
T_{ID}	Indirect trust value
T	Total trust value
N	Corresponding transaction N times in total
h	Transaction factor

In order to deal with the above malicious attacks, the nodes in this model only request the corresponding node reputation from their friend nodes, and through the introduction of transaction factor h, classify the importance of different events, making it more difficult for malicious nodes to obtain high trust value from low transaction factor events. The specific model is as follows:

There are three kinds of social relations among the initial set nodes: ownership, location and community. If the trust value range is (0,1), and the trust value is 0, the node is completely untrusted; if the trust value is 1, the node is completely trusted. Among them, the initial trust value between nodes of the same owner is set to 0.9; the initial trust value between nodes of the same location relationship is set to 0.7; the initial trust value between nodes of the same community relationship is set to 0.6; the initial trust value between nodes without social relationship is set to 0.5.

In a real social network, two nodes in the same community or in the same location are more likely to succeed in transaction than non-social nodes. Therefore, in the simulation of this paper, the closer the social relationship between nodes will lead to a higher rate of successful transaction.

This model uses the trust model between nodes in [14] for reference to define the direct trust value between nodes: after node i requests services from and interacts with node j, node i calculates the direct trust value T_D of node j through the previous transaction experience with node j:

$$T_D = \frac{\alpha_{ij} + 1}{\alpha_{ij} + \beta_{ij} + 2} \tag{1}$$

$$\alpha_{ij} = R * \sum_{l=1}^{N} h_l \tag{2}$$

$$\beta_{ij} = P * \sum_{l=1}^{N} h_l \tag{3}$$

In formula (1), α_{ij} represents the successful transaction between node i and node j, and β_{ij} represents the failed transaction. In formula (2) (3), the calculation method of the two is given, where N represents the corresponding total number of transactions. h_l represents the transaction factor of the corresponding interaction between two nodes at the l th time. R (reward) is set to 1 and P (punishment) is set to 2. The purpose of double punishment for unsatisfied transactions is to deal with the third kind of malicious attack, that is, building trust is more difficult than losing trust. This prevents objects from performing well in low weight services to build good reputation, and then performing poorly in important services.

After the transaction, the node i sends a trust value request to its friend k, and calculates the indirect trust value T_{ID} by combining the trust value of its friends to the node j: (node i has n friends)

$$T_{ID} = \frac{\sum_{k=1}^{n} T_{kj} * T_{ik}}{\sum_{k=1}^{n} T_{ik}} \tag{4}$$

In [14], the indirect trust value acquisition method is to take the average number of recommended trust values of all recommenders, though this is defective in the actual network. Due to the different states of different nodes, the credibility of the recommended trust value given to the service requester is also different, so this model adds the weight of the service requester's trust value to each recommender here.

Finally, the total trust value of node i to node j is evaluated by formula (5):

$$T_{ij} = \lambda T_D + (1 - \lambda) T_{ID} \tag{5}$$

Where $\lambda \in [0,1]$ is used to weigh the direct trust value and the indirect trust value, and keep the total trust between 0 and 1.

Then, the total trust value of node i to node j is obtained by integrating the transaction experience of node i to node j:

$$T_{ij}(t) = (1 - \delta) T_{ij}(t - \Delta t) + \delta T_{ij}(t) \tag{6}$$

$T_{ij}(t - \Delta t)$ represents the total trust value of the last transaction between node i and j. $\delta \in [0,1]$ is used to weight the current and previous trust values.

3.2   Trust Model of SIoT Server-Level

This paper uses the model in [14] for reference, that is, there is a SIoT server and several communities in this social internet of things network, and each community has several nodes.

This paper mainly studies the trust value evaluation of unfamiliar nodes in the social internet of things network (taking the dense network as an example) where the communication may not go well due to the large delay. Therefore, in the simulation, we need to use the improved node-level trust model to simulate several transactions in the community before the trust value evaluation and prediction (10000 random transactions are simulated as training set data because there are many nodes in this paper).

In the simulation process of this model, each node selects the node with the highest trust value of its own trust value evaluation log for task interaction. For the node pairs with more than 10 successful transactions, the SIoT server collects the social relationship between node pairs, the ratio of the sum of transaction weights of previous successful transactions to the sum of transaction weights of all transactions, and the evaluation of the final trust value obtained after the corresponding target node interacts. The SIoT server inputs several groups of information collected as training sets into the DNN deep learning model as shown in Fig. 1.

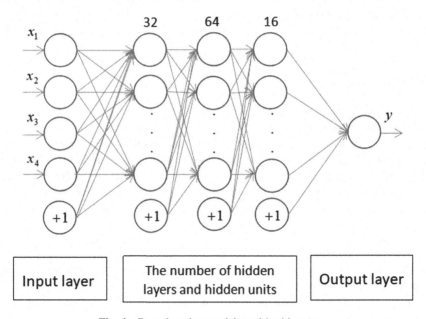

Fig. 1. Deep learning model used in this paper.

In the DNN deep learning model shown in Fig. 1, the input layer on the left is respectively: whether it is the friendship relationship (yes is recorded as 1, no as 0); whether it is the same location relationship; whether it is the same community relationship; the ratio of the sum of the transaction weights of the previous successful transactions of the corresponding interaction node to the sum of the transaction weights of all the transactions. The middle hidden layer is set as three layers: the first layer has 32 units; the second layer has 64 units; the third layer has 16 units. The final output value is the trust evaluation value of the predicted target node.

The social relationship can be expressed as a combination of numbers. For example, they are not only friendship relationship, but also the same location relationship and the same community relationship, which is recorded as 111. Therefore, after a number of random interactions to obtain training set data, all relationship node pairs with social relationships of 111, 110, 101, 100, 011, 010, 001 and 000 can be obtained. We record the ratio of the sum of the transaction weights of these nodes for the first three successful transactions to the sum of the total transaction weights of these three transactions (since the cold start problem often occurs between nodes with less interaction experience, set three times as training set data here), and use this ratio as the fourth input factor of the deep learning model. Finally, the simulation results including the trust value evaluation of the target node are input into the deep learning model shown in Fig. 1, and the model results are trained.

Table 2 shows the parameters of deep learning model:

Table 2. The parameters of training deep learning model

Machine memory	16.0 GB
Computer system	Win 10
Video card	GTX1060
Python version	3.7.4
Pytorch version	1.3.1
Hidden layers of deep learning model	3
The number of units in each hidden layer of deep learning model	32,64,16
Learning rate	0.1

In this model, a total of 100 groups of data of different social relationship node pairs are collected, of which 90 groups are training sets and 10 groups are test sets. The training process of deep learning model is about 5 s.

Through this model, the SIoT server can predict the trust value of the service requester node to the target node in the corresponding environment. In order to make the simulation results clear, when a new node is set to join the community, the service requester can request several services from it (take three times as an example). Then, by providing the corresponding input data for the prediction of deep learning model to the SIoT server, the service requester gets the trust value evaluation of the new node and saves it in its own log. In this way, the service requester node can have the corresponding trust value evaluation even in the face of unfamiliar nodes with poor interaction experience, so that the node with the highest trust value can be directly selected for transaction.

4 Simulation Analysis

In this simulation, the given service requester node is always in good condition. In addition to this node, the state of each other node is dynamic (in the simulation of this paper, there are only two states: good and malicious).

The simulation initially set 40 nodes, 4 different communities, 4 different locations and 4 different owners. The network topology is set in advance, and the ownership relationship, location relationship and community relationship are all randomly selected.

Before each transaction, the service requester randomly selects one of four task types from 1 to 4 and requests services from the relevant interested communities. After randomly selecting the service provider node with the highest trust value of all nodes in the interested community, we start the task of randomly selecting transaction factor as h (the value range of h is (0,1). The larger the value is, the more important the transaction is).

This paper takes dense network as an example. Due to the intensive transaction of nodes in the dense network, there may be too much network load and unsuccessful transaction. The success rate of transaction between nodes is set as 80%.

We do 20000 random transactions and all 40 nodes are good at the beginning. With the increase of interaction times, good nodes become malicious nodes at random, and the number of malicious nodes increases at a constant rate.

Trust value transfer is involved in indirect trust value calculation, and transitivity is one of the controversial properties in trust management related research [8]. At the same time, it has been proved in the simulation analysis of [14] that the use of higher λ value in trust value evaluation can help nodes quickly converge to the real node state. On the other hand, malicious nodes should not rely on their good history to conduct improper behavior, so when new transaction occurs, the proportion of old transaction should be reduced. Overall, this paper considers that the trust value of indirect trust is less reliable than that of direct trust, and in order to compare the simulation results with the model in [14] more clearly, so we use the same weight parameters as the model in [14]: the initial values of parameters λ and δ are set to 0.8.

In this paper, we select two nodes with node numbers of 5 and 22 (set both nodes as good nodes), that is, in 20000 random transactions, only the transaction events of node 5 and node 22 are recorded. In the low malicious node proportion environment (malicious node proportion is 20%) and high malicious node proportion environment (malicious node proportion is 80%), the node-level trust model in [14] is compared with the node-level trust model in this paper. The simulation results are as follows:

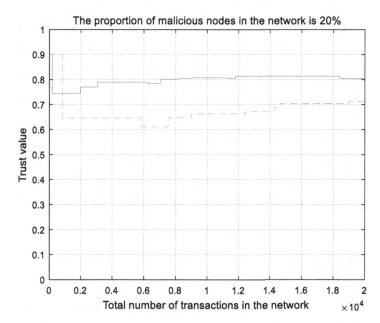

Fig. 2. Comparison of trust values at node-level between two models under the proportion of 20% malicious nodes.

The dotted line in Fig. 2 represents the node-level trust value in the model of [14], and the solid line is the model in this paper. As can be seen from Fig. 2, because the model in this paper gives weight to the trust value of the recommender, the trust value of the good nodes is higher than that of the model in [14] in most simulation time when the proportion of malicious nodes is not very high. A higher trust value also makes it easier for the service provider node to be selected as the next service provider.

The dotted line in Fig. 3 represents the node level trust value in the model of [14], and the solid line is the model in this paper. It can be seen from Fig. 3 that when the proportion of malicious nodes increases to a certain extent, because the indirect recommendation of node-level trust value in the model of [14] is only a simple average of the sum, so when the malicious recommendation increases, the trust value evaluation of a good node to another good node may appear a distrust state of less than 0.5, which makes the good node face the risk of being kicked out of the community and black-listed by the community administrator. However, the trust model in this paper can still maintain a high level of trust value in the high proportion of malicious nodes.

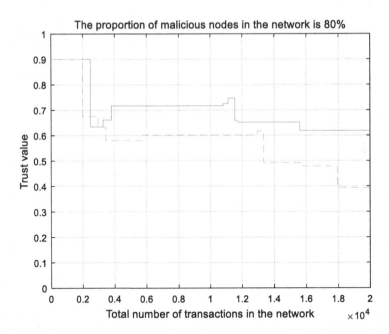

Fig. 3. Comparison of trust values at node-level between two models under the proportion of 80% malicious nodes.

The combination of Fig. 2 and Fig. 3 shows that the node-level trust model in this paper has better protection against malicious recommendation attacks from malicious nodes.

As described in Sect. 3, 10000 transactions are performed as a training set before the simulation starts. In the beginning of the formal simulation, all malicious nodes are initially set up because the malicious nodes have been generated in the training set collection process. New nodes are added to the model in this paper and the model in [14] at the same time to observe the trust evaluation of good nodes to new nodes. Take the proportion of 20% malicious nodes and 80% malicious nodes in the network as an example, we simulate the trust value calculation under the two models. In the simulation, we ensure that in different models of the same transaction, there is the same transaction factor and interested community selection. After each transaction, if the transaction evaluation is successful, it will be recorded as 1; if not, it will be recorded as 0. Count the total number of successful and failed transaction.

We set the node No. 5 and the newly added node as good nodes, and record the trust evaluation of node No. 5 to the new node in the simulation. After 20000 transaction experiments, the comparison results of the two trust models are shown in Fig. 4 and Fig. 5.

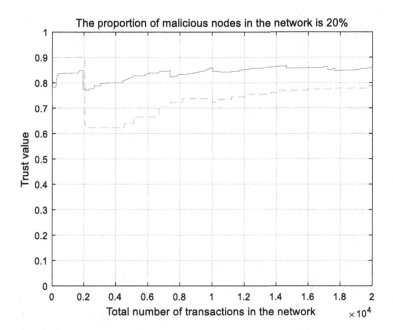

Fig. 4. Comparison of trust values between the two models under the proportion of 20% malicious nodes.

In Fig. 4, the solid line represents the trust value evaluation of the good node to the newly added good node in this model, and the dotted line represents the trust value evaluation of the good node to the newly added good node in the model of [14]. As can be seen from Fig. 4, the trust model in this paper has good trust value prediction, and always selects the node with the highest trust value as the service provider, so after the good node joins the community, it has more opportunities to provide tasks. Providing more good services in Fig. 4 shows that the trust value of the solid line can quickly converge to a higher value, and in most of the transaction process, the trust value evaluation is higher than the dotted line. According to statistics, the total number of successful transactions and failure transactions of this model in this simulation is 12016 and 801; the total number of successful transactions and failure transactions of the model in [14] is 10825 and 1950 (the sum of the number of successful transactions and the number of failure transactions is less than 20000, because when a malicious node requests a service from a good node or other malicious node, the service evaluation given is a fixed value of 0 or 1, regardless of whether the service is good or bad). The number of successful transactions of the model in this paper is significantly higher than that of the model in [14], and the number of failures is also much lower than that of the model in [14].

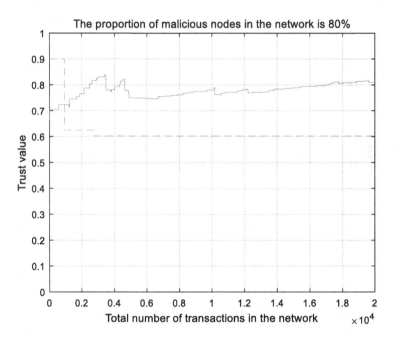

Fig. 5. Comparison of trust values between the two models under the proportion of 80% malicious nodes.

In Fig. 5, the solid line represents the trust value evaluation of the good nodes in this model to the newly added good nodes, and the dotted line represents the trust value evaluation of the good nodes in the model [14] to the newly added good nodes. Comparing Fig. 4 and Fig. 5, the trust model in this paper achieves a high trust value evaluation in the case of a high proportion of malicious nodes, although the trust value evaluation is slightly lower than that in the case of a low proportion of malicious nodes. In the model of [14], malicious recommendation attacks increase due to too many malicious nodes. After the newly added good node completes several transactions, the good node is kicked out of the community due to the malicious recommendation of other malicious nodes in the same community. Therefore, the trust value evaluation maintains the trust value state before being kicked out of the community after several transactions, which is the straight line in the Fig. 5. According to statistics, the total number of successful transactions and the total number of failed transactions in this model are 2420 and 683 respectively. In the model of [14], the total number of successful transactions is 1817, and the total number of failed transactions is 1422. Compared with the low proportion of malicious nodes, the number of successful transactions in the model of [14] is more less than that of the model in this paper.

The model in this paper always selects the node with the highest trust evaluation value for transaction, so good nodes in the model can get more transaction opportunities compared with the [14] model. The more transactions good nodes participate in, the higher the probability of successful transactions. At the same time, because the node with the highest trust evaluation value is always selected to transaction in the model in this paper, it is difficult for the malicious node to appear as the service provider node after obtaining a low trust evaluation value. At this time, the malicious nodes have to quit the community, and because of the "blacklist" system in the administrator and SIoT server, such malicious nodes will have no chance to join the original community. At the same time, for some malicious nodes that may become good nodes, the system in this paper's model also gives them opportunities to transaction instead of directly kicking them out of the community as in the model [14].

5 Conclusion

This paper presents an improved trust prediction model for social internet of things. In view of the "cold start" problem that may occur in the networks with large delay, which may affect the trust value evaluation of new nodes due to the low communication success rate, this paper innovatively proposes the application of deep learning model in the SIoT server-level trust model to evaluate and predict the trust value of corresponding nodes, so that the good nodes can identify the new nodes with good trust value evaluation faster. It can effectively reduce the impact of malicious attacks from malicious nodes. Simulation results show that this model can effectively deal with the network with high proportion of malicious nodes.

Acknowledgements. This work was supported by the Beijing Science and Technology Project (No. Z191100001419001), Key Laboratory of Modern Measurement & Control Technology, Ministry of Education, Beijing Information Science & Technology University(No. KF202011 23202), Shipei Plan of Beijing Information Science & Technology University (2020), Beijing Excellent Talent Support Program (No. 2016000026833ZK08), and Support Plan for the Construction of High Level Teachers in Beijing Municipal Universities (No. CIT&TCD201704065).

References

1. French, A.M., Shim, J.P.: The digital revolution: internet of things, 5G, and beyond. Commun. Assoc. Inf. Syst. **38**(1), 840–850 (2016)
2. Militano, L., Araniti, G., Condoluci, M., Farris, I., Iera, A.: Device-to-device communications for 5G internet of things. http://www.researchgate.net/publication/283327011. Accessed 2015
3. Guinard, D., Fischer, M., Trifa, V.: Sharing using social networks in a composable Web of Things. In: Proceedings of the Pervasive Computing and Communications 2010, pp. 702–707, Mannheim, Germany (2010)
4. Atzori, L., Iera, A., Morabito, G., Nitti, M.: The social internet of things (SIoT) - when social networks meet the internet of things: concept, architecture and network characterization. Comput. Netw. **56**(16), 3594–3608 (2012)
5. Ortiz, A.M., Hussein, D., Park, S., Han, S.N., Crespi, N.: The cluster between Internet of Things and social networks: review and research challenges. IEEE Internet Things J. **1**(3), 206–215 (2014)
6. Mi, B., Liang, X., Zhang, S.: A survey on social internet of things. Chin. J. Comput. **41**(7), 1448–1475 (2018)

7. Geoffrey, H.: Deep learning—a technology with the potential to transform health care. JAMA J. Am. Med. Assoc. **320**(11),1101 (2018)
8. Nitti, M., Girau, R., Atzori, L.: Trustworthiness management in the social internet of things. IEEE Trans. Knowl. Data Eng. **26**(5), 1–11(2014)
9. Eleftherios, K., Orfefs, V., Theodora, V.: TRM-SIoT: a scalable hybrid trust and reputation model for the social internet of things. In: 2016 IEEE 21st International Conference on Emerging Technologies and Factory Automation (ETFA), pp. 1–9, Berlin, Germany (2016)
10. Sherif, E.A.R., Ayman, A., Mohamad, A.: CBSTM-IoT: context-based social trust model for the internet of things. In: 2016 International Conference on Selected Topics in Mobile and Wireless Networking (MoWNeT), vol.1, pp. 1–8, Cairo, Egypt (2016)
11. Saied, Y.B., Olivereau, A., Zeghlache, D., Laurent, M.: Trust management system design for the internet of things: a context aware and multi-service approach. Comput. Secur. **39**(B), 351–365 (2013)
12. Chen, I.R., Bao, F., Guo, J.: Trust-based service management for social internet of things systems. IEEE Trans. Dependable Secure Comput. **13**(6), 684–696 (2016)
13. Carminati, B., Ferrari E., Viviani, M.: Security and Trust in Online Social Networks. Morgan & Claypool, San Rafael (2013)
14. Oumaima, B.A., Mohamed, H.E., Leila, S.: TMCoI-SIoT: a trust management system based on communities of interest for the social internet of things. In: 2017 13th International Wireless Communications and Mobile Computing Conference (IWCMC), pp. 747–752, Valencia, Spain (2017)

An Alarm System Based on BP Neural Network Algorithm for the Detection of Falls to Elderly Person

Wenhui Chen[✉], Xueming Wang, Junfei Chen, Zhiyong Ding, Jianying Li, and Bo Li

School of Electronic Information, Northwestern Polytechnic University, Xian 710072, China
whchen@nwpu.edu.cn

Abstract. With the increase in the elderly population, people pay more and more attention to the harm caused by falls. When people reach old age, various functions of the body will degrade to a certain extent. If the elderly fall down, it may endanger their physical and mental health. In view of the above problems, this system designed a elderly fall detection and alarm system based on the reverse neural network algorithm, specifically using MPU6050 sensor to detect human posture data, the control module using the algorithm for real-time judgment, if the fall behavior, the control alarm module to send alarm messages. This system can be used in nursing home health monitoring system, intelligent home system in the detection subsystem and other intelligent medical aspects, can be used in various aspects to protect the health of the elderly, reduce the risk of accidental injury.

Keywords: Falls in older people · BP neural network · MPU6050 sensor · Wisdom care

1 Introduction

With the improvement of life quality and medical progress, the average age of the elderly has been increased, and the aging of the population has become increasingly obvious. According to statistics, the number of people over 65 will account for about 30% of China's population by 2050 [1]. Accidental falls can cause great harm to the elderly and increase morbidity and mortality among the elderly. Therefore, it is of great significance to develop a system that can detect the daily activities of the elderly in real time and give a real-time alarm after a fall, so as to effectively guarantee the life safety of the elderly [2].

At present, there are two main techniques to detect falls: video image processing and accelerometer detection. Video image processing is the use of cameras to track the daily behavior of the elderly to obtain real-time images and uses a specific algorithm to detect whether there is a fall [3,4]. The technology can

B. Li et al. (Eds.): IoTaaS 2020, LNICST 346, pp. 571–581, 2021.
https://doi.org/10.1007/978-3-030-67514-1_45

only be used in specific places, is computing-intensive and difficult to process, and the images taken can be a privacy risk.

The accelerometer method detects people's attitude changes in real-time through microsensors [5,6]. The system uses a fall detection algorithm to determine whether a fall has occurred. This technology has obvious advantages which it is not limited by space, low cost, and easy to carry. At present, the accelerometer detection method is generally the threshold detection method. For example, LIU Li, Design of MPU6050-based fall monitoring system for the elderly [11], this detection method determines whether a fall has occurred by detecting the acceleration of human body and setting the acceleration threshold of fall. This detection method is simple and easy to operate, but with low accuracy, high error detection rate and easy to make mistakes.

In this paper, we propose a fall alarm system for the elderly based on a neural network algorithm. We use the MPU6050 acceleration sensor to detect the real-time acceleration and attitude angle of human movement, then send the data to the master controller through serial communication and then use the fall recognition algorithm to process the data to get the result of whether the fall has occurred.

2   System Structure Design

The system is mainly composed of the data module, message module, and power module. The data module is composed of MPU6050 sensor and STM32F103 control chip. The message module is connected to the STM32F103 chip through a serial port. The power module is responsible for power supply, 5 V voltage 1 A current. The above modules are fixed and worn on the waist of the elderly for real-time detection. If the fall action is detected, an alarm message will be sent to the relatives or the hospital. The system structure diagram is shown in Fig. 1.

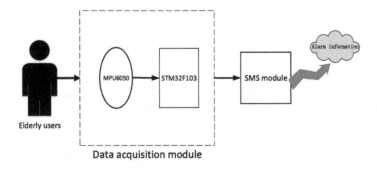

Fig. 1. System structure diagram.

2.1 MPU6050

MPU6050 is integrated with triaxial acceleration sensor and triaxial gyroscope sensor, and contains DMP and ADC module, which can effectively process detected data and transmit it to STM32F103 master controller through IIC bus [7]. Compared with the traditional acceleration sensor, MPU6050 has a strong anti-interference capability and can effectively remove the sensitivity between accelerator and gyroscope axis.

2.2 Controller, STM32F103

The controller is the STM32F103RCT6 chip, which is equipped with 48 KB SRAM, 256 KB FLASH,2 IIC, 5 serial ports, etc. The highest working frequency can reach 72MHz, and the working voltage is between 3.3 V–5 V. The chip has the characteristics of low power consumption and strong functions, which can meet the system design requirements

2.3 Short Message Module

The alarm module of this system adopts the SIM900A, supports RS232 serial port and LVTTL serial port, and has hardware flow control. It supports the ultra-wide working range of 5 V–24 V, and the working frequency band is dual-frequency 900/1800 MHz. It connects with the controller through serial communication, with low working power consumption and stable data transmission, which conforms to the alarm design requirements of this paper.

3 Algorithm of Fall Action Detection

3.1 Data Preprocessing and Network Feature Selection

The fall has abruptness, rapidity and acuteness, it is to fall on the ground that is lower than the human body commonly, produce a violent impact with the ground. In this case, the acceleration and angle of the human body will mutate [8]. Based on this feature, this paper designs an algorithm to distinguish falls from normal activities, such as walking, running, sitting, going up and down a building, etc., so as to detect falls of the elderly and give a timely alarm.

The data sources of this paper are mainly human motion acceleration and attitude angle. How to extract the data and how to process the data into the neural network after extraction is a major problem to be solved in this paper. As shown in Table 1, the part with the largest mass proportion of the human body in the trunk [9]. During normal movement, the activity frequency of the trunk position is small, and the movement data changes steadily. In the process of people fall, the trunk part instantly changes greatly, but after the fall, the data tends to be stable [10]. While in normal activities, legs or arms are frequently used, and the data changes are also very messy, which will make the detection results susceptible to interference and reduce the accuracy. In conclusion, we

Table 1. Proportion of the mass of each part of the human body

Name	The quality of (%) man	The quality of (%) woman
On the trunk	16.33	16.42
Under the trunk	26.27	25.98
Head	9.3	8.60
Arm	2.61	2.62
Hand	0.64	0.49
Thigh	14.00	14.28
Calf	4.00	4.55
Foot	1.50	1.38

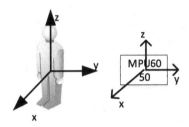

Fig. 2. Coordinate comparison diagram of human body and sensor attitude

put the system at the waist so that the correct data can be collected without affecting the normal activity of the person.

In order to collect correct sensor data, it is necessary to establish a three-dimensional coordinate system in which the human body is in a standing state and the sensor acquisition direction is consistent, as shown in Fig. 2. The MPU6050 sensor detects acceleration along the X, Y, and Z axes in the event of a violent fall. We define the acceleration as $a_x a_y a_z$. We define Ca as the magnitude of combined acceleration, which is an important parameter that distinguishes falling motions from normal motions. The larger the Ca, the more intense the movement. Ca will reach a peak when colliding with the ground when falling [11], so Ca can be used as a feature selection of the BP neural network.

$$Ca = \sqrt{a_x^2 + a_y^2 + a_z^2} \tag{1}$$

The angle of the human body during the fall is also very obvious. When a fall occurs, the body tends to fall forward, backward or to the left and right, that is, the angle changes on the X-axis and Y-axis are relatively obvious, while the angle changes on the Z-axis are not very obvious. Therefore, Pitch in the X-axis direction and Roll in the Y-axis direction is selected as the characteristics of the BP neural network. As shown in Fig. 3, the Pitch and Roll data are significantly changed during the fall. In Fig. 3, the X-axis represents the data length, and the Y-axis represents the angle value. In daily life, the elderly move slowly and the activity frequency is generally no more than 20 Hz. Therefore, the sampling frequency 30 Hz is used to collect data of Ca, Pitch and Roll, and the dynamic Kalman filter is used for denoising. Kalman filter is an optimized autoregressive data processing algorithm, which can well deal with the data noise brought by a real-time sensor[9].

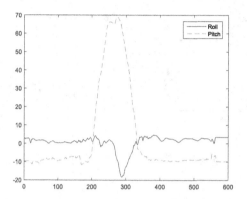

Fig. 3. Change curve of Pitch and Roll data during fall.

3.2 BP Neural Network Algorithm Implementation

Based on the above analysis, this paper designs a three-layer neural network for training sample data [8]. (1) For the input layer, based on feature selection and fall data changes, three neurons can be set on the input layer, namely, acceleration Ca, Pitch and Roll. (2) For the output layer, it only needs to show whether the human body falls, so a neuron is set as a fallen marker. (3) The hidden layer selects two neurons for weight correction. The results show that the model algorithm can train samples quickly with a low error detection rate and good robustness. Figure 4 shows the BP neural network model.

The working principle of this model is as follows.

1) The model is initialized with normal distribution with mean value of 0 and variance of 1.
2) Training samples were collected and divided into Ca, Pitch and Roll data for falls and normal activities, and normalized to make the model more sensitive to data.
3) Do the forward calculation. The induced local domain of the input layer is obtained as follows:

$$net_j^{(1)}(n) = \sum_{i=0}^{3} V_{ji}^{(1)}(n)X_i(n) \quad j = 1, 2 \tag{2}$$

$X_i(n)$ represents the input layer eigenvalues. $V_{ji}(n)$ is the weight from i to j. The activation function selection is sigmoid function, so the input of the

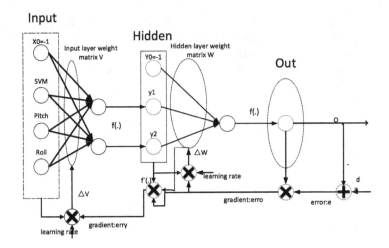

Fig. 4. BP neural network module

hidden layer can be calculated:

$$Y_j(n) = f(net_j^{(1)}(n)) = \frac{1}{1 + exp(-a * net_j^{(1)}(n))} \qquad a > 0 \qquad (3)$$

Similarly, the induced local domain of the hidden layer can be obtained:

$$net^{(2)}(n) = \sum_{j=0}^{2} W_{kj}^{(2)}(n)Y_j(n) \qquad (4)$$

$W_{kj}(n)$ is the weight from j to k. Then the actual output is:

$$o(n) = f(net^{(2)}(n)) = \frac{1}{1 + exp(-a * net^{(2)}(n))} \qquad (5)$$

Calculable error:

$$e(n) = d(n) - o(n) \qquad (6)$$

After the forward calculation, we have set a threshold for the error. If the error is within the threshold range, we can say that training has been completed. If the error is greater than the threshold, the calculation is reversed to adjust the weights on the network for each layer. 4) Reverse training The gradient descent method is used to calculate the optimal weight to minimize the error, and the local gradient of the neural network can be obtained:

$$erro(n) = e(n)f'(net^{(2)}(n)) \qquad (7)$$

$$erry(n) = f'(net_j^{(1)}(n))erro(n)W_{kj}^{(2)}(n) \qquad (8)$$

Using the rule, the weights of the hidden layer can be obtained:

$$W_{jk}(n+1) = W_{jk}(n) + \alpha W_{jk}(n) \tag{9}$$

$$\Delta W_{jk}(n) = \alpha[W_{jk}(n-1)] + \eta e(n)f'(net^{(2)}(n))y_j \tag{10}$$

$$V_{ji}(n+1) = V_{ji}(n) + \delta V_{ji}(n) \tag{11}$$

$$\Delta V_{ji}(n) = \alpha[V_{ji}(n-1)] + \eta erro(n)f'(net^{(1)}(n))x_i \tag{12}$$

Where is the learning rate parameter and is the momentum constant. 5) Iterative calculation After a round of weight adjustment, the forward calculation process is repeated in turn until the error is less than the range of convergence criteria. Then the next set of samples was trained until N samples were trained to detect falls in the body. After all the samples are trained, the overall modeling is completed.

The overall flow chart of the training process is shown in Fig. 5.

After training the samples with neural network algorithm, the weights are obtained, which can be applied to the system. The overall work flow chart of the system is shown in Fig. 6.

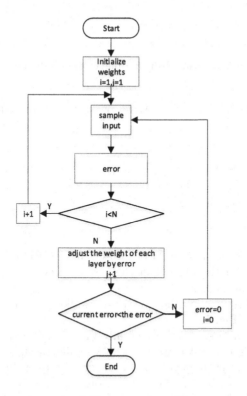

Fig. 5. Overall flow chart of the training process.

4   Experimental Analysis

We apply the above algorithm to this system and carry out a simulation experiment to verify the fall action of the elderly. In this experiment, 10 young students aged 22's–28's were selected to simulate the daily activities of the elderly (walking, jogging, sitting, going up and down the stairs) and falling (falling forward, backward, left and right). Each movement was performed in 50 groups. The experimental results are shown in the Table 2 and Table3.

Table 2. The success rate of fall behavior detection based on the BP neural network algorithm)

Fall of status	Fall times	Alarm times	Success rate
Forward	50	48	96%
Backward	50	50	100%
Left	50	48	96%
Right	50	49	98%

Table 3. The false rate of normal behavior detection based on the BP neural network algorithm

Status	Times	Alarm times	False detection rate
Walking	50	0	0%
Run	50	1	2%
Sit down	50	3	6%
Upstairs	50	2	4%
Go downstairs	50	2	4%

In order to verify the superiority of the system algorithm, we used the threshold based detection method to detect the actions. The experimental results are shown in Table 4 and Table 5.

The tested subjects wear the system for walking, sitting, lying down and falling, as shown in Fig. 7.

The experimental results were basically in line with expectations, and the correct rate of falls reached more than 95%, while the false detection rate of normal activities was around 5%. The fall accuracy rate of threshold comparison method is about 60%, and the false detection rate is about 20%, which is not very practical. This BP algorithm can distinguish the normal activities and fall actions of the elderly very well. As there is a similar place between sitting action and falling action, the range of the human body may be relatively large, so the

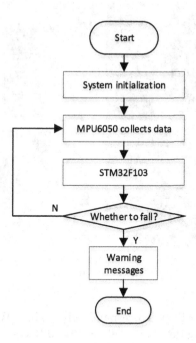

Fig. 6. Overall work flow chart.

Table 4. The success rate of fall behavior detection based on the threshold algorithm

Fall of status	Fall times	Alarm times	Success rate
Forward	50	30	60%
Backward	50	35	70%
Left	50	28	56%
Right	50	25	50%

Table 5. The false rate of normal behavior detection based on the threshold algorithm

Status	Times	Alarm times	False detection rate
Walking	50	8	16%
Run	50	5	10%
Sit down	50	15	30%
Upstairs	50	10	20%
Go downstairs	50	8	16%

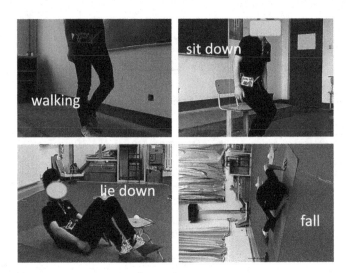

Fig. 7. Action test.

rate of false detection will be correspondingly higher. We set the acceleration threshold to detect lying down and falling action. Because the attitude Angle of lying down and falling is very similar, BP neural network will increase the error. We will continue to improve the system.

5   Conclusion

In this paper, we designed a wearable fall action detection system based on a neural network algorithm, which can more accurately judge fall actions by learning a lot of characteristic data of normal activities and fall actions from the neural network. Moreover, due to the wide source of feature data, the robustness of the system is improved, which is better than the system based on the simple threshold detection method. The experimental results verify the accuracy of the system. The system is simple in design and easy to wear. If the fall is detected, it can send an alarm message to inform the family or the hospital in time, so as to better protect the life and safety of the elderly.

References

1. Jiang, C.: An analysis of the present situation of population aging in China and the strategies and measures in the thirteenth five period. Globalization **2016**(8), 90–105 (2016)
2. Zheng, H., Ju, Y., Shen, D., et al.: Evaluation and prevention for falls in elder people: a leading cause of unintentional injuries. Chin. J. Stroke **8**(12), 1003–1008 (2013)

3. Merrouche, F., Baha, N.: Depth camera based fall detection using human shape and movement, pp. 586–590. IEEE (2017)
4. Bingxia, X.: Research on Multimodal Feature Fusion for Human Fall Detection. Shandong University, Jinan (2015)
5. Peng, L.I.U., Tancheng, L.U., Yuanyuan, L., et al.: MEMS tri-axial accelerometer based fall detection. Chin. J. Sens. Actuators **4**, 570–574 (2014)
6. Cao, Y., Cai, W., Cheng, Y.: Body posture detection technology based on MEMS acceleration sensor. Nanotechnol. Precis. Eng. **8**(1), 37–41 (2010)
7. Guo, Y., Ye, W.: A fall detection algorithm based on MPU6050 sensor. J. Hunan Ind. **32**(3), 77–80 (2018)
8. Wang, R., Zhang, Y., Chen, J.: Design and implementation of fall detection system using tri-axis accelerometer. Comput. Appl. **32**(5), 1450–1452 (2012)
9. He, L.: Design of Human Fall Detection System Based on Acceleration Sensor, pp. 9–12. College of Optoelectronic Engineering Chongqing University, Chongqing (2016)
10. Liu, L., Zhen, D., Liu, X.: Design of mpu6050-based fall monitoring system for the elderly. Chin. J. Med. Dev. **39**(5), 327–330 (2015)
11. Luo, J.: Study on the Fall Detection System of the Elderly, pp. 10–11. Shanghai University of Engineering and Technology, Shanghai (2016)

Satellite Communication Networks
for Internet of Things

The Intelligent Routing Control Strategy Based on Deep Learning

Jinsuo Jia[1]([✉]), Yichun Fu[2], Guiyu Zhang[1], Xiaochen Liang[1], and Peng Xu[1]

[1] China Information Technology Designing and Consulting Institute Co., Ltd.,
Beijing 100048, China
{jiajs5,zhanggy,liangxch,xupeng}@dimpt.com
[2] International School, Beijing University of Posts and Telecommunications,
Beijing 100876, China
2016213048@bupt.edu.cn

Abstract. The rapid development of computer hardware and software provides a suitable platform for machine learning, in which deep learning has become a breakthrough in machine learning technology in various fields in many disciplines. Some recent research efforts have focused on routing control based on deep learning. Therefore, this paper studies the problem of intelligent routing, and aims to propose an intelligent control strategy based on deep learning with the help of Software-Defined Network (SDN) and other new network technologies. The characteristics of SDN network that can easily obtain the network topology have laid the foundation for selecting different routing paths according to the different QoS levels of the flow. Nowadays, the routing modules in commonly used SDN controllers use the shortest path algorithm which is simple to implement and works effectively. However, the best path calculated by controllers may suffer from huge traffic load and result in congestion, and the controllers cannot learn from the previous experiences to intelligently switch to other paths. This paper present intelligent routing control strategy based on Deep Q-Learning (DQN) in SDN, which uses the Openflow to collect information from the network, and aggregates them to the SDN controller, and then uses DQN to generate the specific routing for forwarders.

Keywords: SDN · Deep learning · Routing strategy · Reinforcement learning

1 Introduction

Nowadays, the Internet has become a very important part of people's lives. Driven by strong market demand and the development of modern technology, the Internet has developed more and more rapidly which has been gradually inseparable from other industries. The initial design of the Internet was not considered that it will be so widely used in the future, and its role will be as important as this. Therefore, many designs at that time could no longer adapt to

B. Li et al. (Eds.): IoTaaS 2020, LNICST 346, pp. 585–598, 2021.
https://doi.org/10.1007/978-3-030-67514-1_46

the development trend of modern Internet [9,10]. At present, security, robustness and mobility have become the major problems of the Internet. In recent years, Software Defined Network (SDN) has been sought as the most likely solution of future network, and it has two characteristics: the control plane and data plane are separated, and the network is programmable [1]. Therefore, SDN can provide more effective configurations, better performance and higher flexibility to adapt to the future development of the network [3].

In 2017, the Alphago also announced the arrival of the AI revolution. The term "artificial intelligence" was originally born at Dartmouth society in 1956, and AI has become the hottest research direction in the field of computer currently due to the progress of algorithms and hardware. As the learning algorithm of artificial intelligence, Machine Learning (ML) and Deep Learning (DL) are also accepted to extensive attention and research.

As a branch of machine learning, reinforcement learning is the product of the combination of multidisciplinary. In the field of artificial intelligence, agent is generally used to represent an object with behavior ability, such as robot, unmanned vehicle, human and so on. The problem of reinforcement learning is the task of interaction between agent and environment. The essence of reinforcement learning is a "decision-making" problem, i.e., agent makes a decision by itself. Deep learning is an algorithm proposed after the development of "artificial neural network", which can be regarded as the evolution of traditional neural network. Deep Learning is also a new field in the process of machine learning, and it emphasizes the importance of model depth and feature learning. Compared with the traditional neural network, deep learning has similar structure but obvious improvement. The essence of deep learning is to build a neural network model with multiple hidden layers, and learn more useful features through massive training data, so as to ultimately improve the accuracy of model classification or prediction.

This paper introduces an intelligent SDN routing optimization method based on traffic classification, which is based on the characteristics of SDN, and combined with the advantages of reinforcement learning in strategy optimization and deep learning in data classification: when a network flow reaches a node in the network (Openflow switch), it can use the deep learning model to classify the network flow, and then according to the classification results to judge the QoS level, and then uses reinforcement learning model to plan its forwarding path, so that the flow can reach the destination node (Openflow switch) through the shortest path that meets its QoS requirements [4–8].

The concept of network layered architecture is the key to the rapid development of traditional Internet. However, in recent years, the scale of the network is getting larger and larger, and the traditional network equipment with closed network uses too many complex protocols, which is more and more difficult for major operators to optimize the network, and also difficult for researchers to deploy new protocols in the real environment. At the same time, with the continuous expansion of network scale, the rapid growth of traffic, the emergence of various new services, the improvement of network operation and maintenance costs, the traditional network architecture is difficult to meet the rapid development of network needs.

In order to meet the needs of the next generation of network development, Mckeown proposes the concept of SDN which is a kind of network architecture that the programmable control plane is separated from the data forwarding plane. The control plane is a programmable controller [2]. The R&D personnel and operators can customize the network or deploy new network protocols according to the needs of customers or their own products. The data layer is composed of some Openflow switches, which are different from the traditional two-layer switches. They only provide simple data forwarding function, quickly match data packets, and complete data forwarding to meet the growing network demand.

The most classic description of SDN architecture is the architecture diagram from ONF (Open Network Foundation).

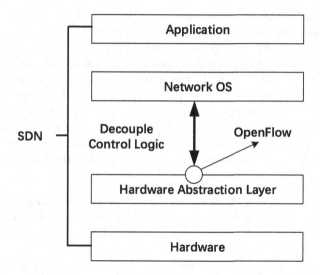

Fig. 1. SDN architecture diagram from ONF.

Figure 1 expresses the concept of hierarchical decoupling of SDN, including the general basic hardware layer, hardware abstraction layer, network operating system, and upper-layer applications. And the basic hardware and hardware abstraction constitute the physical network equipment which is the data forwarding level in the SDN architectures. The network operating system and upper-layer applications form the control level. The data forwarding level and the control level are decoupled with a standardized interactive protocol such OpenFlow. This decoupling architecture shows that the network operating system and network applications (such as routing control protocols, etc.) do not have to run on physical devices, but can run in external systems (such as X86-based servers), thereby achieving flexible and programmability of the network.

At present, the mainstream SDN controllers, such as Ryu, provides modules to complete packet forwarding, and the basic algorithm used is Dijkstra (shortest path) algorithm. Dijkstra algorithm finds the shortest path from the start node to the destination node of packet forwarding every time. However, if the forwarding of all packets only depends on the shortest path algorithm, it will bring a serious problem. The data flow is easy to gather because of choosing the same forwarding path, which greatly reduces the link utilization, and also easily leads to network congestion. In view of the shortcomings of pure Dijkstra algorithm, there are many researches related to SDN routing, and a variety of Dijkstra improved algorithms or new routing algorithms are proposed.

2   Related Work

2.1   Overview of SDN Architecture

The definition of SDN is divided into two types, in narrow sense, SDN refers to the new network architecture based on Openflow proposed by Stanford University. This new network architecture is derived from Ethane project of Stanford University, which has produced the concept of Openflow and has evolved a new network structure called SDN. In the initial SDN network architecture, Open-Flow was its core technology. With the development of the CleanStage project, the SDN network architecture expanded to separate the control plane and data plane of network devices, so as to flexibly control network traffic, develop new network applications on the platform of SDN, and make innovation to network applications. The SDN technology in narrow sense has the following characteristics:

(1) Separation of control plane and forwarding plane: traditional network equipment constitutes the forwarding plane and only forwarding tasks are performed, SDN controller constitutes the control plane to control the forwarding plane.
(2) Centralized control of the network, the SDN controller can obtain the entire network topology of the forwarding plane and the local state of each network device, the SDN controller can achieve centralized control of the entire network with this information.
(3) Open interface: The SDN controller develops different interfaces for the application layer and the device layer, then the application layer and the device layer are logically independent of each other. In this case, when we develop network applications, we just don't need to know the situation of the equipment layer.

As a new type of network technology, the SDN technology based on Openflow has many incomplete places, but shortly after its birth, it has become the top ten cutting-edge technology of MIT. It can be seen from this that the international society is optimistic about the prospects of SDN, and discussions on SDN are also in full swing. At present, the international standards organizations that focus on

SDN mainly include: ONF (Open Network Foundation), Open Daylight, ACM SICGCOM HotSDN Workshop, IRTF SDNRG and IETF.

The SDN architecture based on the Openflow specification was first proposed by ONF which is established in 2011 with objective to formulate SDN related standards and promote its proposed architecture. So far, ONF has proposed the Openflow standard and the Openflow configuration protocol. These work have accelerated the process of SDN standardization, and promoted the rapid development of SDN. The ultimate goal of ONF is to turn SDN into ordinary software, so that SDN can be deployed on general servers and common operating systems. In this way, ordinary programmers can implement network programming on SDN. The SDN architecture are composed of application layer, the control layer and the infrastructure layer. And for the different needs of the data center, access network and bearer network, different SDN architectures are proposed. Based on these architectures, research institutions have developed controllers and network node devices that can be used in SDN networks.

At the same time, for controllers and network devices, as well as controllers and upper-layer applications, there are also available interfaces. At present, the SDN controllers based on Open mainly include NOX, POX, Floodlight, Opendaylight, ONOS and so on. Regarding the switching equipment that can be used in the SDN architecture, NEC first introduced a number of SDN switches that support the Open protocol. Soon after that, companies such as Junifer, Hewlett-Packard, and Huawei also launched network devices such as routers, switches, and wireless network Access Points (AP) that support the Openflow protocol developed by their companies.

2.2   Development Trend of Network Architecture

The core of the SDN architecture is the controller. SDN can be considered as a set of client-server relationships between the SDN controller and other entities (administrators, applications, and SDN controllers, etc.). In its role as a server, the SDN controller can provide services to any number of clients, and the SDN controller acting as a client can call services from any number of servers.

Figure 2 illustrates some of its key functions and interfaces. The introduction of some nouns in the SDN architecture diagram shown in Fig. 2 is as follows:

- Client: Client is an entity that receives services from the server.
- Client context: The conceptual component of the server, which represents all the information of a given client and is responsible for participating the management and control operations with active server clients.
- Server: Server is the entity that provides services to the client.
- Server context: The conceptual component of the client, which represents all information for a given server and is responsible for participating the management and control operations with active server clients.
- Resource group: Network resources are grouped into layers according to a certain technology or management boundary. Different network resources and controllers can be controlled and managed with different protocols.

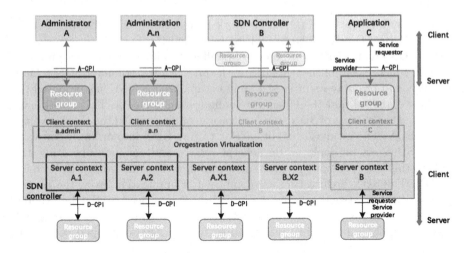

Fig. 2. The core of SDN architecture.

The core work of SDN controller is Orchestration and Virtualization. The control device satisfies client requests through virtualization and collaboration of its underlying resources. As the network environment and customer changes, the SDN controller is responsible for continuously updating the network and business status to achieve optimal policy-based configuration.

An SDN controller controls and manages network resources through a southbound interface (D-CPI, Data-Controller, Platform, and Interface), and through a northbound interface (A-CPI, Application-Control-Control-Control) Internet) to communicate with applications or higher-level controllers. Management and control are regarded as continuous behaviors, in which the role of administrator (Administrator) is different from that of general applications, and it has greater scope and privileges. The administrator has the right to configure the SDN controller itself and Client context and Server context. At present, ONF has defined the standard OpenFlow specification for D-CPI, but A-CPI still lacks industry-recognized standards. The key of SDN is to realize the programmable control of the network, and A-CPI is the basis to realize the programmable. Through A-CPI, network service developers can call various network resources in the form of software programming. At the same time, the upper-layer network resource management system can globally control the resource status of the entire SDN network through A-CPI and uniformly schedule it.

2.3   Routing Algorithms

Routing is the process of selecting a delivery path in a network and has been applied in many types of networks including circuit switched networks and computer networks.

In packet switched networks, routing is a higher-level decision-making which uses a specific packet forwarding mechanism to transfer network packets from their source address to their destination address through intermediate network nodes. Packet forwarding refers to the transmission process of logically processed network packets from one network interface to another. The intermediate nodes are usually routers, switches and other network hardware devices. Routing process usually guides forwarding on the basis of routing table, which maintains records of routes to different network destinations. Therefore, it is very important to build routing table in router memory for efficient routing. Most routing algorithms use only one network path at a time.

In traditional IP networks, routing algorithms are mostly implemented step by step. There are widely recognized and used routing protocols based on link state or distance vector algorithm, such as rip (routing information protocol), IGRP (interior gateway route) protocol, OSPF (open shortest path first), etc. These IP based routing protocols calculate the route and forward the packets only according to the destination address of the packets. The result is that all packets with the same destination address will go through the same network path. Some existing multi-path protocols also do not consider the QoS requirements of different traffic flows. From the perspective of path optimization, this has limitations, because it does not consider the traffic status of the whole network.

Each switching device can obtain manually configured routing table through static routing, or obtain forwarding information through dynamic routing and regularly communicate with other devices in the network to obtain network topology changes, so as to update its own routing table. According to the routing table, the switching equipment forming the network forms a forwarding table. When the IP message arrives at the router interface, the chip in the entrance direction extracts the IP message header, obtains the destination address, and then searches the forwarding table according to the destination IP: if the destination address is the same as the network address connected to an interface of the router, the data will be forwarded directly to the corresponding interface; if the destination address is not found to belong to its own direct network segment, then the router It will check its own routing table, find the corresponding interface of the destination network, and forward it from the corresponding interface; if it is found that the network address recorded in the routing table does not match the address of 0 in the message, it will forward to the default interface according to the router configuration, and return the control message protocol (ICMP, Internet Control Message Protocol) with the unreachable destination address to the user without the default interface configured.

Path selection is to select (or predict) the best route through some route metric parameters among multiple routes. In IP network, routing algorithm is usually used to calculate the metric. This metric information can be divided into bandwidth, network delay, hops, path cost, load, MTU (Maximum Transmission Unit), reliability and communication cost.

In the SDN network, considering that the data plane is separated from the control plane, the switching equipment on the SDN data plane is only responsible for data forwarding according to the flow table issued by the controller, and the forwarding path is calculated by the routing module in the controller. At the same time, SDN is a programmable network, so a corresponding routing algorithm can be developed and loaded on the control plane according to the user's needs.

Based on the above analysis, it can be concluded that the SDN network replaces the routing protocol in the traditional IP network through the centralized control of the controller. The routing strategy of SDN is easier to implement and more flexible.

2.4 Reinforcement Learning

The Basic Principles of Reinforcement Learning. Reinforcement learning is a kind of machine learning and it is different from supervised learning and unsupervised learning. Reinforcement learning is the third machine learning mode in the field of machine learning, which continuously explores the surrounding environment through an agent, and gets a corresponding reward value r for every decision. Reinforcement learning consists of: what to do, how to map between States and actions, and how to maximize reward signals. If the current strategy selected by the agent is correct, a positive feedback signal will be obtained, otherwise a negative feedback signal will be obtained. As a kind of unsupervised learning, the biggest difference between reinforcement learning and supervised learning is that there is no need to label data. Its three important features are: basically a closed-loop form; it does not directly indicate which action to choose; a series of actions and reward signals will have an impact in a long time.

The essence of reinforcement learning is actually a decision-making problem which constantly tries to interact with the environment. Each interaction process will get a different feedback value, and then it will choose the one with the largest feedback value as the best result. Reinforcement learning does not need any label processing in advance. The agent constantly interacts with the environment to get feedback, and then adjusts each attempt strategy through the feedback results. Finally, the whole system will converge, and the intelligent experience will get all the information of the whole environment and make the best choice. Reinforcement learning model mainly includes the following components: system environment (Env), agent (agent), reward function (R), selection strategy (action). As shown in Fig. 3, the agent selects a strategy a at the current time, which is that the agent begins to try the surrounding environment. The agent observes the next state and gets a specific reward value, which may be positive or negative. After a certain number of attempts, the agent can finally make the optimal decision in the current environment.

Reinforcement learning also has its own particularity:

(1) Reinforcement learning is a way of learning without strategy.
(2) Reinforcement learning does not need to know the specific surroundings.
(3) Reinforcement learning, as a weak learning method, constantly tries to get feedback from the surrounding environment through agents. Unlike general

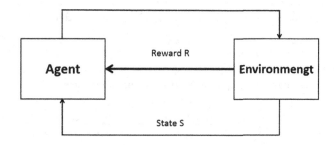

Fig. 3. The interaction of Agent and Environment.

machine learning, it does not even require prior knowledge to train. The feedback information of agent in the process of exploring and learning is presented in the form of reward value, rather than a standard correct answer.
(4) It can be used in combination with other fields such as supervised learning.

Markov Decision Processes. Reinforcement learning is a simple framework from interactive learning to the realization of goals. Learners and decision makers are called agents. What interacts with everything other than agent is called environment and they interact constantly. Agent chooses actions, environment responds to these actions, and communicates new situations to agent. The mathematical framework can be used to summarize reinforcement learning. If the change of state is only related to the previous state and the current action, but not to the previous state and action, then the whole process can be described by Markov decision processes. Most of the research on reinforcement learning methods is based on the theoretical framework of Markov decision-making. The finite state and discrete Markov decision-making process is the basis of the whole reinforcement learning algorithm. When it comes to Markov decision-making process, it is necessary to mention Markov chain and hidden Markov, which are more commonly used in machine learning Hidden Markov model (HMM). In short, once the current state is determined, it is conditionally independent of the historical path of the process, then the process has Markov properties. If a process has Markov properties, then the process is a Markov process. Different from the pure Markov chain, the next state of the Markov decision process system is not only related to the current state, but also to the action to be taken.

A MDP is composed of 4 components $M = (S, A, P, R)$. S represents the state set space, A represents the action set space, P represents the state transition probability matrix, and R represents the expected return value.

The process of simple Markov selection can be represented by Fig. 4. Suppose that the current state of an agent is S_1, and then an action a_1 is selected and executed, and the agent moves to the next state S_2 with probability random P, and then selects an action A, and moves to the next state S_3 with certain probability random, so on.

If action A is selected through state S to obtain MDP state transition process of reward function R, as shown in Fig. 5.

Fig. 4. Simple MDP state transition process.

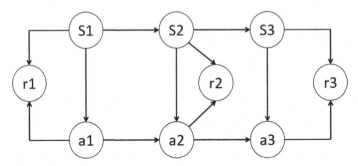

Fig. 5. MDP state transition process with reward function R.

From the MDP process with reward function shown in Fig. 4, it can be seen that the agent will only make decisions based on the reward value under the current decision. In the process of practical application, it is often necessary to consider not only the next step of the current state, but also the next steps of the current state, so the concept of value function is introduced.

Q Learning Algorithm. In real life, the probability of something happening in the environment is usually unknown and Q-learning is just used to estimate an optimal strategy when the system environment is unknown. Q-learning algorithm is a free model Q-value iterative algorithm. The difference is that in sarsa algorithm, the update function of reward value and action value follow different strategies, namely greedy strategy. Q-learning directly uses a Q-valued function that can be calculated iteratively:

$$Q(S_t, a_t) = r_t + \gamma \max_{a_t} \{Q(s(t+1), a_t)|a_t \in A\} \tag{1}$$

The meaning of function is that at time t, the system function is in state s, after action a is taken, the maximum discount reward can be obtained. In Q-Learning algorithm, the update of action value function is different from the policy followed by when selecting action. This update method is also called off-policy.

3   Design and Implementation

3.1   Principle of Routing Planning Algorithm Based on Q-Learning

Q-learning relies on Q-value iteration to achieve the balance between exploration and utilization of strategy selection. In the process of Q-learning algorithm iteration, the direction of Q-value maximum is generally selected. But not every step of iteration will follow this principle. According to the results of many experiments, Q-Learning will distribute with a certain probability, and it will try to go on in the direction of the biggest Q-value. The aim of Q-Learning is to achieve the maximum reward value through continuous learning i.e. Q-learning iteration.

3.2   The Simulation Design of the Experiment

The routing planning system based on reinforcement learning needs to meet the following requirements:

- It has the function of quickly finding a routing path from the starting switch to the ending switch.
- The selection of routing paths can take into account the QoS requirements of the link. The final selection of routing paths should meet the requirements of the link with large available bandwidth, low delay jitter and low packet loss rate.
- The algorithm has good portability and can be compatible with some of the OpenFlow controllers currently on the market, such as Ryu. In order to solve the routing planning problem in SDN environment, this report designs and implements a routing planning system based on reinforcement learning.

The overall architecture design of the routing planning system based on reinforcement learning is shown in Fig. 6. Mainly divided into the following four modules: link discovery module, link state pre-processing module, reinforcement learning training module and Q matrix delivery module.

The link discovery module mainly uses all the information of the whole global network of the controller in the SDN network. So we can get a topology information of the whole network environment through this module. At the same time,

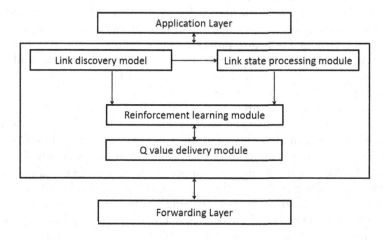

Fig. 6. The architecture of routing plan.

the topology information of the whole link is sent to the reinforcement learning training module.

The link processing module mainly aims at a QoS requirement of the network. The traditional network routing algorithm is basically based on the Dijkstra shortest path algorithm. The selected path only considers the influence of hop number, but ignores other QoS factors such as delay jitter, link available bandwidth and so on. Here, the link state information obtained in advance by the Iperf tool is pre-processed, and then its impact is considered in the reward function of Q learning.

Reinforcement learning training module is the core module of the system. The reinforcement learning algorithm used in this system design is Q-Learning algorithm. Based on the link relationship obtained by the network link discovery module and the link state information processed in advance, the initial Q matrix and the reward function under each link state are established. After training, output a convergent Q value table. The Q-value table distribution module is to distribute the Q-value table obtained after intensive learning training to all OpenFlow switches. SDN controller has two working modes, one is active mode and the other is passive mode. The active mode SDN controller transmits all stream information to the switch at one time; in the passive mode, when the data plane receives a new packet, the control plane will send the relevant information. The first active mode is adopted in this paper. The controller sends the trained Q-value table to all switches. When the switch receives a new packet, as long as you look up the corresponding Q-value table, you can immediately get a route from the start point to the end point.

4   Results and Discussion

This paper introduces the related technologies and principles used in the research process. Firstly, it introduces the basic concept of SDN network topology discovery and the protocol used in SDN network is analyzed. After that, the report introduces the reinforcement learning technology which will be used in the follow-up research. At the same time, most reinforcement learning processes are basically a Markov decision-making process, so this report also introduces several different Markov models and Markov processes in detail to help us understand reinforcement learning algorithm. Then, the current Q-Learning and other reinforcement learning algorithms are described.

In this chapter, we first propose a routing algorithm based on Q-Learning. The implementation principle and algorithm flow of this routing algorithm are introduced in detail. In view of the fact that the route planning algorithm based on Q-Learning needs to design the corresponding features manually, but in the actual application environment, the number of features is often complex, and it is generally unrealistic to extract the required features manually, this paper also puts forward the idea of route planning algorithm based on deep Q-Learning and hopes to use deep-based routing planning algorithm Q-Learning routing algorithm uses neural network model to replace the Q-value table in the conventional Q-Learning algorithm, and learns the design instructions of related functions. Finally, the States and reward functions of reinforcement learning algorithm are described, and a certain network topology is constructed.

5 Conclusion

As a new network architecture, SDN is the focus of the next generation network research, and its biggest feature is the separation of control and forwarding. In SDN network, there is no longer the difference between router and switch. All the work of routing planning is given to the controller, and the switch only undertakes the function of data forwarding. There is no fixed route planning algorithm in the industry at present. The traditional route planning generally adopts Dijkstra shortest path algorithm, which only considers the number of link hops, and does not consider the QoS standard of network links. Therefore, this paper proposes a route planning algorithm based on reinforcement learning, and mainly does the following work around this goal:

(1) The current research status of SDN at home and abroad and the research status of routing planning under SDN network architecture are studied and analyzed. It is concluded that the routing planning in SDN network is actually a very broad research topic, and every aspect of routing aggregation, traffic engineering and so on is worthy of in-depth study. In this paper, only routing algorithm is chosen as the research direction.
(2) In this paper, reinforcement learning is applied to SDN network routing planning. The routing algorithm based on Q-Learning sum is studied. In this process, the network link QoS standard is mainly considered. Obviously, this algorithm can make full use of the network link.
(3) There is a disadvantage in the routing algorithm based on Q-Learning: it needs to design the corresponding characteristics manually. However, in the practical application environment system, the features are often various and complex, so it is very difficult to extract design features by human, and the effect is not very good. Therefore, this paper combines neural network with reinforcement learning and proposes a routing planning algorithm based on deep reinforcement learning. The approximate function trained by neural network is used to replace the Q value table. The experimental results show that the routing algorithm based on deep Q-Learning also has good performance in routing.

References

1. Benzekki, K., Fergougui, A.E., Elalaoui, A.E.: Software-Defined Networking (SDN): a survey. Secur. Commun. Netw. **9**(18), 5803–5833 (2016). https://doi.org/10.1002/sec.1737
2. Bosshart, P., et al.: Forwarding metamorphosis: fast programmable match-action processing in hardware for SDN. In: Chiu, D.M., Wang, J., Barford, P., Seshan, S. (eds.) ACM SIGCOMM 2013 Conference, SIGCOMM 2013, Hong Kong, China, 12–16 August 2013, pp. 99–110. ACM (2013). https://doi.org/10.1145/2486001.2486011

3. Chica, J.C.C., Imbachi, J.C., Botero, J.F.: Security in SDN: a comprehensive survey. J. Netw. Comput. Appl. **159**, 102595 (2020). https://doi.org/10.1016/j.jnca.2020.102595

4. Fu, Q., Sun, E., Kang, M., Li, M., Zhang, Y.: Deep q-learning for routing schemes in SDN-based data center networks. IEEE Access **8**, 103491–103499 (2020). https://doi.org/10.1109/ACCESS.2020.2995511

5. Guo, X., Lin, H., Li, Z., Peng, M.: Deep-reinforcement-learning-based QoS-aware secure routing for SDN-IOT. IEEE Internet Things J. **7**(7), 6242–6251 (2020). https://doi.org/10.1109/JIOT.2019.2960033

6. Henni, D., Ghomari, A., Aoul, Y.H.: A consistent QoS routing strategy for video streaming services in SDN networks. Int. J. Commun. Syst. **33**(10) (2020). https://doi.org/10.1002/dac.4177

7. Liu, Z., Zhu, J., Zhang, J., Liu, Q.: Routing algorithm design of satellite network architecture based on SDN and ICN. Int. J. Satellite Commun. Netw. **38**(1), 1–15 (2020). https://doi.org/10.1002/sat.1304

8. Lu, Y.-H., Leu, F.-Y.: Dynamic routing and bandwidth provision based on reinforcement learning in SDN networks. In: Barolli, L., Amato, F., Moscato, F., Enokido, T., Takizawa, M. (eds.) AINA 2020. AISC, vol. 1151, pp. 1–11. Springer, Cham (2020). https://doi.org/10.1007/978-3-030-44041-1_1

9. Mao, B., et al.: Routing or computing? the paradigm shift towards intelligent computer network packet transmission based on deep learning. IEEE Trans. Comput. **66**(11), 1946–1960 (2017). https://doi.org/10.1109/TC.2017.2709742

10. Tang, F., et al.: On removing routing protocol from future wireless networks: a real-time deep learning approach for intelligent traffic control. IEEE Wirel. Commun. **25**(1), 154–160 (2018). https://doi.org/10.1109/MWC.2017.1700244

Distributed Opportunistic Channel Access with Optimal Single Relay Under Delay Constraints

Wei Sang, Zhou Zhang$^{(\boxtimes)}$, and Tongtong Wang

Tianjin Artificial Intelligence Innovation Center (TAIIC), Tianjin, China
zt.sy1986@163.com

Abstract. In this paper, we study distributed scheduling with different delay constraints for each user in a heterogeneous collaborative network with multiple relays, and the relay assists transmission under AF mode and DF mode, respectively. Considering the case that the winner source has full CSI, that is, the winner source in a contention has CSI of links from itself to relays and from relays to its destination. After research, it is found that this is a pure threshold strategy. In it, the threshold selection of each user is regarded as a non-cooperative game, and the existence of Nash equilibrium is proved. This paper maximizes the throughput by using the optimal stopping theory, and validates the correctness through numerical and simulation results.

Keywords: Delay constraints · Heterogeneous collaborative network · Optimal stopping theory

1 Introduction

With the rapid development of the times, modern society has increasingly higher requirements for the communication quality of wireless networks, which leads to the increasingly serious problem of insufficient spectrum resources. In order to solve this problem, while vigorously developing a new blank spectrum, it is a better solution to efficiently improve the spectrum efficiency.

In traditional wireless network, MAC layer and physical layer are designed independently. Therefore, most of the research [1–3] achieve multi-user collaboration focuses on single layer. The physical layer is only responsible for solving the channel fading problem, while the MAC layer only considers how to avoid collision when multiple users share the channel, and does not consider the channel state information of the physical layer users. According to the viewpoint of joint design, the transmission opportunity can be used for channel transmission more efficiently, so a concept of cross-layer design is produced, i.e. the MAC layer controller dynamically schedules multiple users for channel access according to the channel state information sensed in the physical layer. This special channel access mode is called opportunistic channel access.

© ICST Institute for Computer Sciences, Social Informatics and Telecommunications Engineering 2021
Published by Springer Nature Switzerland AG 2021. All Rights Reserved
B. Li et al. (Eds.): IoTaaS 2020, LNICST 346, pp. 599–610, 2021.
https://doi.org/10.1007/978-3-030-67514-1_47

In the past work, opportunistic scheduling strategies have been studied in both centralized [4–6] and distributed networks [4, 7–9], but in practical applications, many video applications and voice applications have different delay requirements, and some have extremely low tolerance for time. Specifically, when the effective time of real-time video data packet is reduced to zero, it will become a useless data packet and be discarded immediately, Which seriously reduces the video quality. Moreover, with time delay constraints, the system is prevented from endlessly searching for better channel conditions, thus affecting QoS performance.

In this paper, we study the optimal stopping strategy with delay constraints based on two different relay forwarding models, namely, amplify-and-forward network and decode-and-forward network. The rest of this paper is organized as follows. System model under delay constraints is described in Sect. 2. DOS is studied under AF mode and DF mode respectively in Sect. 3, and an optimal DOS strategy is derived in Sect. 4, Performance evaluation is provided in Sect. 5. Finally, the summary is shown in Sect. 6.

2   System Model

In a wireless network, K source-destination communication pairs (also called users) with L relays under amplify-and-forward (AF) mode and decode-and-forward (DF) mode are considered in a distributed manner. There is no direct link between the source and the destination, and it can only be assisted by the relay. Each user senses and accesses the channel in a competitive manner, as shown in Fig. 1.

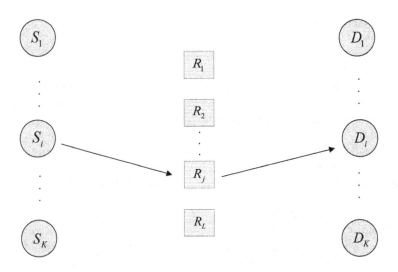

Fig. 1. Relay network model

Opportunistic channel access by multiple pairs proceeds as follows. At beginning of a time slot[1] with duration δ , each source $i = 1,2,...,K$ independently contends for the channel by sending a request-to-send (RTS) packet with probability p_i. There are three situations to consider during this period:

- Idle: If there is no source transmitting RTS in this time slot (with Probability $\prod_{i=1}^{K} (1 - p_i)$), all sources continue to contend in the next time slot.
- Collision: If there are two or more sources transmitting RTS (with Probability $1 - \prod_{i=1}^{K} (1 - p_i) - \sum_{i=1}^{K} p_i \prod_{k \neq i} (1 - p_k)$), a collision happens, and all sources continue to contend in the next time slot.
- Success: If there is only one source, say Source i, transmitting RTS packet(with Probability $\sum_{i=1}^{K} p_i \prod_{k \neq i} (1 - p_k)$), the source is called winner of the channel contention and obtain the channel access opportunity.

When the channel competition is successful, by receiving the RTS of the winner source i, all relays can estimate the CSI between source i and itself, then the relay send RTS to the destination, and the destination replies with a CTS packet after receiving it. At this time, each relay can estimate the CSI between itself and the destination, and the relay sends CTS packets containing information from the source i to relay and relay to destination i to the winner source in turn. At this point, the source i obtains all CSI information. After that, source i has two decisions:

- to *stop*: Source i selects the optimal relay that can reach the maximum rate, and sends the data packet to the optimal relay j^*. Relay j^* forwards the data packet to the destination i, the duration is the channel coherence time τ_d;
- to *continue*: Source i will give up the access opportunity, and a new contention is started among all sources.

After the winner source decides to stop, that is, the channel successfully access, all the source will start one new round of channel contention.

The successful channel contention is regarded as one channel sense. For the nth successful channel sense, let t_n denote the time spent, and the number of channel contentions to be experienced during this period follows a geometric random distribution. There are two cases of time overhead corresponding to channel contention: when the slot is idle due to no user competing for the channel, the time spent is the minimum slot $t_n = \delta$; When there is user competition, the time spent is $t_n = \tau_{RTS}$, that is, the time of using RTS packet for user probe channel. The time expectation of single channel sense t_n is given as

$$\tau_1 = (\tau_{RTS} + \tau_{CTS}) + \frac{\prod_{i=1}^{K} (1-p_i)}{p_s} \cdot \delta + \frac{(1 - \prod_{i=1}^{K} (1-p_i) - \sum_{i=1}^{K} p_{s,i})}{p_s} \cdot \tau_{RTS}, \text{ where } p_s = \sum_{i=1}^{K} p_{s,i}$$

denote the probability of successful user contention, and $p_{s,i}$ is the probability that user i contend successfully, satisfying $p_{s,i} = p_i \prod_{k \neq i} (1 - p_k)$.

---

[1] The time slot is the shortest unit by which the channel availability is sensed.

After each channel access, the winner source will obtain the CSI of the two-hop channel, then calculate the maximum achievable rate and select the best single relay among all relays, and then decide whether to transmit. If it decides to stop, the winner source will transmits through the optimal relay, and if it decides to continue, the winner source will contend for the channel again with other sources.

3   Distributed Opportunistic Scheduling Under Constraints

Based on the optimal stopping theory, the problem of channel access can be modeled as a classical optimal statistical rate of return problem. To simplify the expression, R_n is the mean of achievable transmission rate at the nth observation, given as

$$R_n = \sum_{i=1}^{K} \frac{1}{K} \mathbb{I}[s(n) = i] \max_{j \in \{1,...,L\}} \log_2(1 + \gamma_i). \qquad (1)$$

where $\mathbb{I}[\cdot]$ means an indicator function. Specifically, when relay is selected to help with AF mode, $\gamma_i = \max\limits_{j \in \{1,...,L\}} \frac{P_s P_r |f_{ij}(n)|^2 |g_{ji}(n)|^2}{1 + P_s |f_{ij}(n)|^2 + |g_{ji}(n)|^2}$, and with DF relay mode, $\gamma_i = \max\limits_{j \in \{1,...,L\}} \{P_r |g_{ji}(n)|^2, P_s |f_{ij}(n)|^2\}$.

According to the stopping method, after every successful channel contention, source-destination communication pairs will have two choices: utilize the current channel opportunity for data transmission, or give up this channel to allow others to contend again. Assuming that data transmission is successfully completed t times under this method, let $\{N_1 N_2, ..., N_t\}$ denote the stop time corresponding to multiple transmissions, R_{N_l} denote the information rate of the lth channel access, τ_d denote the time of single channel access, T_{N_l} denote the time spent of lth channel access. Based on Renewal's theorem and the law of large numbers, time-averaged system throughput converges to its statistical value, satisfying

$$\frac{\sum_{l=1}^{t} R_{N_l} \tau_d}{\sum_{l=1}^{t} T_{N_l}} \to \frac{\mathbb{E}[R_N \tau_d]}{\mathbb{E}[T_N]} \quad a.s.$$

where $\frac{\mathbb{E}[R_N \tau_d]}{\mathbb{E}[T_N]}$ is the statistical rate of return of a typical statistical model. The random variables R_N and T_N both depend on the optimal stop time N in this problem.

Considering channel opportunistic access under different user delay constraints, we further analyze the impact of delay constraint conditions on the optimal access method and performance of different users. Specifically, in the optimization problem model, T_N is used to denote the channel access time of each user. According to QoS service requirements, Each user's time expectation needs to satisfy the delay sensitivity constraint condition of $\mathbb{E}[T_N] \leq T_{th}$, and T_{th} denotes the constraint condition of the average service delay. For the method of not waiting for access, the expected access time $\mathbb{E}[T_{N_0}] = \tau_1 + \tau_d$. For $N > 0$,

$\mathbb{E}[T_N] \geq \tau_1 + \tau_d$ is satisfied, Therefore, there is no feasible solution to the above problem when the delay constraint $T_{th} < \tau_1 + \tau_d$.

The optimization problem of statistical throughput of the system can be regarded as the maximum reward problem, mainly seeking the optimal stopping method N^* and the maximum network throughput λ^*, the details are as follows:

$$N^* = \arg \max_{N \in Q_T} \frac{\mathbb{E}[R_N \tau_d]}{\mathbb{E}[T_N]}, \lambda^* = \sup_{N \in Q_T} \frac{\mathbb{E}[R_N \tau_d]}{\mathbb{E}[T_N]}. \tag{2}$$

where $Q_T = \{N : N \geq 1, \mathbb{E}[T_N] \leq T_{th}\}$.

4   Optimal Stopping Strategy

For each user i, the maximum-expected-rate-of-return problem can be equivalently transformed into a standard form of maximum expected return rate. In particular, in order to get N^* of each user, it is necessary to find the optimal strategy that can obtain the maximum expected return

$$V^*(\lambda) = \sup_{N \in Q} \mathbb{E}\left[R_N \tau_d - \lambda T_N\right]$$

$$s.t. \ \ \mathbb{E}[T_N] \leq T_{th}. \tag{3}$$

For the optimization problem of the difference objective function under the delay constraint, the Lagrange duality problem is defined as follows:

$$L^*(\lambda) = \min_{\alpha \geq 0} L(\alpha, \lambda) = \min_{\alpha \geq 0} \left\{V^*(\lambda, \alpha) + \alpha T_{th}\right\}. \tag{4}$$

where $L(\alpha, \lambda)$ is the Lagrangian function, $V^*(\lambda, \alpha) = \sup\limits_{N > 0} \mathbb{E}\left[R_N \tau_d - (\lambda + \alpha) T_N\right]$, α is the Lagrangian multiplier.

The following lemma establishes the relationship between the original optimization problem, the equivalent transformation problem and the dual problem.

Lemma 1. *The above problem satisfies relationship is as follows:*

1) *The inequality relation $V^*(\lambda) \leq L^*(\lambda)$ is satisfied between the maximum value $V^*(\lambda)$ of the objective function of the equivalent transformation optimal problem (3) and the maximum value $L^*(\lambda)$ of the dual optimization problem;*

2) *When the user channel fading follows the Rayleigh model and channel access is performed at the maximum transmission rate, the channel statistical model has sufficient continuity, and there is a strong duality between the equivalent transformation optimization problem (3) and the Lagrange duality problem (4). For any coefficient $\lambda > 0$, $V^*(\lambda) = L^*(\lambda)$.*

3) *When the coefficient $\lambda = \lambda^*$, and λ^* satisfies $V^*(\lambda) = 0$, the optimal solution of the original problem (2) is $\lambda^* = \frac{\mathbb{E}[R_{N^*} \tau_d]}{\mathbb{E}[T_{N^*}]}$, the optimal channel access method is $N^* = N^*(\alpha^*, \lambda^*)$ and α^* is the optimal coefficient solution of the dual problem.*

We assume that the average delay constraint satisfies $T_{th} \geq \tau_1 + \tau_d$, based on the optimal stopping theory and Lagrange duality method, the optimal stopping method under delay constraint is analyzed as follows.

Theorem 1. *The optimal method N^* for distributed channel access has a pure threshold structure. That is to say, after the user contends successfully, the winner source will make the current optimal choice according to the real-time sensed channel quality, access the channel or give up the opportunity. Specifically, when the time delay constraint T_{th} is less than the time delay limit T_{th}^*, the winner source will judge whether the channel achievable rate R_n is higher than the fixed threshold λ_{th} at this time, if it is satisfied, access the channel and transmit at the information rate R_n. Otherwise, the winner source give up the channel opportunity and contend with other users again. Similarly, when the delay T_{th} is higher than the delay limit T_{th}^*, the winner will judge whether the channel reachable rate R_n is higher than the threshold λ^*, and then make a corresponding decision. Therefore, according to the relationship between delay constraints T_{th} and constraint limits T_{th}^*, the optimal channel access method N^* for the optimization problem with delay constraints can be divided into the following two structures:*

1) when time constraints $T_{th} < T_{th}^*$, the optimal access method N^* satisfies

$$N^* = \min\left\{n \geq 1 : R_n \geq \lambda_{th}\right\}, \quad \lambda_{th} = F_R^{-1}\left(1 - \frac{\tau_1}{T_{th} - \tau_d}\right).$$

2) when time constraints $T_{th} \geq T_{th}^*$, the optimal access method N^* satisfies

$$N^* = \min\left\{n \geq 1 : R_n \geq \lambda^*\right\}, \quad \lambda^* \text{ satisfies } \mathbb{E}\left[(R_n - \lambda^*)^+\right] = \lambda^* \tau_1 / \tau_d,$$

where $T_{th}^* = \frac{\tau_1}{1 - F_R(\lambda^*)} + \tau_d$.

Proof. To analyze the Lagrange duality problem, the cost coefficient $\lambda > 0$ and the Lagrange multiplier $\alpha > 0$ are given, the optimal stopping method $N^*(\alpha, \lambda)$ to reach $L(\alpha, \lambda)$ is

$$N^*(\alpha, \lambda) = \min\left\{n \geq 1 : R_n \tau_d \geq V^*(\alpha, \lambda) + (\lambda + \alpha)\tau_d\right\}, \tag{5}$$

where $V^*(\alpha, \lambda)$ satisfies the equation

$$\mathbb{E}\left[\max\left(R_n - (\lambda + \alpha) - V^*(\alpha, \lambda)/\tau_d, 0\right)\right] = (\lambda + \alpha)\tau_1 / \tau_d. \tag{6}$$

Using the strong duality between the original problem and the dual problem, the optimal solution $N^*(\lambda)$ of the equivalent problem (3) and the optimal solution α^* of the dual problem (4) satisfy Karush-Kuhn-Tucker(KKT) conditions as follows:

$$\begin{cases} \alpha^* \cdot (\mathbb{E}[T_{N^*(\lambda)}] - T_{th}) = 0, \\ N^*(\lambda) = \arg\max_{N(\lambda) > 0} \mathbb{E}\left[R_{N(\lambda)}\tau_d - (\lambda + \alpha^*)T_{N(\lambda)}\right], \\ \mathbb{E}[T_{N^*(\lambda)}] \leq T_{th}, \\ \alpha^* \geq 0. \end{cases} \tag{7}$$

The following analyzes the Lagrange multiplier optimal solution α^*, including $\alpha^* > 0$ and $\alpha^* = 0$. Since the optimal solution α^* exists for any cost coefficient λ, and there is a direct mapping relationship between the λ and the revenue function $V^*(\alpha^*, \lambda)$, replacing λ with λ^* that satisfies the $V^*(\alpha^*, \lambda) = 0$ can simplify the KKT condition, i.e. let $\alpha^* = \alpha^*(\lambda^*)$.

For the first case, i.e. $\alpha^* = 0$, the Lagrangian function $L(\alpha^*, \lambda^*) = 0$ can be expressed as

$$\mathbb{E}\big[\max\big(R_n - \lambda^*, 0\big)\big] = \lambda^* \tau_1 / \tau_d. \tag{8}$$

According to KKT condition and expression (5), the optimal stopping method $N^*(\lambda^*) = N^*(0, \lambda^*)$

$$N^*(0, \lambda^*) = \min\big\{n \geq 1 : R_n \geq \lambda^*\big\}, \tag{9}$$

where λ^* satisfies Eq. (8), which is the expected value of maximum throughput without delay constraints.

The time expectation of access method $N^*(0, \lambda^*)$ is

$$\mathbb{E}[T_{N^*(0,\lambda^*)}] = \frac{\tau_1}{1 - F_R(\lambda^*)} + \tau_d \leq T_{th}.$$

For the second case, i.e. $\alpha^* > 0$, according to KKT condition (7), $\mathbb{E}[T_{N^*(\lambda^*)}] = T_{th}$ can be obtained. Since $N^*(\lambda^*) = N^*(\lambda^*, \alpha^*)$, $N^*(\lambda^*, \alpha^*)$ satisfies the expression (5) of the access method, $V^*(\lambda^*, \alpha^*)$ satisfies the Eq. (6). The access time expectation of the optimal stopping method $N^*(\alpha^*, \lambda^*)$ is

$$\mathbb{E}\big[T_{N^*(\lambda^*,\alpha^*)}\big] = \frac{\tau_1}{1 - F_R\big((\lambda^* + \alpha^*) + V^*(\alpha^*, \lambda^*)/\tau_d\big)} + \tau_d.$$

According to KKT condition, the following equation can be derived

$$\frac{\tau_1}{1 - F_R\big((\lambda^* + \alpha^*) + V^*(\alpha^*, \lambda^*)/\tau_d\big)} = T_{th} - \tau_d. \tag{10}$$

In addition, $V^*(\lambda^*, \alpha^*)$ satisfies the equation

$$\mathbb{E}\big[\max\big(R_n \tau_d - (\lambda^* + \alpha^*)\tau_d - V^*(\alpha^*, \lambda^*), 0\big)\big] = (\lambda^* + \alpha^*)\tau_1. \tag{11}$$

and

$$L(\alpha^*, \lambda^*) = V^*(\lambda^*, \alpha^*) + \alpha^* T_{th} = 0. \tag{12}$$

Based on the Eq. (10) and (12), it can be obtained

$$(\lambda^* + \alpha^*) - \alpha^* T_{th}/\tau_d = F_R^{-1}\Big(1 - \frac{\tau_1}{T_{th} - \tau_d}\Big). \tag{13}$$

Combined with Eqs. (11) and (12), it can be derived that

$$\mathbb{E}\big[\max\big(R_n \tau_d - (\lambda^* + \alpha^*)\tau_d + \alpha^* T_{th}, 0\big)\big] = (\lambda^* + \alpha^*)\tau_1. \tag{14}$$

Substituting Eq. (13) into Eq. (14), we can get

$$\mathbb{E}\left[\max\left(R_n - F_R^{-1}\left(1 - \frac{\tau_1}{T_{th} - \tau_d}\right), 0\right)\right] = (\lambda^* + \alpha^*)\tau_1/\tau_d. \tag{15}$$

Based on Eqs. (13) and (15), we can find that the optimal solution α of Lagrange dual problem satisfies

$$\mathbb{E}\left[\max\left(R_n - F_R^{-1}\left(1 - \frac{\tau_1}{T_{th} - \tau_d}\right), 0\right)\right]\tau_d/\tau_1$$
$$- F_R^{-1}\left(1 - \frac{\tau_1}{T_{th} - \tau_d}\right) = \alpha^* T_{th}/\tau_d > 0. \tag{16}$$

It can be seen from the observation that the left function $\mathbb{E}\left[\max(R_n - x, 0)\right]\tau_d/\tau_1 - x$ of Eq. (16) is a monotonically decreasing function with $x \geq 0$. According to Eq. (8), when $F_R^{-1}\left(1 - \frac{\tau_1}{T_{th} - \tau_d}\right) < \lambda_0^*$, i.e. $T_{th} < \frac{\tau_1}{1 - F_R(\lambda_0^*)} + \tau_d$, inequality (16) is valid and λ_0^* satisfies $\mathbb{E}\left[\max\left\{R_n - \lambda_0^*, 0\right\}\right] = \lambda_0^* \tau_1/\tau_d$.

The corresponding optimal stopping method $N^*(\alpha^*, \lambda^*)$ at this time is

$$N^*(\alpha^*, \lambda^*) = \min\left\{n \geq 1 : R_n \geq \lambda_{th}\right\}, \tag{17}$$

where $\lambda_{th} = F_R^{-1}\left(1 - \frac{\tau_1}{T_{th} - \tau_d}\right)$.

When $F_R^{-1}\left(1 - \frac{\tau_1}{T_{th} - \tau_d}\right) \geq \lambda_0^*$, i.e. $T_{th} \geq \frac{\tau_1}{1 - F_R(\lambda_0^*)} + \tau_d$, the inequality (16) is invalid, which contradicts the precondition with $\alpha^* > 0$.

Combining the two cases of $\alpha^* > 0$ and $\alpha^* = 0$, the optimal stopping method has two structures according to the different limits of the time constraint T_{th}: when $T_{th} \geq \frac{\tau_1}{1 - F_R(\lambda_0^*)} + \tau_d$, Lagrange optimal solution satisfies $\alpha^* = 0$, the expression of access method $N^*(0, \lambda^*)$ is shown in (9), λ^* satisfies the Eq. (8). when $T_{th} < \frac{\tau_1}{1 - F_R(\lambda_0^*)} + \tau_d$, the Lagrangian optimal solution satisfies $\alpha^* > 0$, and the optimal method $N^*(\alpha^*, \lambda^*)$ is shown in Expression (17).

Theorem 1 shows that the optimal channel access method exhibits different method structures according to different delay limits T_{th}^*. As the two methods are threshold structures, and the thresholds λ_{th} and λ^* of the method can be obtained by offline calculation, the optimal channel access method has good engineering feasibility.

In summary, the throughput performance of the optimal access method proposed in this paper is as follows:

1) when delay constraint $T_{th} < T_{th}^*$, the average throughput of the optimal access method N^* is:

$$\frac{E[R_{N^*}\tau_d]}{E[T_{N^*}]} = \frac{\tau_d}{T_{th}}F_R^{-1}(1 - \frac{\tau_1}{T_{th} - \tau_d}) + \frac{\tau_d}{\tau_1}(1 - \frac{\tau_d}{T_{th}})E[\max(R_n - F_R^{-1}(1 - \frac{\tau_1}{T_{th} - \tau_d}), 0)]$$

2) when delay constraint $T_{th} \geq T_{th}^*$, the average throughput λ^* of the optimal access
method N^* satisfies

$$E[(R_n - \lambda^*)^+] = \lambda^* \tau_1 / \tau_d$$

5   Performance Evaluation

In this section, system performance for our proposed strategy is investigated
through computer simulations. We consider a wireless cooperative network with
5 source-destination pairs under the help of multiple relays, the channels from the
source to each relay station, from the relay to the destination all experience i.i.d
Rayleigh fading. In it, The channel contention parameters of the source are set as
follows, the contention probability $p_i = [0.2, 0.25, 0.3, 0.35, 0.4]$, $i \in \{1, 2, 3, 4, 5\}$,
the mini-slot duration $\delta = 20\,\mu s$, RTS transmission and CTS transmission duration is $\tau_{RTS} = \tau_{CTS} = 50\,\mu s$, the average SNR of the relay channel for the first
hop and the second hop are σ_f^2 and σ_g^2, respectively.

Based on AF relay forwarding mode, we first investigate the influence of
various average SNR configurations. As shown in Fig. 2, channel coherence time

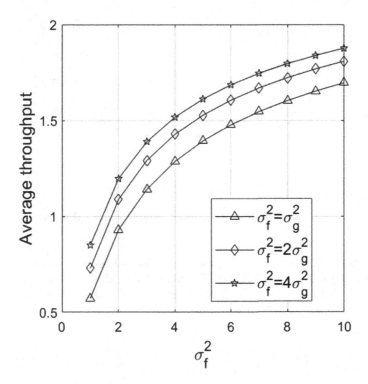

Fig. 2. Performance influence from SNR under AF mode

$\tau_d = 2\,\mathrm{ms}$, the first-hop average SNR σ_f^2 is from $1\,\mathrm{dB}$ to $10\,\mathrm{dB}$, and the second-hop average SNR $\sigma_g^2 = \sigma_f^2$, $\sigma_g^2 = 2 \cdot \sigma_f^2$ and $\sigma_g^2 = 4 \cdot \sigma_f^2$, respectively. We can see that the average throughput increases with the increase of the first-hop average SNR σ_f^2 in the horizontal view, and the average throughput is also improved when the ratio σ_g^2/σ_f^2 increases in the vertical view. Secondly, we studied the influence of τ_d on system throughput as shown in Fig. 3, we can see clearly that the system throughput increases greatly with the increase of τ_d.

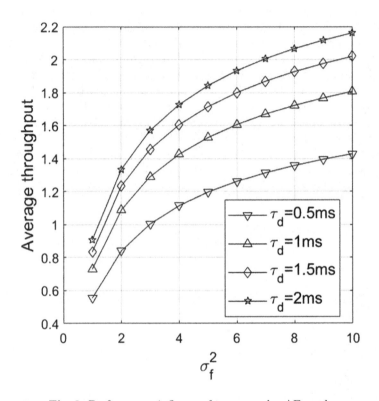

Fig. 3. Performance influence from τ_d under AF mode

Based on DF relay forwarding mode, we also studied the impact of different SNR on the system throughput. In Fig. 4, we can see that the system throughput increases with the increase of σ_f^2. At the same time, with the increase of τ_d, the system throughput also increases significantly.

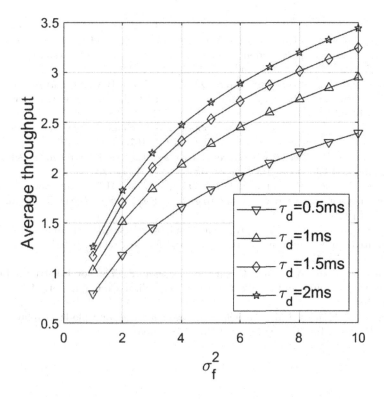

Fig. 4. Performance influence from τ_d under DF mode

6 Conclusion

In this paper, the problem of multi-user channel access in a wireless ad-hoc cooperative network with multiple relaying and no direct link is studied, in which all channels experience independent channel fading. Based on the modeling and analysis of the optimal stopping theory, this paper proposes an optimal single relay strategy with delay constraints, which makes full use of multi-relay cooperative diversity and dynamically determines the channel access time to improve the system performance. The approximate expression of the maximum throughput expectation of the policy system is given in this paper, and all thresholds can be calculated off-line and easy implementation is available. Finally, the optimality of the policy is strictly proved by calculation and simulation.

References

1. Laneman, J.N., Tse, D.N.C., Wornell, G.W.: Cooperative diversity in wireless networks: efficient protocols and outage behavior. IEEE Trans. Inf. Theory **50**, 3062–3080 (2004)

2. Zhang, Q., Jia, J., Zhang, J.: Cooperative relay to improve diversity in cognitive radio networks. IEEE Commun. Mag. **47**(2), 111–117 (2009)
3. Gunduz, D., Erkip, E.: Opportunistic cooperation by dynamic resource allocation. IEEE Trans. Wirel. Commun. **6**(4), 1446–1454 (2007)
4. Gong, X., Chandrashekhar, T.P.S., Zhang, J., Poor, H.V.: Opportunistic cooperative networking: to relay or not to relay. IEEE J. Sel. Areas Commun. **30**(2), 307–314 (2012)
5. Zhang, Z., Jiang, H.: Distributed opportunistic channel access in wireless relay networks. IEEE J. Sel. Areas Commun. **30**(9), 1675–1683 (2012)
6. Viswanath, P., Tse, D.N.C., Laroia, R.: Opportunistic beamforming using dumb antennas. IEEE Trans. Inf. Theory **48**(6), 1277–1294 (2002)
7. Gong, X., Chandrashekhar, T.P.S., Zhang, J., Poor, H.V.: Opportunistic cooperative networking: to relay or not to relay? IEEE J. Sel. Areas Commun. **30**(2), 307–314 (2012)
8. Zhang, Z., Zhou, S., Jiang, H.: Opportunistic cooperative channel access in distributed wireless networks with decode-and-forward relays. IEEE Commun. Lett. **19**(10), 1778–1781 (2015)
9. Dong, L., Wang, Y., Jiang, H., Zhang, Z., Zhou, S.: Two-level distributed opportunistic scheduling in DF relay networks. EEE Wirel. Commun. Lett. **4**(5), 477–480 (2015)
10. Xie, L.L., Kumar, P.R.: An achievable rate for the multiple-level relay channel. IEEE Trans. Inf. Theory **51**(4), 1348–1358 (2005)

Distributed Opportunistic Channel Access Under Single-Bit CSI Feedback

Tongtong Wang[1], Zhou Zhang[1(✉)], and Jing Guo[2]

[1] Tianjin Artificial Intelligence Innovation Center (TAIIC), Tianjin, China
zt.sy1986@163.com
[2] Science and Technology on Complex Aviation System Simulation Laboratory,
Beijing, China
nudtgj@126.com

Abstract. In this research, the problem of distributed opportunistic channel access is investigated under single-bit channel state information (CSI) feedback in ad hoc networks. In finding an optimal strategy achieving the maximum average system throughput, the optimal stopping approach is used, and an optimal strategy is proposed. In it, each winner source decides when to take transmission opportunity based on singe-bit feedback information. Moreover, an optimal quantization vector is also derived for the strategy. Interestingly, it is pure-threshold based, and the optimal quantization vector is fixed. All thresholds can be calculated off-line, and easy implementation is available. Through simulation, the effectiveness and efficiency of the optimal strategy are also verified.

Keywords: Distributed opportunistic access · Single-bit feedback · Optimal stopping approach

1 Introduction

Recent years have witnessed rapid development of wireless network by catering ever-increasing demands. As available spectrum is very limited, emerging innovative techniques improving spectrum utilization receive research attention. In them, the concept of opportunistic channel access is enlightened, designing the link transmission and multiple user channel access in a joint manner. Based on it, centralized opportunistic access has been fully investigated in [1,2]. In these works, a central controller is deployed in the network, and by scheduling the user of best channel condition to access the channel based on global channel state, the multi-user diversity is harvested, which significantly enhances network performance.

However, centralized scheduling does not work in a distributed network. The use of the shared channel and distributed decisions on channel access rises up new challenges due to coupling between wireless transmission adaptation and multi-user collision. Due to independent design of physical and MAC layer strategy,

B. Li et al. (Eds.): IoTaaS 2020, LNICST 346, pp. 611–623, 2021.
https://doi.org/10.1007/978-3-030-67514-1_48

the random and time-varying nature of channel access makes network performance not preferable. Thus, distributed opportunistic channel access is not well addressed.

As a seminal work in resolving the difficulty, authors in [3] proposes an efficient channel scheduling strategy based on optimal stopping approach. The strategy is pure-threshold, and can benefit from easy implementation. Extended from it, work in [4] further investigates opportunistic scheduling under interference channels by allowing multiple users simultaneous access. Moreover, for time sensitive service, distributed scheduling under time constraints is studied in [5]. Optimal scheduling strategies are proposed maximizing average system throughput, respectively.

All the above existing works are based on the assumption that in the wireless distributed network, a winner source has accurate channel state information of the channel. However, in practical network environment, channel state information relies on control channel, where limited feedback is only available. Such quantized CSI is included in control packet from the winner destination, and the winner source has to make its decision on channel access. Furthermore, under limited feedback, the optimal quantization vector with respect to observed CSI needs to design, determining the transmission rate for channel access. In finding the optimal quantization vector for all sources and distributed channel access strategy, the average system throughput is to be maximized.

For optimal design of channel access strategies, this research investigates distributed opportunistic scheduling problem under single bit CSI feedback. In terms of network statistics, homogeneous and heterogeneous wireless channels are considered, respectively. In both cases, the quantized CSI thresholds of single bit feedback are derived for all sources, and can be calculated off-line. Interestingly, based on optimal stopping approach, the optimal strategy is in pure-threshold structure, and maximizes the average system throughput.

The rest of the paper is organized as follows. System model under limited feedback mechanism is described in Sect. 2. The optimal opportunistic channel access strategy is proposed and its optimality is proved in Sect. 3. Simulation analysis is then carried out to validate effectiveness in Sect. 4. Finally, the conclusion is presented in Sect. 5.

2   System Model

Consider K source-to-destination pairs in a single-hop ad hoc network. The transmission power of each source is P_s. The wireless channel follows the Rayleigh fading model. The channel gain from the ith source to its destination is denoted by $h_i, i = 1, 2, ..., K$, which follows a Complex Gaussian distribution with zero mean and variance σ_i^2.

The channel access is operated in a distributed manner. Each source independently contends for transmission opportunities by sending a request-to-send (RTS) packet at the beginning of a time slot with duration δ. The probability of each source sending RTS is p_0, and there are three possible results, which are idle, collision and success. The probability at which the channel is idle is $(1 - p_0)^K$, i.e., there is no source contending the channel in the time slot. The probability of channel collision is $1 - (1 - p_0)^K - Kp_0(1 - p_0)^{K-1}$. It happens when two or more sources contend the channel simultaneously. The probability of successful channel access is $Kp_0(1 - p_0)^{K-1}$ when there is only one source transmitting RTS referred as winner source. When channel is idle or in collision, sources will continue to contend in the next time slot.

In the case of success, upon reception of the RTS, the winner destination, e.g. Destination i obtains instantaneous CSI from Source i. As only a single-bit CSI information is feedback, the destination compares the observed SNR with its local quantization vector, and feedbacks a CTS to the source. In it, a quantized value of instantaneous SNR, denoted as $\omega_{i,j}$ is included. By receiving the CTS, Source i decides to *stop* (i.e. transmit its data for duration τ_d) or to *continue* (i.e. give up its transmission opportunity and re-contend with other sources) (Fig. 1).

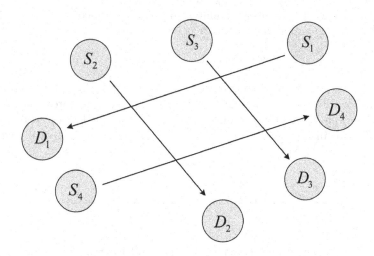

Fig. 1. Network model

time slot

idle	idle	idle	collision	idle	idle	win and give up	win	data transfer

Fig. 2. An example of distributed channel access by multiple sources

An example of distributed channel access in the ad hoc network is shown in Fig. 2. In it, all sources are silent in the first three time slots. Then more than two sources contend the channel, resulting in a collision. After two idle slots, a winner appears, and obtains CSI. Due to bad channel condition, the winner gives up this opportunity and re-starts channel probing in the next slot. Then another winner appears in the new round. After exchange of RTS and CTS, the winner source transmits data to its destination. By doing it, a successful channel access is finished.

Different from existing works with perfect CSI feedback, influence from single-bit feedback mechanism is investigated, and this mechanism makes distributed opportunistic channel access practical. In particular, each winner destination feedbacks a CTS after channel estimation providing tailored information to its source. In the CTS, channel conditions such as channel state, received power and interference level are included, enabling the source to carry out adaptive transmission.

Furthermore, complete channel gain information is known at each destination, limited information is included in the CTS and sent to the source, based on observed SNR. Limited by bit number $\lceil \log_2 B \rceil$, the information available at each source is the quantized counterpart of instantaneous SNR. For Source $i = 1, 2, ..., K$, the quantization vector is denoted as

$$\mathbf{w}_i = [\omega_{i,0}, \omega_{i,1}, \ldots, \omega_{i,B-1}]. \tag{1}$$

The vector $\mathbf{w}_i$ is shared by source-to-destination pair i. Using the vector, when instantaneous SNR h_i satisfies $\omega_{i,j} < P_s h_i < \omega_{i,j+1}$, $\omega_{i,j}$ represents the maximum achievable SNR by accessing the channel. Without loss of generalization, $\omega_{i,0} = 0$ and an increasing order $\omega_{i,0} < \omega_{i,1} < \ldots < \omega_{i,B-1}$ are considered (Fig. 3).

Fig. 3. Example of 2-bits CSI feedback.

3 Optimal Stopping Strategy with Limited Feedback

3.1 Problem Formulation

While quantization vectors $\{\mathbf{w}_i\}_{i=1,2,...,K}$ are fixed, we focus on optimal strategy design for the distributed opportunistic channel access, maximizing the average system throughput.

Define an *observation* as the process of channel contention among all sources until a winner source appears. As sources contend the channel independently, the number of contentions in an observation is a random variable of geometrically distribution with parameter $K p_0 (1 - p_0)^{K-1}$. Among all contentions, the last contention is successful with duration $\tau_{RTS}+\tau_{CTS}$. τ_{RTS} and τ_{CTS} are durations of an RTS and CTS, respectively. An idle slot is with duration δ, and a collision is with duration τ_{RTS}. The mean of the duration of an observation is given as

$$\tau_0 = \tau_{RTS} + \tau_{CTS} + \frac{(1-p_0)^K}{Kp_0(1-p_0)^{K-1}} \cdot \delta + \frac{1-(1-p_0)^K - Kp_0(1-p_0)^{K-1}}{Kp_0(1-p_0)^{K-1}} \cdot \tau_{RTS}.$$

In the nth observation, let $s(n)$ denote the successful source, $h_s(n)$ and R_n represent the corresponding channel gain and maximal achievable rate, respectively. Due to the block-fading channel feature in wireless environment, R_n is random, and can be calculated as $R_n = \log_2(1 + P_s h_s(n))$. Since the limited feedback, the winner source only obtains the quantified SNR as

$$u(n) = \sum_{i=1}^{K} I[s(n) = i] \cdot \log_2(1 + \omega_{i,j}),$$

$$\omega_{i,j} = \max_{l=0,1,\ldots,B-1} I[\omega_{i,l} \le P_s h_s(n) < \omega_{i,l+1}] \cdot \omega_{i,l}. \tag{2}$$

It can be observed that based on quantization vector $\mathbf{w}$, the maximal SNR feedback in the CTS from Destination $s(n)$ to its source will not supersede the instantaneous channel capacity, i.e. $u(n) \le R_n$.

For opportunistic channel access, after observation n, the winner source obtains the rate $u(n)$ and has to make two choices:

- If the channel condition is good, the winner source will stop the observation and transmit data by rate $u(n)$.
- Otherwise, when the channel condition is poor, the winner source will give up transmission opportunity and start a new observation. At the next slot, all sources re-contend the channel.

Based on the optimal stopping theory, this problem can be transformed into a maximum return problem. For the nth observation, the reward Y_n denotes the total traffic volume to be transferred by the winner source, and the cost T_n is the total waiting time for a successful channel access. In particular, when the winner source stops at Nth observation, i.e., stops the observation and transmits data by rate $u(n)$, the instantaneous system throughput is $\frac{Y_N}{T_N}$. The strategy N is also referred as *stopping time*. Following the strategy N for multiple trails of successful data transmission, the average system throughput $\frac{\mathbb{E}[Y_N]}{\mathbb{E}[T_N]}$ is obtained. In particular, $\frac{\mathbb{E}[Y_N]}{\mathbb{E}[T_N]}$ reflects the trade-off between larger transmitted traffic and the time cost.

In the following, we focus on finding an optimal channel access strategy, including an optimal stopping time and quantization vector, to maximize the average system throughput $\sup_{\mathbf{w} \ge 0}\{\sup_{N>0} \frac{\mathbb{E}[Y_N]}{\mathbb{E}[T_N]}\}$. Here $\mathbb{E}[\cdot]$ means expectation.

According to the optimal stopping theory [6], the problem of maximizing the average system throughput can be transformed into an equivalent form with its reward being $\{Y_N - \lambda T_N\}$ and time price λ. To derive optimal strategy N^* given a fixed quantization vector $\mathbf{w}$, we first need to solve the following problem by maximizing the expected reward

$$V^*(\lambda^*(\mathbf{w})) = \sup_{N>0} \{\mathbb{E}[Y_N] - \lambda^*(\mathbf{w})\mathbb{E}[T_N]\}, \tag{3}$$

where $\lambda^*(\mathbf{w})$ satisfies $V^*(\lambda^*(\mathbf{w})) = 0$. $\lambda^*(\mathbf{w})$ is actually the maximal expected system throughput under a given vector $\mathbf{w}$.

Specifically, for nth observation, the reward Y_n and the cost time T_n are calculated as $Y_n = \tau_d u(n)$ and $T_n = \sum_{l=1}^{n} t_l + \tau_d$, respectively. Therefore, the expression (3) is represented as

$$V^*(\lambda^*(\mathbf{w})) = \sup_{N>0} \{\mathbb{E}[\tau_d u(N)] - \lambda^*(\mathbf{w}) \cdot \mathbb{E}[\tau_d + \sum_{l=1}^{N} t_l]\}, \tag{4}$$

where t_l denotes the duration spent in the lth observation.

For a given quantization vector $\mathbf{w}$, the following theorem presents the optimal stopping strategy $N^*(\mathbf{w})$ achieving the maximum expected reward $V^*(\lambda^*(\mathbf{w}))$.

Theorem 1. *The optimal stopping rule $N^*(\mathbf{w})$ maximizing system throughput $\sup_{N>0} \frac{\mathbb{E}[Y_N]}{\mathbb{E}[T_N]}$ exists and is given by $N^*(\boldsymbol{w}) = \min\{n \geq 1 : u(n) \geq \lambda^*(\boldsymbol{w})\}$. The threshold $\lambda^*(\boldsymbol{w})$ is the unique solution such that $\mathbb{E}[\max\{u(n) - \lambda, 0\}] = \frac{\lambda \tau_0}{\tau_d}$.*

Proof. The proof is similar to that in [3]. ∎

While the maximal average system throughput λ^* satisfies the optimal equation in Theorem 1, by the monotonicity of both sides, the problem of maximizing the system throughput transfers to finding an optimal vector $\mathbf{w}^*$ to achieve system throughput $\sup_{\mathbf{w}>0} \lambda^*(\mathbf{w})$.

In the following, we consider the problem where only 1-bit CSI feedback is available, and the problem under multiple bits feedback can be analyzed similarly. Moreover, for wireless channel environments, cases with homogeneous links and heterogeneous channels are investigated, respectively.

3.2   The Case Under Homogeneous Channels

We consider the homogeneous case where all channels between source-to-destination pairs have the same channel statistics. For all pairs, the quantization vector is the same with $\mathbf{w} = [0, \omega_1]$. It thus suffices to find the optimal value ω_1 to maximize throughput λ^*. The optimal strategy is derived in the following theorem.

Theorem 2. *Under homogeneous channels, the optimal channel access strategy with 1-bit feedback is $N^* = \min\{n \geq 1 : P_s h_s(n) \geq \omega_1^*\}$. The threshold ω_1^* satisfies the equation*

$$\frac{\log_2 e}{(1+\omega_1^*)}(1 + \frac{\tau_0}{\tau_d}e^{\frac{\omega_1^*}{P_s \sigma^2}}) - \frac{\tau_0}{\tau_d P_s \sigma^2}\log_2(1+\omega_1^*)e^{\frac{\omega_1^*}{P_s \sigma^2}} = 0,$$

and can be calculated off-line. The optimal average throughput is $\lambda^* = \frac{\log_2(1+\omega_1^*)}{1+\frac{\tau_0}{\tau_d}e^{\frac{\omega_1^*}{P_s \sigma^2}}}$.

Proof. For distributed channel access, in the nth observation, Destination $s(n)$ has two decisions:

- when the instantaneous SNR is less than threshold ω_1^*, i.e., $P_s h_s(n) < \omega_1^*$, the feedback bit symbol is 0, meaning that the practical rate is 0.
- when $P_s h_s(n) \geq \omega_1^*$, the feedback bit symbol is 1.

After receiving the symbol, Source $s(n)$ will compare the practical rate $\log_2(1 + \omega_1^*)$ with λ^*, and decide whether to stop or not.

From the result of Theorem 1, threshold λ^* is the unique solution of equation $\mathbb{E}[\max\{u(n) - \lambda, 0\}] = \frac{\lambda \tau_0}{\tau_d}$. Moreover, the problem of finding ω_1^* such that $\sup_{\omega_1 > 0} \lambda^*(\omega_1)$ is equivalent to solve the solution such that

$$\mathbb{E}[\max\{u_n(\omega_1) - \lambda, 0\}] = \frac{\lambda \tau_0}{\tau_d}. \tag{5}$$

By observing that the left side (LHS) of Eq. (5) is a monotonically increasing function, we focus on finding optimal value ω_1.

The LHS of Eq. (5) can be calculated as follows:

$$\mathbb{E}[\sum_{i=1}^{K} I[s(n) = i] \cdot \max\{u_i(n) - \lambda, 0\}] = \frac{1}{K} \sum_{i=1}^{K} \mathbb{E}[\max\{u_i(n) - \lambda, 0\}]. \tag{6}$$

As link $i = 1, 2, ..., K$ has channel gains $P_s h_i(n)$ following exponential distribution with probability density function $\frac{1}{P_s \sigma^2} e^{-\frac{x}{P_s \sigma^2}}$, expression (6) can be further calculated as

$$\text{LHS} = (\log_2(1 + \omega_1) - \lambda) \int_{\omega_1}^{+\infty} \frac{1}{P_s \sigma^2} e^{-\frac{x}{P_s \sigma^2}} dx$$

$$= (\log_2(1 + \omega_1) - \lambda) e^{-\frac{\omega_1}{P_s \sigma^2}}. \tag{7}$$

Based on it, Eq. (5) is simplified into

$$(\log_2(1 + \omega_1) - \lambda) \cdot e^{-\frac{\omega_1}{P_s \sigma^2}} = \frac{\lambda \tau_0}{\tau_d}. \tag{8}$$

A closed form expression of solution λ^* is derived with respect to ω_1 below:

$$\lambda^*(\omega_1) = \frac{\log_2(1 + \omega_1)}{1 + \frac{\tau_0}{\tau_d} e^{\frac{\omega_1}{P_s \sigma^2}}}. \tag{9}$$

We then analyze the relationship between throughput function $\lambda(\omega_1)$ and threshold ω_1. The first derivative of the throughput $\lambda(\omega_1)$ can be expressed as

$$\frac{d\lambda^*(\omega_1)}{d\omega_1} = \frac{\frac{\log_2 e}{(1 + \omega_1)}(1 + \frac{\tau_0}{\tau_d} e^{\frac{\omega_1}{P_s \sigma^2}}) - \frac{\tau_0}{\tau_d P_s \sigma^2} \log_2(1 + \omega_1) e^{\frac{\omega_1}{P_s \sigma^2}}}{(1 + \frac{\tau_0}{\tau_d} e^{\frac{\omega_1}{P_s \sigma^2}})^2}. \tag{10}$$

Valuing $\frac{d\lambda^*(\omega_1)}{d\omega_1} = 0$, the optimal ω_1^* satisfies the following equation

$$\frac{\log_2 e}{(1+\omega_1^*)}(1 + \frac{\tau_0}{\tau_d}e^{\frac{\omega_1^*}{P_s\sigma^2}}) - \frac{\tau_0}{\tau_d P_s\sigma^2}\log_2(1+\omega_1^*)e^{\frac{\omega_1^*}{P_s\sigma^2}} = 0. \tag{11}$$

And the second derivative of $\lambda(\omega_1)$ at $\omega_1 = \omega_1^*$ satisfies the inequality that

$$\frac{d^2\lambda^*(\omega_1)}{d\omega_1^2}\bigg|_{\omega_1=\omega_1^*} = \frac{-\frac{\log_2 e}{(1+\omega_1^*)^2}(1 + \frac{\tau_0}{\tau_d}e^{\frac{\omega_1^*}{P_s\sigma^2}}) - \frac{\tau_0}{\tau_d P_s\sigma^4}\log_2(1+\omega_1^*)e^{\frac{\omega_1^*}{P_s\sigma^2}}}{(1 + \frac{\tau_0}{\tau_d}e^{\frac{\omega_1^*}{P_s\sigma^2}})^2} < 0. \tag{12}$$

Based on inequality (12), we conclude $\lambda^*(\omega_1)$ is concave and ω_1^* is optimal value satisfying Eq. (12).

Moreover, we prove the uniqueness of ω_1^*. By dividing $e^{\frac{\omega_1}{P_s\sigma^2}}$, Eq. (11) can be transformed into a form that

$$\frac{\log_2 e}{(1+\omega_1)}(e^{-\frac{\omega_1}{P_s\sigma^2}} + \frac{\tau_0}{\tau_d}) = \frac{\tau_0}{\tau_d P_s\sigma^2}\log_2(1+\omega_1). \tag{13}$$

As the left side is monotonically decreasing and the right side is monotonically increasing, the point ω_1^* is unique and maximizes $\lambda^*(\omega_1)$ at $\omega_1 = \omega_1^*$.

Based on the result of Theorem 2, threshold ω_1^* can be calculated off-line. By following the optimal channel access strategy N^*, the transmission rate $\log_2(1 + \omega_1^*)$ is always greater than threshold λ^*, which makes opportunistic channel access efficient. In particular, after nth channel contention, when the winner Source $s(n)$ has channel condition $P_s h_s(n)$ better than threshold ω_1^*, symbol 1 is notified from the destination to allow the channel access. Then, the winner source transmits data by rate $\log_2(1 + \omega_1^*)$. Otherwise, when channel gain is worse than the threshold, symbol 0 is notified, and the winner source actively drops the transmission opportunity and re-contends with other sources in the next slot. In this case, it is found that different from perfect CSI feedback, the optimal decision on when to transmit depends on threshold λ^*.

3.3 The Case Under Heterogeneous Channels

In most wireless networking environment, different links may have different channel characteristics. We consider the heterogeneous case where all channels between source-to-destination pairs have different channel statistics. For pair $i = 1, 2, ..., K$, channel gain h_i follows exponential distribution with expectation σ_i^2.

In this case, each pair has its quantization vector $\mathbf{w}_i = [0, \omega_{i,1}], i = 1, 2, ..., K$. Based on the result in Theorem 1, for given vectors $\mathbf{w}_i, i = 1, 2, ..., K$, the system throughput $\lambda^*((\mathbf{w}_1, ..., \mathbf{w}_K))$ is calculated as

$$\lambda^*((\mathbf{w}_1, ..., \mathbf{w}_K)) = \frac{\frac{1}{K}\sum_{i=1}^{K}\log_2(1+\omega_{i,1})e^{-\frac{\omega_{i,1}}{P_s\sigma_i^2}}}{\frac{1}{K}\sum_{i=1}^{K}e^{-\frac{\omega_{i,1}}{P_s\sigma_i^2}} + \frac{\tau_0}{\tau_d}}. \tag{14}$$

We then focus on maximizing average throughput $\lambda^*((\mathbf{w}_1, ..., \mathbf{w}_K))$ in expression (14).

We define the optimal quantization thresholds as $\{\omega_{i,1}^*\}_{i=1,2,\cdots,K}$. The first-order derivative function can be calculated as

$$
\left[\frac{\partial \lambda^*}{\partial \omega_{1,1}}, \frac{\partial \lambda^*}{\partial \omega_{2,1}}, \cdots, \frac{\partial \lambda^*}{\partial \omega_{K,1}}\right] =
$$

$$
\left\{\frac{\frac{\log_2 e}{1+\omega_{i,1}}(1 + \frac{\tau_0}{\tau_d}e^{\frac{\omega_{i,1}}{P_s \sigma_i^2}}) - \frac{\tau_0}{\tau_d P_s \sigma_i^2}\log_2(1 + \omega_{i,1})e^{\frac{\omega_{i,1}}{P_s \sigma_i^2}}}{(1 + \frac{\tau_0}{\tau_d}e^{\frac{\omega_{i,1}}{P_s \sigma_i^2}})^2}\right\}_{i=1,2,\cdots,K}. \quad (15)
$$

By valuing the derivative as 0, we obtain the stationary point as $(\omega_{1,1}^*, \cdots, \omega_{K,1}^*)$ where $\omega_{i,1}^*$ satisfies that

$$
\frac{\log_2 e}{1+\omega_{i,1}}(1 + \frac{\tau_0}{\tau_d}e^{\frac{\omega_{i,1}}{P_s \sigma_i^2}}) - \frac{\tau_0}{\tau_d P_s \sigma_i^2}\log_2(1 + \omega_{i,1})e^{\frac{\omega_{i,1}}{P_s \sigma_i^2}} = 0. \quad (16)
$$

The point $(\omega_{1,1}^*, \cdots, \omega_{K,1}^*)$ exists uniquely.

Moreover, we derive second-order derivative matrix $\mathbf{J} = [\frac{\partial^2 \lambda}{\partial \omega_{i,1} \partial \omega_{j,1}}]_{i,j}$ as

$$
\mathbf{J} = \begin{bmatrix} \frac{\partial^2 \lambda^*}{\partial \omega_{1,1}^2} & \frac{\partial^2 \lambda^*}{\partial \omega_{1,1}\partial \omega_{2,1}} & \cdots & \frac{\partial^2 \lambda^*}{\partial \omega_{1,1}\partial \omega_{K,1}} \\ \cdots & \cdots & \cdots & \cdots \\ \frac{\partial^2 \lambda^*}{\partial \omega_{K,1}\partial \omega_{1,1}} & \frac{\partial^2 \lambda^*}{\partial \omega_{K,2}\partial \omega_{2,1}} & \cdots & \frac{\partial^2 \lambda^*}{\partial \omega_{K,K}^2} \end{bmatrix}. \quad (17)
$$

By analysis, since each first-order partial derivative depends on variable $\omega_{i,1}$ only, the second-order derivative elements have the following characteristics.

When $i = j$, the matrix element has the form that

$$
\frac{\partial^2 \lambda^*}{\partial \omega_{i,1}^2}\Big|_{(\omega_{1,1}^*,\cdots,\omega_{K,1}^*)} = \frac{-\frac{\log_2 e}{(1+\omega_{i,1}^*)^2}(1 + \frac{\tau_0}{\tau_d}e^{\frac{\omega_{i,1}^*}{P_s \sigma_i^2}}) - \frac{\tau_0}{\tau_d P_s \sigma_i^4}\log_2(1 + \omega_{i,1}^*)e^{\frac{\omega_{i,1}^*}{P_s \sigma_i^2}}}{(1 + \frac{\tau_0}{\tau_d}e^{\frac{\omega_{i,1}^*}{P_s \sigma_i^2}})^2} < 0.
$$

$$(18)$$

When $i \neq j$, $\frac{\partial^2 \lambda^*}{\partial \omega_{i,1} \partial \omega_{j,1}}\Big|_{(\omega_{1,1}^*,\cdots,\omega_{K,1}^*)} = 0$.

Combining the results together, the second derivative matrix $\mathbf{J}$ is diagonal matrix as follows

$$
\mathbf{J}|_{(\omega_{1,1}^*,\cdots,\omega_{K,1}^*)} = \begin{bmatrix} \frac{\partial^2 \lambda^*}{\partial \omega_{1,1}^2}\Big|_{(\omega_{1,1}^*,\cdots,\omega_{K,1}^*)} & 0 & \cdots & 0 \\ 0 & \frac{\partial^2 \lambda^*}{\partial \omega_{2,1}^2}\Big|_{(\omega_{1,1}^*,\cdots,\omega_{K,1}^*)} & \cdots & 0 \\ \cdots & \cdots & \cdots & \cdots \\ 0 & 0 & \cdots & \frac{\partial^2 \lambda^*}{\partial \omega_{K,1}^2}\Big|_{(\omega_{1,1}^*,\cdots,\omega_{K,1}^*)} \end{bmatrix}.
$$

$$(19)$$

Since all diagonal elements are negative, the second derivative matrix is negative definite. The function $\lambda^*(\mathbf{w})$ is thus concave, and points $(\omega_{1,1}^*, \cdots, \omega_{K,1}^*)$ are optimal. Based on the result, the following theorem is obtained, presenting the optimal channel access strategy.

Theorem 3. *Under heterogeneous case, the optimal strategy achieving the maximal throughput* λ^* *is* $N^* = \min\{n \geq 1 : P_s h_s(n) \geq \omega^*_{s(n),1}, and\ u(n) \geq \lambda^*\}$, *and for pair* $i = 1, 2, ..., K$ *thresholds* $\omega^*_{i,1}$ *are fixed such that*

$$\frac{\log_2 e}{1 + \omega^*_{i,1}}(1 + \frac{\tau_0}{\tau_d}e^{\frac{\omega^*_{i,1}}{P_s \sigma_i^2}}) - \frac{\tau_0}{\tau_d P_s \sigma_i^2}\log_2(1 + \omega^*_{i,1})e^{\frac{\omega^*_{i,1}}{P_s \sigma_i^2}} = 0.$$

Moreover, the optimal throughput λ^* *satisfies*

$$\lambda^* = \frac{\frac{1}{K}\sum\limits_{i=1}^{K}\log_2(1 + \omega^*_{i,1})e^{-\frac{\omega^*_{i,1}}{P_s \sigma_i^2}}}{\frac{1}{K}\sum\limits_{i=1}^{K}e^{-\frac{\omega^*_{i,1}}{P_s \sigma_i^2}} + \frac{\tau_0}{\tau_d}}.$$

In accordance with Theorem 3, the proposed optimal stopping strategy N^* is in a bi-thresholds based structure. For each pair, thresholds $\omega^*_{i,1}$ and λ^* can be calculated off-line. Threshold $\omega^*_{i,1}$ is local value for each source-to-destination pair, λ^* is global. All these thresholds can be calculated off-line, which much benefits the strategy implementation.

Following the optimal strategy, channel access by multiple source-to-destination pairs are operated as follows:

After nth successful channel contention, a winner source $s(n)$ appears, and sends a RTS to its destination. Then, the destination estimates the CSI and compares it with its local threshold $\omega^*_{s(n),1}$. Then, if $P_s h_s(n) \geq \omega^*_{s(n),1}$, it inserts symbol 1 in the CTS; otherwise, it inserts symbol 0. Subsequently, the CTS is feedback to the winner source. After receiving CTS, the winner source will make a decision.

- If the feedback in CTS is 1, a winner Destination $s(n)$ compares the practical rate $u(n) = \log_2(1 + \omega^*_{s(n),1})$ with the throughput threshold λ^*. If $u(n) \geq \lambda^*$, it lets Source $s(n)$ access the channel by rate $u(n)$.
- otherwise, it will give up this transmission opportunity, and let all sources re-contend the channel.

Upon a successful transmission, one transmission round is finished and all sources contend the channel in the next slot.

Under the heterogeneous case, all links share the same threshold λ^*. Different from the homogeneous case, the quantization rate is different for each pair. Moreover, due to statistical variety of the wireless channels, probability of channel access by each pair is different. In particular, if a pair has a poor channel condition, it may never access the channel, while others in better channel conditions could obtain more opportunities for channel access.

4   Performance Evaluation

This section carries out numerical simulation to validate theoretic results. Consider 5 source-to-destination pairs in the wireless network, and channels from sources to destinations experience i.i.d. Rayleigh fading. Channel contention parameters of sources are set as $p_0 = 0.3$, $\delta = 25\,\mu s$, $\tau_{RTS} = \tau_{CTS} = 50\,\mu s$.

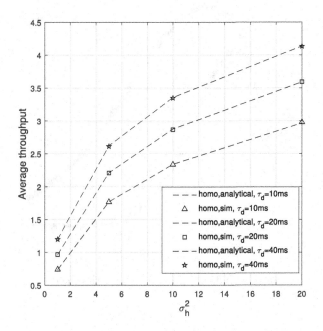

Fig. 4. Performance analysis under homogeneous channels

First, we consider a homogeneous wireless network where average SNR of all channels is σ_h^2. When data transmission time τ_d varies from 10 ms to 40 ms, the average system throughput is analyzed. In Fig. 4, for a fixed τ_d, the statistical average result shown as 'analytical' and the time average result shown as 'sim' are compared. For each value of τ_d, throughput curves match well, verifying the theoretic analysis. Moreover, the relation between average system throughput and quantized threshold is analyzed, as shown in Fig. 5. The two curves represent system throughput when σ_h^2 is 10 and 20, respectively.

Secondly, we consider a heterogeneous wireless network where average SNR of all channels may be different. The channel average SNR parameter of all source-to-destinations are $(0.5\sigma_h^2, 0.8\sigma_h^2, \sigma_h^2, 2\sigma_h^2, 2.5\sigma_h^2)$, respectively. As transmission time τ_d are 10 ms, 20 ms and 40 ms, the average system throughput curves are simulated when σ_h^2 varies from 1 to 10. In Fig. 6, the statistical average result shown as 'analytical' and the time average result shown as 'sim' match well with each other.

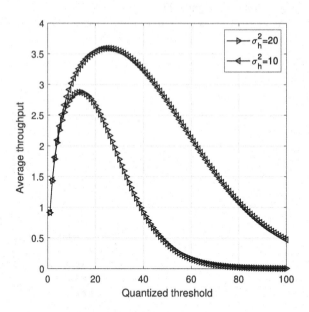

Fig. 5. Influence from quantized threshold

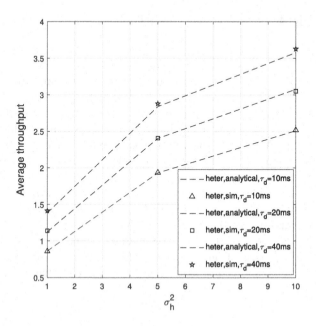

Fig. 6. Performance analysis of heterogeneous channels

5 Conclusion

In practical wireless networks, the channel state information can only be obtained through limited feedback. This research investigates the optimal distributed opportunistic channel access under single-bit CSI feedback. The channel homogeneity and heterogeneity are also studied, and optimal opportunistic channel access strategies are proposed with the optimality rigorously proved. For network implementation, the strategies' structure are analyzed and easy network operation is available. This research should open the potential direction for distributed networking approach under limited CSI.

References

1. Andrews, M., Kumaran, K., Ramanan, K., Stolyar, A., Whiting, P., Vijayakumar, R.: Providing quality of service over a shared wireless link. IEEE Commun. Mag. **39**(2), 150–154 (2001)
2. Viswanath, P., Tse, D.N.C., Laroia, R.: Opportunistic beamforming using dumb antennas. IEEE Trans. Inf. Theory **48**(6), 1277–1294 (2002)
3. Zheng, D., Ge, W., Zhang, J.: Distributed opportunistic scheduling for ad hoc networks with random access: an optimal stopping approach. IEEE Trans. Inf. Theory **55**(1), 205–222 (2009)
4. Ge, W., Zhang, J., Wieselthier, J., Shen, X.: PHY-aware distributed scheduling for ad hoc communications with physical interference model. IEEE Trans. Wirel. Commun. **8**(5), 2682–2693 (2009)
5. Tan, S., Zheng, D., Zhang, J., Zeidler, J.: Distributed opportunistic scheduling for ad-hoc communications under delay constraints. In: Proceedings of IEEE INFOCOM 2010 (2010)
6. Ferguson, T.: Optimal Stopping and Applications. http://www.math.ucla.edu/~tom/Stopping/Contents.html

Spectrum Allocation Algorithm for Energy-Constrained UAV in Interweave Cognitive IoT Network Based on Satellite Coverage

Chao Ren[✉] and Huijie Xu

University of Science and Technology Beijing, Beijing, China
chaoren@ustb.edu.cn

Abstract. Today, the internet of things (IoT) has become an inevitable trend in the development and integration of communication and information technology. The rapid increase of IoT terminals has led to scarcity of spectrum resources. Therefore, if cognitive radio (CR) technology can be added to IoT, it is bound to better meet the frequency requirements of the development of the IoT. In order to solve this problem, this paper uses unmanned aerial vehicles (UAVs) to access cognitive spectrum holes with CR in interweave cognitive IoT network. In the satellite coverage area, the UAV's GPS signal will be stronger. Therefore, this paper comprehensively considers the spectrum hole quality, UAV power limitation and satellite coverage issues, and proposes a spectrum allocation algorithm, which preferentially selects channels with high communication quality, and comprehensively considers UAV power control when implementing the algorithm. Simulation results show that the algorithm improves communication quality and spectrum allocation and realizes power control.

Keywords: IoT · UAV · Satellite coverage · SNR · Spectrum allocation

1 Introduction

The huge scale of the internet of things (IoT), as well as the wireless-based characteristics of information interaction and transmission, are destined to make the IoT a major consumer of spectrum resources. However, today's wireless networks adopt a fixed spectrum allocation policy, that is, the planning and use of wireless spectrum resources are stipulated by government departments, and the use of transceivers by spectrum needs to be authorized by the government department. When the authorized spectrum is free, these resources cannot used by other users. The survey and research of the FCC's Spectrum Policy Task Force show that at any given moment, people use only 2% to 6% of the available spectrum resources and a lot of expensive spectrum resources will be wasted. However, the wireless spectrum is a limited, non-renewable resource. Today, available spectrum resources in many countries and regions have been divided, and China is also facing the threat of depletion of spectrum resources. It can be seen that the lack of spectrum resources restricts the development of the IoT. In order to solve this problem, cognitive radio (CR) emerged as a new type of radio technology. It

B. Li et al. (Eds.): IoTaaS 2020, LNICST 346, pp. 624–632, 2021.
https://doi.org/10.1007/978-3-030-67514-1_49

is based on the allocation of spectrum resources. The basic idea is: Rental User or Second User (RU or SU) continue to detect authorized spectrum resources and ensure that Licensed User or Primary User (LU or PU) give priority to use and under the condition that its performance is almost not impaired, perform spectrum detection and find spectrum holes and dynamically access idle spectrum to realize the secondary utilization of spectrum resources, so as to achieve the purpose of improving spectrum utilization.

The ultimate goal of CR technology is to obtain spectrum resources through cognition and reconfiguration, so finding spectrum holes through spectrum detection is an essential step [1, 2]. The so-called spectrum hole refers to the frequency band that has been allocated to the main user but is not currently used, so it can be used by the perception user. The spectrum detection is to estimate the interference temperature of the observed frequency band. For the interference temperature obtained by spectrum estimation, the interference temperature limit can be given. Through the interference temperature limit, the observed spectrum holes can be selected. Interference or other noise beyond the boundary are all spectrums that do not meet the communication requirements. After that, the spectrum holes mentioned in this paper are all the spectrum that meets the requirements. At the same time, broadcasting can only achieve communication between users accessing holes in the same spectrum. Communication between users accessing holes in different spectrums needs to be achieved through external equipment, which requires a lot of manpower and material resources. The emergence of unmanned aerial vehicles (UAVs) solved this problem.

UAV, as a product of high-tech in the information age, have the characteristics of small size, light weight, and free movement in the air. It has been widely recognized in the world and is currently a hot research topic in the field of communications [3–6]. Therefore, we can combine UAV with CR to give full play to the advantages of low cost and free movement of unmanned aerial vehicles and add the characteristics of cognitive users' active spectrum sensing and spectrum access to the UAV control system. Allowing cognitive users to quickly find and access idle channels can reduce the detection range and increase the success rate. But how to let cognitive users find the optimal spectrum? We can use the Signal-to-noise ratio (*SNR*) to measure the quality of spectrum holes.

In order to improve communication quality, the paper also adds the factor of satellite coverage. In the satellite coverage area, the UAV's global positioning system (GPS) signal will be greatly enhanced. And in the area covered by multiple satellites, UAV interest will increase. At the same time, in order to make the energy consumption of the UAV system as low as possible, this paper comprehensively considers the spectrum hole quality, the limited UAV power and the satellite coverage issues, and proposes an interwoven cognitive IoT network based on satellite coverage. The spectrum allocation algorithm of the restricted UAV improves the communication quality and spectrum allocation and realizes the power control.

2 Related Works

A large number of spectrum allocation algorithms have appeared in spectrum access technology, many of which are based on game theory [7–10] (game theory, studies the interaction between formulaic incentive structures, considers the predicted and actual behavior of individuals in a game, and studies their optimal strategies), and some are based on C-means clustering, deep reinforcement learning [11] and so on.

Ref. [12] uses Nash equalization to solve the problem of spectrum allocation or power control in non-cooperative situations. Ref. [11] designed a dynamic spectrum access algorithm based on Q-learning. Cognitive users learn through continuous interaction with the environment and quickly select the channel with the highest return rate for data transmission, but the algorithm only considers A single cognitive user perceives and accesses the current idle spectrum without considering the priority and competition issues caused by multiple users simultaneously needing to access the network. Ref. [13] proposes a decentralized cognitive MAC protocol, which ensures that in the presence of conflicts and spectrum sensing errors, synchronous hopping in the spectrum between the transmitter and receiver can be used to optimize the performance of secondary users. While limiting the interference perceived by the main user. Ref. [14] designed a spectrum allocation algorithm based on pricing theory. A primary user sells available spectrum to multiple competing secondary users. Ref. [15] establishes repeated games with punishment mechanism, which effectively improves the efficiency of non-cooperative games. Ref. [7] proposed a probability update algorithm based on uncertain network environment for dynamic spectrum access technology, and incorporated the status information of cognitive users within the system into the consideration of model construction, and then proposed user status-based Feedback learning algorithm, but this algorithm considers all authorized users as a whole when constructing the system model, analyzes the situation of cognitive users separately, and does not take into account the actual situation of authorized users. Ref. [8] uses potential games to analyze the game behavior between secondary users, and considers the mutual interference between primary users and secondary users into the revenue function of secondary users, which effectively improves the throughput of the system. Ref. [9] proposes a dynamic spectrum access technology based on C-means clustering algorithm. By establishing a multi-objective matrix model of accessible channels and using multi-object clustering to accurately divide the channel spectrum pool, it can not only meet the different business needs of cognitive users, but also effectively improve the efficiency of spectrum utilization.

Although these algorithms solve the problem of spectrum allocation and improve the spectrum utilization rate, they do not consider the effect of channel quality on spectrum allocation due to their complexity and limited functions. Therefore, this paper proposes a spectrum allocation algorithm for energy-limited UAVs in an interwoven cognitive IoT network based on satellite coverage, which improves communication quality and spectrum allocation, and realizes power control.

When a spectrum hole is detected, the time the user needs to decide whether to access free frequencies, as well as the spectrum hole track, spectrum perception changes, avoiding interference to the primary user. Once the primary users are using channels, other users need to empty out the spectrum and continue to look for spectrum hole to connected to the signal. But when the detection range is larger, the success rate of the is smaller. So a spectrum access algorithm is proposed in this paper, using unmanned aircraft to move this feature, narrow the scope of the detection and effectively detect spectrum hole.

3   System Model

The system model diagram is shown in Fig. 1. When a user of the IoT layer communicates, the frequency band not occupied by the main user is a spectrum hole, so the IoT layer is a spectrum hole layer. To simplify the problem, we assume that all UAVs fly on a certain level. Suppose the position coordinate of a certain spectrum hole is, and the position coordinate of a certain UAV is, then the distance between the UAV and the spectrum hole can be expressed as.

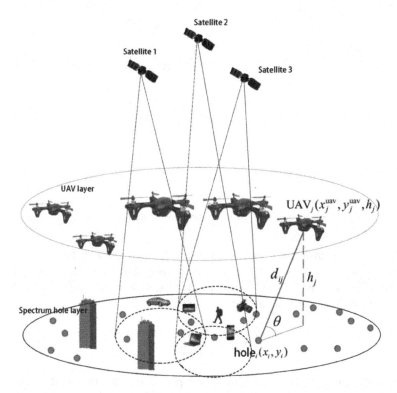

Fig. 1. System model.

$$d_{ij} = \sqrt{(x_j^{uav} - x_i)^2 + (y_j^{uav} - y_i)^2 + h_j^2} \qquad (1)$$

The satellite coverage projection map is shown in Fig. 2. Suppose there are three satellites. In the figure, area A is covered by three satellites at the same time, area B is covered by two satellites, area C is covered by only one satellite and area D is not covered by satellites. In areas covered by satellites, the UAV's GPS signal will increase and in different areas, UAVs have different interests, that is, the UAV's GPS signals in areas A, B, C, and D will gradually weaken and the communication quality will also be reduced. It will fall. Therefore, UAVs in area A will have priority access to spectrum holes. Assuming that the numbers of UAVs in areas A, B, C, and D are a, b, c, and d, respectively, they are numbered: $m_A(i), (i = 1, 2, 3 \ldots, a)$, $m_B(i), (i = 1, 2, 3 \ldots, b)$, $m_C(i), (i = 1, 2, 3 \ldots, c)$, $m_D(i), (i = 1, 2, 3 \ldots, d)$.

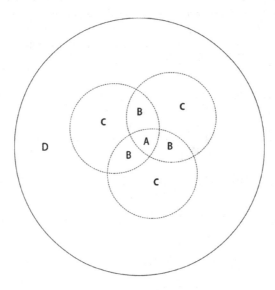

Fig. 2. Satellite coverage projection.

Assuming that there are n spectrum holes in the spectrum hole layer, number these n spectrum holes as $n(i), (i = 1, 2, 3 \ldots n)$; we use *SNR* to measure the quality of spectrum holes. Due to the limited energy of UAVs, the launch power P_t of UAVs must be considered. Therefore, the *SNR* can be expressed as

$$SNR = \frac{P_t \times (h + L)}{N_0} \tag{2}$$

Among them, P_t is the UAV transmission power, h is the small-scale fading, it can be modeled as a normal distribution, N_0 is Gaussian noise, L is the path loss, which is related to d_{ij} and can be expressed as

$$L = \beta_0 d_{ij}^{-2}$$

$$L = \beta_0 \left(\sqrt{\left(x_j^{uav} - x_i \right)^2 + \left(y_i^{uav} - y_i \right)^2 + h_j^2} \right)^{-2} \tag{3}$$

where β_0 denotes the channel power at the reference distance $d_0 = 1$m.

In order to reduce the energy consumption during the flight of the UAV, the power of the UAV must be controlled. Ref. [4] is an initial attempt to conduct energy-efficient UAV communication by optimizing the UAV trajectory to maximize the energy efficiency of the UAV communication system in a given time. To achieve this goal, the UAV power consumption is modeled as a function of UAV flight speed and acceleration, and finally a simplified power consumption model of UAV straight flight is obtained:

$$P = \left| a_1 V^3 + \frac{a_2}{V} + ma'V \right| \tag{4}$$

Among them, a' is the acceleration of horizontal straight flight, V is the speed of horizontal straight line, and a_1 and a_2 are constants related to aerodynamics and aircraft design. It can be seen from formula (4) that with the increase of speed and acceleration, the power consumption of the UAV is gradually increasing, but at the beginning it increases slowly, and the power consumption increases rapidly after a certain point. Therefore, we can call this point the power stability point. At this time, the speed and acceleration of the UAV have been determined. The UAV flying at this point can not only ensure that the speed and acceleration are not too small, but also control power consumption. When the UAV is flying at the speed and acceleration of the power stability point, the flight time depends on the distance between the UAV and the spectrum hole, and the energy consumption of the UAV also depends on this distance. Therefore, the UAV will select $n/2$ spectral holes that are located closer to itself for comparison.

We assume that the transmission power of the UAV is a certain value, then the *SNR* of each spectrum hole can be calculated, which is recorded as $s(i), (i = 1, 2, 3...n)$.

Specifying the value function $R = \{R(i)\}, (i = 1, 2, 3...n)$, $R(i)$ is the final value function of the spectrum hole numbered $n(i)$, then

$$R(i) = \frac{s(i)}{s(i) + s(i+1)} + \frac{d(i+1)}{d(i) + d(i+1)} \tag{5}$$

$$R(i+1) = \frac{s(i+1)}{s(i) + s(i+1)} + \frac{d(i)}{d(i) + d(i+1)} \tag{6}$$

If $R(i) > R(i+1)$, remove $R(i+1)$ from the set R and then continue to traverse the set R. Finally, the spectrum hole corresponding to the remaining value function in R is the spectrum hole that the UAV will choose to access.

4 Algorithm Design

4.1 Source of Algorithm Inspiration

The algorithm is inspired by the 3rd RoboCup Simulation Robot 11VS11 Football League of Beijing University of Science and Technology held in 2019 by the Institute of Advanced Engineers. The rules of the game are that the side with the most goals in the specified simulation time wins.

Here, the stadium can be regarded as a certain frequency domain and the UAV acts as a robot. Certainly, there is only one ball on the field, but let's expand it. Assuming there are multiple balls, the ball can be regarded as a spectrum hole. In the game, the robot closest to the ball has to grab the ball in the direction of a straight line distance, so it can be imagined that the UAV chooses the way to access the spectrum hole close to its own distance. At the same time, the communication quality should be considered, so priority should be given to selecting the spectrum hole access with high comprehensive index.

4.2 Algorithm Steps

Step 1: Number the UAVs in areas A, B, C, and D respectively. Cognitive users in areas covered by satellites will be allocated spectrum first;

Step 2: Calculate the distance between the UAV in area A and the spectrum hole according to formula (1);

Step 3: Calculate the SNR according to formulas (2) and (3);

Step 4: Calculate the value R according to formula (5) and (6). The UAV chooses the R value of $n/2$ spectrum holes that are closer to itself and compares it, and continuously traverses the set R, and finally the remaining value function in R is the spectrum hole that the UAV should choose to access;

Step 5: Repeat steps 2, 3, and 4 to find the spectrum holes that the UAVs in the B, C, and D areas choose to access.

5 Simulation Results

20 UAVs are used in a certain frequency domain, assuming that the number of UAVs in the A, B, C, and D areas are 2, 6, 7, and 5 respectively. Through spectrum detection, six spectral cavities meeting the communication requirements were found. Assuming that the flying height of the UAV is 270 m and the transmitting power is 15 dBm, the SNRs obtained are: -25 dB, -21 dB, -19 dB, -17 dB, -13 dB, -10 dB.

Figure 3 is a channel allocation diagram after the algorithm is executed. It can be seen from the figure that spectrum holes with high SNR are allocated more cognitive users, and most of them exist in satellite coverage areas (A, B, and C areas). Cognitive users who are not covered by satellites (area D) will be allocated to spectrum holes with a small signal-to-noise ratio.

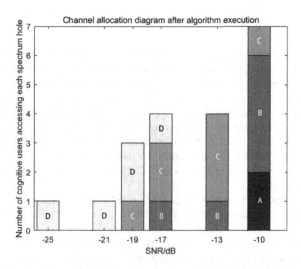

Fig. 3. Channel allocation diagram after algorithm execution.

The simulation results show that the algorithm integrates factors such as the channel quality of the IoT, satellite coverage, and UAV power control, which improves the channel utilization and improves the communication quality and spectrum allocation.

6 Conclusion

This paper mainly discusses the problem of spectrum resource allocation, briefly describes the main technologies of current spectrum resource allocation and points out their shortcomings. In this regard, this paper proposes a spectrum allocation algorithm for energy-constrained UAVs in an interwoven cognitive IoT network based on satellite coverage. The algorithm takes into account the spectrum hole quality, UAV power limitation and satellite Coverage issues, in which the application of UAV technology enables cognitive users to find spectrum holes faster and will be more dominant in the competition for spectrum resources. Simulation results show that the algorithm improves communication quality and spectrum allocation, and realizes power control.

Acknowledgment. This work is supported by Guangdong Province Basic and Applied Basic Research Fund (Grant No. 2019A1515111086) and the Fundamental Research Funds for the Central Universities (Grant No. FRF-BD-20-11A).

References

1. Rahim, V.C.A., Mruthyunjaya, H.S., Kedalya, K.V.: An alternative selection based detection method for spectrum sensing for cognitive radio. In: 2013 Third International Conference on Advances in Computing and Communications, Cochin, pp. 90–93 (2013). https://doi.org/10.1109/ICACC.23
2. Kumar, A., Saha, S., Bhattacharya, R.: Improved wavelet transform based edge detection for wide band spectrum sensing in Cognitive Radio. In: 2016 USNC-URSI Radio Science Meeting, Fajardo, pp. 21–22 (2016). https://doi.org/10.1109/USNC-URSI.2016.7588492
3. Ruan, L., et al.: Energy-efficient multi-UAV coverage deployment in UAV networks: a game-theoretic framework. China Commun. **15**(10), 194–209 (2018). https://doi.org/10.1109/CC.2018.8485481
4. Zeng, Y., Zhang, R.: Energy-efficient UAV communication with trajectory optimization. IEEE Trans. Wirel. Commun. **16**(6), 3747–3760 (2017). https://doi.org/10.1109/TWC.2017.2688328
5. Ghazzai, H., Ben Ghorbel, M., Kadri, A., Hossain, M.J.: Energy efficient 3D positioning of micro unmanned aerial vehicles for underlay cognitive radio systems. In: 2017 IEEE International Conference on Communications (ICC), Paris, pp. 1–6 (2017). https://doi.org/10.1109/ICC.2017.7996485
6. Liu, C.H., Chen, Z., Tang, J., Xu, J., Piao, C.: Energy-Efficient UAV control for effective and fair communication coverage: a deep reinforcement learning approach. IEEE J. Sel. Areas Commun. **36**(9), 2059–2070 (2018). https://doi.org/10.1109/JSAC.2018.2864373
7. Nair, G.R., Moorthy, Y.K., Pillai, S.S.: A novel interference reduction technique in game theory based dynamic spectrum leasing scheme. In: 2016 International Conference on Emerging Technological Trends (ICETT), Kollam, pp. 1–8 (2016). https://doi.org/10.1109/ICETT.7873731
8. Luo, S., Yu, L., Zhou, Y.: Research on spectrum sharing algorithm based on potential game theory. Procedia Comput. Sci. **131**, 1328–1335 (2018)
9. Zhu, X., Liu, X., Xu, Y., Zhang, Y., Ruan, L., Yang, Y.: Dynamic spectrum access for D2D networks: a hypergraph game approach. In: Proceedings of 2017 17th IEEE International Conference on Communication Technology (ICCT 2017). IEEE Beijing Section, Sichuan Institute of Electronics. IEEE (2017)
10. Ni, Q., Zhu, R., Wu, Z., Sun, Y., Zhou, L., Zhou, B.: Spectrum allocation based on game theory in cognitive radio networks. J. Netw. **8**(3), 712 (2013)
11. Das, A., Ghosh, S.C., Das, N., Barman, A.D.: Q-learning based co-operative spectrum mobility in cognitive radio networks. In: 2017 IEEE 42nd Conference on Local Computer Networks (LCN), Singapore, pp. 502–505 (2017). 10. 1109/LCN.80, 2017
12. Sheng, S., Liu, M.: Symmetric Nash equilibrium in a secondary spectrum market. In: 2013 IEEE Global Conference on Signal and Information Processing, Austin, TX, 2013, p. 1133 (2013). https://doi.org/10.1109/GlobalSIP.6737096
13. Zhao, Q., Tong, L., Swami, A., Chen, Y.: Decentralized cognitive MAC for opportunistic spectrum access in ad hoc networks: a POMDP framework. IEEE J. Sel. Areas Commun. **25**(3), 589–600 (2017). https://doi.org/10.1109/JSAC.2007.070409
14. Niyato, D., Hossain, E.: Competitive spectrum sharing in cognitive radio networks: a dynamic game approach. IEEE Trans. Wirel. Commun. **7**(7), 2651–2660 (2008). https://doi.org/10.1109/TWC.2008.070073
15. Niyato, D., Hossain, E.: Competitive pricing for spectrum sharing in cognitive radio networks: dynamic game, inefficiency of nash equilibrium, and collusion. IEEE J. Sel. Areas Commun. **26**(1), 192–202 (2008). https://doi.org/10.1109/JSAC.2008.080117

Edge Network Extension Based on Multi-domains Fusion and LEO Satellite

Chao Ren[(⊠)] and Jingze Hou

University of Science and Technology Beijing, Beijing, China
chaoren@ustb.edu.cn

Abstract. The explosion of heterogeneous devices needs an extended version of edge network. Physical factor, such as time delay and energy cost, is usually used to facilitate resource sensing and neighbor nodes' networking. In fact, other factors from multiple domains may seriously affect the resource selection and edge network extension. Thus, this paper uses multi-domains fusion connect more nodes from multiple domains and expand edge network. In the proposed edge network model, nodes can thus be selected and combined from a single domain to multi-domains. Moreover, low earth orbit (LEO) satellite can act as a relay node providing excess connection for different domains, and further expands the edge network. To formulate the domains fusion, a two-dimensional matrix is used for each domain. The abscissa and ordinate of the matrix exactly correspond to the tasks and nodes of the offloading process in one domain. Finally, the edge network matrix (selected matrix) can be expanded (increasing of non-zero elements) after the fusion operation. Our analysis and numerical results demonstrate that multi-domains fusion and cooperating with LEO effectively extend the edge network with about 9%.

Keywords: LEO satellite · Multi-domains fusion · Edge network extending introduction

1 Introduction

Terminal devices, that can be used for computing, are embracing an explosively increasing number [1]. The Internet of Things (IoT) network continues to expand with heterogeneous devices, which may serve as massive computing resources. Most distributed devices in the IoT have low computing demand and urge for edge computing services. An efficient method to enjoy edge computing service is offloading tasks to other nodes with enough computation resources.

The commonly used methods to select nodes are based on one performance or several related metrics such as time delay and energy cost [2–8]. Most of these metrics belong to physical domain. However, the number of nodes sensed in physical domain may be limited to finish a hug instantaneous task. Can we break away the limitation of a single domain and reexamination the question in view of multi-domains? Besides the physical domain, other domains like social domain and information domain exist in edge network. These domains include various nodes condition and connection information. For example, the owner's willing is the typical factor in social domain. If the

B. Li et al. (Eds.): IoTaaS 2020, LNICST 346, pp. 633–643, 2021.
https://doi.org/10.1007/978-3-030-67514-1_50

owner of a device has no interest to release his device, the node cannot be selected. Therefore, making full advantage of these nodes' information from multiple domains may help extend edge network and finish instantaneous huge computation.

In practical, the issue is how to sense and connect these nodes from multiple domains. Edge computation needs a high speed and low delay connection between nodes, but mobile network may not cover some remote area and important region. The service range of cellular connection is limited by many factors, such a wide range connection's building and low earth orbit (LEO) satellite provides a new choice to serve wide range with low delay and high speed. Starlink and Oneweb have been used in practical to provide a high-speed connection. This paper proposes LEO satellite-based method to find and build connection over large area and extend edge network from one domain to multi-domains.

Node selection for edge computing has careful researched in [2–8]. The authors of Ref. [2] propose an algorithm to offload tasks based on increasing utilization of the network. These related works are able to efficiently utilize the released computation resource from other layers to balance the uneven distribution of computation resources in space, which are also known as task offloading [3–5] or task migration [6–8]. In recent years, there are also some papers trying to integrate the knowledge of multi-domains and to deal with the information of different domains in a unified way. Papers [9] begin to introduce people's part of speech into people's attitude judgment, combining the information domain of people's emotional judgment with domain of humanity emotion. Also, Ref. [10] combined humanity and society to build a system of smart city. In the field of satellite communication, some papers point out that LEO satellite can be used to assist communication by establishing fast and stable links or being a node in edge network. But these are not enough to effectively expand the scope of the edge network because they cannot make full use of all nodes from multi-domains and wide area.

If the nodes' information and connection from multiple domains are fully used, the number optional nodes will be further increased. At the same time, the consideration of multi-domains factors can also reduce the one-sidedness of node selection. The selected nodes may also have a better performance in the macroscopic view.

This paper attempts to describe the information of different domains into three domains, including: physical domain (**PD**), which represents some physical constant parameters like occupying time. Social domain (**SD**), which represents human's attitude or emotion. Information domain (**ID**), which represents some variable parameters of network likes delay. Each domain contains the connect information between nodes and tasks. Such a one-to-one correspondence is suitable to be described by two-dimensional matrix. Through multi-domains fusion, the number of nodes in the edge network increases and the edge network is expanded. After cooperating with the LEO satellite, the non-zero elements will be further increased, and the network will be further expanded. In the actual fusion process, because of the information association between different domains, it will lead to the repeated calculation of part of the information, so this paper reduces the covariance between the information of different domains to 0, so that there is no correlation between different domains. Finally, independent domain information is obtained. The accuracy of fusion is ensured.

In summary, the distinctive feathers and contributions of this paper are as follows:

1. This paper solves the problem of narrow edge network caused by selecting edge network nodes from a single domain, proposes multi domain to expand the scope of edge network, and gives the fusion mode of multi domain information.
2. This paper proposes a LEO satellite-based method to incorporate more nodes and expand the edge network.

2 System Model

The whole system is composed of three different domain information and remote node information connected by satellite. The three domains: **ID**, **SD**, and **PD** are fused to form a selected matrix (**SM**), which contains the information from all the three domains.

Nodes in **PD** can cooperate or offload tasks to other nodes but sometime with the limited information only from **PD** can't provide a good offload plan. For example, some owners don't want their device to serve for the edge computing, but **PD** doesn't contain such an information. Such a condition will cause an invalid offloading. So fusing information from other domains can not only solve these incorrect connections but also can provide some additional node information to extend edge network. Please see Fig. 1.

In order to further expand the network, we need to mine more node information. Because of the limitations of network coverage, remote equipment is always ignored. Some devices are not connected to other domains through wired networks, nor are they covered by wireless networks. If these devices can be found and connected, it will bring more choices for edge computing.

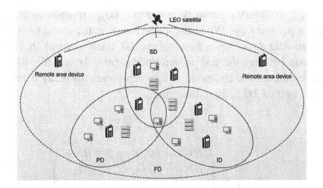

Fig. 1. System model with domains fusion

2.1   Modeling the Three Domains

In edge computing, the computing ability of nodes and task volume are the key parameters. But it doesn't make sense to only measure computing ability or task volume. If the computing ability of a node is very weak, but the volume of computing tasks is also very small, then the node can complete the calculation task. Therefore, the ratio of task volume to computing ability is more meaningful for node selection, which we call occupying time.

Thus, in **PD** computing ability of the nodes donated by *compute* (in CPU cycles per-second) and the volume of computing tasks donated by $volume_m$ (in CPU cycles). Therefore, in an edge internet with N nodes and M tasks, the **PD** can be described as a $M*N$ matrix called **PD**. Each element in **PD** describe the time that task m can be finished by node n ($m \in M, n \in N$). Before the multi-domains fusion, if the node and the task are not in one domain, set the $\mathbf{PD}_{m,n}$ into 0. The unit of $\mathbf{PD}_{m,n}$ is millisecond.

$$D_{m,n} = \frac{volume_m}{compute_n} \tag{1}$$

$$PD_{M*N} = \begin{pmatrix} PD_{1,1} & PD_{1,2} & \cdots & PD_{1,N} \\ PD_{2,1} & PD_{2,2} & \cdots & PD_{2,N} \\ \vdots & \vdots & \ddots & \vdots \\ PD_{M,1} & PD_{M,2} & \cdots & PD_{M,N} \end{pmatrix} \tag{2}$$

The network condition between nodes changes with time, which may lead to the change of connection quality. Delay and BER are the key parameters to describe the network condition. In the edge computing, it can represent the effective calculation proportion in the edge computing. Because delay and *BER* are both negatively correlated with network condition. The smaller the delay and *BER* the better the network condition.

We use $\mathbf{ID}_{m,n}$ to describe network condition. $\mathbf{ID}_{m,n}$ represents the average transmission delay of per error bit. When the value is lower, the current network is in good condition. These data make up a new matrix **ID**. Each element in **ID** describes the network condition between the task m and node n ($m \in M, n \in N$). $BER_{m,n}$ represents the BER between the task m and node n. $T_{m,n}$ represents the delay between task m and node n. and the unit of $\mathbf{ID}_{m,n}$ is millisecond.

$$ID_{m,n} = BER_{m,n} \times T_{m,n} \tag{3}$$

$$\mathbf{ID}_{M*N} = \begin{pmatrix} ID_{1,1} & ID_{1,2} & \cdots & ID_{1,N} \\ ID_{2,1} & ID_{2,2} & \cdots & ID_{2,N} \\ \vdots & \vdots & \ddots & \vdots \\ ID_{M,1} & ID_{M,2} & \cdots & ID_{M,N} \end{pmatrix} \tag{4}$$

Humanity attitude plays a key role in practical application, because the owner of a device may not be willing to release his device completely for edge computing. This is a factor that we must consider, and it is also the most important humanistic factor in edge computing. Owner's will cannot be simply regarded as willing or unwilling. Sometimes there are other influencing factors, such as the compensation of computation and occupation time. Maybe only when the reward is high and the occupation time is short, the owner is willing to release the node.

So, we describe the owner's will as a probability's reciprocal, that is, the probability that the owner will release the existing device for edge computing. The stronger the will of the owner, the greater the probability. All probability values form a new matrix **SD**. Each element in **SD** describe the owner's willing of device n release the device to compute for task m. O_{pre} means the exception occupying time of the node owner. $I_{m,n}$ represents the income of node n compute for the task m and I_{pre} means the exceptional income of the node owner. $(m \in M, n \in N)$.

$$if, \ PD_{m,n} > O_{pre}, SD_{m,n} = 0$$

$$else \ SD_{m,n} = \frac{2}{1 + \frac{I_{m,n}}{I_{pre}} - \frac{PD_{m,n}}{O_{pre}}} \tag{5}$$

$$\mathbf{SD}_{M*N} = \begin{pmatrix} SD_{1,1} & SD_{1,2} & ... & SD_{1,N} \\ SD_{2,1} & SD_{2,2} & ... & SD_{2,N} \\ \vdots & \vdots & \ddots & ... \\ SD_{M,1} & SD_{M,2} & ... & SD_{M,N} \end{pmatrix} \tag{6}$$

2.2 Extended Edge Network with LEO Satellite

Nodes in remote areas are easy to be ignored. Some nodes cannot be covered by the wired network and wireless network, which makes them difficult to connect with other nodes. For example, airplanes and devices on some islands. In recent years, LEO satellites have been able to provide low delay and wide range of network service. This is very important to help these remote nodes establish connections with other nodes. The connection service with low delay can guarantee the good connection performance of these nodes for edge computing. The wide range of LEO satellite services can provide more nodes to expand the edge network (Fig. 2).

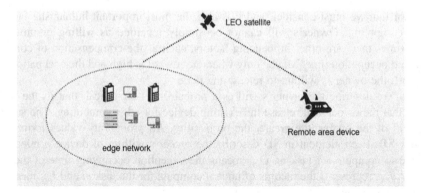

Fig. 2. LEO satellite build a connection between remote device and edge network.

In this model, we divide the device into two parts, one is the local edge network, the other is the remote area equipment. The process we need to describe is to add these remote devices to the local edge network. We define the fusion domain as selected matrix (**SM**), which is defined in the next chapter.

We assume that there are r remote devices that connect to the local edge network via satellite. The information between these *r* devices and *M* tasks is stored in matrix **R**.

$$\mathbf{R}_{M*r} = \begin{pmatrix} R_{1,1} & \cdots & R_{1,r} \\ \vdots & \ddots & \vdots \\ R_{M,1} & \cdots & R_{M,r} \end{pmatrix} \tag{7}$$

The elements in **R** are calculated in the same way with **SM**, which is defined in the following.

2.3   Domains Fusion

Multi domain fusion in edge computing is to integrate the information of multiple domains to expand the scope of edge network. And comprehensively consider the influencing factors in each domain. In order to comprehensively consider the multi-domain factors, after the numerical calculation of the factors of the three domains, the matrix of the three fields should be weighted and calculated. The importance of the selected nodes is weighted according to the information of each domain. This means that the three parameters are variable. When the environment of the problem changes, the value of the parameters can be adjusted to change the ratio of the three domains.

$$\mathbf{SM} = (\alpha\mathbf{PD} + \beta\mathbf{ID}) * \delta\mathbf{SD}, \tag{8}$$

where * is hamard product between two same matrices.

Finally, **SM** is obtained. Each element in the **SM** corresponds to the value of multi-domain factors when a task is offloaded to the node. The smaller the value is, the better the performance will be after integrating the factors of the three domains. When this value is 0, it means that the task cannot be offloaded to the node because it does not meet the owner's expectation the node cannot complete the calculation task.

2.4   Reduce the Relevance

When there is correlation between domains, which will cause too much calculation of one factor in the process of fusion. In order to eliminate the data correlation between different domains, we need to preprocess the data. So that the matrix can store the correct irrelevant information.

One of the quantities that describe the association between data is covariance.

$$Cov(a, b) = \frac{1}{M \times N} \sum_{i=1}^{M} \sum_{j=1}^{N} a_{i,j} b_{i,j}, \tag{9}$$

where $a_{i,j}$ and $b_{i,j}$ represents the elements of any two of the three domains. When the covariance between them is 0, it means that they are not related.

In order to clearly describe the relationship between any two domain elements, we select the corresponding elements in the two domains to form a new contrast matrix $Y(M*N) \times 2$.

$$Y_{(M*N)*2} = \begin{pmatrix} a_{1,1} & b_{1,1} \\ \vdots & \vdots \\ a_{M,1} & b_{M,2} \end{pmatrix} \tag{10}$$

So, we continue to create a covariance matrix $C_{(M*N)} \times {}_{(M*N)}$ to describe the covariance of elements in any number of each two domains.

$$C = YY^{T} \tag{11}$$

The next step is to diagonalize the covariance matrix, so that the off diagonal elements will become zero. The dimensions of the corresponding data matrix are no longer related. Here we assume that the new covariance matrix after diagonalization is Q. The data matrix Y is transformed into a new matrix Z, which is independent of all domains of data.

$$Z = PY \tag{12}$$

And P is the transformation matrix.

$$P = \frac{1}{M * N} ZZ^{T} \tag{13}$$

$$Q = PCP^{T} \tag{14}$$

According to Formula (9), the eigenvalues λ of the matrix can be obtained. Finally, we get the eigenvalue matrix E. Matrix E meets the condition:

$$Z = EY \tag{15}$$

3 Numerical Results

According to the above model, we need to analyze the network expansion after multi domain fusion. We assume an edge network with ten nodes and ten tasks. The node information is stored in different domains. In the actual network, the state of the network is often random, and the owner's attitude towards whether to release the node changes with the change of the task. We use randomly generated matrices instead of data in three fields. In order to make the data easier to process, we set the parameter as the reciprocal of the maximum value of the local value to normalize the data.

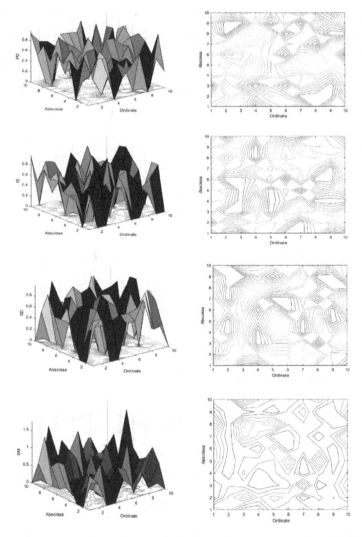

Fig. 3. Numerical results of multi-domains fusion, each picture represents the changing value of elements in each domain. Non-zero element represents a selected node.

Each matrix will generate 30% zero-elements to stimulate the nodes can't be connected in the field. The non-zero values represent the nodes that can be selected in edge computing (Fig. 3).

There are more non-zero elements in **SM** than in **PD** and **ID**, which means that the number of edge nodes that can be selected is increased through multi-domains fusion. Compared with **SD**, because **SD** plays a decisive role in the fusion process (when an element in **SD** is zero, the owner is not willing to release the node), the number of nodes does not increase compared with **SD**. At that time, it was still very important to fuse the information in **SD**, because the introduction of **SD** enabled us to exclude some nodes that could not be released and increase the accuracy of offloading. After three times repeat of these processes, the selected nodes in **SM** is about 9% more than **PD** and **ID**.

When devices in remote areas are connected to the edge network through LEO, the edge network is further expanded. The number of nodes in the network increases further (Fig. 4).

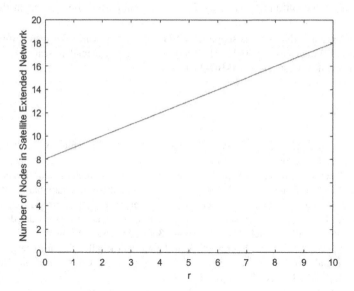

Fig. 4. The number of selected nodes is increasing with more remote devices connect with LEO satellite. The x-coordinate describes the increase of remote device and the y-coordinate describes the number of selected nodes in satellite extended network.

The figure shows the number of devices from remote areas connected to LEO satellite increases, the number of nodes in edge network increases and the edge network is expanded further. Since the zero elements in the matrix are randomly generated according to a certain probability, the non-zero elements in each domain approach to a constant (the probability of generating a non-zero element) after repetitive calculations. When more remote nodes connect edge network by LEO satellite, the number of selected nodes increases and edge network is extended. The selected nodes in LEO extended edge network is formed by the nodes form fusion domain and nodes from remote area. There is a linear relationship between the growth trend of selected nodes and the number of remote nodes.

4 Conclusion

To solve the problem that there are not plenty of nodes in edge network to realize large scale edge computing, this paper fuses the information in different domains. By extending the edge network from a single domain to multi domain, the number of nodes in the edge network is increased and the network is expanded. In addition. This paper also proposes to cooperate with LEO satellite to further expand the edge network and increase the number of optional nodes in the edge network by connecting devices in remote areas. The final numerical results also show that multi-domains fusion and cooperating with LEO satellite can effectively increase the number of nodes in the edge network and expand the network. The research on multi-domains is still in the initial stage and the edge offloading strategy in multi-domains will be studied in the future.

Acknowledgement. This work is supported by Guangdong Province Basic and Applied Basic Research Fund (Grant No. 2019A1515111086) and the Fundamental Research Funds for the Central Universities (Grant No. FRF-BD-20-11A).

References

1. Global mobile data traffic forecast update, 2017 c 2022 white paper, Cisco Visual Networking Index, pp. 1–33 (2019)
2. Lee, S., Cheon, H., Kang, S., Kim, J.: Novel LIPA/SIPTO offloading algorithm according to the network utilization and offloading preference. In: 2014 International Conference on Information and Communication Technology Convergence (ICTC), pp. 314–318 (2014)
3. Chen, M., Hao, Y.: Task offloading for mobile edge computing in software defined ultra-dense network. IEEE J. Sel. Areas Commun. **36**(3), 587–597 (2018)
4. Zhang, Y., He, J., Guo, S.: Energy-efficient dynamic task offloading for energy harvesting mobile cloud computing. In: 2018 IEEE International Conference on Networking, Architecture and Storage (NAS), pp. 1–4 (2018)
5. Boukerche, A., Guan, S., De Grande, R.E.: A task centric mobile cloud-based system to enable energy aware efficient offloading. IEEE Trans. Sustain. Comput. **3**(4), 248–261 (2018)
6. Kong, Y., Zhang, Y., Wang, Y., Chen, H., Hei, X.: Energy saving strategy for task migration based on genetic algorithm. In: 2018 Inter-national Conference on Networking and Network Applications (NaNA), pp. 330–336 (2018)
7. Zhang, W., Tan, S., Lu, Q., Liu, X.: Towards a genetic algorithm-based approach for task migrations. In: 2014 International Conference on Identification, Information and Knowledge in the Internet of Things, pp. 182–187 (2014)

8. Zhu, L., Wang, W. Zhang, Y., Tan, S.: CPN based validation on pervasive cloud task migration. In: 2015 IEEE 12th International Conference on Ubiquitous Intelligence and Computing and 2015 IEEE 12th International Conference on Autonomic and Trusted Computing and 2015 IEEE 15th International Conference on Scalable Computing and Communications and its Associated Workshops (UIC-ATC-Scal Com), pp. 986–990 (2015)
9. Vishnu, K.S., Apoorva, T., Gupta, D.: Learning domain specific and domain independent opinion-oriented lexicons using multiple domain knowledge. In: 2014 Seventh International Conference on Contemporary Computing (IC3), Noida, pp. 318–323 (2014). https://doi.org/10.1109/IC3.2014.6897193
10. Costanzo, A., Faro, A., Giordano, D.: Implementing Cyber Physical social Systems for smart cities: A semantic web perspective. IEEE, Las Vegas (2016)

Completion of Marine Wireless Sensor Monitoring Data Based on Tensor Mode-n Rank and Tucker Operator

Peng Xu[1], Huayang Chen[1], Chunhua Yu[1(✉)], Tongtong Wang[2], and Yechao Bai[1]

[1] Nanjing University, Nanjing 210023, China
yuch@nju.edu.cn
[2] Tianjin Artificial Intelligence Innovation Center (TAIIC), Tianjin 300450, China

Abstract. The marine monitoring system is one of the frontier technologies actively developed by major countries in the world today. The current ocean monitoring system mainly relies on technologies such as positioning, control, and wireless sensors. The buoy equipped with a variety of wireless sensors continuously collects data on the ocean. However, due to natural environmental influences and malicious tampering by the enemy, the data directly obtained by the wireless sensor buoys may contain large errors. Therefore, we construct the obtained original data into a tensor model, and at the same time replace the data with larger errors into null data "0". Based on the tensor mode-n rank, we use the alternating direction method of multipliers (ADMM) framework, combined with the tensor Tucker decomposition, and introduce the tensor Tucker singular value operator to it. The overall data can be completed from the existing original data with missing values, so as to optimize the original ocean monitoring data. The method is compared with the data completion based on tensor Tucker decomposition and the linear regression prediction based on principal component analysis. Numerical experiments are given to confirm the superiority of the proposed method.

Keywords: Marine monitoring · Wireless sensors · Tensor completion · Tucker operator

1 Introduction

Our country is rich in marine resources. Marine environment monitoring is also one of the necessary technical means to study marine resources, which is conducive to safeguarding our country's marine rights and interests, early warning of marine natural environmental risks, and protection of the marine environment.

The monitoring system for the marine environment mainly relies on radar satellite positioning, system control, and wireless sensor [1] buoy technologies. Buoys equipped with multiple wireless sensors are placed on the sea to continuously collect data from the ocean, and then transfer the data to the control center for processing through the relevant equipment. In general, data measured by buoys equipped with wireless

© ICST Institute for Computer Sciences, Social Informatics and Telecommunications Engineering 2021
Published by Springer Nature Switzerland AG 2021. All Rights Reserved
B. Li et al. (Eds.): IoTaaS 2020, LNICST 346, pp. 644–654, 2021.
https://doi.org/10.1007/978-3-030-67514-1_51

sensors have multiple dimensions, including latitude and longitude, temperature, pressure, and salinity, etc. As buoys equipped with wireless sensors are in an open environment and highly independent, they are more susceptible to the impact of natural environment or malicious attacks, resulting in large errors in the monitoring data directly obtained by wireless sensors. In some target sea areas, there will also be insufficient monitoring buoys, resulting in missing data.

At present, there are several commonly used methods to complete missing data at home and abroad, including matrix completion [2], regression prediction based on BP (back propagation) neural network [3], linear regression prediction based on principal component analysis, and tensor completion based on Tucker decomposition, etc. When there are no restrictions on matrix completion, the solution is infinite and unsolvable. It can be seen from [4] that low rank is a prerequisite for good performance of matrix completion. In addition, matrix completion is applicable to low-dimensional data but cannot handle high-dimensional data. The regression prediction based on the BP neural network depends on the number of layers of the network, the number of neurons in each layer, and the initial value. During the training process, the calculations are complicated and the efficiency is low. Linear regression prediction based on principal component analysis is simple and easy to implement, but its accuracy is low, which may cause prediction failure. Tensor completion based on Tucker decomposition extracts the underlying structure between elements, and then extracts the principal components to complete the missing data, but it will lose some high-dimensional information, resulting in a large error.

In this paper, the existing buoy monitoring data is constructed into a tensor model. Based on tensor mode-n rank related knowledge, we combine the alternating direction method of multipliers (ADMM) framework with tensor Tucker decomposition and introduce the Tucker singular value operator for the missing data complement to obtain the finally optimized ocean monitoring data. During the experiment, the error between the data after the final completion and the original data was measured using MATLAB R2017a software to verify the effectiveness of our proposed method. For comparison, the linear regression prediction algorithm based on principal component analysis and the tensor completion algorithm based on Tucker decomposition are considered.

2 Linear Regression Based on Principal Component Analysis

2.1 Principal Component Analysis

The essence of multivariate principal component analysis is a statistical method for reducing dimensions. It converts multiple relevant variables of the research object into a set of linearly uncorrelated variables through orthogonal transformation called principal component. The original variable can be replaced by a linear combination of this group of principal components.

The principal component analysis method is to transform the covariance matrix of the original random variable into a diagonal matrix in algebra. In geometry, it can be regarded as transforming the original coordinate system into a new orthogonal coordinate system that points to the orthogonal direction with the greatest variability in the sample points, and then reduce the dimension of multidimensional variables.

Let $X = (X_1, X_2, \ldots, X_P)^T$ be a P-dimensional random variable, and its principal component Z_i should meet the following conditions.

(1) $Z_i = e_i^T X, e_i^T e_i = 1$, Where e_i is a P*1-dimensional eigenvector.
(2) $Z_i(i = 1, 2, \ldots, k, k \leq P)$ are not related.
(3) The value of e_i makes the variance of Z_i as large as possible.

Corresponding to the eigenvector e_i, the eigenvalue is $\lambda_i, \lambda_1 \geq \lambda_2 \geq \cdots \geq \lambda_P \geq 0$, thus the cumulative contribution rate of the i-th principal component is defined as

$$\gamma_i = \frac{\sum_{k=1}^{i} \lambda_k}{\sum_{k=1}^{P} \lambda_k} \tag{1}$$

If the cumulative contribution rate of the first i factors exceeds the set threshold, the first i factors are selected as the principal components. At this time, the number of factors is reduced from P to i, and they are not related to each other.

2.2 Linear Regression Prediction

The expression of the classical linear regression analysis prediction method [5] is

$$Y = f(B, Z) \tag{2}$$

where B is the parameter variable of the prediction model, Z is the principal component independent variable obtained from Sect. 2.1, and Y is the dependent variable that needs to be predicted.

In the prediction process, the fitting value at time t is set to $\widehat{Y}_t$ and the difference between the actual value Y_t and the fitting value $\widehat{Y}_t$ is

$$v_t = Y_t - \widehat{Y}_t = Y_t - f(B, Z_t), t = 1, 2, \ldots, n$$
$$\min Q = \sum_{t=1}^{n} v_t^2 \tag{3}$$

For linear regression prediction, the expression is shown in (4).

$$Y = BZ = b_0 + b_1 z_1 + \cdots + b_n z_n \tag{4}$$

where $B = [b_0, b_1, \ldots, b_n], Z = [z_1, z_2, \ldots, z_n]$. The specific algorithm is as follows and the final calculation error expression of the algorithm is

$$RSE = 10 * \log 10(\left\| \widehat{Y} - X \right\| / \|X\|), dB \tag{5}$$

Algorithm 1 Linear regression prediction based on principal component analysis (Linear-PCR)

Input: Initial data X and principal component threshold ε

---

1. Standardize X.
2. Remove the rows that contain missing values in the initial data X to form new data X'.
3. Perform principal component analysis on X', find feature values and feature vectors, apply equation (1) to make γ_i greater than threshold ε, and finally obtain principal component Z.
4. The regression analysis method is used to regress the dependent variable on the principal component Z, and the regression model shown in equation (4) is obtained.
5. Substituting the dependent variable of missing values into the model to obtain standardized prediction data Y.
6. Inverse standardization of Y.
7. Compute the RSE (Relative square error).

Output: Predictive value Y and the RSE

---

3 Tensor Decomposition Related Knowledge

Tensors are mathematical tools for studying high-dimensional data, and can be seen as a higher-order generalization of one-dimensional vectors and two-dimensional matrices. In the era of information technology explosion today, more and more attention is paid to it. It makes great contribution to several research fields such as high-dimensional signal processing, data mining and machine learning.

3.1 Tensor Representation

Tensor in this paper refers to a multi-dimensional array, in which one-dimensional vectors and two-dimensional matrices belong to special tensors. The different dimensions of a tensor are called the tensors' mode. The tensor model constructed in this paper is a three-dimensional form. When it is expressed as a vector, the mode-1 vector is a column vector, the mode-2 vector is a row vector, and the mode-3 vector is a depth vector. When it is expressed as a matrix, the slices corresponding to a certain dimension of the tensor are expanded and arranged into a long matrix. The matrix representation on the n-mode is called mode-n matrix expansion of the tensor [6].

3.2 Tensor Rank and Tucker Decomposition

There are multiple definitions of the rank of tensors, which lead to a variety of low rank tensor decomposition methods. The definition of the rank of the tensor is mainly divided into CP rank and mode-n rank, and the low rank tensor decomposition methods determined therefrom are CP decomposition and Tucker decomposition. This paper uses mode-n rank and Tucker decomposition, so only these two methods are described.

The mode-n rank of a tensor refers to the number of maximally linearly independent groups of its expansion matrix in the mode-n form, which is denoted as $rank_n(\alpha)$.

Tucker decomposition, also known as high-order singular value decomposition (HOSVD), is essentially a high-order principal component analysis [7]. For a known tensor $\alpha \in R^{I_1 \times I_2 \times \cdots \times I_N}$, the mathematical expression of its tucker decomposition is

$$\begin{aligned} \alpha &= G \times_1 U^{(1)} \times_2 U^{(2)} \times_3 \cdots \times_N U^{(N)} \\ \alpha &= \sum_{j_1=1}^{J_1} \sum_{j_2=1}^{J_2} \cdots \sum_{j_N=1}^{J_N} g_{j_1,j_2,\ldots,j_N} \left(u_{j_1}^{(1)} \circ u_{j_2}^{(2)} \circ \cdots \circ u_{j_N}^{(N)} \right) \end{aligned} \tag{6}$$

where $G \in R^{J_1 \times J_2 \times \cdots \times J_N}$ is the core tensor, $U^{(n)} \in R^{I_n \times J_n}$ indicates that the tensor $\alpha \in R^{I_1 \times I_2 \times \cdots \times I_N}$ corresponds to the nth order orthogonal transformation matrix (also called factor matrix), and the core tensor G is calculated as follows.

$$G = \alpha \times_1 U^{(1)T} \times_2 U^{(2)T} \times_3 \cdots \times_N U^{(N)T} \tag{7}$$

In the above Eq. (6) and (7), $\times_n$ represents the n-mode product operator, and its expression is

$$\begin{aligned} b_{i_1,i_2,\ldots,i_{n-1}j,i_{n+1},\ldots,i_N} &= \sum_{i_n=1}^{I_n} a_{i_1,i_2,\ldots,i_N} c_{j,i_n} \\ \beta &= \alpha \times_n C, \alpha \in R^{I_1 \times I_2 \times \cdots \times I_N}, C \in R^{J \times I_n} \end{aligned} \tag{8}$$

$A \circ B$ is the outer product, and its expression is

$$[A \circ B]_{m,n,p,q} = a_{m,n} b_{p,q}, A \in R^{M \times N}, B \in R^{P \times Q} \tag{9}$$

3.3 Tensor Completion

The essence of tensor completion is to solve the following convex optimization problem [8].

$$\min \sum_{i=1}^{n} \mu_i rank(X_i) \rightarrow \min \sum_{i=1}^{n} \mu_i \|X_i\|_* \\ subject \quad to \quad P_\Omega(\chi) = P_\Omega(\alpha) \tag{10}$$

where $\|X_i\|$ represents Frobenius norm, which is defined as

$$\|X\| = \left(\sum_{i_1=1}^{I_1} \sum_{i_2=1}^{I_2} \cdots \sum_{i_N=1}^{I_N} x_{i_1,i_2,\ldots,i_N} x_{i_1,i_2,\ldots,i_N}^* \right)^{1/2} = \langle X, X \rangle^{1/2}, X \in R^{I_1 \times I_2 \times \cdots \times I_N} \tag{11}$$

χ is the intermediate tensor variable, Ω refers to the set of non-missing values in tensor α. X_i represents the mode-n expansion matrix of χ. μ_i is a constant set in advance, and needs to satisfy Eq. (12) and $\mu_i = 1/3$ in this paper.

$$\mu_i \geq 0, \sum_{i=1}^{n} \mu_i = 1 \tag{12}$$

Based on tensor tucker decomposition to complete the data, the principle is to use an iterative method to decompose the original tensor α with the missing data, and then reorganize it into a new tensor $\hat{\alpha}$ to achieve the purpose of tensor completion. The specific algorithm is as follows.

Algorithm 2 Tensor completion based on Tucker decomposition (Tucker completion)

Input: The original tensor α , rank $k_1, k_2, ..., k_N$ and the maximum number of iterations Max .

1. Set 0, 1 tensor S and meet

$$s_{i,j,k} = \begin{cases} 1 & (i,j,k) \in \Omega \\ 0 & (i,j,k) \notin \Omega \end{cases} \tag{13}.$$

2. Set initial χ_0 and satisfy

$$x_{i,j,k} = \begin{cases} a_{i,j,k} & (i,j,k) \in \Omega \\ 0 & (i,j,k) \notin \Omega \end{cases}, \chi_0 = S.*\alpha \tag{14}.$$

3. Repeat Max times
4. for n=1: N

$$X(n) = U^{(n)} \sum (n) V^{(n)T} \tag{15}.$$

5. end
6. Update core tensor G :

$$G = \chi_0 \times_1 U^{(1)T} \times_2 U^{(2)T} \times_3 \quad \times_N U^{(N)T} \tag{16}.$$

7. Update intermediate tensor   :

$$\chi_m \tag{17}.$$
$$\chi_m = G \times_1 U^{(1)} \times_2 \quad \times_N U^{(N)}$$

8. Update estimated tensor

$$\alpha : \tag{18}.$$
$$\alpha = \alpha + \chi_m.*(1-S)$$

9. Compute the RSE.

Output: Estimated tensor $\hat{\alpha}$ and the RSE

The above Algorithm 2 removes some minor components in the process of completing data, which reduces its performance when completing data with more detailed features. Therefore, this paper introduces a tensor completion method based on mode-n rank, and on this basis, introduces the tensor Tucker singular value operator. The essence of performing tensor completion based on mode-n rank is to minimize the mode-n rank $rank_n(\alpha)$ of tensor α. The singular value of the tensor expansion matrix is used to update the intermediate variable χ for iterative estimation, and then the missing value of the tensor is completed. In the iterative process, the framework used is the alternating direction multiplier method (ADMM) [9], which combines with the relevant characteristics of tensor Tucker decomposition. The tensor tucker singular value operator $TD_\tau(\bullet)$ is introduced and is defined as follows.

$$\chi \approx G(1:r_1, 1:r_2, \ldots, 1:r_N) \times_1 U^{(1)}(:, 1:r_1) \times_2 \cdots \times_N U^{(N)}(:, 1:r_N) \quad (19)$$

where $r_i = sum(diag(\max(\sigma_i - \tau, 0)))$ and $TD_\tau(\bullet)$ meets the following theorem [10].

$$TD_\tau(y) = \arg\min_\chi \frac{1}{2}\|\chi - y\|_F^2 + \tau\|\chi\|_* \quad (20)$$

Similar to the matrix singular value operator $TD_\tau(\bullet)$ in [10], it can be seen that the tensor Tucker singular value operator is the optimal solution to the tensor complementation convex optimization problem, and because it uses high-dimensional tensor data structure, it can improve the utilization of tensor high-dimensional structure.

In this algorithm, the equation of $TD_\tau(\bullet)$ can be rewritten as

$$\chi = \arg\min \frac{\mu}{2}\left\|\chi - (\alpha + \frac{1}{\mu}y)\right\|_F^2 + \tau\|\chi\|_* \quad (21)$$

From Eq. (20), the intermediate variable χ can be solved as

$$\chi = TD_{\frac{1}{\mu}}(\hat{\alpha} + \frac{y}{\mu}) \quad (22)$$

The values of estimated tensor $\hat{\alpha}$ and auxiliary variable y_m can be calculated from it. The specific algorithm is as follows.

Algorithm 3 Tensor completion based on mode-n rank and Tucker operator (Mode-n and Tucker completion)

Input: The original tensor α, the maximum number of iterations Max and parameter ρ

1. Set 0, 1 tensor S and meet equation (13).
2. Set initial χ_0 and satisfy equation (14).
3. Set auxiliary variable $y_1, y_2, y_3 \in R^{n_1 \times n_2 \times n_3}$ and the elements are all "0".
4. for 1: Max
5.   Update intermediate tensor χ :

$$\chi_m = TD_\tau (\chi_{m-1} + \frac{y_m}{\rho}), m = 1,2,3 \tag{23}.$$

6.   Update estimated tensor α :

$$\alpha = (1 - S). * \left\{ \frac{1}{3} * \sum_{m-1}^{3} (\chi_m - \frac{y_m}{\rho}) \right\} + S. * \chi_m \tag{24}.$$

7.   Update auxiliary variable y_m :

$$y_m = y_m - \rho * (\chi_m - \alpha), m = 1,2,3 \tag{25}.$$

8. end
9. Compute the RSE.

Output: Estimated tensor α and RSE

Among them $\tau = \frac{1}{\rho}$.

4   Experimental Verification

This experiment selects the relevant data of the Argo Real-time Data Center of China (taken from some data in the number 0469). The dimensions of selected data are latitude and longitude, pressure, temperature and salinity. Each dimension has 12 data, and there are 60 in total. This data is constructed as a three-dimensional tensor $\alpha \in R^{6 \times 2 \times 5}$. Among them, the first 24 data belong to the latitude and longitude dimensions, and the last 36 data belong to the dimensions of pressure, temperature and salinity. Randomly select 1–20 of these 36 data (step size is 1) as null data "0", use it to simulate missing data or tamper with data, that is, construct tensor $S. * \alpha$ and then complete it with tensor. Perform 10 experiments respectively to calculate the final average error.

The initial data of the experiment as shown in Table 1 below.

Table 1. Initial data of longitude, latitude, pressure, temperature and salinity

Longitude	110.119	110.114	110.125	109.944	109.849	109.786
	109.637	109.403	109.128	108.813	108.534	108.334
Latitude	17.810	17.837	17.865	18.193	18.437	18.610
	18.707	18.798	18.846	18.814	18.750	18.641
Pressure (DBAR)	1025.200	1063.900	1064.100	1064.000	1064.900	1065.500
	1064.800	1065.000	1064.700	1064.500	1065.300	1064.800
Temperature (DEG C)	5.022	4.913	4.847	4.845	4.957	4.993
	5.012	5.031	4.941	4.938	4.901	4.921
Salinity (PSU)	34.638	34.636	34.638	34.638	34.638	34.634
	34.636	34.632	34.637	34.638	34.637	34.638

4.1   Convergence Experiment

During the experiment, randomly set the S tensor of 6 empty data (two in each of the three dimensions), and then complete the tensor of the missing data, and explore the convergence of Algorithm 3.

The missing position of the tensor data and the RSE of the data completion using Algorithm 3 are shown in Table 2, and the convergence of RSE is shown in Fig. 1.

Table 2. Random missing positions and completion data

	Missing position	Completion value
Pressure (DBAR)	3	992.300
	5	992.900
Temperature (DEG C)	9	4.972
	10	4.972
Salinity (PSU)	1	34.574
	5	34.608

In this experiment, there are 6 missing data (two in each of the three dimensions), and ADMM iteration is performed 1000 times. As can be seen from Fig. 1, in the iterative process, the RSE of data after tensor completion gradually converges, reaching stability after about 350 iterations, indicating that Algorithm 3 has convergences well for tensor data completion.

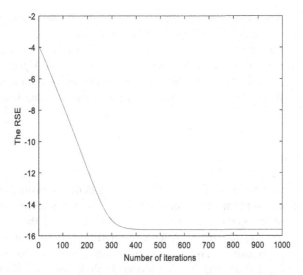

Fig. 1. The RSE during the tensor completion iteration

4.2   Comparative Experiment of Data Completion Effect

This experiment also applies three algorithms to complete the missing data tensor $S. * \alpha$. During the experiment, the missing values are randomly set. In order to make the experimental results more credible, the number of missing data ranges from 1 to 20. Each time a new missing value is added, the last missing value is guaranteed to be unchanged, thereby simulating the effect of initial data tensor completion under different missing degrees. The completion process of each proportion value is iterated 50 times, and finally find the average. The experimental results are shown in Fig. 2.

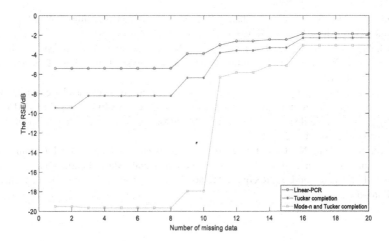

Fig. 2. Comparison of the completion effects of three tensor completion algorithms

It can be seen from Fig. 2 that as the value of "0" in the initial tensor data (that is, the missing value or tampered value in the ocean monitoring data) increases, the RSE after completing the data through the tensor also becomes larger and larger. Overall, compared with the other two algorithms, the tensor completion Algorithm 3 proposed in this paper has a relatively ideal effect on the completion of the monitoring data of marine wireless sensors. In addition, in the process of missing data from 1 to 10, data completion effect is better.

5   Conclusion

In this paper, the marine wireless sensor monitoring data is constructed into a three-dimensional tensor. Using the high-dimensional characteristics of the tensor, the tensor Tucker decomposition operator is introduced on the basis of the traditional tensor mode-n rank completion algorithm. After compared with data completion based on tensor Tucker decomposition and linear regression prediction based on principal component analysis, it is proved that this proposed algorithm can effectively improve the accuracy of tensor completion data, and its convergence is well, which is of great significance for the optimization of monitoring data of marine wireless sensors.

References

1. Wang, J., Zhou, W., Shen, Y.: Research on marine environment monitoring system based on wireless sensor network. Comput. Eng. Des. **2008**(13), 3334–3337 (2008)
2. Shi, J., Li, X.: Meteorological data estimation based on matrix completion. Meteorol. Sci. Technol. **047**(003), 420–425 (2019)
3. Shen, F., Guo, J.: Data fusion method based on BP neural network. Autom. Instrum. **2005** (05), 66–68+71 (2005)
4. Candes, E.J., Recht, B.: Exact matrix completion via convex optimization. Found. Comput. Math. **9**(6), 717–772 (2009)
5. Niu, D., Cao, S., Zhao, L., Zhang, W.: Power Load Forecasting Technology and its Application. China Electric Power Press, Beijing (1998)
6. Cichocki, A., Mandic, D., Lathauwer, L.D.: Tensor decompositions for signal processing application: from two-way to multiway component analysis. IEEE Signal Process. Mag. **32** (2), 145–163 (2015)
7. Zeng, K., He, L., Yang, X.: Support for higher-order tensor machines based on multilinear principal component analysis. J. Nanjing Univ. Nat. Sci. **2014**(02), 113–121 (2014)
8. Wang, L.: Data Collection and Recovery Based on Sparse Representation Theory. Hunan University, Changsha (2017)
9. Boyd, S., Parikh, N., Chu, E.: Distributed optimization and statistical learning via the alternating direction method of multipliers. Found. Trends Mach. Learn. **3**(1), 1–122 (2010)
10. Zhou, J.: Research on Data Recovery Method Based on Tensor. Shaanxi Normal University, Xi'an (2014)

Belief Propagation-Based Joint Iterative Detection and Decoding Algorithm for Asynchronous IDMA Satellite Systems

Shengfeng Li[1], Senlin Li[2], Xiang Chen[2(✉)], and Ling Wang[1]

[1] School of Electronics and Information, Northwestern Polytechnical University,
Xi'an 710072, China
`sf.li@haige.com,lingwang@nwpu.edu.cn`
[2] School of Electronics and Information Technology, Sun Yat-sen University,
Guangzhou 510006, China
`{lislin7,chenxiang}@mail.sysu.edu.cn`

Abstract. In recent years, a new emerging Interleave-Division Multiple Access (IDMA) developed from the Code-Division Multiple Access (CDMA), with its unique advantages, has been introduced into the satellite communication systems to provide a new multi-user access solution. In IDMA satellite systems, the random distribution of the geographical locations of different user ends (UEs) within the coverage of the satellite ground spot beam will cause serious asynchronous transmission. In this case, the computational complexity of MUD will increase sharply compared to the case of synchronization. Unfortunately, although many simplified algorithms were studied, this problem is still not solved effectively. In this paper, inspired by the successful application of the Belief Propagation (BP)-based joint iterative detection and decoding algorithm in CDMA systems, we adopt this method in asynchronous IDMA satellite systems. Analysis and simulations verify that the BP-based iterative algorithm can effectively reduce the algorithm complexity and has better performance than traditional turbo iterative algorithms in the asynchronous IDMA satellite system.

Keywords: Asynchronous · IDMA · Satellite systerm · Detection and Decoding · Belief Propagation (BP)

1 Introduction

Interleave-Division Multiple Access (IDMA) is an new emerging multiple access technology based on Code Division Multiple Access (CDMA) proposed by Li

This work was supported in part by the Guangdong Provincial Special Fund For Modern Agriculture Industry Technology Innovation Teams under Grant 2020KJ122, in part by the State's Key Project of Research and Development Plan under Grants 2019YFE0196400, in part by the NSFC under Grant 61771495, and in part by the Guangdong R&D Project in Key Areas under Grant 2019B010158001.

B. Li et al. (Eds.): IoTaaS 2020, LNICST 346, pp. 655–669, 2021.
https://doi.org/10.1007/978-3-030-67514-1_52

Ping [1]. In the IDMA systerm, users are distinguished by user-distinct inter-leavers instead of user-specific spreading sequences. It simplifies the multi-user detection algorithm and improves the system capacity. Considering the advantages of IDMA and the limitations of satellite communications, many studies have shown that IDMA can be used as a new multi-user access technology in satellite communications, and has better performance than CDMA [2,3].

In IDMA system, turbo manner receivers are traditionally used for detection and decoding. These receivers consist of multi-user detection (MUD) modules and decoders with judicious interleaving in between. The complexity of MUD increases in a linear manner with the number of users and iterations. In recent years, researchers have proposed many methods to reduce the complexity of turbo receivers. In the early works of [4], the turbo receivers utilize the Gaussian Chip Detector (GCD) [5] which is also called Elementary Signal Estimation (ESE). In [6], several simplified algorithms based on the ESE are proposed. The Simplified Gaussian Chip Detector (sGCD) with Probabilistic Data Association (PDA) algorithm is introduced to achieve faster convergence of the iterative MUD [7].

However, the above methods are all analyzed in synchronous IDMA systems. Unfortunately, in the actual satellite communication system, the time synchronization of the system is usually based on the Global Positioning System (GPS) or based on the Timing Advance (TA) mechanism [8]. Although this TA mechanism in the random access process achieves the initial uplink synchronization of different users, due to the large transmission distance between the satellite and the ground and the movement of user ends (UEs), the users cannot obtain the TA value fed back by the ground base station in real time. As a result, the system will inevitably have timing deviations. At present, for the geostationary earth orbit (GEO) satellite system, many studies have shown that the timing deviation can be controlled at about 1 ms [8,9]. Therefore, in the IDMA satellite system, due to the problem of timing deviation, the asynchronous delay of the system is usually on the order of several chips. In this case, the complexity of the above turbo iterative detection algorithms increases approximately linearly with the square of the the maximum of delay.

The Belief Propagation (BP)-based algorithm is another classic method to solve the problem of multi-user detection [10]. In asynchronous LDPC-coded CDMA satellite systems, a BP-based joint chip-level iterative detection and decoding algorithm was proposed in [11]. In recent years, LDPC codes have been widely used in satellite mobile communications [12]. LDPC codes can be easily converted into factor graphs and iterative decoding algorithms are usually used. The BP-based joint iterative algorithm constructs a global factor graph with only global iterations to make better use of the iterative structure of LDPC decoders.

In this paper, we apply the BP-based joint iterative detection and decoding algorithm to asynchronous LDPC-coded IDMA satellite systems considering the inheritance of IDMA and CDMA. The aim of this method is to reduce the complexity of the turbo iterative detection algorithms and improve the BER performance in the asynchronous case. In this article, we have verified the gain of this algorithm through theoretical analyses and simulations under Additive White Gaussian Noise (AWGN) channels.

The rest of this paper is organized as follows. In Sect. 2, the systerm model for asynchronous IDMA satellite systerm are described. In Sect. 3, the joint iterative algorithm for IDMA MUD and LDPC decoding is investigated. Complexity analyses of several joint iterative algorithms are given in Sect. 4. In Sect. 5, we evaluate the BER performance of two types of algorithms through simulations. Finally, the conclusion is drawn in Sect. 6.

2 System Description

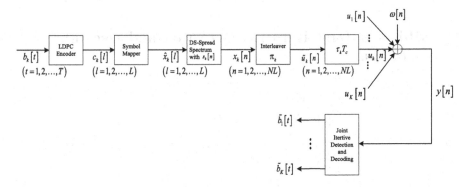

Fig. 1. The asynchronous LDPC-coded IDMA satellite communication system.

In this section, we consider the reverse link of an asynchronous IDMA satellite system, which is an LDPC-coded directsequence binary phase-shift keying (DS-BPSK) IDMA system with K users. In Fig. 1, the k-th user's information bits are marked as $\{b_k[t]; t = 1, 2, \ldots, T\}$ where $k = 1, \cdots, K$, N is the length of each information bit block, $n = 0, \cdots, N - 1$ and $(\bullet)^T$ denotes transposition. $\{c_k[l]; l = 1, 2, \ldots, L\}$ called the coded symbols, where L is the number of coded symbols in a single transmission block of any user after LDPC is encoded. After BPSK modulation, the coded symbols are mapped into modulated symbols with a value space of $\{+1, -1\}$, denoted as $\hat{x}_k[l]$. Assume that $\{s[1], s[2], \ldots, s[L_c]; s[m] = \pm 1\}$ is the spreading code of the k-th user; L_c is the code length. After spreading operation, the spreaded symbols which are also called spreaded chips are denoted as $\{x_k[n]; n = 1, 2, \ldots, NL\}$. The $\tilde{u}_k[n]$ is the output of the chip-level interleaver π_k. These interleavers π_k are generated independently and randomly.

The signal $u_k[n]$ is delayed by the user specific delay $\tau_k T_c$ where T_c denotes the chip time and τ_k is a nonnegative integer. $D_c = max_k\{\tau_k + 1\}$ is defined as the maximum total chip delays plus 1 over all users, where $max_k\{\bullet\}$ says get the maximum τ_k for all users. Because the uplink channel of satellite mobile communication system is usually described as the AWGN model [13], we consider an asynchronous IDMA system in this case. It is assumed that the signal power of each user is perfectly controlled. The received signal can be described as

$$y[n] = \sum_{k=1}^{K} h_k[n]\tilde{u}_k[n - d_k] + w[n], \tag{1}$$

where $h_k[n]$ is the effective channel impulse response. $w[n]$ is the additive Gaussian noise with zero mean and the variance σ^2.

In fact, it is the synchronous IDMA system when the transmission delays $d_k = 0$. Obviously, the existence of asynchronous delay will bring more interference to the system compared to precise synchronization. In this article, we consider the asynchronous model to analyze the robustness of this algorithm.

3   BP-based Joint Iterative Detection and Decoding Algorithm

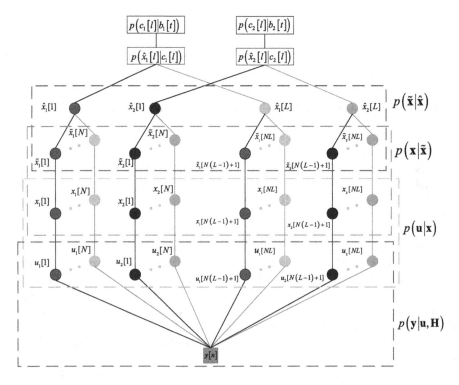

Fig. 2. The factor graph of the IDMA satellite system. For simplification, the number of users K = 2.

In this section, we apply a BP-based joint iterative detection and decoding algorithm in asynchronous IDMA systems. We express the joint probability distribution of information bits from all users as a factor graph, and derive the process of information transmission and update in the joint iterative algorithm.

3.1   The Factor Graph Representation of the IDMA System

In the IDMA system, we can decompose the joint probability distribution as

$$
\begin{aligned}
&p(\mathbf{y}, \mathbf{b}, \mathbf{c}, \hat{\mathbf{x}}, \tilde{\mathbf{x}}, \mathbf{x}, \mathbf{u} | \mathbf{H}) \\
&= p(\mathbf{b})p(\mathbf{y}, \mathbf{c}, \hat{\mathbf{x}}, \tilde{\mathbf{x}}, \mathbf{x}, \mathbf{u} | \mathbf{b}, \mathbf{H}) \\
&= p(\mathbf{b})p(\mathbf{c}|\mathbf{b})p(\hat{\mathbf{x}}|\mathbf{c})p(\tilde{\mathbf{x}}|\hat{\mathbf{x}})p(\mathbf{x}|\tilde{\mathbf{x}})p(\mathbf{u}|\mathbf{x})p(\mathbf{y}|\mathbf{u}, \mathbf{H}) \\
&\propto \prod_{1 \le k \le K} p\left(c_k[l] | b_k[t]\right) \prod_{1 \le k \le K} p\left(\hat{x}_k[l] | c_k[l]\right) \prod_{1 \le k \le K} p\left(\tilde{x}_k[n] | \hat{x}_k[l]\right) \\
&\quad \times \prod_{1 \le k \le K} p\left(x_k[n] | \tilde{x}_k[n]\right) \prod_{1 \le k \le K} p\left(x_k[n] | \tilde{x}_k[n]\right) p\left(u_k[n] | x_k[n]\right) \\
&\quad \times \prod_{1 \le n \le NL} p(y[n] | \mathbf{u}[n], \mathbf{H}[n]),
\end{aligned} \tag{2}
$$

where $\mathbf{H}[n] = [h_1[n], \ldots, h_k[n], \ldots, h_K[n]]^T (n = 1, \ldots, NL)$. The vector $\mathbf{y}$ represents the received symbols, $\mathbf{b}$ denotes the vector of the corresponding information bits $\{b_k[t]\}$ $(k = 1, 2, \ldots, K)$, $\mathbf{c}$ denotes the vector of the corresponding coded symbols $\{c_k[l]\}$ $(k = 1, 2, \ldots, K)$, $\hat{\mathbf{x}}$ denotes the vector of the modulated symbols $\{\hat{x}_k[l]\}$ $(k = 1, 2, \ldots, K)$ before spreading, $\tilde{x}_k[n]$ is obtained by only spreading the modulation symbols at the l-th interval $\hat{x}_k[l]$ by the spreading factor N respectively without multiplying spreading sequences, $\tilde{\mathbf{x}}$ is the vector composed of $\tilde{x}_k[n]$, $\mathbf{x}$ denotes the vector of the spread chip $x_k[n]$, $\mathbf{u}$ denotes the vector of the transmitted chip $u_k[n]$.

According to the factorization of the joint probability distribution as (2), we graphically express the received symbols, transmitted chips, spread chips, spreaded modulated symbols, modulated symbols, coded symbols and information bits by different kinds of nodes. The edges denote that these nodes are related. Therefore, we get the factor graph of the IDMA satellite system as shown in Fig. 2. For simplification, the factor graph with $K = 2$ users is given as an example. The nodes in the factor graph are explained as follow.

1. The top nodes $p\left(c_k[l] | b_k[t]\right), k = 1, \ldots, K$, represent the relation between $b_k[t]$ and $c_k[l]$.
2. The nodes on the second layer $p\left(\hat{x}_k[l] | c_k[l]\right)$, $k = 1, \ldots, K$, represent the relation between the $c_k[l]$ and $\hat{x}_k[l]$. We demap the modulated symbols to the coded symbols or reverse by performing the BP algorithm on these nodes.
3. The nodes on the third floor $p\left(\tilde{x}_k[n] | \hat{x}_k[l]\right)$, represent the relation between the modulated symbols $\hat{x}_k[l]$ and the spreaded modulated symbols $\tilde{x}_k[n]$. By producting every N chips' likelihood ratio on these nodes, we complete the accumulation of the despreading which is multiplied by spreading sequences. N is the spreading factor here. The reason is that the direct spread spectrum operation of modulated symbols in this article includes two processes: 1. Spreading (repeating) the coded symbol sequence according to the spreading factor; 2. Multiplying the spreading sequence. Therefore, in the despreading

process, we will not perform correlation calculations, but will transform it into the following two processes: 1. Multiplying the spreading sequence; 2. Performing accumulation.

4. The nodes in the middle $p\left(x_k[n]|\tilde{x}_k[n]\right)$, represent the relation between the spread chips $x_k[n]$ and the spreaded modulated symbols $\tilde{x}_k[n]$. We will consider the influence of spreading sequence on the information transmitted by these nodes.

5. The bottom-second nodes $p\left(u_k[n]|x_k[n]\right)$, represent the relation between the spread chips and the transmitted chips transmitted from each user. We will use interleavers that distinguish users to process the information transmitted on these nodes.

6. Finally, the bottom-most nodes represent $p(y[n]|\mathbf{u}[n],\mathbf{H}[n])$, the relation between the transmitted chips and the received symbols. The observation node $y[n]$ represent the observation function $g_{k,n}(\mathbf{u}[n])$,

$$g_{k,n}(\mathbf{u}[n]) = p\left(y[n]|u_1[n],\ldots,u_K[n]\right)$$

$$\propto \exp\left\{-\frac{\left|y[n] - \sum_{k=1}^{K} h_k[n]u_k[n]\right|^2}{\sigma^2}\right\}. \tag{3}$$

3.2 Message Passing of Joint Iterative Detection and Decoding Algorithm on the Factor Graph

According to the factor graph, the BP algorithm is adopted to realize the message transfer and update between the variable nodes and the observation nodes. This section will introduce the algorithm process in detail. It is necessary to apply the BP algorithm at the bottom-most nodes to compute $p(y[n]|\mathbf{u}[n],\mathbf{H}[n]), (1 \leq n \leq NL)$. This process is always called MUD. We use $\mu_{u_k[n]\to y[n]}^{t}\left(u_k[n]\right)$ to indicate that the message is transmitted from the variable node $u_k[n]$ to the observation node $y[n]$ at the t-th iteration. $\mu_{y[n]\to u_k[n]}^{t}\left(u_k[n]\right)$ indicates the message transmission in the opposite direction. Therefore, the message transmission process between $u_k[n]$ and $y[n]$ at the t-th iteration is

$$\mu_{u_k[n]\to y[n]}^{t}\left(u_k[n]\right) = \mu_{x_k[n]\to u_k[n]}^{t-1}\left(u_k[n]\right) \times \mu_{y[n]\to u_k[n]}^{t-1}\left(u_k[n]\right), \tag{4}$$

$$\mu_{y[n]\to u_k[n]}^{t}\left(u_k[n]\right) = \sum_{\sim\{u_k[n]\}} g_{k,n}(\mathbf{u}[n]) \prod_{p\in\mathcal{N}(y[n])\backslash k}$$
$$\times \mu_{u_p[n]\to y[n]}^{t-1}\left(u_p[n]\right), \tag{5}$$

where $\mu_{x_k[n]\to u_k[n]}^{t}\left(u_k[n]\right)$ is obtained by transforming the external probability density function (PDF) fedback from the decoder. Observing the calculation process of Eq. (4), the external information feedback from the decoder $\mu_{dec\to\hat{x}_k[l]}^{t}\left(\hat{x}_k[l]\right)$ and the information obtained from the previous iteration $\mu_{y[n]\to u_k[n]}^{t-1}\left(u_k[n]\right)$ are all included, and the traditional turbo iterative MUD algorithm only considers the external information fedback from the decoder. Therefore, the BP-based iterative detection algorithm proposed will be more accurate than the turbo iterative detection algorithm, and will have better BER performance.

Observing the formula (5), we find that the iterative update of information using the BP algorithm will lead to very high computational complexity, so it is infeasible to apply it directly to the IDMA system. In order to be able to perform belief-based iteration in the IDMA system more reasonably, we need to simplify formula (5). The appropriate application of the central limit theorem [65] in the BP algorithm enables the above calculation process to be effectively simplified. First, by minimizing the Kullback-Leibler (KL) divergence $KL\left[\mu_{u_k[n]\to y[n]}^t(u_k[n])\|\hat{\mu}_{u_k[n]\to y[n]}^t(u_k[n])\right]$, we can replace the non-Gaussian distribution PDF $\mu_{u_k[n]\to y[n]}^t$ with the Gaussian distribution PDF $\hat{\mu}_{u_k[n]\to y[n]}^t$ [14], expressed as:

$$
\begin{aligned}
\mu_{u_k[n]\to \mathbf{y}[n]}^t(u_k[n]) &\cong \hat{\mu}_{u_k[n]\to y[n]}^t(u_k[n]) \\
&= \mathcal{N}_c\left(u_k[n], \hat{m}_{u_k[n]\to y[n]}^t, \hat{v}_{u_k[n]\to y[n]}^t\right),
\end{aligned}
\tag{6}
$$

where $\hat{m}_{u_k[n]}$ and $\hat{v}_{u_k[n]}$ respectively represent the mean and variance of $\hat{\mu}_{u_k[n]\to y[n]}^t$, given as follows:

$$
\hat{m}_{u_k[n]\to y[n]}^t = \sum_{\alpha_k\in\{-1,1\}} \alpha_k \mu_{u_i[n]\to y[n]}^t(u_k[n]=\alpha_k),
\tag{7}
$$

$$
\hat{v}_{u_k[n]\to y[n]}^t = \sum_{\alpha_k\in\{-1,1\}} \left|\alpha_k - \hat{m}_{u_k[n]\to y[n]}^t\right|^2 \mu_{u_k[n]\to y[n]}^t(u_k[n]=\alpha_i).
\tag{8}
$$

Therefore, Eq. (5) can be approximated by some simple linear processes, the process is as follows:

$$
\begin{aligned}
\mu_{y[n]\to u_k[n]}^t(u_k[n]) &= \sum_{\sim\{u_k[n]\}} g_{k,n}(\mathbf{u}[n]) \prod_{p\in\mathcal{N}(y[n])\setminus k} \\
&\quad \times \mu_{u_p[n]\to y[n]}^{t-1}(u_p[n]) \\
&\cong \int_{\{u_k[n]\}} g_{k,n}(\mathbf{u}[n]) \prod_{p\neq k} \mathcal{N}_c\left(u_p[n], \hat{m}_{u_p[n]\to y[n]}^t, \hat{v}_{x_p[n]\to y[n]}^t\right) \\
&\propto \mathcal{N}_c\left(h_k[n]u_k[n], \mathrm{mean}_{y[n]\to u_k[n]}^t, \mathrm{var}_{y[n]\to u_k[n]}^t\right),
\end{aligned}
\tag{9}
$$

where $\mathrm{mean}_{y[n]\to u_k[n]}^t$ and $\mathrm{var}_{y[n]\to u_k[n]}^t$ respectively represent the mean and variance of $\mu_{y[n]\to u_k[n]}^t(u_k[n])$, given as follows:

$$
\mathrm{mean}_{y[n]\to u_k[n]}^t = y[n] - \sum_{p\neq k} h_p[n]\hat{m}_{u_p[n]\to y[n]}^t,
\tag{10}
$$

$$
\mathrm{var}_{y[n]\to u_k[n]}^t = \sum_{p\neq k} h_p[n]\hat{v}_{u_p[n]\to y[n]}^t h_p^*[n] + \sigma^2.
\tag{11}
$$

Traditionally, $\mathrm{mean}_{y[n]\to u_k[n]}^t$ and $\mathrm{var}_{y[n]\to u_k[n]}^t$ are computed by summation. Through observation, it is found that a node on the factor graph will receive different information transmitted from other nodes, and there is a certain correlation between these information. Therefore, we can first calculate the sum of messages including a certain node and all other nodes connected to the node, and then each message can be obtained from the sum by means of a subtraction or an addition corresponding to each node. Therefore, formula (7) and (8) can be simplified as

$$
\begin{aligned}
\text{mean}_{y[n]\to u_k[n]}^t &= y[n] - \sum_{p\neq k} h_p[n]\hat{m}_{u_p[n]\to y[n]}^t \\
&= \text{mean}_{y[n]}^t + h_k[n]\hat{m}_{u_k[n]\to y[n]}^t,
\end{aligned}
\tag{12}
$$

$$
\begin{aligned}
\text{var}_{y[n]\to u_k[n]}^t &= \sum_{p\neq k} h_p[n]\hat{v}_{u_p[n]\to y[n]}^t h_p^*[n] + \sigma^2 \\
&= \text{var}_{y[n]}^t - |h_k|^2 \hat{v}_{u_k[n]\to y[n]}^t,
\end{aligned}
\tag{13}
$$

where $\text{mean}_{y[n]}^t = y[n] - \sum_p h_p[n]\hat{m}_{u_p[n]\to y[n]}^t$, $\text{var}_{y[n]}^t = \sum_p h_p^2[n]\hat{v}_{u_p[n]\to y[n]}^t + \sigma^2$.

Therefore, formula (5) can be approximately expressed as

$$
\mu_{y[n]\to u_k[n]}^t (u_k[n]) \propto \exp\left(-\frac{\left|h_k u_k[n] - \text{mean}_{y[n]\to u_k[n]}^t\right|^2}{\text{var}_{y[n]\to u_k[n]}^t}\right).
\tag{14}
$$

The variable node $u_k[n]$ represents the transmission chip after passing through the interleaver of each user and the delay unit, and the node $x_k[n]$ represents the spreaded chip before interleaving. Therefore, the process of message transfer from node $u_k[n]$ to node $x_k[n]$ is expressed as

$$
\mu_{u_k[n]\to x_k[n]}^t (u_k[n]) = \pi_k^{-1}(\mu_{y[n]\to u_k[n]}^t (u_k[n])),
\tag{15}
$$

where $\pi_k^{-1}(\cdot)$ represents the de-interleaving operation using the interleaving pattern of the k-th user.

The process of message transfer from $x_k[n]$ to $\tilde{x}_k[n]$ requires the first step of despreading. It is expressed as

$$
\mu_{x_k[n]\to \tilde{x}_k[n]}^t (x_k[n]) =
\begin{cases}
\mu_{u_k[n]\to x_k[n]}^t (u_k[n]) & \text{if } s[m] = +1 \\
1 - \mu_{u_i[n]\to x_i[n]}^t (u_i[n]) & \text{else.}
\end{cases}
\tag{16}
$$

Further, the process of transferring information from $\tilde{x}_k[n]$ to $\hat{x}_k[l]$ is expressed as

$$
\mu_{\tilde{x}_k[n]\to \hat{x}_k[l]}^t (\tilde{x}_k[n]) = \mu_{x_k[n]\to \tilde{x}_k[n]}^t (x_k[n]).
\tag{17}
$$

After the information at the variable node $\hat{x}_k[l]$ is accumulated, the despreading operation is completed and sent to the decoder. The process is as follows:

$$
\mu_{\hat{x}_k[l]\to\text{dec}}^t (\hat{x}_k[l]) = \prod_{n=1+(l-1)N}^{N+(l-1)N} \mu_{\tilde{x}_k[n]\to \hat{x}_k[l]}^t (\tilde{x}_k[n]).
\tag{18}
$$

In actual algorithm operation, we usually convert $\mu_{\tilde{x}_k[n]\to \hat{x}_k[l]}^t (\tilde{x}_k[n])$ into Log-Likelihood Ratio (LLR), so formula (17) can be transformed into the

Algorithm 1. BP-based Joint Iterative Detection and Decoding Algorithm for the IDMA satellite communication system

---

1: **Initialization**

2: $t \leftarrow 1$, $\mu^t_{u_k[n] \to \mathbf{y}[n]}(u_k[n] = 1) \leftarrow 1/2$, $\mu^t_{u_k[n] \to \mathbf{y}[n]}(u_k[n] = -1) \leftarrow 1/2$, $\text{mean}^t_{\mathbf{y}[n] \to u_k[n]} \leftarrow 0$, $\text{var}^t_{\mathbf{y}[n] \to u_k[n]} \leftarrow 1, \forall k, \forall n$.

3: **Iterative Update of Messages**

4: **while** $t \leq MAXITER$ **do**

5:     **for** $n = 1 \to NL, k = 1 \to K$ **do**

6:        **if** $t > 1$ **then**

7:           $\mu^t_{u_k[n] \to \mathbf{y}[n]}(u_k[n]) \leftarrow \mu^{t-1}_{x_k[n] \to u_k[n]}(u_k[n]) \times \mu^{t-1}_{\mathbf{y}[n] \to u_k[n]}(u_k[n])$

8:        **end if**

9:        $\mu^t_{\mathbf{y}[n] \to u_k[n]}(u_k[n]) \leftarrow \exp\left(-\dfrac{\left|h_k u_k[n] - \text{mean}^t_{\mathbf{y}[n] \to u_k[n]}\right|^2}{\text{var}^t_{\mathbf{y}[n] \to u_k[n]}}\right)$

10:        $\mu^t_{u_k[n] \to x_k[n]}(u_k[n]) \leftarrow \pi_k^{-1}(\mu^t_{\mathbf{y}[n] \to u_k[n]}(u_k[n]))$

11:        $\mu^t_{x_k[n] \to \tilde{x}_k[n]}(x_k[n]) \leftarrow \begin{cases} \mu^t_{u_k[n] \to x_k[n]}(u_k|n]) & \text{if } s[m] = +1 \\ 1 - \mu^t_{u_k|n] \to x_k|n|}(u_k[n]) & \text{else} \end{cases}$

12:        $\mu^t_{\tilde{x}_k[n] \to \hat{x}_k[l]}(\tilde{x}_k[n]) \leftarrow \mu^t_{x_k[n] \to \tilde{x}_k[n]}(x_k[n])$

13:     **end for**

14:     **for** $k = 1 \to K, l = 1 \to L$ **do**

15:        $\mu^t_{\hat{x}_k[l] \to \text{dec}}(\hat{x}_k[l]) \leftarrow \prod_{n=1+(l-1)N}^{N+(l-1)N} \mu^t_{\tilde{x}_k[n] \to \hat{x}_k[l]}(\tilde{x}_k[n])$

16:        $\mathcal{L}^t(c_k[l]) \leftarrow \log \dfrac{\sum_{\chi_k^1} \mu^t_{\hat{x}_k[l] \to \text{dec}}(\hat{x}_k[l])}{\sum_{\chi_k^0} \mu^t_{\hat{x}_k[l] \to \text{dec}}(\hat{x}_k[l])}$

17:        Decoding the encoded bits of the k-th user, and the decoder outputs the external information $\mu^t_{\text{dec} \to \hat{x}_k[l]}(\hat{x}_k[l])$

18:        $\mu^t_{\hat{x}_k[l] \to \tilde{x}_k[n]}(\hat{x}_k[l]) \leftarrow Rep(\mu^t_{\text{dec} \to \hat{x}_k[l]}(\hat{x}_k[l]))_N$

19:     **end for**

20:     **for** $n = 1 \to NL, k = 1 \to K$ **do**

21:        $\mu^t_{\tilde{x}_k[n] \to x_k[n]}(\tilde{x}_k[n]) \leftarrow \begin{cases} \mu^t_{\hat{x}_k[l] \to \tilde{x}_k[n]}(\hat{x}_k[l]) & \text{if } s[m] = +1 \\ 1 - \mu^t_{\hat{x}_k[l] \to \tilde{x}_k[n]}(\hat{x}_k[l]) & \text{else} \end{cases}$

22:        $\mu^t_{x_k[n] \to u_k[n]}(x_k[n]) \leftarrow \pi_k(\mu^t_{\tilde{x}_k[n] \to x_k[n]}(x_k[n]))$

23:     **end for**

24:     $t \leftarrow t + 1$

25: **end while**

---

sum operation. In order to facilitate the decoding, we need to convert $\mu^t_{\hat{x}_k[l] \to \text{dec}}(\tilde{x}_k[n])$ into the LLR of the encoding symbol related to the modulation symbol $\hat{x}_k[l]$ as the prior information of the decoder, expressed as

$$\mathcal{L}^t(c_k[l]) = \log \frac{\sum_{\chi_k^1} \mu^t_{\hat{x}_k[l] \to \text{dec}}(\hat{x}_k[l])}{\sum_{\chi_k^0} \mu^t_{\hat{x}_k[l] \to \text{dec}}(\hat{x}_k[l])}, \tag{19}$$

where χ_k^1 and χ_k^0 are subsets of modulated symbols. χ_k^1 indicates that the information bit corresponding to each symbol is 1, and χ_k^0 indicates that the information bit corresponding to each symbol is 0.

The external information $\mu^t_{\text{dec}\to\hat{x}_k[l]}(\hat{x}_k[l])$ output from the decoder is spreaded (repeated) to obtain the information from $\hat{x}_k[l]$ to $\tilde{x}_k[n]$, which is expressed as

$$\mu^t_{\hat{x}_k[l]\to\tilde{x}_k[n]}(\hat{x}_k[l]) = Rep(\mu^t_{\text{dec}\to\hat{x}_k[l]}(\hat{x}_k[l]))_N, \qquad (20)$$

where N is the spreading factor, and $Rep(a)_N$ means that the element "a" is repeated N times. Considering the influence of multiplying this information by the spreading sequence, the information from $\tilde{x}_k[n]$ to the variable node $x_k[n]$ is obtained, which is expressed as:

$$\mu^t_{\tilde{x}_k[n]\to x_k[n]}(\tilde{x}_k[n]) = \begin{cases} \mu^t_{\hat{x}_k[l]\to\tilde{x}_k[n]}(\hat{x}_k[l]) & \text{if } s[m] = +1 \\ 1 - \mu^t_{\hat{x}_k[l]\to\tilde{x}_k[n]}(\hat{x}_k[l]) & \text{else.} \end{cases} \qquad (21)$$

The information obtained by formula (21) is interleaved to obtain the information transmitted from $x_k[n]$ to $u_k[n]$ as follows:

$$\mu^t_{x_k[n]\to u_k[n]}(x_k[n]) = \pi_k(\mu^t_{\tilde{x}_k[n]\to x_k[n]}(x_k[n])), \qquad (22)$$

where $\pi_k(\cdot)$ represents the interleaving operation using the interleaving pattern of the k-th user. In summary, the algorithm is given as Algorithm 1.

In the traditional Turbo iterative detection and decoding algorithm, the multi-user detection and decoder form an independent, nested iterative structure. The difference is that in order to make more effective use of the iterative structure of decoding, we unify the iterative process of the decoder and detector based on the BP algorithm to form a joint global iterative structure and optimize the overall iterative structure of the algorithm.

4   Complexity Analysis

Figure 3 shows the different iterative structure diagram of 2 kinds of algorithms. In this paper, we organically unite the iterative process of the decoder and the iterative process of the MUD based on the BP algorithm to form a global iterative structure, and update the soft information of the decoder and MUD at the same time during each global iteration. The schematic diagram of the iterative process is shown in Fig. 3(a). In the turbo detection and decoding algorithm, the iterative process of the decoder is nested in the MUD iterative process independently, that is, the external information required for each iteration of the MUD is fed back by the decoder after Q iterations, its iterative structure is shown in Fig. 3(b). In the IDMA system, the traditional turbo iterative detection and decoding structure consists of an ESE mould and K decoders.

For the fairness of the algorithm complexity comparison, we ensure that the total number of iterations experienced by the LDPC decoder in the two types of algorithms is same, that is, assuming that the global iteration number of the joint iterative algorithm is U, the iteration number of ESE in the turbo iteration structure is P, satisfies $U = P \times Q$. Furthermore, we compare the complexity of the iterative process of the LDPC decoder and the iterative process of the MUD.

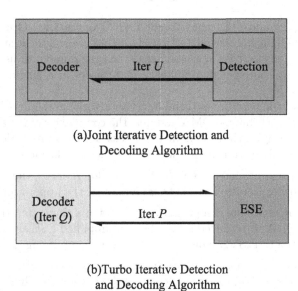

(a)Joint Iterative Detection and
Decoding Algorithm

(b)Turbo Iterative Detection
and Decoding Algorithm

Fig. 3. The iterative structure and complexity comparison.

4.1 Complexity Comparison of LDPC Decoder

In this BP-based joint iterative algorithm, LDPC decoding and MUD form an integral iterative process to run together. However, in the Turbo iterative detection and decoding algorithm, the LDPC decoder operates independently. For the above two types of algorithms, a single user's single LDPC decoding iteration performs the same operation, that is, obtains the external information of a certain information bit and converts it to the LLR output. For the principle of fairness of comparison, the iteration times of the two types of algorithms are made to satisfy $U = P \times Q$ to ensure that the total iteration times of the LDPC decoder are equal. At this time, the computational complexity of the LDPC decoders in the two types of algorithms are equal.

4.2 Complexity Comparison of Iterative MUD

In asynchronous IDMA satellite systems, we compare the complexity of the MUD in Algorithm 1 with a classical detection algorithm in Section IV of [15] which is equivalent to the sGCD algorithm in Section III.C of [7], and simplified ESE algorithms proposed in [6].

In the iterative process, the BP-based iterative detection algorithm uses the factor graph structure to iteratively update the message for each node. It does not require a large number of matrix operations but is composed of simple linear calculations, so its computational complexity is not subject to the system delay in asynchronous systems. At nodes $y[n]$, for K users, the calculations of (14) per chip per iteration include the computation of $\text{mean}^{t}_{y[n] \rightarrow u_k[n]}$ and $\text{var}^{t}_{y[n] \rightarrow u_k[n]}$

expressed by (12) and (13) which needs $O(K^2)$ operations. Other calculation processes in the joint iterative detection algorithm are simple addition or multiplication operations that are not associated with the number of users K. Therefore, the total computational complexity of K users in a single iteration of a single chip is $O(K^2)$.

The MUD of the traditional turbo iterative algorithm requires lots of matrix operations. In asynchronous IDMA systems, the complexity of the algorithm will increase significantly as the system delay increases. The computational complexity of the sGCD algorithm mainly focuses on the calculation of $\sigma^2_{\zeta_k^{(\ell)}[j]}$ in [15]. Since the dimension of matrix $\boldsymbol{H}$ is $K(2D_c - 1)$, for K users, the calculations of $\sigma^2_{\zeta_k^{(\ell)}[j]}$ per chip per iteration needs $O(K(K(2D_c - 1))^2)$ operations. Therefore, the sGCD's computational complexity of K users in a single iteration of a single chip is $O(K^3 D_c^2)$. As introduced in [6], the two simplified ESE algorithms named ESE.SV1 and the ESE.SV2, which are obtained by simplifying the $\sigma^2_{\zeta_k^{(\ell)}[j]}$ in the sGCD algorithm to a constant. Therefore, the computational complexity of K users in a single iteration of a single chip will be reduced to $O(K^2 D_c^2)$.

Compared with traditional turbo iterative algorithm, the BP-based joint iterative detection and decoding algorithm achieves a significant reduction in computational complexity, and this method avoids complex matrix operations, so its computational complexity will not be affected by the asynchronous delay of the system. It is foreseeable that as the number of users and the asynchronous delay of the system increases, this method will have greater gains in reducing complexity and be more conducive to system implementation.

5   Simulation Results

In our simulations, the number of users $K = 4$, the length of the information bit $T = 1024$ and the spreading factor is $N = 4$. The spreading sequences are derived from [16]. We set the code rate $R_c = 1/4$. BPSK modulation is considered in the our simulation. We assume that user delay can be acquired. We also suppose a perfect power control. The following simulations are achieved in asynchronous IDMA systems.

Without loss of generality, we perform simulations in the GEO satellite system with the TA and without the TA. We set the data transfer rate to 4kbps. Firstly, We accomplished the simulations with the TA in IDMA satellite systems, and the user's chip delays are set as $\tau_k = k - 1$, and Fig. 4 shows the results. Further, we do not perform time synchronization based on the TA mechanism in the system, and the maximum user chip delay of the system is $\tau_k = 168$. The results are shown in the Fig. 5. In the process of comparing algorithm performance, it is usually ensured that the total number of iterations of different algorithms is same to ensure the fairness of the comparison. This means $U = P \times Q$. In the case that the algorithms all meet the convergence, we set $U = 50$, $p = 5$ and the number of iterations of the LDPC decoder $Q = 10$ which is not less than the number of iterations required for LDPC decoding to reach convergence [17].

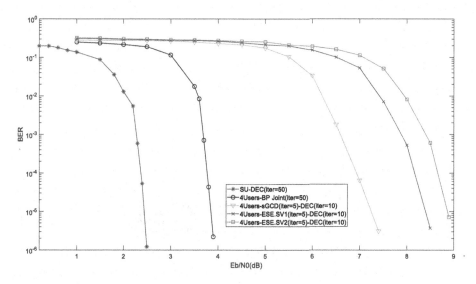

Fig. 4. Performance comparison of the BP-based joint iterative algorithm and turbo iterative detection and decoding algorithms. With TA.

In Fig. 4, the leftmost curve is he performance of the single-user case (SU-DEC(iter = 50)). After 50 iterations, the performance of the BP-based joint iterative algorithm is about 1.4 dB away from that of the SU-DEC. However, at a given BER level of 10^{-6}, the performance of the BP-based joint iterative algorithm outperforms that of the sGCD, ESE.SV1 and ESE.SV2 by 3.5 dB, 4.5 dB and 5 dB respectively. This is due to the MUD of the traditional turbo iterative algorithm only uses the external information fed back by the current iterative decoder to update the LLR, and the external information contained in the received symbol in the previous iteration is lost, resulting in BER performance loss.

Figure 5 shows that the BP-based joint iterative algorithm can save about 4.5 dB, 4.9 dB and 5.4 dB than the sGCD, ESE.SV1 and ESE.SV2 at a given BER level of 10^{-6} with user delay chips get much larger. Comparing the results in Fig. 4, it is obvious that as the asynchronous delay increases, the performance loss of the BP-based joint iterative algorithm is about 0.2 dB, but the performance loss of turbo iterative algorithms exceeds 0.5 dB. The reason is that the information of the previous iteration used by the MUD of the BP-based joint iterative algorithm is the channel information containing the delay information, which reduces the sensitivity of this method to the asynchronous delay.

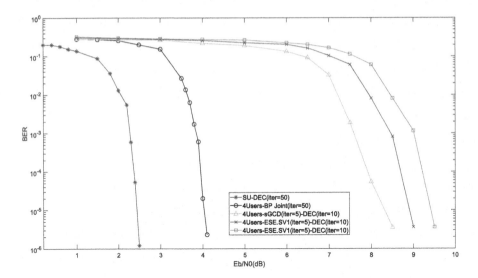

Fig. 5. Performance comparison of the BP-based joint iterative algorithm and turbo iterative detection and decoding algorithms. Without TA.

6 Conclusion

In this paper, we adopt the BP-based joint iterative detection and decoding algorithm in the asynchronous IDMA satellite communication system. This method solves the problem that the computational complexity increases with the asynchronous delay in the traditional turbo method and reduces performance loss. This algorithm breaks the independent iterative structure of the detector and the decoder and forms a global iteration.

On this basis, we established the probability distribution factor diagram of the IDMA satellite communication system, derived the probabilistic message update process using the BP algorithm and simplified it by using the central limit theorem. This algorithm improves the update accuracy of iterative probability information and eliminates the matrix operation in the turbo iterative detection and decoding algorithm, which greatly reduces the computational complexity and makes it immune to system delay. Finally, the simulation results verify that the BP-based joint iterative algorithm has good gains in reducing complexity and improving BER performance in asynchronous IDMA satellite systems.

References

1. Ping, L., Wu, K., Liu, L., Leung, W.: A simple, unified approach to nearly optimal multiuser detection and space-time coding. In: ITW02, Inde (2002)
2. Wang, H., Liu, G.L., Ge, X., Mao, X.P.: Performance evaluation and capacity analysis for IDMA-based satellite communication system. In: 2011 6th International ICST Conference on Communications and Networking in China (CHINACOM), Harbin, pp. 604–608 (2011)

3. Ge, X., Liu, G.L., Zhang, N.: A novel MAC protocol for IDMA-based multi-beam satellite communication systems. Int. J. Commun. Syst. **27**(12), 4038–4058 (2014)
4. Ping, L., Liu, L., Leung, W.: A simple approach to near-optimal multiuser detection: interleave-division multiple-access, vol. 1, pp. 391–396 (2003)
5. Liu, L., Ping, L.: Iterative detection of chip interleaved CDMA systems in multipath channels. Electron. Lett. **40**(14), 884–886 (2004)
6. Mahafeno, I., Langlais, C., Jego, C.: Cth12-4: reduced complexity iterative multiuser detector for IDMA (interleave-division multiple access) system. In: Proceedings IEEE GLOBECOM 2006, pp. 1–5 (2006)
7. Cristea, B., Roviras, D., Escrig, B.: Turbo receivers for interleave-division multiple-access systems. IEEE Trans. Commun. **57**(7), 2090–2097 (2009)
8. Kim, H., Kang, K., Ann, D.S.: Uplink timing synchronization for OFDMA based mobile satellite communications, pp. 831–831 (2009)
9. Kim, H., Hong, T.C., Kang, K., Ku, B.J., Kim, S., Yeo, S.: A satellite radio interface for IMT-Advanced system using OFDM. In: 2010 International Conference On Information and Communication Technology Convergence (ICTC), pp. 303–308 (2010)
10. Guo, Q., Ping, L.: LMMSE turbo equalization based on factor graphs. IEEE Sel. Areas Commun. **26**(2), 311–319 (2008)
11. Gu, N., Wu, S., Kuang, L., Ni, Z., Lu, J.: Belief propagation-based joint iterative algorithm for detection and decoding in asynchronous CDMA satellite systems. EURASIP J. Wirel. Commun. Netw. **2013**, 234 (2013)
12. Pei, Y., Liu, C., Feng, H., Shi, Y.: An LDPC-based physical layer solution in satellite interactive system, pp. 425–430 (2011)
13. Weerackody, V., Gonzalez, L.: Performance of satellite communications on the move systems in the presence of antenna pointing errors. In: IEEE Military Communications Conference, 2006, Washington, DC, October 2006, pp. 1–7. IEEE (2006)
14. Bishop, C.: Pattern Recognition and Machine Learning. Springer, New York (2006)
15. Kusume, K., Bauch, G., CDMA and IDMA: iterative multiuser detections for near-far asynchronous communications. In: IEEE 16th International Symposium on Personal, Indoor and Mobile Radio Communications, Berlin, vol. 2005, pp. 426–431 (2005)
16. Ping, L., Liu, L., Wu, K., Wk, L.: Interleave-division multiple-access. IEEE Trans. Wirel. Commun. **5**, 2869–2873 (2004)
17. Chen, J., Dholakia, A., Eleftheriou, E., Fossorier, M., Hu, X.Y.: Reduced-complexity decoding of LDPC codes. Commun. IEEE Trans. **53**(8), 1288–1299 (2005)

Communications

Modulation Pattern Recognition Based on Wavelet Approximate Coefficient Entropy

Xiaoya Zuo[1(✉)], Donghuan Xu[2], Peng Wang[1], Rugui Yao[1],
Junjie Yang[1], and Lulu Pan[3]

[1] School of Electronics and Information, Northwestern Polytechnical University,
Xi'an 710072, China
zuoxy@nwpu.edu.cn
[2] Shanghai Aerospace Control Technology Institute, Shanghai 201109, China
[3] School of Mathematics and Statistics, Northwestern Polytechnical University,
Xi'an 710072, China

Abstract. Aiming at the modulation pattern recognition of multiple signals in complex electromagnetic environments, a modulation pattern recognition method based on wavelet approximate coefficient entropy is proposed. Based on the traditional wavelet entropy, an improved wavelet entropy, wavelet approximate coefficient entropy, is proposed, which has strong ability to represent the modulation signal characteristics and has good noise suppression effect. The simulation results verify the correctness of the theoretical analysis, and show that the proposed method can effectively realize the modulation pattern recognition of multiple signals at low signal to noise ratio.

Keywords: Modulation pattern recognition · Wavelet approximate coefficient entropy · Signal to noise ratio · Recognition rate

1 Introduction

How to acquire and master the parameters of the complex electromagnetic environment in time is an important and challenging problem in information warfare. In reference [1], J. Mitola proposed the cognitive radio technology, which uses the learning ability of cognitive radio to autonomously sense the surrounding spectrum environment and respond to the actual electromagnetic situation in real time. In electronic counter-measures, the modulation recognition technology is applied to the spectrum sensing of receiver equipment, which can provide more necessary information for battlefield command and decision-making. For example, after intercepting the enemy's information, the first thing is to identify, demodulate and decrypt the enemy's signal, so as to obtain the enemy's confidential intelligence. At the same time, after the enemy's modulation system is proved, the effective communication can be purposefully interfered and the battlefield initiative can be obtained. Wavelet analysis is a local transform of time and frequency, which can effectively extract feature information from the signal, and is conducive to the perception of the surrounding electromagnetic environment. Many cognitive radio technologies are devoted to modulation recognition of communication signals by using cyclic spectrum [2], characteristic parameters and their

B. Li et al. (Eds.): IoTaaS 2020, LNICST 346, pp. 673–684, 2021.
https://doi.org/10.1007/978-3-030-67514-1_53

statistics [3, 4], time-frequency transform [5] and high-order cumulants [6]. These methods are difficult to achieve multi-resolution analysis of modulated signals, which increases the difficulty of obtaining effective information, and the real-time performance of signal analysis and processing is not good. In order to quickly and accurately grasp the current radio spectrum situation, wavelet analysis is applied to the modulation recognition of communication signals. In reference [7], the wavelet coefficients of speech signals after discrete wavelet analysis are used to realize effective recognition of Arabic speech numbers. In reference [8], a recognition algorithm based on wavelet variation coefficient difference and similarity feature is proposed to classify and recognize common digital modulation signals. In reference [9], continuous wavelet transforms (CWT) and multi-layer wavelet decomposition (MLWD) are used to extract the features of signals, and different classification features are adopted for different modulated signals. The algorithm does not need symbol period estimation and synchronization time estimation, which improves the operation speed and recognition rate of modulation signal recognition.

In order to improve the performance of modulation recognition at low signal-to-noise ratio, a modulation pattern recognition method based on wavelet approximate coefficient entropy (WACE) is proposed in this paper. Different from the traditional method, it can effectively extract the relevant features of the signal in the complex electromagnetic environment where the signal-to-noise ratio is low and the accurate modulation parameters are not easy to obtain, so as to realize the modulation pattern recognition of multiple signals.

The following contents are arranged as follows. In Sect. 1, the system model of modulation recognition is given. In the second section, the theory of wavelet analysis is introduced. In Sect. 3, the mathematical definition of WACE is given, and the entropy vector of wavelet approximate coefficient of each communication signal is calculated. In Sect. 4, the simulation analysis of the modulation recognition algorithm proposed in this paper through experiments shows that the algorithm is effective for modulation type recognition, and its performance in noise environment is analyzed. Finally, the conclusions are given.

2 System Model

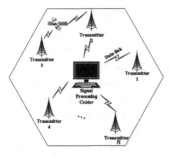

Fig. 1. Model of communication signal modulation recognition system.

In this section, a complete communication signal modulation recognition system model will be established to simulate the communication situation in complex electromagnetic environment, and six representative and widely used communication signal modulation methods will be considered.

Figure 1 shows the communication signal modulation recognition system model, including an integrated signal processing center and n potential modulated signal transmitters. In modern electronic warfare, the signal processing center is the core of the whole combat system. It is responsible for receiving and processing signals of various modulation types from all directions, including our communication signals and the enemy communication signals. At the same time, there are also jamming signals that the enemy intentionally transmits. Whether it is to accurately obtain the information transmitted by our side, or to intercept the enemy signal to obtain intelligence, or to interfere with the effective communication of the enemy, it is inseparable from the modulation recognition technology. In order to better reflect the diversity of communication signal modulation methods in complex electromagnetic environment, six typical modulation methods are selected in this paper, which are Frequency Shift Keying (FSK), Minimum Shift Keying (MSK), Quadrature Phase Shift Keying (QPSK) and 16 Quadrature Amplitude Modulation (16QAM), Offset-QPSK (OQPSK) and Binary Phase Shift Keying (BPSK).

3 Wavelet Theory

Wavelet analysis is a time-frequency analysis method. For any function $f(t) \in L^2(R)$, the continuous wavelet transform is as follows:

$$W_f(a,b) = <f, \psi_{a,b}>$$
$$= |a|^{-1/2} \int_R f(t) \overline{\psi\left(\frac{t-b}{a}\right)} \, dt \tag{1}$$

Where a is the scale factor, b is the shift factor, $a, b \in R$; $a \neq 0$, $\psi_{a,b}$ is the wavelet sequence of basic wavelet $\psi(t)$ after stretching and translation.

In practical application, continuous wavelet must be discretized. Discrete wavelet transform discretizes continuous parameters a, b into m, n. The basic wavelet functions of discrete wavelet transform are as follows:

$$\psi_{m,n}(t) = 2^{-\frac{m}{2}} \psi(2^{-m}t - n) \tag{2}$$

The discrete wavelet transform of any function $f(t)$ is:

$$WT_f(m,n) = \int_R f(t) \cdot \overline{\psi_{m,n}(t)} \, dt \tag{3}$$

After the discrete wavelet transform of the signal $s(n)$, under the j-th decomposition scale, the coefficient of high-frequency component at k-time is $cD_j(k)$, and the coefficient of low frequency component is $cA_j(k)$. The signal components obtained by single reconstruction are $D_j(k)$, $A_j(k)$. The original signal $s(n)$ can be expressed as the sum of the components [10].

$$
\begin{aligned}
s(n) &= D_1(n) + A_1(n) \\
&= D_1(n) + D_2(n) + A_2(n) \\
&= \cdots = \sum_{j=1}^{m} D_j(n) + A_m(n)
\end{aligned}
\tag{4}
$$

In most application scenarios, discrete wavelet transform with multiple scales can reflect the time-frequency distribution of signals. The limit case may be considered. If all the low-frequency components are taken and the high-frequency components are discarded, the anti-noise performance will be greatly improved. However, some key information of the signal will be lost. This paper makes up for this problem by two means. On the one hand, if the original signal is added to the multi-resolution analysis of the modulated signal to form the wavelet domain features together with other scale analysis results, no information of the original signal will be lost. On the other hand, if the appropriate wavelet function is selected to make the energy of each scale more concentrated on the low-frequency components, the denoising effect is better.

dbN wavelet (N denotes the order of wavelet function) is a wavelet function constructed by I. Daubechies, a famous scholar of wavelet analysis in the world. It performs well in the field of signal denoising. Therefore, this paper adopts the wavelet, in which the selection of order n is considered in the following two aspects. Firstly, the N in dbN wavelet corresponds to the vanishing moment of wavelet function. The larger the vanishing moment, the smaller the high frequency coefficient, the more concentrated the signal energy, and the better the noise removal effect. Secondly, with the increase of vanishing moment N, too much noise will be concentrated in the low frequency components, which will affect the denoising effect. At the same time, the support length of wavelet function will be lengthened and the computational complexity will be increased obviously. In this paper, db5 wavelet function is selected to concentrate the signal energy to obtain the best denoising effect.

4   Modulation Recognition Technology Based on Wavelet Approximate Coefficient Entropy

In this section, we mainly analyze two kinds of traditional wavelet entropy, which are wavelet energy entropy (WEE) and adaptive wavelet entropy (AWE).

Combining multi-resolution wavelet transform with information entropy, the definition and calculation method of wavelet energy entropy of signal can be obtained [10].

Suppose that any digital signal $s(n)$ with n sampling points is decomposed on M scales, and on a given decomposition scale m, the wavelet coefficient vector is $\mathbf{A}_m = (a_{m,1}, a_{m,2}, \ldots, a_{m,n})$, $m = 1, 2, \ldots, M$. The wavelet coefficient vectors $\mathbf{A}_1, \mathbf{A}_2, \ldots, \mathbf{A}_M$ of each decomposition scale can form a vector sequence $\{\mathbf{A}\}$. The vector norm of wavelet coefficients is used to describe the closeness of wavelet coefficients at different scales and the energy on scale m can be defined as $E_m = ||\mathbf{A}_m||^2 = \sum_{i=1}^{n} |a_{m_i}|^2$. The

normalized energy $p_m = E_m \bigg/ \sum_{j=1}^{M} E_j$ of each scale wavelet coefficient is taken as the

distribution of energy sequence instead of the probability distribution of signal. Thus, the entropy obtained based on energy distribution is called WEE, which is defined as

$H_{we} = H(p_1, p_2, \ldots, p_M) = \sum_{j=1}^{M} p_j \log_2 p_j$.

The concept of AWE is based on information entropy. In reference [11], the definition of AWE is given by combining the theory of information entropy with discrete wavelet transform.

$$E(S) = \frac{\sum_m |S_m|^P}{N} \tag{5}$$

Among them, the AWE E is a real number. S is the signal after the original signal $s(n)$ is decomposed by discrete wavelet. P is an exponential weight, and its value range is $1 \leq P < 2$. S_m is the m-layer signal of the original signal after discrete wavelet transform and N is the length of S_m.

The two kinds of wavelet entropy mentioned above, including WEE and AWE, have achieved good results in their respective fields. However, if it is used in cognitive radio modulation recognition, especially when the signal-to-noise ratio (SNR) of the modulation signal to be recognized is low, the two kinds of wavelet entropy are difficult to achieve good recognition results. For example, in reference [12], the AWE is used for multi signal modulation recognition. When combined with BP neural network, the average recognition rate is about 95%. However, when the SNR is low, the recognition performance of this method for some modulated signals will decline rapidly.

Based on this, a new improved wavelet entropy, WACE, is proposed in this paper. It is the entropy value calculated from all wavelet approximate coefficients of the signal, and the wavelet approximate coefficient vector can be expressed as

$$W_m = (w_{m,1}, w_{m,2}, \ldots, w_{m,n}) \tag{6}$$

Where, the subscript m represents the decomposition scale parameter, and its value range is $1, 2, \ldots M$. Vector element $w_{m,i}(i = 1, 2, \ldots, n)$ is wavelet approximation coefficient. If the original signal is regarded as W_0, then a new vector sequence $\{W\}$ can be formed from $W_0, W_1, W_2, \ldots, W_M$. Each subsequence in the sequence $\{W\}$ is weighted by 2-norm, and the exponential term in the 2-norm is treated as the weight, and the weighted 2-norm of each scale wavelet approximation coefficient vector is calculated as

$$||W_m|| = \sqrt{\left(\sum_{i=1}^{n} |w_{m,i}|^\gamma \right)} \tag{7}$$

Where, γ is the index weight item. After this step, the vector sequences $\{W\}$ of wavelet approximation coefficients in different scales are transformed into 2-norm weighted sequences $\{\|W\|\}$. After 2-norm weighting, the original signal is added to the vector sequence to ensure that the information of the original signal is not lost in the feature extraction of wavelet domain.

Assuming that the signal is decomposed on M scales, the approximate coefficient vector of wavelet on scale m is $W_m = (w_{m,1}, w_{m,2}, \ldots, w_{m,n})$. The energy on scale m is defined as

$$E_m = \|varvec W_m\|^2 = \sum_{i=1}^{n} |w_{m,i}|^{\gamma}, \ m = 0, 1, \ldots, M \tag{8}$$

In order to increase the number of wavelet entropy features of the signal to be identified, the WACE is given by the following expression according to the concept of AWE.

$$E_m = \frac{E_m}{L_m} = \frac{\|\mathbf{W}_m\|^2}{L_m} = \frac{\sum_{i=1}^{n} |w_{m,i}|^{\gamma}}{L_m} \tag{9}$$

$$\gamma_{approx} = \left(\gamma_{0-approx}, \gamma_{1-approx}, \ldots, \gamma_{M-approx}\right)^{\mathrm{T}} \tag{10}$$

Where E_m represents the entropy of wavelet approximation coefficients at the m-th level of discrete wavelet decomposition, L_m is the length of the m-th wavelet approximation coefficient, and γ_{approx} is the exponential weight vector. In this way, the meaning of WACE is the average energy of wavelet approximate coefficient per length of signal in a certain scale, or the average energy of wavelet approximate coefficient of digital signal at each sampling point. Because this improved wavelet entropy represents the average energy of each wavelet approximate coefficient length in any signal, and reflects the uncertainty of signal at different decomposition scales, so it is called WACE.

For different signals, the WACE at a certain scale can reflect the characteristics of the signal at that scale. When a signal is decomposed in M-level by discrete wavelet transform, the entropy of M + 1 wavelet approximate coefficients can be calculated according to formula (11), in which the approximate coefficient entropy of each layer represents certain wavelet domain characteristics of the signal. In order to make them represent the signal together, the entropy vector is composed of the approximate coefficient entropy of wavelet in each layer and is expressed as

$$E_{approx} = (E_{0-approx}, E_{1-approx}, \ldots, E_{M-approx})^{\mathrm{T}} \tag{11}$$

Where E_{approx} is the entropy column vector of wavelet approximate coefficient when the decomposition scale is M.

Compared with WEE and AWE, WACE has many advantages in modulation recognition. On the one hand, by discarding the high-frequency coefficients after discrete wavelet decomposition and using db5 wavelet with larger vanishing moment, the extracted WACE vector has stronger anti-noise ability; on the other hand, by selecting different weight vectors γ_{approx}, the proportion of low-frequency components is increased, and the high-frequency noise interference is suppressed. Under the same noise environment, the computational complexity can be reduced and the recognition speed can be faster.

In this paper, the unit column vector whose weight vector matrix is 1.5 times is selected. On the one hand, after adding the index term of 1.5, the residual noise in low-frequency coefficients of each scale can be further weakened, and the key information which is conducive to feature extraction can be amplified. On the other hand, if the exponential weight changes in the same direction with the number of decomposition levels, the key information in the lower scale coefficients will be obliterated and the feature extraction of modulation signal will be disturbed, which will lead to the decrease of recognition rate or recognition speed. Otherwise, if the exponential weight vector changes in the opposite direction with the number of decomposition levels, part of the noise in the small-scale coefficients will be amplified, so that the useful features of the modulated signal may not be extracted, which will also lead to the decrease of recognition rate. Of course, according to the different problems to be solved, different exponential weights can be applied to make the WACE achieve better analysis and processing effect, that is, the improved wavelet entropy has good portability in other fields.

5   Simulation Results and Analysis

In this section, six kinds of modulation signals are simulated by using the model proposed in this paper, and the modulation recognition conditions under different SNR are compared. The performance comparison with other literature schemes is carried out to prove the effectiveness of the proposed method.

For AWE, because it is a function of signal, its average value is used as the characteristic parameter of signal recognition; for WEE, the wavelet energy entropy of signal is directly used as the feature parameter of signal recognition; for WACE, each element in entropy vector is used for linear weighting to obtain the characteristic parameter of signal recognition (Table 1).

Table 1. Simulation parameters

Sampling rate	10 MHz	Chip rate	0.5 MHz
Carrier frequency	0–6 MHz	Noise	AWGN
SNR	−5–10 dB	Wavelet basis	db5
Wavelet decomposition level	5	Number of tests	100

It can be seen from Fig. 2 that in the ideal environment without noise, the three kinds of wavelet entropy can distinguish six kinds of modulation signals, and the recognition is completely correct. However, with the decrease of SNR, the recognition performance of AWE and WEE method for six kinds of modulation signals decreases

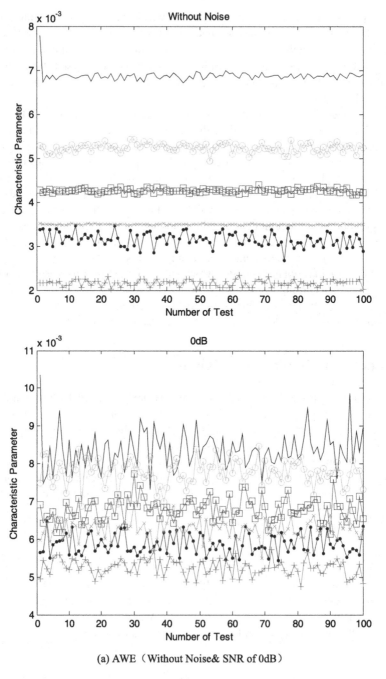

(a) AWE（Without Noise& SNR of 0dB）

Fig. 2. Comparison of characteristic parameters of different wavelet entropy for different modulated signals.

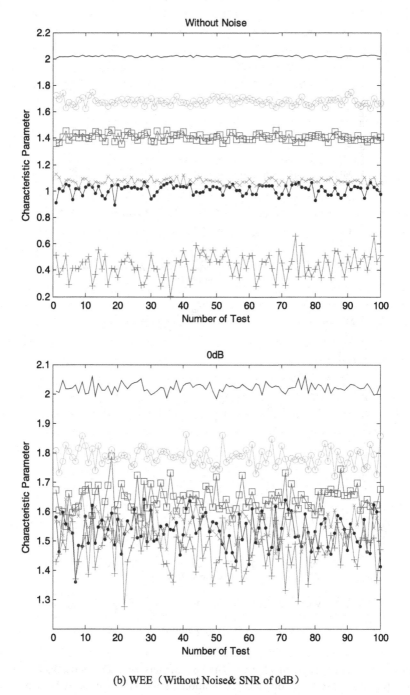

(b) WEE（Without Noise& SNR of 0dB）

Fig. 2. *(continued)*

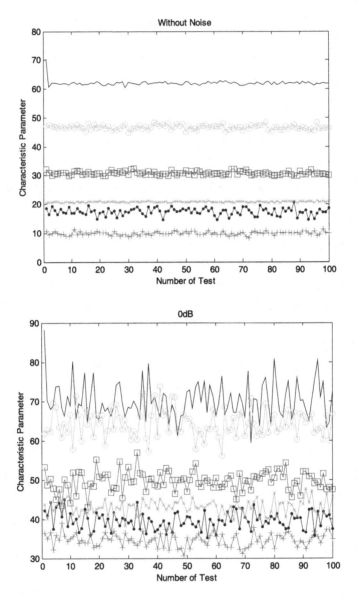

(c) WACE（Without Noise& SNR of 0dB）   Linear weight:[8,16,32,16,8,4]

Fig. 2. (*continued*)

obviously, and the range of characteristic parameters of each signal has significant cross aliasing. In comparison, the recognition performance of WACE is not much reduced. With SNR of 0dB, the probability of correct recognition of all six signals is still above 70%, which is much higher than the other two wavelet entropy recognition methods.

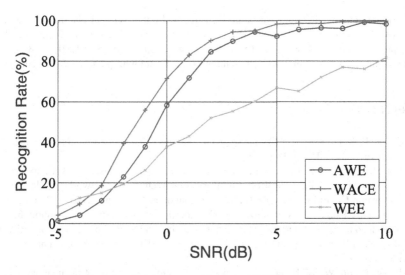

Fig. 3. Comparison curve of recognition rate of different wavelet entropy.

According to the decision tree, the modulation signals are identified in Fig. 3. The recognition rate of the three wavelet entropy methods is very high under high SNR, so we mainly consider the recognition under the condition of low SNR. It can be seen from the figure that compared with AWE, the recognition rate of WACE method is improved by about 15% at low SNR. When the SNR is higher than 2 dB, the correct recognition rate of WACE is higher than 90%. And when the SNR is higher than 5 dB, the recognition rate is stable above 98%. Compared with WEE method, except the recognition rate at − 5 dB, the recognition rate of WACE is much higher than that of WEE method under other SNR. Simulation results show that compared with the existing methods, the proposed WACE has better performance in feature extraction, stronger anti-interference ability, and the computational complexity is almost the same as that of the original method. At the same time, it can optimize the selection of exponential weight vector and linear weight vector to achieve better recognition performance.

6 Conclusions

Based on the traditional wavelet energy entropy and adaptive wavelet entropy, a new improved wavelet entropy, wavelet approximate coefficient entropy, is proposed. It can extract the correlation features from the modulated signal better and has better anti-noise performance. In this paper, the system model of modulation recognition is established and six typical modulation modes of communication signals are selected. The simulation results show that the modulation recognition method based on wavelet approximate coefficient entropy can improve the performance of modulation recognition in low signal-to-noise ratio, and the effectiveness of the modulation recognition method is proved.

Acknowledgments. This work was supported in part by the National Natural Science Foundation of China (No. 61701407 and 61871327), the Aerospace Science and Technology Fund, Shanghai Aerospace Science and Technology Innovation Fund (SAST2019–078) and the provincial undergraduate innovation and entrepreneurship training program (S202010699400).

References

1. Mitola, J., Maguire, G.Q.: Cognitive radio: making software radios more personal. IEEE Pers. Commun. **6**(4), 13–18 (1999)
2. Dong, S., Li, Z., Zhao, L.: A modulation recognition algorithm based on cyclic spectrum and SVM classification. In: 2020 IEEE 4th Information Technology, Networking, Electronic and Automation Control Conference (ITNEC), Chongqing, China, pp. 2123–2127 (2020)
3. Yang, Y., Zhang, X.: A modified method for digital modulation recognition based on instantaneous signal features. In: 2019 3rd International Conference on Electronic Information Technology and Computer Engineering (EITCE), Xiamen, China, pp. 1351–1354 (2019)
4. Huang, Y., Jin, W., Li, B., et al.: Automatic modulation recognition of radar signals based on Manhattan distance-based Features. IEEE Access **7**, 41193–41204 (2019)
5. Bai, J., Gao, L., Gao, J., et al.: A new radar signal modulation recognition algorithm based on time-frequency transform. In: 2019 IEEE 4th International Conference on Signal and Image Processing (ICSIP), Wuxi, China, pp. 21–25 (2019)
6. Zhao, Y., Xu, Y., Jiang, H., et al.: Recognition of digital modulation signals based on high-order cumulants. In: 2015 International Conference on Wireless Communications & Signal Processing (WCSP) , Nanjing, pp. 1–5 (2015)
7. Mohammed, E., Abdwahad, A., Ali, G.: Spoken arabic digits recognition using discrete wavelet. In: 2014 UKSim-AMSS 16th International Conference on Computer Modelling and Simulation, Cambridge, pp. 275–279 (2014)
8. Wang, L., Guo, S., Jia, C.: The digital modulation recognition technique based on the wavelet envelope difference. Appl. Electron. Tech. **43**(2), 95–98 (2019)
9. Chen, J., Kuo, Y., Li, J., et al.: Modulation identification of digital signals with wavelet transform. J. Electron. Inf. Technol. **28**(11), 2026–2019 (2016)
10. Chen, L., Qu, W.: Detection of aero engine instability based on wavelet entropy theory. Microcomput. Appl. **27**(6), 54–57 (2011)
11. Avci, E., Avci, D.: The performance comparison of discrete wavelet neural network and discrete wavelet adaptive network based fuzzy inference system for digital modulation recognition. Exp. Syst. Appl. **35**(1–2), 90–101 (2008)
12. Zhang, C., Yang, L., Wang, X.: Discrete wavelet neural network group system for digital modulation recognition. In: 2011 IEEE 3rd International Conference on Communication Software and Networks, Xi'an, pp. 603–606 (2011)

A New Message Passing Algorithm Based on Sphere Decoding Improvement

Hongwei Zhao$^{(\boxtimes)}$, Yue Yan, and Zichun Zhang

School of Electronics and Information, Northwestern Polytechnical University,
Xi'an 710129, China
13359237963@163.com

Abstract. In a multi-satellite measurement and control system, when multiple satellites transmit data to the ground station at the same time, the ground station needs to efficiently detect the data of each satellite. Large overload access leads to strong mutual interference of satellite signals, and non-positive signals based on sparse codes are used. Cross multiple access (SCMA) technology can provide access and distribution capabilities that exceed the limit of traditional channel capacity, and is suitable for a large number of constellation measurement and control systems. However, the traditional MPA algorithm is extremely complex and has a large processing delay. It has a great test of the complexity and real-time performance that needs to be considered in the application. Therefore, it is of great significance to study the low-complexity space borne reception detection algorithm. A new multi-user detection algorithm based on partial codeword marginalization and sphere decoding, which is called PMSD-MPA, is proposed in this paper. PMSD-MPA considers both the mapping between resource nodes and user nodes and reduce the number of iteration. Proved by simulation, the convergence rate of the iteration process is accelerated, thus reducing the computational complexity of the detection algorithm.

Keywords: SCMA · MPA · Sphere decoding

1 Introduction

The vision of mobile communication is to achieve "anytime, anywhere access to everything", so people put forward many new requirements for 5G system. Compared with 4G, the spectral efficiency of 5G system needs to be increased 5–15 times, the connection density needs to be increased more than 10 times, the end-to-end delay in the system needs to be reduced to the order of milliseconds, and the reliability needs to be close. The new demand of 5G brings new challenges to research and development in many aspects [1].

SCMA is a code-based non-orthogonal multi-access technology with nearly optimal spectrum efficiency, which is designed to meet the requirements of 5G. Overall, SCMA's overall performance is better than NOMA and MUSA's, and its complexity is lower than PDMA's, making it well suited to the 5G standard. Based on the design idea of LDS system, SCMA is a flexible non-orthogonal multi-access scheme to control the complexity of multi-user detection algorithm at the receiving end within a reasonable

B. Li et al. (Eds.): IoTaaS 2020, LNICST 346, pp. 685–695, 2021.
https://doi.org/10.1007/978-3-030-67514-1_54

range through the sparse design of sending end code words [2]. Based on 5G large connection, low latency and low power consumption, as a key technology in the physical layer, the receiver complexity of multi-access technology affects device power consumption, system delay and other indicators from the perspective of underlying devices. Therefore, it is of great practical significance to study low complexity decoding algorithm.

When SCMA technology was first proposed, MPA multi-user detection algorithm was adopted. For the receiving end decoding scheme of SCMA, the message passing algorithm (MPA) can be used to decode the receiving end. MPA can obtain decoding performance close to the maximum likelihood probability criterion on the premise of ensuring reasonable complexity [3, 4]. The complexity of MPA is proportional to the exponential power of constellation size, which leads to limited application in 5G low-delay network. Based on this, scholars at home and abroad focus on reducing the complexity of decoding algorithm. Literature [5] proposed the Log-MPA algorithm, which transformed the messages to be transmitted in the MPA algorithm into the log-arithmic domain, and applied the Jacobian logarithmic formula to further reduce the computational burden, eliminate all exponential operations, and convert about 90% multiplication operations into addition operations, saving at least 20% running time compared with the traditional MPA algorithm. Literature [6, 7] proposed a detection algorithm of fixed complexity based on Partial Marginalization. Literature [8] proposed two improved algorithms. One is the sign flip detection algorithm (SFA). The idea of SFA comes from the bit flip algorithm, which is often used for decoding low density parity (LDPC). The symbol flip algorithm firstly makes local hard judgment on each resource node, then reverses the hard judgment result of the resource node with the lowest reliability, and realizes the reliability update and symbol flip operation through iteration, until the condition of stopping iteration meets. The simulation results show that the computational complexity of SFA is obviously lower than that of traditional MPA algorithm. The other is the dynamic user node marginalization messaging algorithm, which USES the reliability defined in SFA to dynamically decide whether to stop updating the soft information of some user nodes during the iteration of MPA, so as to reduce the complexity. The algorithm is called DPM-MPA. Simulation analysis shows that THE performance and complexity of DPM-MPA are superior to that of PM-MPA.

However, the above literatures only improved the MPA algorithm once, but did not improve it the second time. Through careful study of literature [9], this paper finds that the complexity of the improved MPA algorithm is still high, and there is still room for further improvement, which can reduce the complexity of the MPA algorithm again. Specifically, in message update, the nodes are marginalized first, and then the trusted part of the updated message is updated by using the spherical decoding principle. Simulation results show that when the threshold value is small, the complexity of the algorithm proposed in this paper will decrease again, while BER has no loss.

The structure of the paper is as follows: in Sect. 2, the model of SCMA system and the PMSD-MPA algorithm are presented. Section 3 analyzes the algorithm performance. Section 4 summarizes the conclusions.

2   MPA and Improvement Based on Spherical Decoding

2.1   Basic Model of SCMA System

Basic Model

SCMA is gradually evolved from the combination of OFDMA-CDMA and the idea of sparse spread spectrum. At the transmitting end, the biggest difference between SCMA and LTE systems is that the traditional quadrature amplitude modulation (QAM) is changed to SCMA coding. The key technology of the coding is codebook design. SCMA codebook design can be regarded as multi-dimensional a joint optimization of modulation and sparse spread spectrum. Data of multiple users are superimposed on the air interface to form a superimposed non-orthogonal sequence for transmission. At the receiving end, the SCMA system combines the single-user receiving equalization module, the QAM modulation and the de-mapping module into one, forming a multi-user SCMA detection process. Because SCMA data is non-orthogonal superposition, users cannot be distinguished directly, so the receiving end adopts a multi-user joint detection message passing algorithm for signal detection.

The simplified model of the SCMA system uplink is shown in the Fig. 1 below.

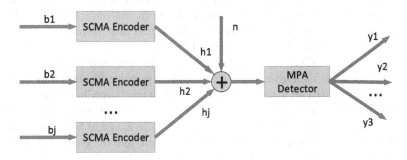

Fig. 1.   Basic model of SCMA system

Assume that the SCMA system contains J users and K orthogonal time-frequency resource blocks, similar to OFDMA orthogonal subcarriers. Each user transmits data to the base station through orthogonal time-frequency resource blocks, and the overload factor can be obtained by

$$OF = \frac{J}{K} \tag{1}$$

At the transmitting end, the input bit stream is SCMA encoded and then mapped into a multi-dimensional complex number domain code-word. The code-word is mapped through physical resources and then transmitted through the channel. The code-words selected by different users are based on the same orthogonal time-frequency resources. The method of sparse spread spectrum is non-orthogonal superposition.

When transmitting data, the SCMA encoder selects code-words from the designed codebook according to the input coded bits. When the code-word is selected, it will carry user data for transmission. To store, it can be represented in the form of a tanner graph. The Fig. 2 shows the tanner graph form of a codebook. In the figure, the 6 data layers are multiplexed on 4 orthogonal resource blocks. The connection point means that the codebook has data transmission on this data layer. There are 3 data streams on each physical resource node, and each data stream is connected. To 2 physical resource nodes. Multiple users superimpose on the air interface to form a non-orthogonal sequence.

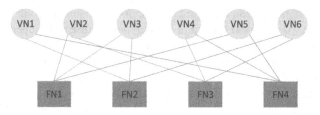

Fig. 2. Tanner graph form of a codebook

In the uplink access system, after the code word is selected, it will carry user data for transmission. Multiple user data is superimposed on the air interface to form a superimposed non-orthogonal sequence, so different user information is superimposed on the 4 resource blocks at the receiving end.

The receiver of SCMA mainly includes two modules: multi-user detector and channel decoder. The multi-user detector is mainly responsible for separating the multi-user data superimposed on the shared channel. The channel decoding module removes the check bits and restores the user's original binary bit stream, which corresponds to the channel encoder at the sending end. Due to the sparse nature of SCMA code-words, a new form of multi-user detection algorithm is given, and the channel decoder can apply the decoding algorithm of the traditional orthogonal system. Therefore, the main purpose is to discuss and study the multi-user detection algorithm.

If all users are synchronized in time and the signal received by the base station is the superimposed signal of all users, the received signal can be expressed as:

$$y = \sum_j diag(h_j)x_j + n \tag{2}$$

Where x_j represents the code word sent by the j user; h_j represents the channel gain vector of the j user; n is Gaussian white noise, and At the receiving end, the SCMA system combines the single-user receiving equalization module and the QAM modulation and demapping module into one, forming a multi-user SCMA detection process. Then the signal received at the resource node K is:

$$y_k = \sum_{j \in \xi_j} h_{jk}x_{jk} + n_k \tag{3}$$

MPA

The multi-user detection algorithm of SCMA system makes use of the sparsity of codebook and adopts MPA algorithm to detect superposition of multiple users on the same physical resource block. However, as the number of access users increases, the constellation map superposed on a single physical resource block becomes more and more dense, and the number of constellation points to be searched for detection will increase exponentially. At the same time, in order to ensure the accuracy of the detection, the number of iterations in the MPA detection process will gradually increase. The increase of computational complexity will lead to the increase of system delay, and a large number of intermediate variables will be generated during iteration, which will also take up more storage space. How to reduce the complexity of detection is one of the key problems in SCMA.

An example is given to illustrate the transmission of 6 users over 4 orthogonal time-frequency resources. There is a one-to-one correspondence between factor graph and mapping matrix. The mapping matrix corresponding to the figure is shown in the following formula:

$$F = \begin{bmatrix} 0 & 1 & 1 & 0 & 1 & 0 \\ 1 & 0 & 1 & 0 & 0 & 1 \\ 0 & 1 & 0 & 1 & 0 & 1 \\ 1 & 0 & 0 & 1 & 1 & 0 \end{bmatrix} \tag{4}$$

The flow chart of MPA decoding algorithm is shown in the Fig. 3. As can be seen from the flow chart of MPA algorithm, the first step of MPA algorithm initializes the conditional probability of factor graph and the probability of each code word of each user. The second step is to update FN and VN nodes of MPA iteratively until the target iteration times or result convergence is achieved. The third step is decision output.

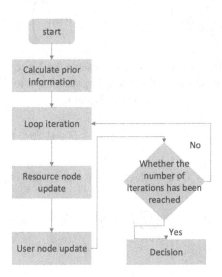

Fig. 3. MPA decoding algorithm process

Use f_k to represent FN, use v_j to represent VN. Each FN corresponds to an orthogonal time-frequency resource, which is a row in F_{K-J}, and each VN corresponds to a user, which is a column in F_{K-J}.

Use $I_{f_k \to v_j}^t(w_{kj})$ to indicate the message from f_k passed to v_j, which is also the updated message on f_k; Use $I_{v_j \to f_k}^t(w_{kj})$ to indicate the message from v_j passed to f_k, which is also the updated message on v_j; w_{kj} indicates the status of the message, $w_{kj} \in \{0, 1, 2, \dots, M-1\}$

The maximum posterior probability criterion is mainly used for the multi-user detection of SCMA using MPA. First, the posterior probability is converted into prior probability through Bayesian formula, and the prior and other concepts are assumed. Then, the message is constantly updated through iteration until the maximum iteration times are reached, and finally the decoding output is achieved. The decoding process of the messaging algorithm can be expressed as follows:

Step 1: Initialization: Assume the prior and other concepts, as shown in the following formula

$$I_{f_k \to v_j}^0(w_{kj}) = 1/M \tag{5}$$

Step 2: Message iteration. Message update on FN, as shown in Eq. (5.3):

$$I_{f_k \to v_j}^t(w_{kj}) = \sum_{w_{kj}^{exit}} \left(I_{f_k \to v_j}^{t-1}\left(w_{kj}^{exit}\right) \right) \tag{6}$$

where w_{kj}^{exit} indicates the information status of other nodes on FN except v_j, $I_{f_k \to v_j}^t\left(w_{kj}^{exit}\right)$ is external information.

$$I_{f_k \to v_j}^t(w_{kj}) = \sum \left\{ \frac{1}{2\pi\sigma} \exp\left(-\frac{1}{2\sigma^2} \left\| y_k - \sum_{l \in \xi_k} h_{kl} x_{kl} \right\|^2 \right) \bullet \prod_{l \in \xi_k/\{j\}} I_{v_l \to f_k}^t(w_{kl}) \right\} \tag{7}$$

t indicates the number of iterations, ξ_k represents the VN collection connected to f_k, $\xi_k/\{j\}$ represents a collection of VNs except v_j connected to f_k

The message update on VN is shown in Equation

$$I_{v_j \to f_k}^t(w_{kj}) = K_j \prod_{p \in \varepsilon_j/\{k\}} I_{f_k \to v_j}^t(w_{pj}) \tag{8}$$

where, K_j is the regulatory factor, which satisfies the following equation

$$\sum_{w_{kj}=1}^{M} I_{v_j \to f_k}^t(w_{kj}) = 1 \tag{9}$$

The ε_j represents the VN collection connected to v_j

Step 3: Decoding detection:

After a finite number of iterations, VN receives the message from FN, which is the guess of the signal sent by the user, and takes it as the detection result, as shown in Eq. (10). The $t_{\max}$ represents the maximum number of iterations.

$$Q_j\left(w_{kj}\right) = \prod_{k \in \xi_j} I_{f_k \to v_j}^{t_{\max}}\left(w_{kj}\right) \tag{10}$$

In order to further reduce the computational complexity of the MPA algorithm, the PM-MPA algorithm introduces the idea of partial marginalization. Since the MPA algorithm needs to traverse the user code words used in each iteration, resulting in a lot of repeated calculations, in order to reduce redundant calculations and reduce the computational complexity, the PM-MPA algorithm selects only those confidences in each iteration. Part of the messages with higher degrees are updated, and the PM-MPA algorithm can achieve a balance between computational complexity and BER performance through reasonable settings of related parameters. The basic principle of the PM-MPA algorithm is: In order to avoid exhaustive traversal in the MPA algorithm, a threshold p needs to be set first. When <, then continue to use the message update iteration process of the previous MPA algorithm; when = , then judge the user information and complete the decoding output; when >, then only select $0 \le \le$ users' messages to participate in the iterative update in subsequent iteration.

2.2   Sphere Decoding and the PMSD-MPA

In order to further reduce the complexity of MPA, based on the theory of spherical decoding and combined with the non-orthogonality of SCMA, this paper introduces the new decision standard of channel quality to screen the user code words and reduce the code words involved in iteration so as to reduce the computational complexity of MPA.

According to the spherical decoding theory, the closer the Euclidean distance of the synthesized constellation point is to the receiving signal point, the more likely it is to be correctly decoded. Then, the user code words participating in the iteration can be reduced by setting the spherical radius, whose expression is:

$$D_k\left(\left[m_j\right]\right) = \left\| y_k - \sum_{j \in \varepsilon_k} h_{kj} x_{kj}\left(m_j\right) \right\| \le R = \beta\sigma \tag{11}$$

Where $D_k\left(\left[m_j\right]\right)$ is the Euclidean distance between the synthetic constellation point and the received signal; β is a real number greater than 0. when $D_k\left(\left[m_j\right]\right)$ is greater than the radius R, the corresponding SCP is discarded and only retained the part of code word that $D_k\left(\left[m_j\right]\right)$ is less than half R to participate in the calculation of MPA. The spherical decoding radius R is determined by the noise power σ^2. A compromise between computational complexity and bit error rate can be achieved by adjusting the size of R. Among them, when $\beta = 1, 2, 3$, the correspondence between the confidence interval and the probability of correct decoding is shown in the table below. when

$R = 2\sigma$, the confidence interval is $(-2\sigma, 2\sigma)$, which can guarantee the probability of correct decoding on resource block K to reach 95.4% (Table 1).

Table 1. Normal distribution.

Confidence interval	Probability value/%
$(-\sigma, \sigma)$	68.3
$(-2\sigma, 2\sigma)$	95.4
$(-3\sigma, 3\sigma)$	99.7

If the filtered code word is substituted into Eq. 7, it can be rewritten as

$$I_{f_k \to v_j}^t(w_{kj}) = \sum_{D_k([m_j] \le R)} \left\{ f\left(y_k | x_k([m_j])\right) \bullet \prod_{l \in \xi_k / \{j\}} I_{v_l \to f_k}^t(w_{kl}) \right\} \tag{12}$$

The setting of radius R value should be reasonable. If it is too small, part of the code words that can be correctly decoded will be screened out, thus affecting the detection result.

The MPA algorithm based on the principle of sphere decoding achieves the goal of reducing complexity by reducing the number of user information superimposed on each resource. If, on the basis of reducing the number of user information superimposed on each resource, the number of iterations of some user information is reduced, the complexity of the algorithm will be more reduced, that is, the PMSD-MPA algorithm proposed in this paper.

3   Results and Discussion

In this paper, six users are multiplexed for transmission on four physical resource blocks, and the code book published by Huawei is adopted. Each user occupies two resources for data transmission. The specific simulation parameters are shown in the Table 2:

Table 2. Simulation parameters.

Parameters	Value
Orthogonal resource number K	4
User number V	6
Codebook dimension M	4
Frame size N	3000
Channel	AWGN

Figure 4 shows the comparison of bit error rate performance with SNR of PM-MPA algorithm and conventional MPA algorithm in 6 iterations. Figure 4 shows that the bit error rate performance of PM MPA algorithm is similar to that of traditional MPA algorithm.

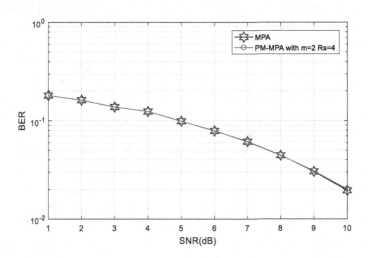

Fig. 4. Comparison of BER performance of MPA and PM-MPA

Figure 5 shows the curve of bit error rate with SNR of traditional MPA algorithm, PM-MPA algorithm, SD-MPA algorithm and PMSD-MPA algorithm proposed in this paper when $t_{max} = 6$.

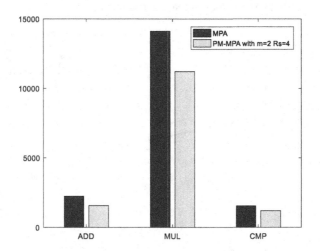

Fig. 5. Comparison of BER performance

When R = 1 and R = 2 are set, the number of iterations is set to 6, and the BER performance of SD-MPA algorithm is shown as Fig. 5: As can be seen from the Fig. 6, the smaller the decision radius is, the worse the BER performance will be, because too small R will over filter the user code word information. When $R = 2\sigma$, bit error rate performance of SD-MPA and MPA is similar, mainly because word screening based on spherical decoding theory ensures the accuracy of multi-user detection with high probability.

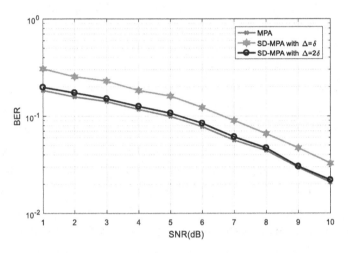

Fig. 6. Comparison of BER performance at different R of SD-MPA

Figure 7 shows the curve of bit error rate with SNR of traditional MPA algorithm, PM-MPA algorithm, SD-MPA algorithm and PMSD-MPA algorithm proposed in this paper when $t_{max} = 6$. When the decoding radius R is set appropriate, the bit error rate performance of PMSD-MPA does not suffer too much.

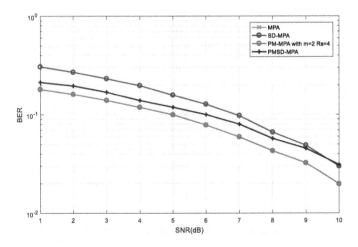

Fig. 7. Comparison of BER performance

Taken together, the algorithm proposed in this paper can achieve a good balance between bit error rate performance and complexity.

4 Conclusions

In this paper, the spherical decoding principle is adopted to implement the MPA algorithm. Based on the partial code word marginalization method, the PMSD-MPA algorithm is proposed. In other words, on the basis of setting the minimum value of the probability density function, constellation points far away from the received signal are discarded again to reduce the complexity of the original MPA again. Simulation results show that the algorithm proposed in this paper is lower in complexity than the algorithm before the improvement, and has no impact on the system BER. The algorithm proposed in this paper is feasible and has practical value.

References

1. Qi, B., Lin, L., Shan, Y.: Non-orthogonal multiple access technology for 5G. Telecommun. Sci. **31**(5), 14–21.2 (2015)
2. Jing, L.: Research on SCMA low-complexity detection algorithm based on information transfer. Beijing University of Posts and Telecommunications. Master's degree thesis (2016)
3. Ning, W.: Research on multi-user detection algorithm in SCMA system. South-Central University for Nationalities (2018)
4. Morrow, R.K., Lehnert, J.S.: Bit-to-bit error dependence in slotted DS/SSMA packet systems with random signature sequences. IEEE Trans. Commun. **37**(10), 1052–1061 (1989)
5. Lian, J., Zhou, S., Zhang, X., et al.: Low complexity decoding method for SCMA in uplink random access. In: Global Communications Conference. IEEE (2017)
6. Mu, H., Ma, Z., Alhaji, M.: A fixed low complexity message pass algorithm detector for uplink SCMA system **4**(6) (2015)
7. Bo, H.: Research on sparse code multiple access technology, Xidian University. Master's thesis (2017), vol. 8 (2017)
8. Jianchao, S., Hua, H.: The structure of LAS code and the advantages of LAS-CDMA over traditional CDMA. Commun. Technol. **40**(12) (2007)
9. Kai, S., Bei, Y., Guangyu, W.: Multiuser detection scheme for SCMA with partial extrinsic information transmission. Syst. Eng. Electron. (2017)

A Novel Codebook Design Scheme for Sparse Code Multiple Access

Huanzhu Wang$^{(\boxtimes)}$, Peihan Yu, and Yue Yan

School of Electronics and Information, Northwestern Polytechnical University,
Xi'an 710129, China
910544662@qq.com

Abstract. The sparse code multiple access (SCMA) technology proposed by Huawei has become a very competitive one of many NOMA solutions due to its high overload capability. SCMA maps the user's binary bit data input by the system's sending end into a multi-dimensional complex number sequence through a pre-designed codebook, instead of the modulation and spreading in the orthogonal multiple access scheme. Based on the sparsity of codewords, the receiving end uses the Message Passing Algorithm (MPA) for multi-user detection. Among them, the excellent SCMA codebook can effectively improve the performance of the system under limited spectrum resources. Therefore, this paper conducts detailed research on the SCMA codebook design scheme. First, this article introduces the principle of the SCMA system in detail, and then proposes a SCMA codebook design method, including the design of the mapping matrix, the design of the mother constellation and the constellation operator. Among them, the mother constellation design adopts a reorganized multi-dimensional constellation scheme. The constellation operator obtains the user constellations of different users through phase rotation, and then maps the designed user constellations into a codebook through a mapping matrix. The simulation results show that the performance of this design is better than the sample codebook given by Huawei.

Keywords: Sparse code multiple access · Codebook design · Mother constellation

1 Introduction

The While the rise of the mobile Internet and the Internet of Things (IoT) has brought unprecedented experience to people, it has also brought massive terminal access to mobile communication systems. New applications and service industries have emerged in an endless stream, providing a broad range of communication systems. Prospects. By 2020, the capacity of mobile communication networks is expected to increase by about 1,000 times compared to 2018. Orthogonal multiple access schemes cannot theoretically reach the maximum capacity of the system, and cannot meet the needs of future mobile communication systems for massive user access. Therefore, the fifth generation mobile communication system (5G) uses non-orthogonal multiple access (NOMA) technology as its core technology. Among them, the SCMA technology proposed by

© ICST Institute for Computer Sciences, Social Informatics and Telecommunications Engineering 2021
Published by Springer Nature Switzerland AG 2021. All Rights Reserved
B. Li et al. (Eds.): IoTaaS 2020, LNICST 346, pp. 696–709, 2021.
https://doi.org/10.1007/978-3-030-67514-1_55

Huawei has become a very competitive one among many NOMA solutions with its high overload capability. The SCMA system directly maps the user binary bit data input by the transmitter into a multi-dimensional complex number sequence through the pre-designed SCMA codebook, instead of modulation and spreading in the orthogonal multiple access scheme. The codewords sent by different users are at the same time frequency. The non-orthogonal superposition of resources allows the system to accommodate more users at the same time. The receiving end utilizes the sparsity of codewords and uses Message Passing Algorithm (MPA) for multi-user detection.

Excellent SCMA codebook can effectively improve the performance of the system under limited spectrum resources. Therefore, it is of practical significance to study the design of SCMA codebook. The design process of SCMA codebook is a non-convex quadratic programming secondary constraint problem. The optimal solution to this problem has not been found so far, so the design codebook has become an open optimization problem. This paper proposes a sub-optimal design scheme for SCMA codebook, which not only effectively reduces the design complexity, but also has good bit error rate performance.

2 SCMA Sender Principle

2.1 SCMA Encoding Process

The traditional CDMA modulation is to pass the input data stream through QAM modulation, and then generate the modulated spread spectrum signal through the spread spectrum sequence $\{s_1, s_2, s_3, s_4\}$, as shown in Fig. 1.

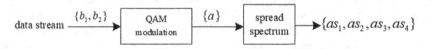

Fig. 1. CDMA modulation

The SCMA system is an improvement of CDMA and spread spectrum technology. The data stream is encoded by SCMA to generate the corresponding codeword. Since the spreading sequence of CDMA is composed of orthogonal codes, and the coding sequence of SCMA is composed of non-orthogonal codes, the SCMA system can accommodate more users (Fig. 2).

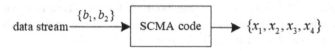

Fig. 2. SCMA modulation

As shown in Fig. 3, the SCMA encoding process can be understood as a process in which a data stream is mapped into a corresponding codeword in a codebook. For example, when data 10 enters the SCMA encoder, it will be mapped to a codeword numbered 10.

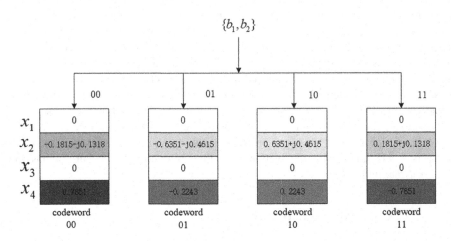

Fig. 3. SCMA codebook

Figure 3 shows the SCMA codebook with $M = 4$-point constellation used by each user. The data comes from the codebook provided by Huawei in the 5G competition [1]. Among them, all users share $K = 4$ orthogonal time-frequency resources. The codebook of each user consists of 4 code words, corresponding to a 4-point constellation. Each codeword consists of 4 blocks, and each block represents an orthogonal time-frequency resource. The squares are divided into white squares and colored squares. White squares represent zero elements, and colored squares represent non-zero elements. Therefore, it can be seen that each user only transmits data on orthogonal time-frequency resources representing non-zero elements. Assuming that the number of non-zero element blocks of each codeword is N, each user in the corresponding figure only transmits data on $N = 2$ orthogonal time-frequency resources.

After the data is mapped into corresponding codewords, the codewords of different users are transmitted after non-orthogonal superposition on the same orthogonal time-frequency resource. Since the codewords of different users interfere with each other when they are superimposed, in order to distinguish the data of each user, the positions of non-zero element blocks in the codebooks of different users cannot be completely the same, that is, N of any two user codebooks Orthogonal time-frequency resources cannot be completely the same. From this, we can get the expression of the maximum user access number J_{max} of the SCMA system as:

$$J_{max} = \binom{K}{N} \tag{1}$$

Figure 4 shows the process of non-orthogonal superposition of codewords of $J = 6$ users on $K = 4$ orthogonal time-frequency resources.

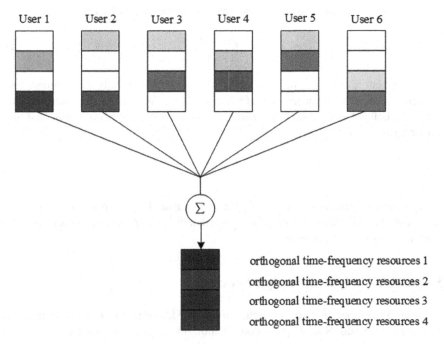

Fig. 4. Overlay of codewords of different users

2.2 Sparse Matrix

It can be seen from Fig. 4 that user 3 transmits data on orthogonal time-frequency resource 1 and orthogonal time-frequency resource 3. The column vector $(1 \ \ 0 \ \ 1 \ \ 0)^T$ can be used to represent its codeword structure, and 1 indicates that data is transmitted on the orthogonal time-frequency resource at the corresponding position. 0 means that no data is transmitted on the corresponding orthogonal time-frequency resource. The matrix $F_{K \times J}$ composed of column vectors of the codeword structure of all users is called a sparse matrix. The sparse matrix corresponding to Fig. 4 is:

$$F_{4 \times 6} = \begin{pmatrix} 0 & 1 & 1 & 0 & 1 & 0 \\ 1 & 0 & 0 & 1 & 1 & 0 \\ 0 & 0 & 1 & 1 & 0 & 1 \\ 1 & 1 & 0 & 0 & 0 & 1 \end{pmatrix} \tag{2}$$

From the sparse matrix of Eq. 2, it can be seen that any two column vectors are mainly non-orthogonal, which reflects the non-orthogonality of SCMA. The sparsity is reflected by the low proportion of 1 in each column. Each user occupies 2 orthogonal time-frequency resources, and the proportion of 1 in each column is 50%. The number of 1 s in each row is 3, which means that each orthogonal time-frequency resource has 3 users' data for non-orthogonal superposition. The number of users d_f superimposed on each orthogonal time-frequency resource can be calculated by Eq. 3:

$$d_f = \frac{JN}{K} \tag{3}$$

The system in Fig. 4 shows that the SCMA system needs only 4 orthogonal time-frequency resources to transmit data of 6 users at the same time, and the overload rate λ of users is defined as the ratio of the number of users to the number of orthogonal time-frequency resources:

$$\lambda = \frac{J}{K} \tag{4}$$

The overload rate of this system is 150%. Compared with the 100% overload rate of the OFDMA system, it can be clearly seen that the SCMA system can accommodate more users in limited resources.

3   SCMA Codebook Design Scheme

Suppose the number of users connected to the SCMA system is J. When transmitting data, if the user adopts an M-point constellation, the SCMA codebook of each user is composed of M codewords, and each codeword contains K orthogonal time-frequency resources, the actual number of orthogonal time-frequency resources occupied by each user is N. SCMA encoding can be regarded as a process of selecting corresponding codewords for $\log_2 M$ bits of data from M codewords containing K orthogonal time-frequency resources. Therefore, the process of SCMA codebook design can be expressed by Equation 5 and Equation 6 [5]:

$$C_j = g_j(b_j) \tag{5}$$

$$X_j = V_j C_j \tag{6}$$

First, the data stream b_j sent by the user j is substituted into the constellation generation function g_j to obtain an N-dimensional user constellation C_j containing M constellation points, and then the mapping matrix V_j is applied to the user constellation C_j, and the SCMA codebook X_j is mapped.

Use V to represent the set of mapping matrices and G to represent the set of constellation generating functions, then there are $V = \{V_j \widehat{u} j \in [1, J]\}$, $G = \{g_j \widehat{u} j \in [1, J]\}$. Then the SCMA codebook design problem can be simplified to find the optimal solution set of V and G under the given conditions of J, M, K, and N. However, the optimal solution for this problem has not been found yet. When designing SCMA codebooks, we usually adopt a sub-optimal solution, which is mainly divided into three links: SCMA mapping matrix design, mother constellation design, and constellation operator design. It is a common scheme for SCMA codebook design.

3.1 Design Mapping Matrix

The purpose of constructing the mapping matrix is to allocate orthogonal time-frequency resources to users. A good mapping matrix can reduce the complexity of MPA decoding at the receiving end, which is equivalent to the spread spectrum function in CDMA. The construction rules of the mapping matrix are as follows:

1.
$$V_j \in B^{K \times N}$$

2.
$$V_i \neq V_j, \forall i \neq j$$

3.
$$V_j^{[0]} = I_N$$

Among them, $B^{K \times N}$ is a matrix of order $K \times N$ consisting of only 0 and 1, I_N is a unit matrix of order N, and $V_j^{[0]}$ is the matrix obtained by removing all 0 rows from V_j.

Define L as the number of orthogonal time-frequency resources occupied by two users. Since the orthogonal time-frequency resources occupied by two users are not completely the same, $L \leqslant N - 1$. When $2N > K$, the number of the same orthogonal time-frequency resources occupied by two users is at least $2N - K$, otherwise it is 0. Therefore, the value range of L is:

$$\max(0, 2N - K) \leqslant L \leqslant N - 1 \tag{7}$$

Take the SCMA system with $J = 6$, $K = 4$, $N = 2$ as an example, at this time $0 \leqslant L \leqslant 1$. The matrix obtained by removing all 0 rows from V_j is:

$$V_j^{[0]} = \begin{pmatrix} 1 & 0 \\ 0 & 1 \end{pmatrix} j \in [1, 6] \tag{8}$$

The six mapping matrices expanded by $V_j \in B^{4 \times 2}$ are as follows:

$$
V_1 = \begin{pmatrix} 0 & 0 \\ 1 & 0 \\ 0 & 0 \\ 0 & 1 \end{pmatrix} \quad
V_2 = \begin{pmatrix} 1 & 0 \\ 0 & 0 \\ 0 & 1 \\ 0 & 0 \end{pmatrix} \quad
V_3 = \begin{pmatrix} 1 & 0 \\ 0 & 1 \\ 0 & 0 \\ 0 & 0 \end{pmatrix}
$$

$$
V_4 = \begin{pmatrix} 0 & 0 \\ 0 & 0 \\ 1 & 0 \\ 0 & 1 \end{pmatrix} \quad
V_5 = \begin{pmatrix} 1 & 0 \\ 0 & 0 \\ 0 & 0 \\ 0 & 1 \end{pmatrix} \quad
V_6 = \begin{pmatrix} 0 & 0 \\ 1 & 0 \\ 0 & 1 \\ 0 & 0 \end{pmatrix}
\tag{9}
$$

3.2   Design Mother Constellation

After the mapping matrix is designed, the SCMA codebook design problem can be simplified to find the optimal solution set of G under the given conditions of V, J, M, K, and N. At this time, it is necessary to design J N-dimensional constellations containing M constellation points. We can design a mother constellation first, and then obtain the constellations of other users through operations such as phase rotation. Define the matrix operation that converts the mother constellation to other user constellations as a constellation operator. The user constellation can be expressed as:

$$C_j = (\Delta_j)C, \forall j \tag{10}$$

Among them, C represents the mother constellation, and Δ_j represents the constellation operator.

Use $C^{(n)}$ to represent the nth dimension of the mother constellation, and its length is M, that is, each dimension contains M constellation points:

$$C^{(n)} = (c_{n1} \quad c_{n2} \quad \cdots \quad c_{nN}) \, \forall n \in [1, N] \tag{11}$$

The mother constellation is composed of vectors of N dimensions:

$$C = (C^{(1)}, C^{(2)}, \cdots, C^{(N)})^T \tag{12}$$

Substitute Equation 11 into Equation 12 to get:

$$C = \begin{pmatrix} c_{11} & c_{12} & \cdots & c_{1M} \\ c_{21} & c_{22} & \cdots & c_{2M} \\ \vdots & \vdots & \ddots & \vdots \\ c_{N1} & c_{N2} & \cdots & c_{NM} \end{pmatrix} \tag{13}$$

We use the method of reorganizing the real and imaginary axes of the N-dimensional constellation to design the mother constellation. As shown in Fig. 5, we first rotate the A and B constellations, and project the constellation points vertically to the dimensional axis of the constellation. Then, the k-th dimension axis of the A constellation is taken as the real axis, and the k-th dimension axis of the B constellation is taken as the imaginary axis to form the k-th dimension recombined constellation of the mother constellation. The N reorganized complex constellations correspond to N orthogonal time-frequency resources respectively.

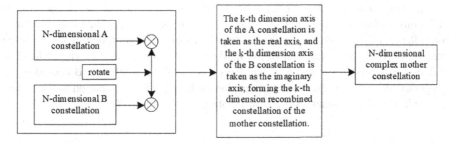

Fig. 5. Mother constellation design process

Next, follow the above design method to design an SCMA system with $J = 6$, $K = 4$, $N = 2$, and $M = 4$.

In the first step, we use two BPSK constellations as A constellation and B constellation (Fig. 6):

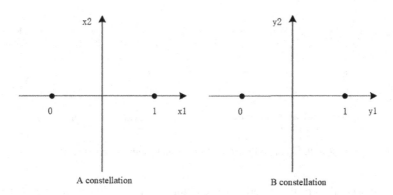

Fig. 6. Original constellation

The second step is to rotate the A and B constellations by the same angle θ (Fig. 7):

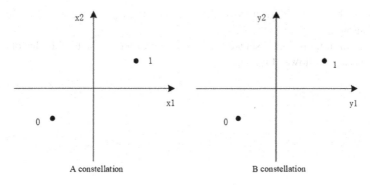

Fig. 7. Constellation after rotation

The third step is to project the rotated constellation points of the A and B constellations on the coordinate axes to obtain new coordinate points. The x1 axis of the A constellation is used as the real axis, and the y1 axis of the B constellation is used as the imaginary axis to form the first of the mother constellation. The x2 axis of the constellation A is used as the real axis, and the y2 axis of the constellation B is used as the imaginary axis to form the second dimension of the mother constellation to generate a reorganized 2-dimensional mother constellation, as shown in Fig. 8.

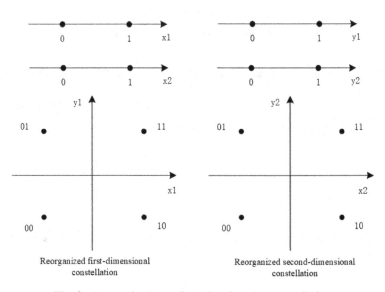

Reorganized first-dimensional constellation

Reorganized second-dimensional constellation

Fig. 8. Reorganized two-dimensional mother constellation

In the second step, the criterion of maximizing the minimum product distance is used to find the optimal rotation angle θ [2]. Define the product distance d_p as:

$$d_{P,i} = \prod_{\substack{N \\ x_i \neq y_i}} |x_i - y_i| \tag{14}$$

Among them, x_i and y_i are two different points in the reorganized same constellation diagram.

The minimum product distance diagram under different rotation angles obtained by simulation is as follows (Fig. 9):

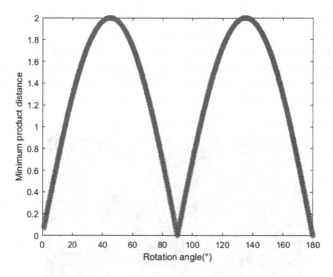

Fig. 9. The minimum product distance of different rotation angles

Through simulation, the optimal rotation angles of the SCMA system with $J = 6$, $K = 4$, $N = 2$, and $M = 4$ are 45° and 135°. When the value of θ is 45°, We choose 45° as the optimal rotation angle.

3.3   Design Constellation Operator

After the mother constellation design is completed, the SCMA codebook design problem can be further simplified as finding the operation matrix that converts the mother constellation into each user constellation. This operation matrix is the constellation operator.

In the SCMA system with $J = 6$, $K = 4$, $N = 2$, $M = 4$, we can get that the number of users superimposed on each orthogonal time-frequency resource is 3 from Eq. 3. Let C^1 and C^2 respectively denote the two mother constellations obtained in the previous section, and suppose that the phase rotation angle of the mother constellation of user j on the k-th orthogonal time-frequency resource is θ_{kj}, then a mother constellation allocation scheme can be designed as follows [4]:

$$
\begin{pmatrix}
0 & C^1 \cdot e^{j\theta_{12}} & C^1 \cdot e^{j\theta_{13}} & 0 & C^2 \cdot e^{j\theta_{15}} & 0 \\
C^2 \cdot e^{j\theta_{21}} & 0 & C^2 \cdot e^{j\theta_{23}} & 0 & 0 & C^1 \cdot e^{j\theta_{26}} \\
0 & C^2 \cdot e^{j\theta_{32}} & 0 & C^1 \cdot e^{j\theta_{34}} & 0 & C^2 \cdot e^{j\theta_{36}} \\
C^1 \cdot e^{j\theta_{41}} & 0 & 0 & C^2 \cdot e^{j\theta_{44}} & C^1 \cdot e^{j\theta_{45}} & 0
\end{pmatrix}
\tag{15}
$$

Since the rotation angle of the constellation diagram of different users has different effects on the decoding complexity of the MPA algorithm, we use the criterion of maximizing the minimum Euclidean distance to find the optimal rotation angle of the user constellation diagram [3].

Taking orthogonal time-frequency resource 1 as an example, a total of 3 users are superimposed on this orthogonal time-frequency resource, they are user 2, user 3, and user 5. The rotation angle of their constellation diagram is represented by θ_{12}, θ_{13}, and θ_{15} respectively. Assuming that the rotation angle of user 2 is $0°$, the contours of the minimum Euclidean distance corresponding to different phase rotation angles obtained through simulation are shown in Fig. 10:

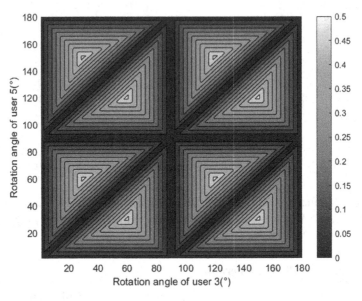

Fig. 10. Contours of the minimum Euclidean distance corresponding to different phase rotation angles (Color figure online)

The blue area in Fig. 10 indicates that the minimum Euclidean distance of the corresponding rotation angle is small, and the yellow area indicates that the minimum Euclidean distance of the corresponding rotation angle is large. It can be seen from the figure that there are eight groups of optimal solutions for rotation angles. The specific optimal rotation angle is obtained by accurate solution as follows:

-
$$\theta_{12} = 0°, \theta_{13} = 30°, \theta_{15} = 60°$$

-
$$\theta_{12} = 0°, \theta_{13} = 30°, \theta_{15} = 150°$$

-
$$\theta_{12} = 0°, \theta_{13} = 60°, \theta_{15} = 30°$$

- $\theta_{12} = 0°, \theta_{13} = 60°, \theta_{15} = 120°$

- $\theta_{12} = 0°, \theta_{13} = 120°, \theta_{15} = 60°$

- $\theta_{12} = 0°, \theta_{13} = 120°, \theta_{15} = 150°$

- $\theta_{12} = 0°, \theta_{13} = 150°, \theta_{15} = 30°$

- $\theta_{12} = 0°, \theta_{13} = 150°, \theta_{15} = 120°$

4 Performance Simulation

A total of eight schemes of user constellation rotation angles are obtained by maximizing the minimum Euclidean distance criterion. The following firstly compares the performance of these eight schemes. From the analysis in Fig. 10, we can use symmetry to select three asymmetric solutions, and reduce the eight solutions to three as follows:

1.
$$\theta_{12} = 0°, \theta_{13} = 30°, \theta_{15} = 60°$$

2.
$$\theta_{12} = 0°, \theta_{13} = 30°, \theta_{15} = 150°$$

3.
$$\theta_{12} = 0°, \theta_{13} = 60°, \theta_{15} = 120°$$

The codebook calculated from the above three phase rotation angles is simulated for bit error rate performance and the result is shown in Fig. 11. The specific simulation parameters are shown in Table 1:

Table 1. Simulation parameters

Parameter	Value
M	4
J	6
K	4
d_f	3
λ	150%
Number of iterations	6
Codebook 1 phase rotation angle	0°, 30°, 60°
Codebook 2 phase rotation angle	0°, 30°, 150°
Codebook 3 phase rotation angle	0°, 60°, 120°
Channel model	Rayleigh channel

It can be seen from Fig. 11 that when the signal-to-noise ratio is low, the simulation curves under the three phase rotation angles are not much different, but with the increase of the signal-to-noise ratio, the three schemes have some subtle differences. When the signal-to-noise ratio reaches 8 dB, the error rate of codebook 1 and codebook 3 is almost the same, and both are lower than codebook 2. When the signal-to-noise ratio reaches 10 dB, the bit error rate decreases sequentially from codebook 1 to codebook 2 to codebook 3.

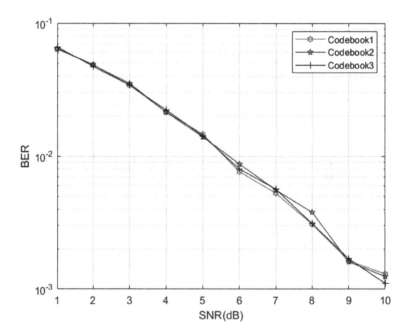

Fig. 11. BER comparison chart for different phase rotation angles

Compare and analyze the codebook design proposed in this section with the codebook disclosed by Huawei in the 5G competition. We use the codebook 1 above for comparison, and the simulation results are shown in Fig. 12:

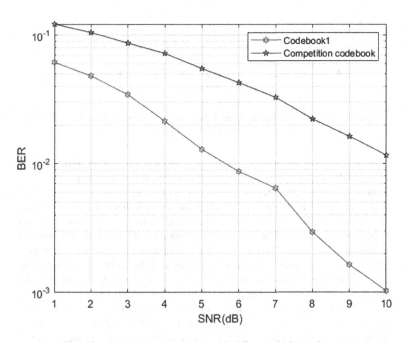

Fig. 12. BER comparison chart of different design schemes

It can be seen from Fig. 12 that as the signal-to-noise ratio increases, the bit error rate of codebook 1 will be significantly reduced compared to the competition codebook, and the performance will be significantly improved.

References

1. SCMA: massive connectivity & low latency. http://www.innovateasia.com/5g/gp2.html. Accessed 15 June 2016
2. Boutros, J., Viterbo, E.: Signal space diversity: a power- and bandwidth-efficient diversity technique for the Rayleigh fading channel. IEEE Trans. Inf. Theo. **44**(4), 1453–1467 (2002)
3. Zhi-Xin, L., Jing, L., Ling, Y.: Optimal design of APSK constellation for satellite channel. Aerosp. Shanghai **023**(005), 33–37 (2006)
4. Shao, K., et al.: SCMA codebook optimization method based on phase rotation. Xi Tong Gong Cheng Yu Dian Zi Ji Shu/Syst. Eng. Electron. **40**(10), 2354–2362 (2018)
5. Taherzadeh, M., et al.: SCMA codebook design. In: IEEE Vehicular Technology Conference. IEEE (2014)

Multi-view Polarization HRRP Target Recognition Based on Convolutional Neural Network

Mengyuan Ma[1,2(✉)], Kai Liu[1,2], Xiling Luo[1,2], and Tao Zhang[1]

[1] School of Electronics and Information Engineering, Beihang University,
Beijing 100191, China
qihuanbuke@163.com
[2] Hangzhou Innovation Institute, Beihang University, Hangzhou 310051, China

Abstract. This paper proposes a multi-view polarization high-resolution range profile (HRRP) target recognition method based on convolutional neural network (CNN-based MVPHRRP), which combines high-resolution technology with polarization technology to extract radar signal features. Using the feature layer fusion method, the intensity of scattering centers, the ratios of odd and even scattering extracted by Pauli decomposition constitute a three-dimensional feature tensor. On the basis of retaining the time-domain distribution characteristics, the multi-polarization characteristics and the target's structural composition are fitted. Then we build a CNN for radar target recognition. The simulation results show that the use of CNN-based MVPHRRP for radar target recognition has a good effect, and the classification accuracy is less affected by the signal-to-noise ratio (SNR). Increasing the number of multi-views plays a positive role in improving the recognition performance, and the introduction of multi-view multi-polarization information can effectively increase the average recognition probability of target recognition.

Keywords: Polarization radar · Target recognition · Convolutional neural network · High-resolution range profile · Scattering center

1 Introduction

Smart cars need the capabilities of perception, decision-making and control. Millimeter-wave radar is one of the core sensors for intelligent driving. It has a measurement distance farther than that of lidar or camera, and can work normally in bad weather. The mobility of objects is related to the type of target. Therefore, it is necessary to obtain information such as the type, size and weight of the measured object. Robust target recognition technology has a positive significance for ensuring the safety of autonomous vehicles.

The feature extraction of wideband radar echoes has been a hot topic in radar target recognition over the world. The large bandwidth provides a higher target resolution. When the range resolution of the radar is much smaller than the target size, the scattering centers of the target are separated in the radial direction, occupying several distance units to form an HRRP, as shown in Fig. 1. The broadband polarization

B. Li et al. (Eds.): IoTaaS 2020, LNICST 346, pp. 710–720, 2021.
https://doi.org/10.1007/978-3-030-67514-1_56

sensitive array has high resolution both in distance and angle, which can obtain multi-view HRRP in an angular range.

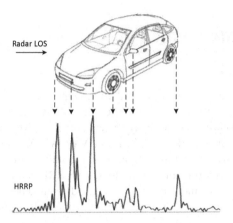

Fig. 1. HRRP formed by a radar.

CNN is widely used in image recognition. The multi-level structure and convolution calculation method can obtain a classifier with better performance. In recent years, deep learning has also been introduced in the field of radar target recognition to extract higher-level features of radar data [1]. The acquisition method of radar HRRP is simple. The one-dimensional geometrical theory of diffraction (GTD) model can be used to extract the scattering centers of the target's fully polarized echo, and obtain the corresponding polarization scattering matrix. The polarization decomposition technology can be used to analyze the characteristics of the scattering centers. Combining polarization technology with high-resolution technology is an idea to improve target recognition performance, and has broad application prospects. Existing technologies for HRRP identification only consider the HRRP amplitude [2], phase, and shift sensitivity. Most of them eliminate the adverse effects caused by the sensitivity and do not use complementary information among related angular domains [3]. In addition, the use of polarization HRRP mostly ignores the relative position relationship of the scattering centers, and the features of different polarization decomposition may be redundant.

In view of above problems, to make full use of the advantages of deep learning in adaptive feature extraction, the multi-view polarization HRRP target recognition based on CNN (CNN-based MVPHRRP) is proposed in this paper. First, we use high resolution technology to obtain more accurate HRRP in the angular range. Then we combine the one-dimensional GTD model and Pauli decomposition to extract the target parameters and form the feature tensor of the target. Finally, CNN is used to train the classification network to obtain a classifier with higher accuracy.

The remainder of the paper is organized as follows. Section 2 introduces the feature extraction of multi-view HRRP and polarization decomposition based on the scattering center model, and then proposes the CNN-based MVPHRRP. Section 3 uses the civilian vehicle (CV) data domes provided by the Air Force Research Laboratory (AFRL) for experimental analysis. Simulation results are given under different multi-view angles and signal-to-noise ratio (SNR). Section 4 concludes this paper.

2   CNN-Based MVPHRRP

2.1   Multi-view HRRP

Array radar can separate the multiple scattering centers of the target in distance and direction with high resolution. The distribution of scatters and target size is included in HRRP. Wideband multi-polarization radar can obtain HRRP under four kinds of polarization configurations (HH, HV, VH and VV) [4]. As shown in Fig. 2, HRRP under different polarization configurations has a certain correlation, and the combination of polarization information and multi-view HRRP can improve target recognition performance. Meanwhile, HRRP between adjacent angles is similar, and two dimensional imaging result of the target contains more information.

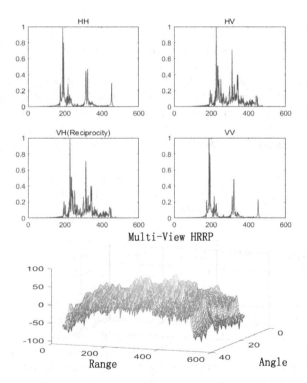

Fig. 2. Multi-polarization and multi-view HRRP.

In this paper, the multi-view full polarization information in the fixed azimuth domain is obtained at first. Secondly, the multi-view HRRP is solved, the target area is detected, and the position of scattering centers is calculated. Then the GTD model is used to calculate the scattering matrix, and the multi-view polarization distance matrix feature tensor is constructed. Finally, CNN is used to train the classifier.

2.2 Feature Tensor Construction

The CP-GTD is used to calculate the scattering matrix, it is expressed as [5]:

$$z_{pq}(n) = \sum_{m=1}^{d} s_{m,pq} \left(j\frac{f_n}{f_c} \right)^{a_m} e^{-j\frac{4\pi r_m}{c} f_n} + u_{pq}(n), n = 1, 2, \ldots, N \tag{1}$$

Where, c is the speed of electromagnetic wave propagation, N is the number of step frequency points, f_n is the frequency of the nth frequency point, d is the number of scattering centers, p and q represent the type of polarization channel, r_m is the position of the mth scattering center, $s_{m,pq}$ is the polarization scattering matrix element of the mth scattering center, $p, q \in \{H, V\}$, u represents noise, a_m is the frequency-dependent factor, and f_c is the center frequency.

The matrix of the GTD model is expressed as:

$$z = AS + u \tag{2}$$

Single-station polarization radar usually satisfies reciprocity, $S_{HV} = S_{VH}$. Under the condition of reciprocity, z is the $N \times 3$ dimensional echo matrix. S is the polarization scattering matrix. A is the $N \times d$ dimensional steering vector matrix, $a(\alpha_m, r_m)$ represents the steering vector corresponding to the mth scattering center and u is an $N \times 3$ dimensional measurement noise matrix. Specifically expressed as:

$$z = [X_{HH} X_{HV} X_{VV}] \tag{3}$$

$$A = [a(\alpha_1, r_1) a(\alpha_2, r_2) a(\alpha_d, r_d)] \tag{4}$$

$$S = [S_{HH} S_{HV} S_{VV}] \tag{5}$$

$$u = [u_{HH} u_{HV} u_{VV}] \tag{6}$$

The polarization scattering matrix is a complex matrix, which is related to the electromagnetic wave frequency, incident attitude, polarization mode and target structure. When two types of linearly polarized waves are sent and received, the data of the four channels obtained by the polarized radar sensor can be represented by the Sinclair scattering matrix S [6]:

$$S = \begin{bmatrix} S_{HH} & S_{HV} \\ S_{VH} & S_{VV} \end{bmatrix} \tag{7}$$

Where, H and V represent horizontal and vertical polarization respectively. S completely describes the polarization characteristics, amplitude and phase characteristics of object scattering. Without considering noise, the scattering matrix is solved by the least square method as:

$$S = \left(A^H A\right)^{-1} A^H z \tag{8}$$

The formula for calculating the intensity of the scattering centers is:

$$span\left(\widehat{S}_m\right) = \left|\widehat{S}_{m,HH}\right|^2 + \left|\widehat{S}_{m,HV}\right|^2 + \left|\widehat{S}_{m,VH}\right|^2 + \left|\widehat{S}_{m,VV}\right|^2 \tag{9}$$

Under the condition of satisfying the reciprocity theorem, Pauli decomposition is simplified as:

$$S = \begin{bmatrix} S_{HH} & S_{HV} \\ S_{VH} & S_{VV} \end{bmatrix} = a \cdot S_a + \beta \cdot S_b + \gamma \cdot S_c \tag{10}$$

The Pauli vector is solved as [6]:

$$\vec{k} = \begin{bmatrix} \alpha \\ \beta \\ \gamma \end{bmatrix} = \frac{1}{\sqrt{2}} \begin{bmatrix} S_{HH} + S_{VV} \\ S_{HH} - S_{VV} \\ 2S_{HV} \end{bmatrix} \tag{11}$$

α, β and γ respectively represent the components of odd-bounce scattering, even-bounce scattering, and the components of a diplane oriented at 45°. Choosing α and β to be the characteristic parameters.

Combined with the GTD model and Pauli polarization decomposition [7], the feature tensor of radar target is formed as $T \in R^{I_1 \times I_2 \times I_3}$, as shown in Fig. 3. Where, I_1 is the unit length of HRRP, I_2 is the number of multi-views, and I_3 is the feature number. In this paper, $I_3 = 3$, which is composed of the intensity of scattering centers, α and β of Pauli decomposition.

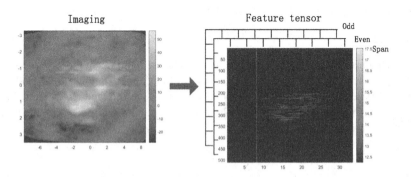

Fig. 3. Feature tensor of a target.

2.3   CNN-Based MVPHRRP Model

At the stage of constructing the data set, the multi-view polarization echoes of the target at the 360° azimuth were captured at a fixed pitch angle. The data of N small azimuth positions near θ is obtained, and the obtained azimuth domain is as follows: $\theta - \left[\frac{N}{2}\right] \times \Delta\theta, \theta - \left[\frac{N}{2} - 1\right] \times \Delta\theta, \ldots\ldots, \theta + \left[\frac{N}{2}\right] \times \Delta\theta$, where $\Delta\theta$ indicates the interval between adjacent angles. The echo data in this angular domain is called multi-view polarization echo. The multi-view polarization echo is processed to obtain the characteristic tensor T mentioned before, and then the T is divided into 70% train samples and 30% test samples for training and recognition probability statistics.

Classical CNN usually consists of convolutional layer, pooling layer, fully connected layer and classifier. We use the feature tensor extracted from the targets as the input of CNN to train our CNN-based MVPHRRP model. As shown in Fig. 4, we build a CNN model consisting of 2 convolutional layers, 2 maximum pooling layers, 1 fully connected layer and 1 classifier layer. The convolutional layer is used to obtain a new feature map. Then we select the largest pooling layer to reduce the dimension of the feature map to avoid over-fitting. The Adam algorithm is used to optimize and update the weights. The initial learning rate is 0.001, the mini-batch is 16, and the number of iterations is 50. On the basis of the classical CNN model, rectified linear units (ReLU) activation function, L2 regularization and dropout technology are added to suppress over-fitting. Finally, the fully polarized radar echo feature tensor of vehicles is trained to obtain a target classifier.

The target feature tensor dimension of the input is $33 \times 512 \times 3$, representing 33×512 features of three channels. The first convolutional layer depth is 16, the convolution kernel size is $5 \times 5 \times 3$, and the output is a feature matrix with a dimension of $33 \times 512 \times 16$. After passing through the first maximum pooling layer, the dimension of the characteristic tensor is $16 \times 256 \times 16$. Then, it is put into the convolutional layer whose depth is 32 and the convolution kernel size is 4×4. After passing through the second pooling layer, the dimension of the feature tensor becomes $8 \times 128 \times 32$. After flattening, the convolutional layer passes through the fully-connected layer with 1024 points and then is sent to the softmax layer, 3 output nodes are obtained, corresponding to the probability of each category.

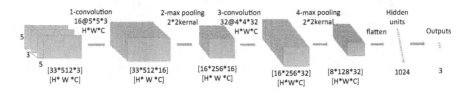

Fig. 4. CNN-based MVPHRRP model.

3   Simulation Results

The data used in this article comes from the AFRL CV data domes [8, 9]. The number of vehicle samples used for identification is 10. Simulation measurement parameters are shown in Table 1.

Table 1. Simulation measurement parameters

Parameter	Value	Parameter	Value
Center frequency	9.6 GHz	Number of samples	512
Bandwidth	2 GHz	Frequency step	≈ 0.48 MHz
Train azimuth	[0:1:359°]	Polarization	HH, HV, VV
Test azimuth	[0.25:3:357.25°]	Multi-view domain	0.25/0.5/1/2°
Elevation	30°		

In an ideal situation, the completeness of the multi-view HRRP sample library determines the recognition performance [10]. However, the performance is limited by the amount of data storage and computing overhead. When building the target database, find the fully polarized echo every 1° and extract the feature tensor according to the method proposed in this paper to obtain the sample set under different azimuth angles. Then expand the data set by adding noise. Figure 5 shows the vehicle imaging under different azimuth (Azis) with a multi-view angle of 2°.

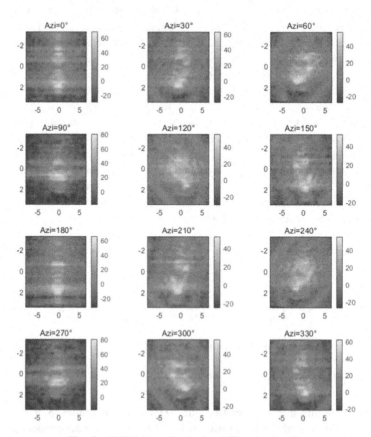

Fig. 5. Vehicle imaging under different azimuths

We choose Tensorflow framework to implement CNN construction, training and testing. And then we use the trained model to identify and verify the test data set. In order to illustrate the effectiveness of the feature tensor modeling method proposed in this paper, we compare the performance of multi-view single-polarization and multi-view multi-polarization target recognition. The method proposed in this paper is compared with multi-view HRRP intensity sequences of different polarization modes. And we verify polarization information extracted from Pauli decomposition is effective for enhancing the recognition performance.

First we select the multi-view multi-polarization feature modeling method in this paper to compare with the multi-view single-polarization feature method. We use the same CNN for training and conduct the experiment under the condition of multi-view angle of 2°. Unless otherwise specified, the multi-view angles selected in the experiment are all 2°, and the type of vehicles is 3. Without considering noise, Fig. 6 shows the relationship between the number of training epochs and the average recognition probability. It can be seen that the recognition effect of HV is the worst, lower than HH and HV. As the number of training epochs increases, the CNN learns more, and the recognition probability rises accordingly. Because the feature extraction technology of this method fits the multi-view and multi-polarization features, it can better characterize the target, which not only improves the probability of target recognition, but also reduces the training complexity. When the epoch number is 10, the method proposed in this paper has a performance improvement over single polarization, and multi-polarization information plays a positive role in target recognition.

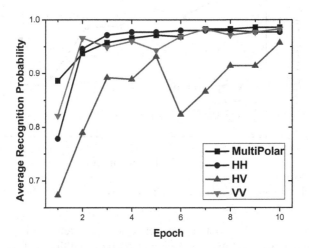

Fig. 6. Comparison of multi-view multi-polarization and single-polarization recognition.

Then we verify the influence of the number of targets on the recognition probability. Under the condition without noise, we select 3–10 types of vehicles for recognition, and verify the relationship between the recognition probability and the number of targets. As the number of training epochs increases, the probability of recognition is improved because of CNN learning. As shown in Fig. 7, the convergence is achieved when the epoch is 50 with the recognition probability of about 99%. And the accuracy is less affected by the change in the type number of targets. Therefore, CNN-based MVPHRRP has a strong robustness in the number of target categories.

To test the sensitivity of this method to noise, add Gaussian noise to the original echo and test the recognition performance under different SNR. As shown in Fig. 8, when the SNR is low, the recognition performance is poor. If the epoch is 50 and the SNR is 10, the recognition probability is 75.28%. When the SNR is higher than 20 db, the recognition probability is above 95%. CNN-based MVPHRRP has noise robustness, even in a noisy environment, it can still guarantee a certain recognition probability.

To compare the classification performance of the CNN-based MVPHRRP method with the traditional SVM classification method. Figure 7 and Fig. 8 also show the result of the comparison with the SVM method when the input parameters are the same. It can be seen that the classification performance of traditional SVM method is worse than the proposed method in the case of different number of targets and different SNR.

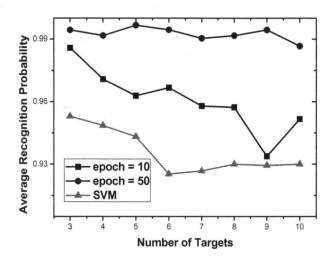

Fig. 7. Relationship between recognition probability and number of target categories.

Finally, we verify the relationship between multi-view angle and recognition probability. The experiment was conducted under the condition that the SNR is 30 db and the multi-view angle was 0.25, 0.5, 1.0 and 2.0°. As shown in Fig. 9, the results show that when the number of viewing angles increases, the recognition probability will increase. When the viewing angle is 2°, the recognition probability is above 98%.

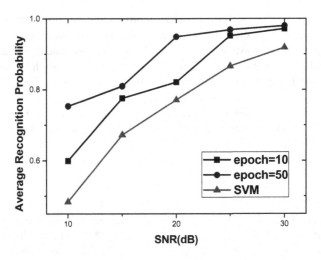

Fig. 8. Relationship between recognition probability and SNR.

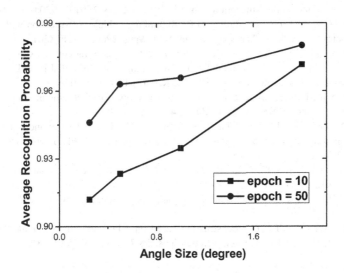

Fig. 9. Relationship between recognition probability and multi-view angle.

4   Conclusion

This paper uses polarization multi-view HRRP for complex target recognition. First, the feature tensor of the target is extracted, and a neural network classifier with strong separability is designed. It has the advantages of small storage capacity, fast calculation, high recognition accuracy and wide application range. The feature tensor modeling method in this paper comprehensively considers the deep joint of multi-view and polarization, which can extract the characteristics of radar echo more than the traditional method and reduce the training complexity. Through simulation experiments, it can be seen that CNN-based MVPHRRP improves the performance of radar target recognition with the characteristics of deep learning and this method has noise stability and strong robustness. However, the use of electromagnetic calculation as a means of simulating radar observation data needs to be further extended to the measured data to verify the feasibility of the method and contribute to visual radar perception.

Acknowledgments. This work was supported by the National Key R&D Program of China under Grant No. 2016YFB1200100, and the National Nature Science Foundation of China under Grant No. 91638301.

References

1. Zhao, C., He, X., Liang, J., Wang, T., Huang, C.: Radar HRRP target recognition via semi-supervised multi-task deep network. IEEE Access **7**, 114788–114794 (2019)
2. Du, L., He, H., Zhao, L., Wang, P.: Noise robust radar HRRP target recognition based on scatterer matching algorithm. IEEE Sens. J. **16**(6), 1743–1753 (2016)
3. Guo, C., He, Y., Wang, H., Jian, T., Sun, S.: Radar HRRP target recognition based on deep one-dimensional residual-inception network. IEEE Access **7**, 9191–9204 (2019)
4. Saville, M.A., Jackson, J.A., Fuller, D.F.: Rethinking vehicle classification with wide-angle polarimetric SAR. IEEE Aerosp. Electron. Syst. Mag. **29**(1), 41–49 (2014)
5. Dai, D., Ge, J., Xiao, S., Wang, X.: Full-polarization scattering center extraction based on coherent polarization GTD model. In: Proceedings of 2011 IEEE CIE International Conference on Radar, pp. 1386–1389. CIE-Radar, Chengdu (2011)
6. Cloude, S.R., Pottier, E.: A review of target decomposition theorems in radar polarimetry. IEEE Trans. Geosci. Remote Sens. **34**(2), 498–518 (1996)
7. Tao, M., Zhou, F., Liu, Y., Zhang, Z.: Tensorial independent component analysis-based feature extraction for polarimetric SAR data classification. IEEE Trans. Geosci. Remote Sens. **53**(5), 2481–2495 (2015)
8. Dungan, K.E., Austin, C., Nehrbass, J., Potter, L.C.: Civilian vehicle radar data domes. SPIE **5**(7699), 731–739 (2010)
9. The AFRL. https://www.sdms.afrl.af.mil/index.php?collection=cv_dome11. Accessed 1 May 2020
10. Ding, B., Wen, G.: Target reconstruction based on 3-D scattering center model for robust SAR ATR. IEEE Trans. Geosci. Remote Sens. **56**(7), 3772–3785 (2018)

Millimeter-Wave Communications with Beamforming for UAV-Assisted Railway Monitoring System

Shiyu Su[✉]

School of Electronic and Information Engineering, Beihang University,
Beijing 100083, China
1902ssy@buaa.edu.cn

Abstract. Railway is an important means of transportation for passenger and freight, and the maintenance and repair work is essential. Unmanned aerial vehicle (UAV) can be deployed along the railway track for monitoring, reconnaissance and ensuring the safe operation of the railway because of its flexible mobility and low labor cost. In this paper, a railway monitoring system based on aerial platform is formed, which takes UAV monitoring as the main body. In order to solve the problem of long-distance and wide bandwidth backhaul communication, this paper adopts mmWave array communication scheme, and designs the large antenna array beamforming on the base station receiver with zero-forcing (ZF) and minimum mean square error (MMSE). Finally, the simulation results show that the minimum mean square error method is effective, and the simulation results also provide a reference for the UAV deployment along the railway.

Keywords: UAV · Beamforming · ZF · MMSE · Railway monitoring · Uplink transmission

1 Introduction

As an important transportation system, the railway's daily stable operation determines the normal operation of national production and life. In order to ensure the track components are in good condition, the railway line must be monitored, regularly inspected and maintained. At present, manual inspection is the most common method of railway line maintenance. The patrol officer uploads the railroad track picture, the latitude and longitude coordinates through the terminal installed on the mobile phone [1]. However, such a line-traveling process is time-consuming and labor-intensive.

This work was supported in part by the National Key Research and Development Program (Grant Nos. 2016YFB1200100), and the National Natural Science Foundation of China (NSFC) (Grant Nos. 61827901 and 91738301).

B. Li et al. (Eds.): IoTaaS 2020, LNICST 346, pp. 721–731, 2021.
https://doi.org/10.1007/978-3-030-67514-1_57

With the reform of the operation system, the railway development should take quality first and efficiency first as the measurement standard [2]. Therefore, the railway patrol inspection requires limited manpower and advanced technical means to fully control the situation along the railway. Combining image monitoring, GPRS wireless communication and automatic control technology, reference [3] actualised the monitoring and data transmission of railway crossing. However, it's well known that the coverage of outdoor cameras is so small that it is impossible to monitor the entire railway from the ground. The authors in [4] introduced the research and development overview of East Japan Railway's line detection device, and put forward a monitoring method of installing inspection devices on trains. However, the applicable speed of the device is below 120 km/h. Inspired by the previous works, this paper proposes a railway surveillance system based on an aerial platform, where multiple unmanned aerial vehicles (UAVs) simultaneously patrol along the railway line, uploading image data to a high-altitude airship in real time.

In recent years, the UAV industry has developed rapidly. Thanks to its flexible mobility and low labor cost, UAVs are widely used in various fields such as communications, reconnaissance, surveillance, remote sensing, aerial photography, disaster relief, and agricultural irrigation [5,6]. Compared with the ground monitoring, the air-based railway monitoring system has a more flexible inspection mode, but it still needs to solve the problem of wide bandwidth backhaul. Due to the need to monitor the entire railway, there are many pictures and large amounts of data. But the bandwidth requirements cannot be met in the sub-6G frequency band. In order to alleviate the shortage of low-band spectrum and further improve the system's communication and monitoring capabilities, one of the most effective ways is to use the Millimeter-Wave band [7]. Compared with current cellular band (3G or LTE) signals, mmWave signals will experience severe path loss, penetration loss and rain attenuation [8]. Therefore, it is necessary to use a large-scale array antenna to perform beamforming on the receiving end of the airship to obtain a beam pointing to the UAV along the railway. At the same time, in the mmWave band, shorter wavelengths enable more antennas to be compressed in the same size, thus allowing large-scale spatial multiplexing and high directional beamforming.

At present, there have been some studies on beamforming of microwave band systems. The authors in [9] proposed a three-dimensional beamforming algorithm applied to the downlink multi-input multi-output (MIMO) system, which performed multi-user grouping and inter-user interference suppression. In [10], the author proposed a three-dimensional beamforming strategy based on area division to ensure that all users can obtain a fair beam gain. The authors in [11] studied the design of hybrid beamforming in the mmWave MU-MIMO system of high-speed railways. And a two-stage algorithm of hybrid beamforming at transmitter and receiver was proposed, which could still have high total throughput in mmWave channel with time delay and doppler effect.

In this paper, the uplink transmission scenario of UAVs is established, and two commonly used beamforming algorithms of different microwave band systems are compared. Besides, the application of the better scheme is extended to provide reference for UAV detection deployment along the railway. The remainder of this paper is organized as follows. The system model is described in Sect. 2. Hybrid beamforming designs are elaborated in Sect. 3. Section 4 presents the simulation results. Section 5 concludes this paper and discusses the deployment of UAVs.

Notation: a, $\mathbf{a}$, $\mathbf{A}$ and $\mathcal{A}$ denote a scalar, a vector, a matrix and a set, respectively. $\|\mathbf{a}\|$ denotes the Frobenius norm of $\mathbf{a}$. $[\mathbf{A}]_{i,j}$ denotes the entry in the i-th row and j-th column of matrix $\mathbf{A}$.

2   System Model

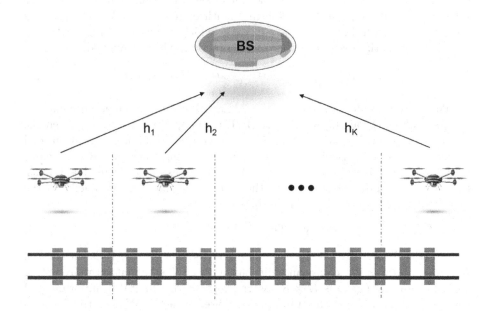

Fig. 1. Scene along the railway.

The schematic diagram of the scene along the railway is shown in Fig. 1. In a section of the railway line with a total length of L, there are K tethered drones, and an airship is used as a base station (BS) above the middle section of the railway. The airship equipped with large-scale antenna arrays, needs to serve the UAV group in the target area. The flying height difference between the airship and UAVs is h, and the number of antennas is N. The channel between the user and the BS is regarded as a millimeter wave channel with spatial sparsity. Since the occlusion and scattering in the link are relatively weak, the line-of-sight(LOS) transmission path is significantly stronger than the non-line-of-sight (NLOS) transmission path [12]. Because ground obstacles will seriously affect the line-of-sight transmission path, the receiving end does not use ground base stations but high-airships. Due to the limited scattering in the mmWave band, the multipath is mainly caused by reflection. Since the number of multipath components is usually small, the mmWave channel has directivity and spatial sparsity occurs in the angle domain. Different multipath components have different angles of arrival. Without loss of generality, we use the directional mmWave channel model, then the channel between each UAV and the base station can be expressed as [13,14]:

$$\mathbf{h}_i = \sum_{\ell=1}^{L_i} \lambda_{i,\ell} \mathbf{a}(N, \Omega_{i,\ell}) \tag{1}$$

where λ is the channel gain complex coefficient of the transmission path, Ω is the cosine of the pitch angle of the line-of-sight transmission path, and the subscripts i and l represent the l-th multipath of the i-th UAV. L_i represents the total multipath number of the i-th UAV, which includes one LOS path and $L_i - 1$ NLOS path. $\mathbf{a}(\bullet)$ refers to a vector function, which is defined as:

$$\mathbf{a}(N, \Omega) = \left[e^{j\pi 0\Omega}, e^{j\pi 1\Omega}, e^{j\pi 2\Omega}, \cdots, e^{j\pi(N-1)\Omega}\right]^T \tag{2}$$

The system model is shown in Fig. 2. Each UAV has a single antenna and sends signals to the airship with power $\mathbf{P}$. The airship's receiver has N antennas, and each antenna is connected to K phase converters to form the front-end analog beamforming. Behind the analog beamforming, there are K RF chains (equal to the number of users). Each RF chain receives signals from all antennas. Finally, after digital beamforming, the received signal $\mathbf{y}$ is obtained. So the expression of the received signal can be written as:

$$\mathbf{y} = \mathbf{D}^H \mathbf{A}^H \left[\mathbf{HPs} + \mathbf{z}\right] \tag{3}$$

where, $\mathbf{H} = [\mathbf{h}_1, \ldots, \mathbf{h}_K]$ is the channel matrix, $\mathbf{s} = [s_1, \ldots, s_K]^T$ is the data of K UAVs, and $\mathbf{z}$ is the Gaussian white noise. $\mathbf{A}$ is $N \times K$ matrix, representing analog beamforming; $\mathbf{D}$ is $K \times K$ matrix, representing digital beamforming. $\mathbf{P}$ is a diagonal matrix, and the transmission power of each UAV is on the diagonal of it, i.e,

$$\mathbf{P} = \begin{pmatrix} p_1 & & 0 \\ & \ddots & \\ 0 & & p_K \end{pmatrix} \tag{4}$$

After obtaining the expression of the received signal, the achievable rate of the k-th UAV can be calculated according to the Shannon formula:

$$R_k = \log_2(1 + SINR_k) \tag{5}$$

where,

$$SINR_k = \frac{\left|\mathbf{d}_k^H \mathbf{A}^H \mathbf{h}_k\right|^2 P}{\sum_{j \neq k} \left|\mathbf{d}_j^H \mathbf{A}^H \mathbf{h}_j\right|^2 P + \|\mathbf{D}^H \mathbf{A}^H\|_2^2 \delta^2} \tag{6}$$

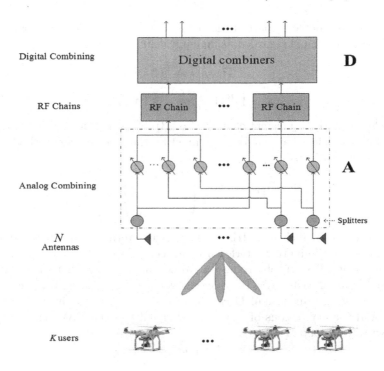

Fig. 2. System model.

Therefore, the problem of this scenario is using beamforming to design two appropriate matrices of **A** and **D**, so that the sum of the achievable rate of the UAVs is maximized. In order to increase the array gain of the analog domain, the analog beamforming should match the channel. Therefore, the phase of each column of the **A** matrix is the corresponding phase of each UAV channel, which is shown with formula (7). The commonly used beamforming algorithms are zero forcing (ZF) and minimum mean square error (MMSE). Next, we will use these two methods to calculate **D**, and compare their performance through simulation.

$$[\mathbf{A}]_{i,j} = \frac{[\mathbf{H}]_{i,j}}{\left|[\mathbf{H}]_{i,j}\right|} \tag{7}$$

3 Hybrid Beamforming

3.1 ZF Beamforming Design

The zero-forcing (ZF) algorithm is the most basic and simplest algorithm in linear precoding. Under the premise of knowing the channel matrix, it can eliminate the interference between multiple channels [15]. Since this paper is directed to the **D** matrix for zero-forcing beamforming, the **A** matrix at the front end needs to be considered as part of the channel matrix. Therefore, the part before digital beamforming is regarded as an equivalent channel $\mathbf{H}_{eff}$:

$$\mathbf{H}_{eff} = \mathbf{A}^H \mathbf{H} \tag{8}$$

$$\mathbf{y} = \mathbf{D}^H \mathbf{H}_{eff} \mathbf{P} \mathbf{s} + \mathbf{D}^H \mathbf{A}^H \mathbf{z} \tag{9}$$

After obtaining the equivalent channel, Eq. (3) can be rewritten as shown in Eq. (9). Assuming a feasible matrix $\tilde{\mathbf{D}}$, defined by the zero-forcing method, the $\tilde{\mathbf{D}}$ matrix should satisfy:

$$\tilde{\mathbf{D}}^H \mathbf{H}_{eff} = \begin{pmatrix} x_1 & & 0 \\ & \ddots & \\ 0 & & x_K \end{pmatrix} \tag{10}$$

In this way, the coefficient matrix of the previous term of Eq. (9) is a diagonal matrix, thereby eliminating interference between UAVs. Where $x_1, x_2, ..., x_K$ are real coefficients. Then by observing Eq. (6), we can find that when calculating the achievable rate of each UAV, the diagonal coefficients of Eq. (10) are cancelled, so the conjugate transpose of $\tilde{\mathbf{D}}$ can be directly equal to the inverse matrix of $\mathbf{H}_{eff}$. And the expressions of the received signal and the UAV achievable rate are rewritten as follows:

$$\mathbf{y} = \mathbf{P} \mathbf{s} + \tilde{\mathbf{D}}^H \mathbf{A}^H \mathbf{z} \tag{11}$$

$$SINR_k = \frac{P}{\left\| \tilde{\mathbf{D}}^H \mathbf{A}^H \right\|_2^2 \delta^2} \tag{12}$$

3.2 MMSE Beamforming Design

The basic principle of beamforming technology based on the minimum mean square error (MMSE) criterion is consistent with MMSE precoding [16]. It is a algorithm to make the received data as close as possible to the transmitted data. This method can Effectively ensure the fairness of each user. Therefore, the purpose of MMSE is to find a matrix $\mathbf{D}$ to make $\mathbf{y}$ closer to $\mathbf{s}$. According to the definition, we take the difference between the received signal and the transmitted signal and take the average value, which can be obtained from Eq. (9):

$$E[\left\| \tilde{\mathbf{D}}^H (\mathbf{H}_{eff} \mathbf{P} \mathbf{s} + \mathbf{A}^H \mathbf{z}) - \mathbf{s} \right\|_2^2] \tag{13}$$

If the minimum value of the above formula is required, the $\mathbf{D}$ matrix needs to be derived first, and then the derivative function is zero to obtain the solution of the $\mathbf{D}$ matrix. Here, assuming that the transmission power of each UAV is equal and all are $\mathbf{P}$, derivation of Eq. (13) can be obtained (see appendix for specific derivation):

$$\tilde{\mathbf{D}} = \sqrt{P} \mathbf{J}^{-1} \mathbf{H}_{eff}$$

$$where, \mathbf{J} = (P \mathbf{H}_{eff} \mathbf{H}_{eff}^H + \delta^2 \mathbf{A}^H \mathbf{A}) \tag{14}$$

4 Simulations

In the simulation, we use the channel model as shown in formula (1). The amplitude of the complex coefficient $\lambda_{i,\ell}$ of the Los channel gain is inversely proportional to the distance, and the average strength of $\lambda_{i,\ell}$ is set to be 1 when the distance between the airship and the UAV is 20 km. In addition, it is assumed that there are four NLOS paths, and each complex coefficient is generated by Gaussian random function, but the gain is 20 dB smaller than that of Los path. The height difference h between UAV and airship is 20 km, the total number k of UAV is 5, and the total length L of UAV reconnaissance track is 100 km. The simulation results of the two methods are as follows:

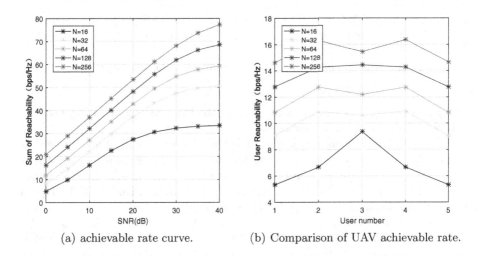

(a) achievable rate curve.   (b) Comparison of UAV achievable rate.

Fig. 3. Simulation results of beamforming with ZF algorithm.

Overall comparison of Fig. 3 and Fig. 4 shows that the beamforming designed by the MMSE algorithm is superior to the ZF algorithm. The simulation results of the MMSE show almost five parallel lines. Both the increase in the number of antennas and the increase in SNR can significantly improve the reachability. The curves of the ZF method are more sparse than the former. As the number of antennas increases, the reachability does not increase linearly. And as the SNR rises, the curve also tends to slow down, indicating that the ZF algorithm may appear saturated at high signal-to-noise ratios. The figure on the right shows the reachability curve of each UAV with an SNR of 40 dB. It can be seen in Fig. 4 that the achievable rate is a straight horizontal line regardless of the number of antennas. It shows that the MMSE algorithm makes the achievable rate of each UAV almost equal, which can ensure the fairness of each UAV. This is because the MMSE method pursues the smallest error between the received signal and the transmitted signal, regardless of the location of the UAV. And the fairness

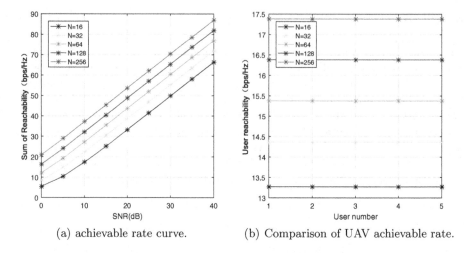

(a) achievable rate curve.   (b) Comparison of UAV achievable rate.

Fig. 4. Simulation results of beamforming with MMSE algorithm.

under this beamforming can just ensure that the UAV inspection at any position will not affect its uplink transmission.

In general, the zero-forcing method has low complexity and simple implementation. Although it can eliminate the interference between multiple signals, it ignores the influence of noise during the operation, resulting in a decrease in the reachability. The MMSE beamforming method is fair and can be well adapted to the space-based platform monitoring system.

In addition, on the basis of adopting the MMSE algorithm, this paper also explores the optimal number of UAVs. Figure 5 shows the effect of the number of UAVs on the total efficiency rate on a fixed-length railway line. It can be seen from the figure that the more UAVs deployed, the more information can be transmitted. But more UAVs mean more energy consumption and RF link requirements. Figure 6 shows the influence of the number of UAVs on energy effectiveness. Energy effectiveness is the ratio of total power consumption and total achievable rate, where the total power consumption includes the power of the receiver on the base station, and the power of all antennas and phase converters.

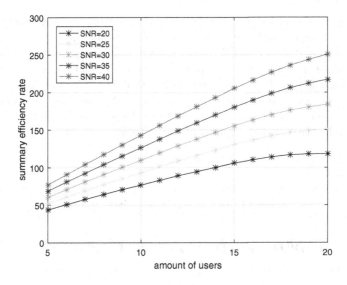

Fig. 5. Influence of UAV number on summary efficiency rate (MMSE).

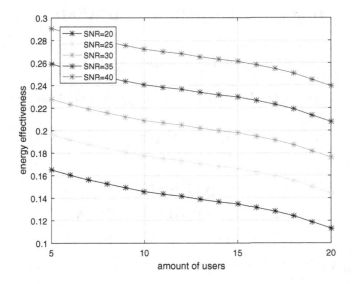

Fig. 6. Influence of UAV number on energy effectiveness (MMSE).

5   Conclusions

This paper proposed a railway monitoring system based on an air-based platform. An uplink transmission scenario for railway UAV inspection was established, and beamforming was designed at the receiving end of the system. The digital beamforming matrix was calculated using the zero forcing algorithm and

MMSE algorithm, and the transmission performance of the two methods were compared through simulation. The simulation results showed that the beam-forming designed by the MMSE could achieve a higher achievable rate, and at the same time, it could well guarantee fairness. Simulation results show that with the increase of UAVs, it could ensure that the information transmission capacity increases steadily. However, too many UAVs reduce the overall energy efficiency, so the number of UAVs needs to be determined based on the speed of the UAV inspection and the length of the railway.

Appendix

Equation (14) derives the $\tilde{\mathbf{D}}$ matrix as follows. First, convert Eq. (14) to expression:

$$f(\tilde{\mathbf{D}}) = Tr\{E[(\tilde{\mathbf{D}}^H \mathbf{H}_{eff} \mathbf{P}\mathbf{s} + \tilde{\mathbf{D}}^H \mathbf{A}^H \mathbf{z} - \mathbf{s})(\mathbf{s}^H \mathbf{P}\mathbf{H}_{eff}{}^H \tilde{\mathbf{D}} + \mathbf{z}^H \mathbf{A}\tilde{\mathbf{D}} - \mathbf{s}^H)]\} \quad (15)$$

Then expand the above formula and simplify:

$$f(\tilde{\mathbf{D}}) = Tr(P\tilde{\mathbf{D}}^H \mathbf{H}_{eff} \mathbf{H}_{eff}{}^H \tilde{\mathbf{D}} - \tilde{\mathbf{D}}^H \mathbf{H}_{eff} \mathbf{P} + \delta^2 \tilde{\mathbf{D}}^H \mathbf{A}^H \mathbf{A}\tilde{\mathbf{D}} - \mathbf{P}\mathbf{H}_{eff}{}^H \tilde{\mathbf{D}} + \mathbf{I}) \quad (16)$$

Derivative the above formula to $\tilde{\mathbf{D}}$ and make it equal to zero

$$\frac{df}{d(\tilde{\mathbf{D}}^H)} = P\tilde{\mathbf{D}}^T \mathbf{H}_{eff}{}^* \mathbf{H}_{eff}{}^T - \sqrt{P}\mathbf{H}_{eff}{}^T + \delta^2 \tilde{\mathbf{D}}^T \mathbf{A}^T \mathbf{A}^* = 0 \quad (17)$$

$$\Rightarrow \tilde{\mathbf{D}}^T (P\mathbf{H}_{eff}{}^* \mathbf{H}_{eff}{}^T + \delta^2 \mathbf{A}^T \mathbf{A}^*) - \sqrt{P}\mathbf{H}_{eff}{}^T = 0 \quad (18)$$

$$\therefore \tilde{\mathbf{D}} = \sqrt{P}\mathbf{J}^{-1}\mathbf{H}_{eff}$$
$$where, \mathbf{J} = (P\mathbf{H}_{eff}\mathbf{H}_{eff}{}^H + \delta^2 \mathbf{A}^H \mathbf{A}) \quad (19)$$

References

1. Jiang, W.: On railway comprehensive inspection and safety management. Technol. Startup Mon. **024**(17), 146–148 (2011)
2. Huang, M.: Reflection on railway development and reform in the new era. China Railw. Corp. **041**(006), 1–8 (2019)
3. Sun, J., Song, H., Zhou, Y.: Using wireless communication to monitor railway crossings. Railw.Tech. Superv. **1**, 48–50 (2010)
4. Ryo, T.: (Japan): monitoring technique for track conditions of east japan railway. JR-EAST **053**(1), 35–40 (2016)
5. Xiao, Z., Xia, P., Xia, X.G.: Enabling UAV cellular with millimeter-wave communication: Potentials and approaches. IEEE Commun. Mag. **54**(5), 66–73 (2016)

6. Jian, W., Gao, F., Wu, Q., Shi, J., Yi, W., Jia, W.: Beam tracking for UAV mounted SatCom on-the-move with massive antenna array (2017)
7. Cui, Y., Fang, X., Fang, Y., Xiao, M.: Optimal non-uniform steady mmWave beamforming for high speed railway. IEEE Trans. Veh. Technol. **67**, 4350–4358 (2018)
8. Haider, F.: Cellular architecture and key technologies for 5G wireless communication networks. J. Chongqing Univ. Posts Telecommun. **52**(2), 122–130 (2014)
9. Li, X., Jin, S., Suraweera, H.A., Hou, J., Gao, X.: Statistical 3-D beamforming for large-scale MIMO downlink systems over Rician fading channels. IEEE Trans. Commun. **64**(4), 1529–1543 (2016)
10. Zhang, Z., Chan, K., KwokHung, L.: Study of 3D beamforming strategies in cellular networks with clustered user distribution. IEEE Trans. Veh. Technol. **65**, 10208–10213 (2016)
11. Gao, M., Bo, A., Niu, Y., Zhang, Z., Li, D.: Dynamic mmWave beam tracking for high speed railway communications. In 2018 IEEE Wireless Communications and Networking Conference Workshops (WCNCW) (2018)
12. Xiao, Z., Zhu, L., Choi, J., Xia, P.: Joint power allocation and beamforming for non-orthogonal multiple access (NOMA) in 5G millimeter-wave communications. IEEE Trans. Wirel. Commun. **17**, 2961–2974 (2018)
13. Ding, Z., Fan, P.: Impact of user pairing on 5G nonorthogonal multiple-access downlink transmissions. IEEE Trans. Veh. Technol. **65**(8), 6010–6023 (2016)
14. Xiao, Z., Xia, P., Xia, X.G.: Codebook design for millimeter-wave channel estimation with hybrid precoding structure. IEEE Trans. Wirel. Commun. **16**(1), 141–153 (2016)
15. Taesang, Y., Goldsmith, A.: On the optimality of multiantenna broadcast scheduling using zero-forcing beamforming. IEEE J. Sel. Area Commun. **24**(3), 528–541 (2006)
16. Bahrami, H.R., Le-Ngoc, T.: MMSE-based MIMO precoder using partial channel information. In: IEEE International Conference on Wireless and Mobile Computing, Networking and Communications, 2005. (WiMob'2005) (2005)

Improved Pulse Shaping Algorithm for Reducing PAPR in OFDM System

Menghao Lian[✉] and Hongwei Zhao

School of Electronics and Information, Northwestern Polytechnical University,
Xi'an 710129, China
944700080@qq.com

Abstract. Orthogonal frequency division multiplexing (OFDM) is the most widely used modulation technology because of its high spectrum efficiency and strong anti-interference ability, and it is a typical representative of multicarrier transmission technology. With the application of OFDM technology more and more common, OFDM also began to face the problem of high peak to average power ratio (PAPR). In this paper, pulse forming technology is mainly used to suppress the problem of too high peak average power. Pulse forming technology is to produce a new sequence by multiplying the formed pulse matrix and the original data sequence, so that each subcarrier symbol has a certain correlation, so as to improve the peak to average power ratio of the signal. Compared with the traditional pulse forming algorithm, the improved Nyquist pulse forming algorithm has better effect on the PAPR suppression, lower algorithm complexity and practicability.

Keywords: OFDM · PAPR · Pulse forming technology

1 Introduction

With the rapid development of science and technology, the application of intelligent products is more and more extensive, such as autopilot, UAV and so on. Therefore, the research of high-speed, efficient and high-quality information transmission system is becoming more and more important in communication. At the same time, OFDM technology came into being. OFDM is a kind of parallel signal transmission technology, which has the advantages of high spectrum efficiency, strong anti-multipath interference ability and strong anti inter symbol interference ability. OFDM signals are generated by superposition of multiple subcarrier signals. When the phases of multiple signals are the same, the instantaneous power of the superposition signal will be much higher than the average power of the signal, resulting in a large peak to average power ratio. In this way, the signal may be distorted, the spectrum of the signal will change, and the orthogonality of each sub channel will be destroyed, which will worsen the performance of the system [1].

At present, there are three main methods to reduce the PAPR of OFDM signals: signal distortion, coding and signal space expansion [6].

© ICST Institute for Computer Sciences, Social Informatics and Telecommunications Engineering 2021
Published by Springer Nature Switzerland AG 2021. All Rights Reserved
B. Li et al. (Eds.): IoTaaS 2020, LNICST 346, pp. 732–742, 2021.
https://doi.org/10.1007/978-3-030-67514-1_58

Signal distortion technology includes compression expansion transformation and limiting technology. Compression transformation is a very simple technology, and it will not increase the number of modulation subcarriers and increase the additional computation. Compression expansion transform is a kind of nonlinear transform function based on μ rate non-uniform quantization, which amplifies the power of the smaller part of the original signal, and keeps the larger part unchanged. By increasing the power of the whole system, the peak to average power ratio is suppressed. The disadvantage of this method is the increase of the average transmit power and the distortion of the signal. Amplitude limiting is the simplest way to reduce the peak to average power ratio. It uses a nonlinear process to reduce the PAPR value of the signal directly in or near the peak amplitude of the OFDM signal. The method of amplitude reduction has strong adaptability and can be applied to any number of subcarriers system. Limiting is equivalent to adding a rectangular window to the original signal. If the signal amplitude is greater than the preset threshold value, a rectangular window with a value less than 1 will be added; if the OFDM signal amplitude is less than the preset threshold value, a rectangular window with a value of 1 will be added to the signal. Because the amplitude of the added rectangular window is not all 1, the OFDM signal will be distorted after passing through the rectangular window. Due to the distortion of the signal, one of the disadvantages of limiting amplitude is that it will produce a kind of self interference, which will cause the BER performance of the system to decline. In addition, because the signal goes through a nonlinear process, it will cause spectrum leakage. At present, there are many ways to solve spectrum leakage by adding no rectangular window function, but the effect is very weak.

The coding methods mainly include block code, gray complementary code and multiple complementary sequences. The coding technology mainly uses different code groups generated by different codes to select the code group with smaller PAPR as OFDM symbols for data transmission, so as to avoid signal peak value. This technology is a linear process. Using coding technology to reduce the PAPR will not cause distortion of the original signal, but the process of coding and decoding is relatively complex, and the calculation complexity is very high, so this kind of technology can be used when the number of subcarriers is relatively small. There are many advantages to reduce PAPR by coding, for example, the system is stable and simple, and the effect of reducing PAPR is very good. But the technology also has many disadvantages.

In this paper, the peak to average power ratio is suppressed by improved pulse forming technology. The pulse shaping technology multiplies the original data and the shaping pulse matrix to produce a new sequence, which makes the subcarriers have a certain correlation, so as to reduce the peak to average power ratio of the signal. This method only needs to select the time-domain waveform of each subcarrier properly, so it can avoid the inverse process of the additional FFT. It can also leave room for channel coding while effectively maintaining the system bandwidth efficiency. Therefore, pulse forming technology is a very effective method to suppress the peak to average power ratio.

1.1   OFDM System Composition

The composition block diagram of OFDM system is shown in the figure below. It mainly consists of transmitter link and receiver. The system mainly includes channel coding/decoding, modulation/demodulation, FFT/IFFT, digital up and down conversion [5]. The flow chart is shown in Fig. 1.

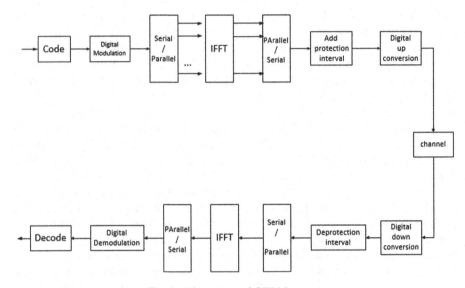

Fig. 1. Flow chart of OFDM system

After the channel coding of the input signal sequence is completed, the modulation is completed according to the modulation mode of the system, and the sequence $\{X(n)\}$ is obtained. The inverse Fourier transform is performed on the $\{X(n)\}$, and the sampling sequence in time domain of the modulated signal of orthogonal frequency division multiplexing is obtained. The cyclic prefix is added, and then the digital up conversion is carried out. The receiver first down converts the received signal, removes the protection interval, and obtains the sampling sequence of the modulated signal of OFDM, then carries on the FFT transformation, and then obtains the $\{X(n)\}$.

1.2   The Basic Principle of OFDM System

OFDM is a multicarrier modulation technology. Its principle is to use N subcarriers to divide the whole channel into N subchannels, N subcarriers with equal interval in frequency are modulated and added to transmit at the same time, so that n subchannels can transmit information in parallel. In this way, the spectrum of each symbol only occupies 1/N of the channel bandwidth, and each subcarrier keeps the spectrum orthogonality within the symbol period T of OFDM.

Figure two shows an example of an orthogonal frequency division multiplexing symbol containing four subcarriers. All subcarriers have the same amplitude and phase. It can also be seen from the figure that each subcarrier contains an integer multiple cycles in an OFDM symbol cycle, and the difference between adjacent subcarriers is one cycle. This characteristic can be used to explain the orthogonality between subcarriers. From the perspective of time domain, orthogonality meets the following formula (Fig. 2):

$$\frac{1}{T} \int_0^t e^{jau} \cdot e^{-jev'} \mathrm{d}t = \begin{cases} 1, & n = m \\ 0, & n \neq m \end{cases} \tag{1}$$

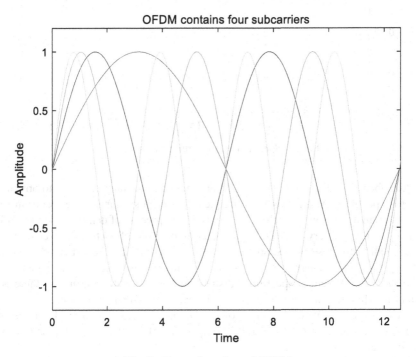

Fig. 2. Four subcarriers of OFDM

Figure three shows the spectrum diagram of four orthogonal subcarriers in an orthogonal frequency division multiplexing symbol. From the diagram, we can see that the four subcarriers reach the peak value in the same frequency, and the frequency value attenuates to 0 at the same time, that is, their spectrum changes are always consistent (Fig. 3).

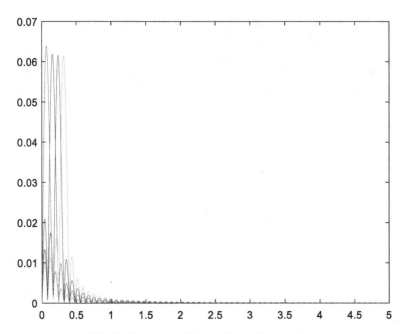

Fig. 3. Spectrum of four orthogonal subcarriers

All subcarriers of a symbol in OFDM are shaped by rectangular wave to obtain sinc function spectrum. At the maximum frequency of each subcarrier, the spectrum value of all the remaining subchannels is exactly 0. In the process of demodulation of OFDM symbols, it is necessary to calculate the maximum value of each subcarrier frequency corresponding to these points, so each subcarrier symbol can be extracted from multiple overlapping subcarrier symbols without interference from other subchannels. Since the OFDM symbol spectrum satisfies the Nyquist criterion, that is, there is no mutual interference, so the interference between carriers can be avoided.

There are three main advantages of the OFDM system, which are high spectrum efficiency, strong ability to resist ISI, frequency selective fading and narrow-band interference.

In the traditional frequency division multiplexing multicarrier modulation technology, the frequency spectrum of each subcarrier does not overlap with each other, but it is necessary to keep enough frequency interval to avoid the interference between each subcarrier. In the OFDM multicarrier modulation technology, the spectrum of each subcarrier overlaps with each other, and meets the orthogonality in the whole symbol period, which not only reduces the mutual interference between the subcarriers, but also reduces the frequency protection interval and improves the spectrum utilization.

The OFDM system inserts a protection interval greater than the channel impulse response time between each transmitted data block, so it effectively reduces the inter code interference. In a single carrier system, a single fading or interference will lead to the failure of the whole link, but in OFDM system, there are multiple subcarriers, and the fading at a certain time can only affect a part of the molecular channel. OFDM can enhance the resistance to impulse noise and channel fast fading by joint coding of subcarriers.

OFDM has many advantages, but it inevitably has some disadvantages. It is easy to be affected by frequency deviation and has high peak to average power ratio.

2 PAPR Suppression Algorithm Based on Improved Pulse Forming Technology

2.1 Definition of PAPR

Compared with the single carrier system, since the OFDM symbol is composed of multiple independent and modulated subcarrier signals, such a composite signal may generate relatively large peak power, which will result in a large peak to average power ratio. The definition of peak to average power ratio in the OFDM system is as follows:

$$\text{PAPR(dB)} = 10\lg\frac{\max\left\{|x_n|^2\right\}}{E\left\{|x_n|^2\right\}} \tag{2}$$

Where a is the output signal after IFFT operation,

$$x_n = \frac{1}{\sqrt{N}}\sum_{k=0}^{N-1}X_k W_N^{nk} \tag{3}$$

For OFDM systems with N subchannels, when n subchannels are summed with the same phase, the peak power of the signal obtained is n times of the average power, so the peak to average ratio of baseband signal can be: PAPR = 10log10n.

2.2 Principle of PAPR Suppression in Pulse Forming

The pulse shaping technology is to multiply the original data sequence and the shaping pulse matrix to produce a new sequence, so that the subcarrier symbols of the multi-carrier have certain correlation, so as to improve the PAPR characteristics of the signal [3].

The flow chart of OFDM system transmitter based on pulse forming technology is shown in Fig. 4.

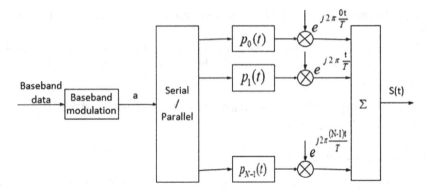

Fig. 4. Flow chart of OFDM system transmitter

After serial/parallel conversion, the baseband data sequence is multiplied by N shaping pulses, and N orthogonal subcarriers are modulated. The symbol period of OFDM is T, $a_n(n = 0, 1, \ldots, N - 1)$ represents the modulation data of each subcarrier, f_n represents the frequency of the nth subcarrier, and $p_n(t)$ represents the shaping pulse of the subcarrier f_n whose period is t. The OFDM complex signal in $0 \leq t \leq T$ is expressed as:

$$s(t) = \sum_{n=0}^{N-1} a_n p_n(t) \exp(j2\pi f_n t) \quad 0 \leqslant t \leqslant T \tag{4}$$

Sub carriers $f_n = n/T$. The real part and the virtual part of $s(t)$ correspond to the orthogonal component and the in-phase of the OFDM signal respectively. In the actual system, they can be multiplied by the in-phase component and the orthogonal component of the corresponding subcarrier respectively to synthesize the final OFDM signal [2].

Forming pulse $p_n(t)$ with period T must meet the following two conditions:

1. Orthogonal:

$$\int_0^T p_m(t) p_n^*(t) \exp[j2\pi(f_m - f_n)t]dt = \begin{cases} T, & m = n \\ 0, & m \neq n \end{cases} \tag{5}$$

2. Equal energy:

$$\int_0^\tau |p_n(t)|^2 dt = T \tag{6}$$

Another expression of PAPR of OFDM signal is:

$$\text{PAPR} = \max_{0 < 1 < T} |s(t)|^2 \Big/ \underset{0 < 1 < T}{E} \left[|s(t)|^2 \right] \tag{7}$$

When the subcarrier modulation phase is the same, the peak value of OFDM signal will be superposed to produce a large peak power, resulting in a high peak to average power ratio. If there is a certain correlation between the subcarrier symbols, the PAPR will be suppressed by reducing the probability of phase congruence.

From the perspective of the sampling values of OFDM symbols, the $R_S(t_1, t_2)$ cross-correlation function is as follows:

$$R_s(t_1, t_2) = \sum_{n=0}^{N-1} \sum_{m=0}^{N-1} E\left[a_n a_m^*\right] p_n(t_1) p_m^*(t_2) \exp[j2\pi(nt_1 - mt_2)/T] \tag{8}$$

From Eq. 8, we can see that the cross-correlation function $R_S(t_1, t_2)$ is a function of shaping pulse waveform and baseband data. We can introduce the correlation between baseband data by encoding the input information. But this will introduce redundant information and reduce the efficiency of system bandwidth.

2.3 Improvement of Nyquist Pulse Forming Technology to Suppress PAPR

The Nyquist pulse set is:

$$p_m(t)e^{j2\pi\frac{m}{T}t} = p_n(t - \tau_{m-n})e^{j2\pi\frac{n}{T}(t - \tau_{m-n})}, \quad n, m = 0, 1, \cdots, N - 1 \tag{9}$$

Where $\tau_{m-n} = [(m - n) \bmod N]T_s, p_n(t)$ (n = 0, 1,..., N − 1) is Nyquist pulse, which has no ISI property:

$$p_n(kT_s) = \begin{cases} 1, & k = 0 \\ 0, & k \neq 0 \end{cases}, k \in \mathbf{Z} \tag{10}$$

The maximum PAPR value of OFDM signal corresponding to Nyquist pulse set defined by the formula is:

$$\text{PAPR}_{\max} = \frac{1}{N} \max_{0 < \tau < T} \left(\sum_{n=0}^{N-1} |p_n(t)| \right)^2 \leqslant \frac{1}{N} \left(\sum_{n=0}^{N-1} \max_{0 < \tau < T} |p_n(t)| \right)^2 = N \tag{11}$$

The maximum value of PAPR is n when and only when rectangular pulse. The derivation of the above formula is based on the no ISI property of Nyquist pulse. It is shown that all Nyquist pulse sets constructed according to the above formula can be used for PAPR suppression of OFDM signals [4].

Since the pulse forming $p_n(t)$ (n = 0, 1,..., N − 1) is a time limited signal within the symbol period T, it can be approximated by Fourier series, that is:

$$p_n(t) = \sum_{i=-l}^{N+L-1} c_{n,l} e^{j2\pi \frac{l}{T}t}, \quad 0 \leqslant t \leqslant T \tag{12}$$

$L = N\beta/2$, $c_{n,l}$ is the coefficient of the Fourier series of $p_n(t)$:

$$c_{n,l} = \frac{1}{T} \int_0^T p_n(t) e^{-j2\pi \frac{l}{T}t} dt = \frac{1}{T} P_n\left(\frac{l}{T}\right) \tag{13}$$

Substituting Eq. 12 into 9, we can get:

$$p_n(t) = \sum_{i=-L}^{N+L-1} c_{n,l} e^{-j2\pi \frac{nl}{N}} e^{j2\pi \frac{l-n}{T}} \tag{14}$$

By substituting the subcarrier waveforms of expression 14 into expression 4, we can get:

$$
\begin{aligned}
s(t) &= \sum_{n=0}^{N-1} a_n p_n(t) e^{j2\pi^n t} \\
&= \sum_{n=0}^{N-1} a_n \sum_{l=-L}^{N+L-1} c_{n,l} e^{j2\pi \frac{nl}{N}} e^{j2\pi \frac{l-n}{T}t} e^{j2\pi n \frac{t}{T}} \\
&= \sum_{n=0}^{N-1} a_n \sum_{l=-L}^{N+L-1} c_{n,l} e^{-j2\pi \frac{nl}{N}} e^{j2\pi \frac{l}{T}t} \\
&= \sum_{l=-L}^{N+L-1} \left[\sum_{n=0}^{N-1} a_n c_{n,l} e^{j2\pi \frac{nl}{N}} \right] e^{j2\pi \frac{l}{T}t} \\
&= \sum_{l=L}^{N+L-1} b_l e^{j2\pi \frac{l}{T}t} \\
&= \text{IFFT}(\mathbf{b})
\end{aligned}
\tag{15}
$$

Where $b_l = \sum_{n=0}^{N-1} a_n c_{n,l} e^{-j2\pi \frac{nl}{N}}$ and $b = \{b_l\}$ is the vector containing N + 2L elements. $p_{n,j} = c_{nj} e^{-j2\pi \frac{nl}{N}}$ (n = 0, 1, ..., N − 1, l = − L,...,...N + L − 1), Then the orthogonal matrix representing $N \times (N + 2L)$ is called the shaping matrix, and B = AP is the new sequence after transformation.

The frequency response and time domain signal of the improved Nyquist pulse are as follows:

$$
P_2(f) = \begin{cases}
1, & |f| \leqslant B(1-\alpha) \\
e^{\lambda[B(1-\alpha)-|f|]}, & B(1-\alpha) < |f| \leqslant B \\
1 - e^{\lambda[|f|-B(1+\alpha)]}, & B < |f| < B(1+\alpha) \\
0, & |f| \geqslant B(1+\alpha)
\end{cases}
\tag{16}
$$

$$p_2(t) = \frac{1}{T_s} \sin c\left(\frac{t}{T_s}\right) \frac{4\lambda\pi t \sin(\pi\alpha t/T_s) + 2\lambda^2 \cos(\pi\alpha t/T_s) - \lambda^2}{(2\pi t)^2 + \lambda^2} \quad (17)$$

Where parameter $\lambda = \frac{\ln 2}{\alpha\beta}$.

Nyquist pulse is a real symmetric signal, and it is zero at Nyquist sampling frequency. From formula 17, it can be seen that the time-domain waveform tailing of the improved pulse is gradually attenuated, and the interference to other values caused by superposition of different sampling times is less.

3 Simulation Results and Analysis

In this paper, the simulation is carried out in the MATLAB environment. QPSK modulation is adopted, the number of subcarriers is n = 128, and the roll off coefficient of Nyquist pulse is $\alpha = 0.3$. The following figure shows the comparison of PAPR suppression between the traditional pulse forming technology and the improved Nyquist pulse forming technology. From the Fig. 5, we can see that the improved Nyquist pulse forming algorithm has better inhibition effect on PAPR than the traditional pulse forming algorithm

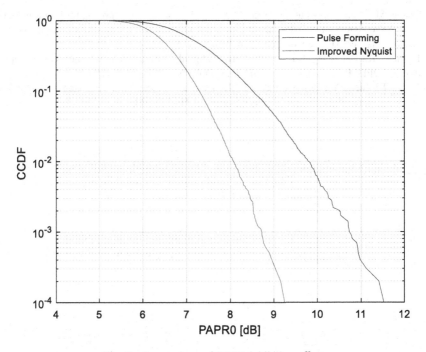

Fig. 5. Comparison of PAPR inhibition effect

4   Conclusion

In this paper, an improved Nyquist pulse shaping algorithm is proposed to solve the problem of high peak to average power ratio in OFDM system. In this algorithm, a pulse is circularly shifted to form a pulse set, which effectively avoids the phenomenon that the peak value of each subcarrier appears at the same time. The results show that compared with the traditional pulse forming algorithm, the improved Nyquist pulse forming algorithm can reduce the inter symbol interference, and it has a very good inhibition effect on the peak to average power ratio. This algorithm has greatly reduced the computational complexity, so this algorithm has certain research value.

References

1. Van Nee, R., Prasad, R.: OFDM for Wireless Multimedia Communications. Artech House, Norwood (1999)
2. Hao, M.-J., Lai, C.-H.: Pulse shaping based PAPR reduction for OFDM signals with minimum error probability. In: 2008 International Symposium on Intelligent Signal Processing and Communications Systems, Bangkok, pp. 1–4 (2009)
3. Jian, Y., Zang, Z., Yan, W.-Y.: PAPR distribution analysis of OFDM signals with Pulse Shaping. In: 2005 Asia-Pacific Conference on Communications, Perth, WA, pp. 473–477 (2005)
4. Zhang, M., Wang, Z.: Joint improved Nyquist pulse shaping and clipping for PAPR reduction of OFDM signals. In: 2011 7th International Conference on Wireless Communications, Networking and Mobile Computing, Wuhan (2011)
5. Bahai, A.R., Saltzberg, B.R.: Multi-Carrier Digital Communications: Theory and Applications of OFDM. Kluwer Academic/Plenum Publishes, New York (1999)
6. Jiang, T., Imai, Y.: An overview: peak-to-average power ratio reduction techniques for OFDM signals. IEEE Trans. Wireless Commun. 56–57 (2008)

Image and Information

Information Optimization for Image Screening and Transmission in Aerial Detection

Jieqi Li[1(✉)], Xi Liu[2], Lefan Wang[3], Fu Kong[4], Zhengxue Li[1], and Geling Yin[1]

[1] China Academy of Lunch Vehicle Technology, Beijing 10076, China
sxtyljq@163.com
[2] Unit 95899 of PLA, Beijing 100085, China
[3] School of Electronics and Information, Northwestern Polytechnical University, Xi'an 710129, Shaanxi, China
[4] Beijing Mechanical and Electrical Overall Design Department, Beijing 100854, China

Abstract. In aerial detection, photoelectric sensor as the main detection form, can usually obtain a large number of image data in the detection target area, however, the communication bandwidth is often limited. As a result, the contradiction between powerful image acquisition and limited bandwidth causes the massive detected images cannot be completely transmitted. To address this problem, an effective method of acquisition information optimization for image screening and transmission in aerial detection is proposed in this paper. This proposed method is mainly based on the principle of sparse coding, in which the key information is extracted and can reconstruct the other information well via a linear combination. It can autonomously select and transmit the most valuable images without the requirement of prior information. As a result, the transmission of redundant information is greatly reduced, and the requirement for communication bandwidth of detection system is also reduced.

Keywords: Information optimization · Image screening · Aerial detection

1 Introduction

Aerial detection uses aircrafts to conduct scientific detection of areas that are not easy for humans to reach to obtain information about the detection target area. It plays an important role in military, civilian and other fields. In modern war, information dominance is the key factor affecting the overall strategic situation. The requirement of intelligence information in combat is higher and higher, and reliable intelligence information has become the fundamental guarantee of precise strike. In the civil aspect, aerial detection also plays an important role. For example, the aerial detection technology combined with remote sensing has been widely used in basic geological survey, mineral resources exploration, environmental geological exploration, geological disasters and other fields, and has broad development prospects.

With the continuous development of photoelectric sensors, the existing detection technology is developing towards the direction of multi/hyperspectral, high-resolution and all-weather detection. It can obtain a large number of detection images in the target

B. Li et al. (Eds.): IoTaaS 2020, LNICST 346, pp. 745–754, 2021.
https://doi.org/10.1007/978-3-030-67514-1_59

area, however, the bandwidth of the downlink channel is usually limited for such large volume of image data. It has been an increasingly significant problem for the detection system to screen the detected massive images to realize the information optimization and to transmit the most effective information back to the ground information center for response.

At present, there are few researches on the screening and transmission of aerial detection images. The simplest approach is uniformly sampling and transmission, however, the content of images is ignored. Hu *et al.* proposed a SAR image filtering method based on bit plane bit-plane characteristics [4], which is for the typical target of interest and requires the prior knowledge of targets. In addition, image deduplication technology [7, 10], that is to delete duplicate images, can also be thought as an information optimization technology, but it has not been applied to the field of image screening and transmission of detection system.

Based on the keyframe extraction technology in the field of video summarization [1, 3], an acquisition information optimization method is proposed for image screening transmission in aerial detection is proposed. The method does not aim at specific targets and does not need prior knowledge. Through the feature representation of the aerial detection image, the most informative image is selected for transmission according to the characteristics of the image. In each subsequent transmission, the image which is mostly different with the transmitted image is selected. Through the proposed information optimization method, the transmitted data amount and the captured information redundancy is significantly reduced, and the effectiveness of information under the limited bandwidth is improved.

2   Image Screening and Transmission System

The aerial detection image screening and transmission system is shown in Fig. 1. Firstly, the detection sensor detects the target area and collects a large number of aerial detection images. Next, the optimization of image screening and transmission is performed on the detected image sequences, and the most valuable images can be screened from all images. Finally, the screened image is transmitted and returned to the ground information center through the communication system. In this process, the most important part is the optimization of image screening and transmission of massive detection images. Furthermore, the major difficulty is the criterion of image screening, that is, how to choose a small number of key images from the massive detection images without specific targets and prior knowledge.

This proposed method in this paper selects the key images need to be transmitted from the massive detection images based on the principle of sparse representation. The main idea of sparse representation is to select a small number of atoms from an over-complete dictionary to form a sub-dictionary, which is required to reconstruct the original signal with a extremely small error. As well as for the screening and transmission of detection images, a small number of images are selected from the mass detection images to form a key image set. If this key image set can reconstruct the mass detection images without losing the important information carried by the original mass detection images, such a key image set is our need.

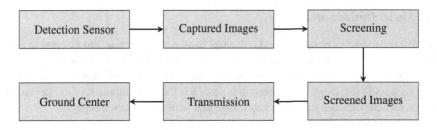

Fig. 1. Aerial image screening and transmission system.

3   Autonomous Screening and Transmission Algorithm

3.1   Screening and Transmission Model

Let $\mathbf{F} = [\mathbf{f}_1, \mathbf{f}_2, \ldots, \mathbf{f}_n] \in \mathbb{R}^{d \times n}$ denote the massive detection image sequence acquired by the aerospace detection system, where $\mathbf{f}_i (i = 1, 2, \cdots, n)$ represents the feature vector of the i-th detection image. Based on the principle of sparse reconstruction, the key image $\mathbf{F}_K = \left[\mathbf{f}_{k_1}, \mathbf{f}_{k_2}, \ldots, \mathbf{f}_{k_p}\right]$ that best covers all of its information is selected from the original detection image sequence for transmission. Once the key image set is selected, so that the original detection image sequence $\mathbf{F}$ not only can be accurately reconstructed but also contains as small as possible columns. Therefore, the aerial detection image screening and transmission model we established is shown in Eq. (1):

$$\min_{\mathbf{S}} : \frac{1}{2} \|\mathbf{F} - \mathbf{F}_K \mathbf{A}\|_F + \lambda \cdot \sum(\mathbf{S}),$$

$$\text{s.t.} \quad \mathbf{F}_K = \mathbf{FS},$$

$$\mathbf{A} = f(\mathbf{F}, \mathbf{F}_K), \tag{1}$$

in which $\mathbf{S}$ is the key image selection matrix, its diagonal elements are '0' or '1', the other elements are all '0', and '1' means that the corresponding detection image is selected as the key image for transmission, vice versa. In addition, $\mathbf{A}$ represents the reconstruction coefficient when key image set $\mathbf{F}_K$ is used to reconstruct the original image sequence $\mathbf{F}$, and $\sum \mathbf{S}$ represents the number of key frames $\mathbf{F}_K$, namely, the number of transmitted detection images.

In the objective function of Eq. (1), the first term is the error when the original massive detection image sequence is reconstructed by the extracted key image set, and the second term is as small as possible to constrain the extracted key images. In order to acquire the reconstruction coefficients $\mathbf{A}$, we use Orthogonal Subspace Projection (OSP), which projects all the detection images to the subspace determined by the key image set. Therefore, the reconstruction coefficient is obtained as follows:

$$\mathbf{A} = \left(\mathbf{F}_K^T \mathbf{F}_K\right)^{-1} \mathbf{F}_K^T \mathbf{F}. \tag{2}$$

3.2   Model Optimization

To solve the model defined in Eq. (1), the key issue is to determine the key image selection matrix S. After obtaining S, the reconstruction coefficient A can be calculated by Eq. (2), then the reconstruction error can be obtained to determine whether the selected key image set is sufficient. The determination of S is the determination of the key images to be screened, including the first key image and subsequent key images.

Determine the First Key Image. The first key image is always the one whose feature vector is nearest from the average or the one who has maximum amplitude.

$$\mathbf{f}_{k_1} = \arg \min_{\mathbf{f}_j \in \mathbf{F}} \left\| \mathbf{f}_j - \bar{\mathbf{f}} \right\|_2, \tag{3}$$

where $\bar{\mathbf{f}} = \frac{1}{n} \sum_j \mathbf{f}_j$ means the average of all image feature vectors, or

$$\mathbf{f}_{k_1} = \arg \max_{\mathbf{f}_j \in \mathbf{F}} \left\| \mathbf{f}_j \right\|_2. \tag{4}$$

Equation (3) indicates that the feature of the first key image is closest to the average feature of all detected images, and Eq. (4) means the first key image has maximum amplitude.

Determine the Subsequent Key Images. When the first key image is determined, the image that has the most differences with the transmitted ones is selected as the next key image. In other words, we use the currently transmitted detection image set to reconstruct all non-transmitted detection images, and select the image with the largest reconstruction error to transmit. This is due to the larger the reconstruction error is, the less information of the image is contained by the transmitted image set.

Assuming $\mathbf{F}_K = \left[\mathbf{f}_{k_1}, \mathbf{f}_{k_2}, \ldots, \mathbf{f}_{k_m} \right] \in \mathbb{R}^{d \times m}$ denotes detection images that have been transmitted, the next detection image to be transmitted is:

$$\mathbf{f}_{k_{m+1}} = \arg \max_{\mathbf{f}_j \in \mathbf{F}/\mathbf{F}_K} \frac{\left\| \mathbf{f}_j - \mathbf{F}_K \mathbf{a}_j \right\|}{\left\| \mathbf{f}_j \right\|_2}, \tag{5}$$

in which $\mathbf{a}_j$ represents the reconstruction coefficient of the j-th detection image, which can generally be obtained by orthogonal projection algorithm:

$$\mathbf{a}_j = \left(\mathbf{F}_K^T \mathbf{F}_K \right)^{-1} \mathbf{F}_K^T \mathbf{f}_j. \tag{6}$$

After obtain $\mathbf{f}_{k_{m+1}}$, the key image set can be updated as

$$\mathbf{F}_K = \mathbf{F}_K \cup \mathbf{f}_{k_{m+1}}. \tag{7}$$

According to the above analysis, the designed image screening and transmission process is shown in Fig. 2.

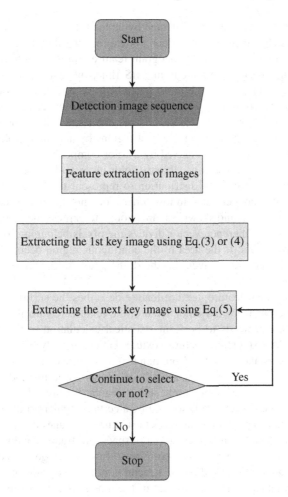

Fig. 2. The proposed aerial detection image screening and transmission process.

4   Feature Representation of Detection Images

As mentioned above, during the screening of massive detection images, how to characterize each image in the detection image sequence directly affects the final screening and transmission effect. If the processing is directly based on the pixel data of the
original image, the similarity of the image is easily affected by factors such as illumination, geometric deformation, etc., and the computation is usually time-consuming.
Features representation can accurately describe the information that users care about
in the image, thereby, the impact of factors such as illumination on image similarity
is reduced. Commonly used image features include color, texture, shape and spatial
relationship.

Color is a global feature that describes the surface properties of the scene corresponding to the image or image area. The most commonly used method to express

color is color histogram, that is not affected by image rotation and translation changes. However, the disadvantage is that it does not express the distribution information in color space. Commonly used color histogram feature representation methods include: RGB (red, green, blue) space histogram, HIS (hue, intensity, saturation) space histogram, HSV (chroma, purity, lightness) space histogram, etc. The color set [8] is an approximation to the color histogram. Firstly, the RGB color space is transformed into a visually balanced color space (HSV), and the color space is quantized into several bins. Then, the image is divided into several regions by automatic color segmentation technology, and each regions is indexed by a color component of the quantified color space, so the image is expressed as a binary color index table. Color moment uses the mathematical moments of color distribution to represent the image [11]. Since color distribution is mainly concentrated in low-order moments, the first, second, third-order moment (mean, variance, and skewness) are enough to express the color distribution of the image. The color coherence vector divides the pixels belonging to each bin of the histogram into two parts. If the area of the continuous region occupied by some pixels in the bin is larger than a given threshold, the pixels in the region are regarded as coherence pixels.

As a kind of global feature, texture feature describes the surface properties of the image area. Different from the color feature, the texture feature is not based on the feature of pixels, and needs to perform statistical calculation in the area containing multiple pixels. As a statistical feature, texture features usually have rotational invariance and strong resistance to noise. Common texture feature extraction methods include structural analysis methods, statistical methods, model based methods and signal processing based methods [12]. Only applicable to regular textures, the structural analysis method assumes that the texture is formed by a certain regular arrangement of texture primitives. The statistical method analyzes the texture of images from the perspective of regional statistics, which can be carried out in space and frequency domains. The main methods include edge histogram, autocorrelation function, edge frequency, gray-level co-occurrence matrix, etc. Based on the structural model of the image, the model based method take advantage of the parameters of the model as the texture feature. Typical methods are random field model methods, such as Markov Random Field (MRF) model and Gibbs Random Field model. Generally, signal analysis based methods utilize filter, such as spatial filter, frequency domain filter, and Gabor filter, to extract texture from the filtered image.

There are two types of representation methods for shape features, one is contour features, and the other is regional features. The contour feature of the image principally focused on the outer boundary of the object, while the regional feature of the image is primarily related to the entire shape area. The typical methods for shape description include boundary feature method, Fourier shape descriptor method, and moment invariant feature method. The boundary feature method obtains the shape parameters of the image by describing the boundary feature, and the representative algorithm includes the Hough transform method for detecting parallel lines and the boundary direction histogram method. The Fourier shape descriptor method uses the Fourier transform of the object boundary as the shape description, and utilizes the closure and periodicity of the region boundary to transform a two-dimension problem into a one-dimension. Invariant

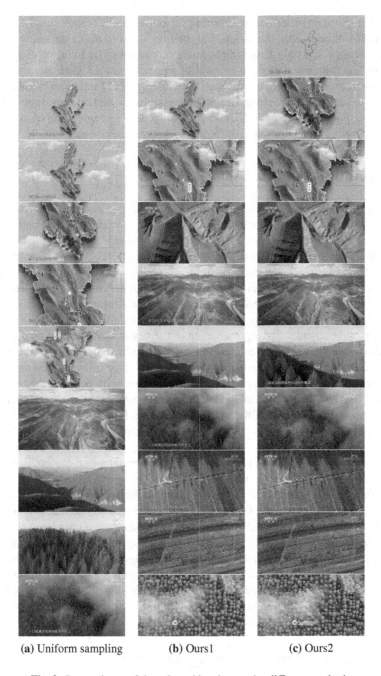

(a) Uniform sampling   (b) Ours1   (c) Ours2

Fig. 3. Comparisons of the selected key images by different methods.

moments exploit the moments in statistics to characterize the geometric characteristics of the image area, which have the invariance to rotation, translation, and expansion.

In order to obtain better image screening performance, the features used should own invariance to illumination, translation and rotation, so as to avoid screening out some detection images that only have simple rotation, translation or light intensity change. Therefore, combined features can be used to represent images, such as a 360 dimensional descriptor consisted of census transform histogram [9] and color moment, which has achieved satisfactory performance in the research of video summarization [2, 6]. In recent years, with the development of deep learning, deep features based on convolution neural networks [5] can also be used for image feature description.

5 Experiment and Discussion

In the experiment, the processed video frames are used to simulate the detection image sequence. The video used in our experiment is from episode 10 of "Aerial China3", which is aerial documentary with 10 episodes. The video is down-sampled every five frames to reduce the computation, and the resolution is 1920×1080. For the feature representation of images, the experiment uses 360-dimensional features, consisting of 252-dimensional CENTRIST features and 108-dimensional color features. In the experiment, 15 key images are selected from 600 images for transmission, and the results of the algorithm proposed in this paper are compared with uniform sampling.

We first give a qualitative representation of the key images selected by our method and uniform sampling, and the comparison results are shown in Fig. 3, in which 'Ous1' and 'Ous2' indicates our method selects the 1st key image using Eq. (3) and Eq. (4), respectively. According to the results of Fig. 3, the similarity between the transmitted images filtered by the proposed method in this paper is obviously small, which indicates that the information content of the transmitted images filtered by our method is more sufficient and abundant. However, it can also be observed that the images selected by uniform sampling have large similarities, for example, the 2nd, 3rd, 4th, 5th and 6th images have certain similarity. This shows that uniform sampling can not consider the content changes of image sequences.

For further observation, the experiment is quantitatively evaluated, and the average correlation defined in Eq. (8) between each currently screened transmission image (image to be transmitted) and the previously transmitted image is calculated. The experimental results are shown in Fig. 4. According to the quantitative evaluation in Fig. 4, the average correlation between the newly selected image and the images that have been selected and transmitted through the proposed algorithm is significantly lower than the correlation through uniform sampling and filtering. In summary, the detection image screening and transmission algorithm proposed in this paper can not only reduce the transmission data volume, but also transmit the most informative images.

$$Cor_{avg} = \frac{1}{|kf^{(pre)}|} \sum_i cor(kf^{(now)}, kf_i^{(pre)}), \qquad (8)$$

where $kf^{(now)}$ denotes the newly selected keyframe at current time, $kf_i^{(pre)}$ denotes the i-th key image that is previously selected and transmitted, $|kf^{(pre)}|$ is the length, i.e., the number of previous key images.

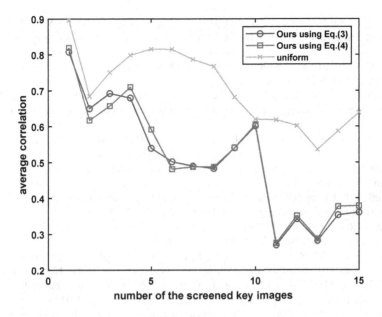

Fig. 4. Comparisons of the selected key images by different methods.

6 Conclusion

In order to effectively solve the contradiction between the massive images of the target captured by the sensor and the limited transmission bandwidth of the communication system, information optimization method for screening and transmission of detection images is proposed in this paper. The proposed method is based on sparse representation principle, which assumes than the screened key image set can reconstruct all the important information in the original image sequence. On the premise that there is no specific target and prior information, the most valuable images are selected and transmitted in the aerial detection system, so as to realize the optimization of information acquisition. Experimental results prove that the proposed method can select more informative images and reduce the transmission of redundant information. Accordingly, the requirement for communication bandwidth of the detection system is reduced under the same detection image acquisition capacity.

References

1. Ajmal, M., Ashraf, M.H., Shakir, M., Abbas, Y., Shah, F.A.: Video summarization: techniques and classification. In: Bolc, L., Tadeusiewicz, R., Chmielewski, L.J., Wojciechowski, K. (eds.) ICCVG 2012. LNCS, vol. 7594, pp. 1–13. Springer, Heidelberg (2012). https://doi.org/10.1007/978-3-642-33564-8_1
2. Cong, Y., Liu, J., Sun, G., You, Q., Li, Y., Luo, J.: Adaptive greedy dictionary selection for web media summarization. IEEE Trans. Image Process. **26**(1), 185–195 (2017)

3. De Avila, S.E.F., Lopes, A.P.B., da Luz, A., de Albuquerque Araújo, A.: VSUMM: a mechanism designed to produce static video summaries and a novel evaluation method. Pattern Recognit. Lett. **32**(1), pp. 56–68 (2011)
4. Hu, C., Liu, F., Zhou, J.: SAR images screening based on bit-plane characteristics. J. Comput. Appl. **29**(11), 3021–3026 (2009)
5. Krizhevsky, A., Sutskever, I., Hinton, G.E.: ImageNet classification with deep convolutional neural networks. In: Advances in Neural Information Processing Systems, pp. 1097–1105 (2012)
6. Ma, M., Mei, S., Wan, S., Hou, J., Wang, Z., Feng, D.D.: Video summarization via block sparse dictionary selection. Neurocomputing **378**, 197–209 (2020)
7. Rashid, F., Miri, A., Woungang, I.: Secure image deduplication through image compression. J. Inf. Secur. Appl. **27**, 54–64 (2016)
8. Smith, J.R., Chang, S.F.: VisualSEEk: a fully automated content-based image query system. In: ACM International Conference on Multimedia, pp. 87–98 (1997)
9. Wu, J., Rehg, J.M.: CENTRIST: a visual descriptor for scene categorization. IEEE Trans. Pattern Anal. Mach. Intell. **33**(8), 1489–1501 (2010)
10. Xu, J., Zhang, W., Zhang, Z., Wang, T., Huang, T.: Clustering-based acceleration for virtual machine image deduplication in the cloud environment. J. Syst. Softw. **121**, 144–156 (2016)
11. Yu, H., Li, M., Zhang, H.J., Feng, J.: Color texture moments for content-based image retrieval. In: International Conference on Image Processing, pp. 929–932 (2002)
12. Zhang, J., Tan, T.: Brief review of invariant texture analysis methods. Pattern Recognit. **35**(3), 735–747 (2002)

Method of Quality Assessment for BOC Navigation Signal Based on Multi-correlation Receiver

Xia Luo[1(⊠)], Li Xu[1], Peihan Yu[2], and Hongwei Zhao[2]

[1] Beijing Research Institute of Telemetry, Beijing 100076, China
justluoluo219@163.com
[2] School of Electronics and Information, Northwestern Polytechnical University,
Xi'an 710072, China

Abstract. The integrity of navigation signal can be reflected on the correlation curve, so the quality of the signal can be evaluated by analyzing the correlation curve of navigation signal. Aiming at the binary offset carrier (BOC) modulation used in the navigation signal, and Taking BOC (1,1) as an example, the acquisition and tracking algorithm of the BOC signal is given first in this paper. Then the software receiver based on the multi-correlator is designed, and the performance of the correlation curve is analyzed from the aspects of pseudo-range difference value, multiple correlation value difference and multiple correlation value symmetry. The simulation results show that the BOC signal synchronization method proposed in this paper can be effectively captured and tracked, and the output results of the multi-correlator can accurately reflect the quality performance of the navigation signal, so it is suitable for signal quality assessment of BOC receiver.

Keywords: BOC navigation signal · Quality assessment · Multi-correlation receiver

1 Introduction

The basic task of navigation is to determine the position of the carrier, and guide the users from the current location to the destination, according to the given time and route. With the rapid development of the Global Navigation Satellite System (GNSS), the military, aerospace, transportation, surveying and mapping, seismic monitoring and other industries have a growing need for high-precision positioning and navigation. However, measurement errors caused by satellite clock errors, satellite ephemeris errors, ionospheric delay [1], tropospheric delays, and multipath effects have seriously affected the measurement accuracy of the GNSS. Among them, the first four types of errors are systematic errors, which can be eliminated by differential or modeling methods. While multipath errors are difficult to eliminate through differential technology due to their time-varying and environment-dependent characteristics, and become the most important factor affecting high-precision ranging.

Multipath effect means that in addition to the direct navigation signal, the receiver also receives various other indirect signals at the same time. These indirect signals are

© ICST Institute for Computer Sciences, Social Informatics and Telecommunications Engineering 2021
Published by Springer Nature Switzerland AG 2021. All Rights Reserved
B. Li et al. (Eds.): IoTaaS 2020, LNICST 346, pp. 755–767, 2021.
https://doi.org/10.1007/978-3-030-67514-1_60

called multipath signals. Multipath signals will distort the correlation function between the synthesized signal (direct signal plus multipath signal) received by the receiver and the local reference signal generated by the receiver. What's more, multipath signals will also cause distortion of the received signal's synthesized carrier phase. Errors are introduced in the measured values of pseudo-range and carrier phase (different signals transmitted by different satellites have different values), resulting in positioning, speed fixation, and timing errors. In severe cases, it can also cause code phase lock-lose, carrier phase lock-lose, and missing the satellite signal. Therefore, suppressing multipath errors effectively is a key technology to improve the navigation and positioning accuracy of the global navigation satellite system.

Since the spread spectrum modulated signal used in the navigation system has good autocorrelation, and its lead-lag correlation curve is symmetrical, it is possible to consider setting up multiple correlators in the receiver and use the correlation curve to monitor whether multipath or distortion exists in the navigation signal. In this paper, the new system BOC modulation signal is studied. Taking BOC (1,1) as an example, a suitable synchronization receiving algorithm is proposed by analyzing its frequency spectrum and autocorrelation function. Then the quality of navigation signals will be monitored and evaluated by setting multiple correlators, and performing pseudo-range difference detection, correlation value difference detection, symmetric ratio detection and other methods.

2   Signal Model and Synchronization Method

2.1   BOC Signal Model

The BOC signal adds square wave subcarrier modulation on the basis of pseudo code modulation. As a result, the original BPSK spectrum is split into two symmetrical spectrums about the carrier frequency, and there is no energy distribution on the center carrier frequency. This split-spectrum feature allows it to share the frequency band with the original signal on the satellite system. In addition, the BOC modulated signal has a sharper correlation peak than the original BPSK signal, so it has better positioning accuracy, higher anti-multipath and anti-narrowband interference capabilities. The BOC modulated navigation signal can be expressed as:

$$s(t) = e^{-i\theta} \sum_k a_k \mu_{nT}(t - knT - t_0) c_T(t - t_0) \tag{1}$$

In the formula, a_k is the spreading code after data modulation with unit amplitude. μ_{nT} is the spreading symbol (pseudo code symbol), the length of chips is nT, where n is a positive integer, representing the ratio of a pseudo-code chip length to half the subcarrier period, also known as the BOC spreading ratio [1]. $c_T(t)$ is the subcarrier, which is a square wave with a period of $2T$. Usually $c_T(t) = \text{sign}(\sin(2\pi f_s t))$ or $c_T(t) = \text{sign}(\cos(2\pi f_s t))$, where $f_s = 1/2T$ is the subcarrier frequency, and $\text{sign}(\bullet)$ is the sign function. θ and t_0 are the phase and time offsets relative to a reference respectively. The modulation process can be expressed as Fig. 1:

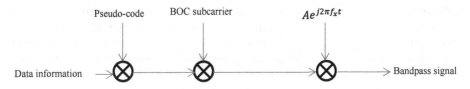

Fig. 1. The process of the BOC modulation

In satellite navigation systems, the BOC modulated signal is usually abbreviated as $BOC(\alpha, \beta)$, where α represents the subcarrier frequency $\alpha \times 1.023\,\text{MHz}$ and β represents the pseudo code rate $\beta \times 1.023\,\text{MHz}$, besides $n = 2\alpha/\beta$.

2.2 BOC Signal Synchronization Method

Taking BOC (1,1) signal as an example, its acquisition method can use ASPeCT (autocorrelation side-peak cancellation technique) algorithm, which is suitable for BOC (n,n) signal acquisition. The specific process is as follows: First, the input IF signal Is multiplied by the local carrier of the in-phase and orthogonal branch to carry out carrier stripping. Then each branch signal is divided into two groups. One group is correlated with the spreading code modulated by the subcarrier, and the other group performs correlation operations with spreading codes of unmodulated subcarrier [2]. Finally the calculation results are squared, and then the processing results of the four branches are combined in a certain manner. The process is shown in Fig. 2.

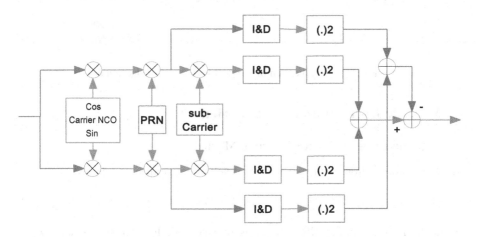

Fig. 2. Block diagram of ASPeCT algorithm

BOC signal includes subcarrier modulation and pseudo-code modulation, so it is proposed to use three-loop tracking algorithm. The main idea of the three-loop tracking algorithm is: the autocorrelation of the BOC signal is obtained by multiplying the autocorrelation result of the pseudo code and the autocorrelation result of the subcarrier. Then the pseudo code and subcarrier can be tracked separately to obtain the phase of the pseudo code rough estimation and precise estimation [3]. Finally combining the phase measurement values of the code tracking loop and the subcarrier tracking loop can get a more accurate code phase tracking result. The specific process is shown in Fig. 3:

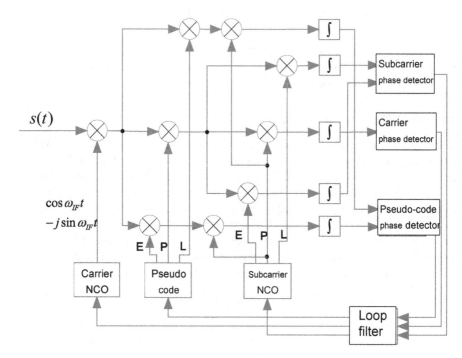

Fig. 3. Block diagram of the dual-loop tracking algorithm

3   Multiple Correlators Detection Method

3.1   Pseudo-range Difference Detection Method

The pseudo-range from the receiver to the satellite i is defined as follows:

$$\rho_i = c[T_R(n) - T_{Ti}(n)] \tag{2}$$

In the formula, $c = 299792458$ m/s is the speed of light in the vacuum. $T_R(n)$ represents the receiving time corresponding to the n epoch of the GNSS receiver clock. $T_{Ti}(n)$ represents the launch time based on the satellite i clock.

Under ideal conditions, the pseudo-range measurement values obtained by the code tracking loop at different correlation intervals are equal, and the difference value should be zero. Once the correlation function is deformed, the difference between the pseudo-range measurements will no longer be zero. If the receiver is configured with multiple channels with different correlation intervals, it can be judged whether the navigation signal is abnormal by observing the difference between the pseudo-range measurement values of each channel. The measurement values are as follows:

$$\beta_\rho = \max \begin{bmatrix} \frac{\Delta\tau_a(d_1,d_2)-\Delta\tau_{nom}(d_1,d_2)}{MDE_{d_1,d_2}} \\ \frac{\Delta\tau_a(d_1,d_3)-\Delta\tau_{nom}(d_1,d_3)}{MDE_{d_1,d_3}} \\ \vdots \\ \frac{\Delta\tau_a(d_1,d_n)-\Delta\tau_{nom}(d_1,d_n)}{MDE_{d_1,d_n}} \end{bmatrix} \tag{3}$$

As long as this metric value is greater than 1, it is considered that the navigation signal is abnormal. The difference of the pseudo-range measurement values between different correlation intervals in the above formula is expressed as:

$$\Delta\tau\left(d_i, d_j\right) = \tau(d_i) - \tau\left(d_j\right) \tag{4}$$

$$\tau(d) = \arg[R\left(\tau + \frac{d}{2}\right) - R\left(\tau - \frac{d}{2}\right)] = 0 \tag{5}$$

Among them, $q = a$ or norm. a means abnormal signal, and norm means ideal signal. $R(d)$ represents correlation value. d_i represents different correlation intervals. $MDE\left(d_i, d_j\right)$ is the minimum detection error threshold corresponding to the correlation interval d_i and d_j.

This method requires each channel to track the satellite independently, and each channel is configured with a correlation interval. Therefore, a large number of channels are needed to obtain the pseudo-range of the same satellite, which leads to a complex system and higher requirements for monitoring receivers. In addition, it can be found that this method cannot identify the flat-top effect of the correlation function from Eqs. (4) and (5).

3.2   Correlation Value Difference Detection Method

Generally speaking, the pseudo-range value is obtained based on the output value (correlation value) of the correlator. Therefore, monitoring can also be achieved by using relevant values. The use of correlation values for detection also requires multiple correlation intervals, but only one lead-lag code tracking loop is required to track the correlation peak. While other lead-lag correlators with different correlation intervals do not participate in loop tracking and output correlation values directly.

$$\gamma_\Delta = \max \begin{bmatrix} \dfrac{\left(\Delta_{a,1}-\Delta_{a,ref}\right)-\left(\Delta_{nom,1}-\Delta_{nom,ref}\right)}{MDE_{1,ref}} \\ \dfrac{\left(\Delta_{a,2}-\Delta_{a,ref}\right)-\left(\Delta_{nom,2}-\Delta_{nom,ref}\right)}{MDE_{2,ref}} \\ \vdots \\ \dfrac{\left(\Delta_{a,n-1}-\Delta_{a,ref}\right)-\left(\Delta_{nom,n-1}-\Delta_{nom,ref}\right)}{MDE_{n-1,ref}} \end{bmatrix} \tag{6}$$

$$\Delta_m = R\left[\tau_{ref} - \frac{d_m}{2}\right] - R\left[\tau_{ref} + \frac{d_m}{2}\right] \tag{7}$$

$$\tau_{ref} = \arg\left\{R\left(\tau - \frac{d_{ref}}{2}\right) - R\left(\tau + \frac{d_{ref}}{2}\right) = 0\right\} \tag{8}$$

In the formula, there are n correlation pairs (one of them is used for tracking). τ_{ref} is the maximum correlation peak position estimated by the tracking correlation pair. A more straightforward description is that $R\left[\tau_{ref} \pm \frac{d_m}{2}\right]$ is the correlation value of the relative output with a correlation interval of d_m, which can be directly obtained.

It is worth noting that $\Delta_{a,ref} \neq 0, \Delta_{nom,ref} \neq 0$ for non-ideal signals. It is guessed that the above expression is complicated to ensure the accuracy of the expression. When the phase tracking is locked, the detection amount can also be expressed by the real part of the normalized correlation output:

$$\Delta_m = \frac{I_{early,m} - I_{late,m}}{2I_{prompt}} \tag{9}$$

In the above formula, 2 is the phase discrimination gain, which needs to be changed for the BOC signal.

3.3 Symmetry Ratio Detection Method

The ideal correlation function is not only symmetrical, but also the slope of the curve is definite. The deformation of the correlation function will change the slope of the curve. Therefore, observing the slope of each point of the correlation curve can detect signal abnormalities [4]. This method uses the ratio of the leading and lagging branch measured values to the instant branch measured values, which is divided into bilateral detection and unilateral detection. The metric for bilateral detection is:

$$R_{double} = \frac{I_{early} + I_{late}}{2I_{prompt}} \tag{10}$$

The metric for unilateral detection is:

$$\begin{cases} R_{single,early} = \dfrac{I_{early}}{I_{prompt}} \\ R_{single,late} = \dfrac{I_{late}}{I_{prompt}} \end{cases} \tag{11}$$

In the above formula, there is only one instant branch, and there are multiple lead-lag correlators. For a receiver channel containing n lead-lag correlator pairs, the metric can be expressed as:

$$\gamma_R = \max \begin{bmatrix} \dfrac{R_{a,1} - R_{nom,1}}{MDE_{R_1}} \\ \dfrac{R_{a,2} - R_{nom,2}}{MDE_{R_2}} \\ \vdots \\ \dfrac{R_{a,n} - R_{nom,n}}{MDE_{R_n}} \end{bmatrix} \tag{12}$$

Since some signal anomalies only affect one side of the correlation curve, unilateral detection is helpful to improve the sensitivity to such distortions. The composition of the formula is flexible. If only the bilateral or one-sided unilateral detection is performed, substitute the corresponding detection amount into the formula. The bilateral and two-sided unilateral detection can also be performed at the same time [5].

4   Performance Simulation and Analysis

4.1   Signal Synchronization Performance

The BOC (1,1) signal is first generated in the simulation. The carrier intermediate frequency $F_c = 1.023\,\text{MHz}$, and the carrier Doppler $F_D = 2500KHz$. The rate of pseudo code is $1.023Mcps$. In addition, the number of bits of the signal becomes longer due to BOC (1,1) modulation. In order to reduce the calculation time, we set the sampling rate of the pseudo code to $F_s = 19.437\,\text{MHz}$; carrier ratio $C_{N0} = 70$; signal-to-noise ratio $SNR = C_{N0} - 10 * \lg(F_s) = 62.4$.

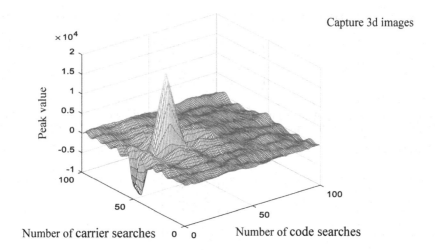

Fig. 4. BOC signal acquisition

The signal acquisition result is shown in Fig. 4. In the figure, the C/A code shifted 53 chips to the right, and the carrier is shifted by 2.5 kHz. There is a peak at x = 51 and y = 25.

The following is the curve of tracking the pilot signal when the satellite number is 18 (Fig. 5).

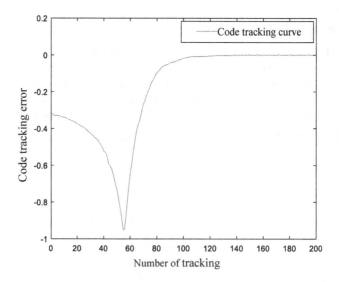

Fig. 5. BOC signal code tracking curve

We can see that after about 110 cycles, the C/A code was successfully tracked (Fig. 6).

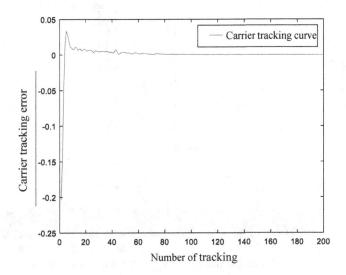

Fig. 6. BOC signal carrier tracking curve

It can be seen that after approximately 70 cycles, the carrier was successfully tracked.

4.2   Performance of Pseudo-range Difference Detection

Since the calculation of the pseudo-range requires real and reliable GNSS data, here we use the actual collected GNSS signals for simulation. The Fig. 7 is the satellite captured. We can see that the signals of the 03, 06, 09, 15, 18, 21, 22, and 26 satellites have been captured.

We take the 18th satellite signal for pseudo-range simulation. First set up four tracking channels, and the intervals (lead minus lag) of the four tracking channels are respectively 0.1 chip, 0.06 chip, 0.07 chip, and 0.08 chips. The tracking result obtained by each tracking channel is used to calculate the pseudo-range.

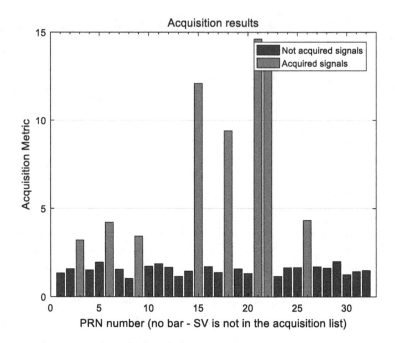

Fig. 7. Satellite capture image

Then we got the signal propagation time T of each channel, the values of T are 69.338 ms, 69.339 ms, 69.338 ms, 69.338 ms respectively. The pseudo-range values of the four channels calculated from $\rho = T \times c$ are 20787143 m, 20787190 m, 20787143 m and 20787143 m. As shown in Fig. 8.

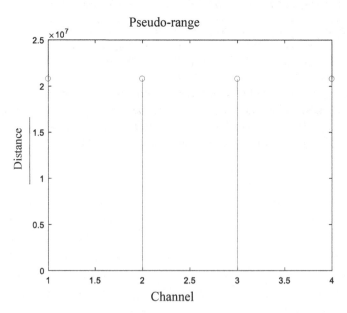

Fig. 8. Pseudo-range difference image

From Fig. 8, we can see that the pseudo-ranges calculated by tracking channels with different tracking intervals is slightly different, among which the pseudo-ranges measured by the middle second channel is the largest. We can see that the tracking channels are different, and the difference is not very significant. The difference here mainly comes from satellite clock errors, satellite ephemeris errors, channel noise interference and so on [6]. Under ideal conditions, the pseudo-range measurement values obtained by the code tracking loop at different correlation intervals are equal, and the difference should be zero. Once the correlation function is deformed, the difference between the pseudo-range measurements will no longer be zero.

4.3   Performance of Multi-correlation Value Difference Detection

We used correlation values to detect, and 21 correlation intervals were configured with only one tracking channel. Among them, with the instantaneous code as the center, there are 10 related channels on the left and right. Adjacent channels are separated by 1/19 chips. The following curve is obtained by accumulating the values of each channel.

Among them, the formula for calculating the correlation value of each relevant channel is as follows (only take the most advanced channel as an example): calculate the cumulative sum of the I and Q branches respectively, and then take the square root of the arithmetic sum of the two.

$$I\_E(t) = \sum earlyCode(t) \times iBasebandSignal(t); \tag{13}$$

$$Q\_E(t) = \sum earlyCode(t) \times qBasebandSignal(t); \tag{14}$$

$$y = \sqrt{(I\_E \times I\_E + Q\_E \times Q\_E)}; \tag{15}$$

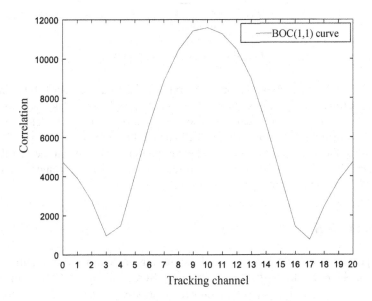

Fig. 9. BOC signal correlation curve

As shown in the Fig. 9, the curve has a peak at x = 10. Since x = 10 is the location of the instant code channel, the peak appears here. It can be found that the correlation curve is similar to the BOC (1,1) signal correlation curve. From the simulation results, we can see that the sharp part of the curve in the middle is not straight, but slightly jittered, and the jitter becomes more serious the higher the top is, then analysis shows that the signal is abnormal. However, compared with BPSK signal, its curve jitter is smaller, which can also reflect the benign nature of the BOC signal.

4.4   Performance of Symmetry Ratio Detection

The slope of each point of the sharp part of the correlation curve was simulated with MATLAB, as shown in the following Fig. 10:

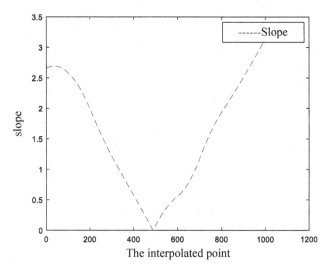

Fig. 10. BOC signal slope curve

First perform spline interpolation on the relevant curve and obtain 1000 points, then the values of the slope obtained after a differential of each point. The ideal correlation function is not only symmetrical, but also the slope of the curve is determined. The deformation of the correlation function will change the slope of the curve. Therefore, by observing the slope of each point of the correlation curve, we can see that the slope is changing. It can be concluded that the correlation curve is not a straight line but may be a multiple curve, so the signal is abnormal.

5   Conclusion

This paper proposes a navigation signal monitoring method based on multi-correlator for the GNSS navigation signal modulated by BOC. Taking BOC (1,1) modulation signal as an example, the paper first studies the acquisition and tracking algorithm of

BOC signal, then analyzes the pseudo-range difference performance of each tracking channel under different correlation intervals based on multiple tracking channels. What's more, this paper analyzes the multi-correlation value difference and the symmetry performance of the correlation curve. The simulation results show that the BOC synchronization method proposed in the paper can capture and track effectively. The signal monitoring method based on multi-correlator can effectively detect the distortion and interference of the navigation signal, thereby providing a reliable method for detecting the integrity of the navigation signal.

References

1. Huangfu, S.T., Cui, Y.J., Liu, B.: Research on modulation quality analysis and test method of BOC modulated signal. In: Proceedings of the 7th China Satellite Navigation Conference (2016)
2. Zhao, H., Zhang, Z., Luo, X., et al.: Quality monitoring and biases estimation of BOC navigation signals. J. Syst. Eng. Electron. **30**(3), 474–484 (2019)
3. Jingyuan, L., Xiangwei, Z., Feixue, W.: Performance analysis of multiple-access interference suppression algorithms for PN code tracking using multicorrelator. Sig. Process. **30**(12), 1510–1516 (2014)
4. Sujuan, Q., Xinfu, Y.: Research on ASPeCT-based acquisition and tracking of BOC modulating signal. Mod. Electron. Technol. **39**(21), 65–69 (2016)
5. Feng, M.: Research on anti-multipath technology of GNSS receiver. Sci. Technol. Inf. **13**, 117–118 + 57 (2014)
6. Peng, Z., Liu, H., Xi, H.: Analysis of satellite navigation signals anti-interfere ability. Wirel. Internet Technol. **16**(11), 1–2 + 9 (2019)

Satellite Navigation Software Receiver Design

Peihan Yu[✉] and Huanzhu Wang

School of Electronics and Information, Northwestern Polytechnical University,
Xi'an 710129, China
1095484794@qq.com

Abstract. The establishment of the Global Navigation Satellite System can provide users with precise navigation information, including speed, three-dimensional position and precise time. In this paper, the signal structure of Beidou B1I is introduced firstly. Then, based on the known rough carrier Doppler frequency shift and pseudo-code phase, this paper analyzes the different forms of carrier loops, including FLL, PLL and FLL+PLL carrier loops. The advantages and disadvantages of their performance are compared. Finally, the simulation and data demodulation results are given.

Keywords: Satellite navigation software receiver · BDS · Tracking

1 Introduction

The satellite navigation uses satellites to broadcast radio signals, and users on the surface of the earth can obtain navigation and positioning information after processing the signals. Satellite navigation has the advantages of not being restricted by distance, little affected by weather conditions, and high accuracy of navigation and positioning. At present, there are multiple satellite navigation systems in the world, which can be divided into global systems and regional systems. The global systems include the United States' Global Positioning System (GPS), Russia's Global Navigation and Positioning System (GLONASS), the European Union's Galileo System (Galileo), China's Beidou System (BDS). The regional systems include Japan's Quasi-Zenith Satellite System (QZSS), and The IRNSS system in India [1].

With the construction of global satellite navigation systems, such as GPS, GLONASS, Galileo, and BDS, the number of satellites will increase significantly, along with the emergence of new modulation methods and signals at various frequencies, which will greatly promote the development of satellite navigation and the upgrading of navigation receiver equipment.

The research of software receiver technology has been relatively mature abroad, among which the United States first started the research of GPS receiver software. In 1995, Dr. Clifford Kelley of the United States designed the first GPS software receiver and made the project public [2]. The U.S. Data Fusion Corporation developed a GPS single - frequency L1 intermediate frequency software receiver and signal source tool based on MATLAB/C in 2001 [2]; Standford University in the United States and Lulea University of Science and Technology in Sweden have developed a GPS L1 four-channel real-time software receiver. The receiver is all realized by software programming from the

B. Li et al. (Eds.): IoTaaS 2020, LNICST 346, pp. 768–782, 2021.
https://doi.org/10.1007/978-3-030-67514-1_61

acquisition of IF signals to the localization solution, and then they continued to cooperate and developed GPS/Galileo multi-frequency compatible software receiver [3]. In 2004, the Ledvina team at Cornell University designed the first dual-frequency GPS receiver based on the Linux system, which satisfies the real-time positioning of signals in the L1 and L2C frequency bands [2]; The GPS Center of the University of Alborg in Denmark developed GPS software based on MATLAB accepted the test prototype, and published GPS and Galileo software receiver development plans and monographs in 2005 and 2007 [4]. ZAHIDUL et al. of Finland designed the software receiver of Beidou B1 frequency point in 2014 with positioning accuracy within ±5 m; the U.S. university of Texas proposed a graphical implementation method for GPS receiver, including two modes of acquisition and tracking [2].

In 1998, the team of Professor Zhang Qishan designed the first GPS L1 single frequency point software receiver in China in 1998 on the platform of PC machine [5]. In 2004, Dr. Lu Yu, a GPS senior software engineer, wrote a complete set of GPS receiver programs in C language, and released it as an open source [2]. In 2012, Zhao Pu of Fudan University developed a software receiver of Beidou B2 frequency based on FPGA + host computer. By processing the signal with baseband digital signal, it can achieve very good accuracy, verifying the practicality of Beidou platform. ZHANG et al. developed the first open source dual-frequency software receiver in china in 2014, which can be compatible with GPS signals of L1 and L2C frequency points simultaneously [5]. In 2015, YIN et al. of Beijing Institute of Microelectronics Technology proposed a dual-mode vector software receiver compatible with four frequency points, It can support GPS L1, L2 signals and Beidou B1, B3 signals at the same time, the positioning results It shows that the performance of vector tracking technology is better than that of ordinary tracking loop [6].

This article will study from BDS system. First introduce the basic overview, including the composition and structure of their satellite signals. The core of this article is the software implementation of digital baseband signal processing such as tracking. The chapters of the paper are organized as follows:

(1) BDS B1I signals. The Beidou Satellite Navigation System is introduced firstly, then the structure of BDS B1 signals are introduced in detail, which includes three levels: data code, ranging code and carrier wave.

(2) Research on signal tracking algorithm. This chapter first briefly introduces the basic principles of tracking, and then analyzes the carrier loop and code loop used in the tracking process. Three implementation forms of the carrier tracking loop are analyzed. Finally, the tracking and data demodulation are realized, and the simulation results are given.

2 BDS B1I Signal

2.1 Introduction to the BDS

The Beidou Satellite Navigation System (BDS) is a self-developed global satellite navigation system with independent intellectual property rights. BDS has now developed to the third generation, and the Beidou-3 system officially provides global services in September 2019.

2.2 Signal Structure

The Beidou-2 satellite signal consists of navigation messages, ranging codes and carrier waves. In this paper, B1I signal of BDS-2 is simulated, and the B1 signal structure is shown in Fig. 1.

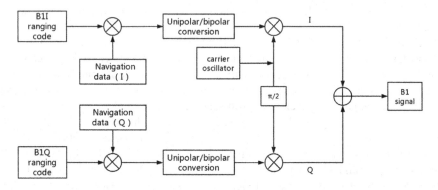

Fig. 1. B1 signal structure of Beidou-2

The expression of B1 signal is as follows.

$$S^j(t) = A_I C_I^j(t) D_I^j(t) \cos(\omega_0 t + \phi_I^j) + A_Q C_Q^j(t) D_Q^j(t) \sin(\omega_0 t + \phi_Q^j) \qquad (1)$$

In this formula, two orthogonal I and Q branches form the signal at frequency B1. The I branch is open for use, and the Q branch is not open to the outside. $C_I^j(t)$ and $C_Q^j(t)$ are the ranging codes of the in-phase and orthogonal branches of the j satellite respectively. A_I and A_Q are the amplitudes of the I and Q ranging codes. $D_I^j(t)$ and $D_Q^j(t)$ are the data codes of the I and Q channels of the j satellite. ω_0 is the angular frequency of the carrier of the signal. ϕ_I^j and ϕ_Q^j are the initial phases of the carrier of the I and Q branches of the j satellite respectively.

2.2.1 Carrier

The Beidou system currently has three carrier frequencies. B1 frequency: 1559.052–1591.788 MHz; B2 frequency: 1166.22–1217.37 MHz; B3 frequency: 1250.618–1286.432 MHz. Based on the above three frequencies, selecting a dual-frequency signal can make use of the difference in the ionospheric delay between the two carrier frequencies of the signal, thereby reducing and eliminating the ionospheric delay.

The use of three-frequency signals has faster carrier convergence speed, smaller ionospheric delay errors, and more accurate positioning effects than dual-frequency signals [6].

2.2.2   The Structure of Ranging Code

The Beidou B1 signal modulates different ranging codes on the I and Q branches. The I branch is modulated C_{B11} Code, P code is modulated in the Q branch. C_{B11} code is similar to C/A code, both of them can be generated by linear feedback shift registers. C_{B11} code also belongs to a Gold code, which is 2046 chips in length and is repeated one period per millisecond. It can transmit 2.046 M symbols per second. The satellite can generate C_{B11} code by a linear combination of two 11-stage feedback shift registers of its internal circuit, and the structure of its generator is shown in Fig. 2.

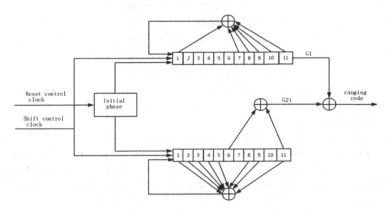

Fig. 2. C_{B11} code generator structure

The C_{B11} code can be generated by truncating one chip from the balanced Gold code obtained after modulo 2 sum of two linear sequences G_1 and G_{2i} [7]. The characteristic polynomials are as follows:

$$\begin{aligned} G_1(x) &= 1 + x + x^7 + x^8 + x^9 + x^{10} + x^{11} \\ G_2(x) &= 1 + x + x^2 + x^3 + x^4 + x^5 + x^8 + x^9 + x^{11} \end{aligned} \qquad (2)$$

The initial phases of the sequence G_1 and G_2 are both 01010101010. Similar to the C/A code, two different register units are selected in the generator, corresponding to the C_{B11} code of different satellites. The following figure shows the phase selector distribution of C_{B11} codes corresponding to different satellite PRN numbers (Table 1):

Table 1. PRN number and corresponding G_{2i} select

PRN	Satellite type	G_{2i}
1	GEO	$1 \oplus 3$
2	GEO	$1 \oplus 4$
3	GEO	$1 \oplus 5$
4	GEO	$1 \oplus 6$
5	GEO	$1 \oplus 8$
6	MEO/IGSO	$1 \oplus 9$
7	MEO/IGSO	$1 \oplus 10$
8	MEO/IGSO	$1 \oplus 11$
...	...	...
...	...	...
33	MEO/IGSO	$8 \oplus 10$
34	MEO/IGSO	$8 \oplus 11$
35	MEO/IGSO	$9 \oplus 10$
36	MEO/IGSO	$9 \oplus 11$
37	MEO/IGSO	$10 \oplus 11$

2.2.3 Data Code

The B1 signal on the MEO and IGSO satellites is modulated with navigation messages D1 with a rate of 50 bps, and also has a secondary encoding, which is modulated by a 20-bit NH code with a rate of 1 kbps [3]. The signal transmitted on the GEO satellite does not use secondary coding, but its navigation messages is different from D1, and the transmission rate of the navigation message D2 is 500 bps.

Secondary encoding refers to the modulation of Neuman-Hoffman codes (NH codes) on D1 navigation messages. NH code transmits 1k bits per second, and repeats for one period every 20 ms. In one period, it contains 20 ranging code period (ranging code period is 1 ms). Each chip in the NH code has the same width as the ranging code period. NH code has 20 bits in total, its sequence is 00000100110101001110.

3 Research on Signal Tracking Algorithm

3.1 The Fundamentals of Signal Tracking

When the acquisition is completed, the value of the carrier Doppler frequency shift and code phase of a certain satellite signal can be obtained. But these values are rough, so the carrier and ranging code cannot be completely stripped. Therefore, after the acquisition, it is necessary to use the loop to keep the tracking of the signal, and get more accurate carrier Doppler frequency shift and code phase values. For Doppler frequency shift, a carrier tracking loop is usually used to keep tracking, and the carrier signal copied by carrier generator is adjusted according to the Doppler shift until the copied carrier is as same as the received signal carrier. After mixing, the carrier can be completely stripped and the Baseband signal can be obtained. For the code phase, the code tracking loop is usually used to track, and the phase of the copied ranging code is adjusted according to the obtained code phase value. When the copied code is aligned with the code phase of the received signal, the ranging code can be stripped completely after multiplying. At this moment, only the navigation messages are left in the signal, and the information required for navigation can be obtained.

3.2 Carrier Tracking Loop

The carrier tracking loop tracks the Doppler shift of the received signal, and adjusts the copied carrier signal by the carrier generator according to the Doppler shift, until the copied carrier is as same as the received signal carrier. The carrier tracking loop usually has two forms: phase locking loop PLL and frequency locking loop FLL. This paper will introduce PLL and FLL respectively, then discuss a compound carrier loop with FLL to assist PLL.

3.2.1 Phase Lock Loop (PLL)

In the tracking process, there is a difference between the copied carrier and the carrier of the received signal. If the phase difference is used as the feedback amount to adjust the phase of the copied carrier, this loop is called phase locked loop (PLL) [7]. In the satellite signal, the navigation data will flip, causing the carrier to produce a 180° phase flip. Therefore, the phase-locked loop is generally a Costas loop, which is not sensitive to phase reversal. The structure is shown in Fig. 3.

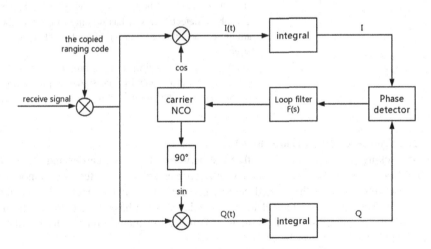

Fig. 3. The structure of Costas loop

In the Costas loop, the carrier generator is used to generate the copied sine-cosine carriers with frequency close to the intermediate frequency. Then the ranging code generator is used to generate the copied ranging codes with certain code phases of the satellite. (Here it is assumed that the copied ranging code is consistent with the phase of the received signal ranging code). The received signal is multiplied by the copied ranging code to realize the ranging code stripped. Then the obtained signal is multiplied and mixed with the sine and cosine carriers respectively, where the sine branch is the in-phase branch (I branch), and the cosine branch is the orthogonal branch (Q branch). Because the received signal contains noise, and the noise power is generally greater than the useful signal power. Therefore, coherent integral filtering with time T is needed to filter out the high frequency components and improve the SNR at the same time. After that, the integral results are sent into the phase discriminator. Different phase discriminator algorithms can be used to obtain the phase difference between the copied carrier and the received signal carrier. Then the phase difference is taken as the feedback quantity to adjust the phase of the copied carrier [8]. Common phase discriminator algorithms are shown in Table 2.

Table 2. Common phase discriminator algorithms

Phase discriminator algorithms	Output phase difference	Characteristic
$I(t) \times Q(t)$	$\sin(2\varphi(t))$	It still has good performance when the signal-to-noise ratio is low, but its phase discrimination result is proportional to the square of the signal amplitude, and the amount of calculation is moderate
$\arctan(\frac{Q(t)}{I(t)})$	$\varphi(t)$	The work of the phase detector remains linear, and the phase detection result has nothing to do with the signal amplitude, and the amount of calculation is the largest
$\frac{Q(t)}{I(t)}$	$\tan(\varphi(t))$	The phase detection result has nothing to do with the amplitude, and the calculation amount is relatively large
$Q(t) \times \text{sgn}(I(t))$	$\sin(\varphi(t))$	The phase discrimination result is proportional to $\sin(\varphi(t))$ and also related to the signal amplitude, so the amount of calculation is minimal

3.2.2 Frequency Lock Loop (FLL)

In the tracking process, there is a difference between the copied carrier and the carrier of the received signal. If the frequency difference is used as the feedback amount to adjust the frequency of the copied carrier, this loop is called frequency locked loop (FLL) [7]. The frequency locked loop is similar to the phase locked loop. The difference between them is the discriminator. This section focuses on the discriminators used in FLL.

Before introducing a variety of frequency discriminators, first define a few parameters.

$$\begin{aligned} P_{dot} &= I_P(n-1)I_P(n) + Q_P(n-1)Q_P(n) \\ P_{cross} &= I_P(n-1)Q_P(n) - Q_P(n-1)I_P(n) \end{aligned} \tag{3}$$

In the formula, P_{dot} is the dot product. P_{cross} is the cross product. $I_P(n)$ and $Q_P(n)$ are the I/Q coherent integration results obtained from epoch n. There are three main frequency identification methods used in FLL.

① Four-quadrant arctangent frequency discriminator

$$\omega_e(n) = \frac{\arctan 2(P_{cross}, P_{dot})}{t(n) - t(n-1)} \tag{4}$$

In the formula, $\omega_e(n)$ is the angular frequency error. $t(n) - t(n-1)$ is the time T of coherent integration. This method has a large amount of calculation, but it is the most accurate frequency discrimination method. The frequency discrimination result has nothing to do with the amplitude of the signal. Therefore, it is often selected in practice. The frequency pulling range is $\left[-\frac{1}{2T}, \frac{1}{2T}\right]$.

② Cross product discriminator

$$\omega_e(n) = \frac{P_{cross}}{t(n) - t(n-1)} \tag{5}$$

This method has a small amount of calculation, but the frequency discrimination result is proportional to the product of the signal amplitude, and its frequency pulling range is $\left[-\frac{1}{2T}, \frac{1}{2T}\right]$. However, this method is sensitive to the jump of the navigation messages, so some processing is required in application.

③ Symbol Dot Cross Product Discriminator

$$\omega_e(n) = \frac{P_{cross} \cdot sign(P_{dot})}{t(n) - t(n-1)} \tag{6}$$

This method has a small amount of calculation, and the frequency discrimination result is proportional to the square of the signal amplitude. The frequency pulling range is $\left[-\frac{1}{4T}, \frac{1}{4T}\right]$. Because $sign(P_{dot})$ can detect the phase reversal caused by the data bit jump, this method is not sensitive to the data bit jump.

3.2.3 Comparison and Combination of FLL and PLL

Both phase-locked loop and frequency-locked loop are often used in the tracking process. Their structures are similar, but the difference is the discriminator, which results in differences in noise and dynamic performance [9].

① The noise bandwidth of the phase-locked loop is narrow. The phase-locked loop can generate a signal with the same frequency and stable phase error. The signal can be closely tracked and the output phase value is accurate. Although the phase-locked loop has many advantages, its disadvantages are also obvious. In the case of high user dynamics, it is easy to lose lock.

② The noise bandwidth of the frequency-locked loop is wide. The frequency-locked loop can generate a signal with stable frequency error. It has a strong tolerance to dynamic stress. It can track low-power signals even when the noise is strong, and is insensitive to data bit jumps. However, the tracking accuracy is low, and it is difficult to obtain accurate carrier phase values.

In the case of high dynamics and low signal-to-noise ratio situation, the use of a frequency-locked loop can lock the signal firmly, which is convenient and fast to pull in the signal; in the case of low-dynamic situation, the use of a phase-locked loop can track the signal more closely and obtain a more accurate carrier phase value [6]. Based on these, this article discusses a compound loop that combines a frequency-locked loop and a phase-locked loop to track the signal.

In the composite loop, the phase-locked loop and the frequency-locked loop are not independent of each other. The second-order frequency-locked loop is usually used to assist the third-order phase-locked loop to achieve tracking. The principle structure is shown in Fig. 4.

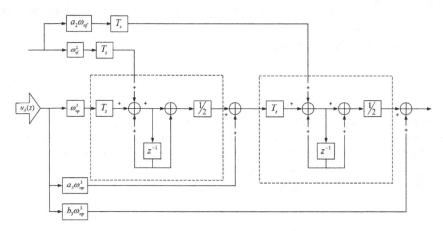

Fig. 4. The structure diagram of the combined loop of the second-order frequency-locked loop and the third-order phase-locked loop

The design has better flexibility. First of all, a rough carrier Doppler frequency shift estimate is obtained after the received signal acquisition. In the initial stage of tracking, due to the inaccuracy of the carrier Doppler shift value, it is difficult to directly use the phase-locked loop to quickly pull into the frequency lock range, and it may cause loss of lock. In this case, the frequency-locked loop can lock the signal more firmly, and can pull into the frequency locking range faster than a phase-locked loop. Therefore, select the pure frequency-locked loop when starting tracking, until the signal is drawn into the stable tracking state. Since the output phase measurement accuracy of the pure frequency-locked loop is low, the carrier loop is gradually transferred from the pure FLL to the FLL assists PLL, and finally enter the mode of the pure phase-locked loop. The pure phase-locked loop can track the signal more closely, and the accuracy of the output phase value has also been improved. In addition, when the phase-locked loop loses lock, the carrier loop can be switched to a pure frequency-locked loop, and the above process is repeated to maintain signal tracking.

3.3 Code Tracking Loop

The function of the code tracking loop is to track the ranging code phase values of the received signal, and adjust the copied ranging code phase by the ranging code generator according to the obtained code phase value until the copied ranging code is the same as the received signal. The ranging code can be completely stripped after multiplying. Usually delay locked loop (DLL) is used to realize code tracking. The general code tracking loop structure is shown in the Fig. 5.

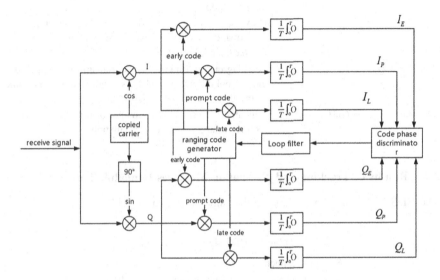

Fig. 5. The general code tracking loop structure

The carrier generator is used to generate the copied sine-cosine carriers with frequency close to the intermediate frequency. Then the ranging code generator is used to generate the copied ranging codes with certain code phases of the satellite. Subsequently, the received signal is multiplied and mixed with the sine and cosine carriers respectively, where the sine branch is an in-phase branch (I branch), and the cosine branch is an orthogonal branch (Q branch). The mixed signal is correlated with the copied ranging code. The ranging code generator replicates three codes with different phases, Early, Prompt and Late Code [9]. The expression is as follows.

$$
\begin{aligned}
x_E(t) &= C(t - \tau + \tfrac{d}{2}) \\
x_P(t) &= C(t - \tau) \\
x_L(t) &= C(t - \tau - \tfrac{d}{2})
\end{aligned}
\tag{7}
$$

In the code tracking loop, there are many forms of code phase discriminators. Common discriminators are shown as follows (Table 3).

Table 3. Common phase discriminator algorithms

Discriminator Algorithm	Characteristic
$D = I_E - I_L$	This algorithm is the simplest discriminator, no Q branch is required, but it has strict requirements on the carrier tracking loop
$D = \frac{(I_E^2 + Q_E^2) - (I_L^2 + Q_L^2)}{(I_E^2 + Q_E^2) + (I_L^2 + Q_L^2)}$	Universal lead-lag energy difference discriminator, performance is still good when the symbol difference is greater than 1/2 symbol
$D = (I_E^2 + Q_E^2) - (I_L^2 + Q_L^2)$	Lead-lag energy difference discriminator, the output at the symbol difference of $\pm 1/2$ symbol is almost the same as the first discriminator algorithm
$D = I_P(I_E - I_L) + Q_P(Q_E - Q_L)$	This algorithm requires the output of 6 integrator, which requires a large amount of calculation

3.4   Results of Tracking and Navigation Messages Demodulation

The BDS B1I signal parameters are the same as shown in Table 4.

Table 4. BDS signal parameters

Satellite number	31
The code phase of the signal source	1000
Carrier doppler shift of signal source	4700
The initial carrier phase of the signal source	0
The signal-to-noise ratio of the signal source	5 dB

① The carrier loop is FLL, using a four-quadrant arctangent frequency discriminator algorithm.

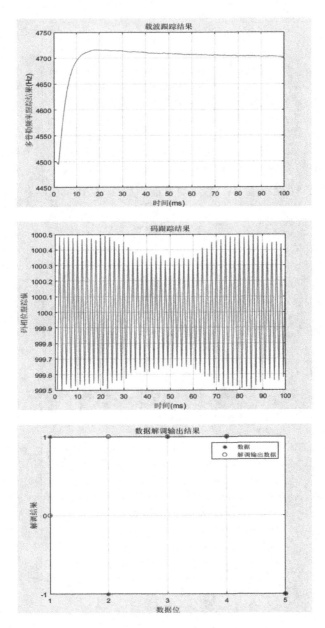

Fig. 6. The carrier loop is FLL

From the above figure, we can see that using the FLL loop can get a stable Doppler frequency shift output and code phase tracking value, but it takes a longer time to track to a stable state (Fig. 6).

② The carrier loop is PLL, which uses a two-quadrant arctangent phase detector algorithm (Fig. 7).

780   P. Yu and H. Wang

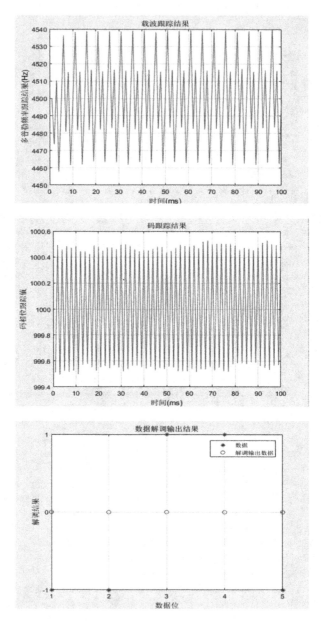

Fig. 7. The carrier loop is PLL

From the above figure, we can see that using the pure PLL loop will cause the carrier loop to lose lock. The stable Doppler shift output and the demodulated output data cannot be obtained.

③ The carrier loop is the second order FLL to assist the third order PLL composite carrier loop. The four-quadrant arctangent discriminator is used in the FLL and the two-quadrant arctangent discriminator is used in the PLL (Fig. 8).

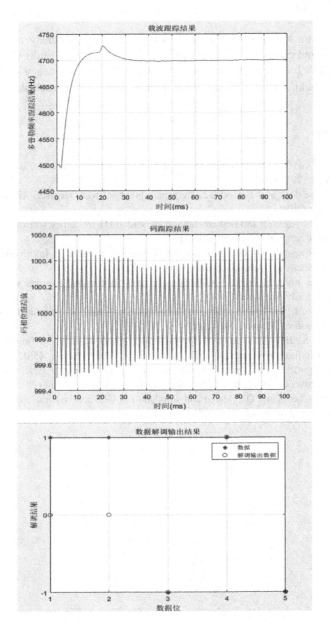

Fig. 8. The carrier loop is FLL to assist PLL

From the above figure, we can see that using the FLL and PLL combined loop can get a stable Doppler frequency shift output and code phase tracking value. What's more, it takes less time to reach stability.

4 Conclusion

Aiming at the tracking part of B1I navigation signal, this paper analyzes three different carrier loops and compares their performance. The simulation results show that using the FLL and PLL combined loop can get a stable Doppler frequency shift output and code phase tracking value. What's more, it takes less time to reach stability.

References

1. Zhang, X.: GPS key technologies research based on software receiver. Beijing Institute of Technology (2017)
2. Tan, Y.: The design of Beidou B2a frequency point software receiver. Xi'an University of Technology (2019)
3. Dong, J.: The research and implementation of Beidou B1 frequency software receiver based on matlab. Chang'an University (2014)
4. Yue, X.: Research on GPS/BD integrated navigation receiver information processing algorithm. Shenyang Aerospace University (2017)
5. Yu, D.: The study of satellite (GPS/Beidou) navigation signal simulation. Civil Aviation Flight University of China (2014)
6. Zhao, Y., Su, J.: Ionospheric refraction error correction method for multi-frequency GNSS. Aerosp. Measure. Technol. 36(01), 42–46 (2016)
7. Li, L., Xin, S., Jing, L., Jinxian, Z., Guo Rui, W., Xiaoli, H.F.: The definition and usage of Beidou basic navigation messages. Sci. China Phys. Mech. Astron. 45(07), 62–68 (2015)
8. Guo, J.: Algorithm and implementation of baseband processing of Beidou 2nd navigation receiver. University of Electronic Science and Technology of China (2015)
9. Meilin, H., Chengfang, Q.: Design and simulation of GPS receiver tracking algorithm. Ship Electron. Eng. 38(09), 45–48 (2018)

A Novel Pansharpening Method with Multi-scale Mutual-structure Perception

Zhenzhen Fan, Xu Li$^{(\boxtimes)}$, and Xugang Wu

School of Electronics and Information, Northwestern Polytechnical University,
Xi'an 710129, China
lixu@nwpu.edu.cn

Abstract. Network geographic information system (WebGIS), a branch of Internet of Things (IoT), is the extension and development of traditional GIS on the network, which integrates and upgrades many remote sensing information processing tasks such as pansharpening, mapping, classification, etc. Pansharpening technology allows a detailed redisplay of the earth surface by fusing a panchromatic (PAN) and a multispectral (MS) image acquired over the same area. The extraction of the details from the PAN image and their subsequent injection into the MS image are still the key points for the pansharpening design. In this paper, we propose a novel pansharpening method which considers the multi-scale mutual-structures of the PAN and MS image pair as a new reference for details extraction and applies a weighted details injection strategy to generate the fused MS image. The experimental results show that our proposed method can obtain high-quality sharpened results and has superior performance with respect to some recent approaches.

Keywords: Pansharpening · Remote sensing · Mutual-structure

1 Introduction

WebGIS is the development of traditional GIS technology in the IoT, in which the task of remote sensing information visualization is one of the key technologies. Nowadays with the rapid development of Earth Observation technology, many high-performance commercial satellites such as QuickBird, GeoEye-1, WorldView-2/3/4 when capturing the same scene, can provide the panchromatic (PAN) image and multispectral (MS) image at almost the same time. Due to the physical constraints of the acquisition devices, PAN and MS images usually have different resolutions, although both of them contain the same scene [1]. PAN band without spectral diversity often covers a wide spectral range (usually from visual to near infrared) and has very high spatial resolution. In contrast, MS image has lower spatial resolution but higher spectral resolution. Therefore, PAN and MS images contain similar or common structures but inconsistent details such as fine edges or textures. Pansharpening has been an important tool in remote sensing field whose aim is to enhance the spatial resolution of the MS image with the aid of the PAN spatial information and the pansharpened products are dedicated to many applications [2, 3] such as Google Earth, classification, change detection, etc.

B. Li et al. (Eds.): IoTaaS 2020, LNICST 346, pp. 783–792, 2021.
https://doi.org/10.1007/978-3-030-67514-1_62

To date, a large number of pansharpening methods have been proposed which can be roughly classified into three major categories, i.e., the component substitution based methods, the multi-resolution analysis based methods, and the variational optimization based methods [4]. Essentially, the effective extraction of the details from the PAN image and the accurate details injection into the MS image always play the key roles in the pansharpening approaches. In recent years, the popularity of the filtering-based pansharpening methods is attributed to the powerful performance of feature-aware filters. Some pioneer attempts with edge-preserving filters are representative [5–7]. However, classical edge-preserving filters process only a single image to either preserve edges or remove textures, which can hardly separate structure from details since edge strength and object scale are completely different concepts. Joint filters such as guided filter (GF) [8], rolling guidance filter (RGF) [9] are more suitable for structural features perception. Li et al. proposed a fusion strategy based on GF, which decomposes the input image into a base layer having large scale structures and a detail layer with small scale details [10]. A method adopting RGF has been developed, aiming to sharpen the large-scale agricultural fragmented landscapes [11]. Mutual-structure refers to the common structural information shared in both images. Shen et al. explicitly defined the concept of mutual-structure and proposed a joint filtering process, a.k.a. mutual-structure for joint filtering (MSF), to extract the common structure from depth and RGB image pair [12]. Then, Liu et al. first introduced MSF to their pansharpening method, which enforces a direct multi-scale MSF to decompose PAN and MS images into high frequency and low frequency sub-bands and implements different fusion rules to obtain the integrated sub-bands [13]. Since PAN and MS images have different spatial resolutions, during the details extraction process, it is important to recognize the objects with different sizes or the structures of various scales. How to accurately extract the details from PAN image compared with MS image is still a core question regarding pansharpening performance. Motivated by this, we propose a novel pansharpening method which takes common multi-scale structures between the PAN and MS images into account and tries to filter out their mutual-structures as a new reference for details extraction. A weighted details injection is designed to guarantee the proper injection and faithful spectral preservation. The experiment is carried out on WorldView-3 data set. The subjective and objective evaluations show that the proposed method can produce high-quality pansharpened results and outperform some recent methods.

2   Methodology

The original MS images are upsampled to the size of the PAN image using bicubic interpolation. The upsampled N-band low-resolution MS images are denoted as LRM_i, where $i = 1 \dots N$. The flowchart of the proposed method is shown in Fig. 1. It consists of three main parts: multi-scale structure filtering, mutual-structure perception, and weighted details injection.

2.1   Multi-scale Structure Filtering

Although MSF has the capability of capturing the mutual-structures from an image pair, it sometimes introduces halo artifacts to the filtering outputs due to its local filtering formulation. It is believed that conducting direct multi-scale MSF to the PAN and MS image pair will accumulate more artifacts and may result in poor pansharpened result. Different from the method [13], we first carry out a multi-scale structure filtering to the PAN image before the mutual-structure perception. In scale-space theory [14], the variance (σ^2) of Gaussian filter is referred to as the scale parameter. When applying Gaussian with varying σ to an image, the structures are suppressed differently according to their size. Inspired by this, we perform Gaussian filtering to the PAN image P at small, medium, and large scales, individually. Then the Gaussian filtering outputs are denoted as P_S, P_M and P_L as shown in Fig. 1 which are expected to have the similar structural features to the MS image at different scales. The corresponding deviations are denoted as σ_S, σ_M and σ_L, respectively. The value of deviation becomes higher, the larger structures will be suppressed. Therefore, we set $\sigma_S = 3$, $\sigma_M = 15$ and $\sigma_L = 50$ based on a large number of experiments. Gaussian filtering is calculated as

$$P_{\sigma^2} = g * P \tag{1}$$

in which Gaussian kernel $g(x,y) = \frac{1}{\sqrt{2\pi\sigma^2}}\exp\left(-\frac{x^2+y^2}{2\sigma^2}\right)$ and $*$ denotes convolution.(x,y) is the coordinate.

2.2   Mutual-Structure Perception

In this stage, we employ MSF to capture the mutual-structures between $\{P_S, P_M, P_L\}$ and MS image. MSF is a joint filtering process to extract the common structures from an image pair and has two inputs: target image and reference image [12]. The function of MSF is defined as

$$(T, R) = \text{MSF}(T_0, R_0, \lambda, \beta, \varepsilon_1, \varepsilon_2) \tag{2}$$

in which T and R are the mutual-structures corresponding to the target image T_0 and the reference image R_0, respectively. λ and β control the deviation to R_0 and T_0, respectively. We set λ and β in range 30−300, which satisfy $\lambda_1 > \lambda_2 > \lambda_3$ and $\beta_1 > \beta_2 > \beta_3$. ε_1 and ε_2 control the smoothness of R and T respectively. We set them around 1E-5. Since the MS image has more than one band, the average of N-band MS image is used to represent the intensity component (INT). We take P_S, P_M, P_L as the target image respectively and INT as the reference for MSF under the assumption that the reference image should contain correct structure information at different scales. Specifically, the multi-scale mutual-structure perception process can be implemented as the following:

$$INT = \frac{1}{N}\sum_i^N (LRM_1 + LRM_2 + \ldots LRM_N) \tag{3}$$

$$(T_1, R_1) \; = \; \text{MSF}(P_S, INT, \lambda_1, \beta_1, \varepsilon_1, \varepsilon_2) \tag{4}$$

$$(T_2, R_2) \; = \; \text{MSF}(P_M, INT, \lambda_2, \beta_2, \varepsilon_1, \varepsilon_2) \tag{5}$$

$$(T_3, R_3) \; = \; \text{MSF}(P_L, INT, \lambda_3, \beta_3, \varepsilon_1, \varepsilon_2) \tag{6}$$

Through multiple iterations and setting constraints, we can obtain the desired mutual structures T_1, T_2, and T_3. As shown in Fig. 1, the filtering out images, i.e., T_1, T_2, T_3 correspond to the mutual structures at small, medium, and large scales, respectively. The scale of the small structures in T_1 is as small as the minimum spatial size of the objects in INT, e.g. cars.

2.3   Weighted Details Injection

In order to reduce the spatial and spectral information distortions, we design a weighted details injection to avoid improper "over" or "under" injection. First, we match the PAN image P with the intensity component INT to obtain the histogram-matched PAN image named as P_M:

$$P\_M \; = \; P \times \frac{\sigma_{INT}^2}{\sigma_P^2} + \mu_{INT} - \frac{\sigma_{INT}^2}{\sigma_P^2} \times \mu_P \tag{7}$$

where σ^2 and μ denote the variance and mean of the corresponding subscripted images, respectively.

Then, the PAN details at different scales can be calculated from the difference between P_M and the mutual-structures:

$$D_1 = P\_M - T_1 \tag{8}$$

$$D_2 = P\_M - T_2 \tag{9}$$

$$D_3 = P\_M - T_3 \tag{10}$$

From Fig. 1, it is clear that the extracted multi-scale details D_1, D_2, D_3 represent the spatial details of the PAN image from large to medium, and then to small scales, progressively. To eliminate the redundancy among $\{D_1, D_2, D_3\}$, we use the weighted sum of D_1, D_2, and D_3 to estimate a synthesized details D by (11). The weight coefficients k_1, k_2, and k_3 can be obtained through (12)–(14), in which $()^T$ represents the transpose operation.

$$D = k_1 \times D_1 + k_2 \times D_2 + k_3 \times D_3 \tag{11}$$

$$k_1 = \frac{(D_1 - D_2 - D_3)^T \times D_1}{\left[(D_1 - D_2 - D_3)^T \times (D_1 - D_2 - D_3)\right]} \tag{12}$$

$$k_2 = \frac{(D_2 - D_1 - D_3)^{\mathrm{T}} \times D_1}{\left[(D_2 - D_1 - D_3)^{\mathrm{T}} \times (D_2 - D_1 - D_3)\right]} \tag{13}$$

$$k_3 = 1 - k_1 - k_2 \tag{14}$$

The details injection into each MS band is modulated by a gains matrix which keeps the proportion among the MS bands unvaried. The injection gains matrix is calculated as

$$O_i = \frac{LRM_i}{\frac{1}{N}\sum_{i=1}^{N} LRM_i} \tag{15}$$

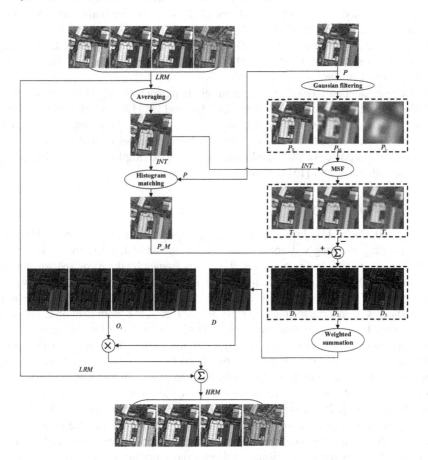

Fig. 1. Flowchart of the proposed method.

Finally, the pansharpened MS image HRM_i is generated by injecting the spatial information D into each band of the upsampled MS image LRM_i by a gains matrix O_i. The sharpened MS image is obtained by

$$HRM_i = O_i \times D + LRM_i \qquad (16)$$

3   Experimental Results

3.1   Dataset and Evaluation Indexes

To validate the proposed method, we use WorldView-3 satellite imagery as the test data which consists of 8-band MS image with 1.24 m spatial resolution and a 0.31 m PAN band. The data set taken in October of 2014 covers the harbor area of Sydney, Australia. The original size of the MS and PAN images are 400×400 pixels and 1600×1600 pixels, respectively. Both images have been registered. Figure 2(a) shows a PAN sub-scene of 800×800 pixels and Fig. 2(b) reports the same area of the resampled MS image.

Three evaluation indexes, i.e., spectral angle mapper (SAM) [15], relative dimensionless global error in synthesis (ERGAS) [16], and Q4 [17], are selected to assess the quality of the results, which are the most widely used in the pansharpening studies because of their robustness to the difference between experimental datasets [4]. For comparison purpose, we also implemented and tested Kaplan's method [6], Dong's method [18], and Liu's [13] method.

3.2   Subjective Analysis

Figure 2(c0-c3)-(f0-f3) show the RGB composition of the pansharpened MS bands corresponding to Dong's, Kaplan's, Liu's and our method, respectively. In order to facilitate observation and comparison, three parts framed by three colored-squares (red, yellow, green) are zoomed up and shown in rows 3–4, rows 5–6 and rows 7–8, respectively. The order of the row arrangement is roughly according to the scale of the main features from large to small. In rows 3–4 of Fig. 2, the prominent object is the big white roof. It is easy to find that Fig. 2(d0-d3) and (e0-e3) present more blurring compared with Fig. 2(c0-c3) and (f0-f3) especially around the contour of the roof. In addition, the light blue part on the roof disappears in Fig. 2(c0-c3) which mean Dong's method produces the worst spectral distortions. In rows 5–6, most ground objects are presented on medium scale such as the red roofs and crowns of trees. Compared with Fig. 2(b0-b3), Fig. 2(c0-c3)-(e0-e3) show the spectral distortions more or less in which the yellow roof in Fig. 2(c0-c3) appear too bright, and the color of the vegetation part in Fig. 2(d0-d3) are distorted from dark to bright. Furthermore, Liu's method (Fig. 2 (e0-e3)) generates the worst visual result especially on the red roofs. Our method in rows 5–6 present the high-quality in terms of the spectral fidelity. Although Fig. 2(d0-d3) have sufficient spatial details, their color distortions are obvious. Rows 7–8 of Fig. 2 display the ground scene full of small objects including the unfinished building

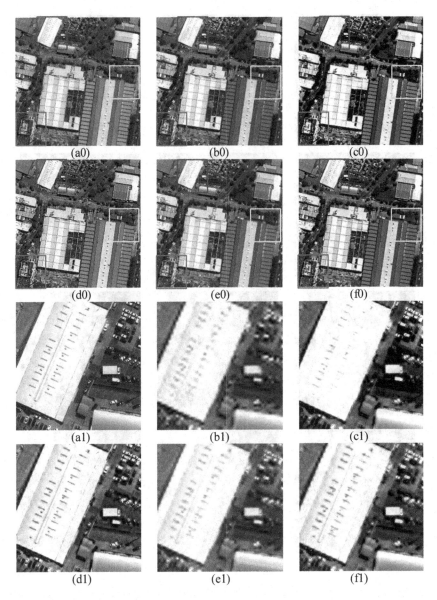

Fig. 2. A sub-scene of the test WorldView-3 dataset with 800×800 pixels: (a0-a3) PAN image, (b0-b3) MS image, (c0-c3) Dong's method [18], (d0-d3) Kaplan's method [6], (e0-e3) Liu's method [13], (f0-f3) our method. In order to observe more clearly, three color (red, yellow, green) boxed parts of the results are zoomed up and shown in rows 3–4, rows 5–6 and rows 7–8, respectively. (Color figure online)

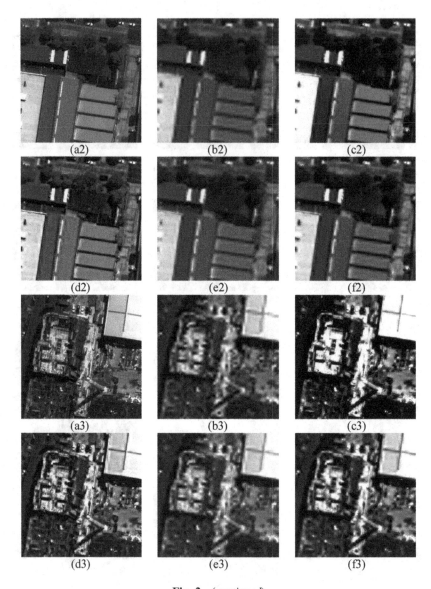

Fig. 2. (*continued*)

site and cars. It is clear that Liu's method (Fig. 2(e0-e3)) is the most blurred partly because of the accumulated artefacts from the direct multi-scale MSF process. Figure 2 (d0-d3) have blurred parts around the fine details which indicate the insufficient details injection of Kaplan's method. Dong's method (Fig. 2(c0-c3)) show better visual effect than Fig. 2(d0-d3) and 2(e0-e3), but it still presents the evident spectral distortions concentrated on the high reflection area. Our method (Fig. 2(f0-f3)) in the rows 7–8 obtains the best visual result compared with the other three methods. From the subjective analysis and comparison of Fig. 2, we can see that our method produces high-quality result at different scales and outperforms the compared methods.

3.3 Objective Analysis

Table 1 lists the quantitative evaluation of the pansharpened results. The values in parentheses are the ideal values for the evaluation indexes. Kaplan's method has the worst performance in terms of all indexes which is consistent with the visual analysis. The advantage of edge-perception seems not obvious. According to SAM and ERGAS scores, Liu's method obtains good results in the second place. The Q4 index shows that Dong's and our method are better, which indicates multi-scale GF and MSF are helpful to improve the spatial quality. Our method achieves the best scores which demonstrates that its multi-scale mutual-structure perception and weighted details injection are more effective for the spatial improvement and spectral preservation than the compared methods.

Table 1. Quality indexes of the pansharpened results.

Index	Dong's method [18]	Kaplan's method [6]	Liu's method [13]	Ours
SAM (0)	6.019	7.045	5.741	**3.514**
ERGAS (0)	15.711	31.009	13.593	**9.620**
Q4 (1)	0.815	0.809	0.814	**0.823**

4   Conclusion

We propose a novel multi-scale mutual-structure perception based pansharpening method focusing on the accurate details extraction and the following injection. The characteristic of MS and PAN image pair having similar structures and inconsistent details motivates us to combine Gaussian filtering and MSF to achieve the purpose of the multi-scale mutual-structure perception. A weighted details injection is also designed to guarantee that the PAN details can be properly injected into the MS image. We conduct the experiment on WorldView-3 satellite imagery and our method performs well both visually and objectively. The experimental results demonstrate that the proposed method can produce high-quality pansharpened results and outperform some recently published methods.

Acknowledgements. This research is supported by the Seed Foundation of Innovation and Creation for Graduate Students in NPU (No. CX2020016), Key R&D Plan of Shaanxi Province (No. 2020GY-034), and Shanghai Key Laboratory of Multidimensional Information Processing in East China Normal University (No. 2019KEY001).

References

1. Alparone, L., Aiazzi, B., Baronti, S., Garzelli, A.: Remote Sensing Image Fusion. CRC Press, New York (2015)
2. Li, S., Kang, X., Fang, L., Hu, J., Yin, H.: Pixel-Level image fusion: a survey of the state of the art. Inf. Fusion **33**, 100–112 (2017)
3. Wang, T., Fang, F., Li, F., Zhang, G.: High-quality Bayesian pansharpening. IEEE Trans. Image Process. **28**(1), 227–239 (2019)
4. Meng, X., Sheng, H., Li, H., Zhang, L., Fu, R.: Review of the pansharpening methods for remote sensing images based on the idea of meta-analysis: practical discussion and challenges. Inf. Fusion **46**, 102–113 (2019)
5. Yin, H., Li, S.: Pansharpening with multi-scale normalized non-local mean filter. IEEE Trans. Geosci. Remote Sens. **53**(10), 1–12 (2015)
6. Kaplan, N.H., Erer, I.: Bilateral filtering-based enhanced pansharpening of multispectral satellite images. IEEE Geosci. Remote Sens. Lett. **11**(11), 1941–1945 (2014)
7. Song, Y., Wu, W., Liu, Z.: An adaptive pansharpening method by using weighted least squares filter. IEEE Geosci. Remote Sens. Lett. **13**(1), 18–22 (2016)
8. He, K., Sun, J., Tang, X.: Guided image filtering. IEEE Trans. Pattern Anal. Mach. Intell. **35**(6), 1397–1409 (2013)
9. Zhang, Q., Shen, X., Xu, L., Jia, J.: Rolling guidance filter. In: Fleet, D., Pajdla, T., Schiele, B., Tuytelaars, T. (eds.) ECCV 2014. LNCS, vol. 8691, pp. 815–830. Springer, Cham (2014). https://doi.org/10.1007/978-3-319-10578-9_53
10. Li, S., Kang, X., Hu, J.: Image fusion with guided filtering. IEEE Trans. Image Process. **22**(7), 2864–2875 (2013)
11. Lillo-Saavedra, M., Gonzalo-Martin, C., Garcia-Pedrero, A., Lagos, O.: Scale-aware pansharpening algorithm for agricultural fragmented landscapes. Remote Sens. **8**(10), 1–19 (2016)
12. Shen, X., Zhou, C., Xu, L., Jia, J.: Mutual-structure for joint filtering. Int. J. Comput. Vision **125**(1), 19–33 (2017)
13. Liu, S., Li, X., Zhang, X.: Remote sensing image fusion algorithm based on mutual-structure for joint filtering using saliency detection. J. Electron. Imaging **28**(3), 033007 (2019)
14. Lindeberg, T.: Scale-space theory: a basic tool for analyzing structures at different scales. J. Appl. Stat. **21**, 225–270 (1994)
15. Palsson, F., Sveinsson, R., Ulfarsson, M.O., Benediktsson, J.A.: Quantitative quality evaluation of pansharpened imagery: consistency versus synthesis. IEEE Trans. Geosci. Remote Sens. **54**(3), 1247–1259 (2016)
16. Ranchin, T., Aiazzi, B., Alparone, L., Baronti, S., Wald, L.: Image fusion – the ARSIS concept and some successful implementation schemes. ISPRS J. Photogram. Remote Sens. **58**, 4–18 (2003)
17. Alparone, L., Baronti, S., Garzelli, A., Nencini, F.: A global quality measurement of pansharpened multispectral imagery. IEEE Geosci. Remote Sens. Lett. **1**(4), 313–317 (2004)
18. Dong, W., Xiao, S., Qu, J.: Fusion of hyperspectral and panchromatic images with guided filter. SIViP **12**(7), 1369–1376 (2018). https://doi.org/10.1007/s11760-018-1291-z

A New Fusion Method for Remote Sensing Images

Xugang Wu, Xu Li$^{(\boxtimes)}$, and Zhenzhen Fan

School of Electronics and Information, Northwestern Polytechnical University,
Xi'an 710129, People's Republic of China
lixu@nwpu.edu.cn

Abstract. As a branch of Internet of Things (IoT), network geographic information (WebGIS) has the task of enhancing remote sensing images, including correction, fusion, mapping, etc. Remote sensing images captured by different satellite platforms often present earth objects with various scales. Due to the different spatial resolutions of imaging sensors, the same object will appear in different sizes. Usually panchromatic (PAN) image, without spectral diversity, has high spatial resolution and multispectral (MS) image has lower spatial resolution but more spectral information. Fusing MS and PAN images, also known as pansharpening, will increase the spatial resolution of MS image without changing its spectral information. In the fusion process, inaccurate perception and extraction of the spatial details will lead to spectral and spatial distortions in the fused image. A new multi-scale structure perception based fusion method is proposed in this paper. Firstly, an improved structure-preserving filter is designed by using MS imagery as the reference to capture the structures in the PAN image. Then the structures having different scales are progressively perceived through a multi-scale decomposition scheme and the spatial details are accurately extracted from the PAN image. Finally, the details weighted by the band-dependent gains are injected into each band of MS images. Experimental results are compared with some recently proposed edge-preserving filtering based fusion methods. Visual analysis and objective evaluations demonstrate that the proposed method can produce high-quality fused output and achieve better performance than some state-of-the-arts.

Keywords: Fusion · Remote sensing · Filter · Multispectral image

1 Introduction

With the fast development of IoT, WebGIS integrates more remote sensing applications and migrates tasks from traditional GIS. Increasing the spatial resolution by fusion technique is one of the tasks of remote sensing information visualization enhancement. The high-resolution remote sensing imagery collected by spaceborne imaging sensors, such as QuickBird, IKONOS, WorldView2/3/4 are often made up of a high-spatial resolution PAN image and serval low-spatial resolution MS images [1]. The fusion of PAN and MS images aims at increasing the spatial resolution of MS images with the aid of the spatial details from the PAN image. Thanks to the development of computer vision technology, more and more image filters are employed in the fusion design and

B. Li et al. (Eds.): IoTaaS 2020, LNICST 346, pp. 793–804, 2021.
https://doi.org/10.1007/978-3-030-67514-1_63

the filtering-based fusion methods have evolved into an important branch in the pan-sharpening field. Kaplan [2] et al. estimated the missing fine spatial details extracted by the bilateral filtering decomposition of the PAN image and proposed a bilateral filter luminance proportional method. Joshi [3] et al. took advantage of the edge preserving and detail transferring capabilities of the joint bilateral filter to design a multistage pansharpening algorithm. Yin and Li [4] presented a two-step fusion approach based on a multiscale normalized nonlocal mean filter aiming to address the spatial distortion issues in multi-resolution analysis-based methods. Upla et al. [5] took the advantage of the guided filter and extracted the details from PAN and MS images using a multistage guided filter. However, it may result in details over-injection due to the improper parameter selection. Recently, Dong et al. [6] introduced the guided filter into the hyperspectral pansharpening to reduce both spectral and spatial distortion. In 2014, Zhang et al. [7] proposed an effective scale-aware filter called rolling guidance filter (RGF) which can extract small-scale structures while preserving other content, parallel in terms of importance to previous edge-preserving filters. Then, Lillo-saavedra et al. [8] designed a new RGF-based fusion method for agricultural fragmented landscape. However, it depends more on the input images having objects with large-scale struc-tures or edges. Most of the existing filtering-based methods mainly focus on capturing the edge features by using different edge-aware filters and rarely describe spatial details from the geometric structure perspective.

Generally, in an earth observation image, complex earth objects are widely pre-sented in different spatial/spectral resolutions. Therefore, in the pansharpening, it is important to recognize the objects in different size or the structures of various scales during the detail extraction. The structure-preserving filter (SPF) in [9] have shown great potential in image processing applications, such as image abstraction, image composition, and seam carving, etc. This paper firstly modifies the SPF in [9] to describe the structures more accurately by considering the spatial correlation and similarity between the PAN and MS images. Then a multi-scale filtering decomposition is designed to extract the sufficient details from the PAN image. Finally, such details are modulated by gains matrix and injected into each MS band. The benchmark datasets from several satellites are used to verify the effectiveness of the proposed fusion method. Both subjective analysis and objective evaluations are conducted on the fused results.

The rest of this paper is organized as follows. Section 2 describes the structure-preserving filter. Section 3 presents the multi-scale structure perception based fusion method in details. Section 4 explains the experimental results and evaluations, and conclusion are drawn in Sect. 5.

2 Structure-Preserving Filter

Structure-preserving filter is a simple image smoothing operator designed to extract the structure from the texture via region covariance. Using image features as patch descriptors can capture the local structure and texture information implicitly and makes the approach particularly effective for structure extraction from texture. Due to the outstanding structure-aware capability, it benefits a variety of image processing applications.

First, let $F(x, y)$ denote a 7-dimensional feature vector representing a pixel located at (x, y) in an input image G:

$$F(x, y) = \left[G(x, y), \left| \frac{\partial G}{\partial x} \right|, \left| \frac{\partial G}{\partial y} \right|, \left| \frac{\partial^2 G}{\partial x^2} \right|, \left| \frac{\partial^2 G}{\partial y^2} \right|, x, y \right]^{\mathrm{T}} \tag{1}$$

where $G(x, y)$ denotes the intensity of the pixel, $\left| \frac{\partial G}{\partial x} \right|, \left| \frac{\partial G}{\partial y} \right|, \left| \frac{\partial^2 G}{\partial x^2} \right|, \left| \frac{\partial^2 G}{\partial y^2} \right|$ are the first and second derivatives of the intensity in both x and y directions. In the feature image F, a patch R with the size of $k \times k$ can be described with a 7×7 covariance matrix C_R as follows:

$$C_R = \frac{1}{n-1} \sum_{j=1}^{n} (Z_j - \mu)(Z_j - \mu)^{\mathrm{T}} \tag{2}$$

with Z_j denoting every 7-dimensional feature vector inside the patch R and μ being the mean of these feature vectors. For two image pixels p and q, the corresponding distance measure is defined as:

$$d(\mathrm{p,q}) = \sqrt{(\mu_p - \mu_q)(C_p + C_q)^{-1}(\mu_p - \mu_q)^{\mathrm{T}}} \tag{3}$$

in which μ_p, μ_q, C_p and C_q denote the means and covariance matrixes of features extracted from these patches centered at pixels p and q, respectively. Based on this measure, the adaptive weight of pixels p and q can be defined as:

$$\omega_{\mathrm{pq}} = \exp\left(-\frac{d(\mathrm{p,q})^2}{2\sigma^2} \right) \tag{4}$$

The structure component of a pixel p is defined as:

$$S(\mathrm{p}) = \frac{1}{H_{\mathrm{p}}} \sum_{\mathrm{q} \in N(\mathrm{p},r)} \omega_{\mathrm{pq}} G(\mathrm{q}) \tag{5}$$

where $N(p, r)$ denotes a squared neighborhood with the radius r centered at pixel p, and $H_p = \sum_q \omega_{pq}$ is a normalization factor.

3 The Proposed Method

3.1 Modified Structure-Preserving Filtering

In the PAN and MS images, even same object often presents in different structures with various scales. However, the SPF only focus on the filtering input itself without considering the spatial and structural similarities in image pair. It is necessary to consider such similarity measurements in the filtering process of the PAN image. To more accurately perceive the structure information of the PAN image, the original SPF is improved by substituting the spatial correlation coefficient (SCC) [10] and the structural similarity (SSIM) [11] for the second derivatives in (1):

$$F(x, y) = \left[G(x, y), \left| \frac{\partial G}{\partial x} \right|, \left| \frac{\partial G}{\partial y} \right|, \text{SSIM}, \text{SCC}, x, y \right]^{\text{T}} \tag{6}$$

To calculate SSIM and SCC, the original MS images are interpolated to the same size as the PAN image P through bicubic interpolation. Let LRM_i ($i = 1...N$) represent the upscaled N-band low-resolution MS images and the average of all LRMs is used as the intensity component I. The modified PAN image [12] matched with I is denoted as MP. Then the SCC and SSIM are calculated from the MP and I image pair. The more spatially similar the two images are, the more accurate the structure-perception is. As a result, the modified SPF (MSPF) regards an image pair as the filtering input in which one is the high-spatial resolution PAN image, the other (MS image) provides the structural reference to the PAN.

3.2   Multi-scale Structure Perception

With reference to the MS imagery, the MSPF decomposes the matched PAN image MP to obtain its structure component S and texture component T. A multi-scale decomposition scheme can capture the structures with different scales by varying the covariance window size parameter k and structure patch size parameter r. Specifically, the filtering input is smoothed by increasing k and r at each decomposition. In each decomposition, the extracted structure component is used as the filtering input for the subsequent decomposition. For the Lth decomposition, the multistage filtering process can be described as:

$$T_t(\text{p}) = S_t(\text{p}) - S_{t+1}(\text{p}) \tag{7}$$

$$P(\text{p}) = \sum_{t=1}^{L-1} T_t(\text{p}) + S_L(\text{p}) \tag{8}$$

in which T_1, T_2 ... T_{L-1} represent the texture components that scale up gradually, and S_L is the final structure component having the coarsest scale. Figure 1 illustrates a 2-level decomposition of WorldView-3 (WV-3) satellite image filtered by the proposed MSPF. Figure 1(a)–(c) show that the MSPF can effectively separate texture from structure. By multi-scale filtering the input PAN image (Fig. 1 (a)) guided by the reference image I (Fig. 1(d)), the structures from small to large are successfully perceived step by step. Correspondingly, the details from fine to coarse are extracted effectively shown in Fig. 1(a) and (c).

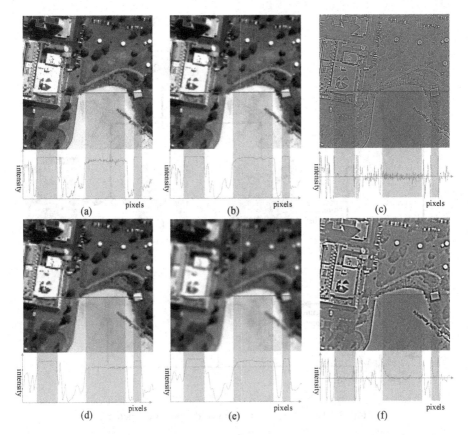

Fig. 1. The 2-level multi-scale structure perception of WV-3 PAN image. (a) The histogram-matched PAN image MP. (b) The 1st level structure component S_1 of (a). (c) The 1st level texture component T_1 of (a). (d) The intensity component I. (e) The 2nd level structure component S_2. (f) The 2nd level texture component T_2.

3.3   The Proposed Fusion Method

The diagram of the proposed method is displayed in Fig. 2. As the aforementioned denotations, LRM_i, I, and MP represent the ith unsampled MS channel, the average of all LRMs, and the histogram-matched PAN image, respectively. Similarly, the PAN image P is matched with each LRM_i to obtain MRM_i. $MSPF_{k,r,\sigma}(A,B)$ is used to represent the MSPF process in which A is the filtering input and B is the reference.

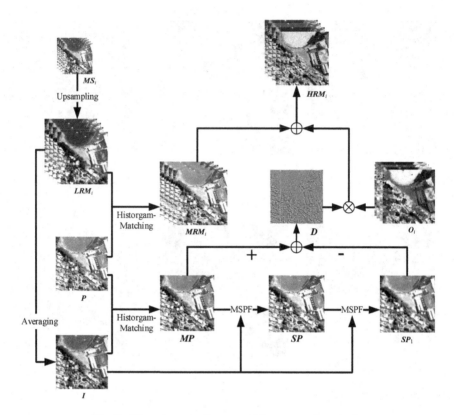

Fig. 2. The schematic diagram of the proposed method.

The fusion procedure can be simply summarized as the follow two steps:

- 1) Multi-scale decomposition
  Generate the 1st and 2nd level structure component images by MSPF with $k_2 = 2k_1 + 1$, $r_2 = 2r_1$, and $\sigma_2 = \sigma_1$:

$$SP = MSPF_{k_1, r_1, \sigma_1}(MP, I) \tag{9}$$

$$SP_1 = MSPF_{k_2, r_2, \sigma_2}(SP, I) \tag{10}$$

Then extract the detail component image D as:

$$D = MP - SP_1 \tag{11}$$

- 2) Details injection
  Compute the band-dependent weighting matrix O_i for each LRM_i:

$$O_i = N \times \frac{LRM_i}{\sum\limits_{i=1}^{N} LRM_i} \qquad (12)$$

The total details D is modulated by the gains matrix and then injected into each MS image MRM_i. Then the final fused image is produced and denoted as HRM_i.

$$HRM_i = O_i \times D + MRM_i \qquad (13)$$

4 Experimental Results

4.1 Experiment Setup

The images acquired by IKONOS, GeoEye-1 (GE-1), and WV-3 are adopted as the test dataset to evaluate the proposed method. IKONOS dataset, which consist of four 4-m MS bands and 1-m PAN band, was built in 2001. It presents part of San Diego urban area, California. GE-1 imagery consists of 2.0-m MS imagery (4 bands) and 0.5-m PAN image, which was taken in February of 2009, shows part of Hobart, Australia. WV-3 dataset contains eight 7.5-m SWIR bands and a 0.3-m PAN band. It was taken in November, 2015 and covers part of the rural area in France. Four indexes are adopted for quantitative evaluation, including spectral angle mapper (SAM), Q4, ERGAS ("relative dimensionless global error in synthesis" in French) [11], and QNR [13]. The ideal value of SAM and ERGAS indexes is 0, the ideal value of Q4 and QNR indexes is 1. For comparison purpose, several state-of-the-art fusion methods, including RGF [8], APS [14], and NND [15], are adopted.

4.2 Selection of the Parameters k and r

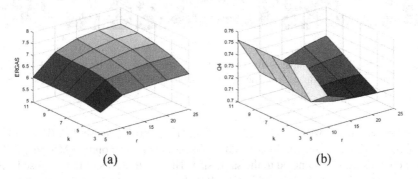

Fig. 3. Change of (a) ERGAS and (b) Q4 with respect to k and r variations.

Since the performance of the MSPF process depends on the choice of the filtering parameters k and r, different parameter selection may affect the quality of the sharpened results. In this paper, these two parameters are tuned by selection the best ERGAS and Q4 values. Figure 3 shows the ERGAS and Q4 of the fused IKONOS images with different k and r. It is observed that ERGAS index increases and Q4 index decreases continuously with the growth of k and r. When $k = 3$ and $r = 5$, ERGAS index reaches its lowest point corresponding the best value of 5.876 and Q4 obtains its highest value of 0.762 for IKONOS dataset. Additionally, similar trends are also verified for GE-1 and WV-3 datasets.

4.3   Comparison Among Different Methods

4.3.1   Experiment 1—IKONOS Dataset

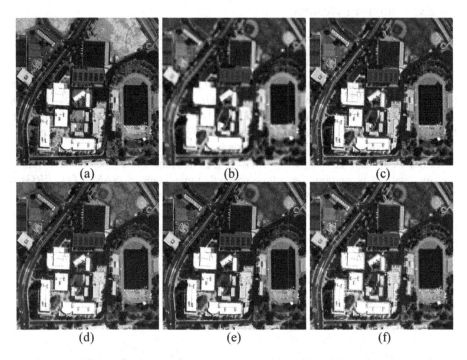

Fig. 4. IKONOS satellite images fusion result. (a) The high-spatial resolution PAN image. (b) The upsampled MS image. (c) The proposed method. (d) APS method. (e) NND method. (f) RGF method.

In this experiment, we set $k_1 = 3$, $r_1 = 5$, and $\sigma_1 = 0.5$. Figure 4(a)-(b) show the IKONOS PAN sub-scene of 400×400 pixels and the corresponding MS image (True color composition) upsampled to the same size. The fused results of the proposed, APS, NND, and RGF method are listed in Fig. 4(c)-(f), respectively. Compared with the MS image (Fig. 4(b)), APS method exhibits severe color distortions, especially on the green grass parts. RGF and the proposed methods preserve more spectral information than NND method. Furthermore, the proposed method looks clearer than RGF and shows the best visual effect. The objective evaluations for the four fusion methods are given in Table 1. It can be seen that NND obtains the 2nd scores in SAM but the worst score in Q4 and ERGAS indexes. Compared with RGF method, APS shows better in SAM and ERGAS. The proposed method achieves the best performance as underlined in the table among all the indexes.

Table 1. Evaluation indexes of IKONOS dataset.

	SAM	Q4	ERGAS
APS	8.050	0.753	6.410
NND	4.344	0.638	11.856
RGF	9.179	0.753	7.124
Proposed	5.759	0.779	5.735

4.3.2   Experiment 2—GeoEye-1 Dataset

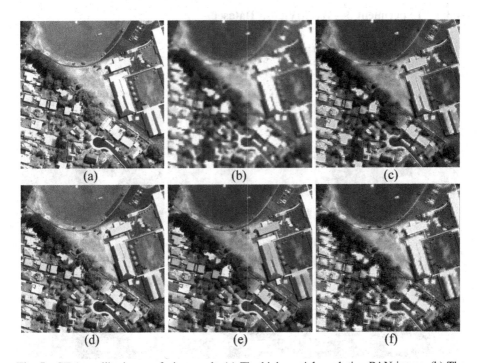

Fig. 5. GE-1 satellite images fusion result. (a) The high-spatial resolution PAN image. (b) The upsampled MS image. (c) The proposed method. (d) APS method. (e) NND method. (f) RGF method.

In Experiment 2, we set $k_1 = 3$, $r_1 = 5$, and $\sigma_1 = 0.5$. Figure 5(a) shows a 400×400 pixels PAN sub-scene and Fig. 5(b) is the corresponding upsampled MS scene. Similar to Experiment 1, APS method (Fig. 5(d)) introduces the obvious color distortions in vegetation area. The highly reflective area at roofs is distorted to gray in NND method (Fig. 5(e)). RGF shows the blurred effect and changes the color around the edges of the red roofs. Although the proposed method produces slight spectral distortions, it looks like the best among the 4 methods. The objective evaluations are listed in Table 2. RGF has the poorest performance in terms of SAM and ERGAS partly due to the higher spatial resolution of GE-1 images. All the evaluation indexes show that the proposed method is optimal, which is consistency with the visual analysis.

Table 2. Evaluation indexes of GE-1 dataset.

	SAM	Q4	ERGAS
APS	9.866	0.712	8.345
NND	8.837	0.698	9.913
RGF	10.606	0.738	10.730
Proposed	3.872	0.792	8.669

4.3.3   Experiment 3—WorldView-3 Dataset

Fig. 6. WV-3 satellite image fusion result. (a) The high-spatial resolution PAN image. (b) The upsampled SWIR image. (c) The proposed method. (d) APS method. (e) NND method. (f) RGF method.

In this experiment, WV-3 PAN and SWIR images are selected and fused together. The original PAN image is 1200 × 1200 pixels while the SWIR is 48 × 48. Figure 6(a) displays the 400 × 400 pixels sub-scene of the PAN image and Fig. 6(b) is the corresponding SWIR image (Band 8-4-1 composition) resampled to the same size. Since there is no spectral response overlap between the PAN and SWIR bands, the intensity component in APS method is built by averaging all the 8 SWIR bands. It is easy to find that APS method still introduces severe color distortions although the clarity is significant. NND method preserves more spectral information than RGF. The proposed method performs well in both spatial enhancement and spectral preservation. Table 3 reports the assessment result in terms of QNR index. Since the great difference of spatial resolution between PAN and SWIR images, QNR is selected as an appropriate index for quality evaluation. In QNR, D_s and D_λ represent the spatial and spectral distortion, respectively. The ideal values of them are 0. APS method obtains the best values in D_s and RGF has the worst result in D_λ. The proposed method achieves the best values in D_λ and QNR, which means it has the best overall quality in the four methods.

Table 3. QNR evaluation of the fused WV-3 images.

	D_S	D_λ	QNR
APS	0.056	0.398	0.568
NND	0.077	0.400	0.554
RGF	0.069	0.715	0.715
Proposed	0.077	0.114	0.818

5 Conclusion

A new fusion method based on multi-scale structure perception is proposed in this paper. Facing the mutual structure characteristics in the PAN and MS image pair, a modified structure-preserving filter (MSPF) is designed to capture the structure information from the PAN image. With the help of the multi-scale decomposition scheme of MSPF, the structures from small to large are effectively perceived and the corresponding spatial details are extracted accurately. Then the extracted details are injected through a gains matrix. Experiment results over IKONOS, GeoEye-1, and WorldView-3 datasets demonstrate that the proposed method performs well in sharpening high resolution remote sensed images regardless of the relative spectral response between PAN and MS images. The proposed method has better capabilities in preserving spectral information and increasing spatial resolution compared to existing state-of-the-art fusion methods.

Acknowledgements. This work is supported by the Seed Foundation of Innovation and Creation for Graduate Students in NPU (No. CX2020016) and Key R&D Plan of Shaanxi Province (No. 2020GY-034).

References

1. Aiazzi, B., Alparone, L., Baronti, S., Carla, R., Garzelli, A., Santurri, L.: Sensitivity of pansharpening methods to temporal and instrumental changes between multispectral and panchromatic data sets. IEEE Trans. Geosci. Remote Sens. **55**(1), 308–319 (2017)
2. Kaplan, N.H., Erer, L.: Bilateral filtering-based enhanced pansharpening of multispectral satellite images. IEEE Geosci. Remote Sens. Lett. **11**(11), 1941–1945 (2014)
3. Joshi, S., Upla, K.P., Shah, P.K.: Consistent pan-sharpening based on multistage joint and dual bilateral filters. In: 2014 IEEE International Geoscience and Remote Sensing Symposium, Quebec City, QC, Canada, pp. 2522–2525. IEEE (2014)
4. Yin, H., Li, S.: Pansharpening with multiscale normalized nonlocal means filter: a two-step approach. IEEE Trans. Geosci. Remote Sens. **53**(10), 5734–5745 (2015)
5. Upla, K.P., Joshi, S., Joshi, M.V., Gajjar, P.P.: Multiresolution image fusion using edge-preserving filters. J. Appl. Remote Sens. **9**(1), 096025 (2015)
6. Dong, W., Xiao, S., Qu, J.: Fusion of hyperspectral and panchromatic images with guided filter. SIViP **12**(7), 1369–1376 (2018). https://doi.org/10.1007/s11760-018-1291-z
7. Zhang, Q., Shen, X., Xu, L., Jia, J.: Rolling guidance filter. In: Fleet, D., Pajdla, T., Schiele, B., Tuytelaars, T. (eds.) ECCV 2014. LNCS, vol. 8691, pp. 815–830. Springer, Cham (2014). https://doi.org/10.1007/978-3-319-10578-9_53
8. Lillo-Saavedra, M., Gonzalo-Martin, C., Garcia-Pedrero, A., Lagos, O.: Scale-aware pansharpening algorithm for agricultural fragmented landscapes. Remote Sens. **8**(10), 1–19 (2016)
9. Karacan, L., Erdem, E., Erdem, A.: Structure-preserving image smoothing via region covariances. ACM Trans. Graph. **32**(6), 1–11 (2013)
10. Zhou, J., Civco, D.L., Silander, J.A.: A wavelet transform method to merge landsat TM and SPOT panchromatic data. Int. J. Remote Sens. **19**(4), 743–757 (1998)
11. Wang, Z., Bovik, A.C., Sheikh, H.R., Simoncelli, E.P.: Image quality assessment: from error visibility to structural similarity. IEEE Trans. Image Process. **13**(4), 600–612 (2004)
12. Laben, C.A., Brower, B.V.: Process for enhancing the spatial resolution of multispectral imagery using pansharpening. U.S. Patents, 6011875 (2000)
13. Alparone, L., Aiazzi, B., Baronte, S., et al.: Multispectral and panchromatic data fusion assessment without reference. Photogram. Eng. Remote Sens. **74**(2), 193–200 (2008)
14. Tu, T., Hsu, C., Tu, P., Lee, C.: An adjustable pan-sharpening approach for IKONOS/QuickBird/GeoEye-1/WorldView-2 imagery. IEEE J. Sel. Topics Appl. Earth Obs. Remote Sens. **5**(1), 125–134 (2012)
15. Sun, W., Chen, B., Messinger, D.W.: Nearest-neighbor diffusion-based pansharpening algorithm for spectral images. Opt. Eng. **53**(1), 013107 (2014)

Author Index

Printed in the United States
By Bookmasters